ADORNO

Theodor W. Adorno was the leading philosopher of the first generation of the Frankfurt School and is best known for his contributions to aesthetics and social theory. Critics have always complained about the lack of a practical, political, or ethical dimension to Adorno's philosophy. In this highly original contribution to the literature on Adorno, J. M. Bernstein offers the first attempt in any language to provide an account of the ethical theory latent in Adorno's writings.

Bernstein relates Adorno's ethics to major trends in contemporary moral philosophy. He analyses the full range of Adorno's major works, with a special focus on *Dialectic of Enlightenment, Minima Moralia,* and *Negative Dialectics.* In developing his account Bernstein lays particular stress on Adorno's contention that the event of Auschwitz demands a new categorical imperative.

This book will be widely acknowledged as the standard work on Adorno's ethics and as such will interest professionals and students of philosophy, political theory, sociology, history of ideas, art history, and music.

". . . a valuable and groundbreaking contribution to the literature on Adorno."
– Thomas Huhn, Wesleyan University

J. M. Bernstein is University Distinguished Professor of Philosophy in the Graduate Faculty at the New School University, New York.

MODERN EUROPEAN PHILOSOPHY

Some Recent Titles

Daniel W. Conway: *Nietzsche's Dangerous Game*
John P. McCormick: *Carl Schmitt's Critique of Liberalism*
Frederick A. Olafson: *Heidegger and the Ground of Ethics*
Günter Zöller: *Fichte's Transcendental Philosophy*
Warren Breckman: *Marx, the Young Hegelians, and the Origins of Radical Social Theory*
William Blattner: *Heidegger's Temporal Idealism*
Charles Griswold: *Adam Smith and the Virtues of the Enlightenment*
Gary Gutting: *Pragmatic Liberalism and the Critique of Modernity*
Allen Wood: *Kant's Ethical Thought*
Karl Ameriks: *Kant and the Fate of Autonomy*
Alfredo Ferrarin: *Hegel and Aristotle*
Cristina Lafont: *Heidegger, Language and World-Discourse*
Nicholas Wolsterstorff: *Thomas Reid and the Story of Epistemology*
Daniel Dahlstrom: *Heidegger's Concept of Truth*
Michelle Grier: *Kant's Doctrine of Transcendental Illusion*
Henry Allison: *Kant's Theory of Taste*
Allen Speight: *Hegel, Literature and the Problem of Agency*

ADORNO

Disenchantment and Ethics

J. M. BERNSTEIN

New School University

PUBLISHED BY THE PRESS SYNDICATE OF THE UNIVERSITY OF CAMBRIDGE
The Pitt Building, Trumpington Street, Cambridge, United Kingdom

CAMBRIDGE UNIVERSITY PRESS
The Edinburgh Building, Cambridge CB2 2RU, UK
40 West 20th Street, New York, NY 10011-4211, USA
10 Stamford Road, Oakleigh, VIC 3166, Australia
Ruiz de Alarcón 13, 28014 Madrid, Spain
Dock House, The Waterfront, Cape Town 8001, South Africa

http://www.cambridge.org

First published 2001

Printed in the United States of America

Typeface New Baskerville 10/12 pt. *System* QuarkXPress 4.04 [AG]

A catalog record for this book is available from the British Library.

Library of Congress Cataloging in Publication data

Bernstein, J. M.
Adorno: disenchantment and ethics / J. M. Bernstein.
p. cm. – (Modern European philosophy)
Includes bibliographical references and index.
ISBN 0-521-62230-1 – ISBN 0-521-00309-1 (pbk.)
1. Adorno, Theodor W., 1903–1969 – Ethics. 2. Ethics, modern – 20th century. I. Title.
II. Series.

B3199.A34 B48 2001
170′.92 – dc21 00-065175

ISBN 0 521 62230 1 hardback
ISBN 0 521 00309 1 paperback

To Jess and Dan
for every day teaching me what matters most

CONTENTS

PREFACE

Readers of Adorno are inevitably struck by how everything he wrote was infused with a stringent and commanding ethical intensity. As a consequence, his patent eschewals of praxis, ethical action, his constant defenses of both philosophical reflection and the claims of aesthetic experience in opposition to praxis, and the vivid absence of a philosophical ethics have not only been weapons in the hands of those who think his version of critical theory betrayed the Marxist tradition from which it sprang, but to those of us moved by his thought a continual source of bafflement, embarrassment, and regret. How could such ethically sensitive writing be so remote from actual ethical experience? How could a philosophy committed to the need for historical transformation be so silent, so abysmally reluctant when it came to political and ethical issues? That constellation of issues formed one side of the pressures leading to this book. The other side was my sense that Adorno's focus on the role of philosophical aesthetics, and within philosophical aesthetics his reflective championing of artistic modernism, was of a kind that made his thought all but inaccessible to a philosophical tradition in which no area could be more marginal to the central questions of philosophy than philosophical aesthetics. Of course, for Adorno himself philosophical aesthetics is fundamentally concerned with issues rationality and knowledge; but, however much I remain convinced by Adorno on this matter, and I have continued over the years to explore his aesthetic theory, my experience has been that my writing on these matters tends to speak only to the converted. Hence, again, I felt the need, the pressure, to break out from the narrow confines of textual commentary and engage in a more reconstructive project.

Since I always interpreted Adorno's aesthetic theory as having an emphatic ethical moment, it was natural to respond to the dual sets of pressures by attempting to construct or reconstruct in Adorno's voice a philosophical ethics without making essential reference to his aesthetic theory – some references to it were inevitable. When I began this book my assumption was that it was going to have to be *very* reconstructive given the void it was attempting to fill. Although a few chapters of this work are reconstructive in that way, particularly the critique of Kant's moral philosophy and my elaboration of Adorno's concept of the concept, in fact, by the time I finished my work it seemed to me that patient analysis and common sense without either much subtlety or hermeneutic violence led quite naturally to an intriguing and I hope compelling ethics. Adorno's commitment to modernism in philosophy and art naturally enough, when unpacked with eye toward ethical matters, turns into something that deserves to be called ethical modernism. Because I have developed this conception of the ethical without reliance on Adorno's aesthetics, then although I feel the label of "modernism" fits, the analysis proceeds without any assumptions about modernism, and the label itself simply affixed to the result – which is equally what happened in the writing: only at the last minute was the name "ethical modernism" given to the notion produced.

Ethical modernism might not be enough to satisfy Adorno's left-wing critics since it is a conception of ethical action and not a prescription for doing such action. But in a philosophical environment in which skepticism about the role of *theory* in ethics is widespread, the incapacity of a philosophical ethics to legislate right action should be able to find for itself an audience better prepared to hear its claims than Adorno's traditional atavistic critics.

This book is as long as it is, and it is long, because in constructing my account I have wanted to be responsive to two distinct pressures: to provide an account that would reach out beyond the narrow confines of Adorno aficionados and speak to any philosophers working in ethics, and, at the same time, to show in detail how the view proposed is indeed *Adorno's* and not a thing apart from his philosophy. The latter demand entailed a great deal of patient commentary and rational reconstruction; the former demand entailed framing commentary and reconstruction in terms familiar to the Anglo-American reader. Both audiences will need to do some stretching since Adorno's philosophy is laced with curiosities that have no analogue in contemporary philosophical practice, and those elements of contemporary practice that I have felt were most pertinent for framing Adorno's thought are, at least formally, quite remote from his preferred angle of approach. This is a plea for patience from the reader: Adornoian curiosities that matter to the final account will be translated into more familiar terms eventually; my appropriation of alien philosophical vocabulary will be eventually textually resituated. Ethical modernism is, I believe, the philosophical ethics latent in Adorno's texts; it is equally, I believe, a conception of the ethical that more than bears comparison with the best of contemporary ethical thought. The gamble involved in proceeding in this double way will have paid off if, in the future, ethical modernism can be viewed as a compelling voice in contemporary ethical debates.

There is much that was in earlier drafts of this manuscript that has not survived, above all elaborate comparisons of Adorno with a variety of other thinkers: Heidegger, Gadamer, Lyotard, Charles Taylor, Alasdair MacIntyre, Wittgenstein, and Stanley Cavell. I hope future occasions will enable me to resuscitate some of these. Another consequence of this work having gone through a variety of drafts is that many of my references to other writers on Adorno disappeared as my explicit engagements with their work disappeared; this is especially the case for writing on Adorno before 1990. To those concerned I here express my gratitude; if they espy an unacknowledged use of their thought, I hope they will inform me so I can make good on the lapse.

This book has been a long time in the making, nearly ten years. And nearly everything that might have interrupted progress toward its completion did so: illness, death, domestic upheaval, moving from one continent to another, and spending years in work responsibilities that were all but incommensurable with doing any research whatsoever. As a consequence, the writing of this work was done in small snatches of time punctured by large expanses of emptiness. The result, almost certainly, is a thing composed of various geological layers that hold together probably rather less seamlessly than I hopefully imagine that they do. For the fault lines in this mass, in anticipation, I apologize to the reader.

The present work is the promised companion to *Recovering Ethical Life: Jürgen Habermas and the Future of Critical Theory*. To those who have been patiently awaiting this book (since 1994), I apologize for the delay. That this book exists at all, that it was ever begun, is in part due to the insistence of William Outhwaite that I say something about Adorno's practical philosophy to mirror my critical view of Habermas' practical philosophy.

My gratitude to the writings of those philosophers that were pivotal in the formative stages of this book. On things Adorno: Marty Jay and Susan Buck-Morss. On matters of moral philosophy: Bernard Williams, Alasdair MacIntyre, and, at a crucial moment, Sabina Lovibond.

I have been extremely fortunate in the quality and quantity of criticism and advice I have received. First I must thank the anonymous reader and the not so anonymous Tom Huhn who first read the manuscript for Cambridge. Their criticism of both the detail of the original argument, and above all, its structure has proved invaluable. Simon Jarvis seemed to know what I wanted to say even before I did and pushed in the appropriate direction. At a later point, his own fine book on Adorno proved an indispensable resource. Above all, however, I must here express my deepest gratitude to Bob Pippin. We have been friends for more than thirty years; in taking on the role of editor, critic, and intellectual conscience he must have at times felt that the claims of friendship were being stretched. If he did think that, he certainly never said so. On the contrary, he has been tireless in encouragement, support, and the kind of fine-grained and reflective criticism that cannot help but make responding to it improve the result. His detailed commentary on an early draft, an extended and penetrating reflection on the problems of modern moral thought in its own right, more than any other advice, helped me shape the final product.

It is for me devastating that the two readers of the earliest draft of this work are not here to share in its completion. Gillian Rose shared her enthusiasm for Adorno with me, starting me on the longer road, and then, with the unspeakable intellectual passion and esprit that was her very self, worried every thought of his with me, those she welcomed and those she despised. That she is not here to comment on the final thing is a great sorrow. As is the absence of Deborah Fitzmaurice. Debbie listened patiently as I read out to her every single sentence of the first draft. It is she who made me see that if I were to make Adorno available to those not already drawn to him I would need to paint on a larger canvas. The larger canvas I have provided is in no small measure a product of her understanding and generosity. To Gillian and Debbie I have a sense of indebtedness I know nothing will ever repay.

Other debts are a pleasure to acknowledge. Mark Sacks and Lucy O'Brien moved across the street at what was for me a dark hour and quickly became perfect friends and wonderful interlocutors. With endless of cups of tea and heartening whiskey, we talked and argued night after night into the wee hours. If ever the presumptive iron curtain between analytic and continental philosophy could be seen to be a flimsy thing of no account it was in their Alma Street home. At a moment when I thought it impossible, and well beyond that moment, they made life warm and philosophy vital. To Sara Beardsworth's encouragement and faith in this project, I remain grateful.

At very different moments, I found myself rather more fortunate than anyone deserves to have first Ståle Finke and then Liz Goodstein as students. Their Adorno radar was remarkable. For years at the University of Essex, I was lucky to have Simon Critchley and Peter Dews as colleagues. But especial mention is necessary for Onora O'Neill, also an Essex friend and colleague. My fascination with Kant's moral philosophy was sustained for more than a decade through reading her works, and, above all, having the benefit of being able to discuss Kant with her day in and day out. No one, I think, has offered a better defense of Kant's moral philosophy than she. Her intellectual integrity and, a different matter, her courage have been a constant inspiration. I hope she will forgive me if, despite all that, I have still found it necessary to take issue with Kant's moral thought root and branch.

Arriving in Nashville I discovered an exquisite friend and ideal critic in Gregg Horowitz. His sane judgement has spared the reader having to plod through thousands of unnecessary words; his acute understanding of the project gave the final draft a more telling shape than I imagined it could have; his power of giving gave me the gift of knowing that my work was done.

Graça Peixoto has made the past few years something more than I ever imagined they would or could be. In my little study in her apartment on Avenida Alexandre Ferreira the best pages of this book took form. I save for a private moment the chance to express my gratitude in full.

A not minor leitmotif of what follows contends that we would do well to consider ourselves learners as well as knowers, and that the standpoint of the neophyte is fundamental for a full appreciation of our situation. For me this thought is not a matter of abstract philosophical argument, but a bit of practical wisdom that I gathered from my everyday interactions with my most demanding, relentless, and loving teachers: my daughter Jessica and my son Daniel. This work must be dedicated to them for truly it would not be without what they have given me.

J.M. Bernstein
Nashville, Tennessee
June 2000

LIST OF ABBREVIATIONS

Adorno

AE — *Against Epistemology,* trans. Willis Domingo (Oxford: Blackwell, 1982)

DoE — *Dialectic of Enlightenment,* trans. John Cumming (New York: Seabury Press, 1972)

EAA — "Education After Auschwitz" in *Critical Models: Interventions and Catchwords,* trans. Henry W. Pickford (New York: Columbia University Press, 1998)

HTS — *Hegel: Three Studies,* trans. Shierry Weber Nicholsen (Cambridge, Mass.: The MIT Press, 1993)

MM — *Minima Moralia: Reflections from Damaged Life,* trans. E.F.N. Jephcott (London: New Left Books, 1974) Citations marked MM, A__, refer to a numbered aphorism. When only a number appears it is a page reference to the Dedication.

ND — *Negative Dialectics,* trans. E.B. Ashton (London: Routledge, 1973)

NL1 — *Notes to Literature,* vol. 1, trans. Shierry Weber Nicholsen (New York: Columbia University Press, 1991)

NL2 — *Notes to Literature,* vol. 2, trans. Shierry Weber Nicholsen (New York: Columbia University Press, 1992)

QF — *Quasi uni Fantasia: Essays on Modern Music,* trans. Rodney Livingstone (New York: Verso, 1992)

SO — "On Subject and Object," in *Critical Models: Interventions and Catchwords,* trans. Henry Pickford (New York: Columbia University Press, 1998)

As appropriate, I have altered the translations from *Dialectic of Enlightenment* and *Negative Dialectics.*

Kant

CJ *Critique of Judgment,* trans. Werner S. Pluhar (Indianapolis: Hackett Publishing Company, 1987)

CPrR *Critique of Practical Reason,* trans. Lewis White Beck (Indianapolis: Bobbs-Merrill, 1977)

G *Groundwork of the Metaphysics of Morals,* trans. H.J. Paton, as *The Moral Law* (London: Hutchinson, 1948)

No abbreviation is used for references to the *Critique of Pure Reason,* trans. Norman Kemp Smith (London: Macmillan, 1933); rather, I refer directly to the standard "A" and "B" page numbers. Other page references to Kant's work are to the Prussian Academy edition, which appear variously in the translations either at the margin or top of the page.

Other

ES Max Weber, *Economy and Society,* trans. Ephraim Fishoff et al. (Berkeley: University of California Press, 1978)

MW John McDowell, *Mind and World* (Cambridge, Mass.: Harvard University Press, 1994)

INTRODUCTION

> Nature, in ceasing to be divine, ceases to be human. Here, indeed, is just our problem. We must bridge the gap of poetry from science. We must heal this unnatural wound. We must in the cold reflective way of critical system, justify and organize the truth which poetry, with it quick naïve contacts, has already felt and reported.
>
> John Dewey[1]

No reading of the works of T. W. Adorno can fail to be struck by the ethical intensity of his writing, sentence by sentence, word by word. Whether he was writing about questions in epistemology, aesthetics, social theory,

1 Dewey, "Wandering Between Two Worlds," quoted in John Patrick Diggins, *The Promise of Pragmatism: Modernism and the Crisis of Knowledge and Authority* (Chicago: Chicago University Press, 1994), p. 4. Chapter 1, "The Disenchantment of the World," documents how emphatically early pragmatism was shaped by the problem of disenchantment that is the leitmotif of this work. Diggins does not believe that, at the end of the day, the pragmatists faced up to the challenge of disenchantment. Hence the heroes of his book are not the pragmatists themselves, but the "historian" Henry Adams. Diggins anticipates his conclusion in these words: ". . . pragmatism shares with Marxism and capitalism the assumption that the meaning of history and the purpose of life are no longer matters of thought but of action. . . . With pragmatism in particular, the use of experience only prepares for further experience, without experience itself being immediately self-illuminating or self-rewarding. The assumption that truth and value are produced in further action rather than revealed in present reflection holds out the promise of success, and as such pragmatism becomes not so much a philosophy as a story of the upward movement of life, a hopeful vision that appeals to America's romantic imagination" (p. 20). I see nothing in Diggins's diagnosis of disenchantment (which like Adorno's is heavily indebted to Max Weber) nor in the precise emphases of his critique of pragmatism (along with Marxism and capitalism) with which Adorno might disagree. On the contrary, Adorno shares with Henry Adams the "anxiety of truth" that cannot be dissipated by indefinite deferral to the future. The question of truth raised by Dewey in the epigraph cannot be side-stepped.

If pragmatism has become the de facto philosophy of our time, Diggins's fine study reveals the extent to which both its classical and current formation fails and forgets the problem situation with which it began. His book has encouraged me in thinking that an unswerving focus on the problem of disenchantment remains the correct one for examining the ethical predicament of the present.

literature, or music, one senses that these were vehicles for his sombre ethical vision of a world grown inhuman in which the primary task of the intellectual had become critical vigilance; all accommodation was exacerbation of the worst: "It is the sufferings of men that should be shared: the smallest step towards their pleasures is one towards the hardening of their pains" (MM, A5). However, if even in the worst world, there are joy, love, acts of courage, and decency, then in relentlessly focussing on what distorts and corrupts what is of worth Adorno is adopting a partial and limited perspective. While this partiality is the evident *risk* of Adorno's philosophising, it is a risk he thought ethically compelled to make without believing it could be unconditionally justified: "We shudder at the brutalization of life, but lacking any objectively binding morality we are forced at every step into actions and words, into calculations that are by humane standards barbaric, and even by the dubious values of good society, tactless" (MM, A6). Adorno does not believe vigilant critique is unproblematically right, just, or epistemically privileged – there is no binding morality because a "wrong life cannot be lived rightly" (MM, A18);[2] his partial perspective, its "coldness" (MM, A6), wrongs what is warm in human life. The margin of hope and hence the justification for this partiality is that through it we can gain an insight into (acquire knowledge of) our ethical predicament that cannot be had in any other way. This book attempts to underwrite and convey this insight.

To be more precise, my working hypothesis is that despite the fact that Adorno did not produce a work of moral philosophy,[3] his oeuvre as a whole is driven by an ethical vision, and hence that in order to do justice to his philosophy it is necessary to disentangle and elaborate the always presupposed ethical contours of his thought. In part, then, this work attempts to tease out the normative presuppositions and ideals governing Adorno's writing so that how they are fed through his diverse output can become perspicuous. It might reasonably be complained, however, that such an elucidation, no matter how perspicuous, would remain internal and bound to a conception of theory at some distance from the sort of questions we now employ in evaluating normative concepts and ideals. For reasons that become apparent below, while the distorting and perspectival character of Adornoian critique cannot be fully mitigated or circumvented, I attempt to draw out from Adorno's work an account of his "ethics" that is, at least in part, responsive to the kinds of expectations about an ethical position now current. This naturally means going be-

2 Unpacking this thesis is the primary task of Chapter 1 below.

3 However, his lectures on moral philosophy have recently been published: *Probleme der Moralphilosophie* (Frankfurt am Main: Suhrkamp, 1996); *Problems of Moral Philosophy*, trans. Rodney Livingstone (Oxford: Polity Press, 2000). Although I shall occasionally make reference to these lectures from 1963, at best they only adumbrate the "Freedom" chapter of *Negative Dialectics*.

yond the text of Adorno's writing; as a consequence, there are significant stretches of this work that are not about Adorno but rather pursue what I take to be an Adornoian analysis of a particular problem. The final position for which I argue, ethical modernism, is something that Adorno never stated or anticipated, although I argue it is fairly directly implied and anticipated by what he did say. It is my account of what an Adornoian ethic comes to, and it is written in part as a critique of what he did say.

In the first part of this Introduction I very briefly sketch in broad outline, employing conceptual frameworks external but directly adjacent to Adorno's own, a conception of our ethical situation and make a first attempt at connecting it to the framework of contemporary moral philosophy. The result of this overview will look philosophically ominous; from the position arrived at there will not appear to be any normatively substantive possibilities on offer. In Section 2 of the Introduction it is argued that this appearance derives from looking at Adorno's philosophy at the wrong level of analysis; while questions of reason and rationality are pervasive in Adorno's thought, it is the nature and status of *concepts,* and hence of human conceptuality, that is his primary object of analysis throughout his major writings. To better appreciate what Adorno wants to say about concepts, I first provide a wholly formal analysis of moral insight, and then go on to anticipate how Adorno's account of concepts both answers to the predicament outlined in Section 1 and fulfils the constraints outlined in the formal analysis of moral insight. The Introduction as a whole provides a framework rather than an anticipation for what is to follow.

Adorno, like numerous other critics of modernity, understands the predicament of ethical life to be a consequence of the overlap and convergence of the domination of scientific rationality in intellectual life and, let's say, the bureaucratic rationalization of practical life in the context of indefinite economic (capital) expansion. These converge in assuming similar if not identical conceptions of reason and rationality, and in securing as never before the *means* for human existence. The result of this convergence is a disenchantment of the world which drains from it the sources of meaning and significance that traditionally anchored ethical practices.[4] However, unlike romantic critics of the modern world, Adorno does not believe we can displace the claims of modern rational-

4 Here, for example, is Dewey, who in contradistinction to Adorno (and Weber) ignores the question of convergence, and instead emphasizes two seeming antinomies of modernity: "Man's increasing intellectual command over science . . . seems to reveal mankind absolutely caught and helpless within a vast unrelenting mechanism which goes its way without reference to human value or care for human purpose; Man's command over the means of life, his industrial conquest, seems only to have sharpened prior existing social inequities, to have led to devotion to the means of life at the expense of its serious and significant ends – a noble, free and happy life in which all men participate on something like equal terms." Quoted in Diggins, *The Promise of Pragmatism,* p. 5.

ism through the suppression of reason in the name of sentiment or emotion or desire or will or faith or taste or some nostalgic conception of community. He unswervingly affirmed the values of Enlightenment, and believed that modernity suffered from a deficit rather than a surplus of reason and rationality. Because one of the central places in which Adorno works through his critique of modern rationalism is in his writings on art and aesthetics, it is widely believed that his project is to displace reason with aesthetic praxis and judgement. This is a massive misunderstanding and distortion of his thought. Adorno believes that scientific and bureaucratic rationalism are, in their claim to totality, irrational in themselves, and hence that the meaning deficit caused by the disenchantment of the world is equally a rationality deficit. Only an expanded conception of reason which derives from a reinscription of conceptuality can lead to a restoration of ethical meaning. But for Adorno to expand reason is to expand the scope and character of cognitive life, of knowing. It is toward a more capacious sense of cognition and thus reason that Adorno's struggles with the concept lead us. Thus the distinct and unique character of his project: Adorno pursues romantic ends (a quest for the renewal of ethical meaning) through hyper-cognitive means.

1. Nihilism, Disenchantment, and the Problem of Externalism

The project of modernity has failed politically and ethically. Politically it has failed at least to provide all the inhabitants of the democratic states of Europe and North America with liberty, equality, and the freedom from fear and hunger it promised in its founding. Even if true, it could be argued that this failure is contingent and conditioned; while the institutional forms of liberal democracy and a market economy have thus far not secured what they apparently promised, there is now no viable or available alternative to them, nor is there a sufficient reason to believe that present failure is intrinsic to the character of those forms. And even if it could be shown, as I intend to do, that these institutional forms cannot, in principle, deliver what was promised and hoped, in the absence of a rationally plausible and practically possible alternative, there is no reason for not adhering to them, ameliorating their deficiencies as best we can. So qualified, the claim for the political failure of modernity must remain equivocal.

Modernity's ethical failure is more radical, and impacts on its equivocal political failure. The simplest, most widely recognised, and most economical way of stating the ethical failure of modernity is through Nietzsche's notion of nihilism: "What does nihilism mean? *That the highest values devaluate themselves.* The aim is lacking; 'why?' finds no answer."[5] By

5 *The Will to Power,* trans. Walter Kaufmann and R. J. Hollingdale (New York: Random House, 1967), p. 9.

seeking to produce a wholly secular form of life we have espoused, above all, the values of scientific rationality and truth; in pursuing these values, in ordering our intellectual and practical lives in accordance with their dictates, all other values and ideals tendentially lose their rational appeal until, eventually, even the worth of scientific rationality and truth become problematic for us. Modern, secular reason is self-undermining. Its self-undermining character has impacted on our practical life not only because it makes suspect the ethical ideals we employ to orient ourselves through the world, but because they are suspect they lose their *force,* their power to (rationally) motivate and guide. The condition of nihilism is the interpenetration of these two factors: the increasing rational incoherence of modern moral values and ideals, and their consequent increasing practical inadequacy for the purpose of regulating – orienting and giving meaning to – everyday life.[6] Nietzsche explicates this interpenetration of rational and practical inadequacy in the following terms:

> But among the forces cultivated by morality was *truthfulness*: this eventually turned against morality, discovered its teleology, its partial perspective – and now the recognition of this inveterate mendaciousness that one despairs of shedding becomes a stimulant. Now we discover in ourselves needs implanted by centuries of moral interpretation – needs that now appear to us as needs for untruth; on the other hand, the value for which we endure life seems to hinge on these needs. This antagonism – *not* to esteem what we know, and not to be *allowed* to esteem the lies we should like to tell ourselves – results in a process of dissolution.[7]

We do not esteem what we know – what the natural and human sciences have revealed to us about the world – because there does not appear to be anything in what is known that is or could be worthy of esteem. Conversely, what we *need* to esteem, what would give meaning and significance to our lives, has been shown not to be a valid component of the known or knowable world, and thus becomes an illegitimate or delegitimated object of veneration. As a consequence of the practical and rational success of modern science, truth and truthfulness have become our highest values.[8] But if what pursuing them reveals is not worthy of esteem, and what we need to esteem is not true, then even the *good* of truth and truthful-

6 For this way of stating the meaning of the crisis of nihilism see Mark Warren, *Nietzsche and Political Thought* (Cambridge, Mass.: The MIT Press, 1988), p. 37. Chapter 1 of Warren is a generally acute and accurate account of Nietzsche's conception of nihilism. He contends that structurally nihilism can be defined as referring to "*situations in which an individual's material and interpretive practices fail to provide grounds for a reflexive interpretation of agency*" (p. 17; emphasis Warren's).

7 *The Will to Power,* p. 10.

8 Of course, for Nietzsche our veneration of science, scientific rationality, and truth is, shall we say, a rationalized successor from our veneration of an all-good creator God. In this sense, for Nietzsche we do not yet inhabit and have yet to achieve a truly secular under-

ness becomes opaque. The "process of dissolution" (*Auflösungsprocess*) to which Nietzsche refers concerns the way in which the rational and practical inadequacies of the present reenforce one another: not only does our framework of rationality delegitimate all extant moral and ethical goods, but in leaving no space for esteeming generally (because, again, nothing scientifically uncovered is worth esteeming), it equally undermines its own worth as our highest value.

Because what is undermined is the worth of our highest values, their meaningfulness for us, there arises the question of why we should pursue these values – what conceivably could motivate us to do so? Because this is clearly a different question from the rational coherence of a value framework, it deserves a different name; let's call it *affective scepticism*. Affective scepticism specifies a situation in which agents can find no good reason, no motive, for pursuing a particular form of practice (intellectual or practical) that can be separated, at least in principle, from the question of the internal coherence of the practice. Typically, affective scepticism is a consequence of cognitive scepticism; but it is possible for a framework to be cognitively coherent while the conditions of affective adherence remain absent. Nietzschean nihilism intends to depict a situation of potentially universal affective scepticism in which we utterly lack the motivation for pursuing significant ends.[9]

However the details of this situation are fleshed out, Adorno follows Nietzsche in regarding present practices as lacking rational coherence and, feeding back into and reenforcing that rational incoherence, practical adequacy. Hence the same conditions that dissolve the *ethical meaningfulness* of human existence simultaneously, in so doing, undermine the conditions of *rational agency, of goal-directed meaningful action* as such. In the next section we begin elaborating the internal connection between the problem of (ethical/moral) meaning and the structure of rational

standing of the world. Our belief in science is the last remnant of Christian theology and culture. Hence his various calls to complete the process of nihilistic undoing, to replace being by becoming, and his espousal of the doctrine of eternal return should all be interpreted as his attempt to locate and secure a wholly secular form of life. Whatever one's worries about Nietzsche's philosophy as a whole, his insistence that the question of what is to *count* as a wholly secular form of life be thought of as an ongoing problem seems to me a pointed and uncomfortable reminder.

9 In the second half of the nineteenth and the beginning of the twentieth century the lack of motivating reasons for action was consistently figured in terms of fatigue, ennui, melancholy, and above all boredom, which hence became – in Flaubert, Baudelaire, Nietzsche, Kierkegaard, Simmel, Heidegger, and so on – central reflective concepts for interpreting the *experience* of modernisation. For a superb articulation and defence of this deployment of the concept of boredom, see Elizabeth S. Goodstein's *Experience Without Qualities: Boredom and the Democratization of Scepticism in Modernity* (Stanford: Stanford University Press, forthcoming). If we were more alert to the problem of boredom and its evasion, diversion, what below I specify as flights from the world, then the skeptical disposition of present society would become wildly more perspicuous.

agency. Nonetheless, it is central to understanding the scope of what Nietzsche and his successors analyse in terms of nihilism that it cannot be restricted to an anachronistic concern for ultimate meaning in a godless universe, but rather relates to the constitutive conditions of human agency. The worry expressed in the nihilistic analysis of late modernity is that the twin pressures of rational incoherence and practical inadequacy threaten the very possibility of recognizable human agency. Universal affective scepticism looms.

Adorno's own understanding of this situation is more heavily indebted to Max Weber's sociological elaboration of Nietzsche than it is to Nietzsche himself.[10] For Weber the nihilism complex is denominated "rationalization," whose two interlocking elements – the disenchantment of the world as a consequence of the development of modern science ("intellectualisation") and the bureaucratisation of everyday life leading to the "iron cage" – are evident successor versions of Nietzsche's two part rational/practical analysis. According to Weber, "intellectualist rationalization" means

> . . . the knowledge or belief that if one but wished one *could* learn at any time. Hence, it means that principally there are no mysterious incalculable forces that come into play, but rather that one can, in principle, master all things by calculation. This means that the world is disenchanted. One need no longer have recourse to magical means in order to master or implore the spirits, as did the savage, for whom mysterious powers existed. Technical means and calculations perform the service.[11]

Intellectualism is the reflexive belief that the domain of scientific rationality – what can be known through the causal analysis of quantifiable law-like processes subject to experimental manipulation – is in principle universal in scope. Modern science became paradigmatic for all claims to

10 My emphasis here and throughout on Weber may, if one wishes, be taken as a simplifying, heuristic device. In providing this emphasis I do not mean to deny the importance of, above all, volume 1 of Marx's *Capital* on Adorno. But since Adorno's appropriation of Marx tends to be through the Weberian reading of *Capital* provided by Georg Lukács's *History and Class Consciousness* (1923), trans. Rodney Livingstone (London: Merlin Press, 1971), and his own position seems to develop more out of Weber's than Marx's, then there is at least a prima facie case for seeing this emphasis as non-distorting.

It is one of the curiosities of present philosophy that despite the continuing fascination with Nietzsche's account of asceticism, the ascetic priest, et al., in the formation of modern rationalized culture, almost no attention is paid to Weber's far more theoretically sophisticated and empirically documented development of Nietzsche's thesis. From the point of view of critical theory, this appears as a massive sociological deficit in the attempts to vindicate or appropriate Nietzschean ideas for contemporary philosophy. For an exception to this lack of attention, see David Owen, *Maturity and Modernity: Nietzsche, Weber, Foucault and the Ambivalence of Reason* (London: Routledge, 1994).

11 "Science as a Vocation," in *From Max Weber: Essays in Sociology*, trans. and ed. H. H. Gerth and C. Wright Mills (London: Routledge, 1948), p. 138.

rationality and theoretical knowledge by relentlessly defeating "rival claimants, such as philosophy, theology and history, and in the course of more than three centuries of controversy, by delegitimating their respective reality-principles (reason, God, and experience)."[12] While in its beginnings modern science was conceived of as a *way*, a spiritual path that would reveal the meaning of the being of the universe or the meaning of life or God's handicraft ("Here I bring you the proof of God's providence in the anatomy of a louse"[13]), its reiterated application shows it to be capable of indefinite progress. However, because indefinite, unlimited progress methodically voids the significance of what is discovered along the way except as a means to further discovery, then the meaning of scientific progress becomes increasingly unintelligible even in narrow instrumental terms.[14]

Once it is recognized that the unlimited scope of intellectualism threatens to undermine the intelligibility of *pursuing* science, of *commitment* to scientific analysis and rationality, then the contours of Weber's historical and theoretical researches become intelligible, namely, to limit knowledge in order to make room for faith, or, in Weber's own terms, to uncover the "vocational" presuppositions of the practice of modern science: the pursuit of science is only intelligible *as a vocation,* as a commitment to the internally legitimated ideals of scientific rationality.[15] Neither modern science nor rationalized social practices would have become so dominating had it not been for Puritan asceticism: "Science, and modern rationality more generally, represents the Puritan obsession with calculation, impersonal rules and self-discipline without the Puritan belief in their divine origin. It is Puritan epistemology without Puritan ontology."[16] The espousal of Puritan epistemology without Puritan ontology inflects the account of nihilism in a significant way: for Weber disenchantment is a condition or cause of nihilism since it is responsible for dissolving any intelligible connection between reason (and its objects) and affective self-understanding. As practices become more rational and orderly, the objects (and subjects) of practice become increasingly mean-

12 Sheldon Wolin, "Max Weber: Legitimation, Method, and the Politics of Theory," in William Connolly (ed.), *Legitimacy and the State* (Oxford: Basil Blackwell, 1984), p. 66.

13 Weber quoting Swammerdam, "Science as a Vocation," p. 142.

14 In putting forward this thesis Weber cites what has become a typical conundrum of the present: while modern medicine continues to discover new ways of preserving and extending life, it is constitutively insensitive to the question of whether the patient regards his or her life as worth being preserved. "Yet the presuppositions of medicine, and the penal code, prevent the physician from relinquishing his therapeutic efforts. Whether life is worthwhile living and when – this question is not asked by medicine." Ibid., p. 144.

15 This way of construing Weber goes back to Karl Löwith, *Max Weber and Karl Marx* (1932), trans. Hans Fantel (London: George Allen & Unwin, 1982), pp. 28–67.

16 Jeffrey C. Alexander, "The Dialectic of Individuation and Domination: Weber's Rationalization Theory and Beyond," in Sam Whimster and Scott Lash (eds.), *Max Weber, Rationality and Modernity* (London: Allen & Unwin, 1987), p. 191.

ingless. Puritanism provides a natural bridge to a disenchanted world because asceticism's bracketing and refusal of sensuousness permits the world to become imaged in the same terms as the denaturalised subject.

Puritan asceticism is equally central to Weber's analysis of societal rationalization. The Puritan took the self-disciplining, selfless, and methodical ordering of life out of the monastery and into everyday existence. To make himself perfectly the tool of God, the Puritan had to depersonalise his relations to himself, to subject his behaviour to impersonal rules of conduct; and to carry out this conduct he simultaneously had to depersonalise and objectify his relations with others, make them calculable and orderly; to reveal and prove himself through his "works," to make these works a success, he needed to make the institutions in which he worked calculable and predictable in their operations. In the same way in which modern science triumphed as it progressively dispensed with the religious zeal that brought it into being, so the "iron cage" of rationalized society came into being in the same way. Because it eloquently describes the meaning of Weber's conception of the "iron cage" in a manner that harmonises with Adorno's own picture of modern society, let me cite at length Sheldon Wolin's account.

> The cage is iron because the main forces of modern life, science, capitalism, and bureaucratic organisation are triumphs of rationality and so the mind has no purchase point to attack them. They are mind incarnated in legal codes and administrative organisations that promise order, predictable decisions, regularity of procedures, and responsible, objective, and qualified officials; into economics that operate according to principles of calculated advantage, efficiency, and means-ends strategies; into technologies that promote standardisation, mechanical behaviour, and uniform tastes. The advantages of rationalization in terms of power and material satisfaction are so overwhelming that the historical process which has brought that system into being is "irreversible." But, finally, the cage is iron because the "fulfilment of the calling cannot directly be related to the highest spiritual and cultural values." Instead of being fired by religious, ethical, and political ideals, action has become simply a response to "economic compulsion" or to "purely mundane passions."[17]

This image of modern society is one Adorno shares: he too believes there is a convergence between the intellectualist disenchantment of the world

17 "Max Weber: Legitimation, Method, and the Politics of Theory," pp. 77–8. The quotations in this passage are from *For Max Weber*, pp. 137, 138. As is well known, the Weberian analysis overestimates the importance of Calvinism and Puritanism in the emergence of capital and modern society – an emergence that was clearly overdetermined. However, whether the story is told in narrow functionalist terms or through Weber's more complex conception of religious rationalization, the structural issues depicted in the notion of the "iron cage" require acknowledgement and addressing.

and societal rationalization which tendentially subjects institutions to the norms of instrumental rationality (efficiency, calculability, standardisation, etc.). Indeed, Adorno believes, like Weber, that for all intents and purposes it is the *same* conception of reason and rationality that governs scientific rationalism as governs societal rationalization. Adorno calls this conception of reason and reasoning "identity thinking." But while the image is shared, Adorno does not agree with (some of) the presuppositions governing either the Weberian or Nietzschean analysis; because he does not agree with (some of) the presuppositions directing the Weberian analysis, he equally does not believe that the process depicted by it is in principle irreversible (although he is far from sanguine about the prospects for reversal). I explain something about why this is the case in Section 2 below.

Now the diagnosis of modern society in terms of nihilism, disenchantment, and rationalization does not cohere in any obvious way with the technical problems of modern moral philosophy. Yet the dominant agent-oriented leitmotif running through the diagnosis has been the story of how the self-undermining dialectic of scientific rationalism begets a generalised crisis of motivation: scientific rationalism delegitimates traditional moral norms and values, making their pursuance increasingly irrational and without appeal. Why bind oneself to norms and values one knows to be illusory or, at best, tenable only as a private act of commitment? Why bind oneself to norms and values one knows are unrelated and irrelevant to the protocols governing the dominant institutions of the social world? Why bind oneself to norms and values one knows will disadvantage one in acquiring the "goods" that those dominant institutions are capable of providing? Why, other than out of self-interest, bind oneself to outmoded (fictional, mythological, irrational) norms and values at all? One partial answer, implied by the reflexive application of scientific rationalism to itself, is that, however irrational, they represent an apparently necessary condition for finding the pursuit of any end, even that of science, meaningful and significant.

Yet, in a sense this partial answer only exacerbates the difficulty: there appears to be an utter detachment or incommensurability between, say, the protocols governing scientific practice and the motivational set of the scientist pursuing it: the *vocation* of the scientist and the rationality of scientific reflection and cognition belong to heterogeneous frameworks of meaning.[18] More generally, within the Weberian picture, there is a sys-

18 Nietzsche's strategy for dealing with this problem was to make rationalized norms themselves (created) values, and thus make value creation the dominant, self-perfecting end. Even if that respects scientific rationality and truth *as* values, one set of values amongst others, it leaves their success too indeterminate and unexplained. Weber simply accepts the duality, but hopes his historical endeavour of showing the constituting role of commitment and vocation to the success of scientific rationalism together with his theoret-

tematic separation between the rational and universalist norms of a rationalized practice, on the one hand, and the concrete, unique agent-specific motivation for pursuing that practice on the other. A version of the problem of the incommensurability between abstract, impersonal norms and the individual motivation for respecting them appears in the analytic discussion of externalism and internalism.

Externalism is the view that there can be justificatory reasons for a moral norm that are independent from the reasons why any particular agent should act on that norm. To put this thought somewhat differently, we can conceive of a path of reasoning which demonstrates why a particular moral norm is valid – for example, all promises should be kept because, *ceteris paribus,* generalised promise-keeping promotes the maximum welfare for the greatest number – which nonetheless leaves it indeterminate as to why I should keep my promises. There are two different angles which make the eventuality of this separation of rational from motivational goodness intelligible. First, the kinds of reasons which are given in the course of justifying a norm may and perhaps should be very general in character, referring only to aspects of agency and features of interaction between and among persons which hold of all agents in all times and places. Unless the justification operated at this level of abstraction, it might be thought, it could not count as a rational demonstration because it could not appeal to all individuals whatever their specific makeup and circumstances. But insofar as the proof of validity is agent neutral, then even if I can follow each step through to the conclusion and find each valid, I may still wonder whether the argument should be overriding for me, bind me to its norm; for example, I do not *care* about this demonstration any more than I care about the demonstration that it is a necessary condition for the survival of any human being that they procure for themselves sufficient quantities of water; for me, the risky adventure of crossing the desert on foot is more enticing than guaranteeing survival. Second, it is a component of what we think morality is that its dictates can require us to act for reasons that are not in our (immediate) self-interest (or better: our present motivational set, however composed), and hence are remote from what we (now) desire to do. If morality enters at the very place our own-interested reasons for action give out, then it is unsurprising that we can find ourselves unmoved by what it demands. Modern moral rationalism's interpretation of the bindingness of moral norms in terms of their overridingness, and securing their overridingness through their universality, is hence precisely what

ical demonstration of its unavoidability (science has practical presuppositions that are extrinsic to its procedural protocols) is sufficient to inspire vocational commitment in others. Such reflexive irrationalism inspires admiration rather than (rational) confidence.

can make them appear remote and/or indifferent to individual desires, concerns, and normative orientations. The detachment and heterogeneity of justifying reasons from motivating reasons seems built into both our conception of rational proof and our understanding of morality generally.

Full-blooded externalists, and they are rare, may even believe that not only are the truth conditions of a moral theory and its acceptance conditions distinct, and must remain distinct, but given a variety of contingent (or even noncontingent) facts about human beings, their typical forms of behaviour and the state of the world, that it is morally better that individuals remain ignorant of the real reasons that make their actions right or good.[19] For example, on one account there is a paradox of hedonism in which "adopting as one's exclusive end in life the pursuit of maximum happiness may well prevent one from having certain experiences or engaging in certain forms of relationships that are among the greatest sources of happiness."[20] By extension, it could be the case that the good of objective or indirect consequentialism is achieved only if individuals do not attempt to calculate what would promote the greatest happiness overall but rather, remaining ignorant of the fact that the rightness of their actions was wholly grounded in the objective consequentialist norm, they pursued ends premised on the false belief that those ends were intrinsically good and not good because they promoted the greatest happiness principle. These apparently paradoxical features of some externalist positions derive from a willingness to endorse the heterogeneity of justifying and motivating reasons that is a consequence of the development of modern scientific rationalism.

Conversely, the internalist believes moral reasons are (or ought to be) intrinsically motivating, their truth conditions and acceptance conditions converging such that coming fully and properly to understand what justifies a moral norm simultaneously involves understanding how it pro-

19 For a defence of this as well as sustaining the separation of truth conditions and acceptance conditions, see Peter Railton, "Alienation, Consequentialism, and the Demands of Morality," *Philosophy and Public Affairs* 13 (1984): pp. 134–71. Railton's position goes back to, at least, Sidgwick who argued that "on Utilitarian principles, it may be right to do and privately recommend, under certain circumstances, what it would not be right to advocate openly"; concluding this run of argument with the claim that "the opinion that secrecy may render an action right which would not be otherwise so should itself be kept comparatively secret; and similarly it seems expedient that the doctrine that esoteric morality is expedient should itself be kept esoteric." *The Method of Ethics,* 7th ed. (1907; Chicago 1962), pp. 489–90, quoted in Bernard Williams, *Ethics and the Limits of Philosophy* (London: Fontana Press/Collins, 1985), p. 109. The gap between Mandeville (who also believed that morality did and could survive only on the basis of illusion promulgated by politicians), Sidgwick, Railton, and Nietzsche is that Nietzsche did not believe such secrets could be indefinitely kept in a democratic, mass society, and that hence a more general response to the duality of dogmatic reason and moral illusion was required.

20 Ibid., p. 140.

vides *me* with a reason for action. One obvious thought in support of internalism is that if the justification of a norm is wholly heterogeneous from its acceptance conditions, then, in a quite colloquial sense, it is not a reason for action.[21] Practical reasons are those that could belong to an agent's motivational set, that is, could figure in the true explanation of an agent's reason for doing what she did. If a reason could not so figure, then it is not a practical reason at all; what makes a reason for action a good one must, by some route, make it a good one upon which to act. If correct, then in virtue of what a reason for action is, justifying reasons must also be motivating reasons. The difficulty with the demand for internalism is that it, arguably, limits legitimate argument to positions continuous with agents' or communities' existing normative self-conception. And while such self-conceptions can be enlarged through argument, there is no reason to believe that such enlargement is indefinite – universal. Thus the procedural requirement for internalist forms of argument would appear to provide justification for narrowly parochial value orientations.

While there are thus evident pros and cons to both internalism and externalism, it is in fact difficult to see what are the stakes in the debate between them. If internalism is true, then, of course, that will place a constraint on theory construction. But that is not a very weighty constraint since, first, an individual's motivational set can contain "dispositions of evaluation, patterns of emotional reaction, personal loyalties, and various projects . . . embodying commitments,"[22] all of which can extend well beyond narrow individual or communal self-interest; motivational sets can be very wide in scope. Second, there is no requirement that the way in which reasons come to belong to a motivational set be through direct cognitive understanding rather than some complex process involving education, training, experience, imagination, and reflection. Arguably, complex processes of socialisation represent the preconditions for the rational appreciation of normative claims. If both these considerations are allowed, and they are hard to disagree with, then almost any set of norms, no matter how external they originally appear to be, can be imagined as eventually being incorporated into an individual's motivational outlook in a manner that satisfies the requirements of internalism.[23] If the inter-

21 See Bernard Williams, "Internal and External Reasons," in his *Moral Luck* (Cambridge: Cambridge University Press, 1981), pp. 101–13.

22 Ibid., p. 105.

23 In a very much more complex way, this is the idea behind Christine Korsgaard's "Scepticism about Practical Reason," in her *Creating the Kingdom of Ends* (Cambridge: Cambridge University Press, 1996), pp. 312–34. In her lexicon, scepticism about the motivational character of a moral theory always devolves into a question of content if for no other reason than because of the diverse routes through which the internalism requirement can be satisfied. So, for example, she concludes a discussion of Bernard Williams by claiming this his "argument does not show that if there were unconditional

nalist requirement does not directly or immediately exclude any externalist theory, where is the debate?

In reality, the complaint or worry about externalism is not formal but content-driven, and while the elaboration of these substantive quarrels with a particular range of purportedly externalist moral theories is stated in appropriately theoretical and analytic terms, behind those elaborations, what makes them intelligible as components of a serious debate, I want to argue, is the *experience* of disenchantment. Said more emphatically and widely, a large expanse of serious debates in modern moral philosophy, including debates about the proper role within such theories of reflection, ratiocination, emotion, decision, communal practice, theory, anti-theory, and so on, are best understood as distorted reflections of our nihilistic condition.[24] Intellectualism drives moral philosophy toward developing universalistic, formal, and procedural *theories* of morals, while the experience of alienation, disaffection, and disillusionment raises reflective protests defending some feature of individual and/or communal experience (emotion, will, concrete ties of affection, sociohistorical embeddedness). Affective scepticism is a response to a range of contents

principles of reason applying to action we could not be motivated by them. He only thinks there are none. But Williams' argument, like Hume's, gives the appearance of going the other way round: it looks as if the motivational point – the internalism requirement – is supposed to have some force in limiting what might count as a principle of practical reason. Whereas in fact, the real source of scepticism is a doubt about the existence of principles of action whose content shows them to be ultimately justified" (p. 329). Where I disagree with Korsgaard is in thinking that the truth of the first sentence of this passage entails the argument of the rest. Trivially, it does not follow from the fact that any principle *could* satisfy the internalism requirement, that all principles of practical reason could satisfy it *equally well.* So there are worries about the relative *availability* of different kinds of principles for incorporation, *how* various principles are incorporated into our motivational sets, the *costs* of incorporation, the *consequences* of incorporation for agents' self-understanding and continuing self-identity, the *coordination* between moral motivation and other components of our motivational sets, and, finally, the *form of their social reproducibility.* It is just these sorts of considerations that are operative in Nietzsche's analysis of nihilism – how certain types of content undermine not just moral motivation but the motivational requirements for non-self-defeating modes of agency – and Weber's concern about the "iron cage." As I state it in the following paragraph: having only rationalized principles available and/or incorporating them into one's motivational set "hurts" and hence damages individual agency. What I term "hurt" is thus the general effect of the *way* in which rationalized moral principles relate to subjectivity, and thus the *way* they satisfy (or fail to satisfy) the various modalities (availability, manner, costs, consequences, coordination, and social reproducibility) of the internalism requirement. While the internalism requirement is thus not a fully independent variable that can be stipulated apart from all content, it is a relative variable for the analysis of formations of practical reason, and its satisfaction is not reducible to "content scepticism" in Korsgaard's sense. Affective scepticism exists; it is what disenchantment brings about.

24 To say that theoretical and analytic considerations are distorted is not to suggest that they are wrong or irrelevant; it is to claim that they can be appreciated and their worth evaluated only in the context of an overall assessment and diagnosis of rationalized modernity.

sharing a body of characteristics. The fundamental objection to externalist theories, what in fact supports the claim that they are external, is not that they cannot in principle be incorporated into individuals' motivational sets (almost anything can), but that they are representative and functional components of a generalised experience of disenchantment and societal rationalization that *hurts*.[25] Symptoms of this hurt are complex, multifarious, and can be experienced directly (as forms of psychic damage) or indirectly (as forms of flight from hurt). Hurt marks the limits of the appeal and claim of rationalized theory and analytic reflection: even if we possess rational reflection only for the purpose of spelling out, explaining, criticising, and proposing alternatives to the condition of damage, it is hurt itself which sustains the debate, and best explains the continuing proliferation of moral conceptions, rationalistic and anti-rationalistic. Hurt is the practical or existential condition through which internalism and externalism come to appear as opposed and irreconcilable value orientations. But if this is correct, then we should not expect rational criticism of moral theories to be themselves value-neutral and formally analytic in character; rather, criticism will have to be a contextual and perspectival elaboration of the experiential dilemmas raised by the process of disenchantment.

Objections to externalist moral theory tend to take two forms: either an objection to certain characteristic *features* of modern moral theory (formalism, proceduralism, abstractness), and/or an objection to the standing of these accounts as *theories*. Both forms claim that rationalized morality is indifferent to, squanders, and distorts individual ethical experience, and thereby the claims of individuality properly understood. Critiques of moral rationalism, then, are made from the standpoint of disaffection and injury, and may, if they intend a justification and immediate restoration of individuality or self-sufficient community, form a prelude to flight. If it is correct to claim that modern moral theory is rationalized in the Weberian sense, then one would expect the standard complaints against them to have the form: rationalized moral reasons are dislocated from the motivating reasons of concrete moral agents. So indeed three typical complaints are: (1) rationalized moral theories offer agents one reason too many for the morality of actions they do perform; (2) rationalized theories are impersonal, sacrificing the good or worth of individuals to an additive good which is distinct from any individual's conception of his or her own good; (3) as theories, rationalized conceptions prohibit a mutually supporting confluence of justifying and

25 Hurt, which is here a general term for the effect of the systematic failure of coordination between justifying and motivating reasons, is one specification of what Adorno's refers to as "damaged life," to be discussed in Chapter 1 below. The issue of "life" in damaged life is taken up in Chapter 4.

irreducibly individual motivating reasons, thereby creating a duality within the moral agent in which the standpoint of justification and evaluation must be kept distinct from the standpoint of action. In each of these there is, at least, an implicit reference to a superseded first-person perspective.

For heuristic purposes, simplifying and exaggerating massively: (1) I go to the hospital to see my friend K. When K inquires as to why I have come to see him, I reply: because he is my friend, *and* because it is a rule of morality that one ought to offer comfort to friends in times of distress. Could not K complain that if my deliberative reason for coming to see him was to satisfy a duty of friendship, and not because he was in distress, then I have wronged the ties of friendship that bind us, subsuming them under a body of rules having nothing to do with him or us? There is, K thinks, something *cold,* chilling and inhuman, in my reasons for coming.[26] (2) Because it seeks the aggregate maximum welfare, it is argued that consequentialism ignores the rights and worth of individuals. K is perfectly healthy; but there are ten patients in the hospital each with urgent needs: a liver transplant, a kidney transplant, a heart transplant, and so on. To produce the maximum welfare, K will be *sacrificed* in order to save and/or improve the lives of the ten.[27] (3) Consider (1) again, but now from my perspective rather than K's. How am I to understand and experience my hospital visit with K? *Either* I am content with the role theory plays in my deliberations, in which case I am foregoing one of the intrinsic goods of friendship, namely, the spontaneous or direct concern for another's welfare (and so not experiencing my role as K's friend; a

26 For a discussion of the "coldness" of rationalized reason, see Chapter 8. Railton, "Alienation, Consequentialism, and Morality," pp. 136–8, broaches this question. The locus classicus of the "one reason too many" complaint for contemporary discussions is Bernard Williams, "Persons, Character and Morality," in *Moral Luck,* pp. 17–18.

27 On the logic of "sacrifice" here, see 4. For this objection to utilitarianism, see the discussion of Bernard Williams in J. J. C. Smart and Bernard Williams, *Utilitarianism For and Against* (Cambridge: Cambridge University Press, 1973); John Rawls, *A Theory of Justice* (Cambridge, Mass: Harvard University Press, 1971), remarks that classical utilitarianism fails "to take serious the plurality and distinctness of individuals" (p. 29), and therefore, by necessarily regarding persons as potentially means to the welfare of others, must "be prepared to impose on them lower prospects of life for the sake of the higher expectations of others" (p. 180). Inevitably this entails some having to make "sacrifices" (p. 180) for the sake of the welfare of others. While any reasonable consequentialist doctrine should be able to simply block a clumsy example like the one above, I am always unclear about how this is to be done without bringing in some nonutilitarian doctrine like inviolable rights or a publicity criterion. Unless a rule or principle is brought in that cannot be traded off against aggregate satisfaction, then somewhere along the line a case like mine, if less extreme, will arise. For this reason, I do not in the course of this work examine consequentialist theories – I have nothing to add to standard critiques. I think the real issue about consequentialism is not its validity, but its entrenchment: its continuing *appeal* relates to its embeddedness within and its convergence with rationalized social practices that leave individuals *no option* but to employ its deliberative mechanisms.

form of the paradox of hedonism); *or* since directness is part of the good of friendship and I want to experience it, then I must keep secret from myself (and keep secret my secret-keeping) that my justifying reason for the visit is its accord with the theoretical requirements for happiness maximising, say, and therefore I must become a divided (or "schizophrenic") moral agent: the deliberating part of me wholly consumed with theoretical calculation as to the best form of life, the acting part blindly and unknowingly pursuing the goods of direct engagement (love, friendship, community, etc.; a form of consequentialism's "secrecy" or "esotericism" problem).[28]

Circulating around these criticisms of rationalized morality there is a curious tension: on the one hand, there is a claim that theory does not belong to morality, that theories have no "right" to legislate moral sentiments, and thus "do not even look as though they were relevant to the question – so soon, at least, as morality is seen as something whose *real existence* must consist in personal experience and social institutions, not in sets of propositions."[29] On the other hand, these very same analyses acknowledge disenchantment, societal rationalization, and the disappearance of morality from the world: " . . . morality itself is problematical, not merely in its content, *but in its supposed existence* as a dimension of practical thought or social evaluation at all";[30] or, the preeminence of duty, rightness, and obligation in moral theory "fits naturally with theories developed in a time of diminishing personal relations; of a time when the ties holding people together and easing the frictions of their various enterprises were less and less affection; of a time when commercial relations superseded family (or family-like) relations; of a time of growing individualism."[31] One cannot directly (and without either nostalgia or blind utopianism) make a plea for individuality and concrete personal and communal attachments while acknowledging that they have lost their place in our world; if rationalized moral theories arise as part of a complex social process, then this must be included in their analysis. Something in the way of a closer fit between the sociological presuppositions of modern theory (their socio-historical belonging) and the critical analysis of their failings is required.[32]

28 See Michael Stocker, "The Schizophrenia of Modern Ethical Theories," in Robert B. Kruschwitz and Robert C. Roberts, *The Virtues: Contemporary Essays on Moral Character* (Belmont, Calif: Wadsworth Publishing Company, 1987), pp. 36–45. For a useful series of essays interrogating the role of theory generally in ethics, including a very useful bibliography, see Stanley G. Clarke and Evan Simpson (eds.), *Anti-Theory in Ethics and Moral Conservatism* (Albany: State University of New York Press, 1989).

29 Williams, *Moral Luck,* Preface, p. x, emphasis mine.

30 Ibid.; emphasis mine.

31 Stocker, "The Schizophrenia of Modern Ethical Theories," p. 43.

32 There are accounts that attempt to provide such a fit between sociological explanation and philosophical analysis, most notably, Alasdair MacIntyre's *After Virtue* (London: Duckworth, 1981), and Ross Poole's *Morality and Modernity* (London: Routledge, 1991).

While Adorno would not want to deny the complaints against externalist theories just canvassed (they are another form of the critique of disenchanted, rationalized society), his own characteristic way of looking at the situation, fully acceding to the sociological conundrum it expresses, is in terms of a *problem*: disenchantment and societal rationalization generate a systematic separation of universal and particular, of which the dichotomy between justifying reasons and motivating reasons, between truth conditions and acceptance conditions, between rationalized practice and vocation, are but articulations – but they *are* articulations of this duality, and hence their separation is actual. The systematic separation of universal and particular distorts both; because both are distorted by their separation, because neither is what it pretends to be without the support of the other (Weber's argument for the continuing relevance of vocation), then the condition of separation may be construed as rationalization dirempting, tearing apart, universal and particular, disfiguring and deforming them both. Said otherwise: there is a nonarbitrary homology or elective affinity between disenchanted theories, on the one hand, and rationalized social practices, on the other. They are abstract universals (the universality of rationalised, abstract, agent-neutral social practices – society as an abstracting universal – and rationalized, universalist moral theories) which, in their different ways (institutionally and theoretically) squander the sensuously particular in its particularity; what is thus squandered and dispensed with, in its deformed state, Adorno calls "the nonidentical." It is because there is something wrong or distorted about the kind of universality and abstractness of rationalized theory, and equally, something deformed about the individual that is produced by rationalized social practices, and hence because what universal and particular have come to mean and be are deformed, that Adorno believes that *both* justifying reasons and motivating reasons as now conceived are deformed; it is because both rationalized universality and particularity are deformed that Adorno believes that modernity suffers not only from a deficit of meaning, but equally from a deficit of rationality.

The dilemma is profound: if the Weberian diagnosis as interpreted by Adorno is correct, then as yet we have nothing approaching a normative account explaining *how a wholly secular form of life can be rationally compelling and intrinsically motivating*. This formula expresses the prereflective animus of the demand for internalism as processed through the sociological comprehension of rationalized moral theories. Better, the formula is the theoretical expression of the dissatisfaction with modern moral theories from the perspective of hurt: affective scepticism is a sign and symp-

In general, Poole tends to marshal nihilism, disenchantment, and societal rationalization in relation to moral theory in much the same manner as I have in this Introduction.

tom of failure. Internalism is not primarily a theoretical demand (again, because in principle it can be satisfied so easily); rather it expresses in theoretical terms a dissatisfaction with what has happened to universality and particularity as a consequence of the disenchanting and rationalizing processes of modernity. Stating the matter this way presupposes there are no safe or privileged subject positions from which an objective account of our dilemma can be posed: all individual standpoints are damaged (hence the necessity of Adorno's analysis being "partial" with which this Introduction began).

Direct expressions of hurt or damage are all too familiar: disillusionment, alienation, disaffection, boredom, despair, anger. The indirect expression of hurt in forms of flight from rationalization are more common, since they are precisely strategies for coping with and escaping hurt, and diverse in character:[33] cynical adaptation to the demands of rationalized society;[34] the redivinization of the world through the making of

33 Both the conception of "flight" and the first three items on my list are derived from Jeffrey Alexander's "The Dialectic of Individuation and Domination: Weber's Rationalization Theory and Beyond," pp. 198–200. In developing his typology, Alexander is following Weber's lead in his account of the "Directions of the Abnegation of the World," in *From Max Weber*, pp. 327–59. It is a good sociological question as to what extent Weber's account can be adapted to current conditions. Toward the conclusion of his essay Alexander offers a Durkheim-inspired suggestion, namely, that "modern social systems . . . can be organized so that irrationality is continually challenged by social movements that embody rational, emancipatory values, and so that domination is confronted by differentiated structures that institutionalize individual autonomy" (pp. 204–5). Something of what I analyse in terms of "fugitive ethics" is at stake in Alexander's deployment here of social movements. In broad terms, I argue that the best we can hope for, about the possibilities for which there is no reason to be sanguine, is that rationalizing processes are repeatedly challenged and transformed by social practices that create havens of symbolic renewal (in which justifying and motivating reasons are appropriately aligned) that nonetheless cannot themselves be fully incorporated into those rationalized systems. Hence, the suggestion is, rather than looking for rational, stable, and systematically reproducible social forms (a coherence model of society), we should be operating with a suitably adjusted anti-utopian (albeit thereby utopian) conflict model of ethics and society.

It is necessary to be careful about being too caustic and damning about forms of flight with respect to individuals. In the absence of alternatives, they represent (subjectively) rational strategies for dealing with affective scepticism despite the fact that they are irrational in relation to rationalized reason. So, despite his eventual genealogical critique, Nietzsche regarded the "advantages" of the Christian moral hypothesis as being that it "prevented man from despising himself as man, from taking sides against life; from despairing of knowledge: it was a *means of preservation*" (*The Will to Power*, p. 10).

Finally, because forms of flight are responses to the pervasive predicament of modern affective scepticism, I do not regard flight as either extensionally or intensionally equivalent to ideology. Of course, particular forms of flight (like cynicism or divinizing scientific naturalism) may partake of ideological strategies of naturalising historical practices, but even that does not make flight itself ideological in character. Not all accusations of irrationality are accusations of ideology. For the most part, I construe ideology as the attempt to naturalise and universalise the claims of rationalized conceptions of reason.

34 For an acute elaboration of cynical reason see Peter Sloterdijk, *Critique of Cynical Reason*, tr. Michael Eldred (London: Verso, 1988).

one fragment of modern life (a political creed, the practice of science) be the one, all-embracing meaning of the whole; a retreat into almost mystical "experientialism" as what, at the psychological level, rationalized society has eschewed (pursued most concretely in a dedication to eroticism or aestheticism); religious fundamentalism and the return of religion generally; obsessive consumerism and a commitment to life-style.[35] While requiring detailing and empirical corroboration, it does not seem untoward to hypothesise that these ideal types of hurt and flight exhaust the possibilities for modern individuals. What would then follow is a claim to the effect that most modern moral philosophy can be seen as being informed by and expressing either hurt or flight, or both. From the position of the victims of modernity, rationalized theories are cynical; sceptical approaches to morality are theoretically mediated expressions of hurt; and affirmative conceptions of anti-theory, virtue ethics, and communitarian positions each represent forms of flight, as do their more cautious nostalgic and utopian correlates. If even our best reflections on ethics are grounded in the distorting lens of hurt or flight, things cannot be better for modern moral agents.[36] While exorbitant, such an hypothesis would explain the disposition and tenor of the debates in modern moral philosophy, and the nagging feeling that these debates are somehow irresolvable.

Adorno's philosophy is routinely interpreted as directly embodying the pessimism implied by the intersection of the sociological picture of rationalized society and the philosophical dilemma of being left without a usable conception of reason. If there is a rationality deficit in modernity, and all subject positions are forms of hurt or flight, damaged, then how might a critical analysis of ethics advance? The acuteness of the social situation and Adorno's own commitment to some form of historicism in which there is no access to forms of reason and rationality that are not historically embodied appears to lead to an ethical cul-de-sac without recuperative possibilities.[37] At best, our ethics can be just a kind of non-

35 This last may, in fact, be thought of as a form of pathological distraction and diversion, in which case it is a modality of boredom, and thus a direct expression of damage. I expect that consumerism and life-style possess both hurt and flight forms.

36 I tend to think of this in terms of the options available for individuals to relate to their own most fundamental moral beliefs (if they have any). Could a modern moral agent avoid being either ironical or cynical or dogmatic (holding their beliefs as a matter of faith) or despairing or what I term a "fragile" moralist, torn between moral beliefs and the claims of desire and self-interest, never sure about the propriety or impropriety of either belief or desire? Typically, I suspect that we each relate to our beliefs in all these ways in different proportions. I work through this suggestion, indirectly, in Chapter 2.

37 The depth and character of critical theory historicism needs consideration below. For the present I am assuming that it minimally involves the Hegelian requirement that all possibilities of human action be grounded in some existing actuality, or, as Bernard Williams states the same thesis, "how a concretely experienced form of life can be ex-

complicity with official culture, while at the same time being an aporetical realisation of there being no possibility (and no real legitimacy) for any serious noncomplicity.[38] Perhaps, then, it can be an ethics which acknowledges the harm it has done to the nonidentical and an expression of guilt for having done so.

2. A Grammar of Moral Insight, a Logic of the Concept

To begin outlining how Adorno seeks to surmount this dilemma or, rather, demonstrate how his philosophy construes the dilemma differently than it originally appears, I again want to proceed indirectly. Because standard moral themes are only rarely directly addressed by Adorno, the problem arises as to how we are to relate what he does say to the problems of moral philosophy. Part of the answer is to relate the process of disillusionment and disenchantment of traditional morality to the structure Adorno and Horkheimer entitle "the dialectic of enlightenment," and to construe this structure in terms of the socially substantive interpretation of the problem of externalism. But this will take us only part of the way since it fails to provide a framework through which these problems themselves and their bearing on issues of reason, rationality, and the like can be processed. For these wider purposes a wider interpretative grid is required.

In his now classic essay, "The Concept of Moral Insight and Kant's Doctrine of the Fact of Reason," Dieter Henrich offers an inductively grounded four-part analysis of the concept of moral insight.[39] Although Henrich does not offer much in the way of empirical evidence for his induction, he presumes that its elements will strike the reader as revealing a formal structure or grammar of moral insight that accurately captures what is shared by the quite different moral theories of Plato, Aristotle, British moral sense theorists, Kant, Hegel, and others. In contemporary parlance, what Henrich's analysis might be said to provide is an account of the formal constraints which any successful account of moral insight must satisfy.[40] By being formal in this way, we are afforded the opportu-

tended, rather than considering how a universal program is to be applied"; *Ethics and the Limits of Philosophy*, p. 104.

38 I owe this formulation to a suggestion of Robert Pippin.

39 Dieter Henrich, *The Unity of Reason: Essays on Kant's Philosophy* (London: Harvard University Press, 1994), pp. 55–87. "The Concept of Moral Insight" was translated by Manfred Kuehn.

40 For an account of such constraints, see Christine Korsgaard, *The Sources of Normativity* (Cambridge: Cambridge University Press, 1996), pp. 16–18. At this formal level, there is not much of a gap between Henrich and Korsgaard. For an analogous presentation, see Jean-Francois Lyotard, "Levinas' Logic," trans. Ian McLeod in Andrew Benjamin (ed.), *The Lyotard Reader* (Oxford: Basil Blackwell, 1989), pp. 275–313. Lyotard's work in this area is not, I think, adequately appreciated.

nity of inquiring whether any of Adorno's substantive views on reason, rationality, knowing, and the self can be seen as satisfying the formal analysis, and thus themselves providing an account of moral insight. Relating Adorno's general philosophical views to this formal framework thus forms a recurrent theme and a central plank in my strategy.

Despite the fact that Henrich's analysis is formal, an abstract grammar of moral insight, and no matter how inductively well based it is, it does not follow that his proposal is wholly neutral. Perhaps nothing we can conceive of could, rationally, satisfy its constraints; perhaps the distinction between theoretical and practical insight which Henrich attempts to elaborate through his analysis cannot be sustained. It is fundamental to Henrich's grammar that there is an intimate connection between truth conditions and acceptance conditions in practical reasoning. In this respect, the entire analysis begs the question against forms of consequentialism which regard their truth as quite independent of their acceptability and hence fit with agents' own motivating self-conceptions. To state the matter more generally, if means-ends reasoning is not truly a brand of practical reasoning in its classical sense, because it is only the *application* of causal analysis and reasoning to practical problems, then perhaps *the ultimate victim of disenchantment is practical reason in its classical or traditional sense.*[41] Nothing like moral insight survives the disenchantment of the world and societal rationalization. This would explain views, like those of Bernard Williams, which claim the very existence of morality is a question and issue for us; and it coheres well with the worries of Nietzsche and Weber. Their view, however, that the way in which truth and scientific rationality have become our highest values undermines the conditions of agency presupposes that something having the formal shape of the traditional doctrine of moral reason is a necessary condition for human agency *überhaupt.* In their different ways, Nietzsche and Weber answer this dilemma by biting the bullet: if something with the formal characteristics of practical reason traditionally understood is *necessary* for the possibility of human agency, and nothing satisfying those formal requirements also satisfies the requirements of our highest values, then something other than truth and reason must, of necessity, be highest for us. The practical contradiction between truth and scientific reason and the requirements for practical agency licenses their nonrationalist qualifications of truth and reason. Again, Adorno broadly shares their analysis of the situation, but not their response to it. Nonetheless, it is important to keep in mind the shape of the problem: what reason has become may, from the perspective of the grammar of moral insight, eliminate the possibility of *practical reason* as such: we have reason but it is not practical;

41 This would be one way of interpreting, albeit not his, Hume's "reason is and ought to be the slave of the passions" doctrine.

we have practice, but it is not rational. So seeing the issue would certainly give force to the overall trajectory of the Nietzsche-Weber analysis of modernity.

Throughout his analysis, Henrich is guided by the belief that there is a categorial distinction to be drawn between theoretical and moral insight. Consider: a deductive or reflective demonstration of the good would necessarily fail because without individual acceptance and approval moral claims lose their capacity to be action-guiding. Part of the meaning of any statement of the form "X is morally good" is the claim that I accept and approve of X as governing (or as the ultimate goal) of my action. To say "X is morally good" and "I am wholly uninterested in X and have no intention of pursuing it or putting my desires and actions into relation with it" is tantamount to saying that X is not good (for me).[42] The morally good can determine action only if it demands and receives approval; hence insight into the morally good includes moments of *demand and approval.*[43] Without demand moral life could not be about claims *on* the self to act in an appropriate manner; all normativity would be lost. Without approval the demand could not be action-guiding. The demand/approval structure is the first element in the grammar of moral insight.[44]

Because moral insight does not occur without *antecedent* approval, it has been denied the status of knowledge – what is ideally available from different starting points through methodologically neutral mechanisms (i.e., proof and demonstration). The structure of demand and approval recapitulates the familiar aesthetic pattern of an imposing perception finding approval in a felt response. This analogy is accurate to the extent to which "the concept of the good cannot be defined without the inclusion of an element of meaning that indicates *the passivity of moral consciousness* in understanding the good."[45] Such passivity is taken as incommensurable with the theoretical affirmation of what is true. The passivity of moral consciousness, the felt character of the response to the demand of the good, the requirement that one has, as it were, always already approved of the good in order to see the demand placed on the self as good, and thus the necessary indexing of insight into the good to the agent having the insight (the constitutive perspectival character of moral insight) are all aspects of moral insight that have led to sceptical doubts about the

42 A neutralization of the claim of the good of this form must be separated from the quite different phenomenon of experiencing the claim of the good and disobeying or acting against it. The sceptic is uninterested in the good while the wrong-doer pulls away from it. It is a reasonable hypothesis that the difference between wrong-doing and scepticism is a matter of degree and hence that there is a continuum in which obedience and skeptical disinterest are the extreme points.

43 "The Concept of Moral Insight," pp. 61–2.

44 I take the first element of Henrich's to encapsulate the central thrust of internalism.

45 "The Concept of Moral Insight," p. 62; emphasis mine.

objectivity of morality. Yet it is evident that these features of moral experience can be considered as grammatical in nature, and hence as identifiable independently of any particular account of the good.

While the demand/approval structure has come to hibernate in the presumed noncognitive sphere of the aesthetic, the demand of the good cannot be reduced to a case of factual being-affected, any more than can the aesthetic. In the case of moral insight, the demand/approval structure is on firmer ground than in aesthetics since despite the moment of passivity, what is approved is necessarily available for discursive articulation, where this articulation itself makes a claim to cognition, to knowledge. Even in the case of Kant's Categorical Imperative, the demand, which is how Henrich interprets Kant's "fact of reason" doctrine,[46] is hermeneutically fleshed out, for example, in terms of nonuniversalisable actions failing to respect the equal autonomy of all agents, and hence as treating others as mere means for the achievement of one's own ends. Hence in approving the Categorical Imperative one would be approving a certain characterisation of agents as autonomous beings, of what the difference amounted to between autonomous beings and mere things, and of what responding to others as autonomous beings as opposed to mere things involves, how, that is, such responding is captured in acting under the guidance of the universalisation formula. Unless, however inarticulately, some such knowledge were at work in responding to the Categorical Imperative, it would not be the Categorical Imperative to which one was responding. Hence, second, *moral consciousness must be a form of insight and knowledge.*

The third element of the grammar of moral insight, according to Henrich, and the one which shows its distinctly modern aspect, concerns the relation between the approval given to the demand of the good and the self which does the approving. We have already begun to broach this claim in noting how the demand of the good is indexed to an agent via the passivity through which it can come to be recognized. But let me quote Henrich at length.

> Although the good does not come into view through a self-reflective act of the individual [i.e., the good is not discovered as a merely reflectively grasped theoretical or transcendental presupposition of the possibility of moral action – a move which would short-circuit the demand/approval structure], it still is a form of self-understanding; indeed, the privileged form of self-understanding. *Approval, without which the good is nothing, is the expression of the good's obligatory character for the existence of the self.* . . . When I know in moral insight what is good, I also know that I understand myself in

46 Ibid., p. 83: "Kant claimed that [moral insight] contains necessity and therefore can be assigned only to reason. The demand of the good is thus the only fact of reason, and it is at the same time the only such fact conceivable."

> relation to it, or that I must understand myself in relation to it in order to become a self. The first is the case in substantial moral relations, the second in moral conflicts.
>
> Accordingly, this approval is a spontaneous achievement of the self. We can say that by means of this approval, the self first constitutes itself as a self. . . . In insight, the mere presence of things, or in the process of the movement of its thoughts, the self as self has receded in order to do justice to thought itself. However, moral insight is also part of the self. Without the consent of the self it cannot come to be; and this self is in turn rooted in its approval.[47]

Henrich is here working within a Kantian frame of reference. He assumes the validity of Kant's thesis that "it must be possible for the 'I think' to accompany all my representations" in order for them to be representations for or to me. The apperception thesis points to the self-awareness that is implicated in any mental act which is discriminable: I could not plausibly be said to be *asserting* or *judging* or *perceiving* unless I am coaware, could become aware, that it is "this" act that "I" am doing.[48] In ordinary perception or representational reflection the "I think" remains recessive, a presupposition which need not itself appear, since the effort of the mind is (apperceptively) directed (direction being the accomplishment of apperception) at its perceptual or thought object. Even if the accompaniment is necessary, it is also muted to the point of silence at the moment of mental activity since were it to sound it would obscure what is to be seen or known. Thoughtful representational attending involves and requires a certain self-forgetfulness. This self-forgetfulness is the apperceptive origin of the claim that true knowing involves the elimination of subjective projection or interference, a removal of the self from the scene represented. From the Kantian perspective, which at this level of generality Adorno accepts, the naturalistic thesis which conceives of the ideal of knowing as one which presents the world as it would be without *any* subjective accompaniment, forgets the self-forgetfulness of representational thought, hence fails to acknowledge how the muting of self is an accomplishment of the self. Recession forgotten becomes reduction and elimination, as we argue below.

How is theoretical apperception to be distinguished from practical apperception? The recessive character of the apperceptive moment of theoretical insight normatively frames the standard epistemological thesis that the object of theoretical insight is subject-indifferent: the object of

47 Ibid., p. 63.

48 For a lucid defence of this thesis, see Robert Pippin, "Kant on the Spontaneity of Mind," in his *Idealism as Modernism: Hegelian Variations* (Cambridge: Cambridge University Press, 1997), pp. 29–55. See p. 41 for a critique of Henrich's own interpretation of the apperception doctrine.

theoretical insight is (ideally) *constituted* as determinate independently of the standing of the self with respect to it. In contrast, moral insight concerns precisely the standing of the self with respect to the good, the morally good formally being just what constitutes relations between the self and its others with respect to what is to be done. Hence, if the morally good exists, it can do so only through the self *taking* it as determinative for itself. Without so taking it, without approving it and making it my good, the good would be indeterminate, or, to use the language of theoretical apperception, without the "I approve it" the good "would be impossible, or at least nothing to me"; but a good that is nothing to me, or by extension, anyone, is no "good" at all. If the meaning of the morally good is what orients or determines action, then it can *appear* only in the context of action-determination. But if it can only appear as what orients action, then it becomes determinate only in relation to what it makes possible. The actuality of the morally good is hence bound to the moral performance which it governs and makes possible.

In the first instance, the binding of moral insight to its performative actualisation derives from its role as action guiding. But this thesis can take on its full sense only if the self is conceived of as itself becoming determinate with respect to its fundamental identity through, at least in part, its own agency. Although human beings are not free to make themselves into anything whatsoever, it remains the case that who I am is in part determined by who I take myself to be; human agency is in part constituted by the conception of agency individuals give to themselves. Each form of human comportment toward the world presupposes a (normative) conception of the self which carries a conception of agency and action with it. To conceive of oneself as a Christian, for example, is to conceive of oneself as possessing an immortal soul and mortal body; one's eternal fate, the fate of one's soul, is determined by how one preserves and responds to the gift of mortal life. That one's soul, one's true self, is immortal, that the self has a fate (saved or damned), that one's future fate is related to one's mortal acts, one's care for mortal life, all belong to the very idea of being a Christian self which forms the horizon within which all one's doings take place and have meaning. But, then, to conceive of oneself as a libertine or a preference maximiser will operate in the same way.

Approval is a "spontaneous achievement of the self" in that the self that does the approving is in part a product of its act of approval. Henrich refers to this modern conception of human identity and agency when he claims that only through approval does the self first constitute itself as a self.[49] Whoever the self is, it is constituted (in part) through its self-con-

49 In Martin Heidegger's *Being and Time*, trans. John Macquarrie and Edward Robinson (New York: Harper and Row, 1962), this becomes the thesis that for Dasein (say, human

ception of what being a self involves. Hence, for any self it is true that it performatively realises (or fails) some conception of the good, that it has always already given its approval to some good: "The self of concrete existence can become itself not by abstractly knowing some idea (the good), but by making a factual choice."[50] Choice presupposes that the demand of the good has been felt (thus providing motive for choice) and approved. While the feeling does not cause the approval (moral knowledge too is involved), feeling must be a component if the demand is going to be sufficient for choice and action. Because the factual choice of the self presupposes what is thereby chosen, no self can emerge without always already having chosen itself, and hence being in permanent cognitive deficit to its conditions of possibility. Nonetheless, the very idea of a human self and human agency operates within the matrix of a normative self-understanding presupposed by or with the act through which the self comes into being. But this is tantamount to claiming that the structural characterisation of moral insight in its differentiation from theoretical insight is necessarily performatively actual and operative insofar as there are human selves at all. Or, to state the point more unequivocally: "Moral insight founds the self."[51]

Finally, then, the concatenation of these three features of moral insight leads to a characterisation of its ontological significance. The key to Henrich's analysis here is the contrast between the recessive character of the self in theoretical cognition and the explicit choice of the self in

being) its very "being is an *issue* for it" (p. 32), that is, something that must be determined in one way or another in order for it to be. Nor is this overlap with this portion of the grammatical analysis of moral insight accidental here; as I hope to show at a future date, the whole of *Being and Time* can be construed as the attempt to transform the formal analysis of traditional moral insight into the deep existential structure of the very possibility of there being human beings inhabiting what they regard as an intelligible world in general. Heidegger signals this intention in denominating Dasein's ontological structure "care," *Sorge*. The strength of this approach is that it builds into the very nature of what it is to be a human being the constraints that have typically been assigned to only moral insight or practical reasoning. Its weakness is that in order to accomplish this, the conception generated remains, however richly articulated, merely formal, a formality which critics of Heidegger's notion of "authenticity" have been quick to point out. Nonetheless, I suspect that Heidegger's general strategy, here and elsewhere, is deeply formative for Adorno.

50 "The Concept of Moral Insight," p. 227, n. 5. In presenting this claim as a wholly conceptual or, as I am terming it, grammatical issue, Henrich is indirectly debunking its transcendental presentation in Heidegger's *Being and Time*. For reasons that become apparent below, the whole question as to whether this thesis should be understood in transcendental or merely grammatical terms is very close to the centre of the debate about the kind of mutual implication that exists between "the good" and the self. In accordance with what one might call his "historicism," Adorno is opposed to any conception of transcendental conditions. For another attempt to give the requirements of moral insight a transcendental status, see Charles Taylor, *Sources of the Self: the Making of Modern Identity* (Cambridge, Mass: Harvard University Press, 1989), chapters 1–2.

51 Ibid., p. 64.

moral insight. Knowledge of the good, and hence the characteristic features of moral insight itself, become available only when performatively realised. Unless the conditions of moral insight (approval, motivational force, and conviction) are satisfied, the good *as* good cannot be *recognised* (known and understood), where nonrecognition means that in employing the basic concepts of ethics "I deal only with empty, incomprehensible formulas"[52] – the concepts of the ethical, again, "would be impossible, or at least nothing to me." In contrast now with theoretical cognition, the self and the good that founds it are not ever-present, necessarily *there* in full clarity, transcendentally presupposed and actual. It is a matter of degree. If moral insight into the good becomes available only with its actually being chosen, which is coextensive with the choice of the self, then where the good is mitigated (under the influence of involuntary forces), refused (wrong-doing or simply acting in accordance with what everyone else does), or indefinitely deferred, then the good can be obliterated or become a representational object (as if available to theoretical cognition), and the individual becomes, as it were, a walking version of the recessive self of theoretical cognition. *If moral insight founds the self, then vice withers self and good.*[53] Under the influence of raw needs and desires, the uncoded play of pleasure and pain, moral insight is blocked; vice destroys principle here in the sense that the self attempts to cut itself off from the *form* of object relatedness required by moral insight. To act otherwise than for the sake of the good is thereby to act under the belief that the good has no place in the world. Conversely, approval "is identical with the affirmation *that* the good exists. The practical contradiction with the demand denies its existence. Therefore moral insight places all being under the condition that the good is possible in it."[54] The *appear-*

52 Ibid.

53 I am here referring to the following passage from Aristotle's *Nichomachean Ethics,* translated by Terence Irwin (Indianapolis, Indiana: Hackett Publishing Company, 1985): "For the sort of supposition that is corrupted and perverted by what is pleasant or painful is not every sort – not, e.g., the supposition that the triangle does or does not have two right angles – but the supposition about what is done in action. For the origin of what is done in action is the goal it aims at and if pleasure or pain has corrupted someone, it follows that the origin will not appear to him. Hence it will not be apparent that this must be the goal and cause of all his choice and action; for vice corrupts the origin [or: vice is destructive of principle]," 1140b13–20. Part of the deep attraction to me of Henrich's formal account is that it makes sense of Aristotle's "vice corrupts the origin" doctrine; and the appeal of that doctrine is that it suggests in terms internal to ethics just how the good, whatever it is (and if there is some), cannot just fail to be seen, but be corrupted, removed from existence not just locally, as Aristotle supposes occurs to the dissolute, but generally. Nihilism is an historical version of the thesis that vice corrupts the origin, and disenchantment the process through which that "vice" takes hold. What the process of nihilism and the vice corrupts origin doctrine share is what I call "the performativity thesis": no ethical good without demand, approval and performative actualisation in experience. It is the performativity thesis that best explains why actuality is prior to possibility.

54 "The Concept of Moral Insight," p. 66; practically: ought implies can.

ing of the good, which is coextensive with both realising and showing how the world includes the good, is conditional upon the performance of activities explicitly enacted within the horizon it makes possible. Moral insight into the good, the choice of the good and the performance of acts it licenses, and the revealing of the world as a place in which the good is actually possible all mutually imply one another.

Now I have wanted to elaborate Henrich's account of the grammar of moral insight at some length because I wanted to give a sense of how *seductive* this grammar is, how, although nothing of any content is being urged, it is almost as if simply by announcing this grammar, above all the way in which it fixes the demand of the good in relation to passivity and feeling, on the one hand, and then identifies what is demanded and felt as what founds the self on the other hand, that the morally good, the ethical, was somehow legitimated and salvaged. Nonetheless, the account is only formal; at most, one might say that we *need* a conception of the good if we are to be the sort of agents we have traditionally thought ourselves to be. The depth of this need structurally underwrites Nietzsche's and Weber's diagnosis of the nihilistic character of modernity. Nothing, however, supports the hypothesis that there is some one good which could, even in principle, satisfy the requirements of the analysis. On the contrary, from the point of view of the present, it is difficult to conceive of any object, material or immaterial, that could fulfil the place of "the good" in this analysis, which makes moral scepticism look plausible.[55] Nor, despite their attempt to non-cognitively approximate the broad contours of the grammar of moral insight, do the Nietzschean or Weberian solutions appear sufficient: they suggest, however differently, that agents give to themselves (by creation or commitment, respectively) the horizon of meaning that is withdrawn through the advancement of knowledge. By so doing they qualify the passivity of moral consciousness, making the first element of the structure, demand and approval, utterly secondary. Despite themselves, Nietzsche and Weber are unable to sustain significant passivity, a passivity of consciousness that is not, eventually, debilitating; hence they cannot make central to their thought a conception of the pervasive and yet rational character of human *dependence*,[56] which is precisely what is required if anything like an unchosen demand upon the self is to be possible.

55 The assertion of a pervasive scepticism should be unsurprising since it is a direct or indirect premise of most liberal political thought. It is indirectly presupposed when liberalism assumes that each individual is in possession of or entitled to their own conception of the good life for man (moral pluralism), without even attempting to ensure that any life deserves to be truly characterised as "good." Which is what leads to the sceptical strategy in the defence of liberalism: assuming we no longer know what is good or that there can no longer be a rational consensus concerning the good, what institutional arrangements can we agree to that do not impose on any individual other individuals' unjustifiable conception of the good?

56 It is no wonder that Zarathustra grows weary of his creations; because they are *his* cre-

Adorno's philosophy is best seen as an inflection of Weber's analysis of disenchantment and societal rationalization. Apart from its sheer success, the central reason why Weber regards the processes of disenchantment and rationalization as irreversible is that their development occurs through a thoroughly historical process. Because there is no "outside" to this historical process, no rational end governing the whole, then there is no reason or rationality that may judge or qualify it; rationalized reason *is* our reason. Adorno continues and yet attempts to go behind the dialectic of nihilism and disenchantment projected by Nietzsche and Weber. Nietzsche indicts modern rationalism as still theological; Weber indicts it as the fate of religious rationalization that fails to acknowledge its own "religious" (vocational) presuppositions. Adorno dialectically reverses this indictment: if religious rationalization degenerates into a self-stultifying modern scientific rationalism, then that end can, must, be projected back into the process through which it emerged: religious and mythic forms of life are already predicated upon the instrumental rationality, identity thinking, they will become. By proposing that we can view the past this way, Adorno is *not* proposing an alternative history or replacing genealogy with a dialectical history of his own. Nowhere does Adorno suggest a narrative of secularisation that is meant to compete with existing narratives. Adorno's concern is with an analytic structure rather than an historical process: if we can come to comprehend religious rationalization as itself already instrumentally rational (enlightening, a form of identity thinking), then what we think of as "religious" and as "secular" are coextensive, and the problem with both, only fully revealed in their present formation, is their conception of reason and rationality. For Adorno this entails that not only does religious and mythic thought contain a rational kernel, but scientifically rational thought contains a mythic core. The rational and mythic core of thought is univocal: identity thinking as the subsumption of individuality (sensuous particularity) under a coherent, unifying, simplifying, explanatory universal (myth, god, natural law, unified science). Rationalization means the comprehension and/or meaning of individuals is increasingly had through their

ations, they ultimately do not demand approval. For a critique of Nietzsche that turns on the lack of constitutive passivity in his philosophy, see Michael Allen Gillespie's immensely useful *Nihilism Before Nietzsche* (Chicago: Chicago University Press, 1995). For my own briefer version of this argument: "Autonomy and Solitude," in Keith Ansell-Pearson (ed.), *Nietzsche and Modern German Thought* (London: Routledge, 1991), pp. 192–215. In opposition to these critiques, one might argue that there is in both Nietzsche and Weber an antecedent moment of, let's call it, "faith" in the potential worth and dignity of human life that motivates each theory.

Two other accounts of modernity that criticise it for its lack of significant passivity are: Bernard Yack, *The Longing for Total Revolution: Philosophic Sources of Social Discontent from Rousseau to Marx and Nietzsche* (Princeton, N.J.: Princeton University Press, 1986), and Amos Funkenstein, *Theology and the Scientific Imagination from the Middle Ages to the Seventeenth Century* (Princeton, N.J.: Princeton University Press, 1986).

location within conceptual schemes whose fundamental terms are invariant and unchanging. Hence, while in accordance with the grammar of moral insight the fundamental relation between universal and particular is *actualisation* (becoming determinate) through individual performance, in theoretical reason the relation is one of *subsumption*, individuals as mere tokens of given types.

By staking his philosophy on a critique of scientific rationalism, Adorno is following what is by now a well-worn path. Almost all critiques of scientific rationalism share the attempt to demonstrate that it possesses necessary conditions that it cannot eschew, take account of, or get on level terms with.[57] However, since in almost all cases what these demonstrations reveal are nonrational conditions for rational thought, then they inevitably suffer from two deficiencies: they leave the gap separating justifying reasons and motivating reasons unbridged, and thereby leave the nonrational exposed to sceptical attack from the perspective of reason (or the inversion of this: simply espouse the cause of the nonrational). Insofar as these deficiencies remain, then an intrinsically satisfying portrayal of a wholly secular form of life has yet to be provided. If scientific rationality eliminates its own motivating conditions (where these are construed as *reasons* for action), then – Adorno can be construed as hypothesising – it is in itself insufficiently rational. Only an expansion of reason, rationality, and cognition will answer the dilemma of disenchantment; and if this expansion is to be keyed to the diagnosis of scientific rationalism as a process of systematically negating particularity in favour of universality (the movement of rationalization as identity thinking), then the direction of expansion will be the inclusion in reasoning of ineliminable moments of dependency and particularity. The depth, pervasiveness, ineliminability, and constitutive role in rationality of dependence on sensuous particulars is, it might be said, Adorno's central thought.

Formally, to think through these moments of dependency and particularity involves having a conception of the elements of practical or ethical reasoning that, minimally, will satisfy the requirements of the Henrich analysis, while noting that in one crucial respect Henrich's proposal evinces an element of identity thinking, namely, his framing of moral insight as being into "the" (one) good. For reasons that become apparent below, Adorno is best interpreted as attempting to preserve the fundamental structural characteristics of moral insight while conceding to en-

57 There have been numerous attempts to delegitimate scientific rationalism, to demonstrate why it is not unconditionally rational: ontological (Heidegger), linguistic (Wittgenstein), phenomenological (Merleau-Ponty), hermeneutical (Gadamer), categorial (Habermas), quasi-transcendental (Derrida), empiricist (Dupré), historical (Kuhn), and so on. Because these all attempt to reveal the conditioning of scientific rationality, then there is much in them that Adorno could and/or would need to affirm.

lightenment rationalization that there is no one good, formally or materially, orienting all human endeavour. Hence, in his account of the disenchanting of the world, Adorno contends that not only does it eliminate previous *objects* of ethical esteem, but more emphatically and importantly it eliminates what I want to call the *forms of object relation* that previously had been manifest in ethical reasoning: *experience, knowledge, and authority.* Disenchantment thus effects not only beliefs (trading in bad ones for good ones), and a transformation of the objects of knowledge (eliminating certain items – starting with the gods and coming to an extinguishing of values as belonging to the furniture of the universe) but even more significantly our *modes* of cognitive interaction with objects. It is in virtue of the enlightenment critique of reliance on experience and authority that ethical cognition too disappears (into sentiment, emotivism, will, etc.); and with the disappearance of ethical cognition the entire structure of moral insight collapses. Experience is shown below to relate to the moment of demand and approval, and authority will relate to both the role of experience in ethical knowing and the necessary deficit in rationality and cognition that dependence on antecedent approval for knowing leaves in its wake.[58] Vindicating the requisite notions of experience and authority is thus central to Adorno's defence of an expanded conception of reason.

These suggestions are provocative and are bound to meet with resistance. If they are going to succeed, then they will need entrenching within some more fundamental aspect of human thought and action. Or better, to demonstrate the centrality of the modes of object-relation that constitute moral insight, Adorno will need to provide an account revealing the primacy of practical reason (moral insight) over theoretical reasoning (scientific insight). Only through so doing can an expanded conception of reason be achieved which would align justifying and motivating reasons. Following Kant, Adorno regards the basic mental act to be the act of judgement, bringing intuitions under concepts. We have already seen that disenchanted reason involves a systematic separation between universal and particular and that this separation best explains the diremption between truth conditions and acceptance conditions in ethical reasoning. Adorno avers that despite claims to the contrary, the Kantian distinction between concept and intuition typifies and exemplifies this diremption. Adorno conceives of the Kantian concept, what I term *the ideal of the simple concept,* as the exemplary product and vehicle of disenchantment.

Knowing and its objects become deformed and distorted when reason and concept are defined in terms radically independent of the objects to

58 Thinking of authority in terms of coping with a "deficit" in rationality is not quite accurate since it thus views ethical reason from the point of view of ideal theoretical reason.

which they apply, where by objects Adorno intends not just objects known but equally the sensory images of these objects, the articulation of these objects and images in language, the entanglement of natural languages in social practices, and the complex history of these practices. Disenchantment is demythologisation, which is the systematic overcoming of anthropomorphism, the critical negation of projections of the indelibly human onto the world. In practice, the withdrawal from anthropomorphism became equivalent to freeing reason and concept from their dependence on and submergence within their "others": object, image, language, social practice, and history. Each of these items could be, and in the course of the emergence of modern, enlightened reason was, regarded as a systematic source of error, from Descartes's sceptical worries about the deliverances of the senses, to Locke's worry as to whether language distorts the meaning of ideas, to Bacon's (and Descartes's) concern about collective prejudices sedimented in linguistic and social practices – tradition as no more than the idols of the tribe. At the core of the charge of anthropomorphism is the claimed discovery of these systematic sources of error; each of them, apart from the object itself, having the characteristics of being both "subjective," of what belongs to human subjects in their engagements with the world, and mediums or forms of mediation for those engagements. Both the ideal of the simple concept and the simple concept itself – the concept conceived as wholly independent from its mediations – are formed through the successful process of demythologisation. Because demythologisation not only overturns beliefs and eliminates a certain range of objects, but equally destroys the forms which had mediated subject and object, *then the disenchantment of nature is at the same time a rationalization of reason.* The simple concept is the result of that process of rationalization; it is the bearer and medium of rationalized thought.

Disenchantment and rationalization, terminating in the simple concept, eliminate the modes of object relation, now identified as the material mediations of and in the concept, that make ethical reasoning possible. Hence, if ethical reasoning is to become possible once more, then what is required is some notion of a "complex concept." We can consider the complex concept as possessing two axes: a logical axis through which thought identifies different particulars (individuals or properties of individuals) as belonging to the "same" concept – hence an axis that is equivalent to the ideal of the simple concept itself; and a material axis composed of the mediating moments of object, image, language, and tradition. Adorno argues that the mediations of the material axis are not mere factual conditions of the concept, but ingredients *in* it, ingredients that do cognitive work. Concerning the dual axes of the complex concept Adorno makes two claims: first, these axes stand in a complex relation of *independence and dependence,* each axis being both independent of and dependent on the other.[59] Second, although always internally dependent on one another, the axes of the concept correspond to two different modalities of understanding: the logical axis, whose ideals are expressed in the simple concept, demands a radical transitivity of understanding, while the material axis aims at a form of intransitive understanding. To capture some notion of intransitive understanding requires defending a notion of non-discursive, or at least not fully discursive, cognition.[60] What is required for this latter notion is that in it cognitive states be in the appropriate sense, object-dependent, or, object-involving. Cognitive states that satisfy this condition can be intrinsically motivating.

What deserves to be called *Adorno's original insight* follows directly from the analysis of the complex concept. *Once elaborated, the elements composing the complex concept will be seen to correspond to and articulate the forms of object relation – authority, knowledge, and experience – which compose the fundamental structures of ethical reasoning and moral insight.*[61] To state the same thesis from the opposing angle: the structures of moral insight (as analysed by Henrich) are nothing other than elaborations of human conceptuality as such. Disenchantment as procedural demythologisation is sceptical and irrational because it operates with an illegitimate, partial concept of the concept; disenchantment is sceptical and destructive because the logic of the simple concept destroys the very structures which make human cognition sensitive to "goods" (and "evils"). By seeking to eliminate the materiality and passivity of the concept, the mechanisms of the simple concept tendentially disintegrate an independent ethical world.[62]

59 In deploying the ideas of independence and dependence in this way, Adorno is seen to be extending the Hegelian recognitive analysis of the concept, first broached in the famous master/slave dialectic in *The Phenomenology of Spirit,* back into subject-object relations. The propriety of this reversion – which is implicitly gestured toward in central Adornoian notions like "mimesis" and "affinity" – is central to my defence of Adorno.

60 In broad terms, I model transitive understanding after the Kantian conception of determinative judgement, and intransitive understanding after the Kantian notion of reflective judgement. Hence showing that something like reflective judgement is presupposed by all determinate judgement, and showing that the former is truly cognitive, forms the crux of my defence of the primacy of practical reasoning; see Chapter 6. I originally essayed an argument of this form, in a way I now think too dependent on the example of aesthetic reflective judgement, in my *The Fate of Art: Aesthetic Alienation from Kant to Derrida and Adorno* (Oxford: Polity Press, 1992), chapter 1.

61 I argue as well that the three aspects or forms of authority (legal-rational, charismatic, traditional) can equally be seen to articulate different moments of the complex concept: legal-rational authority corresponding to the logical moment of the concept; charismatic authority corresponding to sensuous particularity (object and image); and traditional authority corresponding to the mediation of the two previous moments through time.

62 If this is correct, then it explains why Adorno, whose every word reverberates with ethical urgency, did not provide an ethics. If the simple concept is the true bearer of antiethical thought, and its ideals and protocols have become hegemonic for us, then it requires deconstructing in its own terms: the project of *Negative Dialectics.* If the suppressed material moment of the concept, the other of the ideal of the simple con-

Conversely, if the ideal of the complex concept were realised in practice, and presuming that its scope of operation is extensionally limited to what can be effected through natural causal processes (which is one possible interpretation of Adorno's so-called "materialism"), then ethical knowing would simply be the knowing of ordinary states of affairs, events, and happenings. What the model of the complex concept appears to project is hence a heterodoxical and utopian form of particularistic moral realism.[63] The particularism is implied, for example, in Adorno's image of a changed philosophy, a philosophy of the future, whose "substance would lie in the diversity of objects that impinge upon it and of the objects it seeks, a diversity not wrought by any schema; to those objects, philosophy would truly give itself rather than use them as a mirror in which to reread itself, mistaking its own image for concretion. It would be nothing but full, unreduced experience in the medium of conceptual reflection (*unreduzierte Erfahrung im Medium begrifflicher Reflexion*)" (ND, 13). For Adorno, this (utopian) vision is meant to emerge solely from the immanent critique of identity thinking and the simple concept, as what conceptuality enjoins when freed from the distortions of rationalization. His realism is implied in his contention that nonidentity, that in the object which is excised by identity thinking, "is opaque only for identity's claim to be total" (ND, 163). This realism involves a re-enchantment of the world to this extent: empirical ethical predicates are not mere projections of human valuings onto a wholly indifferent object domain, but rather conceptions of things (events, happenings, actions) as conceived in the light of natural human interactions in the world.[64] Further, those predicates are significantly object-dependent. The standpoint of agency,

cept, has in macroscopic terms migrated into the marginalised domain of art, then the logic of art practices require rational redemption: the project of *Aesthetic Theory*. Since these two practices exhaust the moments of the complex concept, the false claim to independence of the simple concept and the immanent claim to rationality of the material moments of the complex concept, then together they reveal the rationality of the complex concept as a whole. The duality between science with its philosophical underlabourer and art is the evacuated space of ethical life; seeing that duality as a duality in and of the concept is to recall us to that now absent space. Because this internal way of reading Adorno's programme raises difficult questions about the status and nature of art and aesthetics, I am here risking a more austere, reconstructive approach.

63 For more orthodox versions of such moral realism, see John McDowell, "Virtue and Reason," in *Anti-Theory in Ethics and Moral Conservatism*, pp. 87–109; Jonathan Dancy, *Moral Reasons* (Oxford: Blackwell, 1993); and Sabina Lovibond, *Realism and Imagination in Ethics* (Oxford: Blackwell, 1983).

64 An argument of this form presupposes what might be called "modest anthropomorphism." Modest anthropomorphism relies on the idea that basic human responses to the environment (things and other humans) are themselves parts of the natural world, albeit, finally, intensely historicised parts. Vindicating modest anthropomorphism, which is at least part of what Adorno means to be defending with his notions of "mimesis" and "affinity," does not overturn but elaborates and extends the enlightenment project of discriminating legitimate from illegitimate concepts.

of ethical reasoning, and the standpoint of the (complex) concept are but one and the same standpoint seen from different perspectives.

3. Outline of the Argument

Chapters 1 through 3 form a relatively continuous argument. No account of Adorno's ethical thought would be complete without exposition of his book *Minima Moralia*; the immediacy of its topics and form of expression equally make it the ideal point of entry into Adorno's philosophy as a whole. In Chapter 1, I offer commentaries on just a handful of the 153 fragments or aphorisms that compose the book. Each fragment offers an objective expression of the subjective experience of ethical life in late modernity. The conundrum diagnosed, summarised by the thought that wrong life cannot lived rightly, informs all that follows. The central target of Chapter 2 is to explain this conundrum in terms of the disenchantment of nature and the rationalization of reason as purveyed in Horkheimer and Adorno's *Dialectic of Enlightenment*. In the second half of this chapter I argue that the rationalization of reason should be construed as involving the destruction of previous forms of mediation between subject and object: knowledge, experience, and authority. In Chapter 3, I offer a genealogical reconstruction of Kant's moral philosophy that demonstrates how each of its fundamental gestures can be interpreted as both a *response* to the disenchantment of nature and the rationalization of reason, and, at the same time and despite itself, a further work of disenchanting and rationalizing. More precisely, I attempt to show how the destruction of knowledge, experience, and authority inform the central turns in Kant's moral project. For reasons that will become apparent, Adorno construes Kantian idealism as the privileged object of philosophical critique; hence throughout my argument engagements with Kant's theoretical and moral philosophy form a recurring letitmotif. In explicating the Kantian reaction to disenchantment, I introduce a further claim about the destructive character of enlightened thought: it dissolves material inferential relations amongst concepts into formally logical relations. One way of expressing Adorno's critical goal hence becomes: reactivating relations of material inference.

All of this, if not exactly formal, is at least relatively austere in keeping to questions of reason, rationality, and knowledge. In Chapter 4, I introduce an altogether new layer of analysis. The self-defeating character of enlightened reason derives in part from its disenchantment of the natural world and its consequent removal of itself, as free, rational, and self-determining, from that world. But this is to argue that the self-defeating character of enlightened reason is not a wholly formal matter, but in part derives from its inability to avow its material conditions of possibility, its being a part of nature. The nature which is at stake here cannot be the nature that is the result of disenchantment, the nature projected by mathematical physics. Progress involves abstraction from *living nature,* and it is thus living nature which is disenchanted by the progress of enlightenment. Because living nature is suppressed in the emergence of rationalized modernity we experience it as damaging, as hurting. For Adorno, I argue, the axiological presupposition governing the possibility of ethical experience are the distinctions between the living and the dead, and the living and mere things. If re-enchantment means anything for Adorno, it is bringing these distinctions back into the core of our ethical self-understanding. Hence, the whole problem of Adorno's philosophy becomes showing how the two sides of his thought, his account of instrumental or enlightened reason and its opposite (some notion of the complex concept and material inference) and his dependence on some notion of living or animal nature fit together. Chapter 4 begins the work of suturing these two sides of Adorno's thought together substantively, while in Chapter 5 I interrogate the methodological status of Adorno's naturalism.

Chapter 6 is highly reconstructive; in it I attempt to defend the requisite notions of the complex concept and material inference to which I have been pointing, and show how the notion of the complex concept can answer both the formal conundrums about reason that have arisen and simultaneously enables a reliance on living nature, our experience of others as what I shall call "animistic auratic individuals," as essential to conceptuality so understood. In making my reconstruction I directly and indirectly engage with Robert Brandom's account of material inference and John McDowell's account of perceptual experience (as one attempt at a notion of a complex concept), as well as pick up a pivotal moment from Wittgenstein's private language argument. While Adorno's accounts of material inference, what he calls constellations, and perceptual experience are contiguous with Brandom and McDowell, they do diverge significantly from them; however, my hope is that in showing both the contiguity and the divergence the precise space of Adorno's concept of the concept will become more perspicuous. Because my account of the complex concept is reconstructive, in Chapter 7 I demonstrate how this notion fits, exactly, with the central expressions of Adorno's theoretical philosophy.

Chapters 8 and 9 are the core of my affirmative moral argument; equally these two chapters together are meant to form an extended commentary on the remarkable concluding section of *Negative Dialectics,* "Meditations on Metaphysics." Chapter 8 falls into two halves: in the first half of the chapter I offer a defence of Adorno's claim that the experience of Auschwitz generates a new categorical imperative, namely, that we should arrange our thoughts and actions such that the like will not happen again. Formally, this imperative is intelligible only in terms of the complex concept. In the second half of the chapter I attempt a defence of Adorno's contention that the affect which he will call *coldness* is the principle of bourgeois subjectivity (it is we might say the all-pervading *mood* of enlightened reason), and that without coldness Auschwitz could not have happened. In working through the idea of coldness I contrast it with compassionate rescue. Compassion can be understood only within the frame provided by a conception of ourselves as injured and injurable animals. Hence, my accounts of coldness and compassion will complete my attempt to support Adorno's understanding of living nature as the presupposition of ethical life.

Chapter 9 tracks Adorno's insistence that if nihilistic despair is not final, and it cannot be without being self-contradictory, then this is because we are in possession of what he terms "metaphysical experience," which exceeds the boundaries of the iron cage of modernity by not fitting into it. He also contends that metaphysical experience is the experience of a complex concept as fulfilled or satisfied. Hence Adorno offers metaphysical experience as the experience of the complex concept satisfied as his proposal as to how a wholly secular form of life can be rationally compelling and intrinsically motivating. By propounding his account of metaphysical experience Adorno offers as a prime candidate works of modernist art. My contention is twofold: once we understand what features of modernist works make them ideal candidates for objects of metaphysical experience, then it is possible to see that ordinary, intramundane objects can also possess these features and that certain types of ethical actions and experiences, ones I call "fugitive," can provide metaphysical experience. This not only claims what is almost always denied, namely, that there are possibilities of ethical action that accord with Adorno's philosophy; it is the more radical claim that *all the rational authority of modern moral norms and principles derives from fugitive ethical action and experience.* Fugitive ethical experiences reveal the becoming modern of the ethical; by "modern" I mean that conception of it which Adorno sees exemplified in modernist works of art. Thus what is revealed by certain rare moments of ethical experience is an ethical modernism, that is, a fully modernist comprehension of the ethical.[65] Ethical modernism in its fugitive appearances provides both the normative authority of secular norms and principles, and the promise of a form of life in which these norms and principles would be fully instantiated. That we live our relation to present and future in the mode of a *promise* is, I argue, Adorno's deepest dis-

65 The only writer who has fully taken up this potential in Adorno is Jean-Francois Lyotard, *The Differend: Phrases in Dispute,* trans. George Van Den Abbeele (Manchester: Manchester University Press, 1988). The absence of Lyotard in these pages is something for which I hope to make amends in the near future. For a small beginning in this direction, see my "'After Auschwitz': Grammar, Ethics, Trauma," forthcoming.

covery about the modal status of our ethical ideals and norms, and hence the one central for understanding his ethics.

When I began this project I had hoped that what I would provide was a full argumentative defence of Adorno's thought. Despite the great length of this work, I have not succeeded to this end. The richness, complexity, novelty of Adorno's philosophy, its entanglement with the thought of others, not to speak of the complex relation between philosophy and sociology in his thought, make a defence something no one work could even hope to provide. There is hardly a chapter in this book which could not have been elaborated into a medium-sized monograph of its own; and there are large areas that are important for Adorno's ethical thought, above all its relation to psychoanalytic theory, which I do not even touch. Instead of a full-dress defence, I offer an argumentative reconstruction that attempts to press Adorno's thought into a form that enables its fuller appreciation and ideally its further extension and elaboration. At the very least, I hope to have provided notice that in Adorno there is found a wide-reaching challenge to contemporary moral thought as well as a substantive alternative to it.

1

"WRONG LIFE CANNOT BE LIVED RIGHTLY"

Minima Moralia's subtitle is *Reflections from Damaged Life.* Adorno's concept of "life" is equivocal: "reflections from damaged life" is certainly intended as the contemporary fate and an ironic inversion of what once was regarded as the true field of philosophy, "the teaching of the good life" (MM, 15); but "life" here equally means to connote the evaluative sense of organic life, the sense of "life" that gives on to vitalism; finally, Adorno intends the Hegelian notion of "ethical life," *Sittlichkeit,* with its conception of social practices, customs, and institutions being the necessary mediums and supports in virtue of which individuals can possess the life they do. To assert that our ethical life is damaged is to claim that for us the good life is no longer possible, and hence that now all philosophy can do is to survey the damage, to read the ruins of ethical life as a negative expression of what has been lost and/or what we intend and hope for. Thus Adorno conceives of *Minima Moralia* as a "melancholy science" (MM, 15) – far removed from Nietzsche's "joyful science" (*fröhliche Wissenschaft*).[1] The dominant leitmotif of *Minima Moralia,* the title itself an inversion of Aristotle's *Magna Moralia,* is the condition of damage; hence Adorno's reiterated expressions of our damaged condition:

> "Life does not live." (Ferdinand Kürnberger; MM, epigraph to Part One)
>
> "Our perspective of life has passed into an ideology which conceals the fact that there is life no longer." (MM, 15)
>
> "There is nothing innocuous left." (MM, A5)
>
> "Dwelling, in the proper sense, is now impossible." (MM, A18)
>
> "Wrong life cannot be lived rightly." (MM, A18)

1 For considerations of *Minima Moralia*'s title, style, and use of inversions, see Gillian Rose, *The Melancholy Science: An Introduction to the Thought of Theodor W. Adorno* (London: Macmillan, 1978), chapter 2.

"The whole is the false." (MM, A29)

"No measure remains for the measure of all things" (MM, A39)

While each of these hyperbolic inscriptions of our condition could provide an entrance into Adorno's ethical thought, the thesis that wrong life cannot be lived rightly articulates the connection between ethical action and its condition of (im)possibility. What is presupposed in claiming that wrong life cannot be lived rightly, and what is it for this thesis to be a "reflection" from damaged life?

Like Aristotle, Adorno presupposes that ethical thought is a reflective articulation of ethical experience, which itself is structured through ethical practices. This assumes that the ethical possibilities open to an individual are delimited by the state of the ethical world this individual inhabits: wrong life (the state of the ethical world) cannot be lived rightly. And this, by itself, assumes that the provenance of the meaning and force of moral terms are the practices of the community deploying them, and that outside these practices, and the history they sediment and report, such terms lose their force. Hence by examining a wide and diverse range of phenomena (I track Adorno's accounts of love, marriage, and dwelling, but he considers as well relations between generations, the position of women, psychoanalysis, the culture industry, the role of high art in society, the task of philosophy, and so on) Adorno is interrogating *spheres* of social practice, forms of practice, and hence the forms of interaction between or among subjects or between subjects and objects encoded by these practices. In this respect, the phenomena considered are aspects of what Hegel called "objective spirit," that is, the anonymous rule systems, laws, customs, practices, and institutions that embody and express the collective identity and ethical orientation of a people.

What distinguishes Adorno's procedure are the phenomena he considers for analysis and his method of presentation. In the "Dedication" he asserts that "what philosophers once knew as life has become the sphere of private existence. . . . " (MM, 15) Without directly arguing the case – it *is* indirectly shown in each analysis – Adorno simply accepts some version of the Weberian/Marxist analysis of contemporary society which claims that the major institutions of society have been rationalised in accordance with the needs and autonomous mechanisms of capital reproduction, and that hence these institutions are no longer available as spheres of ethical practice. To the degree to which it remains, the ethical has retreated into forms of practice that are most remote from and least necessary for capital reproduction – private existence. Private existence, however, is not untouched by the fact of its location within a world dominated by the needs of production nor by the fact that it now must bear (nearly) the *full* burden of being the locale for ethical existence. On the contrary, each of Adorno's analyses insinuates a twofold conditioning or mediation of private existence: as a repository or refuge for ethical life apart from the demands of the economy, its coming to have a status *as* a refuge; and as indirectly but emphatically deformed by productive relations and societal rationalization. Hence, Adorno's *evidence* for the claim that our life is "wrong" devolves down to the way in which what remains of ethical life is deformed and distorted: "He who wishes to know the truth about life in its immediacy must scrutinize its estranged form, the objective powers [economic and societal rationalization] that determine individual existence even in its most hidden recesses" (MM, 15).

But there is a further inflection to Adorno's emphasis on private existence. Because the practices that make up ethical life are deformed, they cannot be trusted to provide adequate guidance on what is morally permissible or impermissible, what is worthy and unworthy, what is the bearer of true happiness or a false pleasure. If social practice itself is not a guide to the correct evaluation of our ethical life, and ethical reflection is unable to detach itself from those practices, then, again in an Aristotelian way, only the reflective experience of the ethical subject is left. In the "Dedication" – a personal gesture of friendship to his sometime collaborator, Max Horkheimer, which stands in for the more usual and "neutral" preface or introduction – which opens *Minima Moralia,* Adorno champions individual experience against its demotion in Hegel's philosophy.

> Compared to the patriarchal meagreness that characterises his treatment in Hegel, the individual has gained much in richness, differentiation and vigour as, on the other hand, the socialisation of society has enfeebled and undermined him. In the period of his decay, the individual's experience of himself and what he encounters contributes once more to knowledge, which he had obscured as long as he continued unshaken to construe himself positively as the dominant category. (MM, 17–18)

Adorno is aware that his reliance upon individual experience is anachronistic (MM, 17), and while this reliance is therefore epistemically risky, he equally believes it is unavoidable. While concentration on individual experience was a block to knowledge of the world when individuals falsely considered themselves as its practical and evaluative centre, now that individuality's metaphysical narcissism has been torn away and the very existence of the highly individuated self is threatened and decaying, at risk, it becomes a distorted fragment of the world through which the processes generating decay might be glimpsed.[2] The decayed life of the individual

2 "The individual owes his crystallization to the forms of political economy, particularly to those of the urban market. . . . What enables him to resist [the pressures of socialization], that streak of independence in him, springs from the monadological individual interest and its precipitate, character. . . . Within repressive society the individual's emancipation

poses both the stakes and the conditions of its articulation. Risk, urgency, and unavoidability thus inflect the stylistic "tone" of each of Adorno's aphorisms. The series of aphorisms which compose *Minima Moralia* are meant to provide a "reflective" and hence objective expression of subjective ethical experience.[3] The reflective element involves the presenting of subjective experience of private existence as objectively conditioned. Because for Adorno "society is essentially the substance of the individual" (MM, 17), then in giving objective expression to ethical life in this form, the individual "calls his substance by its name" (MM, 16), that is, reveals the (deforming) social substantiality composing broken subjective existence.[4]

Because Adorno intends to provide only a reflective articulation of subjective experience, he employs aphorisms as his mode of presentation since from the point of view of both their production and consumption they remain within the ambit of subjective experience without pretending otherwise. Aphorisms are the mode of writing that remain most loyal to the inaccessibility of a wholly objective perspective; they are not arguments but reflective understandings and judgements. Below we must consider what assumptions about rationality their employment makes.

Both substantively and methodologically, there is about all this something utterly at odds with Marxist theory. While Adorno indeed believes that private existence has been "dragged along as an appendage of the process of material production, without autonomy or substance of its own" (MM, 15), so that what was supposed to be the means to private existence has overwhelmed it, thus inverting means and end; he does not

not only benefits but damages him. Freedom from society robs him of the strength for freedom. . . . If today the trace of humanity seems to persist only in the individual in his decline, it admonishes us to make an end of the fatality which individualizes men, only to break them completely in their isolation. The saving principle is now preserved in the antithesis alone" (MM, A97). It is this dialectic that leads Adorno to speak of modern society formed by an individualism without individuals.

3 I am here merely clarifying Adorno's procedure in MM; the effort of defending his reliance on individual experience and explaining how that is compatible with his orientation toward ethical life in its Hegelian sense takes the whole of this work.

4 Throughout the "Dedication" Adorno poses his aphoristic procedure against the dialectical methodology of Hegel's *Phenomenology of Spirit,* contending that now only aphorisms can sustain the Hegelian demand to "penetrate into the immanent content of the matter" and not be beyond it. One way in which this is the case is that the combination of first-person experience and objective reflection is meant to provide an analogue of the dual perspectives in the *Phenomenology*: natural consciousness and philosophical consciousness. However, instead of the philosophical perspective emerging behind the back of natural consciousness, as in Hegel, in MM each aphorism, as well as groups or, as he calls them, "constellations" of aphorisms, is meant to invoke both the internal perspective of the subject and the reflected or external view of the observer. Aphorisms, thus, are meant to inherit the procedure of employing negativity – the immanent cancellation of merely subjective experience – and through so doing to track subject becoming substance, i.e., showing the social constitution of individual experience, with the twist that now social substantiality is as much the cancellation of the subject as it is its support.

believe that ethical life, no matter how deformed and deracinated, is merely an epiphenomenon, a mere appearance: "Reduced and degraded essence tenaciously resists the magic that transforms it into a façade" (MM, 15).[5] By "essence" Adorno means the objective content and truth of ethical life; hence what is ethically essential is to be found, if at all, through the reflective comprehension of the subjective experience of private existence.

Thus in *Minima Moralia* Adorno is attempting to reveal the ethical complexion of the practices of private existence as, we might say, contexts, spheres of practice that possess ethical significance and salience open to ethical judgement independently of the precise moral intentions and willings through which we consciously put ourselves into relation to them. So he is attempting to put himself, and thereby us, his readers, in an appropriate ethical or subjective relation to the phenomena being considered (e.g., love, marriage, homes) in virtue of the facts of the case, that is, in virtue of how choices and regard are constituted as a sphere of practice by the network of relations – social, economic, historical – which make them what they are. Because of the conditioning of the practices composing private existence by productive relations in their widest significance, our intentions and actions must systematically misfire.

I have chosen to begin with an analysis of aphorisms concerning love, marriage, and dwelling (the setting up and having of a home) because the phenomena they consider are domains of private life which are most widely shared and, in ascending order, are increasingly explicitly conditioned by their placement within the dominant structures of the world outside. Love, marriage, and dwelling are practices that contain and express certain ethical ideals; they are locales where, if anywhere, our self-conceptions as agents of a certain kind are fostered, elaborated, and worked out. One might even claim that in the way in which we engage in these practices (and hence implicitly in the practices themselves) there exists a certain utopian insistence: both a conception of our self-realisation in relation to intimate others, and a conception of what ethical regard itself involves and requires. Each practice is a sketch, in miniature, of the "good life"; each practice is an "aphorism" of the good life. In them there is a desire for "real" life.[6]

Yet Adorno's account shows each of these practices suffer from similar deformations and aporiae. In his aphoristic presentations Adorno is thus seeking to do two things apart from articulating the kind of hopefulness and ethical ideality these practices embody. First, he seeks to demonstrate

5 "Magic" implies the thought that the disenchantment of ethical life is, in fact, a new kind of enchantment. The analysis of this thesis begins in Chapter 2.

6 I grateful to Tom Huhn for urging on me this way of locating the place of ethical ideality in these aphorisms.

how these practices are deformed through being forced to carry (nearly) the full weight of ethical existence and ideality, that is, how the intimate sphere is deformed by becoming a refuge for ethical life in general. While the intimate sphere has more or better possibilities for ethical existence than does public life, there is no sharp line to be drawn where one stops and the other starts, which the fate of marriage and homes makes evident. Second, Adorno seeks to show how the *pattern* of deformation these practices suffer, their systematic forms of misfiring, points to a general derangement of modern ethical life: the fatal antagonism or failure of coherent articulation of universal and particular. For present purposes, we can construe what is "universal" to mean the dominant institutions of society and the kind of rules governing their practices; and "particular" in this context means either the practices of private existence or individuals themselves. To say that there is a fatal antagonism between universal and particular is to claim that the anonymous rule systems that are meant to provide the conditions of possibility for individual existence, to be the mediums through which individuals are able to attain self-realisation, have in fact become obstacles. While we might well be sanguine about the fact that the economy is governed by impersonal mechanisms which leave no space for intersubjective engagements of an ethical kind, Adorno believes that the economy and economic rationality have invaded or, to use Jürgen Habermas' term, "colonised" private existence.[7] The objective reflection of the subjective experience of this invasion and colonisation is what the aphorisms in *Minima Moralia* provide. If Adorno is right, if wrong life cannot be lived rightly, then both contemporary debates among opposing and incommensurable moral paradigms and philosophical scepticism about morality are but the shadow caste by the aporetic condition of modern ethical life.

1. A Refuge for Goodness?

How might we frame Adorno's focus on private existence? What set of considerations makes private existence a plausible object of ethical reflection in opposition to existing moral theory? One significant temptation of contemporary moral thought, most perspicuously represented by the reemergence of virtue ethics and certain strands of feminist theoris-

7 For Habermas's discussion of the colonisation of the lifeworld, see his *The Theory of Communicative Action,* vol. 2: *The Critique of Functionalist Reason,* trans. Thomas McCarthy (Cambridge: Polity Press, 1987), especially pp. 367–73, 391–6. While Habermas's analysis here is useful, it remains a fully sociological account of the invasion, thus repeating at the theoretical level the very deflation of individual existence it is analysing. Habermas's objectivism theoretically colonises the individual existence it aims to protect. The aphoristic procedure of *Minima Moralia* can thus usefully be seen as a corrective to theoretical colonisation; it aims to express as well as reflect (on) the experience of the individual.

ing, is to locate the categorial rudiments of true morality in the practices of private life, as if in this sheltered and protected sphere what formally constituted morality as such lived a shadowy afterlife, dimly, if affirmatively, projecting what morality might be and that to which a moral life might amount. What sense can be made of this temptation?

Virtue ethics means to oppose both the morality of intentions represented by Kant and the morality of ends represented by the various forms of utilitarianism. If one were to approach these opposed moral theories from a diagnostic perspective, one would notice their shared premise: the systematic dislocation of moral intentions from consequences. For both types of theory this dislocation is the given of our moral predicament with which a self-reflectively modern theory must cope. Modern moral agents cannot assume that the immediate context of moral action provides a reliable guide to what is morally required. Which is to say that the systematic dislocation of moral intentions from consequences presupposes the moral isolation of the agent from the others most affected by her actions. In both cases, the mode of coping with this isolation and dislocation is to find impersonal rules that will *indirectly* cross the gap separating the agent from her others. These rules – the Categorical Imperative and the principle of utility – reflectively morally align or realign self and other: the former by requiring action types (maxims of action) to be universally sharable and hence aligned to a *possible* moral community; the latter by counting in the happiness of all others as a determinant of the rationality of given actions.

The wager of virtue ethics is that even if the shared premise of the new moral theories is sociologically valid – there now exists a systematic dislocation of self from society – it is morally and rationally invalid: no coherent account of morality (of the rationality of action or moral identity) is possible that goes behind the back of the moral agent and seeks to secure moral relations solely through rule-bound reflective procedures. Such procedures mistake what the emphatic meaning of moral terms must be.[8]

If the duality between the morality of intentions and the morality of ends is a consequence of the dislocation of self from society, then the

8 This is one way of interpreting Alasdair MacIntyre's "disquieting suggestion" that there has been a "catastrophe sufficient to throw the language and practice of morality into grave disorder . . . ." *After Virtue: A Study in Moral Theory* (London: Duckworth, 1981), p. 3. The catastrophe, as a first approximation, is just the dislocation of self from society. A more radical suggestion about the nature of the catastrophe is suggested at the end of the chapter. For a survey of the traditional connection between virtue ethics and feminist ethics, see Rosemarie Tong, *Feminine and Feminist Ethics* (Belmont, Calif: Wadsworth Publishing Company, 1993), chapter 3. Significant recent examples of this connection include: Carol Gilligan, *In a Different Voice* (Cambridge, Mass: Harvard University Press, 1982); Nel Noddings, *Caring: A Feminine Approach to Ethics and Moral Education* (Berkeley: University of California Press, 1984); Sara Ruddick, *Maternal Thinking: Toward a Politics of Peace* (Boston, Mass.: Beacon Press, 1989).

sphere of intimacy may well be thought of as a refuge, as offering "one of the last possibilities of forming human cells within universal inhumanity" (MM, A11). Indeed, it is not implausible to believe that the very idea of morality, its intelligibility, and the possibility of our having rational confidence in it as such all first become manifest in the intimate sphere. In the intimate sphere the task of acting on ends contrary to one's particular interests and strongest private desires, which can seem both difficult and pointless outside it, seems to occur almost "naturally" and "spontaneously," even though we know that this is learned behaviour (albeit the lessons taught might be thought to be the lessons of love, care, and concern rather than moral lessons proper) and can recall our education into this way of acting. Philosophers have sometimes wanted to claim that because acting selflessly, disinterestedly, and compassionately feels almost spontaneous here, that action in the intimate sphere is outside morality, that morality begins where such spontaneous universality, spontaneous benevolence, ends. But this not only overlooks how "unnatural" and learned such action is, and begs the question as to what is to count as moral, but more significantly, this negative thesis deprives us of the most perspicuous representations of moral ideals and actions. If we now believe that there is such a thing as morality, that our moral convictions are more than either emotings or obedience to impersonal rules, then this is because moral values and ideals still appear to flourish here.

If this were the case, it would be important since from it we could, perhaps, extrapolate, beyond the duality of good willing and good ends, the physiognomy of an intelligible morality that entwined both these elements. Perceived through the correcting lens of intimacy, such an entwinement might be perceived as demonstrating that the fragmentation of morality into Kantian and utilitarian strands is itself a function of the distortions incurred by mass society, and that consequently some appropriately reconstructed conception of virtue ethics matched not just our deepest intuitions, but ethical reality itself when distortions are removed. It does not seem implausible to suggest that Kantian and utilitarian morality are moralities for hard times, moralities for a world in which neighbours have become strangers and the coordinating mechanisms for social reproduction are impersonal ones like the market rather than intersubjective, discursive practices. (The gamble of these two moral theories is that our hard times are a permanent state of affairs. Their normalisation of hard times thus anticipates the postmodern hermeneutic that is meant to displace them.) Could we not become convinced, working outward from the ethical unity and integrity of the intimate sphere to the public world, that the two dominant strands of modern moral thought are designed to cope with a world grown indifferent to the claims of morality? Kantian morality answering the need for guidance in personal interactions between strangers, and utilitarianism the need for policies applicable to the institutions that coordinate the public actions of such individuals? Might not the oft-noted difficulties with Kantian morality and utilitarianism derive from the fact that, at bottom, they are remedial moralities, moralities standing in under adverse conditions for morality proper?

Alternatively, if even in the sanctuary of private life, the presumptive home of the voice of care, we cannot perceive how life is to be lived, but find ourselves dealing only with fragments and difficulties, then it would follow that even in the optimal case no guidance on how to act and live could be garnered from *a* morality. But, then, if even in the optimal case we are unsure of what morality requires, of what moral goodness *looks* like, of how moral reason might guide action or at least make experience morally intelligible, then the very idea of a rational morality collapses, at least as traditionally conceived. This result could not harbour an absolute scepticism toward ethical life since, even in the making of a diagnosis that reveals a complexity unable of being accommodated within existing systems of thought, we must be relying on some kind of ethical understanding of the phenomena in question. Rather, all a negative result would demonstrate is that given moral thought falls short of what is required for true ethical understanding.

About the possibility of finding models of undeformed moral life in the intimate sphere, Adorno is less than sanguine. In one sense intimate relations are a refuge, but not as such, in and of themselves; they are not uncorrupted or unmediated just because, again, they are enclaves, refuges. Even romantic love, in practice and idea, is formed and deformed by what it is not.[9]

> Everywhere bourgeois society insists on the exertion of will; only love is supposed to be involuntary, pure immediacy and feeling. In its longing for this, which means a dispensation from work, the bourgeois idea of love transcends bourgeois society. But in erecting truth directly amid general untruth, it perverts the former into the latter. . . . The very involuntariness of love . . . contributes to the whole as soon as it is established as a principle. If love in society is to represent a better one, it cannot do so as a peaceful enclave, but only by conscious opposition. This, however, demands precisely the element of voluntariness that the bourgeois, for whom love can never be natural enough, forbid it. Love means not letting immediacy wither under the omnipresent weight of mediation and economics, and in such fidelity it becomes itself mediated, as a stubborn counterpressure. (MM, A110)

9 The best sociological study of this process of formation is Niklas Luhmann's *Love as Passion,* translated by Jeremy Gaines and Doris L. Jones (Cambridge, Mass.: Harvard University Press, 1986).

For us the involuntariness of love models ethical passivity, the sense that our responses to others can be awakened by them, and that their unique, nonsubstitutable being is sufficient to engender a fully particular response from us. Passivity captures an aspect of ethical objectivity in that it signals a fidelity to the *object* as opposed to the needs, wants, and desires of the self or to some extrinsic ideal norm, hence it is a fidelity that comes not from us but from the claims of the other. In its immediacy and feeling love presents ethical objectivity – our concern for the welfare, interests, and flourishing of the beloved – as heightened subjectivity, our deepest concern as flowing from the sheer thisness of the loved one. For Adorno this is the moment of ethical truth in the bourgeois idea of love, a component of the value of loving and of what in loving is valuable.[10]

However, if an aspect of ethical objectivity is salvaged by the involuntariness of love, then this very fact bespeaks the formation of the idea of love as a protest and a refuge. Thus when this same involuntariness becomes too insistent, too emphatic, a matter of right or principle, the loss of its moment of truth is threatened. Which is why Adorno believes that involuntariness can be what it intends only by the supplementation of the voluntariness – the exertion of will love opposes – represented in the notion of fidelity. Fidelity is the conscious willing of the involuntary relation, even when it is no longer involuntary. Love without fidelity becomes a plaything of pure chance: "Passive without knowing it, it registers whatever numbers come out in the roulette [wheel] of interests."[11] Pure or principled passivity would make love unethical, the demands or claims of feeling through its very randomness trumping the claims of the object as revealed through it. Love must not only salvage sentiment in opposition to the will, but if it is to make good its "erecting of truth amid general untruth," then it must achieve truth's permanence: "It is the test of feeling whether it goes beyond feeling through permanence, even though it be as obsession." However blind obsession is, its truth moment, as it were, resides in the semblance of permanence it provides. Obsession is the af-

10 If Michael Allen Gillespie is even only partly correct in his claim that "nihilism arises in the context of a new revelation of the world as the product not of reason but of will" – originally the will of the God of late medieval nominalism and then of the modern subject – and further that "the solution to nihilism thus lies not in the assertion of the will but in a step back from willing" (*Nihilism Before Nietzsche,* p. xxiii), then the continual recourse to love within modernity as a refuge for involuntary experience that simultaneously provides an ethical counterweight to nihilistic freedom makes good structural/functional sense.

11 Throughout this chapter all quotes that lack a reference are from the same aphorism as the previous quote. No attempt is being made here to defend Adorno's views, only to more fully elaborate what he says. Of course, in making the claims of his aphorisms more fully discursive, they become more vulnerable to argument and counter-argument, which immediately raises questions about the kind of *claiming* these fragments do. My mode of elaboration intends, just here, to leave Adorno's form of claiming intact, and so for the duration of this chapter to bypass the question of status.

fective and irrational analogue of what has value beyond whim and fancy. Erotic obsession and agapic devotion, which arguably are meant to be entwined in the bourgeois ideal of romantic love, come to appear to us as possessing ethical substantiality because they simulate an objectivity that exploits rather than denies feeling while remaining in thrall to their object. Yet in abstracting from the exertions of will and choice, the "work" of love, they become (negatively) subjective and private once more. Imagining that by heeding solely the spontaneous "voice of the heart" one is sustaining the integrity of love therefore involves blinding oneself to what society has made of love, how the spontaneity of feeling has come to invoke only a (real) semblance of objectivity. By maintaining the "supreme independence" of the feeling of love one becomes "precisely the tool of society."

"In betraying the loved one," as one's feelings spontaneously change and take a new object, entails love, in its spontaneous ethical claim, "betray[ing] itself." In contrast, fidelity self-consciously holds the judgement of love in place against the arational spontaneity and immediacy of the feeling of love. This is not to assert that fidelity is an unproblematic virtue, as if it were not imposed by society as a way of keeping the anarchy of human emotions in order, and keeping the latent conflict of interests between lovers or husbands and wives from issuing into open competition: "The fidelity exacted by society is a means to unfreedom, but only through fidelity can freedom achieve insubordination to society's command."

For Adorno the idea and practice of love are in constant tension: its unreflective spontaneity and receptivity, which is love's approximation to cognition as opposed to the exertions of desire and will,[12] are essential to what gives love ethical substance, its claim; yet this claim is accomplishable only self-consciously, as an act of will. Love's self-conscious and willed moment, fidelity, however, is itself "exacted" by society for its own sake, independently of the individual's particular (if momentary?) good. Fidelity is the voluntariness of love, but it is also, especially for women, a societal demand for subordination masquerading as an ethical virtue. Love is "forced" into involuntariness, and hence immediacy, in order to salvage meaningful passivity: we want some of our regard for others to be antecedent to choice since, even to ourselves, our choosings are all capable of having the stigmata of self-interest ascribed to them. Hence the surprise of love: desiring the good of the other as one's own good. But the forcing of love into involuntariness is already a mediation, a social

12 Love approximates cognition to the extent to which the evaluation of the beloved appears to derive from a full and attentive (perceptual) response; which is what gives rise to the converse thesis, namely, that the most accurate and just perception of an other is given through a "loving" regard. For a suspiciously transcendent reading of the converse thesis, see Iris Murdoch, *The Sovereignty of Good* (London: Routledge, 1970), pp. 17–23.

forming, of ethical passivity, its construction through modernity's intensified individualism that narrows the scope of intelligible involuntary concern for others almost to the point of extinction. So the straightening, forcing of involuntariness requires activity in order to sustain itself; and that activity is itself forced, "exacted" by society, and thus requires a self-conscious doubling in order to be differentiated from its given social form – we are faithful despite the fact that our feeling of love has dissolved and that we are socially required to be faithful; we perceive the goodness of fidelity in relation to our loving independently of the feelings that prompted it and in opposition to its overt social utility.

The ethical ideality of love is complex and antinomical because it is formed and deformed at the same time: "If love in society is to represent a better one, it cannot do so as a peaceful enclave, but only by conscious opposition." The ideality of the involuntariness of modern love is formed in opposition to society's requirements of willing, choice, work, in opposition to the idea that goods are consequences or the results of action (as governed by instrumental reasoning), and hence even in opposition to subjective interest and desire. Fidelity's willing explicitly contradicts the presumed good of love's involuntariness; but this good is betrayed even more by a lack of willing. If there is no fidelity to the good of love except through fidelity, then the good of love is sustained only by what explicitly opposes it. There is no direct path here. The aporiae of love bespeak the incommensurability and disequilibrium between activity and passivity in ethical life, a disequilibrium that echoes the duality between a morality of intentions (activity) and a morality of ends (passivity). Adorno's result is negative: we know that ethical activity and passivity are out of joint, but we are unable to form a positive image of how they are to be rejoined. Modern love thus comes to reiterate the dislocations of modern ethical life in the very gesture that originally made it appear as an antidote to them.

Because it is so emphatically a bearer of ethical ideality and so firmly entrenched in the mechanisms of societal reproduction, marriage is, if anything, more palpably problematic than love; something that has become a good deal more evident now than it was when *Minima Moralia* was written (1944–1947).[13] Again, Adorno is intent on underlining the reflective structural tensions that underlie even the best and most well-intentioned partnerships and not dismissing the refuge of the intimate sphere outright. He therefore reminds us of the "whole sombre base on which the institution of marriage arises, the husband's barbarous power over the property and work of his wife, [and] the no less barbarous sex-

13 While critiques of marriage are legion, recent philosophy has been consistently silent on its moment of ideality. Perhaps the only sustained attempt is Stanley Cavell's *Pursuits of Happiness: The Hollywood Comedy of Remarriage* (Cambridge, Mass: Harvard University Press, 1981).

ual oppression that can compel a man to take life-long responsibility for a woman with whom it once gave him pleasure to sleep" (MM, A11); and that "marriage as a community of interests unfailingly means the degradation of the interested parties, and it is the perfidy of the world's arrangements that no-one, even if aware, can escape such degradation" (MM, A10).

Economic realities distort marriage twice over: in making both parties necessarily self-interested, and their union thus an "enforced . . . community of interests"; and by creating and sustaining, traditionally and for the most part although decreasingly now, male domination. The effects of the first distortion become manifest in divorce where, despite intentions and good will, "the alienated orders of rights and property" take their revenge, forcing both parties into self-protective and self-preserving strife: "Those who once experienced the good universal in restrictively belonging to each other, are now forced by society to consider themselves scoundrels, no different from the universal order of unrestricted meanness outside" (MM, A11). Because, one is tempted to say, there is no viable ethical community, no stopping place between the *extremes* of affective intimacy, monogamous bliss, and purely contractual arrangements between strangers in the marketplace, between the voluntary doubling of love in fidelity (of which the marriage "contract" is an elaborated extension) and the self-interest of individualised wills, then the meeting of these extremes in divorce, the lapse of one sphere into the other, reveals the distortions consequent upon their mutual conditioning and normative division which exacerbate the human failure involved into something worse. So Adorno concludes this aphorism: "The universal is revealed in divorce as the particular's mark of shame, because the particular, marriage, is in this society unable to realise the true universal." Marriage, like love, becomes deformed by becoming a refuge, its goodness formed by what it is not; the goodness of marriage too much, say, like the goodness of homes for battered wives.

Aphorism 111 (entitled "Philemon and Baucis") works the issue of male domination, the second economic distortion of marriage, in terms of a master/slave dialectic.[14] Adorno's interest here is not in tackling male domination head on, but rather in tracing the strategies of collusion in standard marriages that attempt to correct, compensate, avoid, or overturn inequality while simultaneously recognising the illusory character of male power. The tone of the aphorism is well represented in the first two sentences: "The domestic tyrant has his wife help him on with his coat. She eagerly performs this service of love, following him with a

14 For an attempted critique of the use of the master/slave structure to analyse marital relations, which in fact tallies well with Adorno's argument, see Ulrich Beck and Elisabeth Beck-Gernsheim, *The Normal Chaos of Love,* trans. Mark Ritter and Jane Wiebel (Cambridge: Polity Press, 1995), pp. 150–5.

look that says: what else could I do, let him have his little pleasure, that is how he is, only a man." The indulgent "only a man" both self-deceptively turns enforced subordination into choice, while simultaneously registering the hollowness of patriarchal authority. Adorno provides this latter with a triple declension: (1) his "power rests on money-earning trumped up a human worth"; (2) "in the sphere of consumption the stronger party is the one who controls the commodities" – which makes modern wives repressed matriarchs, but because "repressed," dependent, not true matriarchs; and (3) "The hen-pecked husband is the shadow of him who has to go out to face the hostile world." Neither (2) nor (3) undermine patriarchy as such, they only reveal the dependence which makes patriarchal authority hollow (as authority, which is not to deny its reality). Dependence can give wives the power only of Hegelian slaves, not of equals. So Adorno writes: "In the incongruity between his authoritarian pretensions and his helplessness [because powerless in the work world and only titular in the home], that emerges of necessity in the private sphere, there is something ridiculous. Every married couple appearing together is comic, and this the wife's patient understanding tries to offset." The bitter comedies traditional marriages enact derive from the intention of establishing and sustaining meaningful equality implied by their romantic origin against a background of systematic inequality and economic domination. Hence each small, caring gesture of solidarity between husband and wife simultaneously carries with it a coded correction of the deforming powers of society against which the intimate society of marriage arises. The correction, like fidelity's correcting of love, tokening and recapitulating what it means to deny.

Nothing Adorno says here should be news, nor should his conclusion. The mistake would be to read these familiar complications in individualistic terms, say, as part of the battle between the sexes, where the competition is strictly for individual power within the neutral framework of marriage. Nothing any individual party within a marriage can do, no contrivance of will or desire, can altogether offset its structural and functional placement as an economic unit within a repressive economic system. Hence Adorno's conclusion: "No emancipation without that of society."[15]

15 With respect to the issue of sexual equality, this claim is too strong. Nonetheless, what writers like Anthony Giddens overlook is that while there has been a democratisation of personal life, from another angle what has occurred is a shift of aspirations for democratic control from the public to the private sphere, and hence a further burdening of private existence with ideals that have lost their public meaning. If the democratisation of personal life evinces a gain in self-determination and autonomy, by that very underlining of individual agency, the whole passive or object-oriented aspect of private existence gets elided. For Giddens's argument, see his *The Transformation of Intimacy: Sexuality, Love and Eroticism in Modern Societies* (Cambridge: Polity Press, 1992), chapter 10, "Intimacy as Democracy." For a critique of Giddens akin to the one suggested here, see Keith Tester, *The Inhuman Condition* (London: Routledge, 1995), pp. 116–22.

Finally, in "Refuge for the homeless" (MM, A18) Adorno presents the fate of our relationship to our homes as the allegorical realisation of the fate of private life and the intimate sphere in bourgeois societies. Or, as he states his thesis: "The predicament of private life today is shown by its arena. Dwelling, in the proper sense, is now impossible." He begins his account thus: "The traditional residences we grew up in have grown intolerable: each trait of comfort in them is paid for with a betrayal of knowledge, each vestige of shelter with the musty pact of family interest." The bitterness in tone of this aphorism is a consequence of its dual perspective: the nostalgic insider view, which remembers home's "comfort" and "shelter," and the outsider's disillusioned comprehension of the wider set of conditions which made sheltering homes possible. Again, it is a question of ethical ideality and its limitation and conditioning. This sentence is a judgement and a reminder: of the sources of family wealth, and the kind of economic unit the bourgeois family was as represented by its sheltering (from what and whom?). Comfort and shelter then were equally tokens of self-interest and injustice; this is the knowledge betrayed by comfort. Nonetheless, one may find Adorno's "intolerable" overstated and implausible; maybe there is some truth to the judgement, but does that entail that homes and what they represent are inevitably tainted, inevitably caught within histories and structural inequalities that their present occupants neither desire nor intentionally promote? Adorno appears to avoid these questions, turning directly to the homes available to us. Modern homes are "factory sites that have strayed into the consumption sphere, devoid of all relation to the occupant"; while seeking refuge from such in period-style houses one "embalms himself alive." And we are the fortunate ones, those for whom there are houses. The fate of the homeless is another knowledge to be betrayed.

Again, Adorno's judgement may appear both nostalgic and too harsh: who is he blaming for the fact that modern homes lack the grace, comfort, and human proportions of the "intolerable" homes in which he and his cohort were raised? Certainly, he is *not* blaming us for living in such homes (if we do); nor is he blaming architects, builders, land developers (although there may be some blame to be apportioned here). The questions of blame and guilt, which so naturally arise in this context, are wrongly posed. Homes are the "arena" of private existence, their character inflecting the practices of "dwelling" that occurs in them. Hence, the stakes are again those of a practice and our relationship to it in virtue of a reflective grasp of the relevant factors that make it possible. So, in the face of a world where there are the "intolerable" residences of the past, blank estate or tract housing that reduces the idea of a home to sheer utility (even though we necessarily invest more), and deceitful period-style homes, in a world where the choices available each token injustice and either ignore the human needs of their inhabitants or satisfy them on the basis of deceit and illusion, Adorno suggests the best mode of conduct is an "uncommitted, suspended one: to lead a private life, as far as the social order and one's needs will tolerate nothing else, but not to attach weight to it as to something still socially substantial and individually appropriate." Dwelling would be individually appropriate if its individual achievement could be wholly detached from its nonachievement by others; it would be socially substantial if my dwelling could be conceived as a component of a justly distributed social good. Neither condition is now met.[16] In echo of Nietzsche's comment that it was part of his good fortune not to be a home-owner, Adorno considers his "suspended" stance answerable to a new moral requirement: "not to be at home in one's home."

Inevitably in the background when stating this requirement are the issues of property rights and economy; in this instance Adorno brings his views to the fore, putting them into a bland, paradoxical formulation that occurs immediately following his statement that it is now part of morality not to be at home in one's home.

> This gives some indication of the difficult relationship in which the individual now stands to his property, as long as he still possesses anything at all. The trick is to keep in view, and to express, the fact that private property no longer belongs to one, in the sense that consumer goods have become potentially so abundant that no individual has the right to cling to the principle of their limitation; but that one must nevertheless have possessions, if one is not to sink into that dependence and need which serves the blind perpetuation of property relations.

The issue here is not the large one of private property, but rather our stance toward it, the difficulty of having a stance that does justice to the complexity of private need and public context. Note how modest are the assumptions that support the thought that private property no longer belongs to one: "consumer goods have become *potentially* so abundant that no *individual* has the right to cling to the *principle* of their *limitation*." It is being asked of us to have a sense, an ethical awareness, of this state of affairs and to let this sense color our stance toward property, while ac-

16 The strength of this conclusion says much about Adorno's aphoristic procedure since typically one would expect such strong normative claims to emerge out of an elaborated normative system. In terms of its normative assumptions (about the worth and value of having a home, of what makes for dwelling), "aesthetic" judgements (most estate housing is architecturally brutal and indifferent to what it aims to achieve), and reflective awareness (the possibility of decent housing is not a fairly and justly distributed good), Adorno intends to tap only a relatively modest set of intuitions. The force of his claim depends solely on his aphoristic marshalling of these thin resources. In responding we are (reflectively) judging a (reflective) judgement rather than evaluating a formal argument.

knowledging that having this stance and expressing it does not involve disowning or giving up our property since that would both worsen our real and legitimate entitlement to a private existence and, in fact, make us even more dependent on unjust circumstances. Adorno's paradoxical formulation should not be surprising since in his aphoristic portraits of love and marriage he was equally arguing that "dwelling, in the proper sense, is now impossible."

Nonetheless, the paradoxical formulation of stance is not, as stated, sufficient to the dilemma. It is both too quick and too easy. A truly suspended relationship with things would become "a loveless disregard for things which necessarily turns against people too." How could we utterly suspend our relationship to home and property, show them neither concern nor care, be utterly indifferent to their intrinsic and extrinsic qualities, and not expect this stance to affect our relations with others? Would not having things, homes, and their furnishings, on the basis of need and necessity only (with no claim to "right" beyond that) involve the adoption of a stance that disallowed things as the bearers of historical attachments (like family heirlooms) or expressions of our taste and concern for our living environment? How could such a reductive relationship with objects, detaching them utterly from the history of their making and use, not erode our relations with makers and users themselves? And would not agreeing to this line of reflection be tantamount to conceding that to be "owned," prized and celebrated as extensions of ourselves, is the means through which we extend our concern into the world at large?

All of this does require consenting to, but it should not be thought of as a justification for embracing the opposite standpoint, as licensing the unavoidability of the principle and goodness of private property. If there are good reasons for denying the abstract denial of private property, then these reasons, as soon as they are uttered, become "an ideology for those wishing with a bad conscience to keep what they have." Adorno's conclusion is the hard thought that acknowledging the aporia here requires: "Wrong life cannot be lived rightly."

The depth, parameters, causes, components, and conceptual undergirding of wrong life are all matters to which we come in other chapters. Arguably, the thesis that wrong life cannot be lived rightly instructs the whole of Adorno's philosophy. If his analyses are true, then there is no morally correct way of acting, even in the intimate sphere, except a suspended one that refuses to claim legitimacy for itself beyond its unwillingness to settle for the moral choices on offer; the moral choices on offer are themselves "immoral," not consonant with what we take morality to be. And to the degree to which this is the case, to the degree to which we can be neither good wills nor utility maximisers nor concretely envision the confluence of these two moralities in a new or renewed virtue ethics with its caring voice, then the very idea of morality evades us.[17] By taking a suspended, aporetic stance we affirm the possibility of ethical life by denying its present, empirical and conceptual, embodiments.

There is something ethically compelling about Adorno's stance, but equally something awkward and rebarbative; like the limitless demands of some utilitarian moralities, it appears to lack a sense of the limits of what can be ethically demanded: Is my loving *distorted* because it requires active fidelity? Why measure marriage by its relation to divorce, or perceive it through structural inequalities rather than what individuals do under such conditions? And if as an individual I am powerless to shift the distribution of wealth and goods, why should I not celebrate my moral good fortune for having a home in which I can dwell rather than feel compromised or undeserving? These thoughts echo the standard complaints that have been lodged against Adorno's philosophy as a whole: it provides no room or guidance for modes of action that might remedy the situation he analyses; it is inattentive to the pragmatic demands on action, seeking a false or utopian purity; it is secretly a negative theology that in fact denies the complexities and compromises that form the human condition in general, measuring it against a standard that is in fact unattainable. Adorno asks too much, or asks in a way that makes attainment appear impossible. He draws us away from historical existence, and thus away from concrete engagements and attempts to enforce a hyper-reflective stance. His aporetic stance leaves no room for living and acting, or at least no living and acting that is not at every stage reflectively qualified.

Yet against what might be regarded as the unforced reasonableness of the microanalyses just given, these criticisms appear to be both apologetic and exaggerated. Must not the structural complexities of ethical life have some inroad into our moral stance regarding these phenomena? How can we regard the screening off of the qualifications and complexities Adorno adduces as anything other than self-deception or pretence? Surely love, marriage, and homes are caught within a web that implicates them in what they mean and hope to resist? And must not that matter to how we live these components of our lives? If it is the case that life has become identified with private existence, then must not this already be a derangement of it, and hence a radical abridgement of the very idea of

17 Adorno is not claiming that there is no "correct" way of acting; for example, he clearly thinks that a certain fidelity is "correct" and that a complex, suspended stance toward property is "correct." Hence his position, even at this level, is not sceptical or unknowing or indifferent. What is denied is that here and now our actions can be unconditionally good or worthy, uncompromised, not a further abetting of what they mean to resist, and consistent with their own normative presuppositions and insistences. And to the degree to which this is the case, at least at this juncture, we must say that the nature of rightness, worthiness, goodness is opaque.

the "good life" for persons? Alternatively, turning the matter over again, against the standard of Adorno's conclusion – wrong life cannot be lived rightly – the criticisms of it have point: the relentless negativity of Adorno's thought appears to reduce ethical thought to contemplation, politely termed "critique," which produces only praxial paralysis and offers nothing in the way of even an utopian vision.

To get the true measure of Adorno's position, to come to think and feel that his uncompromising stance is not a self-deceiving moral puritanism, but, even if partial, fully rationally motivated, we need a broader canvas than that provided by textual commentary, that is, we need to see his position emerge as a response to problems that can be fleshed out in terms external to those in which he was wont to frame the problems he addressed. In framing my consideration of his thought on love, marriage, and home in terms of the contemporary moral triumvirate of Kantianism, utilitarianism, and virtue ethics my concern was to demonstrate, however quickly and inadequately, that the aphorisms of *Minima Moralia* and the theory of *Negative Dialectics* belong to our moral world. As a way deepening the analyses already given, making more explicit their metaethical presuppositions, and in anticipation of what comes below, I want to turn to a contemporary formulation of the debate concerning the relative merits of thinking about ethics in terms of ethical life (*Sittlichkeit*) as opposed to thinking about it in terms of abstract principles of moral rightness (*Moralität*) which implicitly lies behind the debate between internalism and externalism canvassed in the Introduction, and to relate these considerations to some further aphorisms in *Minima Moralia*.

2. The Death of the Good Life for Man: Ethical Life versus Moral Centralism

> Is morality itself growing old?
> Paul Valéry

In *Minima Moralia* Adorno is not providing a sociology of marriage or love but taking the pulse of the moral possibilities and hence the *rationality potential* latent in them. Adorno's reflections are normative and critical, insinuating without stating ideals which issue from the valuations, qualifications, and contradictions which the practices themselves enact. Adorno's detection of aporiae in these spheres is hence precise: these practices do not provide a path to right living, rather they prohibit what they promise, and do so in a way that suppresses the moment of prohibition, thereby substituting moral illusion for moral truth. By detecting the illusion, say, by coming to comprehend and distrust love's involuntariness, one is not thereby able to live in truth, live rightly; the deformations of feeling and will, subject and object, remain. Perceiving the systematic disjunction of motive (feeling) and will (reason), which is what Adorno's fragments reveal, does not presage their future harmonisation except as "idea"; but the status of this idea is equivocal, perhaps only as real as the concrete potentialities that stretch out from the practices themselves. But it is just such a concrete "stretching out" toward a determinate, different future which Adorno demonstrates as lacking in these practices. Even their internal forms of correction collude with what they deny. In the first instance, what Adorno underlines are the aporiae of ethical life itself.

If the possibilities and impossibilities in ethical life denote the rationality potential within it, then the aporiae of ethical life must infect and determine Adorno's philosophising about it. He attaches the possibility of philosophical or theoretical reflection on ethical life to the same states of affairs that determine the possibilities of ethical action. So the suspended stance of the agent necessarily binds the theorist. This, however, requires only the assumption that reflection upon moral life is continuous with it; but if continuous with it, then philosophical reflection itself becomes a certain kind of ethical activity. For Adorno the dilemmas facing the philosophical theorist mirror the dilemmas of ethical life itself.[18] How tight the bond is between ethical life and reflection on it, and thus the kind of activity Adorno takes reflection to be, we come to below.

These general assumptions, which by themselves begin to delimit Adorno's general views on ethical life, say very little toward explicating and explaining his aporetic stance. What do we need to claim about the nature of ethical life such that it can become intelligible that the possibilities of dwelling, living rightly, can have substantively dried up? And why should this drying up make positive ethical or moral teaching impossible? All moral theories should be able to concede that not all circumstances are equally propitious for fully realising moral life; but in itself this does not entail the impossibility of either morally right action or positive moral teaching. Adorno never explicitly elaborates the assumptions that would form an answer to the first question, perhaps because he believed doing so would provide solace or edification rather than ethical insight itself and thus abrogate his abstinence toward substantive teaching. Nonetheless, given what he says, his meta-ethical views are not difficult to reconstruct; indeed, his views here begin to provide an historical context for the debate between internalism and externalism.

We can begin with a sketch of two ideal type meta-ethical perspectives: moral centralism and ethical life, the former embedding the theoretical presuppositions that lead it to be labelled as externalist, and the latter a representation of the antitheoretical assumptions behind some internal-

18 Which is why scattered throughout *Minima Moralia*, but most clearly at the end of Part 1 (MM, A41-A50), there are aphorisms concerned with the nature of philosophy and the activity of philosophising.

ist views. Although moral centralism and ethical life tend to appear as competing moral *theories*, as theoretical options open to the moral philosopher, for Adorno this appearance is illusory, another aspect of the deformation of ethical life itself. For the moment, let us put this thesis aside. There can be a positive moral teaching irrespective of the configuration of empirical circumstances only if there are moral principles whose validity logically transcends their employment in particular cases; ideally, such principles enable the performance of morally right actions even when the complete set of events they prescribe for their actualisation is not empirically possible. Although there are a variety of ways in which such transcendence can be satisfied, the most plausible way contends that there is some one *central* term, like "right," "good," or "ought" whose meaning is prior to and independent of the more specific terms through which concrete descriptions of cases are given, like "generous," "prurient," "selfish," "cruel," "vicious," or "sincere," and that it is in virtue of their relation to a central concept that specific terms that cannot be applied to all moral situations acquire (moral) reason-giving status. For the holder of this view, that cases can be described "as" moral and that our descriptive vocabulary comes to possess moral significance both depend upon the vertical relation between a central concept and our apparently merely descriptive concepts. Let us hence call those who believe that good reasons operate vertically, top-down, from a basic moral concept to the concepts through which cases are to be described as "centralists," and their doctrine "centralism."[19] Although he is often interpreted as meaning and emphasising a version of moral individualism with his concept of *Moralität,* Hegel's concept is better construed as denoting moral centralism.[20]

19 I am borrowing the notion of "centralism" from Susan Hurley, *Natural Reasons* (Oxford: Oxford University Press, 1989), chapter 1. Inspired by Wittgenstein and Davidson, the whole of Hurley's book is a defence of non-centralism. In the course of the first chapter she usefully canvases centralism with respect to color (where the concept of color itself would be prior to and independent of particular color concepts), law (where the concept of law is prior to specific legal concepts), and logic (where validity or truth-preservingness is prior to and independent of particular logical principles like *modus ponens*). What might motivate centralism about colors, for instance? Perhaps something like the fact that our phenomenological experience of particular colors can so easily go astray, and that we can now buttress our normative account of color perception (what ordinary perceivers would perceive under standard conditions) with a tougher causal account in terms of wavelengths. Color centralism thus would represent a disenchanted view of colors. For Adorno the cases of moral and color centralism would be deeply analogous. Centralism is one version of what Adorno entitles "identity thinking," and our engagement with moral centralism is thus a first engagement with identitarian habits of thought.

20 While centralism conduces to moral individualism, they are separate doctrines; one might believe that mentality is socially constituted, and still be a centralist. For Hegel's "official" view on *Moralität* see his *Elements of the Philosophy of Right,* ed. Allen W. Wood, trans. H. B. Nisbet (Cambridge: Cambridge University Press, 1991), paragraphs

Conversely, those who take our specific, "thick" descriptive and evaluative concepts as logically prior to central concepts believe that ethical life is a matter of acquiring an elaborate discriminatory vocabulary whose terms, which possess reason-giving force, ideally harmonise sufficiently such that, appropriately articulated, they hang together to envision a "good life." On this conception, the correct employment of thick concepts orients the correct usage of centralist concepts; so, for example, if to do φ is cruel or callous or vicious, then one ought not to do φ, or φing is wrong. These concepts are "thick" in a dual sense: they are bound to particular ranges of objects, properties, states of affairs; and they are partially constituted in their capacity to pick out such worldly items by their connection to other similar concepts. Hence they are dependent for their meaning upon "objects" and upon their horizontal, same-level connections with other concepts – one knows the meaning of a thick concept only through knowing it in relation to the field of concepts of which it is a part.[21] In broad terms, the notion of ethical concepts as thick and horizontal equates with Hegel's conception of ethical life (*Sittlichkeit*).

The thick concepts view conduces to a form of moral realism that consequently would make much of ethical life cognitive.[22] On this account, acquiring an ethical awareness or taking up the moral point of view is continuous with learning a language and the practices of a linguistic community. In learning to use the term "vicious" one is being taught both the kinds of cases that are to be regarded as vicious and simultaneously being taught not to act in a manner that could be such a case. Once we have learned the correct usage of a term, then the issuing of linguistic responses to circumstances where this term is appropriate happens in the same way as our linguistic responses to material objects and ordinary empirical events: through perception. This puts ethical and nonethical predicates on a par; and if it makes sense to say that my linguistic responses to ethical and nonethical circumstances are occasioned in the same way, then it must be correct to say that ethical terms refer to properties or kinds of actions or states of affairs. Prescriptive and descriptive aspects of ethical terms are intertwined; actions *are* rude or callous or kind or spiteful – and this is what we see them *as*. If there is no going behind the reality revealed through our linguistic practices of sorting, classifying, and responding to the world, if there is no vantage point outside language

105–41; for a full evaluation of Hegel's critique of Kantian morality see Robert B. Pippin's "Hegel, Ethical Reasons, Kantian Rejoinders," in his *Idealism as Modernism: Hegelian Variations* (Cambridge: Cambridge University Press, 1997), pp. 92–128.

21 For this initial characterisation of thick ethical concepts, see Bernard Williams, *Ethics and the Limits of Philosophy* (London: Fontana Press, 1985), chapter 8.

22 For the version of moral cognitivism at stake here, see: John McDowell, "Virtue and Reason," *The Monist* 62 (1979): pp. 331–50; and Sabina Lovibond, *Realism and Imagination in Ethics* (Oxford: Basil Blackwell, 1983), pp. 69–82.

that would permit us to distinguish the real from the apparent (other than the routine internal ways we do), then ethical discourse is realist in character. From this it follows that ethical knowledge is neither knowledge of what is right or good in general nor a priori knowledge of what makes certain actions right and others wrong; ethical knowledge is the knowledge we have *of* circumstances in virtue of having the thick concepts we do, just as one knows about electrons in virtue of having a language and theory that allows certain states to be registered as "electrons going through the cloud chamber now." So one knows an act to be vicious, say, and not that doing vicious acts is wrong. The latter claim would require us to rationally ground rightness and wrongness apart from all the ways we have of responding to and picking out the sorts of phenomena in question. Our unsurprising inability to do this opens the door to scepticism.

At this juncture a centralist might intervene with a query as to whether material object language and ethical language are on a par. Is there not something "second"-level about ethical predicates? Might it not be more precise to say, for example, that he hit her and this was a vicious thing to do? Are not all ethical predicates like that, second-order ascriptions? (Notice how this question replicates the question whether or not there is a theory-neutral observation language in science.) But how are we to understand this second-orderness other than by saying that in themselves actions are neither cruel nor kind, say, but we learn to evaluate them this way? Even in teaching the use of thick ethical concepts our promptings are parasitic upon actions that can be described quite neutrally (hitting, tripping, giving or taking a toy, etc.). What makes some hittings the wrong thing to do ("being a bully") and others the right thing to do ("protecting a friend" or "finally standing up for yourself")? From here it becomes tempting to claim that there are certain "right" making principles, like the Categorical Imperative or the principle of utility, which rationally *explain* valuings. Nor is the search for rational grounding dogmatic: the world of thick concepts is – or was when fully operative – a closed and parochial world where the ruling consensus rules (ruled) the way everyone is (was) to live. Not only may such a consensus come to appear arbitrary, apparently having no firmer basis than "that's the way we do things around here," but for many this way may be (is and was) oppressive or worse. To restrict ethical discourse to thick descriptions may thus come to appear as a way of shoring up the prejudices and outlook of a particular group or tradition that possesses no independent moral authority.

This centralist response to the thin description of ethical life can be construed as the first move in what has become a fierce theoretical debate, one that brings in its train views not only about ethics but about the philosophy of language, the privileges of the scientific perspective (or at least material object language), the nature of rationality, and so forth. Although it would not be incorrect to say that for the most part Adorno's position tallies with the ethical life perspective with its attendant commitments to an expressive conception of language, a curbing of the claims of natural science and a parochial conception of rationality,[23] he rarely broaches these questions directly, and never in a manner that would make them theoretically self-sufficient. He does not believe we can defend the claims of one position against another through purely theoretical or a priori argumentation. The belief that we can determine the philosophical truth about these matters, including the teaching of the good life, apart from the ethical possibilities actually available to us belongs to centralism. If meta-ethical positions are substantive through having significant repercussions on what ethical conceptions get licensed, and if reason-giving is an activity, and if the kinds and range of reasons one can offer or to which one can respond are themselves a function of the ethical space one inhabits, then the "conduct of thought" in philosophy is coextensive with ethical conduct in general. There is no neutral space for inquiry to inhabit. If a positive teaching of the good life were possible, this could only be because the living of a good life were possible. But it is just this that Adorno denies.

If, however, all of this is true, then centralism and ethical life are *not* analytical, theoretical options, not self-sufficient conceptual types, but in their scope, meaning, and possibility they are socio-historically determined.[24] By concluding that wrong life cannot be lived rightly Adorno is claiming that the thick concepts that made a substantial ethical life possible, where "the good life for man" was conceived as a real possibility, are no longer sufficiently available (if they ever were), or more precisely, no

23 All these matters are elegantly discussed by Lovibond in her *Realism and Imagination in Ethics*. Her few but pointed references to *Minima Moralia* lead me to think she would, rightly, include Adorno in the position she seeks to defend. I am not aware of any other critic who has included Adorno within the moral realist camp.

24 Precisely how this claim is best stated is difficult to specify. MacIntyre, in *After Virtue*, argues that "a moral philosophy . . . characteristically presupposes a sociology" (p. 22). While Adorno would certainly agree with that claim, he is in fact urging a closer or more intimate relation than a moral philosophy "presupposing" a sociology, since, stated in that way, the evaluative moral philosophy and the descriptive sociology are conceived of as analytically distinct but causally connected. For Adorno the emergence of a value-neutral sociology (which MacIntyre too doubts the existence of) is as much a precipitate of the destruction of ethical life as centralism. The difficulty in stating this matter correctly derives from the fact that, at least to a certain degree, there really has been a collapse, a draining from the practical world (in some quarters) of normative qualifications, and hence the emergence of an "object" (e.g., the economy) that is not axiologically saturated. One might state the thought in this way: in Hegel's *Philosophy of Right*, for example, the normative and the descriptive are still seamlessly connected, hence the philosophy and sociology of right are one and the same. Whether or not Hegel was right about this, Adorno takes our situation as one in which such a seamless relating is no longer possible. Our aporetic ethical condition is that separation: philosophical reflection can qualify the meaning of empirical theories; and empirical theory can qualify and explain philosophical claims, but there is no sustainable univocal perspective which harmonises or unifies the two perspectives.

realm of social life is free from the kind of aporiae we saw affecting the practices of love, marriage, and dwelling. Affirmative ethical life has disintegrated, and with it the knowledge that was available through the deployment of thick concepts, a position that has recently been forwarded in slightly different terms by Alasdair MacIntyre and Bernard Williams. If no social determination of a practice can be detached from its historical formation (deformation and reformation), then Adorno's account of the aporiae infecting love, marriage, and dwelling equally tracks a process of disintegration and disappearance. By forwarding the claim that affirmative ethical life has disintegrated Adorno is not contending that the state of affairs from which things departed was ethically or morally superior to our own: the historical forces that generated moral centralism were, in part, progressive, enlightening; and the traditional world of ethical life was hierarchical and repressive. Hence the unavoidable equivocality of disintegration, in part, is going to make ethical reflection on the present aporetic rather than positive.

Still within the narrow, aphoristic parameters of *Minima Moralia,* in "On the Dialectic of Tact" (MM, A16), by focussing on a pivotal moment of transition between the metaphysical past and the nominalist present, Adorno manages to insinuate a history of disintegration and collapse that begins to reveal centralism as a precipitate of this process, as well as deepening the stakes of the loss involved. The aphorism opens with the instancing of Goethe's attempt in *Wilhelm Meister's Years of Travel* to present tact "as the saving accommodation between alienated human beings" in emergent industrial society. For Goethe this accommodation was "inseparable from renunciation, the relinquishment of [the romantic ideal of] total contact, passion and unalloyed happiness." As a form of self-limitation, tact is a form of respecting and acknowledging others in contexts where no determinate guidelines for respect are available. Tact as the "discrimination of differences," consisting in "conscious deviations,"[25] was suited to a rising individualism since it mimicked traditional courtesy, manners – modes of honouring others – without formalism. A culture of tact would be a culture of virtue without any actual, determinate rules or practices being required by specific types of occasions; it would represent

25 In "Tact: Sense, Sensitivity, and Virtue," *Inquiry* 38/3 (1995): 217–31, David Heyd defines tact "in contradistinction to both morals and manners," as dealing with "concrete situations in a way guided not by rules but rather by sensitive perception and intuitive response. This sensitivity has both a cognitive or perceptual dimension and an emotive or sympathetic one. It combines attentiveness (a skill) and considerateness (a motive)" (p. 218). He goes on later in the article to relate tact to Kant's conception of reflective judgement and Aristotle's conception of practical reason (*phronesis*). In ably defending tact as accomplishing something which neither manners nor morals can, Heyd nonetheless ignores the historical emergence of tact as an attempt to cope with the lapse of the force of both manners and morals.

a culture of virtue without any plural configuration of virtues being available to guide action.

Tact, Adorno contends, has "its precise historical hour":

> It was the hour when the bourgeois individual rid himself of absolutist compulsion. Free and solitary, he answers for himself, while the form of hierarchical respect and consideration developed by absolutism, divested of their economic basis and their menacing power, are still just sufficiently present to make living together within privileged groups bearable. This seemingly paradoxical interchange between absolutism and liberality is perceptible . . . in Beethoven's attitude toward traditional patterns of composition, and even in logic, in Kant's subjective reconstruction of objectively binding ideas. There is a sense in which Beethoven's regular recapitulations following dynamic expositions, Kant's deduction of scholastic categories from the unity of consciousness, are eminently "tactful." The precondition of tact is convention no longer intact yet still present.

The moment of tact was the moment when thick concepts lost their religious, metaphysical, and political anchoring but were still available as forms of action and perception. Under these conditions, tact meant the use of thick concepts tailored to the claims of the individual – which is the claim behind Adorno's references to Kant and Beethoven: they "tactfully" gave concepts or forms that had been metaphysically grounded an emphatic relation to the nascent individual. And this makes sense in a transitional state since apart from some thick concepts there was no way of acknowledging the claims of individuality; by diverting those concepts from their hierarchical setting to the "discriminating" judgement of the individual they lost their original metaphysical coerciveness. Conversely, however, the tactful deployment of a particular set of thick concepts, above all those used in public and quasi-public occasions to show "courtesy," "respect," "trust," and "regard," and which were the acknowledging of others as having standing or worth, had no measure other than the concepts themselves: "Convention represented, in however etiolated form, *the universal which made up the very substance of the individual claim*" (emphasis mine). Without some moment of universality, some general concepts whose descriptive/evaluative grid constituted a form of *recognition,* there was no practised route to claiming and showing respect. To designate thick concepts as "convention" is to capture them at a moment when their usage began to appear as *merely* conventional (which is what the efforts of Kant and Beethoven were attempting to resist). This made the exercise of tact both paradoxical and impossible; it demanded the reconciliation between "the unauthorised claims of the convention and the unruly ones of the individual." Tact represented an impossible compromise formation; neither side of the equation, neither individual nor disintegrated thick concepts, could support the other since both were attempting to derive their *authority* from the other. Convention was meant to signify the worth of persons conceived as independent of and prior to conventional forms. Hence, the whole weight of tact was had through the intentions of the user and the intended object. But if conventional forms were construed as wholly empty bearers of meaning, then intentions lacked any vehicle for their outward expression. Conversely, to consider conventional forms as the necessary means toward expressions of respect would make these forms have meaning prior to and independently of the claims of the individual, as if, say, god-given. Tact, Goethe believed, was the negotiation of this paradoxical situation, an ethical balancing act that attempted to halt the slide into either arbitrary conventionalism or unregulated individualism. The terms of the situation, however, undermine any stable solution: tact was asked to give each side of the equation (convention and individual) what only the authority of the other could provide. Tact is the attempt to hold together the ground of authority and the social expression of authority when they have in fact become incommensurable.

Having isolated the historical emergence of tact, Adorno quickly shifts focus in order to reflectively indicate the eventual fate of Goethe's compromise. Because tact remains unsupported, insistence on it *comes* to be felt by the individual as coercive or indifferent to his claims as the old conventions felt to the nascent individual under absolutism. When emancipated, tact "confronts the individual as an absolute, without anything universal from which to be differentiated, it fails to engage the individual and finally wrongs him" – a sentence compressing a century or more of historical development. How are we to interpret tactful remarks and questions when they no longer automatically invoke the sense of "this is my being respectful to you"? Without an interpretative key, tactful remarks can reasonably be construed as either invasively prying or as brusquely indifferent, as too personal or too distancing: "The question as to someone's health, no longer required and expected by upbringing, becomes inquisitive or injurious, silence on sensitive subjects empty indifference, as soon as there is no rule to indicate what is and what is not to be discussed." With this ambiguity manifest, individuals comprehensibly begin to react antagonistically to tact: "a certain politeness, for example, gives them less the feeling of being addressed as human beings, than an inkling of their inhuman conditions, and the polite run the risk of seeming impolite by continuing to exercise politeness, as a superseded privilege. In the end emancipated, purely individual tact becomes mere lying." Tact becomes lying because rather than revealing respect for the other, it comes to appear as a veil or a bit of social machinery that stands between individuals; its use appears as a replacement for being engaged or open or direct.[26] Not that openness or directness is truth; as rules against discrimination and difference, they tend to collapse distinctions by means of which the social world was navigated: pertinence and impertinence, respect and disrespect, friendship or acquaintanceship, and so on. "You needn't look so hurt, " the open one says, "I am only telling you what I think." Tact was the buffer between individuals which intended to halt the collapse of the metaphysics of respect (for both self and other) into unalloyed self-interest. Adorno concludes: "The nominalism of tact helps what is most universal, naked external power, to triumph even in the most intimate constellations. To write off convention as an outdated, useless and extraneous ornament is only to confirm the most extraneous of all things, a life of direct domination."

To perceive tact in its "precise historical hour" is thus to follow an idealised history of disintegration: the transition from ethical concepts as elements of a hierarchical, metaphysical conception of society to the moment when they lost their metaphysical support but were able to be reconfigured – by means of tact – as modes of individual comportment to the moment when tact itself became suspect, viewed as another element of a surpassed hierarchical system that now can be seen only as conventional and unearned privilege. The moment of suspicion, of course, requires qualification since it is impossible not to regard the forms of inferential binding at work in Adorno's aphorisms as themselves forms of logical or semantic tact, which thus becomes a mode of intellectual comportment. To echo a thought of Schiller's: tact is never more necessary than at the moment of its perceived collapse. Thus the "precise historical hour" of tact is equivocal: Goethe's time and our own.

If Adorno's sombre assertion of "a life of direct domination" as all that remains sounds melodramatic, then it is, from a more familiar angle, not unprecedented. What he traces in the fate of tact was already construed by Hobbes, "one of the dark writers of the bourgeois dawn" (DoE, 90), as the truth of the aristocratic virtues. For him "Worth, Dignity, Honour and Worthiness" – the final four items mentioned in the title of chapter 10 of *Leviathan* – are reformulated as tokens of social recognition that *are* the "Power" – the first item in the title of the chapter – of the individual to achieve his ends. In making his reformulation, Hobbes was being both

26 David Heyd (ibid.) is alert to these complexities in tact, but not perceiving the historical figure in the carpet of the practice, interprets them as simply structural: "Tact is an impressive virtue just because it involves a measure of *risk*, a selective silence which would not be interpreted as indifference, a remark which would deflect the conversation without sounding over-protective or humiliating. The overtactful person too easily avoids the risk altogether" (p. 228). For an historical measuring of tact akin to Adorno's, see Hans-Georg Gadamer, *Truth and Method*, trans. T. Weinsheimer and D. G. Marshall (London: Sheed and Ward, 1989), pp. 16–17.

descriptive and prescriptive; he was contending that the classical aristocratic virtues were no longer what they metaphysically pretended to be, but that until the individual came to view them as they truly were, as forms of social power and domination, he would lack true moral self-consciousness, that is, awareness of himself as caught in a struggle for power with other self-interested, desire-driven vulnerable selves which would lead to a war of all against all and the threat of violent and sudden death unless all submitted to the rule of law. While the dialectic of tact marks a moment of equivocation between metaphysical sociality and society's reinscription in terms of relations of power, Hobbes's affirmative naturalism begins explaining how this state of affairs could occur. For him, good and evil no longer refer to objective states, but are code names for individual desires and aversions; as a consequence, ethical questions devolve down to practical questions, the discovery of adequate means for desired ends. Hobbes, we might say, disenchants moral categories and the aristocratic virtues, replacing the former with (natural) desires and aversions, and replacing the latter, the concepts that traditionally mediated between persons, with relations of power.

This Hobbesian moment is implicitly diagnosed toward the end of a long fragment (MM, A116; "Just hear, how bad he was"), in which Adorno is defending "micrological moral myopia," that is, a resolute focus on the minutiae of private existence where "we still get the feel of morality in our very skin – when we blush –," as opposed to "news" of moral catastrophes, a murder somewhere, which can leave us strangely cold in the midst of our moral disapprobation. He reads civilisation, the long history of human socialisation, as a fragile synthesis of civilisation as self-preservation and civilisation as humanity, as answerable to both instrumental and non-instrumental ends, as providing a response to the need for order and co-operation, on the one hand, and to a moral conception of human worth and dignity, on the other. This fragile synthesis comes under siege in the modern period when what was a synthesis comes to be and be interpreted in terms of civilisation as humanity (the unconditioned end) becoming the instrument for the realisation of civilisation as self-preservation. The instrumental ends become unconditional by subtending the ends of humanity; means and ends are inverted. Or rather, this is the story Hobbes offers. Equally, however, this same story, the dissolution of the internal connection between the two civilisations, can be scanned another way: once the natural world is construed as wholly subject to a causal understanding, then civilisation as humanity can and must be isolated from its embeddedness in empirical experience and provided with an autonomous sphere of operation. If tact is a moment of avoidance of this dissolution, moral centralism is a precipitate of the uncoupling of the two civilisations, with its sustained attempt to give to us, our humanity, a worth or dignity not reducible to the now naturalised empirical world. This is the moment of Kant's moral philosophy, the object of Chapter 3 below.

From the inside, as it were, the precipitous event marking our moral modernity – an event subject to competing rationalizations – is the uncoupling of material and nonmaterial culture.[27] When this historical situation is viewed directly and internally, the meta-ethical orientation of ethical life does *not* appear: rather the immediate consequence of the uncoupling of material and nonmaterial culture is a debate between naturalism (in all its forms, right down to emotivism) and the centralism of moral rationalism, civilisation as self-preservation and civilisation as humanity. Those two civilisations in separation from one another come to appear as the dominant meta-ethical perspectives of the modern period, each articulating a now autonomous aspect of what was once an all but seamless metaphysical whole. The perspective of ethical life was thus not an item or option initially appearing within the moral horizon of modernity. Only genealogically, perhaps beginning with Herder or Hegel, do both naturalism and centralism come to appear as precipitates and inflections of our broken ethical life, and only micrologically, within private existence, is a refuge for affirmative ethical life to be found. So Adorno completes his sentence about the little offences that cause us to blush by asserting that morality is "assimilate[d] to the subject, who looks on the gigantic moral law within himself as helplessly as at the starry sky, of which the former is a poor imitation." For now, the moral law is not sublime and inspiring, but is as endlessly remote as the disenchanted starry sky; the blush is a surer sign of attunement to the moral than awareness of the moral law. Of course, to *find* in blushing, say, the remnant of ethical life is far from obvious – it takes a kind of "myopia" to see it there. Which is in part why the remoteness of the Categorical Imperative can be reassuring in a way that blushing is not. A sense of "helplessness" before the moral law – which is the secret of the complaint against "externalism" – leads back to the small things forgotten by moral centralism.

This is why Adorno focuses on private life and the intimate sphere in *Minima Moralia*; there presumptively decoded individuals, who are without the civilisation of thick concepts supporting them, attempt to recoil from the reduction of civilisation to self-preservation that holds gener-

27 There is no unique narrative telling of this precipitous event, in part because it is not a single event, but a discontinuous series of events that is variable in its palpability across different geographical regions. In a recently discovered manuscript from 1941, "A History of the Doctrine of Social Change," *Constellations* 1/1 (1994): 116–43, Herbert Marcuse and Franz Neumann argue that the crucial change "takes place in the period in which the French middle class overthrew the rule of feudal absolutism and set out to adapt the social and political institutions [nonmaterial culture] to the actual state of material culture" (p. 118).

ally, and to attain their "humanity" through forms of immediacy: love, friendship, marriage, high and popular culture, and so on. And there is much humanity here. What Adorno insists upon, however, is that we perceive in the reduction of humanity to immediacy the violence being done to individuality as such. Speaking of the man who "conforms his reactions to social reality," rather than "myopically" attuning them to private existence, Adorno says:

> Where civilisation as self-preservation does not force on him civilisation as humanity, he gives free rein to his fury against the latter, and refutes his own ideology of home, family and community. It is this that is combatted by micrological myopia. It detects in the formless familiarity and slackness a mere pretext for violence, a show of being nice in order to be nasty to our heart's desire. It subjects the intimate sphere to critical scrutiny because *intimacies estrange, violate the imponderably delicate aura of the other which is his condition as subject. Only by the recognition of distance in our neighbour is strangeness alleviated: accepted into consciousness.* The presumption of undiminished nearness present from the first, however, the flat denial of strangeness, does the other supreme wrong, virtually negates him as a particular human being and therefore the humanity in him, "counts him in," incorporates him in the inventory of property. Wherever immediateness posits and entrenches itself, the bad mediateness of society [as self-preservation only] is insidiously asserted. The cause of immediacy is now espoused only by the most circumspect reflection. This is tested on the smallest scale. [emphasis mine]

For now civilisation as self-preservation can still force upon individuals the rules and regularities of civilisation as humanity, permitting the further Marxian and/or Nietzschean suggestion that perhaps the force of moral humanity has always been held in place by its consonance with civilisation as self-preservation, that morality has been in league with, underwritten and supported by, the human pursuit of prudential ends. For example, where there are conflicts of interest, it can be instrumentally rational to adopt second-order rules of conduct that espouse "agreements to differ." By agreeing to differ, and by taking on the stance of the one for whom this is a principled response to certain types of conflict, out of self-interest a space is opened up in which respect, or at least a semblance of respect, is shown for the views and interests of others. In comparison with naked self-interest directly pursued, the evolution of such second-order rules of conduct are morally progressive. Civilisation as humanity would interpret this same evolution as one in which we came to appreciate or understand the independent worth of others and adopted second-order rules of conflict resolution as a consequence. So long as the two civilisations harmonised, then the espousal of humanity aided the ends of the individual and no decision between the two was necessary;

they are "two" civilisations only in retrospect. Only when the two civilisations are sundered can it appear, as it did for Hobbes, that the goods of humanity are themselves illusory existences until understood as instruments for furthering individual self-interest.

This is not to deny the actuality of civilisation as humanity, as Marx and Nietzsche do, but rather to point out the social dynamic through which the ethical inversion of the two civilisations occurs and becomes intelligible, as well as to remind us of the equivocality of the ideals of humanity, that historically they have been also repressive, requiring sacrifice and self-denial in order to secure the necessary repression of immediate desires that made self-preservation possible, and thus that there has been about them something against which the individual could, rightly, feel fury. The repressive dimensions of civilisation as humanity, right down to the Categorical Imperative,[28] give point to the claims of the individual against society, the claims of natural desire against morality, and the claims of immediacy against the mediations of convention.

Adorno's micrological myopia nonetheless reveals the categorial inadequacy of the naturalistic and instrumental framework in the newly won immediacies of the intimate sphere. The intimacies that estrange us are, finally, the intimacies of Hobbesian man, natural man, at home. These "violated" intimacies rehearse the inversion whereby, for example, one loves for the sake of personal gratification, egoistically, and thereby betrays and forfeits the good of love. By probing the violence of the claims to immediacy, Adorno here introduces both a deeper worry about the aporiae of private existence and an elaboration of the ethical orientation of his reflective approach. In opposition to the claims of immediate feelings, desires, wants, and needs, Adorno tactfully asserts, almost as a counterpoint and with apparently nothing but the justness of its rhetorical dissonance to support him, the *claim* of distance: the "other's delicate aura" which is his "condition as subject." What is this imponderability? Is it essential or only contingent? And why employ a term like "aura" in this context? Is it meant to adumbrate the return of a religious outlook? Above all, why claim that this aura is the individual's "condition" as subject?

The contrast Adorno draws out in this passage is a familiar one: it is the distinction between seeing and treating an other as an end in him- or herself, and treating him or her as a means, a piece of property. But at least here Adorno is giving this familiar Kantian distinction a perceptual or phenomenological slant: the other's condition of being an end is given through her aura. Although the character of aura, the experience and

28 "The august inexorability of the moral law was this kind of rationalised rage at nonidentity . . . " (ND, 23). "Nonidentity" is here another term for the "strangeness" and "aura" of the other. Precisely why Adorno construes the moral law this way is taken up in Chapter 3.

perception of aura, is a matter that we begin detailing in the next chapter, even at this juncture it is worth noting how even Kantians draw upon some version of it when attempting to explicate deontological reasons for action. So Christine Korsgaard comments: "It is the particular badness of treating someone as a means that explains the badness of deontological reasons. It is the horribleness of looking into a pair of human eyes, while treating their owner like a piece of furniture or tool."[29] How are we to make intelligible to ourselves the precise "horribleness" of looking into a pair of human eyes and yet treating their owner as a thing to be used? What sort of "looking" is this? And those eyes, they are looking back at us and yet, somehow, are not seen; they are ignored, crushed in their plea or defiance, their vulnerability and reproach. For Adorno, this exchange of looks, of seeing and not seeing, of being seen and disregarding this seeing, is very near the centre of the intelligibility in principle of ethical life; unless the "horribleness" of this scene can be or become intelligible (in principle) the ethical as such will be lost to us. Deontological reasons may recapitulate or express the horribleness; but what is that horribleness itself? Why horrible?

As Adorno conceives of it, our world is riven with the horribleness of this scene; the same deformations to social practice that generate the aporiae of love, marriage, and dwelling simultaneously infect our experience of others: their aura decays, the look they return is unseen, or even worse, their eyes no longer look back at us because they no longer possess any moral uniqueness. The moral substance of individuals is disappearing with the transformations of the practices that supported and gave point to it. In the context of the mini-history suggested thus far, this can be stated as the thesis that the perceptual experience of others, the experience of their aura, as a consequence of the naturalisation of the world became, at best, and for as long as they last, deontological reasons; they became the reflective question of rules or the constraints on rules for treating others as ends in themselves. Which is not to claim that whatever was or may be significant in perceiving the aura of another is a matter of simple or direct perception, a raw experience beyond all conceptualisation, rules, or norms. Aura could not decay, evaporate, or wither if that were the case. The disenchantment of the world, its rationalization, among other consequences, drains persons and things of their auratic particularity and thereby transforms questions of value into *reflective* ones concerning the character and status of rules (reasons) for action. And while the distancing work of reflection represents the standpoint of disenchanted morality, above all of centralist morality, it contains a potentiality for going beyond this standpoint.[30]

29 Korsgaard, *Creating the Kingdom of Ends*, p. 297.

30 Stated differently: the transformation of auratic individuality into rules discriminating

If nothing else, Adorno wants to insist that the "natural" immediacies of Hobbesian man themselves "violate" subjectivity, and that the cause of immediacy, what it truly wants and what would support it against repressive morality, is salvaged not in the immediacies of practice but through circumspect reflection. At one level, the move to reflection is just the acknowledgement of a practical impasse – the satisfactions desired cannot be had through the means available. At another level, however, reflection intends the recovery or discovery or institution of, again, "the universal which [makes] up the substance of the individual claim" (MM, A16). Adorno's reference here to "the universal" is equivocal, referring back to the mythological and theological categories that once gave auratic substance to the claims of individuals (e.g., their being God's creatures), to the secularisation of these categories (e.g., Kant's conception of individuals being ends in themselves), to the social practices through which persons were given the status of, say, right-holders, and, finally, referring forward to whatever categories or concepts that will figure as the replacement for those failed claims to substantiality while satisfying the requirement for individuals to possess aura. In its forward reference, reflection can be considered an ever tactful continuation and replacement of tact, challenging rather than colluding with modernity's nominalistic self-conception, which reads all universality as Hobbes read the old virtues: as ideological disguises for hierarchical domination, as if all normative universality and rationality were antithetical to the claims of singular subjects.[31] To the degree to which the Hobbesian claim is true,

between others as ends in themselves or as means can be interpreted both progressively as an enlightening rationalization of previous moral experience, and critically as the reflective memory of previous moral experience. To insist upon a both/and formulation of this situation, rather than an either/or, is required in order to sustain Adorno's aporetic perspective.

31 Although lacking the element of ideological critique, Hobbes's detection of illusion is carried forward in J. L. Mackie's *Ethics: Inventing Right and Wrong* (Harmondsworth: Penguin, 1977), in which it is argued that nothing in the world corresponds to assertoric moral judgements – there are no such peculiar items in the world as moral facts about which such judgements could be true or false to. As opposed to the mere falsity of moral realism, arguably the dominant trend in modern moral thought has been some form of "emotivism" or ethical expressivism. For contemporary defences of the latter, see Simon Blackburn, *Spreading the Word* (Oxford: Oxford University Press, 1984), chapter 6; and Alan Gibbard, *Wise Choices, Apt Feelings* (Cambridge, Mass.: Harvard University Press, 1990). In chapter 3 of *After Virtue*, "Emotivism: Social Content and Social Context," MacIntyre pursues a line of argument concerning the breakdown of the relation between civilisation as humanity and civilisation as self-preservation that is strongly analogous to Adorno's. So, for example, he states: "[E]motivism entails the obliteration of any genuine distinction between manipulative and non-manipulative social relations. . . . The sole reality of distinctively moral discourse [according to emotivism] is the attempt of one will to align the attitudes, feelings, preferences and choices of another with its own. Others are always means, never ends. . . . For one way of re-envisaging the emotivist self is as having suffered a deprivation, a stripping away of qualities that were once believed to belong to the self. The self is now thought of as lacking any necessary social identity"

nominalism and the claims of immediacy have point. Reflection, responding to the violences of immediacy, the disappearance of aura, must be "circumspect," tactful, however, because the reason and universality that would not be at one with domination and would, knowingly, respond to the individual claim through acknowledging the "distance" that would allow the other to be accepted into consciousness as other are not directly available, not elements of existing practices. Conversely, immediacy in practice, which is here taken as coextensive with nominalism, because it recognises no distance, not only leaves the claims of individuality unsupported but engenders an unbroken continuum between immediacy in its moral and immoral senses, for example, the collapse of love into frenzied, erotic possessiveness. The local vandal, the date-rapist, the wife-beater realise the ethical truth of Hobbesian man; in them the "withering of experience" (MM, A33), the withering of the "imponderably delicate aura" becomes palpable.

If the first three fragments we examined propose a retreat of the ethical from public into private, and reveal private existence as constitutively aporetic, these second two fragments take the analysis further by suggesting not only that the practices of the intimate sphere are deformed, but that contributing to that deformation is an even profounder loss: a disintegration of those elements that make us moral subjects – an event described somewhat mysteriously in terms of the destruction of aura. Further, Adorno implies, the loss of moral subjectivity is coordinated with fundamental issues in moral rationality. The destruction or decay of aura occurs simultaneously with the emergence of the conceptual frameworks of naturalism and centralism, which are the competing rationalities of this disintegrated state of affairs. Yet if Adorno's story about ethical life is true, then these rationalities are also rationalizations (in the critical rather than Weberian sense) of our disintegrated ethical world, and there is hence a *rationality deficit* in our ethical life. If progress in understanding this is to be made, then it is to an analysis of the destruction of aura and experience, and the processes that brought about this destruction, that we must turn.

(pp. 22, 23, 32). Adorno must believe that more has been stripped away than social identity; or better, more is lost in the stripping away of social identity than that identity itself. The question raised by his reflective procedure and his employment of the term "aura" is, what has been stripped away and how? Responding to these questions is the work of the next chapter.

2

DISENCHANTMENT: THE SCEPTICISM OF ENLIGHTENED REASON

How can we begin to comprehend what is involved in the destruction of aura? Adorno borrowed the notion of the destruction of aura from his friend, Walter Benjamin, and associated it with another and more central Benjaminian theme: the destruction of experience. In the opening section of the "The Storyteller," Benjamin describes soldiers returning home from the First World War shell-shocked, grown silent, not richer but poorer in experience: "A generation that had gone to school on a horse-drawn streetcar now stood under the open sky in a countryside in which nothing remained unchanged but the clouds, and beneath these clouds, in a field of force of destructive torrents and explosions, was the tiny, fragile human body."[1] Commenting on this passage, Giorgio Agamben states:

> Today, however, we know that the destruction of experience no longer necessitates a catastrophe, and that humdrum daily life in any city will suffice. For modern man's average day contains virtually nothing that can still be translated into experience . . . it is this non-translatability into experience that now makes everyday existence intolerable – as never before – rather than an alleged poor quality of life or its meaninglessness compared with the past (on the contrary, perhaps everyday existence has never been so replete with meaningful events). . . . [E]xperience has its necessary correlation not in knowledge but in authority – that is to say, the power of words and narration; and no one now seems to wield sufficient authority to guarantee that truth of an experience, and if they do, it does not in the least occur to them that their own authority has its roots in an experience. On the contrary, it is the character of the present time that all authority is founded on what cannot be experienced, and nobody is inclined to accept the validity of an authority whose sole claim to legitimation was experience.[2]

1 In *Illuminations,* translated by Harry Zohn (London: Collins/Fontana Books, 1970), p. 84.

2 *Infancy and History: Essays on the Destruction of Experience,* trans. Liz Heron (London: Verso: 1993), pp. 13–14. I take it that Agamben's conception of authority "founded on what cannot be experienced" is meant to refer to what Weber termed legal-rational authority.

A rational and cognitive relation to auratic individuality would require not, or not only, different beliefs than we now possess, but fundamentally different cognitive resources, different forms and types of relations between persons, different mechanisms mediating subject and object. Agamben suggests three relational forms that have disappeared or are disappearing from rationalized modernity: *experience*, rational and legitimate *authority* grounded in experience, and emphatic truth; but since, *pace* Agamben, there cannot be truth without knowledge, then what has disappeared is that *form* of knowledge that could be coordinated with experience and authority in the appropriate sense.

In their *Dialectic of Enlightenment* Adorno and Horkheimer provide a genealogy of modern enlightened reason that seeks to demonstrate, first, that it is through and through a form of instrumental reason, and, second, that this formation of reason now structures the dominant practices of social life. This work thus provides Adorno and Horkheimer's version of the Weberian account of the disenchantment of the world through intellectualism, and modern society's becoming an "iron cage." Since the writing of *Dialectic of Enlightenment* partially overlaps with the writing of *Minima Moralia*, it is reasonable to assume that the theoretical framework of the former structures the aporetic account of ethical life in the latter. The "dialectic of enlightenment," which at least in one of its construals refers to the rationalization of reason, is thus responsible for the destruction of experience, non-legal-rational authority, and ethical knowledge, whose joint destruction explains the destruction of auratic individuality. This thesis cannot be extracted from a reading of either *Dialectic of Enlightenment* or *Minima Moralia*, but only from reading these two works together.

After explicating the three fundamental features of modern moral thought, I present the focal argument of *Dialectic of Enlightenment*, namely, that instrumental reason is inherently negative and critical, and therefore sceptical; and then go on to elaborate that scepticism in terms of the destruction of ethical knowledge, experience, and authority. The account of the destructions is inferential; they are implied but rarely thematic in Adorno's writing; and when they are thematic, it is in contexts removed from the text of *Dialectic of Enlightenment*. Hence, although the account of the destruction of knowledge, experience, and authority is free-standing, the full evidence that it belongs to Adorno's thought emerges only as we progress. Part of the reason for this is that on its own *Dialectic of Enlightenment* does not possess the conceptual resources to adequately back the assumptions about the destruction of experience, authority, and knowledge as cognitive forms; on the contrary, a variety of confusions bedevil the text which prohibit it from satisfactorily achieving its intended end. And this entails that the case *for* experience, authority, and knowledge as intrinsic ingredients in ethical life cannot be inferred from the terms which describe or explain their destruction. Only an "analytic" reconstruction of the dialectic of enlightenment in narrowly epistemic terms will ultimately support its focal argument. Adorno does not achieve clarity about the necessity for this epistemic orientation until he writes *Negative Dialectics.*

1. Disenchantment, Rationalism, and Universalism

> Liberation from superstition is called *enlightenment* . . . it must be very difficult to preserve or instil in someone's way of thinking (especially the public's) that merely negative element which constitutes enlightenment proper.
>
> Kant

The process of disintegration implied by Adorno's micrological analyses of the intimate sphere, his accounts of tact and the decay of aura project an historical movement from thick concepts to centralism, from ethical life lived in terms of a complex of practices expressive of a conception of "the good life for man" to its being supported by some anchoring first principles ideally susceptible to a priori theoretical legitimation. For Adorno the relation between these two ideal type ethical situations is one of cause and effect: the disintegration of premodern *Sittlichkeit* engenders theoretical reflection in search of a priori foundations, which itself then contributes to the further disintegration of ethical life and a further rationalizing of reason. If it was once the case that rational reflection upon ethical life meant its codification or harmonisation with some privileged, canonical texts, it has since become the attempt to a priori ground or found the moral point of view, to give it pertinence and significance apart from the contingencies of communal practice. Modern centralist thought transforms ethical reflection into moral theory.

Historically, three pressures converged to make the search for rational foundations for morality necessary and intelligible. The first pressure was the explosive emergence of natural science. Its mathematical, quantitative depiction of the world challenged the view that ethical predicates could be descriptive. Once it was conceded, for example, that color predicates (as exemplars of secondary qualities) do not refer to anything that is mimetically like red sensory impressions and that the look of the visible is in fact a product of the action of invisible particles (composed of only primary qualities) upon our sensory apparatus, then there could be no hope that predicates like "cruel" or "generous" referred to real properties of worldly events like actions. Second, and directly continuous with this, there developed the privilege of reason-giving or theoretical justification itself. If the truth of canonical texts could be challenged by a theoretical physics resting on axiomatic first principles, there was no reason to believe the truth claims on moral issues of canonical texts (and the traditionalist practices they supported) were any firmer. It thus became urgent to supply nonconventionally or nontraditionally backed reasons for the existence of any moral norm or practice, and ideally to propound a conception of moral truths and moral reasoning that would operate on analogy with mathematical (geometrical) reasoning.[3] Finally, the growth of religious, economic, and political individualism within a world in which the first two pressures were already operative stripped the last remnants of legitimacy from the belief that social roles constituted the moral substance of persons. When this new individualism was harnessed with the new rationalism of moral theory, it generated, with the backing of previous Christian thought, a demand for universalism as the "flip side" of individualism.[4] *Disenchantment* (of the natural world), *rationalism* (the demand for theoretical justification) as the rationalization of reason, and *universalism* as the flip side of *individualism* converge to instigate the belief that morality could be salvaged only by a priori argumentation since, clearly, no socially constituted or factual evidence could be shown to be legitimate against these characterisations of the world and demands on reflection.

The identification of disenchantment, rationalization, and universalism as fundamental ingredients in the evolution of enlightened modern moral thought is meant to be a relatively benign and neutral characterisation. Adorno and Horkheimer's *Dialectic of Enlightenment* can be conceived as possessing two interlocking analytical motives: first, to explain the profound inner unity of disenchantment, rationalization, and universalism by elaborating their joint conceptual presuppositions; and, second, to demonstrate how these same conceptual presuppositions explain the dual character of enlightened thought as simultaneously progressive and disintegrating. As stated this second claim is ambiguous since even Kant is content to characterise enlightenment as critical and negative, or,

3 The equating or analogising of moral truths with mathematical truths was one, prominent response to disenchantment and the rationalization of reason, forming at least one limb of the Kantian settlement I take up in the next chapter. But the possibilities of response and hence the narrative of the emergence of secular morality is immensely complex; in particular, I am here downplaying the intervention of the "sceptical method" of the British moral sense tradition. Both the natural law/intuitionist tradition and that of the moral sense tradition are brought into some kind of synthesis in Kant. For a useful account of the emergence of secular morality with Kant's moral theory as its endpoint, the view explicitly upheld by Adorno, see J. B. Schneewind, *The Invention of Autonomy* (Cambridge: Cambridge University Press, 1998).

4 "The idealizing supposition of a universalistic form of life, in which everyone can take up the perspective of everyone else and can count on reciprocal recognition by everybody, makes it possible for individuated beings to exist within a community – individualism as the flip-side of universalism." Jürgen Habermas, *Postmetaphysical Thinking: Philosophical Essays,* trans. William Mark Hohengarten (Oxford: Polity Press, 1992), p. 186.

as Rüdiger Bittner states it, a work of "desecration."[5] To call enlightened thought disintegrating involves a stronger thesis, namely, that the formation of reason that eventuates from the process of enlightenment is partly constituted by the negativity from which it evolves, which is to claim that *enlightened reason is itself intrinsically sceptical.* Enlightened reason cannot shake or eliminate from itself the negativity that permits it to accomplish its fundamental tasks of disenchantment, desecration, rationalization, and universalisation.

Making out this claim, however, is more complex and difficult than it may at first appear since the very same formation of reason which Adorno and Horkheimer identify as sceptical is widely interpreted, including by Kantian moral philosophies, as progressive and rational, which is in part what was implied by terming the characterisation of modern disenchantment, rationalism, and universalism "neutral." Before turning to *Dialectic of Enlightenment,* in order to better appreciate the stakes here, it will prove helpful to outline a version of the enlightenment that possesses the elements of disenchantment, the rationalization of reason, and universalism but while acknowledging the sceptical moment nonetheless construes the process as progressive.

In *Moral Consciousness and Communicative Action,* Jürgen Habermas potently focuses the experience of the historical collapse of ethical life into moral reflection and theory into the image of the phase of adolescence concentrated into a single moment of time in which the adolescent adopts, for the first time, a hypothetical attitude "towards the normative contexts of his life-world which enables him to see through everything unmercifully." Under his unmerciful gaze, the world he unproblematically has inhabited is "suddenly deracinated, stripped of its natural validity,"[6] disenchanted. If this adolescent is to avoid returning to the prejudices of the community he must reconstruct his world by distinguishing between norms that are factually held from those norms that deserve to be held. Ultimately, Habermas argues, he will come to recognise that there remain *only* the idealised procedures of rational argumentation itself (Habermas's intersubjective and communicational version of Kant's formula of universal law) that are rationally and motivationally satisfying. Rationalism is necessary.

5 Rüdiger Bittner, "What Is Enlightenment?," in James Schmidt (ed.), *What Is Enlightenment? Eighteenth-Century Answers and Twentieth-Century Questions* (London: University of California Press, 1996), p. 352.

6 Jürgen Habermas, *Moral Consciousness and Communicative Action,* trans. Christian Lenhardt and Shierry Weber Nicholsen (Cambridge, Mass.: MIT Press, 1990), pp. 126–7. In concentrating enlightenment into the phase of adolescence, Habermas is picking up Kant's statement that "Enlightenment is mankind's exit from its self-incurred immaturity."

> When measured against the moral actions of everyday life, the change of attitude which discourse ethics with respect to the procedure it singles out (i.e. the transition to argument) retains something unnatural; it signifies a break with the naivety of spontaneously held validity claims upon whose intersubjective recognition the communicative practice of everyday life depends. This unnaturalness is like an echo of that developmental catastrophe which the devaluation of the world of tradition signifies historically – and which is what prompts us to attempt a *reconstruction on a higher plane.*[7]

Habermas's critical adolescent discovers through his rebellion that the only reliable thing is rational argumentation just as the Kantian agent discovers that the only rationally reliable thing is the procedure for maxim testing. But by making unperturbable reliability central, the adolescent finds himself cut off from the contingencies that constituted the possibilities of ethical experience for him and those around him. "Reconstruction on a higher plane" is precisely the movement from experience into theory; in conceiving of reflection as argumentation governed by a priori rules both the arguer and norms lose their cultural-historical place, the urgencies of the present and the weight of memory (all of which traditionally motivated ethical action). Habermas's communicative version of the moral law "generalises, abstracts, and stretches the presuppositions of context-bound communicative actions by extending their range to include competent subjects beyond the provincial limits of their own par-

7 Ibid. Habermas's theory possesses two aspects: a conception of the pragmatic presuppositions of communicative interaction and an associated moral principle. Consensual speech acts, he contends, rest on a background consensus which is formed from the implicit mutual recognition of four validity claims: (1) that what is said be linguistically intelligible and comprehensible; (2) that the propositional content or the existential presuppositions of what is said be true; (3) that the speaker be truthful (honest or sincere) in what she says; (4) that what the speaker says (and hence does) is right or appropriate in the light of existing norms and values. Habermas's universalisation principle (U) is meant to provide a rule for the impartial testing of norms for their moral worthiness. It states that a norm is valid only if: "All affected can accept the consequences and the side effects its general observation can be anticipated to have for the satisfaction of everyone's interests (and these consequences are preferred to those of known alternative possibilities" (p. 65).

It is not to the point to here rehearse in detail objections to Habermas's proposal; for this, see my *Recovering Ethical Life: Jürgen Habermas and the Future of Critical Theory* (London: Routledge, 1995), and Albrecht Wellmer, "Ethics and Dialogue: Elements of Moral Judgement in Kant and Discourse Ethics," in his *The Persistence of Modernity,* trans. David Midgley (Oxford: Polity Press, 1991), pp. 113–256. Two objections, both of which circulate around the problem of rationalized reason and its abstraction from the concreteness of ethical experience, are worth mentioning at this juncture. First, Habermas makes an error that I argue Kant also makes, namely, conflating norms of rationality (which are norms for argumentation in Habermas's case) with moral norms. As Wellmer nicely states the point, "obligations to rationality are concerned with arguments regardless of who voices them, whereas moral obligations are concerned with people regardless of their arguments" (p. 185; see also p. 187). Second, Habermas is unable to close the gap between norms that have been found intersubjectively valid and those that are true.

ticular form of life."[8] As Habermas thus concedes: rationalized moral theory decontextualizes and demotivates.

Finally, the consequence of the interaction of sceptical *disenchantment,* the *rationalism* of reconstructing morality on a higher plane, and *universalism* is the production of the isolated individual, on the one hand, and, on the other, the discovery that there "*are no shared structures preceding the individual except the universals of language use,*"[9] just as there are no moral norms preceding the Kantian moral subject except those of reason itself. On this account, but for reasons that as yet are opaque, the critical gaze of the enlightenment subject marks a movement from a complexity of beliefs binding subjects to one another and their objects to reason itself; the only stable objects for rationalized, enlightened reason are its own norms and procedures. Hence, under the "moralising gaze" of the rationalized moral subject the ethical totality loses its "quality of naïve acceptance, and *the normative power of the factual [is] weakened.*"[10] Within the scope of the weakened normative power of the factual, we should include the eyes, now deadened, of the once auratic individual.

Although Habermas would prefer to regard his discourse ethics, properly speaking, as only a continuing complement and corrective to the ethical substance of the life-world, his image of sceptical adolescence and the security provided by rationalized reason make this position difficult to sustain. Is it not just the initial and ground intelligibility in general of ethical life that the unmerciful gaze of his adolescent and our historical community that he represents dissolves, placing him and us within the impossible space of an unlivable scepticism and undischargeable rationalism? Can we make sense of the "unnatural" shift to argumentation unless we regard the telescoped moment of adolescence as invoking the "historical catastrophe" of the utter dissolution of conventionally held and backed beliefs, and thus as invoking a moment or the threat of a moment of radical moral scepticism? The phase of adolescence signifies not a moment in which we are forced to choose among a range of potential moral norms or ethical codes, wherein it might seem plausible to subject the going options to some form of reflective coherentising, but rather, precisely as encapsulated by the narrative of tact, a moment in which the fact that moral norms, codes, and conventions suddenly appear as merely conventional generates a general quandary as to what morality really *is* beyond, say, the paternal or communal imposition of order, or the "etiquette" of our community, or a mutual back-scratching arrangement that

8 *Moral Consciousness and Communicative Action,* p. 202.

9 Ibid., p. 203; emphasis mine.

10 Ibid., p. 108; emphasis mine. This weakening of the normative power of the factual is the pivotal aspect of disenchantment, and hence what I argue is most in need of being reversed.

allows everyone to follow their self-interest without undue interference, or an arbitrary code for keeping unruly desires in check (or males or elders in power), or just the unreflective dead-hand of tradition.

Pressing Habermas's story in this way cannot yet be taken as a criticism of it. Rather, it means to regiment this account in order that three features of it become perspicuous. First, because traditional ethical life is the victim of progressive enlightenment, we must construe Kantian reason, whether as a procedure of maxim testing or a procedure of argumentation, in a centralist manner, as founding or grounding the moral point of view, and hence as determining what makes or constitutes a reason for action moral; this is what it means to reconstitute ethical life on a higher plane. Second, in tandem with this shift to reason itself, we must take literally Habermas's statement that for purposes of moral deliberation there are no longer any shared structures preceding the individual except the universals of language use. Finally, and slightly more problematically, we should see in the result of the rationalizing of morality a continuation rather than a dissolution of the inaugurating sceptical moment since the "unnatural" shift to argumentation never does return the modern moral agent to an ethical life-world. To state the same point another way, there is an alliance between the moment of original scepticism and the kind of reflectiveness appropriate to rationalized reason; by its perpetual detachment from concrete experience, the reflective distancing of rationalized reason, its being the rationality of reason, embeds and recapitulates the dissolving gaze of the adolescent; such reason is sceptical.

This last thesis is less contentious than it initially appears. In both "Discourse Ethics" and "Morality and Ethical Life," Habermas concedes that discourse ethics itself cannot conceivably be regarded as making up the meaning deficit left by the transition into reflectiveness, a deficit that involves moral norms losing "the thrust and efficacy of empirical motives for action."[11] He continues:

> To become effective in practice, every universalist morality has to make up for this loss of concrete ethical substance, which is initially accepted because of the cognitive advantages attending it. Universalist moralities are dependent on forms of life that are rationalized in that they make possible the prudent application of universal moral insights and support motivations for translating insights into moral action. Only those forms of life that meet universalist moralities halfway in this sense fulfil the conditions necessary to reverse the abstractive achievements of decontextualization and demotivation.[12]

11 Habermas is here thus conceding what Kant did not, namely, that pure practical reason is not essentially motivating.

12 Ibid., p. 109.

Communicative reason can accomplish its rationalizing work (its "cognitive advantage") only through abstraction; it is this abstraction which generates decontextualization and demotivation; and decontextualization and demotivation must be compensated for if universalist morality is to be effective in practice. Let us assume that this is not a vicious or self-defeating argument; rather, Habermas is conceding, in his own way, that the labor of enlightened reason is progressive and regressive at once. As I have argued elsewhere and say more about later, enlightened moral universalism conflates a number of different senses of universality.[13] For present purposes, two perspectivally distinct implications of Habermas's statement should be stressed. On the one hand, if universalist morality requires a form of life to meet it "halfway," which is to say, to contextualize it and thereby give its norms and requirements a motivational anchoring in everyday practices, then communicative reason is not self-sufficient – it requires, as Weber informed us, commitment and conviction in order to be carried through. Or, we could say, by inference, that although communicative reason is self-sufficient *as reason,* modern rationality is not self-sufficient but requires the cooperation of the nonrational for its effectiveness. Rationalized reason and enlightened moral universalism are *dependent upon* what is extrinsic to them. On the other hand, if the abstractive achievements of decontextualization and demotivation are required to be reversed if ethical life is to be possible, then we must regard the absence of ethical substance as implied by the unmerciful, reflective gaze of enlightenment as permanent, and hence the cold gaze as a constitutive feature of the rationalized reason it precipitates. The cold gaze synthesises (or is the synthesis of) rationalization, disenchantment, and universalism in what is called moral or communicative reason. Enlightenment reason is thus contentful (because truly a form of reason and rationality) and sceptical at once.

2. The Principle of Immanence

If this characterisation of enlightened reason is accurate, then in the first instance what is required is a critical explanation of why the process of enlightenment produces a rationalization of reason that leads it to claim self-sufficiency, and why this reason in its claimed self-sufficiency is sceptical. Notoriously, Adorno and Horkheimer claim that enlightened reason is instrumental reason, the constituting action of which is abstraction and the consequent identifying and subsuming of different particulars under some common universal (concept or law), and that the sceptical negativity of instrumental reason is carried through by its work of abstraction and subsumption. It would be perverse in the extreme to flatly

13 See *Recovering Ethical Life,* pp. 191–6; and Chapter 3, section 3, below.

assert that instrumental rationality is intrinsically sceptical; nor is this what Adorno and Horkheimer say. Rather, they claim that enlightened reason and rationality as a whole are only instrumental, and that the scepticism of instrumental rationality occurs only when it claims to be total and self-sufficient.[14] And while this thesis might sound anodyne, it is not because the claim to totality and self-sufficiency is not accidental but rather is a consequence of the essential negativity of instrumental reason; enlightening critique necessarily includes other formations of reason amongst its critical targets. Rationalization is necessarily the rationalization of reason; rationalized reason is sceptical, and because sceptical it is thereby irrational. If the self-sufficiency of instrumental reason renders it sceptical, and the claim to self-sufficiency is intrinsic to its movement, form of claiming, and formation, then this would explain how and why our highest value, critical reason, devaluates itself. Of course, reason as instrumental is also dominating and repressive. But unless there is a cognitive and rationality deficit in instrumental rationality, rationalization becomes simply the Weberian iron cage (or Foucauldian discipline) to which the only response is nonrational rebellion.

It is tempting to read *Dialectic of Enlightenment* as telling a counter-history to the progressive, demythologising philosophy of history provided by writers like Kant and Habermas. From Rousseau's "Second Discourse," in which "progress has been so many steps in appearance toward the perfection of the individual, and in effect toward the decrepitude of the species,"[15] critiques of enlightenment have taken the form of proposing

14 Within their genealogical strategy, Horkheimer and Adorno argue that what became instrumental rationality emerged through the cunning of reason as exemplified by Odysseus. This entails, genealogically, that rationality includes within itself the deceptions and deceit through which it was formed. Because the role of the cunning of reason argument is to enable us to see the overlap between Odysseus, who is presented as a proto-bourgeois right down to his penchant for do-it-yourself (in his bed building), and ourselves, then its textual function is to make us feel the deceptions in our submission to rational authority. And this is continuous with a general intention of *Dialectic of Enlightenment,* namely, to enable us to perceive the power of modern reason, its authority, *as* domination by matching the opaque present with a past in which the domination was visible. That reason is dominating does not by itself show that it is irrational or sceptical, alas. And while the cunning of reason argument does, I think, demonstrate irrationality, because its intention is to transform the reader's self-understanding, to charismatically engender a conversion, it proves insufficient as immanent critique. Nonetheless, it is worth noting the argument I pursue here is a component of a more complex argumentative and critical strategy. In his useful essay "The Possibility of a Disclosing Critique of Society: The *Dialectic of Enlightenment* in the Light of Current Debates in Social Criticism," *Constellations* 7/1 (March 2000): 116–27, Axel Honneth catalogues the rhetorical strategies (narrative metaphor, chiasmus, exaggeration) that enable the text to performatively disclose our social world in new way; strangely, however, he detaches the effort of world disclosure from the more austere task of providing a metacritique of formal reason.

15 *The First and Second Discourses,* trans. Victor Gourevitch (New York: Harper and Row, 1986), p. 177.

inverted or regressive philosophies of history. And passages of *Dialectic of Enlightenment* sound as if they were proposing such a regressive philosophy of history.

> Mythology itself set off the unending process of enlightenment in which ever and again, with the inevitability of necessity, every specific theoretic view succumbs to destructive criticism that it is only belief, until even the very notion of spirit, of truth and, indeed, enlightenment itself have become animistic magic. The principle of fateful necessity which brings low the heroes of myth and derives as a logical consequence from the pronouncement of the oracles, does not merely, when refined to the stringency of formal logic, rule in every rationalistic system of Western philosophy, but itself dominates the series of systems which begins with the hierarchy of gods and, in a permanent twilight of the idols, hands down an identical content: anger against insufficient righteousness. Just as myths already realise enlightenment, so enlightenment with every step becomes more deeply engulfed in mythology. It receives all matter from myths, in order to destroy them; and even as judge it comes under the mythic curse. (DoE, 11–12)

This passage does not represent a turn to the philosophy of history in order to unseat an intransigent abstract rationalism. Rather, the historical endpoints inscribed within it are dictated by the enlightenment conception of reason itself: it opposes myth. What appears as a developmental history to Habermas and Kant is thus dependent upon a structural or conceptual dualism: enlightenment versus myth. The mythic-dominated origin of culture and civilisation is a posit of enlightenment rationality itself (DoE, 8). This posit raises a wholly *conceptual* question: what are the logical parameters of myth and enlightenment which could explain how the project of overcoming myth, a project that in its self-conscious form is uniquely modern (however much anticipated by Greek philosophy), could eventuate in the nihilistic present? That we should conceive of this conceptual issue historically, as a process of overcoming, is demanded by enlightened reason, whose modern hegemony indeed comes to create the very process it projects onto the historical past. It is the coming-to-be of an historical necessity as project and process postulated by enlightenment philosophies of history, from Bacon and Kant to Marx, that Adorno and Horkheimer are seeking to undo not by substituting a regressive history for a progressive one but by dismantling the conceptual dualism of enlightenment and myth, and thereby the idea of history it grounds.[16]

16 In pursuing this project they were patently following the lead of Walter Benjamin's "Theses on the Concept of History," which had insisted that "there is no document of civilisation which is not at the same time a document of barbarism" (*Illuminations*, p. 258) and that by reifying the entwined process of civilisation and barbarism into a progressive philosophy of history the barbarism of civilisation is ideologically legitimated –

The thesis animating *Dialectic of Enlightenment* is not the historical proposition that civilisation has been a continual growth in the development of instrumental reason leading to a regression into mythology, barbarism, and the threat of total annihilation (but see ND, 320). We have already seen that for Adorno up until the commencement of modernity, and after, civilisation as self-preservation and civilisation as humanity were united, and thus that there has occurred throughout history a real progressive development in individuality and the ideals of enlightenment (freedom, equality, etc.), amongst other items. Horkheimer and Adorno refer to these ideals when they state that their task is to continue the process of reflection, forcing enlightenment to "examine itself": "The task to be accomplished is not the conservation of the past, but the redemption of the hopes of the past" (DoE, xv); and hence that the goal of their enterprise is "to prepare the way for a positive notion of enlightenment which will release it from blind domination" (DoE, xvi). Through reason's self-examination the most general aims of enlightenment are preserved: emancipation from fear and the establishment of humankind's sovereignty. Further, in the only place where he explicitly takes up the notion of regression, Adorno denies that it can intelligibly refer to a relapse into either an earlier phase of the individual's development or an earlier phase of collective development. But if regression is neither ontogenetic nor phylogenetic, then it does not refer to a developmental history at all. Regression is from an "existent possibility";[17] hence, historical regression refers to processes that displace extant possibilities of thought and action. If the dualism of enlightenment and myth inscribes a history, it is a history of the present: progressive and regressive tendencies within it are in accordance with the practices and ideals it furthers.[18]

it is part of the cost of progress – permitting the process it signifies to continue unabated. Again, the entwinement of civilisation and barbarism is not a thesis an enlightenment thinker need deny; nor that the costs of progress should be remembered. Benjamin's contention can have force only if he can demonstrate that barbarism is not an accidental accretion but intrinsic. But how could barbarism be intrinsic to reason? For Benjamin the answer to this question is that progressive philosophies of history, in virtue of conceiving of history in wholly teleological terms, must regard each present as only a means to the posited end, and thus can deny it significance in itself; philosophies of history instrumentalize history for the sake of its endpoint. And while this is pointed against historicism and strongly teleological theories, it does not touch the breadth of modern, enlightened rationality. Horkheimer and Adorno translate Benjamin's thesis into a narrower conceptual thesis; in place of barbarism they put instrumentality and scepticism. It is the effects of these features of enlightened reason which explain the entwinement of civilisation and barbarism.

17 Theodor W. Adorno, "On the Fetish Character in Music and the Regression of Listening," in his *The Culture Industry: Selected Essays on Mass Culture,* ed. and introduced by J. M. Bernstein (London: Routledge, 1991), p. 41.

18 That the *Dialectic* was ever read as a regressive philosophy of history is surprising; the implausibility of this reading was already demonstrated by Susan Buck-Morss, *The Origin of Negative Dialectics* (Hassocks, Sussex: Harvester Press, 1977), pp. 59–62. For excellent

Because enlightenment has so demonstrably failed to realise its fundamental aims and ideals, Adorno and Horkheimer turn with the third sentence of the text to its actual "programme": enlightenment understands itself as progressive demythologisation, "the disenchantment of the world; [t]he dissolution of myths and the ruin of fancy through knowledge" (DoE, 3). Because some mythic claims really were illusory and were a function of uncontrolled and naïve anthropomorphism, the programmatic and methodological negativity of enlightenment is not historically groundless. Nonetheless, this programme, so defined, is the critical object of Adorno and Horkheimer's analysis; there has been a mismatch between the aims and ideals of enlightenment, and its method of progressive demythologisation. Progressive demythologisation has yielded disenchantment but not liberation. *Dialectic of Enlightenment* rejects the conceptual dualism of enlightenment and myth upon which the project of progressive demythologisation relies: "already myth is enlightenment, and: enlightenment reverts to mythology" (DoE, xvi). The "already" and the "reverts" indicate that myth and enlightenment are being speculatively identified: myth contains a central moment of enlightenment and therefore is not its opposite; and enlightenment, in reifying itself against myth, falls prey to a fundamentally mythic principle.

The constitutive principle of mythic thought is the *principle of immanence*: "the explanation of every event as repetition" (DoE, 12). It is the principle of immanence – what Adorno will later call "identity thinking" – that is the joint between myth and enlightenment; equally, it is the hinge connecting rationality and instrumentality. The principle of immanence turns on a series of familiar platitudes: an item (object, event, property, etc.) is neither known nor explained by giving it a proper name; rather, an empirical item is recognised, and so cognised, only when it is classified in some way, when it is shown, via subsumption, to share characteristics or features with other items. Analogously, and by extension, an event is explained if it can be shown to fall within the ambit of a known pattern of occurrence, if it falls within the ambit of a known rule or is deducible from (subsumable by) a known law. What holds for empirical items equally holds for the concepts, rules, and laws that classify and explain them: they become cognised, rationalized, when subsumed under or shown to be deducible from higher-level concepts, rules, or laws.

The work of classification, subsumption, explanation, deduction each permits the item in question to be detached from its immediate sensory impact upon the cognising subject: classification and explanation negate

recent rebuttals, see: Robert Hullot-Kentor, "Back to Adorno," *Telos* 81 (Fall 1989): 5–29; and Christopher Rocco, "Between Modernity and Postmodernity: Reading *Dialectic of Enlightenment* Against the Grain," *Political Theory* 22/1 (February 1994): pp. 71–97.

immediacy and thereby objectify experience. Only when an item is objectified, detached from the subjective states to which its presence gives rise, can it be regarded as belonging to the furniture of the world; and only what belongs to the furniture of the world is a candidate for being manipulated and controlled. Conceptualisation accomplishes the minimum of objectification necessary for cognition. But since many, if not most, ordinary empirical concepts classify objects merely in accordance with their phenomenological appearance to subjects, most empirical concepts are anthropomorphic in the precise sense that makes anthropomorphism a source of illusion: order is gathered from how things affect and appear to embodied, sensuous subjects. Hence few empirical concepts are robustly objective or permit manipulation and control. What is objective must be detachable from the subjective effects to which it gives rise; and what is truly objective, non-anthropomorphic, out there, must be what can maximally be detached from the attitudinal effects it produces. But a subject matter is most compellingly detachable from the attitudinal effects to which it gives rise if "citing the kinds of states of affairs with which it deals is potentially contributive to the explanation of things *other than,* or *other than via,* our being in attitudinal states which take such states of affairs as object."[19] States of affairs having this characteristic are said to possess a wide cosmological role.[20] Although the idea of strong objectivity as involving a "wider range of intelligible and legitimate uses of the relevant" subject matter cited than its role in explaining the state of a subject does not restrict such objectivity to either explanatory contexts or, within those, "discourses dealing with causally active states of affairs," explanatory contexts dealing with causally active states of affairs are almost paradigm cases of such objectivity.[21]

Disenchantment is the extirpation of what is subjective, or, as expressed in a formulation to which we need to return, "the extirpation of animism" (DoE, 5). Disenchantment progresses through the operation of the two dominant, albeit logically distinct, features of the platitudinous principle of immanence: reiterability and instrumentality. If an item is cognised by being subsumed under a concept, rule, or law, then this concept, rule, or law is further cognised, rationalized, by being subsumed under a more general concept, rule, or law. Cognition is subsumption, subsumption is necessarily reiterable, and reiteration occurs through cognitive ascent from concrete to abstract, from particular to universal, from what is relatively universal, and thereby still in some respect particular, contingent, and conditioned, to what is more universal. If sub-

19 Crispin Wright, *Truth and Objectivity* (London: Harvard University Press, 1992), p. 196.
20 Wright contends (ibid., pp. 197–8), plausibly enough, that moral facts are unable to play a wide cosmological role.
21 Ibid., p. 198.

sumption is a necessary condition for objectification, and objectification a necessary condition for manipulation, then what provides for greater objectivity, a further detachment from subjectivity, ideally provides for greater control and manipulability. The anti-anthropomorphism that moves the demand for seeking items with an optimally wide cosmological role is realised in the platitudinous principles of reason implied by the principle of immanence. The idea of a unified science which would be deterministic, hierarchical, theory reductionist (our understanding of everything derivable from our understanding of the smallest structural components of the universe), and essentialist is the fullest expression of the convergence of the two aspects of the principle of immanence.[22]

Here are some indicative passages from Horkheimer and Adorno elaborating the principle of immanence as reiterative subsumption and instrumentality.

> There is no difference between the totemic animal, the dreams of the ghost-seer, and the absolute idea. On the road to modern science, men renounce any claim to meaning. They substitute formula for concept, rule and probability for cause. (DoE, 5) ... the Enlightenment recognises as being and event only what can be grasped in unity: its ideal is the system from which all and everything follows. The rationalist and empiricist versions do not differ on that. Even though the individual schools may interpret the axioms differently, the structure of scientific unity has always been the same.... The multiplicity of forms is reduced to position and arrangement, history to fact, things to matter. (DoE, 7) To the Enlightenment, that which does not reduce to numbers, and ultimately to the one, becomes illusion; modern positivism writes it off as literature. Unity is the slogan from Parmenides to Russell. The destruction of gods and qualities alike is insisted upon. (DoE, 7–8)

The platitudes of the principle of immanence – subsumption, reiterability, and instrumentality – are sufficient to explain the disenchantment of the world and its ramified consequences for even the most minimal forms of anthropomorphism. Since, however, subsumption on its own is logically compatible with anthropomorphism, the negativity of the principle of immanence must be accomplished through the cooperation of reiteration and instrumentality. Logically, reiteration, the cognitive ascent to more embracing forms of unification, is the methodological activation of the normative element of subsumption: if collection of the diverse under

22 For an exposition of this claim, see John Dupré, *The Disorder of Things: Metaphysical Foundations of the Disunity of Science* (Cambridge, Mass.: Harvard University Press, 1993), pp. 2–7. Dupré's critique of this ideal in the remainder of his book is instructive. While Wright is not a proponent of the ideal of a unified science, nonetheless if my twining of his conception with the principle of immanence is correct, then his strong conception of objectivity inherits the ideals of the now overtaken enlightenment program.

the one objectifies the diverse, then higher-level acts of unification are more objective. We realise the normative presupposition of subsumption through reiteration. In fact, however, reiteration will not put an end to anthropomorphism; gods can be principles of unity just as well as laws or theories, and the positing of ever more abstract gods was certainly intended as an effort toward an anti-anthropomorphic rationalization of experience. Since the gods can be and usually were causally active explainers, then what causally explains can plausibly be regarded as a component of the principle of reiteration itself, part of what gives reiteration its cognitive bite; playing a wider cosmological role is most directly realised when the role is causal. Instrumentality shifts the idea of causal explanation from the wholly contemplative, which still lets in the gods, to the interventionist; only ascents that provide for increased predictive power and potential control over natural events truly escape from the anthropomorphic web. Thus the reiterative operation of subsumptive thinking entails cognitive ascent, which thereby generates an emphatic pull toward universalism. Universalism becomes optimal when reason's own principles of subsumption and reiterability become self-conscious, thus rationalizing reason; the rationalization of reason will necessarily engender a claim for its self-sufficiency; and self-sufficient reason becomes fully or properly disenchanting when reiteration is harnessed to instrumentality. The platitudes of the principle of immanence are thus sufficient to explain how disenchantment, self-sufficient rationalism, and universalism become the constitutive features of enlightened reason.

Instrumentality in fact belongs to both the lowest and highest levels of the process since, self-evidently, conceptualization and mythic telling are both driven by the need for control and are assumed to be forms of control; instrumentality is thus written into subsumption and reiterative ascent. The pattern of control through understanding through subsumption is refined when it is discovered that understanding without the power of intervention is insufficient.

3. Enlightenment Depends on Myth

For Adorno and Horkheimer enlightenment refers not to an historical epoch but to "a series of related intellectual and practical operations which are presented as demythologising, secularising, or disenchanting some mythical, religious or magical representation of the world."[23] Their identification of the principle of immanence with instrumental reasoning is intended as an *explanation* of one of the cognitive achievements of mythic thought – how myths helped conquer fear by giving terrifying events an intelligible structure as recurring events within a cyclically struc-

23 Simon Jarvis, *Adorno: A Critical Introduction* (Oxford: Polity Press, 1998), p. 24.

tured natural world, thereby providing for a potential linkage between enlightenment and myth: "Myth intended report, naming, the narration of the beginning; but also presentation, confirmation, explanation . . . " (DoE, 8). Myth is indifferently or indiscriminately authoritative narration and instrumental knowledge. To say that myth indifferently contained these two aspects suggests that they were not clearly differentiated within mythic telling; hence the modern question whether myth and ritual were protoscience or "religious" representations enabling the acknowledgement of what could not be controlled presses for a cognitive discrimination wholly extrinsic to myth. The syntax of myth appears as an interweaving of narration and explanation, meaning and cause, and since there are no grounds short of enlightened reason's own sharp, evaluative discrimination of the cognitive difference and worth of them, it must be presumed that traditional myth contains them both. Further, because the mythic world was cyclical and ahistorical in character, the principle of myth as a whole was the principle of immanence – even mythic narration cognised events as repetitions of older events. While myth was always more than this principle, by being authoritative narration, it was the principle of immanence that was picked up and exploited by enlightenment. Yet this development would not have occurred without the modern conceptual dualism between myth and enlightenment – identificatory or subsumptive thinking was not, after all, exhaustive of mythic conceptuality.

Enlightenment, as a self-conscious project, defines itself as the critique of anthropomorphic myth; which is the claim that enlightenment is, in accordance with its own original understanding, *essentially critique,* without a positive content of its own and receiving "all its matter" from myth.[24] *The sceptical premise of enlightenment is its self-constitution as the abstract (because indefinite) negation of myth.* While in the first instance enlightenment took the basic principle of myth to be anthropomorphism, "the projection onto nature of the subjective" (DoE, 6), since neither the notion of projection nor that of subjective ever received a positive definition, then neither did myth; hence there existed no natural terminus to critique short of the principles of reason which make critique itself possible. What began with the critique of religion and the removal of the gods is carried through in the disappearance of values and secondary qualities (DoE, 8). But this is too mild a statement. If what counts *as* pro-

24 This definition is defended by Bittner in his "What Is Enlightenment?" The proximate origin of Adorno and Horkheimer's characterisation of enlightenment as critique and pure negativity is the Enlightenment chapter of Hegel's *Phenomenology of Spirit* (especially pp. 328–49), where "pure insight," relentless negativity, opposes itself to "pure faith," blind trust (p. 334). Trust here is blind because Enlightenment can only affirm itself, reason affirm itself, through its lack of trust. Proleptically, trust can be regarded as a figure for our always presupposed dependence on the world that rationalized reason seeks to excise from itself.

jection and *as* subjective are not defined, if there does not exist positive criteria for what is subjective or anthropomorphic, then there is no reason to attribute a positive end or goal to critique. Once projection becomes the *formal* rather than substantive object of critique, then whatever appears in a definite and therefore conditioned relation to the knowing subject becomes subject to critique. In this way conditionality itself becomes the mark of the anthropomorphic; finally, then, only what is unconditioned, fully detachable from the projecting subject, can count as objective. But conditionality is equally a mark of a defect from the perspective of the principle of immanence. Hence the sceptical movement of the critique of anthropomorphism and the reiterative ascent of the principle of immanence converge. If enlightenment is critique, and critique is realised through cognitive ascent, then in the final analysis, at the end of the negative process, the process of negation, the human itself, and hence truth and enlightenment themselves, are also myths and projections. Trivially, reiterative cognitive ascent and sceptical critique are the same process viewed from different angles. By seeing in each objective configuration something still too subjective, still too bound to the subjective affects to which it gives rise, sceptical critique seeks items with a wider cosmological role, and by seeking for items with a wider cosmological role it performs the operations of reiterative cognitive ascent. But one good reason for seeing items as still too subjective is the presumption of the principle of immanence; without it contingency and conditionedness could not give rise to epistemic anxiety or systematic doubt, to the need for further ascent and rationalization. The final picture of a disenchanted world is projected by the presupposition that the human is a projecting animal caught in the mirror of itself, hence the "true" world is a world without the human, the human becoming only a distorting perspective on a physical universe forever independent of it – after all items with the widest possible cosmological role ideally will not be coordinated with meaningful attitudinal affects.[25] The perfection of enlightenment scepticism is, exactly, one which surmounts the human and leaves it behind, a perspectival take on a world without perspective, a view from nowhere (which, of course, cannot be a "view" at all).[26] The construal of mathematical physics as paradigmatic for knowing and the correspon-

25 This dialectical movement is formalised in Kant's contention that reason has the task "to find for the conditioned knowledge obtained through the understanding the unconditioned whereby its unity is brought to completion" (B365 = A307). The understanding cannot accomplish its explanatory task without the guidance of reason; hence the effort of reason is the rationalization of the understanding till (ideally) it, the understanding, becomes identical with the normative constitution of reason itself.

26 See Thomas Nagel, *The View from Nowhere* (Oxford: Oxford University Press, 1986), chapter 5.

ding belief in reason as autonomous and self-legislating have their roots and legitimation in the mythic principle of immanence.

Enlightenment and myth each contain, at least, a double signification. Enlightenment is (1) positively, the overcoming of fear and the establishment of sovereignty through explanation; and (2) methodologically and formally, a negativity with respect to all contents. (2) is the means for realising (1). Myth is hence (1) substantively, the dogmatic (because mimetic) presentation (narration) of content in accordance with the principle of immanence; and (2) formally, that content itself, the *indeterminate* object of critique. Myth in sense (1) is already enlightenment in sense (1) because it is motivated by and includes an explanatory moment; while enlightenment in sense (2) reverts to myth in sense (1): its dynamic and critical activity is finally for the sake of a stable and closed order of understanding. Enlightenment must so revert because it has no space for myth in sense (2): all presumptive content, if conditioned, is formally equivalent to a projection. What counts as myth at any juncture is defined formally as what remains outside the reach of progressive negation. For this reason "the very notions of spirit, of truth, and, indeed, enlightenment itself become animistic magic," mere beliefs, further anthropomorphic illusions; or, in a similar vein, enlightenment "treats its own idea of human rights exactly as it does the old [Platonic] universals" (DoE, 6). Of course, the negativity of enlightenment which is not its reversion to myth, but the dogmatic consequence of reiterative cognitive ascent: "The world as a gigantic analytic judgement, the only one left over from all the dreams of science, is of the same mold as the cosmic myth which associated the cycle of spring and autumn with the kidnapping of Persephone" (DoE, 27). Hence the conclusion: "The absorption of factuality, whether in legendary prehistory or into mathematical formalism . . . makes the new appear as the predetermined, which is accordingly old" (ibid.). Reiterative cognitive ascent necessarily entails weakening the normative power of the factual; or rather, *it entails that only reason and not factuality can have normative power.*[27]

The dialectical entwinement of enlightenment and myth is dependent upon their mutual formation because of their mutual dependency in sense (2) of each: critique is always of a conditioned, determinate content; conditionality will always harbor the threat of something unseen distorting what is understood, thus the threat that what is understood is

27 This is implicit in the dialectic of understanding and reason mentioned in note 25. Its fullest expression is Kant's claim that "[r]eason does not here follow the order of things as they present themselves in appearances, but frames for itself with perfect spontaneity an order of its own according to ideas, to which it adapts the empirical conditions, and according to which it declares actions to be necessary, even thought they have never taken place, and perhaps never will take place" (B576 = A548).

merely subjective. Enlightenment originally took this to refer to the objects of knowledge, but in its modern formation it soon turned its focus upon the mediums of knowing itself: sensory images, the objects of sensory knowing, language, the practices in which linguistic activity is embedded, the history these practices undergo. In principle, there is no division to be drawn between illusory objects of knowing and the always conditioned mediums of knowing. Enlightenment as the pure light of reason, whose purity is constituted through its negative self-definition, and hence in its constitution through the practice of abstract negation, needs and *depends* upon myth in sense (2) as the material condition of what in the end will become its processual self-affirmation. Structurally, enlightenment instrumentalises the object and mediums of critique for the sake of its own self-possession and self-affirmation: each successful critical encounter further legitimates both enlightenment's scepticism and rationalism. And if all contents and mediations are conditioned, then each encounter will be successful. Because myth (2) material remains material-to-be-negated, indeterminate stuff for the light of reason to shine upon, then the progressive marriage of enlightenment and myth is the dissolution of both: enlightenment into abstract, self-sufficient reason and myth into a meaningless world – events and practices as, at best, only meaningless instances of natural law. Reiterative cognitive ascent and disenchantment as demythologisation are, again, the same effort of reason seen from competing perspectives; from the perspective of reiterative cognitive ascent, enlightenment reverts to mythic stasis, for example, the laws of pure reason, the universals of language use, the method of natural science: form can be its only content when any "external" content can be regarded as a projection. From the perspective of progressive demythologisation the negativity of reason overtakes all the objects and mediations it forms (or acknowledges) along the way, including itself. Reiterative cognitive ascent progresses toward the self-sufficiency of reason in relation to any content; while sceptical demythologisation, the active form of the negative principle, progresses toward the autonomy of the will, pure will, will to power; that is, if the point of reiterative cognitive ascent is demythologisation, then it must become the attempt to remove passivity, dependence, conditionality; the cognitive version of that achievement would be either an ideal physical theory or the principles of a self-legislating reason, while the volitional one would be a free, self-determining will. The process that leads to both of these ideal forms when continued one step further leads to their sceptical displacement: the devaluation of truth and self-legislation without rational law (Nietzschean self-making). The claim to self-sufficiency of reason or will, the inability of enlightened reason to avow its material conditions of operation, demonstrates its *scepticism* is equally a form of *irrationality*.

The contention that rationalized reason is intrinsically sceptical – because it is without an intrinsic end or purpose, and reflectively bound to dissolving its own meaning and worth – goes some of the way toward delegitimating "the modern version of independent theoretical curiosity, utility, self-knowledge, progress in research, and so on."[28] However, the charge of scepticism by itself could, conceivably, leave enlightened reason in the aporetic predicament which Nietzsche and Weber, for instance, place it, that is, as truly and rightfully all the reason there is or could be and yet self-stultifying in its operation. In giving their account of the formation of the self-sufficiency of instrumental reason through the course of its critical endeavours, Adorno and Horkheimer thus continually underline the *dependence* of critique on the objects it seeks to desecrate. If the objects of critique are in some weighty sense a condition of critique that reason cannot avow – they are only occasions of self-affirmation – then enlightened reason is not self-sufficient in the manner it presumes. Enlightenment *depends* upon myth, it depends upon the entire range of anthropomorphisms for the possibility of enacting its sceptical reflections. Without material to negate, there can be no enlightenment; without the material mediations of reason in sensory states and its objects, language and its social conditioning, reason could not rationalize itself; if these are neutral as historical theses, they become performatively self-defeating as a characterisation of reason as a whole. *If rationalized reason is constituted essentially by the principle of immanence, then it cannot avow its conditionality.* Enlightened reason's intrinsic claim to independence and self-sufficiency rationally prohibits it from acknowledging its dependency on its object. The "dialectic" of enlightenment is a dialectic of claimed independence and disavowed dependence; and thus in the same way in which the master in Hegel's version of the dialectic of independence and dependence, through and in virtue of his claim to absolute independence, becomes the slave of the slave, so in Adorno and Horkheimer's rationality version of this dialectic enlightenment "reverts" to myth, to mythic stasis, to the inertia of the master: a final physical theory, the principles of reason, a will without anything worth willing.

In brief, the dynamic of rationalization that Horkheimer and Adorno uncover operates in the following way: the experience of terrifying nature leads us to mythically explain the occurrence of the events in question; some mythic beliefs are discovered to be wholly anthropomorphic, mere projections. Adopting the platitudinous principles of immanence is discovered to be the most effective tool in combating naïve anthropomorphism and simultaneously controlling fearful nature. As we become

28 The phrase here is from Robert Pippin's critical account of what Hans Blumenberg was attempting to legitimate in his *The Legitimacy of the Modern Age* (Cambridge, Mass.: MIT Press, 1983): "Blumenberg and the Modernity Problem," in *Idealism as Modernism,* p. 283.

increasingly aware of the claims of the principles of immanence, it becomes rational to adopt them as principles of reason in general, which in its turn enables enlightenment to become a generalised practice opposing all anthropomorphism. Because no beliefs can withstand the dissolvent rationality of enlightened criticism, enlightened reason is forced to regard itself as self-sufficient, and thus as incapable of regarding any material conditions as intrinsic to it. In the end we are left with only pure reason or pure will, which in turn can be dissolved through the same process of critique through which it arose.

What makes this argument less than fully satisfactory is its generality: What material *exactly* is it that rationalized reason cannot avow? What are the material conditions of its operation that rationalized reason cannot acknowledge? And what makes Adorno and Horkheimer believe that the material conditions of reason are *intrinsic* to it? There is a looseness of fit in their argument between, on the one hand, the demonstration of the self-defeating nature of reflexive rationalization, and, on the other, the panoply of objects they cite as its defeated victim: sensory states, the correlatives of sensory states in objects, anthropocentric nature, language and social practices, tradition, history, particular objects, and so on. In the eventual formation of reason Adorno proposes, the role of each of these items will require vindication, but if the argument concerning the constitutive dependency of enlightened reason is to be effective, then Adorno and Horkheimer need to show how reason must not simply avow but must *contain* these dependent moments as elements of itself. The lack of such a demonstration can make the argumentative strategy of the book appear to contain the *petitio principii* to which they admit in the "Introduction" (DoE, xiii). If the destructive element of enlightened reason is its relentless negativity, and the critique of enlightenment requires the activation of this same power of reflective negation (DoE, 194–5), then critique is self-stultifying – something which the critics of *Dialectic of Enlightenment* have been eager to insist upon.[29] To state the same point an-

29 Jürgen Habermas, *The Philosophical Discourse of Modernity,* trans. Frederick Lawrence (Oxford: Polity Press, 1987), p. 119; and Steven Vogel, *Against Nature: The Concept of Nature in Critical Theory* (Albany: State University of New York Press, 1996), pp. 66–71. It must be mentioned here that there is a direct and obvious way in which these criticisms fail, namely, Horkheimer and Adorno's contention that *there is a moment of objectivity in all the mediating forms that comprise the actuality of instrumental reason that is not irreducible, and hence nondominating:* "Domination, ever since men settled down and later in the commodity society, has become objectified as law and organization and must therefore *restrict itself.* The institution achieves independence: the mediating instance of the spirit, independently of the will of the master, modifies the directness of economic injustice. The instruments of domination, which would encompass all – language, weapons, and finally machines – must allow themselves to be encompassed by all. *Hence in domination the aspect of rationality prevails as one that is also different from it.* The 'objectivity' of the means, which makes it universally available, already implies the criticism of that domination as whose means thought arose" (DoE, 37; emphasis mine). To date, all the medi-

other way: the demonstration that, broadly speaking, some of the objects dissolved in the course of enlightened progress are material conditions for that progress occurring does not, by itself, transform the abstract negation of enlightened reason into the hoped-for determinate negations of dialectical reason (DoE, 27). If this diagnosis is correct, then the argument of *Dialectic of Enlightenment* is not false or self-defeating, but simply incomplete.

Nonetheless, however benighted about itself, however irrational and untrue, enlightenment thought is necessarily "stronger," logically and critically, than whatever might oppose it;[30] a thought that will eventually lead us to want to separate logical strength from truth. We will fail to understand the modern hegemony of enlightened reason and its continuing appeal unless we can comprehend it as actually logically stronger and critically more powerful than any competitor. Enlightened reason possesses the strength of a dogmatic scepticism that shapes itself as the whole of reason. Because what opposes it is either myth, dogma, or argument, it cannot lose.

> Every spiritual resistance [enlightenment] encounters serves merely to increase its strength. Which means that enlightenment still recognises itself even in myths. Whatever myths the resistance may appeal to, by virtue of the fact that they become arguments in the process of opposition, they acknowledge the principle of dissolvent rationality [*zersetzenden Rationalität*] for which they reproach enlightenment. Enlightenment is totalitarian. (DoE, 6)

Enlightenment's rationalized scepticism, scepticism rationalized as reason, secures an abstract, determinate syntax – universalisation, the procedures of communicative rationality, deductive formalism, pure logic, bivalence (true or false as the logical expression of the choice between life and death, dominating nature or submitting to it), the methodologism of positivistic science, and so on – against all, essentially indeterminate semantic claims, say, the kinds of claims that emerge in narrative.

ums (mediations) of domination contain a rational excess that implicitly critically delimits what their dominating actuality accomplishes; it is this nondominating moment in reason which the self-reflection of enlightenment employs against its dominating moment. Thus instrumental reason can criticise itself without self-contradiction because it is not unconditionally dominating or homogeneous, but rather already implicitly self-critical. While it should be evident that law and economy contain claims to justice and equality that there actuality blocks, I exemplify this duality of reason in my account of Kant on universality in Chapter 3.

30 Again, Bittner's "What Is Enlightenment?" draws this conclusion: ". . . to call superstition what enlightenment fights against is to imply that in any case its opponent is wrong. . . . Yes, enlightenment is always right against its opponent . . . " (p. 351). What Bittner fails to consider in his defence of enlightenment as critique is the formation of reason, the rationalization of reason, that is a consequence of that practice.

Because the latter can only *claim* by giving themselves a syntactic, argumentative shape, and in argumentative form are partial, perspectival, conditioned, then the claims of syntactical reason will always trump what seeks to oppose it – which is what Adorno and Horkheimer mean by the claim that enlightenment is "anger against insufficient righteousness": no contingent claim is true enough. The trumping power of enlightened reason is "dissolvent" because it forces claims to declare themselves, show their righteousness, in argumentative and hence syntactic (formal, procedural) terms alone. In this respect, Habermas's concession that the advance of procedural reason has meant a "weakening" of the factual is an understatement: "In myths everything that happens must atone for having happened. And so it is with enlightenment: the fact becomes null and void, and might as well not have happened" (DoE, 12). How can the fact *matter* if, for example, moral sense and meaning is *exhausted* by its fitness for either universal legislation or rational communicative consensus? Fitness and consensus trump.

The weakening of the factual, making its moral meaning dependent upon rules and reasons that derive from reason's own rationalized self-understanding, vanquishes auratic individuality from *sight*. From here it does not seem untoward to claim that the unmerciful gaze of Habermas's adolescent is just an expression of rationalized reason. Adorno and Horkheimer offer Sade's Juliette as the sceptical fate of the moral reason that takes itself to be truly enlightened. She is a rational demythologiser, bent upon employing reason to demonstrate that what has been superstitiously believed is empty, and what has been reviled only superstition. In demythologising the taboo against extreme forms of sexual behaviour she takes seriously the decay of aura that eventuates if one regards others only as aids or obstacles to one's own ends. If Sade's thought-experiments go beyond the organisation of bodies and pleasures, they do so only on the basis of a wholly demythologised conception of others which leads to a scepticism about even instrumental rationality: how much is its validity premised upon the desire for stable conditions for the pursuit of ends, and thus upon risk averseness? Is not the requirement to acknowledge and believe in reason or logic as superstitious as belief in religious commandments and taboos? Because rationalized reason cannot answer these questions without turning against its own principles, attempting to circumscribe and curtail their field of operation, it becomes a short step to the Nietzschean admonition to live dangerously and obey no law except that which one prescribes for oneself (DoE, 99).

4. The Destruction of Knowledge

In its baldest form, and disregarding ethical and moral issues, the central claim of *Dialectic of Enlightenment* is that the very same rationality which provides for humankind's emancipation from the bondage of mythic powers and allows for progressive domination over nature engenders, through its intrinsic modes of operation, a return to myth and new, ever more absolute forms of domination. The feature of enlightened reason accounting for this reversal is its identification of rationality and understanding with abstraction from immediacy and sensuously particularity generally, and the subsumption of particulars under ever more abstract universals. Here is a version of the dialectic of enlightenment stressing its implications for ethical life.

> Each step forward on it [viz., the line of both destruction and civilization] represents some progress, some enlightenment. But whereas all earlier changes, from pre-animism to magic, from the matriarchal to a patriarchal culture, from the polytheism of the slaveowners to the Catholic hierarchy, replaced the older mythologies with new – though enlightened ones – , and substituted the god of legions for the great mother, the adoration of the lamb for that of the totem, *the brilliance of enlightened reason banished as mythological any form of devotion which claimed to be objective and grounded in actuality.* All previous obligations therefore succumbed to the verdict which pronounced them taboo – not excluding those that were necessary for the existence of the bourgeois order itself. (DoE, 92–3; emphasis mine)

This passage occurs in a paragraph in which Horkheimer and Adorno, as part of their preparation for the discussion of Juliette's perversion of enlightened reason, are attempting to specify the "radicalism" of the historical Enlightenment in a manner which distinguishes it from earlier stages of demythologisation (DoE, 92). The break occurs when reason displaces its object as the ground of objectivity. Ethical experience was always grounded in some actuality, devotion (*Hingabe*) to some object independent of the collective. Formally, the concept of the object "worthy of devotion" is the counter-thesis to the concept of the object as mythic projection. If the latter concept of an object generates scepticism, it has appeared to modern rationalism that the former must degenerate into dogmatism. At the level of conflicting concepts of an object, there is nothing to choose between the two – scepticism and dogmatism. Which is why enchantment and disenchantment remain aporetically connected at the substantive level of world-views. Only at the level of the concept, philosophically and reflectively, can we hope to resolve the debate between them.

The path of moral enlightenment, the rationalization of moral life, involved the substitution of more "rational" objects of devotion for less so. What made the substitutions more rational was that each could be retrospectively seen as less an anthropomorphic projection than its predecessor, and simultaneously and progressively more consonant with standard canons of rational belief, that is, each was more universal, more epistemically plausible and more consonant with the values grounded by it than its predecessor. The canons of rational belief emerged out of progressive demythologisation as criterial for non-anthropomorphism, and hence as non-mythological; they thus became the sedimented bearers of the non-anthropomorphic (with mathematics becoming the ideal type). Still, as objects of devotion pre-enlightenment foundations for morality grounded ethical life in some actuality, in some real or ideal object that was thought to transcend the subject and place it in its world. While from a Kantian perspective, say, such devotion appears as heteronomy, one could equally say that it bespoke a concern for moral truth. Nonetheless, such a truth conception, as devotional, could still be accused of anthropomorphism and projection, and hence in need of further rationalization and systemisation. And if rationalization was to extend beyond the priestly, it would have required obedience to the emergent canons of rational belief, autochthonous standards of rationality; but these canons themselves recognise no outside, no standards but their own formal ones: consistency, coherence, unity, universality, non-arbitrariness, and so on. Thus their reiterative application ends up voiding all objects – including other humans as ends in themselves – as worthy of devotion; all goods and objects other than reason itself are, in their devotional sense, totems. This is the sorrow of rationalized reflection: reason shorn of any constitutive relation to actuality becomes the self-determining measure of meaning and experience. But since this measure recognizes no meaning other than its own formal sense, then the rational meaning of the objects over which it rules and measures becomes imponderable. Reason without devotion is empty.

This way of portraying the consequence of disenchantment is intended to make plausible the continuity from the modern interrogation of premodern beliefs to the radical questioning of bourgeois beliefs and values. Without wanting to gainsay that plausibility – the continuous movement from Cartesian doubt to Nietzschean nihilism – there is a disproportion in Horkheimer and Adorno's emphasis on the question of devotion and actuality, on the one hand, and their focus on higher order, foundational objects (the gods), on the other. This is all of the more the case if their ultimate worry relates to the fate of persons and objects. Ultimate objects are poor exemplars of actuality; thus, while Horkheimer and Adorno's account directly implies the weakening of the normative power of the factual, because it focuses on founding or transcendent objects, it leaves the lost character of such normative factuality opaque. An account of the disenchantment of the world which directly parallels the one they offer but focuses on the fate of ordinary events and objects is forwarded by Bernard Williams. If enlightened reason disenchants the world (simultaneously with enchanting it under the spell of reason), and this disenchantment involves, via abstraction and reiterative subsumption, peeling off from the world its qualitative density on the presumption that the characteristics providing that density are only anthropomorphic projections, then, Williams contends, what was *known* by means of the concepts specifying qualities is no longer known. This knowledge, ethical knowledge, has disappeared. Williams presents the conclusion of this process of the destruction of ethical knowledge thus:

> Earlier I said that reflection might destroy knowledge, because thick ethical concepts that were used in a less reflective state might be driven from use by reflection while the more abstract and general ethical thought that would probably take their place [e.g., the moral law or the principles of communicative rationality] would not satisfy the conditions of propositional knowledge. To say that knowledge is destroyed in such a case is not to say that particular beliefs that once were true now cease to be true. Nor is it to say that people turn out never to have known things they thought they knew. What it means is that these people once had beliefs of a certain kind, which were in many cases pieces of knowledge; but now, because after reflection they can no longer use concepts essential to those beliefs [or use them in the same way], they can no longer form beliefs of that kind. A certain kind of knowledge with regard to particular situations, which used to guide them round their social world and helped to form it, is no longer available to them. *Knowledge is destroyed because a potentiality for a certain kind of knowledge has been destroyed*; moreover, if they think about their earlier beliefs, they will now see them as the observer saw them, as knowledge they do not share.[31]

Williams intends his account of how reflection destroys knowledge to be an inference or elaboration of Weber's disenchantment theory, but for precisely this reason he believes it plausible to describe the premodern employment of thick ethical concepts as providing propositional knowledge. As he puts the thesis: "They [premodern subjects and communities] may not have been wrong in thinking that their social order [including the constitutive use of thick ethical concepts] was necessary for them. It is rather the way in which they saw it as necessary – as religiously or metaphysically necessary – that we cannot now accept."[32] Given the state of their knowledge of the world, their technology, what we now know about long-term patterns of development relating to beliefs about social roles, social order and values, they might not have been able to order their social worlds in significantly different ways than they did; hence, there may have been a necessity and hence legitimacy to their ethical practices even if they were wrong in their foundational beliefs. Nonetheless, reflection, societal rationalization, has made it impossible for the

31 *Ethics and the Limits of Philosophy* (London: Fontana Press/Collins, 1985), p. 167; emphasis mine.
32 Ibid., p. 165.

concepts which formerly provided ethical knowledge to do so now. In accordance with an argument from the previous chapter, we could say that centralist concepts have arisen that have disabled thick, empirical ethical concepts from being fully epistemic or, thereby, fully action guiding.

Rather than attempting to progressively track the disappearance of ethical knowledge, I want to approach the disappearance thesis indirectly by demonstrating exactly what *now* makes insupportable the belief that one may have ethical knowledge. My argument is not about the philosophical truth of moral realism, but the intelligibility of it being presently available. *The precise way in which we now cannot be moral realists makes it plausible to regard it as our surpassed ethical past.* Consider again the thesis that empirical ethical predicates appear to have a second-order character, an abstractness, about them when compared with factual predicates ranging over strictly material objects, events, and what can be objectified like material objects and events. The optimistic moral realist who believes that realism remains in force despite enlightenment disenchantment will respond by claiming that so long as metaphysical empiricism and its attendant philosophy of language have been disposed of, then metaphysically ethical and material object discourse are on a par even if our particular language games concerning material objects and ethical life themselves obey different grammars of description. If, let's say, an expressivist theory of language and corresponding communal construction of ethical life are true, then statements like "It was a vicious attack" can be true or false in the usual way. Although our ethical vocabulary is perhaps not as rich or unified as it once was, the hope of the realist depends upon our acknowledging and becoming rationally confident that there are a significant bundle of terms – callous, vicious, generous, patient, kind, mean, aggressive, indifferent, taunting, teasing, bullying, and so on – in which no line can be drawn between their factual and evaluative components, and that for the most part we do, unreflectively, use these concepts to provide propositional knowledge of states of affairs. It might further be urged that it is a necessary condition for learning our way around the world ethically that we do originally regard ethical discourse as delivering propositional knowledge on pain of the phenomena revealed by ethical concepts becoming (being) indescribable. So stated, this position might be considered a version of a kind of philosophical communitarianism; the necessity once provided by the gods has been replaced by the necessity of communal practice for linguistic meaning.

This optimistic construal of our ethical predicament is subject to a three-pronged critique, which attempts to weave together philosophical and sociological considerations. One of the accomplishments of our reflective culture is that, under the influence of the enlightened critique of myth as modelled by the natural sciences, we have learned for nearly the whole range of ethical predicates to which the realist points that we *can* discriminate a purely factual component, say, by isolating basic actions from more complex act descriptions, or by providing more nearly behavioural descriptions, or by separating ethical intentions from unconscious psychological motivations, or by showing that other communities would describe the same act differently, or by turning particular ethical actions into tokens of sociological types thereby making the original fact-value into a social fact.[33] Nor are these strategies of discrimination and isolation purely technical procedures since they underlie much everyday moral argument and dispute in the sense that no one can, for the vast majority of cases, close a dispute with a factual or descriptive claim (or where this is possible within a narrowly bounded community there is some larger community of which the first is a part where the closure can be relativised or objectified in accordance with one of the four strategies just noted).[34] Being able now even if only problematically to draw a fact/value distinction is just the destruction of ethical knowledge even for those who are philosophically committed to communitarian conceptions of ethical life. The diverse reflective strategies of redescription undo the necessity and so embeddedness and objectivity of the original fact/value predicates. Thus even if the fact/value distinction turns out to be metaphysically false, our collective ability to draw it in nearly all cases *de facto* subjectivises values or turns them into projections whose objective ground, if there is any, lies elsewhere, thus turning cases of moral truth into mere or rational agreement: the ethical predicates no longer *adhere* to the practices and phenomena as they did previously. (This can be thought of as what the Habermasian adolescent discovers, what enjoins his merciless gaze.) Disenchanting reflection has, minimally, privatised value (to individuals or communities) to the extent they can one and all appear *as* mere projections in need of (vertical) support or backing.

Nor is it the case that values peeled off from the phenomena, like a layer of flesh peeled from a living body, are left undissected. The evaluative component of previously unified concepts is relocated and explained. Some of these explanations are subjectivist and sceptical (emo-

33 These strategies for relativizing the evaluative component of states of affairs operate in a wider context of public institutions (economic, commercial, medical, educational, legal, etc.) where to a large extent practices have been rationalized in manner that either eliminates or makes marginal the space for ethical/moral evaluation and action. And where such space remains, it does so on the *presumption* that the moral choices on offer are subjective, matters of private conscience. This presumption (roughly that rational choice is instrumentally rational, and moral judgement and choice a wholly subjective space within objective practice) inevitably feeds into the reflective considerations taking place within remnant spaces of ethical life quite irrespective of how the rationalization of public practices itself deforms the practices of private life (as diagnosed in *Minima Moralia*).

34 There are some counterexamples to this, mostly of an exorbitant kind: certain types of rapes, murders, terrorist acts. I explicate how these slip past the neutralization of ethical experience in Chapter 9.

tivism, existential decisionism, communal relativism), while others are rationalist and objective (utilitarianism and Kantianism). For the latter type, again, the moral syntax of theory prohibits the quasi-empirical ethical predicates from being properly evaluative in themselves: they derive their evaluating force, their force as providing reasons for action, from the moral syntax of the theory. Hence the two streams of explanation secure the former evaluative component of ethical concepts in a framework that is either explicitly non-cognitive or is cognitive in a manner incompatible with their delivering propositional knowledge. Again, it is important to notice that these strategies are not just philosophical accounts of the moral, but routine, if often confusedly employed, moves available to everyday moral argument and discourse: for example, your conscience says you must *w*, while I claim you must not *w*, invoking the moral principle *p*, and she states that in her community people generally do *x* (and not *w* or *p*), while he thinks we are all just espousing our private opinions. And other voices may enter. The concatenation of meta-ethical voices is the sociohistorical actuality of disenchantment, its presence to and in reflection now.

Hence even where there appear to be descriptions that ideally can close an argument – "brutal attack," "vicious rape," "blatant act of torture" – instances where the best description of the case appears to contain its evaluation, nonetheless the loss of authority infecting ethical discourse generally comes to infect them as well. As we see in the next chapter, for the modern moralist even for cases of murder and mayhem, rape and torture, their precise wrongness is not rationally transparent, not an empirical fact, not given in the way low-level empirical claims are given through their descriptive tokening. If the wrongness of a "vicious rape" is past argument, the location and meaning of "wrongness" itself isn't, and that reflective, quasi-theoretical quandary infects how we *hold* or sustain our first-order beliefs. This points to the third prong of the critique of modern moral realism.

The combination of reflective enlightened peeling or stripping off of values from the world together with the diversity of common sense and philosophical strategies for relocating and explaining these values progressively lead the destruction of ethical knowledge to terminate in nihilism: we no longer can unconditionally "believe," possess faith and have confidence in, our own moral beliefs – they lack unproblematic *authority*. Demotivation, which Kant, Habermas, and objective consequentialists all concede is a consequence of reflective rationalization, and which Nietzsche analyses as the decadent malaise infecting bourgeois culture to which his conceptions of will to power and eternal return are intended as a response, should be understood as a *reflective distancing between agents and their own beliefs that occurs with the withering of authority.* The modern movement into reflection, enlightenment desecration, generates a conflict of voices within the reflective sphere which causes a draining of rational authority from norms, which itself causes a transformation in how we *can* relate to our own most fundamental beliefs. If demotivation is the general form of this transformation, it is not the only expression of the weakening of authority and the opening up of a reflective distance; just as there are various modes of flight from disenchantment, so there are various forms of moral self-relation: most commonly, the absence of compelling authority manifests itself in a *fragile* holding of moral beliefs such that there is a continual tension between them and the claims of self-interest and desire (whether the desire for sexual satisfaction or for self-realisation). As I say more about below, agents' sense of the fragility of their moral beliefs can make these beliefs appear or feel external to them, to what they most want and desire; which in turn transforms the meaning or question of morality from "What is to be done? What is the best course of action here?" into a question of self-control, of ordering, curbing, silencing, or forsaking desires and preferences. Disenchanted desire becomes the problem, the problem of fitting my subjectively comprehended desires into a world of others who have different and competing desires, and morality the answer to the problem, providing rules for the regulating of desires among indifferent agents. Under this condition, morality can come to feel remote, external, a challenge to wants and needs, and hence continuously threatening them and under threat from them. How can moral norms feel compelling when they appear and claim no more for themselves than they enable the coordination among competing preferences? Saying that the rules of coordination are fair or just by itself does not remove from them the sense that they are, because for the sake of coordination, not moral but merely instrumental.

But we can respond to the threat or sense of fragility through a retreat from reflection into dogmatic conviction (political, religious, personal). Agents may, that is, take the fragility of moral self-relations as a sign that something is untoward in the secular moral world, and attempt to compensate for this fragility by immersing themselves in a less reflective moral universe; but since any moral framework now will be but one amongst others, and thus already reflectively dissociated from everyday practice, then the immersion can work only through dogmatic affirmation. Or, accepting the lack of rational authority as permanent, agents can take up a cynical, disillusioned stance in which moral norms are construed as no more than useful social fictions, which are seen through but obeyed anyway (cynicism as the generalised instrumentalisation of morality).

Doubtless there are other and more complex forms of self-relation; but for us the significance of these self-relations is unequivocal: they are symptoms of the decay of authority from which the realist cannot be immune. The classification of belief self-relations into the cynical, the desperate, and the fragile – the best lacking all conviction – is one way of invoking the now all but universal condition in which moral values are in competition with other goods and values, and hence, again, no longer worldly items in the way they were before. It is because there is such competition that the moral theorist is first led to claim that the criterion of the moral is its overridingness (it must have the capacity to trump competing claims), and hence that at the core of a theory of morality is a theory of obligation. The fact that these are issues at all, the fact that moral theory is faced with demonstrating overridingness, as I argue more fully below, is the reflective record of the disappearance of the authority of the ethical as a form of knowledge, and hence a record of the disenchanted state of the world. The optimistic moral realist fails to take seriously the *sociological* significance of the existence of competing moral theories, competing moral perspectives, the problems of belief self-relation, the fact that there is a question about the overridingness of moral norms. Once moral realism must prove itself against other *theories* of morality, where those competing theories do possess rational force, and hence are real practical alternatives, then moral realism cannot be actual. Conversely, the way moral realism depends for its intelligibility upon screening its beliefs off from the corrosive effects of highly reflective approaches to morality is good evidence that it represents an historically superseded moral outlook. The rational appeal of philosophical moral realism is that it represents a highly reflective defence of a simpler, more direct and immediate form of ethical life – one we can no longer share.

The way we must consider moral realist claims now, I am suggesting, is good evidence for the historical thesis that thick ethical concepts were once mediums of propositional knowledge, and hence that disenchantment destroys such knowledge. To this extent Williams's diagnosis of the ethical present converges with that of Horkheimer and Adorno. Nonetheless, and despite his forceful critiques of modern moral theory (which equally converge with the Adorno's position as I want to construe it), at least in *Ethics and the Limits of Philosophy,* Williams urges this fate of ethical knowledge as permanent and irreversible in a way that is incompatible with the critical utopian element in Adorno's thought.[35] Consider two theses of Williams: (1) "ethical reflection becomes part of the practice it considers, and inherently modifies it;" and (2) "there is no route back from reflectiveness."[36] The conjunction of (1) and (2) may make

35 If I am reading him correctly, Williams has changed his mind now allowing for *local* ethical knowing to survive and continue, albeit having a different (foundationless) status than it had before. See "Who Needs Ethical Knowledge?" in his *Making Sense of Humanity and Other Philosophical Papers 1982–1993* (New York: Cambridge University Press, 1995), pp. 203–12. Williams's late strategy of what might be called "refuge ethics" suffers from failing to consider how the local is conditioned by what surrounds it. Refuge ethics is possible only if *Minima Moralia* is wrong in root and branch.

36 *Ethics and the Limits of Philosophy,* pp. 168, 163.

Williams's position appear thoroughly Weberian: the destruction of ethical knowledge produces the iron cage of modernity; once in place, only Nietzschean affirmation, what Williams (ironically?) calls "confidence," can, at least, but also at best, diminish its most pernicious consequences.[37] While Adorno would wish to dissent from the Weberian/Nietzschean conclusion, it nonetheless looks as if he must affirm both theses. Since Horkheimer and Adorno accuse enlightenment reason of a lack of reflectiveness (about its conceptions of reason and reflection), since they claim that only further reflection ("disenchanting the concept") can begin undoing what enlightenment thought has produced, and, as we see below, since Adorno is committed to a very strong conception of self-consciousness as a constitutive element in ethical belief and practice, then even if there was a nondesperate, noncoercive route back to unreflectiveness, which anyway seems unlikely, it is not one Adorno could endorse. The first claim also appears in order; unless reflection did "inherently" modify ethical practices, it would not be the case that reflection destroyed ethical knowledge, transforming the meaning of the ethical thereby into something else (say, moral theory). However, it does not follow from the conjunction of Williams's two theses that ethical knowledge is "inherently unreflective," which is the most obvious proposition needed to draw the bleak Weberian conclusion and to raise the question as to whether what premodern practices demonstrated was propositional knowledge.[38]

What is required for the strong Weberian conclusion is the thesis that the reflective process generating the disenchanted iron cage was itself inherently rational, and hence essentially progressive and developmental. But it is just this thesis that the argument of *Dialectic of Enlightenment* denies. Again, the unity of rationalism, disenchantment, and universalism

37 Ibid., pp. 170–1. In context, confidence replaces ethical knowledge and conviction. However, on p. 200 Williams asserts the possibility of the continuance of ethical knowledge locally, and it is this local ethical knowledge that comes to be grounded in "confidence" in "Who Needs Ethical Knowledge?," p. 209. For present purposes, my interest is solely in opening up an intelligible route back to ethical knowledge from within the confines of a critical portrayal of the set of assumptions that produced its destruction. Williams's own route back is through the employment of Edward Craig's ingenious pragmatist, advisory conception of knowledge in *Knowledge and the State of Nature* (Oxford: Clarendon Press, 1990). Even if this view of knowledge is preferred to a truth conditions approach, I think there are questions about the adherence of ethical predicates in their objects which this line simply side-steps (and covers over the side-stepping with "confidence"). Williams fails, I think, to sufficiently align his general critique of moral theory with a critique of the rationalization of reason that brought it into existence. Like traditional moral realists, Williams believes that, at bottom, the only sort of defence of realism possible is fending off sceptical challenges to it. Adorno's claims for the nonidentical, while ending up in a position contiguous with Williams's, permits a fuller vindication.

38 Pace A. W. Moore, "Can Reflection Destroy Knowledge," *Ratio* 4/2 (December 1991): 97.

as produced by abstraction and reiterative subsumption entails the sceptical constitution of rationalized enlightened reason: "The self-satisfaction of knowing in advance and the transfiguration of negativity into redemption are untrue forms of resistance against deception" (DoE, 24). Enlightened reason is a form of resistance to deception, but an inherently sceptical one which transforms its critical procedures, its indefinite capacity for abstract negation, into the meaning of reason, as if only in acts of critique and negation can we be assured that our reasoning is ours and thus truly reasonable. By transforming itself into critique, reason overreaches itself. If we can be satisfied that the form of reflection that dissolved premodern belief structures was itself sceptical, then even if we believe that some of what was dissolved deserved to be dissolved, we cannot rationally affirm that everything found by reflection to be illusory is illusory. Indeed, it is just this view of reflection that Williams needs to support his contention that while the premoderns were wrong about the grounds of the necessity of their ethical beliefs, they were not necessarily wrong in operating with their thick ethical concepts. For us to be able to say that they had valid beliefs (ethical knowledge) that we cannot share requires that what destroyed those beliefs is *also* irrational, and hence that our belief system is committed to a conception of reason that is in part irrational. Hence while there may be forms of practical knowledge that are essentially incompatible with reflection (activities which as soon as you *think* about them you can no longer *do* them), nothing that has been said about what ethical knowledge might have been, if there ever was any, entails that it was like that, although such presumptive knowledge is incompatible with wholly rationalized reason.

"But if knowledge is what it claims to be," an objector might urge at this juncture, "then it is knowledge of what is there anyway."[39] If there was ethical knowledge, then it must have been knowledge of what is there anyway; hence the fact-values which were known could not be banished, leaving only a factual component. A potentiality for knowledge is not the kind of thing that can be lost. That only a factual component has remained is thus good evidence that knowledge can be only of facts, not values, and therefore there was no propositional ethical knowledge in premodern societies. Despite appearances, this argument is only the other side of the previous objection. If propositional knowledge was had through the employment of thick ethical concepts, it must have been local knowledge, knowledge that aided a particular people to find their way around their social world.[40] So much is built into the *thickness* of such concepts. If

39 This conception of knowledge is one Williams defended in his *Descartes: The Project of Pure Enquiry* (Harmondsworth: Penguin, 1978), p. 64. It is used against his thesis concerning the destruction of ethical knowledge by Moore, ibid., pp. 104–6.

40 To forestall a certain misguided worry, let me state immediately that even the most lo-

knowledge *is* of what there is there anyway, then a moment's reflection will puncture the claim that thick ethical concepts deliver knowledge. How else could reflection permanently undermine the now only illusory character of premodern epistemic claims? Not reflection, but enlightened rationalizing reflection is at issue. And rationalized reflection determines the *scope* of "what is there anyway" as subject transcendent.

By demonstrating that the enlightenment critique of myth possessed an inherently sceptical premise, Adorno and Horkheimer were explicitly contending that its scope "is an anthropomorphic projection" (which is the formal definition of the mythic) became *indefinitely* extended. The indefinite extension determined the scope of "there anyway" as equivalent to what exists independently of human beings and their interactions with the world *as such*. As we saw above, items which can have a wide cosmological role, and thus be maximally detached from the attitudes to which they give rise, are best fitted to satisfy the platitudinous principle of immanence. Fully satisfying the principle of immanence engenders the efforts of abstraction and reiterative subsumption, which in turn make the business of overcoming anthropomorphism indefinite. Finally, only nature as a self-contained, self-sufficient, and ahistorical order can truly be known, if anything can, since only such an object can be characterised as wholly free from the stigmata of possessing features projected onto it. While this may be a legitimate and binding aim for physics and cosmology (since they are concerned with the way the world was before we stepped onto the scene), trivially it appears to bar any other type of objects, even those of biology, from being legitimate objects of knowledge.[41] Put this thought aside for the moment. The deep worry here concerns the worth of the claim that true knowing is bound to a weighty conception of "what is there anyway." If Horkheimer and Adorno are right, then the conception of "there anyway" is generated by a sceptical dynamic that forces all knowledge to systematically detach itself from the *appearing* of things to humans, as if humans and their interactions with the world were not themselves also *parts* of the natural world. In fine, the claim that ethical knowledge was not knowledge turns on a conception of "what is there anyway" – which I am conceding is what knowledge is of – with an ideally

cally embedded thick ethical concept can be logically compatible with the requirements of moral universalism, that is, nothing about its contextual location and nontransferability to other locations prohibits its use from at least satisfying the requirement of universalization. The conflict between the local and the universal is less direct than that.

41 For a sustained defence of biology against the enlightenment conception of knowledge, see John Dupré, *The Disorder of Thing: Metaphysical Foundations of the Disunity of Science* (Cambridge, Mass.: Harvard University Press, 1993). I have tried to show how the Peircean conception of what at first sight appear to be general features of knowledge and truth are intrinsically (and reasonably) bound to physics in my *Recovering Ethical Life*, pp. 106–110. I would want to make the same claim about Wright's notion of states of affairs able to have a wide cosmological role.

maximum scope: there irrespective not of what *anyone* thinks or believes, but irrespective of entanglement with thought and belief generally. On this assumption any facts constituted in part by our valuings cannot be objects of knowledge, and hence there can be no truly value-bound social facts (e.g., in 1998 a Jaguar costs, and hence is worth, $50,000). The weighty conception of "what is there anyway" includes an unregimented and unrestricted anti-anthropomorphism; ideal knowledge follows the path of demythologisation. Unless the objection presumes the weighty, wide cosmological role conception of "what is there anyway" it could not rule out ethical knowledge. Since this conception of "what is there anyway" is generated from a sceptical premise, then it is no more obligatory than the thesis that claims ethical knowledge and reflection are inherently incompatible. They are the same thesis seen from different angles.

If disenchantment of the world occurred in the manner and through the procedures which Horkheimer and Adorno say, and if the disposition of our contemporary ethical world is anything like I have been suggesting, then Williams's thesis that enlightened reflection destroyed ethical knowledge is plausible. From the perspective of the problem of disenchantment, what is important in this narrative is not the account of ethical *knowing* – I have said almost nothing about that to which such knowledge amounted or how it operated – but its presumption about what such knowledge was *of*: a world of fact-values, a world in which values adhered to and saturated objects, events, and persons. Hence, the *destruction* of ethical knowledge primarily relates to the way in which values were peeled off from the body of the world and relocated (in reason, will, affect, desire, agreement, etc.). The world lost its "magic" in the simple sense that the concrete objects of experience lost their axiological colors, their intrinsic worth or awfulness. As far as I am aware, Adorno nowhere explicates the consequences of disenchantment in precisely these terms, nor does he explicitly elaborate his considerations of the ethical in terms of the kind of ethical knowledge operative within a moral realist framework. Moral realism of this kind seems to be something of which he simply was unaware. Nonetheless, Horkheimer's and his account of the procedures of enlightened reason, their analysis of the form of its sceptical character, their account of the way rationalized reason displaces it objects, and, finally, and above all, their complaint that in all of this, ethical valuing loses its binding relation to the *actual,* what is concrete in the world, all make the destruction of ethical knowledge thesis the simplest and most direct expression of what disenchantment is and does. *Enlightenment destroys not just a range of beliefs but a certain previous ethical form of relating to objects: knowing them.*

Wrong life cannot be lived rightly because in order to live rightly one would have to be able to *know* what to do; in order to know what to do, in this privileged sense, there would have to be a field of fact-values about which one could have knowledge. By peeling off values from the world enlightenment has razed this field. Hence in attempting to respond to worldly circumstances morally we now are responding to something very different than that to which we would have been responding were there fact-values. Hence "responding" cannot mean the same thing in the two cases. Responding to fact-values would be to have an experience. Experience, like knowledge, concerns not a particular range of beliefs, but a form of object relation, a mode or way of relating to what is there. With modernity experience too is destroyed.

5. Destruction of Aura, Destruction of Experience

Within the context of the critique of rationalized reason, the discussion of experience has the precise role of trying to capture a mode of cognition in which the passivity of the knowing subject and hence its dependency on the object can become minimally intelligible. Experience is (the beginning of) a counter-concept to abstraction. The destruction of experience is the destruction of significant cognitive object-dependence.[42] Only the destruction and not the possibility of experience is at stake in this section. For both Adorno and Benjamin, the destruction of experience is always connected with the destruction of aura since, if for no other reason than because the notion of experience seems most central in the experiencing of others, their otherness on this scheme being their individuality as somehow of unique worth, so possessing an aura. Hence the withering of experience is thought in relation to the destruction of aura.

For Adorno the paradigm of experiencing auratic individuality is the nonideal case of the eyes of another returning our gaze; the other is not a dead object but a subject who looks back, and hence who announces its subjectivity by taking up a stance *toward me* and so toward the world rather than being merely in it.[43] (Consider for a moment the uncanniness of portraits where the eyes of the painted subject seem to follow us about the room so displacing and decentring us, prohibiting our looking from

42 Andrew Hewitt, "A Feminine Dialectic of Enlightenment? Horkheimer and Adorno Revisited," *New German Critique* 56 (1992): 143–70, argues persuasively that in *Dialectic of Enlightenment* woman is presented less as the subject of experience than as a figure for experience itself, and hence that the destruction of experience is worked through the double movement of male domination and feminine self-alienation.

43 The instance of the gaze of another is not ideal for Adorno's purposes since it so easily and all but unavoidably is subject to interpretation in terms of the subjectivity of another placing and objectifying "my" subjectivity, thus passing over the embodiment issue (the other's *eyes, face, gaze*) it calls for but does not necessitate. It is the wholly mentalistic interpretation of the gaze that emerges in and deforms Sartre's account in *Being and Nothingness: An Essay on Phenomenological Ontology*, trans. Hazel Barnes (New York: Philosophical Library, 1956), part 3, chapter 1. Avoiding recourse to interiority – by ascribing what is important about being alive, being a living thing, to the soul, self, subjectivity – is difficult.

being the organising frame of reference.) Looking back creates the "strangeness" and "distance" that Adorno stipulates as required if the aura of the other is to be accommodated. By making these stipulations he was following Walter Benjamin's lead. For Benjamin, the phenomenon of aura becomes detectable at the very moment and in virtue of its immanent disappearance. So he records how photography was implicated in the decay of aura because in daguerreotypy there was a prolonged looking into the camera without anything occurring in response: " . . . the camera records our likeness without returning our gaze."[44] He continues:

> There is the expectation, when we look at someone, that the recipient of the gaze will return our look. Where this expectation is met . . . , there is an experience of aura in its fullness. "Perceptibility," as Novalis puts it, "is a kind of attentiveness." The perceptibility he has in mind is none other than that of the aura. Experience of the aura thus rests on the transfer of a response common in human society to the relationship between the inanimate or [living] nature and man. The person who is seen, or who believes himself to be seen, returns the gaze. To experience the aura of a phenomenon means to invest it with the ability to look at us in turn.[45]

The experience of auratic individuality would, on this account, appear to be almost the fundamental effect or primary instance of anthropomorphism in its projective sense. But when Benjamin in a later essay offers an instance of experiencing the aura of a natural object, we may begin to wonder: "We define the aura of the latter [natural objects] as the unique phenomenon of distance, however close it may be. While resting on a summer's noon, to trace a range of mountains on the horizon, or a branch that throws its shadow over the observer, until the moment or the hour become part of their appearance – that is what it means to breathe the aura of those mountains, that branch."[46] Aura is the apprehension of an object in its uniqueness, a uniqueness that is temporally and spatially bound, where the spatio-temporal binding of the apprehension is the condition for preserving its uniqueness. Uniqueness is preserved only if it is somehow durable, *if the uniqueness of the object is related to or sustained through the uniqueness of the occasion of apprehension.* Hence, according to Benjamin, when things lose their aura they lose their uniqueness; or better, the decay of aura is the process through which the uniqueness of

44 *Illuminations,* p. 190.

45 Ibid. I have here adopted the translation of this passage offered by Rebecca Comay in her fine essay, "Framing Redemption: Aura, Origin, Technology in Benjamin and Heidegger," in Arleen B. Dallery and Charles E. Scott (eds.), *Ethics and Danger: Essays on Heidegger and Continental Thought* (Albany: State University of New York Press, 1992), p. 144.

46 *One Way Street, and Other Writings,* translated by Edmund Jephcott and Kingsley Shorter (London: Verso, 1985), p. 250.

things is lost: "The stripping bare of the object, the destruction of the aura, is the mark of a perception whose sense of the sameness of things has grown to the point where even the singular, unique, is divested of its uniqueness."[47] This passage, in a sense, reverses the "transfer" and hence projective assumptions of the first passage, since here objects that *are* unique lose their uniqueness and auratic quality in virtue of a form rationalized perception. Benjamin is systematically equivocal here since he does not mean to contend that auratic uniqueness is a quality objects possess in the absence of human apprehension; rather he is insisting, in his own way, that apprehension of auratic individuality cannot be reduced to our apprehending in nature a quality we have put or placed there, and hence, in a sense he is unable to spell out, our apprehension *depends* upon its object: the uniqueness of the object binds the neutral mediums of space and time to it, transforming them into *place* and *moment*.[48]

Benjamin provides two different accounts of the decay of aura, and correspondingly two different evaluations of this decay. In both instances decay is a consequence of rationalization processes; when these occur in the art world,[49] as a consequence of new productive techniques making works indefinitely reproducible, like photography and film. Benjamin conceives of the demise of the auratic, unique artwork as a fact to be celebrated since it tokens a more democratic and critical conception of art. In his essay "On Some Motifs in Baudelaire," however, the decay of aura is associated with a "crisis in perception," and hence, more generally a decay of experience. If aura is a quality of uniqueness had by objects, *"experience" (Erfahrung) is the cognitive mode through which we have that apprehension of uniqueness.* Throughout the Baudelaire essay, Benjamin situates both aura and experience in the Proustian *mémoire involontaire.* Involuntary memory is, according to Benjamin, the locale of experience once it has been dispatched from its place in everyday empirical life; involuntary memory permits the experience of objects that we failed to truly experience on the occasion of our original encounter with them. Involuntary memory is to experience what private existence is in relation to ethical life: a refuge. Benjamin's strategy with respect to experience is analogous to his handling of aura; the phenomenon of experience becomes perceptible and emphatic only on the occasion of its disappearance. Proust's

47 Ibid.

48 This thesis is the leitmotif of Comay's essay cited in note 45. See, esp. pp. 146–50.

49 The auratic quality of a painting, for example, is that uncanny feature of it that would lead us to think that slicing it to bits with a knife was nothing like the destruction of some private property, no matter how valuable, but somehow an act of violation. When Benjamin is being sceptical about aura, he is thinking that this strange way of regarding artworks is bound to cult practices, and hence an anthropomorphic illusion; when he is being non-sceptical about aura he is noting the utter convergence between auratic experience and emphatic experience generally.

centring of involuntary memory is hence meant to capture the experience of the disappearing of experience, which is thus a clue to what has been lost. This is equally how Adorno construes Proust's significance: "Undamaged experience is produced only in memory, far beyond immediacy. . . . Total remembrance is the response to total transience, and hope lies only in the strength to become aware of transience and preserve it in writing."[50] Writing gives empirical transience, a world without aura or experience, the *form* of experience. Benjamin said the same of Baudelaire: " . . . Baudelaire battled the crowd – with the impotent rage of someone fighting rain or the wind. This is the nature of something lived through (*Erlebnis*) to which Baudelaire has given the weight of an experience (*Erfahrung*)."[51] Modernist art provides us with the experience of a world without experience.

In excessively broad terms, to "experience" something is, in accordance with colloquial usage, to have had an "experience." To have an experience is to undergo something, to suffer something, and to do so in such a manner that one is changed thereby. What is experienced is something that one had not anticipated or predicted, something that occurs counter to expectations. Because unexpected exposure to something unprecedented entails that experiences are "undergone," then experience invokes ideas of passivity and even loss of control. Experience is the arena of what we learn through "suffering."[52]

From these uncontentious characterisations of experience, three inferences follow. First, novelty and transformation are intrinsic to the structure of experience; these characteristics make experience contrary to the goals and ideals of scientific knowing. In science, the unexpected is what falsifies a theory; the ideal of science would be to never be surprised and hence for a theory to be complete and determinate independently of the objects and events it explains. (That ideal is roughly what Adorno intends by his notion of identity thinking.) To imagine experience coming to an end, conversely, is to image a world in which nothing would or could matter to an individual, in which the course of events was neutral with respect to subjectivity, in which subjects were beyond meaningful change and transformation. An image of death as somehow an ideal state.

Second, if the transformation undergone in an experience occurs at the behest of a specific object or event, then the state of the subject which eventuates from the experience is determined by its object. From this it

50 "On Proust" in *Notes to Literature,* vol. 2, trans. Shierry Weber Nicholsen (New York: Columbia University Press, 1992), p. 317.

51 *Illuminations,* pp. 195–6.

52 In its root sense of undergone, endured, passed through. The negative sense of the term, that all suffering is the suffering of pain or evil, is perhaps the most perspicuous linguistic consequence of the cultural disenfranchisement of dependence and passivity.

follows that experience always depends on individuals being *present* or directly *exposed* to what they experience, and that the ensuing transformation *remains* a relation between the individual and object or events. Experiences of love, death, war, childbirth, friendship, freedom, desire, beauty, courage, sympathy, and so on, expose individuals to a domain of meaning that nonetheless remain bound to the events and objects precipitating the exposure (all love is but the attempt to recapture our first love). Because experience is bound to the events and objects precipitating it, the inscription and communication of experience tends now to be broadly "aesthetic" and often narrative in character. To give prominence to the aesthetic as Adorno does derives not from a fascination with art, but with a concern for the experiential dimensions of human lives. In comprehending an experience recourse is necessary to the state of the individual prior to it, the context in which it occurs, and what eventuates from it; in brief, the comprehension of experience is necessarily contextual, often in the form of a narrative of some sort, rather than a decontextualizing explanation. The binding of experience to time and place, and the tight link between the affective state of the subject of experience and the event which precipitates it make the objects of experience the exact opposite of those capable of having a wide cosmological role. There can be no experience if context does not possess justificatory significance.

Finally, then, having an experience involves both a transformation of the individual and the emergence of a new object domain for consciousness.[53] And while this conception of transformation or conversion may model what occurs in paradigm changes in natural science, the goal of science is to be done with such changes. The image of life without experience is ultimately the image of life without history, as if the meaning of a life were in its eternal cessation, death. There can be no meaningful historical life without experience; and only lives articulated through experience can be fully and self-consciously historical.

We all have had experiences. In speaking of the withering and destruction of experience, Adorno is not denying the obvious. Rather, he is concerned with the possibilities of experience in modern societies (in virtue of the characteristic structures and practices of those societies, and the types of individuals or subjects such structures and practices require for their reproduction), and, where they occur, the worth or rational authority they are granted. At the commencement of this chapter we noted Benjamin's attempt to model the destruction of everyday experience upon those men suffering shell shock; he sets up this dislocation of experience in modernity in these terms: "For never has experience been

53 This is the notion of experience employed by Hegel in the *Phenomenology of Spirit*. The collapse of *Erfahrung* into *Erlebnis* is pivotal in Hans-Georg Gadamer, *Truth and Method*, (London: Sheed and Ward, 1975).

contradicted more thoroughly than strategic experience by tactical warfare, economic experience by inflation, moral experience by those in power."[54] The image of war is of the incommensurability between the individual and the structuring of the events of which the individual is a part; this incommensurability is "the withering of experience, the vacuum between men and their fate, in which their real fate lies" (MM, A33). The structures that determine the meaning of the events individuals undergo are detached from the experience of undergoing them. The "real fate" of these individuals resides not in what they experience (or fail to experience), but in tactical planning and the even more remote negotiations of statesmen. But this remote determination is built into what is directly lived through: events take on the character of being atomistic, fragmentary, without direct meaning. In the exorbitant form of war, one is aware that there is a massive dislocation between actual combat and "the war." This systematic dislocation and incommensurability between individual and society – which are the sources and causes of the modern social sciences beginning with political economy – mark out modernity's destruction of experience, or so it is claimed.

Even if we are willing to concede that war usefully images the disproportion between individual experience and the structures determining it – or in the case of economics, while inflation as a feature of the economic system has effects on individuals (their money is suddenly worth less), it is not itself "experienced" – nonetheless, it might be objected, that this is not enough to procure the conclusion that experience itself has withered. Might not one simply say that a good deal of what is of real significance for individuals is not available at the experiential level – and can be understood only reflectively and theoretically as is the case with economics – but that experience itself remains the same, and hence the fundamental structures of human subjectivity remain unaltered?

This sanguine view, testifying more to our natural and necessary desire to affirm the worth of our subjectivities, to continue to perceive ourselves as loci of meaning and determination, which arguably includes conceiving of ourselves as centres of experience, ignores the tension in its own pronouncement. If more of the structures that determine the meaning of everyday life increasingly occur outside the ambit of individual experience, then how can what is meant by experience remain the same? Is not "economic experience," a sense of oneself as producing and consuming goods whose value would be intelligibly connected to one's activities and hence proportionally related to them, contradicted by the dominion of macro-economic structures? And the experience of producing itself contradicted by increasing division of labor and automation? Is not

54 *Illuminations*, p. 84.

political experience contradicted by the disappearance of a determining public sphere of active citizens, and the growth of media politics and plebiscite democracy (where occasional voting replaces political activity)? Is not our experience of health and illness, life and death contradicted by the bureaucratisation and rationalization of medicine? And are not Adorno's microanalyses of the private sphere detections of how these objective dislocations enter into the fibres of everyday life? Is not Adorno interrogating how the experiences, and so meaning, of love, marriage, home, and property have been deformed by macro social structures remote from those practices? Without as yet interrogating the depth and density of these transformations, the question raised by them is what is experienced at the individual level, and how is what is so experienced different from what has been or would be experienced if the disproportion between individual and system were not as dominant as it now is?

But if we consider again Habermas's adolescent, then this list of questions might seem belated. For if each of these queries points to an aspect of societal rationalization creating a "vacuum" between individuals and their fates, Habermas's adolescent experiences the same phenomenon from the other side, that is, from the perspective of experience losing its rational authority and weight, and thus no longer being a bearer of truth. From this angle the issue concerning the destruction of experiences is mooted by the epistemological/rational effect of destruction: individuals can no longer rely upon or *trust* their experiences as vehicles for rational cognition, and hence the role of experience in its thick sense disappears from rational accounting and self-understanding. And this is equivalent to saying that rationalized reason has become dominant in determining what is to count as rational and what not.

Scepticism about the scope and validity of the thesis concerning the decay of experience is intrinsic to it since only through retrospection and historical comparison could we become aware of an absence or radical transformation; but if the lived instant and reflective theory have taken over as the authoritative mediums of everyday life, then it follows that "the experience of modernity does not have a tradition, does not stand in any relation to its own origin in the nineteenth century. . . . [t]his means that the experience of modernity is oblivious to itself."[55] A consequence of the decay of experience is that we lack an experience of its dissolution. The oblivion of the transformation of *Erfahrung* into *Erlebnis* is itself part of that transformation and decay. Benjamin thus attempts to use the evidence of writings that most directly and immediately suffered

55 Howard Caygill, *Walter Benjamin: The Colors of Experience* (London: Routledge, 1998), p. 69. Caygill's illuminating and austere study provides an account of Benjamin that makes his thought closer to Adorno's than any other of which I am aware.

this loss as vehicles for presenting it, however necessarily circular such presentations are as evidence for the presumed loss.

In "On Some Motifs in Baudelaire," Benjamin develops a speculative psychology intended to provide a language that can shape and hence explicate the transformations of subjectivity that occur as a consequence of the withering of experience. He employs experiences of shock, of events too frightening and/or traumatic to be fully consciously experienced, as a model for the kind of stimuli faced by individuals, above all inhabitants of modern cities, whose own activities are no longer determinate for the meaning of what they experience. Experiences of shock that leave us numb, unable to absorb what has occurred, testify to a function of consciousness quite different from the standard one of interpreting and recording events, namely, protection *against* stimuli which would disorder the mental system. Hence, instead of recording a traumatic event directly, consciousness screens it out, and sends the undigested event into unconscious memory. Benjamin perceives this operation of exchanging conscious experience for memory (*Errinerung*) as precisely Proust's recognition of what is now the norm with respect to individual experience, and hence what structures the specific narrative programme of *Remembrance of Things Past.* After noting Freud's thought that memory fragments are often most powerful and enduring when the events that occasioned them never directly entered into consciousness, Benjamin comments: "Put in Proustian terms, this means that only what has not been experienced explicitly and consciously, what has not happened to the subject as an experience, can become a component of the *mémoire involontaire.*"[56] Screening stimuli and involuntary memory are proposed as mental capacities which under the changed circumstances of modernity move from being peripheral mental functions to dominant ones. Their centrality is explained by the order of experienced events coming to consciousness in such fragmented and meaningless shapes that they are incapable of absorption in just the way shock experiences are.[57] Indeed, for Benjamin they are shock experiences that are only occasioned differently than the routine horrors we might imagine as the germs leading to the evolution of the system of protection and involuntary memory.

If traditional stories can no longer be told and the novel as evidenced by Proust (or the lyric poem by Baudelaire) is regarded as an accurate registering of a transformation of experience – their new forms of writ-

56 *Illuminations,* pp. 162–3.

57 The idea that shell shock modelled and had become the norm is not unique to Benjamin; it was current at the time of his writing. In *Tender Is the Night* (Harmondsworth: Penguin, 1982), p. 129, F. Scott Fitzgerald intones that whether someone was a combatant "doesn't matter – we have some shell-shocks who merely heard an air raid from a distance. We have a few who merely read newspapers."

ing a response to the unavailability of experience upon which earlier literary forms rested – *then conscious experience is no longer a repository for experience.* If anything deserves to be called a transformation in the structure of subjectivity as a consequence of modernity, it is this.

> The greater the share of the shock factor in particular impressions, the more constantly consciousness has to be alert as a screen against stimuli; the more efficiently it does so, the less these impressions enter experience (*Erfahrung*), tending to remain in the sphere of a certain hour in one's life (*Erlebnis*). Perhaps the special achievement of the shock defence may be seen in its function of assigning to an incident a precise point in time in consciousness at the cost of the integrity of its contents. [58]

The withering of experience is, again, the transformation of *Erfahrung* into *Erlebnis.* Giving events a time in consciousness is both a strategic response to events that can no longer be experienced and a strategy of the shock defence producing *Erlebnis.* This is the strategy of *Erinnerung,* factual remembering, mentioned above. Its destructiveness is accomplished by a form of narration which would bind impressions to their time and place in consciousness as what constitutes and exhausts their possibility of meaning. This is destructive because once an impression has received its narrative spatio-temporal index, its placement as what is emphatically past is confirmed; from hence forward that impression is something over and done with, it has been fully accounted for by being given its time and place. Factual remembering and the modes of narration which accomplish it seek to insulate the present and future from the trouble, the shock and trauma, of past events. They are no longer spaces of hope or despair, promises made, disasters pending; they are what happened then – and that is all. Rather than experiences being turning points and origins which give sense to what follows from them, sense is given to experience by placing each event in a narrative causal order. Thus while we still narrate our lives and identities, the forms of narration adopted bespeak a thinning out of identity as a consequence of the disintegration of experiential meaning we might have supposed (or hoped) our mini-narratives salvaged.

This is how the loss of the "integrity of its contents" is accomplished by consciousness, the mark of the dissolution of experience, and hence the sense in which something can happen to us and yet fail to be experienced. Proust's project is poetically to reverse this collapse by producing experience synthetically. Involuntary memory acknowledges the destruction of experience; Proust's heroic narrative practice employs the resource of involuntary memory as an opportunity for *Gedächtnis,* and

58 *Illuminations,* p. 165.

thereby for the synthetic, writerly production of experience: the provision of an experience of what failed to be experienced at the time of its occurrence. Through Proust's novelistic remembrance, the taste of the madeleine *becomes* a promise (and site) of happiness that reveals the failure and emptiness of Proust's actual life in relation to the indeterminate promise of childhood. Adult disillusionment, the recapitulation of enlightenment disenchantment as a now structural feature of individual life history, is underlined and subverted in the recuperation of past hopes; to fictionally recapture these hopes permits us to experience hope as the ground of disillusionment, and hence as a horizon for it. Hence, the synthetic restoration of experience makes intelligible the disillusionment consequent on its empirical absence.

In the fragment "Out of the firing-line" (MM, A33), Adorno rapidly syntheses Benjamin's insights.

> But the Second War is as totally divorced from experience as is the functioning of a machine from the movements of the body, which only begins to resemble it in pathological states. Just as the war lacks continuity, history, an "epic" element, but seems to rather start anew from the beginning with each phase, so it will leave behind no permanent, unconsciously preserved image in memory. Everywhere, with each explosion, it has breached the barrier against stimuli beneath which experience, the lag between healing oblivion and healing recollection, forms. Life has changed into a timeless succession of shocks, interspaced with empty, paralysed intervals. But nothing, perhaps, is more ominous for the future than the fact that, quite literally, these things will soon be past thinking on, for each trauma of the returning combatants, each shock now inwardly absorbed, is a ferment of future destruction [of experience].

All of this accords with Benjamin except for the denial that now even unconscious memory can preserve the image of what we failed to experience; the Proustian synthesis too is becoming unavailable. The sign of this unavailability is that both *Dialectic of Enlightenment* and *Minima Moralia* are composed of "fragments": modernity's rationalization of experience and dissolution of significant narrative (the narration of experience) is itself unnarratable – which is the distance separating Adorno's philosophy from Benjamin's cultural history. Only the "shock" of the fragment which breaks the uninterrupted flow of lived instants can synthetically produce the experience of the loss of experience. Against the background of the understanding of the Proustian project and its replacement by the writing of fragments, Adorno and Horkheimer's claim that the task of *Dialectic of Enlightenment* is the "redemption of the hopes of the past" becomes comprehensible.

6. The Destruction of Authority

> It is the fate of charisma to recede before the powers of tradition or of rational association after it has entered the permanent structures of social action. This waning of charisma generally indicates the diminishing importance of individual action. In this respect, the most irresistible force is *rational discipline*.
>
> Max Weber[59]

Someone is an authority or has authority only if there is deference to her claims or commands that is not a consequence of either coercion or independent rational evaluation. Authoritative beliefs and commands are accepted on trust or out of respect, and not from self-interest or habit or lassitude or need. In speaking of "deference," "trust," "respect," what is being indicated is a moment in which a belief or command is accepted, taken as worthy and acceptable, without reflective assessment; authoritative beliefs or commands are precisely facts, given statements, possessing intrinsic normative force. Weber states that *Herrschaft* (translated as either "domination" or "authority") refers to a situation in which "the manifest will (command) of the ruler or rulers is meant to influence the conduct of one or more others (the ruled) and actually does influence it in such a way that their conduct to a socially relevant degree occurs as if the ruled has made the content of the command the maxim of their conduct."[60] So one final characterisation of Habermas's adolescent would be that his moral beliefs have lost their authority, their givenness now has become a source or ground for doubt and denial rather than acceptance. Disenchantment and rationalization destroy the authority of moral norms, but since the authority of moral norms would have been, in accordance with the first element of the grammar of moral insight, their demand and the approval of this demand, then it becomes plausible to contend that this destruction best explains why rationalization is demotivating.

If Henrich's grammar of moral insight does adequately limn the nature of practical reason, then the thesis that rationalization begets demotivation portends more than a local difficulty with the force of rationalized moral norms. Demand and approval encapsulated two distinct

59 Weber, *Economy and Society*, trans. Ephraim Fischoff et al., 2 vols. (Berkeley: University of California Press, 1958), pp. 1148–9. Hereafter references to this text will be abbreviated *ES*.

60 Ibid., p. 946. As Weber notes, his awkward "as if" is meant to capture, in a Kantian way, the sense that the ruled accepts or approves of the command as valid in accordance with one of the three modes of legitimate domination, and hence in abstraction from the concrete psychological mechanisms that may be operating in any particular case. I discus the three modes of legitimate domination below.

features of moral experience: the sense that moral norms are in some sense subject transcendent, originating from outside the subject as the condition for their placing a demand upon the self while nonetheless, *at the same time,* providing an internal condition that would *move* an agent to this or that action. Kant calls the internal connection between external demand and motivating power "the philosopher's stone": "When I judge by the understanding that an action is morally good there is still a great deal missing concerning the actual doing of the act that I have judged to be good. However, if this judgement moves me to do the act, then we have a case of moral sense. The understanding can indeed judge, but to give the judgement of the understanding motivating power that moves the will to do the act, that is the philosopher's stone."[61] By tracing the destruction of moral knowledge and experience, the double movement through which the disenchantment of the world transpires through its displacement by rationalized reason, the nature of demand retreats from some ideal or real object or some actual state of affairs as the source of demand to only the formal requirements of reason being demanded; and with the eclipse of the object there disappears as well the capacity of its formal or abstract replacement to be the sort of "object" that might move an individual to action. If, to use Kant's locution, the connection between moral understanding and moral sense is severed, then it becomes unclear in what sense what replaces it is *practical reason* at all.

The disenchantment of the world and the rationalization of reason tends toward the destruction of practical reason – in its constitutive differentiation from theoretical reason – as such. Disenchantment tends in this direction because its sceptical movement must regard significant exteriority as an anthropomorphic projection. The deference structure constitutive of legitimate authority is, at least, extensionally equivalent to the demand and approval aspect of moral insight. Hence, the process through which moral norms tendentially lose their authority is equally the process through which the internal connection between demand and approval becomes severed. However, according to Henrich, it is equally this first element of the grammar of moral insight that lays the foundation for the third element: it is through approval that the self first constitutes itself as a self. Again, the thought here is that every conception of the self as agent presupposes a normative horizon, some conception of the good in order to orient its activities, in order to give it direction and criteria for selection amongst alternative courses of action in its travels through the world. Demand and approval, the experience of the good, is the means through which a conception of the good comes to form an individual's basic motivational set. A self without such a motivating hori-

61 I. Kant, *Lectures on Ethics,* translated by L. Infield (Indianapolis: Hackett, 1980), pp. 44–45.

zon for action is barely a self. As moral norms lose their authority, their understanding and motivational force become dissociated; that dissociation undermines the conditions of coherent agency. And this, of course, is precisely the Nietzschean conundrum: we do not esteem what we know, it has been disenchanted; and what we need to esteem has been delegitimated as worthy of respect or veneration. The dissociation of moral understanding and moral sense undermines the conditions of significant individual action.

Some authors have wanted to identify the tendential collapse of the authority of moral norms with the disappearance generally of authority from the modern world.[62] If the deference structure of authority were intensionally equivalent to the structure of demand and approval, this claim would have some basis. But this is not obviously the case since in modern society we probably base more of our actions on the authority of experts (from garage mechanics and stockbrokers to scientists) than previous peoples; and in the liberal state we defer to those *in* authority minimally as a procedural mechanism for regulating and coordinating action under conditions of equality and dissensus over substantive ends.[63] Nonetheless it may be claimed that these modes of deference and obedience contain a sceptical moment about authority: across the range of cases where we defer to the authority of experts we do so out of convenience; in principle their knowledge is public and available to all. In the latter case, ideally, we can conceive of our deference either as analogous to deferring to expert knowledge[64] or as the result of a prior rational consensus over procedural norms through which authoritative norms are generated. In both cases, then, structures of authority are accepted on a nonauthoritative basis; we accept a structure of authority because it is (instrumentally) rational to do so.

For analytic and diagnostic purposes, it will prove useful to begin diagnosing this outcome in Weberian terms. Nor is a short detour through Weber irrelevant to an understanding of Adorno. *Dialectic of Enlightenment*'s genealogy of instrumental reason is without question a regimented and

62 So Hannah Arendt begins her essay "What Is Authority?" by stating that the title really should have been "What Was Authority?" because "authority has vanished from the modern world." See her *Between Past and Future: Eight Exercises in Political Thought* (Harmondsworth: Penguin Books, 1977), p. 91. In *Secularization and Moral Change* (London, 1967), p. 53, Alasdair MacIntyre states: "In our society the notion of moral authority is no longer a viable one. For the notion of authority can only find application in a community and in areas of life in which there is an agreed way of doing things according to accepted rules."

63 On the first point, see Max Weber, "Science as a Vocation," p. 139. For an excellent and subtlety organised collection of essays on the authority of the law, see Joseph Raz (ed.), *Authority* (New York: New York University Press, 1990).

64 This is the core of Joseph Raz's strategy in "Authority and Justification," in *Authority*, pp. 115–41.

narrowed version of Weber's rationalization theory; as a consequence it makes sense to construe it as tacitly acknowledging Weber's analysis of domination into three modes of authority to which all social action must be meaningfully related: charismatic, traditional, and legal-rational; as well as supporting Weber's conclusion that modern, rights-based societies generate an increase in domination. For Weber the three forms of authority are analytically distinct but co-present in all social arrangements, with the variation between societies a matter of which form is more or less dominant in relation to the others.[65] To say that the distinction among the forms is analytical and that they remain co-present is to imply, first, that in any particular historical instance we cannot fully or completely discriminate the role the different forms are playing; and second, that none of these forms is intrinsically irrational or eliminable. Conversely, by including legal-rational along with charismatic and traditional, Weber is implying the Nietzschean thought that reason is a form of *authority*, hence a value and orientation. Weber's blanket sociological realism hence contests enlightenment's self-understanding which identifies authority with heteronomy, priests and monarchs doing our thinking for us, with autonomy presented as the dissolution of the authority relation in general – a dissolution implicit in the sceptical moment within modern structures of authority that make accepting them either a rationally grounded acceptance of the division of cognitive labor (which itself presupposes a simple but indefinite deferring of a rational evaluation of its results one could, in principle, carry out) or a consequence of a previous rational evaluation. If the payoff of the dissolution of charismatic and traditional authority is the emergence of institutions organised in accordance with wholly impersonal and abstract rules which submerge individuals every bit as much as traditional roles – for example, in the ways in which the previous discussion of how the meaning of practices (economic, political, medical, etc.) become detached from individual experience showed – then from the perspective of the individual agent such institutions are as dominating and heteronomous as previous social forms retrospectively appear. This much of Weber's claim, however complicated the details,[66] should be uncontroversial. The question is whether, employing Weber's typology, a *clue* for an analogous form of argument can be found for the non-institutional case, remembering this it was just this analogy which lay behind the complaint about external reasons?[67]

65 *ES*, p. 216, n. 2.

66 For some of these, see Mark E. Warren's "Nietzsche and Weber: When Does Reason Become Power?," in Asher Horowitz and Terry Maley (eds.), *The Barbarism of Reason: Max Weber and the Twilight of Enlightenment* (Toronto: University of Toronto Press, 1994), pp. 68–96.

67 In making out this clue I will not be considering one significant criticism of Weber's analysis, viz., that he illicitly and wrongly analyses the case of legal rationalization, both for constitutional law and the legal system generally, in precisely the same way as he han-

According to Weber what distinguishes the three pure or ideal types of legitimate domination is the basis of their claim to legitimacy: the basis of legal authority is the rationality (either instrumental or value-rational, or both) of rules and the right of those in authority to propagate and execute those rules. Ideally those rules should be impersonal and abstract, and the obedience of subjects is owed to the "impersonal order."[68] Traditional authority rests on an established belief in "the sanctity of age-old rules and powers" and the "legitimacy of those exercising authority under them."[69] In this context Weber underlines the thought that obedience is "owed not to enacted rules but to the *person* who occupies a position of authority by tradition or whose has been chosen for it by a traditional *master*"; or, again, "*Personal loyalty,* not the official impersonal duty, determines the relations of the administrative staff to the master."[70] Finally, charismatic authority rests on "devotion to the exceptional sanctity, heroism or exemplary character of an individual person, and of the normative patterns or order revealed or ordained by him."[71]

dles bureaucratic and economic rationalization. It is, I think, plainly true that rationalization of the legal system is not only a matter of institutionalizing instrumental and value-neutral mechanisms, but includes the attempt to embed substantive values into a system of rights and legal procedures. This issue can be sidestepped here for two reasons: (1) It is no part of Adorno's case to deny that enlightenment rationalization has been also progressive, and thus the generation of substantive values we cannot rationally forgo; the question is how best to account for and preserve those values, to redeem the hopes of the past. In other words, because Adorno also believes that Weber's paradox of rationalization is in principle soluble, he does not deny the ideals of the enlightenment, only their characterisation as attributes of pure practical (communicative) reason. As I have been implying throughout this chapter and argue for more fully in the next, the Habermas/Kant account that argues for disenchantment providing a real progressive development of reason and only a contingent reification of its institutional bearers (the thesis of the colonization of the life-world) does not provide an adequate account of enlightenment ideals, and colludes with what it means to resist. (2) At *ES,* p. 1209, Weber comments on the depiction of natural rights by Tocqueville and Jellinek: "This charismatic glorification of Reason, which found a characteristic expression in its apotheosis by Robespierre, is the last form charisma has adopted in its fateful historical course." Critics of Weber's analysis of legal rationalization ignore the role he ascribes to the "charisma of reason" in the generation of the modern state and the potential of this analysis for further use. For an exception to this rule, see Wolfgang Schluchter's "Charisma and Counterculture," in Guenther Roth and Wolfgang Schlucter, *Max Weber's Vision of History: Ethics and Methods* (Berkeley: University of California Press, 1979), chapter 3. The "paradox" in Weber, as I shall argue, is only that no one has been able to locate or identify in a persuasive manner the "rational kernel" in his conception of charismatic authority; hence the necessary conditions for resistance to the routinization of reason into legal-rational form always appears to be an existential and irrational irruption. For the now standard critique of Weber on the rationalization of the legal sphere, see Jürgen Habermas, *The Theory of Comunicative Action,* vol. 1, trans. Thomas McCarthy (Oxford: Polity Press, 1984), pp. 345–65. Support for Habermas's account can be found in Mark E. Warren's "Nietzsche and Weber," while in the same volume there is a useful critique by Asher Horowitz, "The Comedy of Enlightenment: Weber, Habermas, and the Critique of Reification," pp. 195–222.

68 *ES,* pp. 215–18. 69 *ES,* pp. 226, 215. 70 *ES,* p. 227; emphasis mine.

71 *ES,* p. 215. Weber repeats the thesis that the actions or character of charismatic indi-

One comes to understand better Weber's strictures on the worth of rationalized modernity when one takes account of the role he ascribes to charismatic authority within history. To simplify, I simply enumerate his findings and theorems.

1. Weber contends that bureaucratic and patriarchal (traditional) order share the characteristic of being rooted in the need to meet the demands of everyday life in a continuous, reliable manner. Bureaucracy, he states, is "merely the rational counterpart of patriarchalism" in that it too is "a permanent structure and, with its system of rational rules, oriented toward the satisfaction of calculable need with ordinary, everyday means."[72]
2. Conversely, all extraordinary needs, needs that arise in times of distress for a community – be it psychic, physical, economic, ethical, religious, or political distress – have been satisfied on a charismatic basis. Charismatic authority interrupts the economic order of everydayness in order to respond to needs that are not satisfiable by routine operations. Charismatic leadership, by dint of the exemplary character of the leader or belief in her divine inspiration, is what enables a community to transcend its instrumentally rational attachment to everyday practices.
3. Hence, Weber contends that charismatic authority has been the dominant revolutionizing force within history. This requires qualification since bureaucracy too revolutionizes society, but it does so through "technical means," and hence "from without": "It first changes the material and social orders, and *through* them the people, by changing the conditions of adaptation." Charismatic authority revolutionizes society "from within": "if it has any specific effects at all, [it] manifests its revolutionary power from within, from a central *metanoia* [change or turning or conversion] of the followers' attitudes." Charismatic authority operates through conversion or transformation; hence, episodes of charismatic authority are paradigmatically experiences. Charismatic authority and experience necessarily refer to one another. What is thus significant here is not the origin of ideas (through intuition or reason), nor their actualization since in all cases ideas gain reality through works, but the *manner* in which ideas and beliefs are internalized by followers. One can either, to use Weber's example, internalise or learn the multiplication tables (and do so to the degree to which they really become one's own), or be turned around by a new idea

viduals are "exemplary" on p. 241, but it is implicit throughout – a point that will be important as we proceed.

72 *ES*, p. 1111. All further quotes in this enumerated account are from *ES*, pp. 1111–17.

(political, ethical, mathematical, scientific) so that it continues to effect one as a creation, an achievement, or breakthrough. In the first case internalization is adaptation, while in the second type of case it is transformative, reorienting. It is the capacity of charismatic authority to revolutionize from within that leads Weber to claim that in a "purely empirical and value-free sense charisma is indeed the specifically creative revolutionary force of history."

4. As a creative force, charismatic authority is what allows for the possibility of not just better rules, more efficacious ways of doing things, but new rules, new ways of ordering experience. In this respect, charismatic authority is itself "self-determined," not bound by existing rules, procedures, or laws. The irruptive or law-breaking character of charismatic performance is thus continued in the empirical or factual display of the new rule. Because the new rules ordained by the charismatic leader are not sanctioned by anything anterior to them, they can authorize themselves initially only through their mode of *appearing*, through the actual (or linguistically rhetorical) performance of the charismatic leader. To use a trope we return to below: charismatic performances are new *facts of reason*. Hence, charismatic authority concerns the subjectively effective moment in which new beliefs are instituted, performatively given, rather than their routinization through institutions.
5. Finally, the authority of the charismatic leader is utterly dependent on its being *recognized* by his followers; without recognition the claim of the leader collapses. However, while utterly dependent on recognition for its reality, the claim itself is not derived from the will of the followers: "it is their *duty* to recognize his charisma." Charismatic leadership thus must reveal itself as having a claim beyond the ordinary, and thus must find a mechanism for making its claiming appear exemplary.

Once the contours of Weber's affirmative sociological characterization of charismatic authority are appreciated, we can better comprehend his construal of the paradox of rationalization. After all, he acknowledges that charismatic authority is fundamentally unstable, and hence must, in time, give way to traditional or bureaucratic institutionalization. And, evidently, the more complex a society is the more it requires the kind of authority that only legal-rational institutions can provide, the fewer the opportunities for and the more marginal will be outbreaks of charismatic authority. But even this is a marginal consideration since *Weber neither can nor does offer any rational characterization of charismatic authority other than its functionally productive effects*. For Weber, charismatic authority is always protoreligious in nature; even the charisma of reason has theological contours: god-given or natural or self-evident rights and duties. Hence, substantive or value-rational beliefs are, from the perspective of rationalized reason, a puzzle.

This puzzle can be nuanced one step further. The central feature that traditional and charismatic authority share, and what separates them from legal-rational authority, is that their bindingness in the first instance is located in the recognition – *love, respect, veneration, trust, loyalty* – of the follower to the *person* of the master or charismatic leader. Hence, the "from within" authority of tradition and charisma depends on their mediation through a *personal relation* of respect or veneration, while the "from without" character of legal-rational authority, its externalism, is precisely its claim to being abstract, formal, impersonal, pure. A reasonable question for the ethicist at this juncture would be: "Who is the charismatic leader or traditional master spelled out in ethical terms?" The answer most consistently given in moral philosophy is the *phronimos,* the individual possessed of practical wisdom whose actions and style of acting provide the benchmark for those within his ethical community. The *phronimos* is the model of the ethical traditional master, a domesticated or routinised charismatic leader. Acknowledging that our communities are not closed in the way Aristotle's was, this figure can be domesticated one step further as "an abstracted, improved, neighbour lodged in one's inner life."[73] However much the image now of an ideal *neighbour* privatises the charismatic leader and traditional master, there is still the thought of a bond of respect to a *person* that gives the idealised other her authority. And it is just this which legal-rational conceptions of authority reject – emphatically:

> Every example of it [morality] presented to me must first be judged by moral principles in order to decide if it is fit to serve as an original example – that is, as a model: it can in no way supply the prime source for the concept of morality. Even the Holy One of the gospel must first be compared with our ideal of moral perfection before we can recognise him to be such. (G, 408)

Trust in the exemplary figure – charismatic leader, traditional master, *phronimos,* ideal neighbour – from the standpoint of autonomous reason appears naïve and heteronomous, while moving to the standpoint of reason appears to de-personalise and disembody ethical life to such an extent that it can naturally seem abstract, inhuman, external. It does not seem untoward to regard the separation of the authority of reason from its embodiment in a concrete individual as the core of Kant's question "How can pure reason be practical?," that is, how can reason detached

73 Bernard Williams, *Shame and Necessity* (Berkeley: University of California Press, 1993), p. 98.

from the mediations of love, trust, loyalty, or respect between persons be a motive for action? Is not that separation precisely the demotivating of reason, its formation as an impersonal structure? This same separation is equally the source of Weber's paradox: if disenchantment delegitimates the mechanisms for individual agency, how can the iron cage of modernity be rationally reformed? Will not what we think as reason necessarily appear as an external constraint on behaviour detached from individual ends and beliefs? How can that reason matter to me? Hence, will not the waning of tradition and charisma entail, as the epigraph to this section claims, a waning of the possibilities of individual action, that is, a waning of the mechanisms through which persons could conceive of themselves as authoring their own actions?

From this perspective, the thesis that disenchantment destroys the authority relation as such, while false, is nonetheless comprehensible. From a sociological standpoint, if legitimate authority traverses a path of routinization from the charismatic through the traditional to the legal-rational, and this path has underwritten the dynamic dialectic of Western rationalization, then with the disenchantment of charismatic and traditional authority, the historic dynamic of the authority relation itself tendentially lapses. Looking back from the standpoint of pure reason, rationalized reason makes it appear as if authority was only charismatic and traditional authority since in them there remains an indissoluble moment of heteronomy, the emergence of facts and demands for reason which when recognized become facts of reason. From the standpoint of rationalized reason, how can the obedience following on from respect, loyalty, love, or veneration not appear as heteronomous and pathological? Hence, what I termed the "sceptical moment" in the modern acceptance of rational authority is intrinsic: as rational it wishes to make no appeal to authority, to any fact or experience subjectively apprehended and mediated, while as designating a command it intends to claim authority for itself and itself alone and so be subjectively efficacious for individual agency. Hence, for Adorno in the same way in which enlightenment's repudiation of conditionality is what explains its reversion to mythic repetition, so for him rationalized reason's repudiation of charismatic authority, the exemplarity of some ethical performances, is what makes it, metaphorically, charismatic: an enchantment or spell (*Bann*) paralysing its subjects.

If the authority relation is fundamentally a personally bound experience of legitimate command, echoing Agamben's thought cited earlier that experience has its necessary correlation in authority, then the dissolution of charismatic and traditional authority entails that we are losing any coherent experience of the authority relation itself. For Adorno the barometer of the loss of the experience of authority is the growing disappearance of paternal authority occurring alongside the collapse of the bourgeois family. Because his critics have assumed the disappearance of the authority relation whose absence Adorno is contesting, they have focused their attacks on the implied approval of patriarchal authority, and on the inconsistencies and ambivalences in his appropriation of psychoanalysis.[74] In *Minima Moralia* the so-called end of internalization thesis is broached aphoristically, subjectively, and reflectively, without direct recourse to either psychoanalytic or sociological theory. The title of the aphorism "Grassy seat" refers to a well-known German song: "The dearest spot I have on earth / is the grassy seat by my parents grave."[75] The sentimentality and melancholy of these lines is their ironic point: the form of generationality which produced the bourgeois individual immanently joined authoritative rationality and love since in it the father, at least, was a charismatic leader and/or traditional master in miniature. While at the time parental authority came to be resented since it spoke with the voice of prudence (the "reality principle") rather than happiness, retrospectively, once the family itself is factually or normatively dissolved, the dynamic of emulation and resistance can be recognized as a debilitated form of transformation "from within." Hence, the joining of reason, love, and resentment made possible, rather than undermined, a dynamic relation between the generations. The disintegration of parental authority, as a token of the collapse of the authority relation,

74 Adorno's appropriations of psychoanalysis were unsteady and uneven, in part because he was at different points trying to explain different things: authoritarianism, growth of aggressivity, susceptibility to conformist pressures, narcissistic regression, etc. His best single piece on these issues is "Psychology and Sociology," trans. Irving Wohlfarth, *New Left Review* 46–7 (1966–7). Still the best analysis and critique of Adorno's writings in this area is Jessica Benjamin, "The End of Internalization: Adorno's Social Psychology," *Telos* 32 (1977): 42–64. Following Benjamin it has become common to criticise Adorno's psychoanalytic thought for being insufficiently intersubjective, that is, he consistently operates with a subject-object rather than a subject-subject structure. As we see below, while true, intersubjectivity for Adorno is not a self-sufficient paradigm since what we need is an account of the character, the epistemology, of our apprehension of others as living beings; and this apprehension had better be consonant with our best of account of knowing, judging, and responding in general. Further, these attacks misfire because they displace the problem of the nature of legitimate authority, the authority of enlightened reason, that is Adorno's real focus of attention. Still, it should be conceded that Adorno needs a social psychology – a workable conception of identification, internalization, projection, etc., in relation to an account of socialization and ego formation – which his own writings fail to provide. I find the beginnings of such an account in Judith Butler, *The Psychic Life of Power: Theories in Subjection* (Stanford, CA: Stanford University Press, 1997). "Power" in Butler almost always corresponds to what I mean by authority.

75 The autobiographical background to this aphorism is almost certainly the Nazi confiscation of property and then imprisonment of Adorno's parents as reported in his letter to Benjamin of February 1, 1939. Hence the thought that the competition between generations is dissolving from the Oedipus complex into parricide: "Such a climate fosters a late, lucid understanding with our parents, as between the condemned, marred only by the fear that we, powerless ourselves, might not be able to care for them as well as they cared for us when they possessed something" (MM, A2).

thus produces a false individualism since the mechanisms of socialization displace emulation with adaptation to either a peer group or neutral rules for navigating the social world (or both). The kitsch image of the grassy seat in the graveyard contains an historic truth behind its sentimental façade, but only the façade and not the truth remains. The typical Adornoian figure of affirmation and critique in the final lines of the aphorism presents the ideal connection between authority and love that make legitimate authority possible, and answers the objection that he was an unconditional supporter of patriarchal familial structures.

> With the family there passes away, while the system lasts, not only the most effective agency of the bourgeoisie, but also resistance which, through repressing the individual, also strengthened, perhaps even produced him. The end of the family paralyses the forces of opposition. The rising collectivist order is a mockery of a classless one: together with the bourgeois it liquidates the utopia that once drew sustenance from motherly love.

Rational authority is ideal here only since its various components are distributed between father and mother, whose differentiation is the source of the distortion of rational authority, the authority of reason, in the micro-charismatic society of the bourgeois family.[76] But this fate of complex authority connects up and converges with the first gesture of this chapter: the destruction of aura. In the same way in which morality becomes abstracted from the person of the leader, so the worth of agents becomes abstracted from their embodied personhood. In both cases there is a movement from responding to an individual toward employing rules to measure that personhood, whether we measure the perfection of the Holy One against the standards of the moral law or deliberate on the maxims of action that enable us to treat others as ends in themselves. The displacement of parental authority is equally a movement through which love is displaced as the mediating mechanism of ethical norms and, by this fact, how these norms take on a life of their own: rules of reason. How costly these abstractions are we come to in the next chapter. Still, the impetus of such rules is worth noting: they intend that our love, care, concern, and respect for others be derived from rational forms abstracted from actual relations of love, care, concern, and respect.

76 As Peter Dews has correctly noted, in *Dialectic of Enlightenment* Adorno and Horkheimer must presuppose a "primordial lack of differentiation between mother and father figures" since only so can they "seek to suggest that the trauma of separation and its sacrificial repetition are not necessary preconditions of subjectivity – that "the institution of sacrifice is the scar of an *historical* catastrophe, an act of force that befalls humanity and nature alike" (DoE, p. 51). The passage appears in Dews's essay "The Crisis of Oedipal Identity: The Early Lacan and the Frankfurt School," collected in his *The Limits of Disenchantment: Essays on Contemporary European Philosophy* (London: Verso, 1995), pp. 231–2. I return to the issue of a logic of sacrifice below.

The losses recorded in this fragment are meant autobiographically and hence reflectively (MM, p. 18); they condition, indeed constitute, the aporetic, loveless, cold rationalism of the modern intellectual that Adorno elaborates in the following seven aphorisms (MM, A3-A9).

It is no accident that Adorno places this aphorism almost at the very beginning of *Minima Moralia* (MM, A2): the whole text, including its fragmentary style, is written under the shadow of the disappearance of the triune authority relation: the appearing and immanent connection between fact and reason, reason and its performance, the power of reason to command belief. Said otherwise, the practice of *Minima Moralia*, like that of *Dialectic of Enlightenment* in its own way, self-consciously inflates the presumption that philosophical argumentation should be tightly logical, appealing only to the force of better reason, by adopting a contrary style of presentation in which premises are not offered, definitions not given, logical connectives dropped, and fundamental ideas elaborated discontinuously. Key theses are emphatically authored and performed. I elaborate the conception of cognition, material inference, and the consequent view of rationality at work in these procedures in Chapter 7. For the present it is sufficient to note how Adorno explicitly opposes the disavowal of the responsibilities and risks of authorship (authoring belief) implied in the ideal that philosophy should provide demonstrations that no one could rationally deny.

> ... instead of reducing philosophy to categories, one would in a sense have to compose it first. Its course must be a ceaseless self-renewal, by its own strength as well as in friction with whatever standard it may have. The crux is what happens in it, not a thesis or a position – the texture (*Gewebe*), not one-track, deductive or inductive, trains of reasoning. Essentially, therefore, philosophy is not expoundable. If it were, it would be superfluous; that most of it can be expounded speaks against it. (ND, 33–4)

What would make philosophy superfluous would be if its theses were beyond dispute. The condition of being beyond dispute is achievable only by dissolving the relation between experience and reason whose synthesis alone can account for the authority of reason. Since that relation cannot, finally, be dissolved, then all that can be beyond dispute are theses either tautologically true or so trivial that their acceptance or rejection does not "matter." In opposition, Adorno attempts to propel his thought into the space – the entanglement of reason and authority – that enlightened reason has been razing, to insinuate an indeterminate contest of reason, authority and writing by refusing the strategies and methods through which that context is systematically disavowed: a priori truths, transcendental deductions, deductive demonstrations, and so on. By so doing he means to call into question the reduction of reason to its legal-rational form. What he seeks to offer his readers is not a thesis, but an experience of the object about which he is writing. But this is to say only that for Adorno *the demands of reason generally are utterly continuous with demands of moral reason, with the connection between the two being the authority of reason.* If reason is to command, practically or theoretically, then it must be in some sense authoritative; but, on the Weberian analysis, a vital and dynamic culture of reason is not possible if the authority of reason is reduced to its ideal legal-rational form.

If correct, this raises more questions than it answers since it presupposes that Weber's sociological and political analysis of legitimate authority has bearing on a viable conception of reason and rationality as such. But this makes the philosophical deficits in Weber's account significant: why are there are only three ideal forms of legitimate authority? Why must a dynamic or viable conception of authority be triune? And why must, and in what sense of must, the three forms of authority be copresent? Put differently, why are the distinctions between the modes of authority analytic? I have suggested that what distinguishes charismatic and traditional authority from legal-rational authority is that the first two but not the latter are mediated through the affective attachment – love, respect, loyalty – of the followers to the leader. While this helps explain both the differentiation between transformation from within and transformation from without, and, consequently, how historically reason and motivation have been aligned, the sheer fact of this sociological thesis tells us nothing about its necessity.

7. Conclusion

The relation of reason to authority is directly homologous with the relation of enlightenment to myth; in both cases the second term is defined negatively, as that which is to be overcome, with the result that both first terms become frozen and deformed. What Adorno and Horkheimer's negative statement of their fundamental thesis – enlightenment reverts to myth – suppresses, and what is directly entailed by the disappearance of authority thesis, is the positive, speculative identification of the concepts in question: enlightenment and myth are "one," they belong together (but they have become separated from one another); reason and authority are "one," they belong together (but they have become dirempted from one another).[77] Our modern hope to be done with authority (like the modern aspiration to eliminate all "myth" from reason), to let reason rule autonomously, is what generates the antagonistic space of reason that is neutral, impersonal, without subjective accompaniment (or, what amounts to the same thing, needs to connect up with a separate

77 Peter Osborne jolted me into seeing my commitment to this speculative thesis.

and antecedent desire to become efficacious), and a regressive subjectivity possessing only its futile spontaneities and privatised feelings and emotions. And while in this form the issue concerns, narrowly, the nature of reason, in its institutional form that very neutral and abstract reason governs institutional practice – economic, political, medical, legal. One cannot make out the depth of the complaint against external reasons in moral thought without seeing the complementarity between bureaucratic rationalization and the rationalization of reason.

I began this chapter with a characterization of enlightenment thought as disenchanting, rationalizing, and universalizing, and claimed that we could ideally trace the emergence of these characteristics to the operations of the principle of immanence: classification, subsumption, reiterability, and instrumentality; and further that these features of the principle of immanence were *platitudes*. Conversely, I have tended to characterize the forms of object relation which the sceptical dynamic of enlightenment undermines in, intentionally, estranging terms. The contrast between the platitudes of enlightened reason and the strangeness of what has been lost (ethical knowledge, auratic experience, charismatic authority) is necessary if we are going to appreciate the resilience of enlightenment and the remoteness of what would be different from it. If ethical knowledge, experience, and authority are possible, they are not easily so either practically (because of the fundamental mechanisms underlying the reproduction of the major institutions of modern society) – the world cannot be re-enchanted by philosophical fiat – or reflectively – what we need to restore reason is not platitudinous.[78]

In making a case for the plausibility of Adorno and Horkheimer's account of the process of disenchantment, it was conceded that, as stated, their argument is troubled by having too indeterminate an account of what precisely the conditions of reason (object, image, nature, language, history) are that would be adequate to their account of what the debili-

78 A good example of a platitudinous dispatching of rationalized reason is John McDowell's "Might There Be External Reasons?," reprinted in his *Mind, Value, and Reality* (Cambridge, Mass.: Harvard University Press, 1998), pp. 95–111. While I admire much in this essay, it supposes that the problem of external reason arises simply in the case of the individual who is deaf to a certain way of seeing the world. In making this assumption McDowell simply assumes that we now can *see* the world (which is the consequence of an imaginative activity of deliberation) aright, and that nothing about the nature of the modern world troubles such seeing. All of the sociology of modernity, and its continuance in a work like *Minima Moralia*, is lost on McDowell. Can we be attuned to an ethical world like that? More important, McDowell copes with the problem of the ethically deaf individual by insisting that what is needed is a process of conversion (pp. 102, 107, et al.). I too think that conversion is what is required; but as my account of Weber has tried to underline, in order to bring conversion into the picture we need a conception of charismatic authority – which is hardly something easily rationally available. McDowell requires then, as part of his conception of reason, to show why, how, and with what right conversion should belong to our repertoire of reason. It is just this that the platitudes of rationalized reason make hard to accept.

tating consequences of their eschewal are. Adding to this problem I noted that simply acknowledging that reason is conditioned is insufficient; what must be shown is that what rationalized reason disavows and destroys is intrinsic to it. By discussing the demise of ethical knowledge, experience, and authority I have complicated this account by claiming that not only is the *world disenchanted,* but *reason,* in terms of forms of object relation, *rationalized.* Only when he turns to the problems and nature of *concepts,* I have suggested, does Adorno find a way of adequately specifying the connection of world and reason in a manner sufficient for explicating the nature of disenchantment and what it would take to overcome it. Before turning to the question of the concept (Chapters 6 and 7) however, and in partial preparation for it, I want to examine Kant's moral philosophy since in his accounts of the autonomy of reason, the universality of the moral law, the primacy of rational deliberation, the authority of the fact of reason we find the fullest and most articulate conception of a disenchanted, rationalized morality.

3

THE INSTRUMENTALITY OF MORAL REASON

In this chapter I want to offer a contextualized reading and genealogical reconstruction of Kant's moral thought in order that it can be understood as both a response to the problem of disenchantment and a continuation of the rationalization of reason under the governance of the principle of immanence. More precisely, my intention is re-cross the terrain of the previous chapter by seeing how the principle of immanence and the destructions it brings about (of knowledge, experience, and authority) form and de-form Kant's moral theory, although the order of reconstruction will not directly follow Chapter Two's order of presentation. Kant's Copernican turn in morals is certainly a continuation of the rationalization of reason. However, more generously, Kant's moral philosophy should first be seen as *responding* to the disenchantment of the natural world that had already occurred, and hence as suffering the loss of traditional and charismatic authority. If the Weberian account of that loss is anything like correct, then it corresponds to the disintegration of the first moment of the grammar of moral insight: demand and approval. If the moment of demand and approval anchors the difference between practical and theoretical reason, then one would anticipate that being left with only legal-rational authority Kant would be unable to demonstrate why rational morality is to be seen as intrinsically motivating, or, what is the same, unable to transform theoretical insight into a practical norm. In Section 2 I argue, in narrow textual terms, that as a consequence of the detachment of the authority of reason from the other sources of authority Kant is unable to demonstrate how pure reason can be practical. In Section 3 moral universalism is shown to be ambiguous between an historic achievement, a substantive piece of inductive moral knowledge, and a formal principle; only the former is truly moral. But here too it is important to see Kant's thought as responding to a disaster that has already occurred. The disaster, as I will interpret the collapse of pre-modern ethical life, is the fracturing of the body of the rules of material inference that were the empirical bond amongst living subjects; this fracturing occurred by the logic of instrumental rationality, narrowly understood, coming to supervene on previous material inference rules; that is, to state the same in more familiar terms, there occurred the imposition of a generalized instrumental rationality on what were formerly moral principles – Hobbes' moment. Hence, Kant faced a situation in which disenchantment and the rationalization of reason had *already* destroyed the older moral culture. If the substance of the earlier moral rules was the victim of the disaster, then the only hope would be to resurrect or reconstruct them on a higher level; and in order to do that one required an account of reason that could itself supervene on the Hobbesian instrumentalization of morality. Kantian moral reason, pure practical reason, is intended as a supervening logic or interpretative grid capable of imposing itself on the narrow instrumental rationality that had already absorbed into itself the substance of antique morality by transforming moral substance into rules of prudential rationality.[1] This saving movement is, nonetheless, a further rationalization of reason operating under the governance of the principle of immanence. In Section 4 I argue that Kant's own logical view of universality is, despite itself, a form of instrumental reason. In the final section of this chapter, through a brief analysis of moral complexity and the problem of the conflict of duties, the question of moral experience and moral necessity are raised. No account of moral conflict can be satisfactory unless the *objects* of moral action are the source of moral demands; but to accede to that thought would involve giving Kant's Copernican turn an axial turn toward the object; which is one of the central ways in which Adorno describes his project as a whole. Hence the point of my genealogical reconstruction is twofold: first, to provide an exposition of modern moral thought that radically underlines how it is constituted by the disenchantment of the world and the rationalization of reason; and secondly, by inference to begin indicating some of the parameters of Adornoian ethical thought. Since, again, Adorno left us very few hints in this domain, orienting the argument through the construction of a reading of Kant's moral thought becomes a plausible strategy. Before, then, beginning the effort of reconstruction let me offer a sketch of the propriety of focusing on Kant's moral philosophy in this context as well as the propriety of reading it genealogically.

1. Axial Turn and Saving Urge

In the short Preface to *Negative Dialectics* Adorno twice describes his project as an immanent critique of Kant's transcendental idealism: first, he states his intention as "to use the strength of the subject to break through the fallacy of constitutive subjectivity," and then, in the next paragraph

1 Theodor W. Adorno, *Problems of Moral Philosophy*, pp. 107–8.

referring to the final chapter of the book, to try "by critical self-reflection to give the Copernican revolution an axial turn" (ND, xx). For Adorno transcendental idealism is the fullest philosophical articulation and expression of rationalized reason; it is what reason is and comes to as a consequence of the dialectic of enlightenment. Traditional and charismatic authority, ethical experience and knowledge each represented ways in which reason was responsive to, formed and informed by what it was not. In the formations of reason in which those modes of object relation still prevailed the gap between reason as embedded in social practice and reason as reflection was marginal; one might consider a condition of such proximity between social/practical reason and reflective reason, a condition in which each explicitly interprets the other, as one version of the perspective of ethical life as opposed to centralism. As those modes of object relation were dissolved so reason rid itself of anything heteronomous, it became autonomous, constitutive: what the meaning of an object is, the very idea, the concept of an object in general is given by reason. The "spontaneity" of reason refers to the power of reason to be self-determining, not determined by anything external to it, and thus to possess the power to specify in advance, a priori, what it is, in general, for something to be an object for me (or us).

For Adorno the disenchantment of the world, the rationalization of society, the hegemony of scientisim and reductive naturalism are all shadows of the rationalization of reason; and the fullest expression of rationalized reason is the idealist conception in which it becomes self-determining and legislative. While in contemporary argument it is normal to think of idealism at itself a form of anthropomorphic projection which a properly naturalist understanding of the world opposes, for Adorno that thought simply leaps over the rational *shape* which the natural world as a closed causal order knowable in mathematical terms is presumed to possess. What *counts* as natural is determined not by what is naturally out there, but by the rational determination of what is out there. Reductive naturalism for Adorno is a conception of the world determined by rationalized reason, and not available otherwise. So, again, the rationalization of reason destroys previous modes or forms of object relation, and it is that which finally disenchants the world, and not the direct replacement of false beliefs by truer and better ones; in its most humdrum elaboration, that is Kant's critique of Hume. And it is that same rationalized reason that construes the natural world as a closed causal order that will be employed to rationalize the major institutions of society into their modern bureaucratic, legal-rational form. Hence it is our reasoning that disenchants nature and creates the iron cage of modernity. Kant's Copernican turn is the attempt to legitimate legal-rational authority against all competitors, to demonstrate why nothing can be true or good or valid for us other than what is determined by self-determining reason to be good or true or valid. Kant does not merely accept, but argues to the hegemony of legal-rational authority as the standpoint of secular modernity. Hence, for Adorno the philosophical critique of modernity can be nothing other than the critique of the rationalized reason of idealist philosophies, most especially Kant's.

Now if the modes of object relation which would curtail the claims of rational autonomy have truly been destroyed, then constitutive subjectivity is not an ideology of reason, a mere conception of reason and subjectivity, but what they actually have (almost) become. If reason has become (almost) autonomous and transcendental subjectivity (almost) constitutive, then, at one level at least, philosophical thinking is bound to those results: it can deploy the powers of constitutive subjectivity to undermine such subjectivity, and it can attempt, from within, a further turn of the subject in order to give priority to the object. But for Adorno it must be the constitutive subject that undoes itself, and it must be by critical self-reflection that the Copernican revolution is given an axial turn toward the object. "The priority of the object," the critical result Adorno aims to establish, is only a meaningful counter to the idealist conception of the object which must be demonstrated from within the purview of the constitutive subjectivity that denies it. Any other mode of procedure would by-pass the historically elaborated authority of autonomous reason.

But this demand for critique to be immanent is historically inflected from the outset: it is only because autonomous reason *historically is* the quintessence of the rationalization of reason that critique must locate itself within its confines; but, equally, the same – historical – necessity forcing critical reflection to be immanent places it outside the self-understanding of such reason. Consistently, Adorno captures this complex of history and necessity as a relation between the ideal of transcendental philosophy and the claims of tradition it seeks to disavow: "While reflecting the transcendental moment, the traditional is quasi-transcendental, not a point-like subjectivity but properly (*eigentlich*) constitutive" (ND, 54). Tradition is quasi-transcendental because, while representing the necessary conditions for the possibility of experience (empirical or reflective), its authority is only historical, and hence subject to further elaboration. Adorno perceives an adumbration, almost a concession, of this thesis in Kant's conception of the reproductive imagination. In order for a present perception to be meaningful the immediately previous moments of experience must be held in mind and coordinated with it; for example, in order to hear the chimes strike "12" I must hold in mind the previous 11 strikes. In this respect the meaning and identity of present perceptions or thoughts are constituted by their internal relation to what immediately preceded them. Adorno interprets Kant's employment of the reproductive imagination as a "trace of historicity," an unconscious acknowledgement that thinking as an "intratemporal, motivated, progressive motion is the microcosmic equivalent of the macrocosmic motion of history internalized in the structure of thinking" (ND, 54). If thinking attempted to eschew its past in order to make knowledge conform to the "idol" of purity and timelessness, it would become at best a tautology, at worst a disconnected, amnesiac solipsism of the present moment, lacking room even for transcendental logic. What holds for the thinking process itself must hence hold for its contents; tradition is immanent in knowledge itself as its formation; all content is sedimented history, carrying with it the processes through which it came to be. Knowledge partakes in tradition as "unconscious remembrance" (ND, 54). Once the requirement of tradition is acknowledged in this way, it can be turned against the procedures of transcendental philosophy. So Adorno contends that missing from the *Critique of Pure Reason*'s initial questions is "the question how a thinking obliged to relinquish tradition might preserve and transform it; for nothing else is mental experience" (ND, 54–5). Kant's turn and hypothesis – asking not whether our knowledge conforms to its objects, but rather if (how and why) objects must conforms to our modes of knowing – is an insufficient acknowledgement of the tradition idealism aimed to relinquish; immanent critique, Adorno avers, is more adequate to the dialectic of relinquishment, preservation, and transformation.

Conceiving of tradition as a necessary condition for the possibility of reflection relocates the demands of tradition from tradition to the conceptuality of autonomy; hence, what is quasi-transcendental is an autonomous demand for a heteronomous content. To consider the *authority* of tradition as quasi-transcendental both exemplifies and constitutes Adorno's relation to transcendental idealism: accepting its form of claiming (e.g., interrogating the necessary conditions for experience) as the mode for undermining the norm of constitutive subjectivity.

Of course, this is both an anticipatory moment – a very short run of argument belonging to the methodological prologue which forms the Introduction to *Negative Dialectics* – and highly abstract: to insist upon the necessity of tradition appears to abstract from any concrete tradition. But that abstraction is the tradition of transcendental philosophy and rationalized reason. Hence, despite the fact that Adorno consistently presses for content, concreteness, contingency, abstraction is the milieu and product of disenchantment, and thus cannot be circumvented. A further consequence of the culture of abstraction is that the mutual implication of social and reflective categories, the processes through which each side interprets the other, dissolves. An expression of that dissolution is, again, the duality between philosophy and sociology. It is in virtue of the duality between the reflective and the social that the social content of reflective categories becomes opaque, and, as a consequence, Adorno's hermeneutical premise concerning the centrality of transcendental idealism appears so suspect. If practically, rationalized reason represents the constitutive mechanisms of capital reproduction and bureaucratization, then transcendental idealism is the reflective version of those mechanisms.

So saying does not itself reveal the social content of Kant's abstract, a priori categories. Their "meta-logical" content, as Adorno calls it, is sublimated within them; in this respect introducing sociological reflections into Kant's classificatory program is not done from the outside. Nonetheless, such reflections do depart from the systematic and argumentative setting in which Kant immerses his fundamental ideas, and it is this which, in each individual case, gives to a meta-logical reflection its tinge of being arbitrary, external. The duality between philosophy and sociology, the historic consequence of the abstractive processes of rationalized reason in theory and practice, makes the tinge of arbitrariness ineliminable. So in discussing the formula of the end in itself – "Act in such a way that you always treat humanity, whether in your own person or in the person of any other, never simply as a means, but always at the same time as an end" (G, 429) – Adorno concedes that Kant's concept of "humanity" has an ideal content that is irreducible to anything empirically extant. He contends that nonetheless there is a factual content in the word that cannot be controlled by Kant's intentions and thus that cannot be shaken off: "that every individual should be respected as a representative of the socialized human species, not [treated as] a mere function of the exchange process" (ND, 257). The distinction between means and ends on which Kant relies in generating his formula is a social difference: "it is the difference between subjects as merchandise, as labor power that can be used to produce value, and the human beings who even in the form of such merchandise remain the subjects for whose sake the whole machinery is set in motion, in which they are forgotten and only incidentally satisfied" (ND, 257). While in the following pages Adorno does attempt to track places in Kant where social content is acknowledged as belonging to systematically defined concepts, he ends this account with a flat pronouncement that without the perspective provided by this meta-logical decoding of "humanity" in terms of the social difference between means and ends this variant of the Categorical Imperative would be "lost in a void" (ND, 257). In our culture the distinctions between the noble and the base, the virtuous and the dissolute, free man and slave, fail to connect with the dominant ways in which our "humanity" is respected and disregarded, and hence with the experiences in which making moral distinctions press themselves on us. Indeed, the dominant experience is one in which "humanity" in the form of labor power is recognized and not recognized at the same time, in which the (moral) worth of individuals is constantly threatening to collapse into or be overwhelmed by what an individual is worth monetarily; but this direct threat extends well outside the economic domain, as we saw in Adorno's treatment of the relation between marriage and divorce. For Adorno, this has been the most *pervasive* threat to human dignity in the modern experience, and hence how our conception of human dignity is formed in resistance; it is not an accident that Kant contrasts the dignity of humans to mere "market" or "fancy" price (G, 434–5). Kant's formula expresses the pervasiveness of the threat, that persons might be treated as exchangeable things, and establishes a reflective form of resistance to it. It is for this reason that Adorno seconds Horkheimer's judgement that the "never simply" (*niemals bloss*) in Kant's formula "is one of those majestically sober turns of speech designed not to spoil utopia's chance at realization" (ND, 257–8). The conundrum of means and ends, whatever its other sources, localizes Kant's formula to a social moment.

Adorno's immanent critique of transcendental idealism is, throughout, logical (as exemplified by the treatment of tradition) and meta-logical (as in the interpretation of the end in itself formula). Both logical and meta-logical critiques depend on the presumption of transcendental idealism being quasi-transcendental for us. It is because idealism is quasi-transcendental that meta-logical critique, and its genealogical extension, are not external imputations, but themselves "logical." While the dominant movement of Adorno's reading of Kant is critical, it is not uniformly so as his take on treating others never just as means but as ends at the same time shows. Indeed, while the controlling moment of Adorno's reading of Kant turns on reiterated attempts to demonstrate how Kant reifies, makes transcendental, what are historical distinctions and problems, thus further engulfing us in them, he consistently acknowledges that the *Critique of Practical Reason* as a whole is motivated by a "saving urge" (*Begierde des Rettens*), namely, to save the residue of human freedom – something Kant himself appears to acknowledge (CPrR, 95). In the light of a social practice that promised freedom but failed to deliver it, Kant was led to construe empirical life as constituted by a thoroughgoing causality, so eliminating freedom from experience. While this is an exorbitant claim on Kant's part, if the arguments of the previous chapter hold, its has an evident truth content: if the ethical mediations connecting subjects with one another have been eliminated, then the empirical world is, so to speak, (ethically) *like* a causal universe. As disenchanted, no values are "in" this world, and therefore no empirical moral bonds can connect its inhabitants. If moral relations exist among the inhabitants of this world, then they must be "abstract," a manner or mode of acknowledging one another without empirical intermediaries. Reflecting back, we have already seen this disappearance of intermediaries in the abyss separating the extremes of marriage and divorce, and in the failure of tact to mediate between individualized selves. Kant's philosophical system makes this abyss systematic and metaphysical: it is the abyss between the standpoint of the understanding that cognizes the empirical world as a law-like causal order without sense or meaning, and the standpoint of a moral reason that produces an intelligible world of rational agents bound to one another through the prescriptive determinations of individual rational deliberation. In fine, Kant makes a radical conception of disenchantment a premise of his reflections, and then, from within the extreme of that premise attempts to salvage enlightenment's progressive meaning. Saving the residue hence became synonymous with saving what enlightenment promised and withdrew.

If Kant's philosophy represents for Adorno the quasi-transcendental condition of our present, then we can best begin approaching his ethical position through tracking, without directly following, his meta-critique of practical reason. A number of qualifications and caveats are necessary before beginning. First, although following Adorno's lead, I will not here expound his own meta-critique of practical reason since its central impetus concerns the abstraction of Kantian reason from nature and human embodiment, especially with respect to Kant's metaphysics of freedom and the will; for Adorno pure reason cannot be practical because it has become to a certain extent and interprets itself as independent of bodily inclinations and drives rather than being a certain formation of inclinations and drives. While the abstraction of reason from the body is relevant to the overall trajectory of my argument, and hence will require instancing Chapter Five, I want to approach it here via and in the context of the presuppositions governing Adorno's handling of normativity. Normative questions, however, are only obliquely dealt with by Adorno, even in the "Freedom" chapter of *Negative Dialectics,* and in his *Probleme der Moralphilosophie.* His explicit, albeit inconsistently stated view is the standard Marxist one, viz., with a state of freedom there would be no "morality," that is, no system of constraints and externally imposed obligations (ND, 285).[2] And while such a disappearance view of morality is plausible with respect to a particular conception of ethical life, it hardly does justice to normativity as such, or to Adorno's own implied conception of the normative.

Second, in what follows Kantian reason is construed formally, that is, wholly apart from his moral metaphysics which makes human beings ends in themselves because, through their freedom, they bring (inject) value into the world by having ends, but as origins of value they cannot

2 For the Marxist critique of morality see Allen Wood, *Karl Marx* (London: Routledge, 1981), chs. 9 and 10. Against his explicit anti-moralism, and following out what his general orientation commits him to, I am construing Adorno's critique of the "moral system" as akin to that of Bernard Williams in *Ethics and the Limits of Philosophy.* That Adorno was himself never entirely clear, in the writings we possess, about the relation between his critique of morality and his own normative commitments I have acknowledged from the outset.

be measured or valued. As we will see more fully in the next chapter, while Adorno clearly thinks there is something important and compelling about the distinction between means and ends in Kant, he equally thinks Kant's way of sustaining that difference must be resisted – despite itself, it furthers the disenchantment it means to dislodge. Here, as the title of this chapter indicates, I am interested in meta-critically demonstrating how Kant's conception of moral reason partakes in the very instrumentalization of reason it was intended to overcome. More exactly, I am interested in pressing Kant's conception of *pure reason:* Can it be practical? If and when it is practical, is it really "moral"? What does its abstract character do to our relations with others?

Third, in thinking through these questions we will need to keep in mind that Adorno does *not* conceive of instrumental reason as restrictedly means-end reasoning. Properly speaking, instrumental reason is defined by Adorno as constituted by the principle of immanence; hence, in his extended sense pure logic is a form of instrumental reason. Instrumental reason is thus best comprehended negatively; it refers to any form of reasoning *that conceives of itself* (necessarily falsely for Adorno) as determined by pure reason itself apart from and independently of content and object. Hence, Adorno will sometimes describe instrumental reason or identity thinking as that conception of reason constituted solely by the requirement of consistency (bi-valence and the law of non-contradiction).

Finally, in pursuing this immanent, logical and meta-logical, critique of moral reason I will also be abstracting from those features of Kant's thought that Adorno takes up and develops for his own purposes: others as ends in themselves, the saving urge in the "Postulates of Pure Practical Reason," the spontaneity of the intellect, affinity, Kant's conception of reflective judgement in the third *Critique.* These, and related notions, will be taken up in later chapters.

2. Authority and the Fact of Reason

I suggested in the previous chapter that there was a persistent ambiguity of rationalized reason in relation to authority: if authority is conceived of as antecedent acceptance and obedience, then enlightened reason must conceive of itself as opposed to authority *überhaupt*; alternatively, since reason aims to be critical as well as normative for us, it must lodge a claim against all competitors, and thus reveal itself as authoritative, as what itself asks for and demands antecedent acceptance and obedience. Further, the question of acceptance and obedience relates to the question of motivation since authority is a mode of address to a subject; traditional and charismatic authority resolve the problem of address and motivation – squaring the circle of how there can be a demand on a subject that is or becomes a motive for her – through the intermediaries of the loyalty, love, veneration, respect for the person of the charismatic leader or traditional master. And while those relations to leader or master raise problems, they at least make intelligible the mediation between normative demand and subjective acceptance. It is the absence of that mediation, I suggested, that is the proximate cause of the problem of externalism, a problem which harbors both the ambiguity problem and the question of motivation. Kant's question "How can pure reason be practical?" should be read as a response to this whole syndrome of problems.

Kant's argumentative strategy in the *Groundwork* is the most insistently rationalist within his moral writings. Although there is some lingering scholarly debate on the issue, in general the most plausible reading of Chapter Three of that work is that it intends to provide a theoretical argument for transcendental or absolute freedom without moral premises, and then on the basis of that conception of freedom to provide a deduction of the objective validity of the moral law. That Kant there so conceived of what was required exemplifies the strong conception of reason as incompatible with authority: nothing requires or demands acceptance independently of rational demonstration. At that juncture, he believed that if he argued to freedom relying on a full moral premise, then the deduction would be viciously or at least narrowly circular (G, 449–50). Yet, his various stratagems – from the requirements of thinking and judging (G, 448), from our membership in an intelligible world based on the spontaneity of reason in the production of non-sensuous ideas (G, 451–3) – for demonstrating transcendental freedom have, almost universally, been found unconvincing: at best they show that we must or are entitled to regard ourselves as free, as participating in a non-moral but normative order, but neither that we are (practically) free as a consequence or that so regarding ourselves is outside the ambit of some version of compatibilism.[3] Worse still, even if some version of Kant's argument to freedom were accepted, it would remain opaque how that theoretical conception of freedom and spontaneity would connect with our conception of ourselves as moral agents; there is no reason why theoretical freedom and agent freedom must be the same freedom.[4] With-

3 For a full and useful discussion of these issues, see Karl Ameriks, "Kant's Deduction of Freedom and Morality," *Journal of the History of Philosophy* 19/1 (Jan., 1981), pp. 53–79.

4 For an insightful reconstruction and critique of the deduction in *Groundwork*, chapter 3, see Henry Allison, *Kant's Theory of Freedom* (New York: Cambridge University Press, 1990), chapter 12; see also Dieter Henrich, "The Deduction of the Moral Law: The Reasons for the Obscurity of the Final Section of Kant's *Groundwork of the Metaphysics of Morals*," tr., Paul Guyer, in Paul Guyer (ed.), *Kant's Groundwork of the Metaphysics of Morals: Critical Essays* (New York: Rowan & Littlefield Publishers, 1998), pp. 303–341. Henrich offers a more complex reconstruction than the one I am suggesting, with the relation between theoretical and practical freedom ever only analogical; and where, in fact if not in intention, the path of argument in *Groundwork* III dovetails with the fact of reason argument of the *Critique of Practical Reason*. Nonetheless, Henrich argues that the "strong de-

out subsuming theoretical cognition under practical reason, making theory a derivative of practice, there is no reason why demonstrating that the freedom necessary for our submission to the norms of thought should segue into free agency.

The purity of Kant's project for a deduction of morality is one indication of how emphatically he construed the demand for *theoretical* legitimation of the moral, where the conception of theory is one which is suitable for defeating the skeptic, and hence one which attains to the full rigor of rational demonstrability as such, granted the weaker conception of rational demonstrability possible when fully deductive demonstration is impossible. A perhaps more illuminating indicator emerges through surveying how exorbitantly he conceived of the necessity of detaching freedom and morality from sensuousness in his brief statements about moral interest. For Kant an interest "is that in virtue of which reason becomes practical – that is, becomes a cause determining the will" (G, 460n.). Because moral interest is non-empirical it necessarily follows that there can be no explanation of it, by which Kant means that although it must be the case that pure reason has the power of "*infusing* a *feeling of pleasure* or satisfaction in the fulfilment of duty" (G, 460), no further elaboration of the causal sequence that generates pleasures from acting from duty is possible since, properly speaking, explanatory causality belongs wholly to empirical experience. But even the question of pleasure in the fulfilment of duty seems wrongly positioned here since it would not approach the issue of our interest in morality in the first place, as Kant seems half-aware.[5] Toward the end of the paragraph in question he thus rephrases his central thought: we cannot explain how and why "the universality of a maxim as a law" (NB, not: the fulfilment of a duty), morality, should interest us. What we can be certain of is that "the law is not valid for us *because it interests us* (for this is heteronomy and makes practical reason depend upon sensibility – that is to say, on an underlying feeling – in which case practical reason could never give us moral law); *the laws interest us because it is valid* for us as men in virtue of having sprung from our will as intelligence and so from our proper self" (G, 460–1; emphasis mine). The stringency of Kant's dilemma here is that he wants our interest in morality, our being moved by the moral law, to flow from its validity, which is equivalent to saying, from a theoretical insight; on the other hand, it is only in virtue of the interest that flows from the insight that reason becomes practical. Nor is Kant's argument aided by what that insight is into since it identifies our "proper self" with the moral law (as the rational essence of the will), and hence with nothing which is any-

duction" of the validity of the moral law itself fails. See also "The Concept of Moral Insight," pp. 80–3.

5 We can be infused by pleasure, however minimally, by satisfying any intended end.

thing *like* a self at all. Because an empirical self remains, come what may, only empirical, the act of identification moves curiously in the narrow circle of the intelligible sphere alone; hence the interest/motive, assuming there is one, has no route by means of which it can infect empirical experience.

Kant knows that for pure reason to be practical there must be an interest, but here at least the problem is irresolvable because pure reason is being understood theoretically, that is in terms of rational insight, and not practically; hence, the issue of interest remains a derivative and an imputation: if the moral law is objectively valid and so the true law of our will, then there must be an interest that flows from that fact since otherwise reason could not be practical; it is not *logical*, theoretically consistent, not to be interested in what can be theoretically shown to be the rational essence of willing. Kant's underlying problem is not, as he supposes, the explanatory one (although, in virtue of the ban on sensuousness, that problem is extreme), but rather that by wanting to radically detach validity from interest, in order to ensure the former's necessity, he has, despite himself, constituted the moral law as an object of theoretical and not practical insight.[6] What Henrich identifies as the moment of demand and approval, which in practical reasoning is supposed to be a *condition* for insight itself, has here disappeared altogether. But that eventuality is fully consistent with a general skepticism about authority since, patently for Kant, anything that might look like authority, anything requiring antecedent obedience, is heteronomous. In order to avoid heteronomy Kant thus makes insight into the validity of the moral law the source or occasion of interest without really being able to make intelligible why interest should track insight. By cutting insight off from interest, the full impact of the rationalization of reason, Kant unsurprisingly has no way of stitching them back together.

Matters do appear to change in the second *Critique* with the introduction of the "fact of reason" doctrine since with it Kant gives up the hope of providing a theoretically neutral deduction of the moral law, and begins instead with our experience of it as authoritative for us as finite yet rational beings. Is this claim any stronger than the concession that pure reason is a form of authority? And is conceding that sufficient to transform the essentially "without" structure of legal-rational authority into an intrinsically motivating structure?

Against the background of the fact of reason doctrine it becomes natural to suppose that Kant has come to a clearer grasp of the difference

6 As will be evident directly, I need not deny that Kant routinely thinks he is beginning from the experience of obligation in which insight, demand and acceptance are fused. Only that in thinking through the meaning of that experience the fused elements fall apart in a manner that does not enable their re-constitution.

of practical reason from theoretical reason, hence the unavoidability of the authority relation. However, if the argument of the previous paragraph but one that in his account of moral interest Kant did no more than *impute* an interest in morality as simply what was required to establish the practicality of pure reason is accepted, then it is not evident that the shift to the fact of pure reason does more than solidify that imputation – however significant that shift is with respect to his surrendering of the hope of providing a deduction of morality. The fact of reason, indeed, says no more than that pure reason is practical, that it can independently of and prior to any desire, impulse, or sensuous motive, determine the will (CPrR, 15–16). And this is continuous with the primary Kantian thought, his version of the principle of immanence, that reason can determine the particular from the universal; in practical terms, this amounts to the claim that the requirement for lawfulness or universality can determine my will to act or not act in a particular way. If our worry is *whether* pure reason is the kind of thing that can be authoritative and truly move us, then this worry remains, although now requiring interrogating from a different angle.

The most natural way to consider the problem is to wonder whether the fact of reason doctrine itself is capable of being stated consistently. After all, Kant cannot construe the fact of reason as equivalent to the claim that we are all explicitly conscious of the moral law (whether acting for or against it) since that is just false. Conversely, he cannot construe the doctrine conditionally, that is as claiming that were we to become aware of it we would see it as a priori binding for us, since that would destroy its universality. Hence the paradox of a fact of reason: how can something universally valid be a practical law since for a law to be practical requires a moment of submission or acceptance, a moment of particularity? Prima facie, it would appear that if an item is universally and unconditionally valid then it must be so independently of its acceptance or rejection by any particular individual (albeit not all individuals), hence an object of theoretical understanding; while if an item is to be a practical law, it must first be accepted, thereby ruining its unconditionality (practically: its inescapability and overridingness). Behind this paradox, as I am presenting it, is an ontological thesis: if acceptance is a *condition* of insight and validity, then acceptance is a condition of *actuality*; hence, the existence of moral norms is non-detachable from their actual employment. Context, again, possesses justificatory significance for non-rationalized reason; but it is just this notion of context which the disenchantment of the world, empirical reality as a universal causal order, has made unavailable to Kant. Moral norms can only be moral norms, *practical reasons,* if they can come to be and cease to be – vice *destroys* principle. Hence, if a priori valid, then not a moral norm. So much is presupposed by the very idea of disenchantment, e.g., the destruction of moral knowledge; but here this thought is emerging, however partially, as an implication of the problem of relating pure reason to interest – its effective authority.

Kant must deny, at least, the second half of the paradox: the first person character of the fact of reason does not destroy its a priori character or unconditionality. For him it is the special character of the moral law as the *ratio cognoscendi* of the will that enables it to escape the paradox: nothing can count as a reason for an action unless I so take it, self-impose it; but the moral law in the form of the universality requirement provides the criterion of what can and cannot be rationally self-imposed. Hence, if I become aware of the moral law in any way – the fact of reason – ,then I must become aware of it as universally binding.[7] This looks susceptible to both universalistic and motivational objections. From the fact that even if I chose to submit to the moral law, I could submit to it, self-impose it, it does not follow that I am capable of acting from reasons that are not interest based since nothing in my acceptance requires that.[8] Only accepting it because it is impartial would ground the required entailment, but at the cost of utter triviality. Secondly, the very way in which Kant conceives of the moral law as making its way into our motivational set is theoreticist in the troubling way noted previously. Consider Henry Allison's statement of Kant's version of internalism: " . . . he holds that the very recognition of the moral law as the supreme norm *implies* the existence of a motive for following its dictates. But to acknowledge that the law is itself an incentive is to recognize that one *can be motivated* by respect for it."[9] The italicized phrases are the source of difficulty. An implication is not a motive in the psychological sense; properly stated, Allison's thesis only states that recognizing the moral law as the supreme norm provides me with a reason for accepting it and therefore including it in my motivational set. Worse, one-half of that reason is negative: acting against the moral law would be rationally self-defeating, destructive of my moral agency. Hence, half of what brings the moral law to my practical attention equally attaches it to interests that are not themselves unequivocally moral (since my reasons for wishing to avoid the destruction of my agency can be, and mostly plausibly are, prudential).[10] This entails that ac-

7 Henry Allison, "Justification and Freedom in the *Critique of Practical Reason*," in Eckart Forster (ed.), *Kant's Transcendental Deductions: The Three "Critiques" and the "Opus Postumum* (Stanford, CA: Stanford University Press, 1989), pp. 114–30.

8 Barbara Herman, "Justification and Objectivity: Comments on Rawls and Allison," in *Kant's Transcendental Deductions*, ibid. p. 135.

9 "Justification and Freedom in the *Critique of Practical Reason*," p. 125; italics mine.

10 I am here applying or drawing out a claim of Dieter Henrich's, "Ethics of Autonomy," in *The Unity of Reason*, pp. 109–112, where he argues that Kant' doctrine of respect collapses into two discrete acts without any unity between them. The first, the act whereby the moral law presents a "check" on the inclinations, so humbling and humiliating our sensible nature; and an act of reverence in which I identify myself with the moral law,

knowledging the law as an incentive is not the same as recognizing that one can be motivated by *it*. And even if the entailment were correct, "can be motivated" still hovers in a psychological void. Again, the best explanation for these failures is that in order for pure reason to be motivating it must produce the incentive to obey from out of its purely rational character; but everything that is going to make it possible for that to be case will equally require the motive to follow from insight into what that rational character is. Hence, the queer sense that a pure rational interest is just an interest that flows from rational insight. What makes it possible to sustain the rationality of the insight makes the motive for acting on that insight ideal – an imputation rather than a fact. This is not to deny that there is some "fact" here, a feeling of right and wrong, an experience of conscience; Protestant conscience is one precipitate of disenchantment, an inwardizing of both formerly external social knowledge and the new coerciveness of rationalized social forms:

> Ripening, rather, in the internalization of social coercion into conscience, with the resistance to social authority which critically measures that authority by its own principles, is a potential that would rid men of coercion. In the critique of conscience, the rescue of this potential is envisioned – not in the psychological realm, however, but in the objectivity of a reconciled life of the free . . . Conscience is the mark of shame of an unfree society. (ND, 275)

The fact of reason does not show reason's authority because in order to do so factuality would have to possess normative force, but it is just the force of the factual which Kant's doctrine of reason dissolves. There is a painful irony in this since transcendental idealism can be interpreted as the doctrine that the claims of factuality and the force of reasons are one.

which is a relation of practical reason to itself. These must be discrete acts since for Kant sensibility cannot be "elevated" in the sense required – only limited, constrained, ordered, made to conform, etc. Not only are these acts discrete, but, Henrich contends, "the facticity of the moral law can be carried out only in concert with the consciousness that inclinations are limited; for that reason it cannot belong solely to the intellectual side" (p. 111) – which is the thesis I am elaborating. However, Henrich continues, if the facticity of the moral law were simply its check on the inclinations, then it would be without rational content in itself. Hence, the fact of reason must be "both in one: judgement of reason and consciousness of being limited. . . Each aspect pointing to the other as the real locus of facticity. The sum of two bad thoughts is not a better, but a worse thought than either by itself" (ibid.). Henrich is thus contending that the fact of reason is not internally coherent but suffers from precisely the *same* failure, albeit in a different form, that invalidated Kant's search for a deduction of morality, namely, squaring the *principium diiudiactionis* with the *principium executionis*. That Kant came to see the requirement for fully integrating moral reason with moral sense is both the incremental gain in the doctrine of the fact of reason, and the ground for attributing to Kant an internalist conception of practical reason. Only the manner and hence failure of his attempted integration grounds entitling the moral law "external."

3. A Short Genealogy of Modern Universalism: How Pure Reason Overtook Empirical Knowing

In one respect, the argument of the previous section is misleading; it implies that pure reason is interest free, and Kant's difficulty derives from the attempt to show how something so pure can be practical. Meta-logically, if pure reason has come to be, then the converse thesis is more plausible: pure reason has too many interests associated with it, and that Kant can only make it subject to his purposes through abstracting reason from its historic constitution, which thence proves troubling when he needs to give it a unique, moral determination. If we inquire into the meaning of modern moral universalism – and it is only Kant's conception of universality that will be at issue for the remainder of this chapter – , we discover it has, at least, a dual genesis: first, it eventuates from the process of disenchantment itself as the realization or completion of the operation of the principle of immanence as applied to moral experience – the rationalization of reason; secondly, moral universalism embodies a series of concrete socio-historical experiences of moral learning which while partaking in disenchantment are not bound by the principle of immanence. These developments occur, more or less, simultaneously, are entwined, and hence are *both* expressed in the formula of universal law. Still, the end result of the first genesis is a form or principle, Kant's formula of universal law, while the end result of the second genesis is a moral content and a utopian aspiration. Because each genetic process, as a complex social practice, is driven by particular desires, hopes, aspirations, interests that are themselves embodied in the practices that were their bearers, then the results of the processes in question equally embody those interests. Contents, however formal or concrete, express interests, interests *formed* through the processes through which their corresponding contents emerge. Hence, modern moral universalism, even in its utterly formal self-presentation, is constituted by interests intended and unintended: instrumental, ethical, and utopian.

As we noted at the beginning of the previous chapter, modern moral universalism arises from the entanglement of the development of civilization as instrumentality and civilization as humanity as driven by the dual processes of the disenchantment of experience and the rationalization of reason. Rationalist universalism *intends* that its principles express only civilization as humanity; but because that expression contains, as sedimented content, both the disenchantment of experience and the rationalization of reason through which it arose, then, despite itself, it expresses, at the same time, the *interest* of enlightenment generally, namely, self-preservation through the control of nature. It is that suppressed interest in self-preservation, in instrumentality in its wide sense (i.e., the principle of immanence), that ruins and undermines the claim of moral rationalism to express, unconditionally, the moral point of view. What are typically regarded as analytic failures in Kantian rationalism, ways in which it fails to correspond to or contradicts our or its own moral intentions, are here to be presented as consequences of its disavowed instrumental genesis. The forms of failure will be familiar, only the understanding of their significance different.

Moral reason is conditioned by the disenchantment of experience it means to resist. Even the criteria we, as Kantians, have come to think an account of moral reason must satisfy are so conditioned. Why believe that moral maxims or judgements need express categorical force unless the context of their employment were one in which we presupposed systematic individualism and mutual indifference, and hence presupposed the ethical isolation of each individual from every other individual?[11] Is not the thought that there are "circumstances of justice," say, minimal altruism and scarcity, a coded way of expressing a condition of universal injustice in which morality is being employed as a remedy, and hence must be attributed with the power to override socially constituted egoism (formally: mutual indifference)?[12] While Kant does not directly employ this Humean conceit in generating his theory, as we shall see it is indirectly implied by the divorce between the empirical reality of a universal causal context, and the sheer ideality of the moral. Second, why believe, even for a moment, that the basis of all correct judgements and maxims must be uniform, single, apart from, on the one hand, the destruction of multiple sources for action determination (G, 420), and, on the other, the rationalization of reason through the principle of immanence? Is centralism, moral and non-moral, intelligible apart from disenchantment? Finally, why believe, even for a moment, that the unitary basis determining the correctness of all judgements, making them a reason for action, must be located in reason itself other than because the skeptical dynamic of the rationalization of reason terminates in reason becoming independent of any content?[13] In fine, once we assume emphatic and anonymous plurality in the form of mutual indifference, and with it a disenchanted social world, then only a self-sufficient reason, which itself has

11 As will become evident below, in saying this I need not deny that ethical reasons do have a certain categorical quality. The point here is rather to see how inescapability and overridingness *become* fundamental to our conception of what a moral reason is like and ought to be. If the distinction hypothetical versus categorical tracks the distinction between empirical and intelligible, where the first term of each pair points to a condition of universal moral indifference (Kantianly: blindness), then whatever else the categorical quality of moral reasons has meant and will mean, it here has a quite specific inflection.

12 For the idea that the circumstances of justice are, in the first place, "so to speak, the circumstances of injustice," see Onora O'Neill, *Towards Justice and Virtue: A Constructive Account of Practical Reasoning* (New York City: Cambridge University Press, 1996), p. 99.

13 For these three criteria, and an interrogation of them, see David Wiggins, "Categorical Requirements: Kant and Hume on the Idea of Duty," *The Monist* 74/1 (Jan., 1991), p. 93.

been negatively or skeptically constituted as authoritative (not a subjective projection), can function as the basis of action determination which is in principle capable of overriding indifference. Once the conditions of disenchantment are accepted, then the requirements for a reason to be moral converge on universality: act only on that maxim of action (the particular, empirically conditioned and thus morally indifferent act specification) which you can at the same time will that it should be a universal law, that is, hold for all rational beings or, equivalently, become through your willing a universal law of nature (G, 421).[14] Stated in this way, as directly conditioned by disenchantment, one might well find Kant's proposal an ideal solution to an intractable situation. But if the situation really is intractable, a world of injustice, then must not the solution drag its unworthy conditions with it?

In two separate passages Adorno urges his standard thesis opposing Kant's repression of the historicity of cognitive contents against the idea of pure reason or the moral law. The first is quite general, in fact nothing more than the standard Hegelian critique of the givenness of rational forms, the second more pointed.

> Pure consciousness – logic – itself is a coming-to-be and a validity that has submerged its genesis. [Its genesis] lies in a moment that Kantian doctrine suppresses (*unterschlagenen*): the negation of volitions (*des Willens*) . . . (ND, 230)

> In the Kantian invective against psychology is expressed not only the fear of losing the laboriously caught scrap of the intelligible world, but also the authentic insight that the moral categories of the individual are more than only individual. What manifests itself in them as universal, after the model of the Kantian concept of law, is secretly social. One of the major functions of the oscillating concept of humanity in the *Critique of Practical Reason* is that pure reason, being universal, is valid for all rational beings: a point of indifference in Kant's philosophy. *The concept of universality was obtained from the multiplicity [or plurality: Vielheit] of subjects and then made independent as the logical objectivity of reason in which all single subjects, as well as, seemingly, subjectivity as such, will disappear.* But Kant, on the narrow ridge between logical absolutism and empirical generality [*Allgültigkeit*], wants to return to that entity which the system's logic of consistency has banned before. (ND, 281–2; emphasis mine)

Implied in the longer passage is a genealogy of universality which offers to it the two, opposing aspects I mentioned above, one logical, the other empirical. For Adorno the moral force of universality depends on its gen-

14 There is no reason to think that the law of nature statement is anything other than a "typic" of the standard formula of universal law; see Philip Stratton-Lake, "Formulating Categorical Imperatives," *Kant-Studien* 84 (1993), pp. 316–40.

esis, what was gathered from the multiplicity of subjects, which is then squandered when raised to the level of form ("logical absolutism"). Hence, Adorno's conception of modern moral universalism construes it as a last bit of moral knowledge, what moral knowing congeals into in the course of its disappearance, which itself disappears into Kant's logical formalism. In this and the next section I want to offer an argumentative reconstruction of this thought.

As I read him, Adorno is contending that universalism substantively concerns an *inductive* claim or discovery about the putative *scope* of moral predicates, viz., the discovery that scope restrictions on the application of moral predicates is not compatible with the best, albeit defeasible, grounds for employing those predicates. Hence for Adorno the positive thesis of universalism, all moral predicates "hold for all," is derived from and bound to those historic occasions when assumed legitimate provinciality was shattered. In proposing that the rational force of universalism is, broadly, empirical Adorno is not suggesting a different history of modern moral universalism than the standard one in which a variety of factors converge: Christian universalism and Protestant individualism, the collapse of feudal hierarchy and its role-bound conception of persons, the new naturalism and the new scientific rationalism, the emergence of the economic conception of the person and its expression in positive law, etc. On the contrary, the best interpretation of that history is that it enables, embeds, or precipitates the inductive generalization, and it is equally the totality of pressures, social and reflective, that explain that induction that simultaneously explain how Kantian universalism became a point of indifference, stranded on the narrow ridge between logical absolutism and empirical generality.

Because universalism is now taken for granted it is natural to believe that the question of scope refers fundamentally to hard cases (fetuses, the brain dead, etc.) to which no theory could reasonably be expected to provide a general answer, and hence that the only universalism that is subject to reflective determination is the one elaborating its pure modal form: maxims must be followable by all.[15] Stating the option in these terms, almost extension versus intension, begs the question against Adorno's historical induction; is not the coming-to-be of universalism itself a question of scope? Historically, the most potent immoral maxims,

15 So in *Towards Justice and Virtue,* Onora O'Neill contends that "a focus on universal principles cannot fix the *scope of ethical consideration*; it cannot show *who* falls within the domain of universal principles" (p. 4). In chapter 4, she goes on to provide an elegant practical construction of scope from the perspective of assumptions about others that are implied in normal activities. She condenses these assumptions into plurality (there are others), connection (who, empirically, must be accounted for in deliberation), and finitude (those others have determinate powers). On my reading, her construction tracks a portion of the experience of empirical generalization, or, equivalently, the translation manual that transforms Christian universalism into normative secular fact.

e.g., "All slaves ought to obey their masters," can pass the universalization test because their proposer denies what "we" take to be a morally relevant *truth*, namely, that race (gender, class, ethnic identity, language, religion, status role, etc.) is a morally irrelevant feature of persons under normal circumstances.[16] Morally relevant features of persons and objects, in this context, are those presumed to regulate the application or the withholding of the application of a range of predicates to an object. Demonstrating the "contradiction" in the immoral maxim *presupposes* demonstrating the falsity of the belief that skin color is a moral relevant property for assigning the entitlement "moral person" or "personality" (CPrR, 87) in Kant's sense of the word (ND, 292–7), and hence worthy of consideration in moral deliberation. But that demonstration can neither be a priori nor constructed; it must, in the first instance, be immanent and empirical, drawing heavily upon the actual beliefs and principles of material (non topic neutral) inference that actually and implicitly operate in the use of moral concepts, and hence, by extension, in the assignment of entitlements.[17] And showing the logical powers of those principles of material inference will inevitably involve arguments from analogy; for example, if the predicates "to be trusted with the care of my children" or "being capable of organizing the harvest" are insensitive to skin color, then what different facts make the predicate "deserves respect" sensitive to skin color? As such arguments and the struggles for recognition around them unfold,[18] the giving and withholding of predicates will be-

16 It cannot be a failure of Kantian universalism that is at issue here since until such time as those regarded as slaves are seen as persons the thought that they could not consent to the obedience maxim is not even up for consideration. With respect to Kant himself, while I see no evidence that he thought moral considerations should be restricted because of gender, race, class, et. al., his views were, at least, equivocal since according to his theory of race racial differences effect moral potential: Africans possess strong feeling and a sense of honor, but while educable, it is chiefly for servitude. See Emmanuel Chudwudi Eze, "The Color of Reason: The Idea of 'Race' in Kant's Anthropology," in E. Eze (ed.), *Race and Enlightenment* (Oxford: Blackwell, 1997), pp. 103–40. That Kant was a universalist and held racist views is perhaps the most direct evidence against logical universalism being sufficient to its own promise, and thus evidence for empirical universalism. If logical universalism is an inflection of enlightened reason, then the former's blindness to its own prejudice must be telling against the presumed neutrality of the latter. My contention is here is not the obviously false thesis that logical universalism and enlightened reason are racist, it is that racism and true universalism operate from elsewhere; which makes logical universalism idle, or worse, where it should matter most.

17 Christian universalism is obviously of no help in explaining the undoing of scope restrictions since the point in dispute is, whether in religion or secular belief, who is a person.

18 If the mini-narrative of this and subsequent paragraphs hold weight, then struggles for recognition occur *through* and in virtue of the patterns of material inference implicit in different social practices. Without those practices and patterns of material inference possessing implications that fail to support exclusionary practices, it would be impossible to explain how struggles could get a foothold in their different social worlds. If honor amongst thieves does actually manifest *honor,* then it really does point beyond it-

gin to cluster as certain more abstract characteristics – abilities (including rational and linguistic ones), sensitivities, forms of awareness, vulnerabilities, and the like – recur as what actually regulate scope restrictions in cases of the disputed type. And while indeed one can think of the breakthrough that occurs when a presumed scope restriction is overturned as the discovery that, for example, *all* human beings should be told the truth, the force of that claim rests on the determinate negation through which it arose: the *experience* that a difference in skin color (or race or class or gender or religion or language) does not provide a differentiating reason between those to whom the truth is owed and those to whom it is not. *The experience of past blindness and its collapse is a part of the content of any "all"* (which is part of the reason why the search for "essential" features in order to ground universal scope application will necessarily fail – apart from the fact that such essentialism is theoretical rather than practical), which is to say that any moral "all," that is any consideration in which it is relevant that "all" be counted in, taken account of, is empirically loaded.[19] While such a demonstration will do nothing in the way of vindicating the employment of the relevant predicate (truth-telling, promising, not injuring, etc.), it does reveal that "we" cannot sustain the rationality of our employment of the predicate while excluding "them" from its extension.

Because the discovery of universalism, the lapsing of antecedently believed scope restrictions, does not directly effect the contents of first-order predicates and rules of material inference, it does become tempting to think that it must relate to their form; and if we think the uncovering of the formal property is substantive, that universality is somehow deep but formal not empirical, then it will suggest the centralist thought that it alone provides the reason-giving force of the predicates that fall under it. A construal that becomes all the more tempting when located in the context of reason being rationalized, the analogy between mathematical truths and moral truths being in the air so to speak. In that second gesture in which the collapse of perceived scope restrictions is transformed into a single truth holding for and thus grounding all empirical moral predicates, universalism detaches itself from the history making it possible, claiming a power for itself that is, strictly speaking, inherited. *Genealogically: (logical) universalism is the moral knowledge that arose through the course of the destruction of moral knowledge.* The process making empirical

self. Of course, coming to see or grasp extensions of a predicate to unfamiliar circumstances is coming to see differently. This is not to deny the role of invention or creation in ethical life, but rather to locate an intelligible middle between blind pragmatic conceptions of progress and Kantian intellectualism. Much more will be said about material inference in subsequent chapters.

19 The rationality and epistemological assumptions in this claim will be backed in Chapter 7, Section 2.

universalism possible is equally the process through which universalism is transformed from knowledge into form. Logical universalism is the optical illusion that arises from the moral collapse of hierarchy and provinciality under conditions in which the empirical bonds connecting subjects were also collapsing. From one perspective, then, logical universalism too expresses a saving urge.

The implicit induction underlying universalism as a form knowledge rests on a variety of assumptions.[20] Comparing of cases and drawing analogies from one domain to another can occur only if the agents involved share a form of life and hence share a wide range of practices (laboring, child rearing, friendship, linguistic practices, etc.); without shared practices there exists no basis for making comparisons between the use of different types of predicates. Against the background of shared practices, however, the question of why a particular range of predicates and material inferences should be assigned to some and not others can become inevitable and urgent, especially for those suffering as a consequence of exclusion. In trying to imagine those cases where this has occurred, what appears to ground the comparing of cases and drawing of analogies is the way in which the practices in question embed material inferences (e.g., "My baby is crying; she needs comforting or changing or feeding"), and how the actual operation of those inference patterns places pressure on their restriction ("You demand your baby be tended to when she cries as I want mine tended to; why then prohibit me from doing now what you demand me to do for your own?"). It is the *actual* operation of the patterns of material inference that ground struggles for recognition; without those patterns of material inference being themselves actually albeit implicitly color- or role- or gender-blind it is unclear how an "all" that practically included some previously excluded group could come into effect. But if universalism is *practically* an issue of scope, then that it is not self-sufficient but tracks suppressed or implicit assumptions in actual moral practices should be unsurprising.

To be sure, the universalism that arises from the lapse of scope restrictions does not by itself permanently fix the scope of moral predicates. The shift from "some" to "all" that is a consequence of the induction implied by the overturning of a restrictive practice (and what else might an induction be but a movement from "some" to "all"?[21]) naturally conceives

20 I am here, anachronistically, including in the historic induction forming Kantian universalism the post-Kantian induction which indicted slavery as a way of making vivid the less perspicuous operations lying behind the original inductive sequence. Since for us the force of Kantian universality is non-detachable from the later inductive sequence, no theoretical harm is done by this inclusion. The genealogical intelligibility of moral idealism cannot be altogether detached from the mediations by which it has reached us.

21 In actual struggles for recognition there does seem to be a putative "all" and an excluded

of "all" as those previously included and the new claimants who were previously excluded together with a reflective acknowledgement that if our previous restriction was baseless, then our new "all" may not be all. "All" is a critical as well as normative concept; but both its critical and normative use seem naturally to attach to its empirical emergence and re-emergence, the history through which "all" comes to morally matter. Moral form is sedimented content; even in its reified employment there is an unconscious remembrance. In saying this, my comments are modeled on Adorno's statements concerning Kant's account of freedom: "Freedom can be grasped only through determinate negation, corresponding to a concrete form of unfreedom" (ND, 231); universality emerges against the background of illegitimate and felt exclusions, and continues to matter because it so evidently is not realized. And thus in the same way in which, according to Adorno, freedom is "essentially historic, and not just as a concept but in its experiential substance" (ND, 218), and thus something which once upon time did not exist and perhaps will not exist in some future, so moral universalism came to be and might disappear (say, because it was realized).

All this falls well short of Kant's connecting of universality with reason. What is the "reason" of Kantian moral reason; how are morality and reason connected? As a partial answer, consider the following: the Kantian can concede that in opposing the maxim of obedience to masters the real work is accomplished by the immanent demonstration that skin color is not a morally relevant feature of persons, that the logical universalism involved in the testing procedure of the categorical imperative presupposes empirical universalism if its results are to be truly universal. But that we should seek to discriminate between the morally relevant and the morally irrelevant, between the arbitrary and the non-arbitrary recognition of characteristics, or between arbitrary and non-arbitrary premises or assumptions in moral argument is not itself an empirical matter. What makes moral reason a form of reason is its ban on arbitrariness, and the consequent demand for consistency in action. So the striving after non-arbitrariness, which is one possible interpretation of the rational kernel of the formula of universal law, becomes the moment of reason in normative practice. If the moment of non-arbitrariness is itself to be non-arbitrary, then it cannot draw upon changing conditions or the desires of the agent. Hence, no empirical features of agents' conditions of agency can themselves provide for what is non-arbitrary. Since the content of agents' maxims are one and all empirical, then only the form of agents' maxims can provide for non-arbitrariness. Since for Kant the contingent

group. Hence the consequence of a breakthrough is a new, *emphatic,* "all." To insist that the process is inductive does not remove the ideality or normativity of the "all"; on the contrary, it is only because such normativity is implicit in the first instance, that the breakthrough can occur.

and non-contingent are discriminated through what is not law-like and what is, then for practical reasoning only what attains to law-likeness can be non-arbitrary (G, 312–13). Still, it is the ban on arbitrariness which captures what Kant has in mind when he seeks to purify morality of empirical and contingent conditions.

In itself this thought is not compelling because an arbitrariness or non-arbitrariness that would matter morally is itself ethical and empirical. If it matters morally to me that persons not be deceived, then it *can* come to matter to me, as a further development or making explicit of my starting point, that in deceiving M because of the color of her skin I am not being consistent (I am deceiving myself) about my principle of non-deception (or: the material inferences governing my employment of truth-telling are themselves color-blind). My *desire* to behave consistently is just my desire to *actually* act on the principle of non-deception. I cannot simultaneously believe that deception is wrong and deceiving M is legitimate once my reasons for withholding the application of my principle to M are discovered to be extrinsic to the reasons that lead me to apply it where I do – whatever the ultimate grounds of the principle are. Thus the ban on arbitrariness is internal to the content and material inferences governing the employment of non-deception simply in so far as it is regarded as other than instrumental (in its narrow sense). At one level, a certain notion of consistency is implicit simply in what it is to participate in a practice and employ the concepts implicated in that practice: to have the practice of private property is to believe that stealing is wrong; to have the practice of promising is to believe that promise-breaking is wrong.[22]

Consistency in action which would bear on my moral life is itself a fully ethical ideal, one which flows from and develops from, say, my desire to respect others in my group; indeed without the multiple pressures enforcing consistent behavior with respect to them, it is unclear how a *desire* for consistency could emerge and matter to beings like ourselves – the creation of an animal that can keep promises, that is, follow inferences consistently, took the longest time. Insofar as respect matters to me, then showing respect can come to involve not making an exception of myself when it suits since that would contradict my concept of respect (and self-respect). In the first instance, inconsistency can matter because it is experienced as practically self-defeating (I am not acting honorably or I am going to lose face or be shamed); its being practically self-defeating locally is what enables it to be experienced as mattering non-locally. Like universality, a consistency that might matter to me can only be conceived of as something that is a development from parochial beginnings, where

22 I interpret Hegel's contention that Kantian universality is tautological in just this way: the relevant universality or consistency is *in* the practice, and hence the universalization requirement does nothing more than say what the practice already says.

those beginnings are not eclipsed in their development, because their grounding is found theoretically suspect, for example, but rather practically unfolded or elaborated through experiences that challenge restrictions. Thus the argument of the previous paragraph but one collapses; in a perfectly anodyne and non-rationalist way, seeking consistency and banning arbitrariness are substantive ethical ideals learned from ethical experience rather than rationalist forms that need to be applied to action from the "outside," from the resources of reason itself.

Or, at least, such might have been the case had not the moment when universality became historically salient equally been the moment when civilization as humanity and civilization as instrumentality became so utterly and systematically separate from one another that it became intelligible for *each* ethical practice to be pursued or conceived of as being pursued self-interestedly: promise keeping, non-injury, keeping contracts, et al., can each be practiced as forms of enlightened self-interest rather than constitutive modes of intersubjective action. This is how Hobbes' dark work of desecration and disenchantment begets the surreal and too real moment of Kant's grocer whose actions may accord with the dictates of duty, conform to its requirements, and still, because not done from the motive of duty, not be truly worthy (G, 397). I take Kant's grocer as *the exemplary figure* in which the experience of disenchantment becomes ethically manifest. Enlightened modernity, from this Kantian perspective, invokes a dual accounting system where each action according with duty may, for all anyone knows (G, 407–8), be chalked up to either side of the moral ledger: moral or self-interested. How could this situation come about? What is actually being here depicted? I take the relevant background to this situation to be the transformation of Hobbesian doctrine into social experience, that is, the sudden subjecting of all traditional moral rules to an individualist, instrumental interpretation. Once the individualist, instrumental interpretation becomes universally possible, it equally overwhelms the older rules: how am I to know whether I am following what morality requires (the old rules) or acting on the basis of self-interest? My presumption is that it is this morally complex self-experience that is the general one which Kant and those around him faced, and hence which his theory is meant to address. I equally assume it is this duality, this sense that any action that accords with the dictates of traditional morality can suddenly and nonetheless be regarded as self-interested, that continues to give Kant's resolution of it salience. What are we to make of this situation, a world in which all moral actions are themselves systematically and routinely capable of being regarded as non-moral, even for ourselves?

I begin with the assumption governing my genealogy of universalism that prior to the onset of this dilemma the relation between object and action was a material inferential one, where the material inferences themselves were embedded in social practices (social practices just being, in part, structures of material inference). *In place structures of material inference were the empirical bonds that connected human subjects.* Although I will say more about material inference in Chapter 6, for the purposes to hand the idea is that practical norms are just conceptual norms, where conceptual norms are just the inferential commitments implied by the actual use of a concept; normative proprieties are embedded in practice and use, and do not require further or higher-order grounding. On this account actions follow perceptions in the same way in which on the epistemic level it follows, for example, from something being red that it is not green. The action of picking the tomato when it is red and not picking it when it is green or picking it and putting it on the windowsill to ripen is what it involved in adequately possessing the concept of tomato. Knowing about tomatoes and possessing the concept of tomato are the same: one possesses the concept of tomato not only when one can distinguish tomatoes from apples, but when knows and obeys the proprieties of action in relation to them (tending, picking, eating, etc.). Analogously, when baby is crying one must either pick it up or feed it or change its diaper or seek out another cause of the distress and relieve it is understanding the concept of crying baby. Hobbes and Kant both write as if once upon time, in the period just preceding their efforts, moral rules operated in the same way: if my neighbor is in distress, and I am the only one about, I aid her; aiding her follows from seeing her in distress because giving aid is an inferential commitment of the concept of someone being in distress. In the same way in which picking the tomato is the appropriate inference to draw from seeing the tomato as red, so aiding my neighbor is what follows from the ordinary perception of seeing her in distress. The concepts used to pick out the phenomena practically entail those actions as a consequence. If you think of concepts as determined by use, and uses are matters of practices, then there is no reason to suppose that, at least once upon a time, the contents of the concepts themselves that descriptively rendered a situation did not simultaneously articulate one's practical commitments *thereby.* My account of the disappearance of moral knowledge in the last chapter was assuming that just this conception of material inference, from perceiving something *as* X to *doing* Y, was how ethical experience could be cognitive – whatever the authority for these rules of inference. In conceiving of ethical knowing as the operation of rules of material inference we can interpret the having and reflective sharing of those rules as being themselves the bonds among individuals, what would make them a community. Focussing on material inferences, as opposed to virtues or practices or a logic of recognition, is fundamental for Adorno's procedure since it will eventually enable us to articulate both the fate of modernity and its critique in terms of competing understandings of the concept.

The dialectic of enlightenment, disenchantment of the world and the rationalization of reason, are forces that dissolve those empirical bonds. Kant's grocer is a figure experiencing those bonds as dissolved, his moral attachments now, as every moral writer in the modern epoch struggled with, somehow subjective, in him as feeling (conscience) or will or intuitive knowledge. But part of what *enforces* that inwardness is precisely the pervasive and unavoidable perspective that says of *any* action that it can be interpreted instrumentally and egoistically. For some, Hobbes and his cohort, the correct interpretation of this phenomena is that the old rules were nothing but repressive fictions, and seeing through that fictionality is a moment of enlightened release, a moral emancipation. Hence, from the Hobbesian perspective the situation is one of the collapse or disintegration of reified beliefs back into their perfectly natural setting. Conscience, if felt by some as possessing more than it Hobbesian sense, could only be an irrational remnant. Because under these conditions each action is subject to this dual perspective interpretation, then the material inferences that might earlier have appeared to self-sufficiently account for the ethical meaning of the practices they were implicated in can no longer be interpreted in the same way; those practices are not what they once might have been or might have become because an alternative logic, that of instrumentality generally, can (always does) supervene on their immanent sense. *Radical disenchantment is the condition in which the logic of instrumental reason supervenes on the material inference structures of formerly ethical practices*; but in order for there to be a universal potentiality for supervenience, then relations among subjects must already be disenchanted, and hence one in which the structures of intersubjective encounter are no longer *constituted* by the original structures of material inference. It is this condition in which the claims of material inference structures of everyday practices are no longer constitutive of an intersubjective world that Hobbes so tellingly showed us and which Adorno surveys in its micrological forms in *Minima Moralia*. Seeing the matter in this second way, that is, seeing instrumental rationality not as the naturalized default position consequent upon the simple collapse of the old order, but rather as a logic supervening on the older principles is the genealogical redescription of the Hobbesian moment that licenses the possibility of a further work of rationalization of practical reasoning. This redescription, from simple collapse to logical supervenience, is the fundamental gesture of Kant's theory that creates the possibility for his own moral project.

It is just this redescription of instrumental rationality (narrowly, Hobbesianly, understood) as a work of universal supervenience on the previous rules of material inference, a condition of constitutive indifference or injustice, that is Kant's starting point; and it is what instrumental reason has already done to ethical relations that calls into operation the three demands on moral reason with which we began this section. If instrumental reason universally supervenes on the material inferences governing everyday practices, then the most plausible strategy for reactivating those blocked inferences, making them intersubjective once more, is to find a logic capable of universally, categorically, and univocally supervening on instrumental reason. Given the now universal scope of instrumental rationality, there is nothing left but reason itself to show another face. As supervening on a logic that itself supervenes on everyday practices and their inference structures, Kantian reason must second, and thus theoretically legitimate, instrumental reason's mechanism for disabling first-order material inferences. Empirical realism, the empirical world as a universal causal context, is the theoretical legitimation, but also theoretical acknowledgement, of modernity's original disabling of the material inference patterns of tradition, and moral centralism the structure of second-order supervenience. Because its aim is to re-activate the material inferences of first order practices "on a higher level," explicitly the intention of Kant's *Metaphysics of Morals,* and the historic induction which exposed those practices as possessing no scope restrictions, moral universalism is indeed an unconscious remembrance and utopian aspiration. However, since its method of reactivation accepts the de-activation of the material inferences of everyday practice, then it colludes with what it means to resist. *Kant's rationalism is the supervening of instrumental reason in its wide sense, the principle of immanence, on instrumentality in its narrow sense.*

Note the acuteness of Kant's difficulty: if instrumentality really is a structure of supervenience, then, if there is anything moral, it is something distinct from the instrumental and own-interested; this is the actuality of the dual accounting system. Hence, if moral reason is to supervene on the instrumental as a separate form for constituting meaning, then it requires agents to deliberatively abstract from their instrumental (prudential) purposes as a condition for acting morally; this is the precise social source behind Kant's novel distinction between hypothetical and categorical imperatives.[23] Further, because its second-order supervening seconds and doubles the disabling of the material inferences of the everyday, moral reason requires agents to abstract from their immediate *moral* intentions, purposes, and affections; these, which come to appear in Kant as the material of subjective maxims of action, represent a historically superceded stratum of meaning.[24] The separation of the instrumental from the moral, as a consequence of instrumental reason's power of universal supervenience, and the abstraction from immediate

23 At any rate, a distinction that is all but non-present in the moral writers preceding Kant with the important exception of Crusius.

24 As we will see in the final section of this chapter, this is the core of Adorno's objection to Kant's conception of obligation and the idea of acting from the motive of duty.

moral intentions, in accord with what instrumentality has already done to them and in order for moral reason to be fully a logic supervening on all else, jointly make the experience of the moral law repressive, dominating and heteronomous. In a passage directly following the one in which Adorno identifies Kantian reason as lodged between empirical general validity and logical absolutism, he interprets the objectivity of the moral law, as conscience, as drawing on the objectivity of society, "from the objectivity in and by which men live and which extends to the core of their individualization." He then continues: "Entwined in such objectivity are the antagonistic moments: heteronomous coercion and the idea of a solidarity transcending the divergent individual interests" (ND, 282). Heteronomous coercion, about which I will say more below, corresponds to the required isolation of the own-interested from the moral that has become a requirement for moral deliberation, and the equally painful abstraction from first-order moral intentions. Oppositely, Kant's moral law does, sometimes, speak to us, address us. If and when we feel moved by the moral law, what we are being moved by, however, is not reason itself, but its sedimented content and utopian aspirations. In those passages in which Kant depicts individuals being stirred by the moral law are they being moved by deliberative thoughts, requirements of reason, or by an image, say, the "glorious solidarity" of all rational beings as depicted in the formula of the kingdom of ends?[25] Kant's failure to synthesize moral reason and sense, and a reasonable genealogy of the moral law together make the latter suggestion compelling.

Still, a Kantian may argue that my genealogical gestures do not dispute or displace Kant for I have yet to show exactly in what sense the saving urge of Kant's second order supervenience does, despite itself and despite its sedimented content, exhibit the very instrumentality it means to surmount. Perhaps reason can no longer be shown to be practical, that it is thus necessary to abstract from motivational issues when presenting a philosophy of morals, and hence that issues of motivation must be dealt with separately; and perhaps second-order supervenience is the most that can be achieved if, as argued, universal instrumentality has already supervened on first-order material inferences of everyday ethical practices. Could not the genealogy of moral reason turn out to be its best defense?[26]

25 David Wiggins, "Categorical Requirements," p. 100. Wiggins' eloquent essay converges nicely with Adorno to the extent that he wishes to deny that Kant makes a convincing case for our having an interest in the requirements of pure reason, and hence that pure reason can be practical; but he is persuaded that, at least, there is a vision of human solidarity in Kant, and that this vision is the true foundation of his morality.

26 I do not mean this as a wholly rhetorical question. It does seem to me that defenses of Kant do his thought an injustice by not taking sufficiently seriously the condition of disenchantment he faced. Only that condition can finally justify his two worlds or two perspectives on a single world doctrine. And if the indictment of disenchantment on experience were final, then perhaps my "dark" Kant would be the best that could be on

4. The Utility of Testing Maxims

In the second excursus of *Dialectic of Enlightenment,* "Juliette or Enlightenment and Morality," Adorno and Horkheimer seek to demonstrate the Kantian moral reason in explicitly requiring consistency in action as articulated in the formula of universal law is amoral in itself, and lacks the internal resources to firmly resist collapsing into the immorality of the libertine. While not convincing in detail, it is nonetheless not an unilluminating run of thought. In outline, the argument of the excursus is composed of five steps.

(1) Kantian moral reason is the practical employment of a reason that is the same reason in both its practical and theoretical employments (G, 391). What makes this reason "enlightened" is its being reflective, autonomous, and unified. Through reflection, the process of becoming enlightened about itself, it achieves autonomy – it becomes self-governing and self-determining – and thus progresses toward systematic unity.

(2) Because reason is autonomous, logically self-sufficient and hence syntactically and semantically independent of its objects, then both knowing and acting attain to reason only to the extent to which objects (intuitions in cognition and maxims in practical reasoning) accord with and are determined by what it prescribes: "The conceptual apparatus determines the senses, even before perception occurs; a priori, the citizen sees the world as the matter from which he himself manufactures it. Intuitively, Kant foretold what Hollywood consciously put into practice: in the very process of production, images are pre-censored according to the norm of the understanding which will later govern their apprehension" (DoE, 84).

(3) If only systematic unity – being part of a lawful whole – is left as the immanent goal of reason with respect to all contents, then reason "is the organ of calculation, or planning; it is neutral in regard to ends [beyond that of unity]; its element is coordination" (DoE, 88). Principles of coordination are to intersubjective life what systematic, practical thinking is to interactions with the natural world: " . . . principles of self-preservation. Immaturity is then the inability to survive" (DoE, 83).

(4) From (3) it follows that affects and emotions are regarded as, in themselves, natural and non-cognitive, their worth (viability) determined by their capacity to accord with reason's prescriptive determination (DoE, 86). But it is the combination of reason's constitutive power with respect to worth and its lack of substantial ends that makes affects and emotions merely natural, disenchanted: "Since reason posits no substantial goals, all affects [which do posit substantial ends] are equally removed

offer. At the very least, the anxiety that even a genealogically reconstructed Kantian picture could be all there was is never far below the surface in Adorno's thought.

from its [intrinsic] governance, and are purely natural [empirical]. The principle by which reason is set over against all that is unreasonable is the basis of the true antithesis of enlightenment and mythology" (DoE, 89). This antithesis is responsible for the eclipse of pity and compassion as fundamental forms of sociation and bonding (DoE, 101–3).

(5) From (3) and (4) it follows that moral autonomy as the coordinating activity of the solitary agent is homologous with the coordinating activity of the libertine: the universalization which enables the coordination of practical agents into a stable whole is the same as that which enables the systematic arrangement of bodies and pleasures in the perfect orgy. Both moralist and libertine are modern stoics committed to demonstrative rationality in opposition to religious belief (DoE, 96).

Argumentatively, this is a mess. Even if the first two steps are recognizable as readings of Kant, step (3) simply asserts what needs to be argued. Step (4) tries to attribute directly to Kant the neutralization of empirical experience that Adorno later recognized as what Kant was responding to. Something like the account of instrumental reason supervening on everyday practices, and moral reason supervening on it is necessary to explicate Kant's curious treatment of affects and emotions, i.e., that they are re-activated on a higher level by becoming practical laws, virtues, rather than being given sentiments. But even so, what Adorno should have argued there is that the emptying of material inference structures of everyday practice disorients moral intentions, and that Kant's second-order re-activation provides them with the wrong sort of object: duty or a principle rather than an object and the token of the type. An argument I will pursue in the next section. Finally, step (5) simply presupposes that ends and objects must be heteronomously supplied (without devotion reason is empty), hence too quickly equates all activities of autonomous reasoning. Yet if something can be made of (3), and (4) is construed as a version of the argument of the previous section, then the suggestive image of (5) will linger. As noted previously, the libertine is only turning enlightenment's own skepticism on its remnant dogmatism; or better, the libertine, draws out the implication of pure reason's not being intrinsically moral, and hence the impossibility of it being intrinsically practical.

What sense can be made of (3)? It has already been conceded that there is something about modern universalism that matters, and consistency as self-binding in its Nietzchean sense is implied in having any full-blown ethical concepts whatsoever. The question relates solely to universality and consistency as exemplified and articulated by the formula of universal law, where the expression of that formula in the procedure of maxim testing is construed – however partially – as exhausting the meaning of the formula. For Adorno, that formation of universality is a higher, more abstract form of instrumental reason, a more consistent expression of what the principle of immanence requires. Because the progress of enlightenment originally entwined civilization as humanity with civilization as instrumentality, the employment of the formula will inherit the "moral" accomplishments of enlightenment: the social life preserved through its employment will be the life of individual agents: "The burgher, in the successive forms of slaveowner, free entrepreneur, and administrator, is the logical subject of the Enlightenment" (DoE, 83). But, of course, this logical subject is the one also and already operative through the fracturing of medieval society; this is the grocer ("free entrepreneur") whose actions have already been disoriented through the supervenience of instrumental reason (narrowly construed) on everyday practice. It is this *agent,* an agent who is already weakly autonomous, independent, having to decide what to do, and not, say, the subject of a totalitarian regime or a traditional society, who is at stake in the Kantian reconstruction.

If moral reasoning injects moral content into experience through deliberation, then it must hence go beyond the fact that those I must cope with are agents not things, since evidently coping with agents is a different kind of activity to coping with things. The Hobbesian copes with other agents but instrumentally (honor or glory or wit cannot be forms of power for or with respect to stones or caterpillars). Agency is thus weakly presupposed even in narrow instrumental reasoning. Hence the issue is not are others agents, but rather in deliberating about what is involved in acting in a space populated by other agents does a distinctly moral conception of their agency emerge? Does the supervenience of universal law provide moral as opposed to instrumental orientation for this agent? What does the deliberative procedure of maxim testing teach the grocer?

Moral reflection, for Kant, involves a further stretch of reasoning beyond what is demanded by the immediate context of action, namely, a relation of one's maxim of action – the underlying intention(s) or principles guiding specific intentions and actions – to its availability to agents in similar situations. If my maxim of action were not so counterfactually available, if the practice would collapse if my maxim were universalized, that would show that in acting on the maxim now I would be making an exception in my own case. In making an exception in my own case, disallowing, as it were, others to do the same and employing them for my purposes, I would be instrumentalizing them and existing social practices, existing patterns of cooperation for the sake of my own ends. From this angle, it certainly looks as if the universalization test reveals when I am free-riding on others, using them, not treating them as they deserve, or, at least, deserving the same sort of regard that I require for myself. In such cases there is a lapse of mutuality and reciprocity, ideals we take as fully moral.

But if all the failure of a maxim to pass the test of universalization demonstrates is non-reciprocal instrumentalizing, then a fortiori all the test *can* reveal, require, is reciprocal instrumentalizing, i.e., what patterns of cooperation must be in place in order for agents like me to pursue any ends whatsoever. Maxim testing tests *policies,* since it is policies which regulate the actions of abstracted agents, just as it is causal laws that regulate the movement of disenchanted objects. In order to *cope* successfully with things, survive and flourish through manipulating them, requires obedience to the truths of causality; in order to cope successfully, survive in interactions with other agents requires heeding the demands of lawful policies. Are there any policies that all agents, qua agents, must have to act successfully in a world inhabited by other agents like themselves? Are there any policies whose general flouting would reverberate back onto my possibility of successfully achieving my indeterminate and as yet unknown ends?[27] Acceding to the claims of the Categorical Imperative thus reveals, at most, the character of my necessary long-term dependence on others, my dependence on certain stable patterns of cooperation (truth telling, promise keeping, non-injury) in order for me, as an isolated or socially abstracted agent, to pursue any ends whatsoever. Hence, calling the resulting principles "obligatory" is explicated as their being practically or instrumentally necessary components of any social space I, and those like me, must share with one another. The difference between hypothetical and categorical imperatives[28] is not a difference between means-ends reasoning and moral reasoning, but between short-term means-ends reasoning with respect to objects and persons, and long-term means-ends reasoning with respect to persons only. The Kantian extra stretch of reasoning is that of the fully enlightened burgher who may comfortably lack all deep regard for specific other agents. To agree that such agents would be "fully" enlightened is to agree that such reasoning is not natural or spontaneous, but then neither is consistent obedience to the requirements of narrow instrumental and prudential rationality.

The sting of the principle of immanence, its visibility, and the way in

27 In formulating the background to what is required in prudential reasoning, Christine Korsgaard states: "The common element in all of these formulations is that they serve to remind us that we characteristically have more than one aim, and that rationality requires us to take this into account when we deliberate. We should deliberate not only about how to realize the aim that occupies us now, but also about how doing so will affect the possibility of realizing our other aims." "The Normativity of Instrumental Reason," p. 217. The second sentence does not require the force of the first for its force. But if the second sentence can survive without the first, that is, without some thought of our overall good, then there is more to "prudential" reasoning, reasoning about our own good, than direct teleological reasoning *toward* it. In essence, that will be the claim of this section: universalizing is non-teleological prudential reasoning.

28 Notoriously, Kant does not adequately distinguish the instrumental (means-ends) from the prudential (what best promotes my overall aims and intentions); sometimes the prudential and the instrumental get collapsed, and sometimes the prudential forms a premise in moral reasoning. Neither is sufficient to the distinctive quality of prudential thought.

which its operation reveals that there is a suppressed interest in instrumental ends, emerges in the way in which universalization makes all constitutive moral failure the *same* – call it negative practical centralism. Or better: the force of universalizing is necessarily exhausted by the mechanism demonstrating why certain maxims fail; and it is the nature of the form of failure that reduces the content of those that pass the test to instrumentality or prohibits them from providing distinctly moral insight. By thinking of failure like *that,* Kant necessarily blocks insight into what is moral. Maxims that fail the test for universality reveal the agent whose maxim it is as intending to be a free rider (G, 424). That this is taken by Kant to be *the* type of moral failure already slants his argument toward the border where instrumentality and morality meet since the question "Is free riding wrong?" is ambiguous between the two types of concern.[29] Kant's way of revealing free riding through the procedure of maxim testing in fact takes the instrumentalist path, *malgré lui.* If free riding is the model of all failure, the paradigm case of making an exception in my own case, then all that can be at issue in maxim testing are my self-interested ends widely framed: given my utter indifference to the lives and fates of those around me, is "this" course of action one which could be pursued by all? (Compare: Given my utter indifference to the things around me, could this course of action – wrecklessly burning fossil fuels, using shabby building materials, driving too fast – be pursued by all or by me indefinitely?) The reflective ascent from the actual social world to a counterfactual possible social world reduces my relations to others to one of practical compossibility – systematic causal thinking in the social as compared to the natural world. Is "this" action type one capable of forming a principle for a compossible set for a plurality of agents of which I am one? If it is not, then it cannot be instrumentally rational for me to pursue it: the long term consequences of what would happen if pursued by everyone, which itself assumes no more than ideally everyone is an isolated agent like me, are self-defeating for my ends; practically speaking, I would be contradicting myself. If the tests for universality pick out compossible and non-compossible sets of arrangements, then all the reasoning in them must be causal and logical. If only compossibility is at issue, then logically only instrumental relations among agents *can* be at issue. Hence, the pro-

29 Or rather, the question is ambiguous if articulated through the way certain maxims fail the test of universality. Hence, my general thesis is that the test is *too* strong, too emphatic about what failure looks likes to be unequivocally moral. It is thus the very *strength* of the testing procedure that is the source of the equivocation. Conversely, for the position I will want to defend, nothing logically or unequivocally reveals an action or its maxim as immoral other than the fact that it flouts what we take to be moral. This does not mean that what we take to be moral is arbitrary or merely conventional, only that lapses from it cannot be detected from the outside, they do not have a distinct logical pattern or form, and hence do not look like anything in particular.

cedures for maxim testing reveal the amoral interest in instrumentality in the formula of universality.[30]

By pressing Kant this way, I am assuming that the procedures for maxim testing, the extra stretch of deliberative reasoning they enable, are intended to *constitute* what is worthy and unworthy; the procedures cannot be merely heuristic devices if moral reasoning is to determine the full rational meaning of a maxim. Hence what is fully rational for such agents is what is revealed through the procedure. So the obvious Kantian objection to the line of thought I am developing will not work: If I could know now that the worse case scenario as projected by the testing procedure would never come about, I would still be Kantianly obligated not to pursue the

30 In commenting on an early draft of this chapter, Robert Pippin objected that I was moving here, at least, too hastily, and that the issue of mutual survivability could not bear the weight I am giving it. He went on to state that "The Kantian idea throughout is supposed to be: in denying others' *freedom* I presuppose for myself, I make my own freedom, for myself, incoherent; I rule myself out as an agent, a true subject. This is the problem it is because freedom's laws . . . must be self-imposed under the assumption of freedom, the freedom I am denying myself in principle. There are of course, empirical assumptions at work in any judgmental reflection on such constraints; esp. about our own dependence and our death etc. But these are always framed within the unavoidable commitment to freedom (the fact of reason); not the other way round! (as if the commitment to freedom were framed within an attachment to such empirical needs and ends)." In opposition to this, I am suggesting that considering ourselves as independent agents who coordinate with one another through policies should be regarded as a non-moral premise of operating with the Categorical Imperative procedure; and that hence it is wrong to think of the destruction of ourselves as agents (weakly understood) as equivalent to denying myself as a "true subject." Secondly, I am construing the fact of reason doctrine as simply the requirement that I universalize, that I go in for the extra stretch of reasoning. This seems to me right since otherwise, again, the deliberative procedure itself could not be constitutive and informative. If everything is packed into the fact of reason – so: I am utterly committed to regarding others as of unconditional worth, where that worth is essentially lodged in their capacity for autonomous choosing – , then I am unclear where practical *reasoning,* of a Kantian sort, is going to enter the picture in a significant way. (And even if we allow that universalization is only the *unique* expression of the commitment to others as free agents, the collapse I am pointing to will still occur so long as we take seriously the thought that agency is uniquely expressed in this way. It is that formation of reason that is the culprit.) Even if some contemporary Kantians want to go this way, it is far removed from the historical Kant and the role he attributed to reasoning via the role of reason. Hence, on the line I am taking, the question is: does deliberative reasoning of the kind Kant enjoins reveal "reasons we could share" (really) or only "policies necessary in order to make coordination of interest-satisfaction possible"? *Pace* Pippin, as some point we need to interrogate Kant's conception of reason and what he claims it can accomplish independently of his intentions, hopes, and aspirations with respect to it. Some interesting recent reconstructions of Kant's moral philosophy that, implicitly or explicitly, withdraw from the centrality of reason and begin with a fundamental commitment to treating others as ends in themselves as the core of Kantian doctrine include: Barbara Herman, "Leaving Deontology Behind," in her *The Practice of Moral Judgment* (Cambridge, MA: Harvard University Press, 1993), pp. 208–40; Allen Wood, "Humanity as End in Itself" and Paul Guyer, "The Possibility of the Categorical Imperative," both in Paul Guyer (ed.), *Kant's Groundwork of the Metaphysics of Morals: Critical Essays,* pp. 165–87 and 215–245 respectively.

unworthy maxim. What is wrong with this counter is that it, non-Kantianly, qualifies the premise of the procedure itself, namely, deliberative reasoning about action – instrumental and non-instrumental. In so qualifying the premise, it necessarily obfuscates and makes idle all systematic, practical reasoning: the typical and expected consequences of what would happen if various action types were pursued. Special contingent knowledge, a kind of empirical version of Gyges' ring, can obliterate the force of any systematic reasoning. The practical force of pure reason, in Kant's own terms, must be derivative from what reason demonstrates and how it does so. If the reasoning shows various courses of action to be practically self-defeating if adopted by all, then that is the logical force of that stretch of reasoning. The more that Kant wants from such reasoning, its moral interest, I have suggested, comes from elsewhere.

Kant identifies two types of practical failure which issue in the two standard tests for universality. Some maxims "cannot even be *thought* as a universal law of nature without contradiction;" while for others that can be so thought "it is impossible to will . . . because such a will would contradict itself" (G, 424). These forms of practical failure yield what are called respectively the contradiction-in-conception test and the contradiction-in-the-will test. Although it is a matter of dispute, from his handling of examples in the *Groundwork* it seems plausible to think that Kant associated with each test a specific type of duty or obligation: the contradiction-in-conception (hereafter: CC) test yields perfect or narrow duties which allow of no exceptions, while the contradiction-in-the-will (hereafter: CW) test yields imperfect or wide duties. These latter also do not directly allow of exceptions; they are "wide" in the sense that the "when, where, and how" of their realization is necessarily indeterminate.

Both tests derive their logical power by showing that agents who transgress upon universal law enter into contradiction with themselves as practical agents with own-interested projects. For the perfect duties that come out of the CC test what gets demonstrated is a contradiction between the maxim of an agent and the institutions or practices making the agent's maxim possible. So, the lying promiser is in contradiction with himself because he cannot rationally pursue his career of lying without simultaneously willing that the institution and practice of promising should work; yet it is just this which he wills not to happen in lying. The test involves asking what would happen if the maxim of lying (as useful) were everyone's maxim. Thinking about what would happen is considering what consequences could be expected to occur given what we know about human psychology (individual and social) in the context of the social practices we now possess. People would stop believing one another's promises, and, in time, promising itself would collapse as an institution. Universalizing thus performs an ideal prediction showing lying promises to be self-defeating with respect to own-interested agency. The contradiction is thus between unenlightened and enlightened self-interest, between myself as a partially rational interest-maximizer and myself as a fully rational interest-maximizer.[31]

Analogously, for the wide duties that are captured in the CW test, in transgressing universal law an agent is removing the conditions she must will if she is to will the means to her own ends. The practical irrationality of not aiding others in distress derives from the fact that, as vulnerable and not self-sufficient, she cannot insure herself from distress and hence, since receiving such aid from others can plausibly be regarded as a necessary means to achieving her ends generally, then in willing never to aid another in distress she is, in the light of the ideal prediction of the universalization test, willing against herself. Here the good will of others takes the place of the institutions and practices that figure in cases covered by the CC test. Given that beneficence is not an institution, we can conceive of a world in which nonbeneficence reigns since in such a world we could *intelligibly* will nonbeneficence; we cannot *will* such a world, however, without forsaking the indispensable means to our ends. Since the latter is a principle of own-interested rationality narrowly construed, then a policy of beneficence is practically necessary. As before, what the testing reveals is the instrumental irrationality of not aiding others, but not what is positively unethical or immoral in not so doing.

An anxiety that Kant's testing procedures in eliciting forms of ideal coordination is not thereby providing moral content can inadvertently make itself manifest. The content in question is murder; in *Dialectic of Enlightenment* it is argued that at the end of the nineteenth century much of

31 Writers on Kant can still get wrong what he is saying. So David O. Brink, "Kantian Rationalism: Inescapability, Authority, and Supremacy," in Garrett Cullity and Berys Gaut (eds.), *Ethics and Practical Reason* (Oxford: Clarendon Press, 1997), complains: "What it shows is that the practice of promising could not be sustained if everyone were to make false promises. But this shows a certain consequence of universal false promising; there is nothing inconceivable about the resulting state of affairs. Moreover, this a consequence not of universal false promising but of universal false promising *only if* each recognizes the promises of other as false. But there seems nothing *self*-contradictory about universal false promising." From the bottom: there is a self-contradiction because I am willing *both* that there be promise keeping and that there be no promise keeping. Secondly, there is no need to contrast universal false promising and each recognizing the promises of the other as false; the test asks after predictable consequences of the universal adoption of a policy. For Kant mutual recognition of unreliability and distrust is a predictable consequence of the universal practice. Finally, Kant is not suggesting the resulting state of affairs is itself inconceivable; it is a CC in the sense that because the consequent, the lapse of the *institution* of promising, is incompatible with my having the maxim of false promising. "Conception" relates me not directly to others, but to practices and institutions I require (and so to necessarily collective goods); while "will" relates me to others' dispositions toward to me. It may be objected that Kant's distinction between the institutional practices and individual dispositions is too rigid since both rely on my having a will of a certain sort. But does that show that he has drawn a line in the wrong place?

the fury of progressives against the likes of Sade and Nietzsche came from their having publicized the impossibility of rational morality's inability to provide any fundamental and compelling argument against murder (DoE, 118). That it is so little mentioned in modern moral philosophy motivates the harshness of Horkheimer and Adorno's judgement. In "Murder and Mayhem: Violence and Kantian Casuistry," Barbara Herman, in attempting to make good Kant's bewildering silence on violence in the *Groundwork* and elsewhere, plausibly suggests that there are significant similarities between nonbeneficence and convenience killing, and the CW argument against the former models an analogous argument against the latter. In both cases something I must want for myself – the good will of others: help in the case of need, and not to be randomly and violently interfered with – is in fact denied by me when acting on maxims of nonbeneficence and convenience killing. Hence, there is a "deliberative presumption" against convenience killing as there is against nonbeneficence. The following, to my ear, sounds Kantianly right.

> Within the CW argument, in willing that maxims of nonbeneficience or killing become universal laws, the agent wills to forgo something (the help of others, their restraint) that he must as a rational agent will that he have (or – not will that he not have). It is because we . . . cannot exempt ourselves from the condition of need (and so cannot withdraw from the possibility or making claims on the help of others), that we may not ignore their claims of need. And, it is because we cannot escape the conditions of mortality and vulnerability that we may not take lives of others as well.[32]

All the argumentation of this passage turns on the agent adopting policies that he cannot forgo without defeating his ends and purposes as a self-interested agent. His vulnerability and non-self-sufficiency (the finite character of his practical powers) generate a condition of indeterminate need that make him practically dependent on the good will of others for the possibility of carrying out his projects. His mortality exposes him to violence that makes him dependent on the good will of others not to use his mortality to accomplish their ends. In each case the agent calculates (deliberates) what policy he is to adopt given his ends and the conditions of his acting.

Unlike narrow pieces of instrumental reasoning, the calculating here does not look toward specific ends but the pursuing of ends as such, not specific means to achieving those ends but the standing conditions and hence general social means which pertain to whatever ends one might have. Because routine pieces of instrumental reasoning begin with "in conditions C" clauses while maxim testing through universalization func-

32 Barbara Herman, "Murder and Mayhem," in her *The Practice of Moral Judgment* (Cambridge, MA: Harvard University Press, 1993), p. 123; and p. 124 for the next quote.

tions to relate maxims to standing conditions of action, the surface grammar of the two deliberative procedures are distinct. Nonetheless, what is revealed through the testing procedure, and does not appear to be rationally calculable otherwise, is that the institutions, policies, and the attitudes of others to the agent are as surely indispensable means to private ends in general as hammers, fast trains, money, or an easy smile can be. Acting on the policies of beneficence and non-killing represent the agent as being fully rational about his wants and needs *whatever* they turn out to be; and that is unequivocally an own-interested matter. Thus the presumptive difference between the Kantian modal "could" and overtly utilitarian forms of generalization's "would" collapses: Kantian universalization does not depend upon contingent desires and thus upon what agents would desire because it uniquely specifies universal rather than contingent means. Outside this domain, as we shall see, all else lies in darkness, the governance of reason exhausted.

Now something like this run of thought must have unconsciously dawned on Herman since just five sentences after the previous passage quoted we find her interpreting her claim in this way:

> The burden of the CW argument as I interpret it is that the agent who would kill in pursuit of his interests fails to acknowledge what follows from the fact that the life he would take is the life of a person. He fails to count the life of the other as in itself providing a reason not to kill – a reason that outweighs (independent of calculation) the reasons for killing derived from the agents pursuit of private ends . . . [T]he CW argument shows that it is impermissible to discount the value of human life to the currency of purposes . . . The correct moral complaint from the victim does not speak of pain or loss, but of the lack of proper regard for him as a rational agent.

This is baffling: in accordance with the CW argument the life of another cannot "in itself" be the reason I do not kill since if the concrete life of another were regarded automatically as trumps – as possessing an "imponderably delicate aura" – , then the testing procedure would be unnecessary.[33] On the contrary, what calls the entire deliberative procedure into being is that the other is another agent, indifferently regarded, who I must deal with somehow; the procedure means to tell me what reason requires in such dealing. What gives the procedure its power and makes it explicitly deliberative and constitutive is hence contrary to seeing the other as possessing immediate intrinsic or unconditioned worth: assume that the lives of others are not in themselves and absolutely of value (as

33 Indeed, perhaps the single most systematic shift from Kant to later idealism – beginning with Schiller and Fichte – is the transformation of respect for the law to respect for another directly confronting us; which is what is meant by the idealist notion of "recognition." It is, somehow, the presence of the other that "checks" our inclinations and reveals our essence to us.

required by disenchantment), it is nonetheless rationally necessary to adopt a policy against convenience killing if you are to will the necessary standing conditions of agency.[34] If maxim testing is to be more than a *heuristic* through which antecedent commitment to the moral worth of others is reflected on, but a discovery of what reason and rationality require, then the "wrong" of faulty maxims cannot be a mistake in "valuing" but in reasoning and calculating (otherwise, again, the process of deliberation could not be informative, Kantianly constitutive). Logically, the sine qua non of reasoning is consistency, and the type of all failure inconsistency; the detection of inconsistency is the detection of contradictions. In practical reasoning, inconsistency in action with respect to the fact of others is what shows the agent to be in contradiction with himself – with the necessary conditions of agency; contradictory maxims are practically self-defeating.[35]

The CW test reveals that I cannot *consistently* want whatever ends I might have but not want my life to be weakly respected, not violently interfered with, since, bluntly, my life is a necessary condition for me pursuing all and any ends. It is "because we cannot escape the conditions of our mortality" that we, self-interestedly, have *reasons* to make policies of not murdering overriding. Were I immortal and all others mortal, then the CW procedure would not work since there would be nothing self-defeating in killing. Hence the value of life constituted through the CW deliberative procedure does not necessitate a moral scruple that the life "he would take is the life of a *person,*" where personhood is taken as a self-sufficient reason for not killing. How could anything like maxim testing show anything like *that*? Other agents matter, unlike squirrels or tigers, because while I might want non-interference from tigers (and not care about squirrels unless suddenly predatory), and causally arrange my life accordingly (building fences, say), other agents (with whom I am potentially connected) act on policies too, and ideally on rational policies like me. So my policies are meant to reflect what policies we, minimally, must endorse as rational agents who share a common social world in which the policies I adopt may be thought of as "ideally" reflecting the policies we

34 Although, as already granted, the formula of ends-in-themselves possesses a moral content that the formula of universal law does not, nonetheless, if it is to be employed *deliberatively,* as Kant requires, then its use, at least here, will yield analogous results. So, for example, Onora O'Neill states that "Ends-in-themselves may provide us with grounds of action not by being the *aim* or *effect* of action but by constituting *limits* to our actions." I read the first clause as implicitly denying that in the case of convenience killing I am overlooking that the other is a *person* (of infinite moral worth). Deliberatively, the emphasis must be on the negative, which is exactly how O'Neill continues her thought: "Not to treat others as mere means introduces minimal, but indispensable requirements for coordinating action in a world shared by a plurality of agents." *Constructions of Reason* (Cambridge: Cambridge University Press, 1989), p. 114.

35 Onora O'Neill, "Consistency in Action," in her *Constructions of Reason.*

can adopt on the premise that, again "ideally," self-interest and the pure reasoning governing its pursuance are the only good reasons anyone can have to adopt any policy. Practical reasoning, on the principles of the hypothetical and categorical imperatives, extends no further than action coordination. Beasts and angels are of no consideration because there is no sense in which I must *coordinate* my actions with theirs if my pursuance of ends is to be possible. Coordination, however, is a logical and causal matter, a question of compossible sets.

By regimenting the meaning of universality and consistency to modes in which maxims *fail* the test for universality, Adorno's contention that the objectivity of the moral law is drawn from the objectivity of society becomes perspicuous. At its extreme, say with a maxim of convenience killing, what is yielded through the CW test, a state in which everyone kills as convenient, converges eerily with Hobbes' state of nature. But to a lesser extent, breaking contracts or promises as convenient, if universalized, while not destructive of any imaginable society, would be destructive, in the sense of introducing an uncontrollable arbitrariness, of a society of burghers. The logical subject of the deliberative procedure is the independent agent who must secure his *social survival* on the basis of reflectively endorsed policies (and not trust, tradition, habit, material necessity, bonds of affection or identification, coercion, etc.); which is why failed maxims are *self*-contradictory: the agent's own legislative intentions contravene what he must want. Hence, while not every failed maxim projects a state of nature, each exposes the agent to arbitrariness. But is this not equivalent to saying that those policies that must be endorsed are criterial for membership of a society of independent agents, and thus what that society must have for *itself*?

5. Moral Experience: Of Urgency and Obligation

Pure reason is not uncontentiously moral, although, by ascending to the level of the logic of consistency, its deliberative procedures do introduce contents not derivable from instrumental reasoning narrowly understood. In the previous chapter we saw how the account of the logical characteristics of the principle of immanence and the way those characteristics project a conception of the rationalization of reason made plausible the thought that pure reason should be interpreted as bound to instrumentality. If universalization is a reasonable extension of the logic of consistency to practical affairs – coping with other agents as opposed to the environment – , then the revelations of non-universalizable maxims underline that claim. Whatever the moral depths of Kant's image of a kingdom of ends, his idea of others as ends in themselves, his conception of autonomy, all those, I have claimed, come from elsewhere and are neither intrinsic to nor transparently compatible with the requirements of pure reason.

Yet, the account offered thus far does not cohere with the standard objections to Kant: formalism, rigorism, emptiness. This should be unsurprising since one premise of those objections must be that pure reason itself is contentless; from a genealogical perspective, that view of pure reason cannot be sustained. Another assumption in those objections is that Kant illicitly abstracts from affections and context; but this blames Kant for instrumental reason's supervening on everyday practice, rather than perceiving him as attempting to provide a second order logic of supervenience which would reactivate, in a wholly enlightened and disenchanted way, the rational kernel of those practices. There is in Kantian morality an abstraction from context and affects, but these are best comprehended as inherited. Kantian deliberative procedures rationalize practices by substituting reflective endorsement through maxim testing (honesty is an indispensable practice for me and those with whom I interact whatever I and we may want) in place of narrowly instrumental reasons for endorsement (honesty is a good, useful policy for me) and the material inferences of the traditional practice that societal rationalization has already supervened on. Again, we should not take lightly the thought that under conditions of radical disenchantment and given what reason has become that this may be all we can say. The genealogical critique of Kant may again be turned around into the best defense of him and reason possible.

However, even so fervent a supporter of Kant as Dieter Henrich acknowledges that there are two objections to the categorical imperative that cannot be answered: " . . . that it does not allow one to derive all those duties which are recognized by moral consciousness, and that even for those duties which do follow from it, it fails to take into consideration the intention of moral consciousness."[36] Even these failures, it should be conceded, originate from ordinary moral consciousness, and thus fail to sufficiently acknowledge the damage done to ethical life that forms the background to and is the presupposition of Kant's endeavors. For this reason, the full backing for these objections, that we can *still* mount them, must wait upon the vindication of the Adornoian alternative. Nonetheless, what makes these objections seem pointed is that they both accord with and can be thus be explained by the instrumental interpretation of the moral law just offered.

36 "Ethics of Autonomy," p. 101. Henrich defends the use of these objections by referring to Kant's statement that his ethics must do justice to the "common moral reason of human beings." That indeed is the ground of the objections, but it is not obvious that a Kantian ought to concede that ground.

If Kant's rationalization and reactivation of traditional morals depends upon showing that some practices and some dispositions (alias: virtues) are indispensable means to whatever ends one has, then predictably it is going to leave untouched a whole range of more specific duties, Henrich cites duties toward oneself (cultivating one's talents, moderation, etc.),[37] that cannot be conceived of as necessary or indispensable in the required way (as universal means). Put another way, Kant can only rationally reactivate those moral notions that can play an indispensable role within a disenchanted society; obligations that are too tied to metaphysical conceptions of the person, the way moderation is bound to "consciousness of the dignity of human nature"[38] and cultivation of talents bound to some picture of self-realization or perfection, are bound to become suspect and be swept aside. When Kant does attempt to squeeze these in, he can, at best, capture only the extreme flouting of the former virtue: I cannot will ruinous excess. But I can will excess short of that, and I can will to use only those talents that require no or only minimal cultivation.

Moving to the second objection, it follows from the disenfranchisement of the material inferences of everyday practices that obligation must track rational necessity. What is rationally necessary, however, is only ever going to be acting on the basis of certain principles or virtues, that is, having and acting on those principles and virtues that are themselves required as forming the fundaments of action coordination for a society of anonymous and independent subjects. For Kant, obligation attaches to "principles of action and not to their particular embodiment in act tokens: they require acts of a certain type, rather than particular act-tokens of that type."[39] This fails the intention of ordinary moral consciousness in that for it actual states of affairs and not act-types are the ground of actions of a given type, and equally it is tokens, not types, that are obligated. As I will say more about directly, for ordinary moral consciousness (that is here depicted as still using remnant material inferences) it is the case that I aid others in need *because* they are in need, from a perception of their neediness, and not because I have a duty of benevolence that emerges through the rational impossibility of promoting my own happiness and ignoring the happiness of others. The point is not, as was stated in the Introduction, that moral reason provides one reason too many for the relevant actions; rather, it transforms what were reasons, the given complex state of affairs, into occasions, making the ground of the action the indeterminate principle or virtue. Form (type) displaces content (token) as the ground of action: "In the intention of my moral will the other person and his need for help are only a case for the application of the

37 Ibid., p. 102. 38 Ibid.
39 O'Neill, *Towards Justice and Virtue,* p. 159. O'Neill is not here explicitly interpreting Kant, but the thought seems to me exactly his.

universal principle and an occasion for confirming the rational universality of the will."[40] In opposition to this, ordinary moral consciousness presumes a self-grounding or ungrounded material inference: he's needy, I will (must) help. Once this inference is blocked, anything like it can only survive by being reconstructed on a higher level. In being reconstructed on a higher level, not the token but only the type survives as having unequivocal necessity. Of course, rational necessity is going to mean something quite other than what was thought in the necessity (the parenthetic "must") of the material inference.

It is with the reduction of others to occasions for moral willing and the displacement of immediate demands by reflective obligations that Adorno rhetorically balks. After contending that in seeking theoretical justification for our actions we fall into the "bad infinities of derivation and validity," he continues: "We criticize morality by criticizing the extension of the logic of consistency to the conduct of men; this is where the logic of consistency becomes an organon of unfreedom. The impulse, naked physical fear and the feeling of solidarity with what Brecht called tormentable bodies (*quälbaren Körpern*), is immanent in moral conduct and would be denied in attempts at ruthless rationalization; what is most urgent would become contemplative again, mocking its own urgency" (ND, 285–6). "Ruthless (*rücksichtsloser*; so also: callous, unfeeling) rationalization" withdraws from the urgency of response, from the *experience* of the other's distress (fear, solidarity, etc.), which are feelings that prompt and are contained in the moral conduct, in order to find grounds which would vindicate generally acting on responses like that. This has a double consequence: the ground or reason for the action is displaced from the object to logical form (the principle the action falls under), and the obligation to perform the action is transferred from the "urgency" of a response to rational necessity. Adorno thinks this is an organon of unfreedom because he conceives of the transformation of the ground of action shifting the requirement for action from "within" to "without," to use Weber's terms; or, my reasons for action in the "urgent" sense are internal to my relation to the object responded to, while they are external to that, specific, relation when rationalized; or, a last gloss, rationalization requires the repression, or at least discounting, of the original "impulse" to action which is, in Adorno's jargon, our "freedom toward" the object. These different locutions pick out different aspects of the transformation that are significant for Adorno: it transforms something concrete and particular into a case of something general; it transforms something that is itself partially corporeal, embodied, into something purely intellectual; it transforms the meaning of "reason" as ground and motive into only ground; it transforms a complex experience involving feeling, imagina-

40 D. Henrich, "Ethics of Autonomy," p. 102.

tion and thought, into thought only. What is left unexplained here, or in any surrounding passages, is precisely how Adorno conceives of "impulse," the fear and the solidarity, as immanent in moral conduct. That is the large knot that will need to be untied in later chapters.

For Adorno, here in tune with ordinary moral consciousness, if the reason (both ground and motive) for an action lies in the object, then equally the particular state of affairs will be the locus of obligation (what must or must not be done). "Urgency" qualifies the situation, thus generating one form of the ethical "must." As will be amplified later, what *must* be done comes out as a consequence of what the situation is, what it is like, how it may be best described; and how I am related to that state of affairs. That it is I that must do what must be done turns on both features of the situation (the state of the object to be responded to, and that I am the only or best positioned person to do something about this situation, for example), and who I am, my character: I could not live with myself, take myself and my claimed beliefs seriously if I did not do this thing. In Adorno's stark phrasing: "Without recourse to the [concrete] material, no ought could issue from reason . . . " (ND, 243).

The apparent weakness of this type of account of obligation is that what is obligated is indelibly first-person, wholly internal to the context, ethical vocabulary, and ethical self-understanding of the agent concerned. At one, extreme level the impossibility of my acting otherwise requires the sense of: without betraying myself, denying myself and you, destroying what I (or we) most value. If the immoral action is self-destructive and self-defeating in any sense, it is so only with respect to my already constituted moral self-understanding. For this very reason, doing the opposite of what I ought to do is "possible," one could do it (without contradiction in the Kantian sense), and perhaps another agent in the same situation could justifiably act differently. In ways that will turn out to have ontological consequences, Adorno believes that acting under an obligation is to acknowledge and take a stand on (become responsible for) the values acted on; my action matters to the being and meaning of the values or ideals implicated in it.[41]

41 For analogous considerations see Bernard Williams, *Moral Luck*, chs. 9–10, "Ought and Moral Obligation" and "Practical Necessity"; and Christine Korsgaard, *The Sources of Normativity* (Cambridge: Cambridge University Press, 1996), pp. 101–113. The idea that, at the limit, acting immorally is destructive of the person is implied by the third element of Henrich's grammar of moral insight; and from that element it does follow that there must be some *general* relation between practical necessity and the moral or practical identity of agents. But it had better not turn out to be the case that every act I "must" do has as its corollary an act I must not do on pain of practical self-destruction, or as Korsgaard does want to affirm: "An obligation always takes the form of a reaction against a threat of a loss of identity" (p. 102) . One quick way of seeing why this must be wrong is to remind ourselves that even if individual acts are the locus of deontic accounting, practical identity – having a "good will" or being a person of integrity – "is conveyed in

Once we perceive how Kantian obligation discounts the intentions of ordinary moral consciousness twice over, by making principle not object the ground of action and locating types not tokens as the locus of deontic accounting, then, prima facie, there must be a third type of objection that dialectically connects the two previous ones: because the domain of what is obligatory for Kant is narrower than before, much of what ordinary moral consciousness counts as obligatory, because singular, is removed into the space of the merely permitted or morally indifferent.[42] Kant categorizes maxims into the morally worthy (obligatory), morally indifferent (merely permissible), and morally unworthy (forbidden). For Kant, because the domains of the obligatory and the forbidden capture only those act-types either required for or incompatible with the minimum necessary conditions of coordination, then many more actions, act-types, will fall into the domain of the permissible (neither required nor forbidden). As noted, this means at one level that some previous act-types that were obligatory cannot be accounted for. But it will also mean that act-tokens that appear to the Kantian to be in the domain of the permissible will appear to agents themselves as either required or forbidden. So while lying out of self-interest fails the universalizability test (it is morally unworthy and forbidden), lying for the sake of protecting another from unnecessary hurt is permissible. For the agent these two cases will not appear so different: one in which I ought not to lie and one in which I may lie. If in both cases I decide that I ought to tell the truth, it will be because in both cases I judge that is what the situation demanded. For me, the difference between the cases is *not* one of deontological types, that is, between the case where truth-telling is required and where it is only permitted (because lying too is permitted); for me it is a difference in the

the continuity of a lifetime rather than in isolated acts" (ND, 226n.). Said another way, acts and agents can be worthy or unworthy, but they are so in different ways. That the *durée* of individual worth is extended is one reminder about the role of time; another would be that it is only a philosophical fiction that acts have narrow temporal boundaries, even if decisions more plausibly do. Finally, a reminder: while the occasion of discovering what I must do is useful for illuminating the existence of a connection between obligation and practical identity, one must not conflate the experience of obligation or my becoming aware of, what I will be calling, *claims* on me with their existence; claims can accrue without my willing, desire, say so, endorsement. Of course, from this it trivially follows that there can be claims I am unaware of or am indifferent to; but equally, my practical identity can be destroyed, my life emptied, without my knowing much about it. For Adorno (or Kierkegaard or Nietzsche) this is in fact the norm rather than the exception, and at one level must be the norm rather than the exception if the account of disenchantment is true.

42 "Prima facie" because most of the cases that fall under this description turn on conflicts of duty, and there is not an orthodox or widely agreed view on what Kant should say here. As a consequence, I run three different Kantian lines. Even if my argument should fail by not locating the best Kantian account, it moves my argument forward, and there is no reason to think this failure could alter that status of the previous two objections that I am here attempting to connect up.

ease or difficulty of *knowing* what I ought to do. In discovering what to do, what I have most reason to do, I discover, sometimes painfully and uncomfortably, what I *must* do.[43] In the case where lying too is permitted, the moral exigencies of the situation are, if anything, higher; hence, coming to the decision that I must tell the truth is more, not less, significant, more, not less, proximate to what I as a moral agent perceive as necessary for according the other respect.

On one plausible reading, then, the exigencies of morally complex situations are opaque from the perspective of Kantian moral reasoning because there is either a conflict of principles or a real inscrutability about which principles apply or about likely consequences; that is, if complex situations are really like this, really conflicted, inscrutable, indeterminate, then it would appear that complexity of the relevant maxim of action would fall into the class of the morally indifferent.[44] But, apart from Kantian scruple, this is counter-intuitive, since there is no reason to think that complexity should obviate necessity; on the contrary, if the elements or potential elements that contribute to making the situation complex would be, taken separately, members of the extreme deontological classes (obligatory or forbidden), then why believe their clustering, and the relevant maxim of action that is a consequence of that clustering, entails a weakening rather than deepening of demand?

But the Kantian cannot really go in the opposite direction either. It is empirically implausible to suggest that moral complexity is only ever an appearance, and that when the correct interpretation of the situation is finally hit upon, when a universalizable interpretation of the situation is provided, then since the remaining interpretation(s) is (are) by definition non-generalizable, it is deonotologically forbidden.[45] Such an argu-

43 See Williams, *Moral Luck,* pp. 128–30.

44 See Albrecht Wellmer, "Ethics and Dialogue: Elements of Moral Judgement in Kant and Discourse Ethics," in his *The Persistence of Modernity: Essays on Aesthetics, Ethics and Postmodernism,* translated by David Midgley (Oxford: Polity Press, 1991), pp. 199–202.

45 Ibid., p. 202. This line of thought, which Wellmer is elaborating, is closer to the one Kant himself suggests than the one just canvassed. In the *Doctrine of Virtue,* translated by Mary J. Gregor (Philadelphia: University of Pennsylvania Press, 1964), Academy p. 224, he states:

> A conflict of duties would be a relation of duites in which one of them would annul the other (wholly or in part). – But a conflict of duties and obligations is inconceivable. For the concepts of duty and obligation as such express objective practical *necessity* of certain actions, and two conflicting rules cannot both be necessary at the same time: if it is our duty to act according to one of these rules, then to act according to the opposite one is not our duty and is even contrary to duty. But there can be, it is true, two *grounds* of obligation . . . both present in one agent and in the rule he lays down for himself. In this case one or the other of these grounds is not sufficient to oblige him . . . and is therefore not a duty. – When two such grounds conflict with each other, practical philosophy says, not that the stronger obligation takes precedence . . . , but that the stronger *ground of obligation* prevails . . . (MM, p. 23)

ment assumes that what appears originally as indeterminately complex is in reality morally determinate and simple apart from any relation I or any other may have to it. This seems wrong-headed in two different ways. First, it assumes so-called moral complexity is always mere appearance, hence akin to what an opaque physical situation would be for a natural scientist; and just as a scientific realist presupposes that there is a determinate structure underlying the opaque appearances which the methodology of scientific reasoning can approach, so here it is assumed that some understanding of the situation through the methodology of rational argumentation is generalizable without remainder, generalizable moral interpretations of situations thus producing a semblance of objectivity akin to the scientific. There is no reason to think moral reality *is* determinate in this way; nor is there any reason to think that an ideal procedure for coming to an *agreed* interpretation makes it the right one; nor any reason to believe the method of argumentation somehow uniquely conduces to uncovering the correct simple one, even assuming there was such.

But all of these failures point to a second trouble. Let us ignore the problem that it is difficult to comprehend what the locale for this procedure is meant to be; it looks like it is intended to uncover "what must be done," but that cannot be right since complex situations are ones requiring some decision now and therefore there is no *time* for the interpretation game, especially an idealizing one. Maybe, the idea of a generalizable interpretation is meant as a model for individual reflection. But how is that really different from just my judging what to do? Individual judgement, here and now, cannot be replaced by anything else. If, however, the procedure is retrospective, then it detaches the obligatory and the forbidden from their role in determining action. Yet this quandary – where is this procedure? – does point to the way in which it moves practical reasoning from a first to a third person perspective, thereby making the practical a species of the theoretical. The idea that through a normatively governed argumentative procedure we could come to agree which interpretation of the situation is correct, valid, reflectively distances agent from circumstances, making her specific relation to it contemplative. Hence, even before a universalizable interpretation of the situation is reached, it has been reduced to something external, describable apart from the agents' possible responses to it, so excising part of what makes it truly complex, viz., the differential claims that different features of the situation have on her. In so doing it assumes that situations are determinate apart from or prior to what agents do in them, and that what values come to circulate and have force in a social world are determinable

The clearest elaboration and defense of this I know is found in Barbara Herman, "Obligation and Performance: A Kantian Account of Moral Conflict," in her *The Practice of Moral Judgment* (Cambridge, MA: Harvard University Press, 1993).

apart from what agents do. Practical reasoning, at this level, is thus reduced to the question of application: making principle and circumstance determinate through generalized interpretative procedures. Because principles are indeterminate apart from circumstances, on any account, and circumstances here only apparently indeterminate and complex (making the circumstances simple is making them determinate and thereby enabling a "simple" application of rule to case), then the whole apparatus can be seen as designed to make practical "urgency" into theoretical rightness. Hence, while this account salvages moral complexity from falling into the abyss of the merely permitted, it does so at awful cost.

A more natural account of how Kant handles moral complexity will not have quite these exorbitant consequences, but, come what may, it will reduce the complex to the simple: if ought implies can, then I cannot really be obligated to do both of two incompatible acts. In coming to see that I cannot do both, and there are no further bases for discriminating the cases left to me, then in doing one rather than another I have done what is obligated and I have not left anything undone. The non-Kantian, it is charged, in making performance what is obligated rather willings that are the outcome of deliberation, sustains complexity at the cost of making agents obligated to do impossible things.[46] But this reads back into ordinary moral consciousness a conception of obligation, and its centrality for ethical life, that it does not possess. If states of affairs, their complexion, and an agent's relation to them provide the grounds for ethical action, then those grounds remain in force no matter what the agent does. We need a word here, other than obligation, to describe the way in which states of affairs ground actions and can give rise to actions that an agent *must* do without either denying complexity or requiring an agent to do something impossible. What we normally say is that a state of affairs inscribes a field of *responsibility* or a field of *claims.*[47] In a complex state of affairs, an agent cannot act on all the claims on her at once; but why should that fact mitigate the reality of the claims? Hence, in acting one way rather than another the agent alters the complexion of the field; the field will now be described differently, re-aligning responsibilities and claims, but they *and their former complexion* remain – they are her morality reality. In doing what she must do, she nonetheless does not do all that needs (needed) doing. And the most natural way of describing this, new, situation is to say that her actions disposed of, met, some claims on her and not others, and that new ones have arisen.

46 This, I hope, is a fair two sentence summary of Herman's "Obligation and Performance."

47 Throughout the final lectures recorded in *Problems of Moral Philosophy,* Adorno keeps pointing to the idea of a morality of responsibility ("towards empirical existence, self-preservation and the fulfilment of the species to which we belong . . . " p. 146) as the alternative to Kant. Alas, Adorno never moves beyond the pointing stage.

The immediate consequence of giving priority to the ethical object in this way is that it makes ethical action and deliberation intrinsically historical and temporal, forward looking only in the context of being backward looking. In giving equal weight to the ethical past as to the ethical future, it gives what have been marginal categories of ethical life centrality, namely, what Barbara Herman has nicely termed "the three Rs: remorse, restitution, and remainders."[48] Because claims are the focus, then the dominant category here is that of remainders; that these should be called "remainders" already bespeaks the present-future configuration of this conception of moral consciousness. A better description of remainders (I will continue to use the term) is of *continuing and transformed claims*. Claims do not suddenly lapse because I did not act upon them when I could have; they continue, although what continues will doubtless be transformed as a consequence of my not acting in the first instance, sometimes radically so. And when the alteration of the claim is radical, then sometimes all that is left to me is remorse and the complex forms of expression through which it is enacted (apology, confession, atonement). Restitution is required when the other suffers an increment in damage as a consequence of my non-action, although normally, in cases of moral complexity, that increment is minor compared to the continuing claim. To employ Sartre's well-known example, if I choose to stay and nurse my sick mother rather than join the resistance, I *still* owe the resistance, and hence my country, something, a claim remains; the part played by the damage caused by my not choosing it is minor in comparison to the original claim. Guilt, *Schuld,* needs to be re-externalized into its original sense of indebted to and responsible for, and not let lapse into the notion of a bad feeling with respect to acts of omission. Restitution, normally, belongs to cases where I was or we were responsible for the original damage, or where I or we continue the damage through ignorant or intentional non-action. And in such cases, where I or we have caused the damage, then the primary requirement is to repair it, make reparation and amends.

By a circuitous route we have returned to the starting place of this chapter. An immanent critique of transcendental idealism requires that

48 Ibid., p. 324; the following discussion, pp. 324–33, which attempts to minimize without denying the significance of these categories, is worth consulting. In a telling footnote, Onora O'Neill has commented that while remainders of feeling (remorse, regret, guilt) have recently figured in philosophical discussion, remainders of action have not, while clearly being as if not more important. "Rectifactory action other than punishment (which is oriented only to perpetrators, rather than to victims or to the relationship between perpetrators and victims) is surprisingly little discussed in secular ethics. It may include forms of apology, confession, atonement, forgiveness, reconciliation, compensation, reparation, restitution, recognition, penance, and not doubt other acts and activities." *Towards Justice and Virtue,* p. 160. The middle terms of O'Neill's list – reconciliation, reparations, restitution, recognition – , at least, are pivotal for Adorno's ethics.

it be understood genealogically and historically. While the mid-point of this critique is the detection of an instrumental interest subtending the moral in the Kantian elaboration of moral reason, the terminus for the genealogical critique of moral reason is the discovery that a reasonable account of moral complexity requires giving priority to the object, the very form of an axial turn that Adorno construes as the end-point of his critique of idealism. That moral complexity should form an Achilles' heel for moral rationalism derives from the inevitable thought that while complexity must appear to agents, its reality concerns the shape of the world, its various forms of destitution and neediness. The plural demands that are the source of moral complexity necessarily displace moral agents as constituting, from within their deliberative outlook, what is and is not to count as a demand. Without an axial turn the actuality of moral complexity is denied, as it is in all three of the Kantian accounts canvassed. But this cannot be for us a merely technical matter since the premise of my analysis has been that Kantian moral thought is a response to disenchantment. It now turns out that it is a response that cannot acknowledge the damage done to persons and things by disenchantment, that is, it is necessarily blind to the injurious condition that calls it into being in the first instance.

To sustain the intuitions of ordinary moral consciousness against the trespass of moral reason the object must be the ground of moral action; in order for objects to be grounds they must be the locus of claims; if it is a configuration of objects, a state of affairs, in which a claim is lodged, then claims can and will endure past the moment of action that passes them by. Ethical encounter itself is temporal and historical. In order for ethical encounter to be temporal and historical, it is the object of ethical awareness, its claim, that must be the ground of ethical action. To hear or perceive this claim requires us to experience the object. For this experience of the object to be possible, and hence to acknowledge the object's claim demands an "axial turn" in moral consciousness. The consequence of such a turn would be to give, at least, equal weight to moral remainders, to restitution and remorse. It would not be an exaggeration to say that for Adorno the process of disenchantment is historically a collective damaging of objects, persons and things; and hence for him each object now faces us as the damaged face of what we have done to it. That is the object's claim. In this situation, restitution – confessing, repairing, making amends, reconciliation – becomes the dominant ethical *orientation*. If the ethical and the philosophical are as entwined for Adorno as I have been implying, then it should be unsurprising to discover that he is prepared to consider this orientation the one proper to philosophy now: "While doing violence to the object of its syntheses, our thinking heeds a potential that waits in the object, unconsciously obeying the idea of making amends (*wieder gutzumachen*) to the fragments for what it has done to them; in philosophy, this unconscious tendency becomes conscious" (ND, 19). The tug of the past that will always make Adorno's thought appear nostalgic is in reality not the ideality of past states of affairs, but that pervasive state of the world as disenchanted, and as disenchanted damaged. What faces us, calls to us, are nothing but remainders, but remainders created by our own doing, hence demanding restitution and remorse. It is with this experience that Critical Theory begins.

4

MASTERED BY NATURE: ABSTRACTION, INDEPENDENCE, AND THE SIMPLE CONCEPT

> The individual is left with no more than the morality which Kantian moral theory, which accords affection, not respect, to animals, can muster only disdain: to try to live so that one may believe oneself to have been a good animal.

1. Bringing Nature Back In

The ethical impulse of Adorno's thinking, what it is to think the world as disenchanted, is fundamentally oriented by remorse, the need to make restitution, to repair the damage done, to seek reconciliation, to make amends. Only that backward-looking impulse, when elaborated, can do justice to the present in a manner that would redeem the hopes of the past. Before I can give substance to this ethical impulse (I conclude this chapter with an account of it), I must begin making amends for leaving out of account a major item in Adorno's argument: the role of nature. In a manner that is difficult to provide with conceptual clarity, Adorno consistently reads the dualisms implied in the Kantian contrast of concepts with intuitions – form and matter, universal and particular, spontaneity and passivity[1] – as themselves darkly mirroring, in an epistemological register, the more fundamental duality of culture and nature. For Adorno and Horkheimer, rationalization desocializes nature (disenchantment) and denatures society, which is the explanation for society itself becoming desocialized, that is, an iron cage dominating persons. In a way from which he never deviated, Adorno regards culture as a *part* of the natural

1 In *Making It Explicit,* Brandom summarizes these three dualities thus: "In the first, the conceptual is distinguished from the *material,* that which provides *content,* as opposed to form (more specifically the *normative* form or rulishness), which is the contribution of concepts. In the second, the conceptual is distinguished from the particular, as what *classifies* to what is *classified.* In the third, the conceptual is distinguished from what is imposed on from without, as what *we do,* as opposed to what is *done to* or imposed on us" (p. 616).

world, albeit an intensely historicized part whose fundamental forms of activity cannot be reduced to their natural origins or counterparts, but whose origins and counterparts provide the conditions of possibility of their cultural elaboration as well as their genealogical intelligibility. Conversely, he always conceives of nature, or at least those portions of nature (our bodies and practical environment) that we routinely and as a matter of necessity incorporate into our practical activities, as not an atemporal system of lawful regularities, empirically real in Kant's sense, but as in themselves historical. Not only do our concepts of things change, but the things themselves change and alter, have a history: air, the very stuff, *becomes* polluted; animal species *become* extinct (on their own and through our intervention), mineral resources *become* depleted, new natural kinds are intentionally *developed*. What is true of external nature is more emphatically true of human nature: our biologically given attributes are continually being formed, determined, and elaborated through cultural practice. As Adorno states the thesis in *Negative Dialectics*: "The traditional antithesis of nature and history is both true and false; true, in so far as it expresses what the moment of nature underwent; false, in so far as it apologetically recapitulates, by conceptual reconstruction, history's concealment of its own natural outgrowth [*Naturwüchsigkeit*]" (ND, 358).[2] History is a natural outgrowth above all because instrumental rationality is the rational/cognitive expression of the drive to self-preservation; it is the mechanism for coping with the natural environment for an animal species that can no longer reproduce itself through nature-implanted instinctual routines. There is an antithesis between history and nature insofar as the nature that is necessary for undeformed ethical practice is not evident or available; but this social and historical fact is misrecognized when it elevated to a conceptual truth, say, in the distinction between an autonomous and self-moving space of reasons or culture in contrast with a space of causal law. Neither conception is accurate: history is also a part of nature and a "natural outgrowth" from it; and the nature that is the actual material substratum of human lives is other than the law-governed whole it is depicted to be. The methodological presuppositions of this way of thinking are discussed in Chapter 5. For the present I ignore these methodological questions in order to focus on some substantive ones.

Perhaps the dominant difficulty in thinking through Adorno's deployment of nature is that, as he is intensely aware, there is very little, if any, "nature" in evidence; all the nature we come across has already been, inevitably, socially mediated. And while his complaint about the repression of nature within and without is not that it has been so mediated, but that it has been mediated and used *wrongly* (it has become the Other of

2 My translation of this passage follows Jarvis, *Adorno: A Critical Introduction,* p. 40.

culture), because all the nature we know is of the wrongly mediated kind, it can certainly appear that in asking for a reconciliation between nature and culture he is asking for unmediated nature to be restored. To avoid that impression, and to find leverage from within culture to unlock the natural, in *Negative Dialectics the thought of nature as conditioning history is primarily construed epistemologically: repressed nature is expressed in the silencing or, better, the formation of the second components of concept-intuition dualism: matter, particularity, passivity (receptivity).* Intuition, so defined, as lacking the rulishness of conceptual norms, as lacking the generality of the concept, as lacking the (self-determining) power of the freedom of the concept to impose order, is the remnant or remainder of sensuous particularity after it has been formed, classified, imposed on, and done to in a way which makes its role in cognition imponderable.[3] Hence dominated nature becomes nonidentity: that in the object which is missed (squandered, eliminated) by the regime of identity thinking as expressed in concept-intuition dualism (i.e., everything that might be thought of as belonging to "empirical reality" – circumambient nature – that is excluded by Kant's account of it). Yet, at first glance, there is no obvious reason why we should associate conceptual dualism with a disavowal of nature, or why we should think that overcoming those dualisms is going to be equivalent to giving priority to the object, or why giving priority to the object in that epistemological way is equivalent to seeking reconciliation with nature. Spelling out these equations is the effort of Adorno's late thought.

As a very brief first pass at them that will require the rest of this work

3 I am here assuming that intuitions without concepts are blind, that is, on their own or independently of concepts intuitions lack a representational dimension; and hence that it is by means of being brought under concepts that intuitions come to represent particular objects. But it is just this fact that drives the mystery: if the functional role of intuitions is actual only once they are conceptualized, then in what sense are they able to provide a rational constraint on conceptualization? It would appear that the gesture through which intuitions are given their role in cognition, that is, as being finally within the space of reasons, is what denies them sufficient independence from reason to place a check on, guide, its operations, hence fulfill the very function they were assigned. For the orthodox interpretation of how intuitions operate in Kant, see Henry Allison, *Kant's Transcendental Idealism: An Interpretation and Defense* (New Haven: Yale University Press, 1983), pp. 65–8. Although I do not here have the space to develop the claim, I am throughout assuming that intuiting, in Kant's sense, is the rationalized version of mimetic response, and hence that mimesis functions in Adorno's thought not in opposition to conceptual response, but in opposition to intuiting. Intuitions are representations of individuals seen wholly through their rationalized concepts; anthropocentric or circumambient nature is the object of concepts whose original sensuous presentation occurs through mimetic reaction. Roughly, then, I want to say that reiterative abstraction and ascent requires the transformation of mimetic response, however eventually theorized, into intuition. But intuition is only the systematic relegation of mimetic identification beneath conceptual identification. Hence, mimetic response was also for Adorno a primitive notion of nonpredicative identification. Mimetic response, such as a baby smiling in response to a mother's smile, is now thought of as a proto-cognition by developmental psychologists. Nonetheless, I have chosen to treat the mimetic moment in terms of reflective judgement.

to become remotely convincing, we should ask: what does Adorno mean by "nature" in all this? There is a formal and a substantive answer to this question. The formal answer should at this juncture be unproblematic. Recall that myth was defined by enlightenment as anthropomorphism: the projection of the human onto nature. Hence the project of enlightenment, demythologization, is the overcoming or elimination of anthropomorphic nature, the elimination of anything that might look like it is a part of nature solely because we have collectively placed it there, where this goal can be expressed positively in the thesis that no state of affairs is *objective*, is truly out there as a piece of the world, unless it can form part of an explanatory system composed of items possessing the widest possible cosmological role. The conclusion of this process is adequately expressed in Kant's domain of empirical reality: an ideally conceptually closed system of law-governed substances. For Adorno the incoherence of this idea of objectivity is that it denies that human nature is a part of nature, that seeing things in relation to our size and projects, perceiving things as colored, in our practices of eating, copulating, and reproducing our kind, even in being speaking animals, we are behaving *naturally* (we are hard-wired that way). To be sure, all of these doings are subject to cultural elaborations, to historical formation and transformation, in ways that outrun their natural condition of possibility. Nonetheless, perceiving middle-sized objects in the environment as bearers of significance (*as* living, hurt, damaged, needy) is not, or so Adorno wants to argue, a mere projection of the human onto nature, at least not a projection onto nature in the way in which perceiving a tree as inhabited by a god is. *Because*, in virtue of our embodiment, we are parts of nature, albeit intensely historicized parts, then the circumambient nature which is the proximate object of our doings is historical nature. And it is this historical nature – the nature whose appearing to us is conditioned by our belonging to it, whose parts necessarily lack the possibility of playing a wide cosmological role because they are, as parts of a living system, mutually dependent upon one another (at least locally, and perhaps globally), and are bound to our contingent and historically conditioned practices – whose constitutive role in thought and practice has been dominated or repressed to the point of cognitive disappearance. It is, precisely, anthropomorphic nature that is explained away in the progress of enlightened knowing and supervened upon in the rationalization of social practices.

The substantive answer to what is meant by nature could not be simpler except for the fact that its cognitive and rational status is both difficult and obscure: nature refers what is living as opposed to what lacks life. Adorno's epigraph to Part One of *Minima Moralia* is "Life does not live"; in *Dialectic of Enlightenment*, Adorno and Horkheimer flatly claim that the "disenchantment of the world is the extirpation of animism" (DoE, 5). I take these two claims to be convergent if not equivalent. Animism attributes life, a living soul, to even the nonliving, spiritualizing it thereby. Animism is gross anthropomorphism. The systematic and methodological terms that enabled enlightened thought to overcome animism, namely, the displacement of objects' sensuous particularity, necessarily "removed" life from living things as well since life belongs essentially to the *individual* organism; individuals live, die, decompose, return to the inorganic material world. Life cannot be an accidental property of an individual since were it to lose its life, it would no longer be "it." The mechanisms of abstraction, subsumption, and cognitive ascent necessarily discount from the individual the one feature that defines it as the organism it is, *its* life; its life is not a property had by an individual in the way in which its size or color is, it is the condition of it being an individual as opposed to stuff. Individuality and sensuous particularity are given their original sense through and made possible by the living organism. If the principle of immanence makes individuality a function of something that is not the individual – spatiotemporal location, a qualitatively unique concatenation of properties – then it will discount life. Any piece of natural stuff is the same as any other piece of natural stuff apart from spatiotemporal location and surrounding causal field; stuff lacks intrinsic individuality; individuality is essential to the living. Hence, everything that has been said thus far about how instrumental rationality and societal rationalization disenchant nature must now be read as saying how they assimilate the living to the nonliving, thereby not simply treating the living as if it were not living, but in so doing in some sense to be explained sapping from the living its life.

In *Dialectic of Enlightenment* the extirpation of animism thesis is elaborated in two stages: first in terms of the epistemology of animism itself, and then in terms of its epistemological antithesis. The speculative epistemology of animism has a direct bearing on moral issues. The idea of things having ends "for themselves" is the nonprojective core of animistic thought, and it is that idea which Horkheimer and Adorno are attempting to make prima facie plausible. Hence their tracking this idea back to earliest times: "The separation of the animate and the inanimate, the occupation of certain places by demons and deities, first arises from this preanimism, which contains the first lines of the separation of subject and object. When the tree is no longer approached merely as tree, but as evidence for an Other, as the location of mana, language expresses the contradiction that something is itself [a phenomenally appearing item] and at one and the same time something other than itself [the excess expressed as deity], identical and not identical" (DoE, 15).[4] Whatever the

4 In the accompanying footnote to this sentence Horkheimer and Adorno cite a passage from Hubert and Mauss's "General Theory of Magic" contending that just this experience of something as both identical and not identical (with what language calls it) is how

empirical status of this bit of speculative anthropology, the thought it contains is suggestive, namely, that coordinated with the subsumptive conception of the objectivity of the object (the one that matures into the thesis concerning items with a wide cosmological role) there is a more primitive one in which what makes something objective, other, an object out there in the world is its individuated intricacy and power in excess of its simple phenomenal appearing and thus in excess of its empirically grounded designation. In this, genealogical, sense the "object" as opposed to the subject is the nonidentical excess (the deity "in" the object) beyond what is captured in the ordinary concept of a thing. In this ideal history, in which animism itself is the metaphysical rationalization of an earlier wholly religious stage, it is "through the deity," the identification of mana, that "language is transformed from tautology," the mere repetition and tracking of the appearing world, to "language," the expression of an order beyond its mere appearance for or to a subject. Animism is the metaphysical doctrine that enables the linguistic doctrine to be held in place; animism is the ascription to individuals of an excess in virtue of which they become nonsubstitutable for one another.

Both the subsumptive and the animistic concern an objectivity beyond phenomenal appearings to the subject, but in the first case objectivity is associated with what is detachable from its immediate phenomenal appearance via sharable properties, while in the second case the excess beyond phenomenal appearing relates to what has *powers* of resistance to the subject and it own ends, possesses a "life" of its own (and thus, so to speak, turns away from the subject as its mode of appearing to the subject). This dual and contrasting conception of objectivity adds a level of complexity to the development of the concept: "The concept, which some would see as the sign-unity for whatever is comprised under it, has from the beginning been the product of dialectical thinking in which everything is always that which it is, only because it becomes that which it is not" (DoE, 15); for example, as "this" tree is objectified under the concept *tree*, making it essentially a tree, it loses its animistic otherness, an otherness that remains implied by the identification through which it is suppressed (DoE, 16). Whether there is an intelligible and plausible account of conceptuality that can track this complexity we shall investigate later.

The antithetical epistemological moment is expressed in these terms: "The *ratio* [viz., instrumental reason] that supplants mimesis is not simply its counterpart. It is itself mimesis: mimesis of what is dead. The subjective spirit which abolishes animation from nature, can master this

they interpret sympathy or mimesis: "*L'un est le tout, est dan l'un, la nature triomphe de la nature.*" The concept of mana, which is coordinated with experiences of surprise and fear ("terror as sacredness"), expresses "not a spiritual as opposed to a material substance, but the intricacy of nature in contrast to the individual" (DoE, 15).

inanimate nature only by imitating its rigidity, and abolishing its own animism in turn" (DoE, 57). The basic idea here is a continuation of what is involved in the discounting of affective states as required by reiterative cognitive ascent. Assume that as a consequence of ascent, we no longer respond to items in a manner which acknowledges their possessing powers distinct from those captured and codified in their empirical concept: all sense of their having a "life" of their own has been excised. Hence, the forms of cognition necessary in order to register and respond to life require mental capacities that themselves get excised, fall into disuse. Hence thinking is confined to "rigidly" formal activities. If the items with the widest cosmological role are those whose relations are fully lawlike and mechanical, then the thought processes apprehending them will themselves be increasingly formal and mechanical. More generally, means-ends reasoning, say, makes fewer calls on our capacities for affective response, imaginative identification, attentiveness to individual items. It is these processes which, it is being implied, are the "animism" of mental life. Hence, even in narrowly epistemic terms, that is, from the point of view of the subject doing the extirpating, the adaptation of the self to a lifeless world requires a discounting of the subject's own "inner life." It is presumed that this requirement is exacerbated to all but unbearable extremes in the transition from puritan self-ordering to inhabiting rationalized social forms.

Passages like these in Adorno point to a constellation of issues which talk of disenchantment, subsumptive reiterability, instrumentality, and the like passes over, namely, that no doubt incoherently but emphatically the distinction between living and nonliving structures and orients Adorno's theorizing. Adorno's scepticism about moral theory and modern moral reason does not derive from a desire to disparage the attempt to provide rules of reasoning that would tell us what counts as treating a person as a mere means, a dead thing, and what counts as treating them as an end in themselves, it is that insofar as we think that distinction is *constituted* by those second-order rules and reasons, then the very thing at issue, that it is a living being before us, is necessarily discounted – necessarily because in thinking in this way we are "abolishing our own animism in turn." The propriety of employing a concept like "animism" in this context is modest: a conception of what counts as treating something as a mere thing will, minimally, assume that mere things are not alive and hence do not possess any ends for themselves – even the minimal one of staying alive. Hence, the living/nonliving distinction is necessary to even begin making the kinds of discriminations necessary for ethical life. But to say this is equally to claim that the living/nonliving distinction is for Adorno not only antecedent to the distinction between consciousness and being, but that for adequate conceptions of knowledge, rationality, and normativity the living/nonliving distinction is the fundamental one.

More obviously, but following on from what has just been said, for Adorno in order for an individual to possess auratic individuality he or she must be apprehended as living. An object's aura is necessarily animistic.[5]

If paradigmatically the search for objectivity involves searching for items with a wide cosmological role, then objectivity is purchased at the price of eliminating from the repertoire of items that explain our affective states those which are irreducibly anthropocentric. Hence the search for items with the widest possible cosmological role involves a rational mimesis of what is dead. Because he believes that rationalized reason has become hegemonic for us, Adorno always approaches the question of living/nonliving indirectly, by means of circumspect reflection. Following Marx,[6] Adorno does believe that the rationalization of modern society – bureaucratisation, capital exchange, technology, and so on – tendentially deforms social practices so that they become increasingly nonresponsive to the living/nonliving distinction – it is precisely this that the account of the Hobbesian subject at home who misses the other's aura was picking out – but it is not that which makes his writing so disconcerting. It is rather his overly acute sense that any *direct attempt* to register the normative and rational weight of that distinction would necessarily fall short of what for now counts as a good reason; and that any indirect account of the distinction, like the very ones offered in *Dialectic of Enlightenment,* betray the phenomena.[7] From within the confines of rationalized reason, not only would it be true to say that the *emphatic* life of things eludes direct cognition but, in the same way in which it is true to say that anthropomorphic nature has all but disappeared, so Adorno believes that the supervening of instrumental reason on earlier structures of material inference in some sense actually petrifies the living. How this can be literally true emerges in Chapter 9. Because it is all but impossible for us to consider ourselves

5 I am here assuming that the auratic is partly constituted by something being a unique living being. I employ the term animism because I assume that for Adorno nonorganic things can have auratic qualities in virtue of their relation to "life."

6 For a still powerful account of the living/nonliving distinction in Marx, see Michel Henry, *Marx* (Paris: Gallimard, 1976). For a brief discussion of the relevant Marxian materials in Adorno, see Jarvis, *Adorno: A Critical Introduction,* pp. 67–71.

7 Adorno's circumspect procedure is pointed since an overly hasty and direct appropriation of the mana thesis could quickly collapse into the kind of philosophy of nature espoused by the young Schelling, who took the lessons of Kant's *Critique of Judgement* to include a positing of *living nature* as the condition of possibility for mechanistic science whose abstraction from the living Schelling construed in much the same way as do Horkheimer and Adorno. So, for example, Schelling states: "The completed Science does not rely on dead faculties, which have no reality and exist only in an artificial abstraction; it rather much more relies on the *living unity of the I,* one which remains the same in all the external manifestations of its activity." *Sämtliche Werke,* ed. By F. W. J. Schelling (Stuttgart: J. G. Cotta'scher, 1856–61), I: 238, quoted by Robert Pippin, "Avoiding German Idealism: Kant, Hegel, and the Reflective Judgement Problem," in his *Idealism as Modernism,* p. 135. As I suggest in Chapter 6, the best way of construing the core argument of *Negative Dialectic* is as a version of the reflective judgement problem.

as anything other than simply alive, our being alive unqualified, dealing with the issue directly would be all but impossible. Only reflectively and conceptually can the distinctions that matter be brought to bear.

At the conclusion of the discussion of the destruction of knowledge thesis in Chapter 2 I noted that despite being the most immediate and direct consequence of disenchantment, it is not a thesis that Horkheimer and Adorno discuss, and that at least for Adorno this is odd given his extensive cognitivist commitments. If I am right about the centrality of the living/nonliving distinction, and the penumbral but central role of auratic animism, then perhaps this lacuna is intelligible after all. Even if one is inclined toward moral realism,[8] there is nothing in its ancient or modern presentation that explicates how standard ethical predicates such as *cruel,* or *vicious,* or *agony* (not to speak of non-ethical ones like *delicate lips, flushed,* and *hungrily*) involve, invoke, or depend on cognitive experiences flatly incommensurable with, qualitatively unlike, seeing something as red or square or larger than the item next to it; and further, nothing that shows how the former set of concepts are, somehow, elaborations or determinations of the experience of perceiving living things.[9] Explicating the animistic content of such predicates has not played a noticeable role historically; on the contrary, the dominant tradition has manifested a calculated rush to distinguish us from the rest of living nature, above all our fellow animals. Hence the fact-values that moral knowing was taken to be of were construed as belonging almost wholly to the human/cultural side of the culture-nature distinction. In this respect, nothing within the tradition of moral realism, even if Adorno had been aware of it, looks as if it could provide direct support to the narrative of *Dialectic of Enlightenment.* As a consequence, he and Horkheimer leap over, or at least side-step, the fine-grained cases that moral realism hints at (perceiving and responding to X's *distress,* say) toward, on the one hand, a concept like *mana* which exorbitantly summarizes the perception of living nature and hence the complexity of the more ordinary empirical concepts just mentioned and, on the other hand, the differentiated cognitive mode in or through which the objects of such concepts are encountered: experience.

Adorno's philosophical project is to resurrect a legitimate anthropomorphism, an anthropomorphic nature that is somewhere between the

8 In "Moral Cognitivism, Relativism and Beliefs," *Proceedings of the Aristotelian Society,* 91 (1990/91): 62–5, David Wiggins argues that we should prefer the notion of moral cognitivism to moral realism since the latter is open to a wide variety of misunderstandings, above all being caught in the dispute over realism and anti-realism in semantics, not to speak of forms of metaphysical realism (Platonism) which moral realists are systematically opposing. The reminders are worth noting. Nonetheless, I have stayed with moral realism in order to appropriately sustain the difference between Adorno and Kant.

9 I am taking it that seeing someone *flushed* (from running, say, rather than from shame or with pride) is more intermediate and experientially bound, and therefore more recalcitrant, than, say, seeing something as an apple or a hippopotamus.

mythic extremes of myth, "which compounds the inanimate with the animate," and enlightenment, "which compounds the animate with the inanimate" (DoE, 16). Again, what is mythic is cognitively taking the new as the old, whether that oldness is cyclic nature or nature as a law-governed system. An anthropomorphic nature would be part of a wholly secularized and truly historical "enchanted" world.[10] Yet there is no direct way of mapping the terrain that lies between the extremes of myth and enlightenment. Adorno's gamble, the gamble animating his late works, is that the immanent critique and correction of the dualisms of idealism's concept of the concept, as the philosophical apotheosis of identity thinking, will bring anthropomorphic, living nature into view. Or, more austerely, *the immanent critique of the idealist concept is, epistemologically, the bringing of anthropomorphic, living nature into view.* For Adorno concept-intuition dualism, which itself supports the categorial distinctions between mind and body, consciousness and matter, the free and the determined, structurally dissolves the distinction between the living and the nonliving ("compounds the animate with the inanimate") which provides the orientation for ethical experience. That is the underlying premise of Adorno's late works.

All this complicates an already complicated argument since now the claims of ethical practice against moral centralism involve more than logical and conceptual issues. But then, they never were just that: if the problem of externalism cannot be made intelligible without explaining why particular rational regimes *feel* imposed, why resistance to externalism is an expression of hurt and damage, then there must be an explanation of how those practices can damage and be hurtful – why the language of damage and hurt is the bottom line for ethical thought. Conceptual problems and ruined lives rise and fall together. Damaged lives are the consequence of irrational practices. And while this has been assumed all along, to here the conception of damage has been the thin one of what does not conduce to a rationally coherent ethical life, where the latter has been for the most part defined in terms of practices that can sustain a convergence between cognitive and motivating reasons for action. This remains a good formal criterion for success. What Adorno's conception of the suppression of anthropomorphic nature does is to frame the abstraction from motivating reasons that defines externalism in a wider and more substantial setting. By adding in a conception of anthropomorphic nature, within and without, of some requirement that our *animal* nature essentially belongs to our "humanity" such that the failure to adequately give place to the for-

10 For the purposes to hand, an objected is suitably "enchanted" if *it* can make or lodge or have *claims* upon me that *demand* recognition, acknowledgement, granting, independently of and prior to my self-imposing those claims and demands; its claims and demands would arise because of how things were with the object, what had and was happening to it, and how I am related to those occurrences.

mer is destructive of the latter, at least the possibility of disenchantment as a form of damage, being something individuals *suffer*, something that might *pain* them is opened.[11] The pain of externalism, that external reasons are impositions and take effect from "without," cannot be understood in formal terms because what underpins those claims is the substantial if obscure issue of how reasoning practices relate to our animal nature. Only filling in something of the character of that animal nature can provide rational support for the critique of externalism.

Because no positive vision of anthropomorphic nature is to be had, then Adorno must provide the rudiments of an account that would weld together conceptual inadequacy with what is existentially self-defeating, where comprehension of the latter is for the most part found – in terms of marks, signs, exemplifications – through the spelling out of the former. As I understand his strategy, and as I intend to reconstruct it, this is best conceived through a two-step process. In the first, at a very high level of abstraction, Adorno provides a series of arguments that seek to directly align, interpret, the fundamental features of rationalized reason and its corollaries (constitutive subjectivity, the rational will, etc.) with the misbegotten and self-defeating attempt to eliminate anthropomorphic nature. In the second step, having thus exposed rationalized reason as fundamentally a self-defeating process of abstraction from anthropomorphic nature, he returns to the purely conceptual issue of concept-intuition dualism as a way of attacking that abstraction at its micrological core. Negatively, the project is to demonstrate how the rationalized concept indeed encapsulates a drive to independence from the natural world. Positively, the goal is to undo the series of dualisms that constitute concept-intuition dualism: in order to dismantle the duality between a normative concept and its material content, it must be shown how that content is already normative or rulish in itself; in order to undo the distinction between universal and particular it is necessary to show how particularity can be identified other than being classified; in order to dissolve the distinction between spontaneity and passivity it must be shown that the conceptual is not merely what imposes order from without, that what is imposed on us can itself be conceptual (freedom and reason/meaning are not equivalents). Undoing those dualisms in the appropriate manner anticipates a form of cognition appropriate to the sensuous particularity of objects belonging to an anthropomorphic natural world. Only the negative argument is to be pursued in this chapter; the positive argument belongs

11 Because modern moral thought for the most part eschews animal nature as the fundament of meaningfulness, it must eschew the roles of pain, suffering, damage, and injury as pivots for moral thought and replace them by some broader notion of moral wrongness. Since the separation of consciousness from animal embodiment goes back to the earliest form of philosophical thinking, it is not surprising that suffering should play such a marginal role.

to Chapter 6. The two steps of the argument – the genealogy of rationalized reason and autonomous subjectivity in the suppression of anthropomorphic nature, and the two-sided (negative and positive) analysis of concept-intuition dualism – can be aligned and seen as parallel to one another, but no further synthesis of them is possible. The impossibility of directly connecting the two aspects of the argument – which is just the logical shadow of the unavailability in practice of anthropomorphic nature – is the source of why it has appeared so unsatisfactory over the years.[12]

In the next section I outline how the notion of abstraction that is the pivot of the principle of immanence can be fitted, via a conceptual employment of Hegel's dialectic of independence and dependence, to demonstrate how the growth of reason is equally an existentially self-defeating detachment of the human from nature. In section 3 I show how Kant's argument for our taking ourselves to be ends in ourselves exactly recapitulates the self-defeating claim for independence. After that brief excursion, I turn to Adorno's own account of the logic of self-defeat implied in Kant's idea of constitutive subjectivity. Jointly those analyses mean to show how the notions of self-determining rationality and constitutive subjectivity in their claims to independence from the natural world become all the more dependent on and entrapped within it. Section 5 then has the mild task, in preparation of what is to follow, of exploring how the ideal of independence is inscribed in the Kantian concept: what are the logical features of the concept that generate the dualities between concept and content, universal and particular, spontaneity and passivity? I complete the chapter with a first essay at an ethics of dependence.

2. From Instinctual Renunciation to Abstraction

Horkheimer and Adorno's first go at demonstrating the existentially self-defeating character of enlightenment follows in the footsteps of Nietzsche, Weber, and Freud: civilization is the path of instinctual renunciation, and it is only through instinctual renunciation that reason and subjectivity can emerge. While this story is reasonably consistent, it falls far short of what Adorno requires. Nonetheless, since some of its conceptual figures have already appeared, above all the suggestion that renunciation is a continuation of the logic of sacrifice in which the pattern of sacrificing present happiness to ideal future happiness is transformed

12 A good deal of the theoretical and rhetorical energy of *Dialectic of Enlightenment* derives from Horkheimer and Adorno's belief there that the two stages of the argument could be immediately aligned. In *Negative Dialectics* and *Aesthetic Theory* Adorno pursues only the second stage of the argument, and retrospectively interprets *Dialectic of Enlightenment* as concerned primarily with its first step.

into the sacrifice of the particular to the universal, it is worth citing its core formulation at length.

> In class history, the enmity of the self to sacrifice involved self-sacrifice because the price of this enmity was the denial of nature in men and women for the sake of domination over extra-human nature and over other men and women. Precisely this denial, the quintessence of all civilizing rationality, is the germ cell of the proliferating mythical irrationality: with the denial of nature in men and women, not only the *telos* of the external domination of nature, but the *telos* of men's and women's lives becomes opaque and confused. In the instant in which men and women sever the consciousness of themselves as nature, all of the aims for which they struggle to preserve themselves, social progress, the intensification of material and intellectual forces, indeed consciousness itself, are vitiated. . . . The domination of the [animal] self, on which the [intelligible] self is based, is inevitably the destruction of the subject in whose service it is undertaken because the substance that is dominated, repressed, and dissolved by self-preservation is nothing other than that very life by which the efforts of self-preservation are exclusively defined; that very life that is to be preserved. . . . The history of civilization is the history of the introversion of sacrifice. In other words, it is the history of renunciation. He who renounces gives up more of his life than is given back to him, and more than the life that he defends. (DoE, 54–5)[13]

In one respect, this passage wildly misrepresents what Adorno and Horkheimer think. According to the logic of the passage, it sounds as though they are claiming that if we could stop renouncing nature within and without, stop repressing inner nature and stop dominating external nature, then we could realize what we have lost. Civilization, they appear to be saying, is a system of surplus repression, repression beyond what is required for the ends for which renunciation was undertaken. Alas, all these are vacuous claims since who we are and how we understand and comport ourselves in the world are formed through this process of renunciation and domination: instinctual renunciation is equally the processes of socialization and individualization, individualization through socialization; which, indeed, is a crucial component of Horkheimer and Adorno's argument. There is no pristine inner nature awaiting release from repression. Suddenly not acting on the moral law or the socially formed superego will not directly enable some repressed or unknown self to emerge.

The fundamental conceptual error of the simple instinctual renunciation story is that, despite itself, it assumes a fundamental separation between nature and culture, as if inner nature was a qualitatively and quan-

13 I am here following the translation of this chapter by Robert Hullot-Kentor which appeared in *New German Critique* 56 (Spring/Summer, 1992): 119.

titatively given about which it would make sense to say renouncing "this" much of it is necessary for the activities of reason while repressing "that" is not so necessary. This is not to argue against the idea of renunciation and repression, or, conversely, in favor of the thought that because cultural formation does, in a way, go all the way down, then all we can talk about are different cultural practices.[14] One broad reason for urging an association between asceticism (Puritanism) with its explicit, self-defeating attempts at abstraction from embodiment[15] with the refinements of idealism and rationalized reason is to enable us to perceive the lineaments of the former in the latter; and hence perceive that in their most extreme manifestations, rationalized regimes of practice are self-defeating in a manner analogous to the way in which the identification of one's true self with a disembodied God is self-defeating. Extreme cases tell a story, but not one which can easily be shown to be coextensive with our own.

The analysis of this process through the image of instinctual renunciation examines it, naively, from the perspective of the ascetic. If reason is also a part of nature, and its power nature's, as Adorno argues, and further, if individualization is a process belonging to natural history, then the elements of the story cannot be approached as if coming from different realms. It is the coming from different realms thesis that, ironically, makes the cognition of nature imponderable. What, thus, makes this account idle is that nothing within it helps explicate what would *count* as not denying nature within ourselves, or what would count as not trying to dominate extra-human nature (showing that embodiment must be acknowledged is no help in explaining how). Hence, while this narrative enables us to understand how the anthropogenesis of subjectivity might be self-defeating, and hence how adopting a wholly instrumental stance toward inner and outer nature strategically misfires (it is instrumentally irrational), apart from the logic of sacrifice, its terms are too remote from the conceptual materials of which they are meant to be the anthropological version.

In Chapter 2 I suggested that the dialectic of myth and enlightenment was best conceived on analogy with the dialectic of master and slave: enlightened rationality claims to be radically independent, disavowing its dependence on the mythic materials whose negation provides it with its claim to superior rationality.[16] Since we now know that some of those

14 This latter, understandable, mistake is the one Michael Foucault commits in *The History of Sexuality*, trans. Robert Hurley (New York: Pantheon Books, 1978), part 2.

15 For a powerful interpretation of Hegel's critique of asceticism that focuses on this issue, see Judith Butler, *The Psychic Life of Power: Theories in Subjection* (Stanford: Stanford University Press, 1997), chapter 1.

16 For a quick presentation of the thesis that it is the dialectic of master and slave that governs Adorno's treatment of the dialectic of concept and object, see Willem van Reijen,

mythic materials are, in the first instance, anthropomorphic materials (their representational equivalents), legitimate and illegitimate, then in denying, excising, and subsuming those representational materials we would have been excising our own anthropomorphic nature, our animal nature, we would have been denying ourselves. What those mythic materials were and represented, as well as the cognitive processes involved in apprehending them, explains why rationally removing them is existentially self-defeating. However, what that process of denial amounts to just is the processes of abstraction and reiterative subsumption through which rationalized reason and disenchanted nature are formed. *Abstraction* is the fundamental operation making the employment of the principle of immanence possible since it provides the necessary condition for subsumption (equalizing the different) and reiterative ascent.[17] Rationalization proceeds through abstraction; hence, abstraction *becomes* the nonrecognition of dependence as its results are systematized and reified into the rule of reason, the priority of the general over the particular, the claim that subjectivity, as given through the spontaneity of the intellect, is *constitutive* of the meaning of nature within and without.

Adorno's fundamental strategy is to appropriate Hegel's analysis of the dialectic of master and slave, independence and dependence, by turning it back into logic of concept and object. Concept depends on object. The initial anti-idealist premise of this transposition is that so-called intersubjective practices are forms of interacting between beings that are, also and ineliminably, *objects* of a certain kind. Recognition is always, at least, the recognition of another bodily being. Whatever else is involved in recognizing another, the minimum of recognizing is *perceptual* and *sensible*. If the concepts employed in giving recognition necessarily pass over this perceptual and judgmental beginning, or acknowledge it only in terms of the application of what is already conceived of as moral or rational in itself, as I have claimed Kantian moral reason does, then what is recognized will be misrecognized at the same time. Rationalized reason is systematic misrecognition.

All that is assumed by this is that conceptual strategies are the strategies of persons, hence in Hegelian terms, social practices. Conversely, however, the stances available to persons are determined by the concep-

Adorno: An Introduction, trans. Dieter Engelbrecht (Philadelphia: Pennbridge Books, 1992), pp. 36–40.

17 Once this mechanism is in place, then it becomes possible to redescribe the economic model of instinctual repression accordingly since, with respect to nature within, subsumption and ascent describe the path of unification whereby the strong, unified ego can emerge. When it comes to the self, abstraction presupposes repression as opposed to the case of nature without where repression, that is, control, presupposes abstraction. Here, more than anywhere else in the argument, is the presumption that the unity of the concept and the unity of the self are the same necessary for its intelligibility. This becomes perspicuous in section 4.

tual regimes available to them. For Adorno, the image of Hegelian mastery is the stance or strategy internal to the meaning of rationalized reason, hence the stance implied by the employment of that reason whoever uses it. As we see below, any rushed attempt to bypass the moment of perceiving and judging in favor of social practice will a fortiori displace the role and significance of embodiment even if the moment of perceiving and judging is a socially mediated practice. Hence, Hegel was wrong to believe, as he is widely interpreted as believing, that the logic of concept and object could be sublimed into a logic of recognition and misrecognition where the latter is conceived of, finally, in terms of wholly self-determined social practices among essentially self-conscious agents.

Adorno's second assumption is that the vehicle of enlightenment misrecognition is abstraction. Nothing is wrong in abstraction itself; it is a necessary feature of any conceptual practice. However, when the results of abstraction are systematically detached from what they have been abstracted from, and thereby, what is the same thing, reified as independent, then the forms of knowing and reasoning that result are themselves a mastering of the object, approaching the object as nothing other than what the concept *determines* it to be, hence as *merely* a token or case or example of what is already known. What I termed the "platitudes" of the principle of immanence incline reasoning activity to this reification of abstraction.

Finally, however, what separates this lament over abstraction from the nominalist critique of universals with which it is in league, is that both the activity of abstraction and what is abstracted from are, indeterminately, rooted in or parts of anthropomorphic nature. With this thought Adorno returns the dynamic of independence and dependence to Hegel's early formulation of it as a logic of "life." Here is how Hegel originally formulated his doctrine of independence and dependence:

> In the hostile power of fate, universal is not severed from particular in the way in which the law, as universal, is opposed to man or his inclinations as the particular. Fate is just the enemy, and man stands over against it as a power fighting against it. Only through a departure from that united life which is neither regulated by law nor at variance with law, only through the killing of life, is something alien produced. Destruction of life is not the nullification of life but its diremption, and the destruction consists in its transformation into an enemy.[18]

In this confused account, Hegel opposes the logic of universal and particular, against which he is bringing the same accusation as Adorno does, to a logic of life where, roughly, the notion of life is being used to figure

18 "The Spirit of Christianity and Its Fate," in *On Christianity: Early Theological Writings*, trans. T. M. Knox (New York: Harper and Row, 1961), p. 105.

human communities as organic communities, literally and metaphorically, of a certain kind. Hence, in acting against the other (suppressing her) I act against myself, removing myself from the organic totality of which I am a part and which gives me my life. Hence what I as criminal suffer is nothing other than "the reactive force of a life that has been suppressed and separated off."[19]

There is no need to oppose a logic of conceptuality to a logic of life, once life is interpreted as anthropomorphic nature, and the issue of universal and particular concerns not them as such but a particular regime of concept and object, namely, one in which the concept is taken to be and operates in accordance with the notion that it is independent and self-determining. Once these substitutions are made, then the logic of life and the logic of independence and dependence can be thought together: instrumental reasoning, as the rational expression and means securing the desire for self-preservation, misrecognizes itself when its reifies the process of abstraction through which it proceeds, when it comes, finally, to think of itself as reason as such. In so doing it separates itself from anthropomorphic nature, conceiving itself as independent and separate, and nature as its alien other – an other whose shape, as a system of objects governed by mechanical laws, shares nothing with it. Finally, what it suffers in terms of fate, now the debilitating consequences of rationalized modernity, our iron cage, is still the "reactive force of a life that has been suppressed and separated off." Broadly speaking, this is Adorno's narrative.

His explanation of how it occurred that men and women severed consciousness of themselves as parts of nature thus ultimately follows the path of rationalization, that is, the path through which cultural formations come to assert their independence from their immersion in the natural world.[20] The utter denial of dependence, however anticipated in Judeo-Christian soul doctrine, is a *late* corollary of culture's necessary assertion of its relative independence from nature that is precipitated by the emergence of modern enlightenment thought.[21] And while it will re-

19 Jürgen Habermas, *The Philosophical Discourse of Modernity*, trans. Frederick Lawrence (Cambridge: Polity Press, 1987), p. 28. For my critique of Habermas's handling of Hegel's causality of fate doctrine, see my *Recovering Ethical Life*, pp. 82–7, 176–91.

20 Instinctual renunciation is thus to be comprehended *through* cultural formation, that is, through the practices a culture develops to explicate its independence from but relation to the natural environment (without and within) as its limiting condition and horizon. Horkheimer and Adorno's reading of the *Odyssey*, above all the Sirens episode (DoE, 32–4, 58–9), remains powerful because it aligns instinctual renunciation with the abstractive processes of cultural formation and self-assertion.

21 Although Adorno does not explicitly say so, I am assuming that traditional religious and related practices were not flat denials of dependence on nature, but complicated ways of acknowledging and disavowing that dependence at the same time – a thesis requiring a work far larger than this to spell out. I think this thesis is implied by Horkheimer and Adorno's statement that "the Enlightenment of modern times advanced from the

main the case that what counts as acknowledging anthropomorphic nature, within and without, can be approached only via what is required to heal the divisions in the idealistic concept of the concept, so long as enlightenment is accepted as demythologization, where myth is identified with anthropomorphism, then a conceptual and normative logic of independence and dependence should be able to bind together logical and existential stratums of meaning. A snapshot of this process can be seen in Kant's argument for our considering ourselves ends.

3. Abstraction and Ends in Themselves

> Now as the original way of producing physical entities is by creation, so the way in which moral entities are produced can scarcely be better expressed than by the word *imposition*. For they do not arise out of the intrinsic nature of physical properties of things, but they are superadded, at the will of intelligent entities, to things already existent and physically complete, and to their natural effects, and, indeed, come into existence only by the determination of their authors.
>
> Samuel Pufendorf

Even moralists suspicious of Kant's universalization procedure find attractive the formula to "act in such a way that you always treat humanity . . . never simply as a means, but always at the same time as an end" (G, 428). Yet the argumentation for this principle, the argument designed to show that we are ends in ourselves, is built on precisely the mechanisms of abstraction, object independence, and dematerialization that are central to the formation of the reified, abstract concept and rationalized reason; the end result of the argument is a rationalized version of the impositional theory of value so eloquently stated by Pufendorf. I construe the impositional theory of value to be the singular manifestation of the third element of the concept-intuition dualism, spontaneity and passivity. It is then not Kant's doctrine I am concerned with here, but the structure of his argument for it; it is difficult not to read the structure of Kant's argument as an allegory of the coming to be of a disenchanted world since it is the world that is abstracted from in the course of the argument, generating, on the one side, a wholly denaturalized rational subject and, on the other, a wholly valueless, empirically real object-world; or, better, the path of argument is for the sake of generating that duality which would then support the impositional theory. Although, I suggest below,

very beginnings under the banner of radicalism; this distinguishes it from any of the earlier stages of demythologization" (DoE, 92). Needless to say, the utter denial of dependence occurs at the very moment in which it becomes equally plausible to state that we are nothing but members of a disenchanted natural world. If Hobbes, apparently, surrenders everything, he does so with perverse consistency and integrity; which is exactly what Adorno and Horkheimer appreciate in him.

the impositional theory is as much presupposed as argued for. Needless to say, from the outset, the subject of reflection is conceived monadologically, as solitary; the questions raised are raised about its choosings. So from the outset the subject is the agent and chooser, and no other subjects enter the picture until the argument is complete; above all, neither animals or other persons are ever *seen* in the unfolding of this argument, so whatever resistance they might offer to the abstractions performed is nullified from the beginning.

The core of the argument for the formula of humanity is a regressive one from conditioned to unconditioned, where the conditional goodness of objects, desires, and maxims are *all* without goodness in their own right, and come to receive their worth only from the value-conferring power of rational choice; that value-conferring power is our "humanity," and hence what makes us ends-in-ourselves.[22] Regressing from conditioned to unconditioned is, however, a movement of abstraction. So Kant begins: "All objects of inclinations have only a conditional worth, for if the inclinations and the needs founded on them did not exist, their object would be without worth." Objects' properties are without value in themselves since without our desiring or needing, our presence, the ascription of value to them would be pointless, idle. The plausibility of this thesis depends on a stark contrast: the world as it would appear without humans, and the world as it appears in the light of our presence. Only thus can the inference be made that things are good because I desire them rather than I desire them because they are good. While both inferences are faulty, as we see below, in making his Kant has already abstracted the human subject from the natural world, and through that abstraction disenchanted the world itself, as if there were not other animals with needs and inclinations, or, indeed, a functional interdependence of living nature. To state the point another way, objects are here already being considered wholly as means to the satisfying of our natural ends, hence our desiring and needing has already become the perspective or point of view from which nature is regarded. The very idea of things as having "relative worth" is a work of relativizing them to us and our needs; and this relativization can proceed only through the contrast between the world as it would be in itself and the world as it appears in the light of human desiring and needs.

Kant's second step is equally radical: "Inclinations themselves, as sources of needs, are so far from having an absolute value to make them desirable for their own sake that it must be the universal wish of every ra-

22 My account closely tracks the reconstruction of Kant's argument offered by Christine Korsgaard, "Kant's Formula of Humanity," *Kant-Studien* 77 (1986): 183–202, and in her *Creating the Kingdom of Ends* (Cambridge: Cambridge University Press, 1996), pp. 106–32. All quotes in this section are from G, 428 unless otherwise noted.

tional being to free himself completely from them." From which it follows that objects produced to satisfy inclinations are also of conditioned and only relative value. Kant's abstractive hyperbole leads him from a plausible thesis, there are some needs we would rather be without (say, my desire to smoke) or ones that are bad, to the ascetic and world-hating "universal wish" to be completely free from them all. Kant does not really believe in this universal wish since he regards our desire for happiness, sensual satisfaction, to be legitimate in itself and, finally, a necessary end belonging within the formulation of the "highest good" as the ultimate object of moral striving. Kant nonetheless here needs to empty inclinations and desires of intrinsic worth if the demonstration of their utter conditionedness is to succeed.

Such an emptying is impossible to accept. Our judgement of the sadness of the eunuch depends not on the thesis that having certain appetites, it is permissible to satisfy them under certain conditions; but, rather, it is of value to have those appetites, and having them to indulge them.[23] Appetite here forms the ground of the rational valuation; those lacking the appetite are barred from rational reflection not from the lack of the power of choice but from an absence of nature. To be without sexual appetite, to never know the longing or the pleasure of satisfaction, is to be without something we have come to value on the ground of possessing the appetite in the first instance. Even if natural appetite requires to be valued, as an act of spontaneity, the ground of the valuing is not confined to spontaneity but necessarily depends on what was never chosen or willed.

This assignment of dependency can work its way back to objects themselves: if the appetite for apples in part grounds the choice of eating them, then equally the apples' sweetness, firmness, juiciness and nutritiousness are elements grounding the goodness of the desire. Consider a possible dystopic world in which everything we needed tasted foul and poisonous, and everything we desired and delighted in was poisonous. Suddenly there appears an apple. Despite the fact that individuals' desires and inclinations have not changed in the interim, there now exists the possibility of a worthwhile activity that was not there previously, namely, finding pleasure in the same activity that provides sustenance. Does the apple have value only through those desires and inclinations; do they confer value on the apple, make it good? Or does the apple, its unique configuration of properties, generate the valued activity? The dystopic world makes the first hypothesis invalid, while the consideration of an array of properties without that array being for any being makes the second idle. Thus both "good because desired" and "desired because

23 Gary Watson, "Freedom of the Will," in Gary Watson (ed.), *Free Will* (Oxford: Oxford University Press, 1982), p. 103.

good" appear to lack unproblematic validity. No intentional set (desires and inclinations) can constitute the value of an object independently of the conditioning material properties which are the support grounding the array of properties being properties of a material object. Identity thinking, the value conferring power of reasons, depends on and lives off the nonidentical object which its activities of value-conferment recognize and misrecognize.

What can be said about the case of the apple can be extended. What Kant apparently wants to claim is that "to set an end is to attribute objective goodness to it and that we can regard this good as originating only in the fact that we have those ends according to reason."[24] Hence, it will follow that "an action is *good as a means* if it is represented by reason (in a hypothetical imperative) as necessary for the attainment of an (actual or possible) end."[25] For the case apple, this just looks false: my action of eating the apple is not good because it can be represented as a necessary means for attaining the end of nutrition since my action would be objectively good for that end even if it were never so represented (all my apple eating is done for pleasure). The objective goodness of the action can occur behind my representational back; but this is so because the goodness of the action is objective in a way in which the value-conferment thesis misidentifies. Where reason might be thought to enter is in regulating, aligning, and ordering my needs and actions with things antecedently found good or valuable. Hence, in the conceptual space that I have planted with sexual desire (as a stand-in for having natural needs and desires generally), on the one hand, and the array of properties apples possess (representing the worldly contribution to my ends) on the other, one could substitute a quite indefinite variety of items. As Robert Pippin states the thought: "But while 'value' might be 'conferred' as a result of some deliberation that involves reasoning, in finite, sensibly affected situations, it surely cannot be wholly set by appeal to reason alone, but must be responsive in various ways to on-going commitments, traditions one has inherited and carries on almost habitually, desires and lacks already in play."[26] The goodness of my commitments and my willingness

24 Allen W. Wood, *Kant's Ethical Thought* (Cambridge: Cambridge University Press, 1999), p. 129.

25 Ibid., p. 127.

26 Robert B. Pippin, "Kant as Value Theorist," p. 19; forthcoming in *Inquiry*. This is a critical review of Wood's book. In criticizing Wood, Pippin is in part criticizing the interpretation of Kant as value theorist (as having his position grounded in an antecedent commitment to others as ends in themselves), and, as here, the moral theory implied by that interpretation. While I agree with both limbs, I equally think that Kant believed that the value-conferment thesis itself is at one with the rationalism of the first two formulations of the Categorical Imperative. Which is to say the value-conferment thesis is not itself directly tied to non-deontological readings of Kant. There are of course weaker versions of Kantian deontology: reason as placing negative constraints on permissible

to hold to them come what may – Pippin instances commitment to the welfare of one's children – cannot plausibly be thought as deriving either their objectivity or force from how attached I am to my worth as a rational end-setter. On the contrary, it is their antecedent worth that governs, brings into play and makes significant, whatever stretches of reasoning are involved in determining what to do with respect to them. So, again, it appears appropriate to say that my reasoning lives off its objects rather than being the "source" of their worth.

Blocking Kant's regress in this manner blocks his question: what is of unconditioned worth, good in itself, good not because of anything else, and hence the ultimate *source* of value?[27] That question is not obviously a good one. On the contrary, in relativizing the world to our needs and desires in his first step, Kant has already framed the problem in terms of items that are good as means versus those that are good in themselves; and while that is not a wrong question in itself, it is unclear why it should be the question of value. Why should it not be the case that there are many and incommensurable sources of value – how the world is, our power of choice, the contingent development of certain practices, commitments, desires, and so on? Why cannot a negative test of sufficiency be enough; namely, "the fact that something is pleasant or desired or intrinsically good is a sufficient reason for as long as there is no extrinsic reason why not"?[28] The fact that a conditional good in the sense of there being no extrinsic reasons not to pursue it is not, by that fact, absolutely or unconditionally good, does not vitiate the negative stance. (Which is why Kant's argument needs the "universal wish" of being rid of desires completely: desires we do not wish to have and desires found not worth having can both be overridden by extrinsic reasons.) Further reasons are required to get the question of unconditioned goodness going; and those further reasons need to be stronger and/or differently posed than the question of extrinsic reasons since extrinsic reasons of the sort that can show that having a particular desire is not good in all respects or in all times and places prima facie can carry all the burden that that Kant wants to assign to reason. Things can be intrinsically good without being unconditionally good, and the conditioning of intrinsically good items does not obviously require unconditional goodness for the possibility of rational criticism. What would set all these assumptions into motion is the Hobbesian disenchantment of intrinsic goodness, relativizing it to what I find good, pleasurable, or desirable. So, again, behind the back of the

courses of action. My argument in the previous chapter implied that the actual employment of the procedures for maxim testing accomplished no more than constraint. But that does not aid Kant's cause.

27 For a defense of the question and Kant's answer to it, see Christine Korsgaard, "Aristotle and Kant on the Source of Value," in her *Creating the Kingdom of Ends,* pp. 225–48.

28 Ibid., p. 227.

Kantian analysis there is an anterior sceptical disenchantment of nature and value which makes even desire satisfaction normatively vacuous. It is that vacuum that Kant is simultaneously argumentatively reproducing and overcoming. For present purposes we can put these genealogical claims aside.

It is on the basis of the double abstraction from object and inclination/need that Kant performs his separation of those items whose existence does not depend on our will, which, having now only relative worth, are means and "therefore called 'things'" from those rational beings who are designated "persons" because "their nature indicates that they are ends in themselves." Note that the very designation of something as a "thing" is *derived* from its status of being a mere means, which is another way in which the perspective of subjective use constitutes the meaning of "things." For Kant the very idea of things that are mere means and persons who are ends in themselves derives from abstraction. But this is equivalent to saying that the a priori distinction between persons and things, hence even between moral reason and instrumental reasoning, is a consequence of that double abstraction.[29] Kant's abstractive gesture, his disingenuous regress from conditioned to unconditioned, itself will turn into the categorial and so transcendental distinction between mere things and persons opening the door to the instrumental disregard for things that his project was in part designed to block.[30] What is worse, persons are not here living beings, animals, with rational capacities; the abstraction from inclination and desire has already revealed them to be on a par with their objects – of only relative worth. Our humanity is to be contrasted with our animality; humanity's distinguishing feature is the "power to set ends." Hence, it is not the case that for Kant living persons are ends, but "humanity in persons is an end."[31] Persons' suffering, their living and dying, has shifted from intrinsic goods and evils that might be

29 One cannot have a distinct or isolatable domain of instrumental reasoning unless it is contrasted with something. But if there is no such thing as distinctly moral reasoning, a moral as opposed to an instrumental regard for things, then arguably the instrumental would disappear too. If the idea of instrumental reasoning is parasitic on the point of view that transforms things into means, their being means just the perspective of a misbegotten rationalization of reason, then the conception of instrumental reasoning as such belongs to an irrational conception of reason. This is not to deny that means-ends considerations are components of practical reasoning, only that practical reason does not necessarily possess any such autonomous aspect. I am minded to say here what Adorno says about the distinction between nature and history, that it is true and false: it is true historically that the instrumental and the moral have separated out, but false when reflectively hypostatized as an intrinsic ingredient of practical reasoning.

30 Further, as we have already commented upon, our (Kant's) distinction between means and ends is, arguably, a social and historical distinction. The twist of treating others as never mere means cannot be easily abstracted from the sense in which in capital production they are means, their labor power a commodity to be purchased.

31 Thomas E. Hill, Jr., "Humanity as an End in Itself," in his *Dignity and Practical Reason in Kant's Moral Theory* (Ithaca: Cornell University Press, 1992), pp. 39–40.

conditioned to things of merely relative worth, really of no worth but the value placed upon them by rational choosing.

In accordance with the interpretive hypothesis offered in Chapter 3, we can comprehend Kant's desperate gesture, his desperate humanism here as one demanded of him: if instrumental reason had already disenchanted the world by supervening on the material inferences grounding everyday ethical practices, thus demanding each individual to take up the perspective of acting on the basis of their disenchanted desires for happiness, then only a logic capable of supervening on this universal egoism could save the worth of such beings. Because, instrumentalism had already, so to speak, claimed proprietary rights over desires and happiness, their ethical claim, the normative claims of embodiment, had to be logically forsaken. Prudential goods, even the happiness of a life, had *become* nonmoral goods, natural goods. Hence the strategic elimination of the desire for happiness, and the forcing of the question of an unconditioned value. And equally, thus, the tensions in Kant's account of happiness: while even universal happiness is not competent to serve as a law of the will (CPrR, 36), nonetheless virtue is "a worthiness to be happy" (CPrR, 110).

For all that, Kant's defence recapitulates and provides an allegory of the dialectic of enlightenment. The isolation of "humanity" is the independence that is achieved through the regress of conditions. But the regress of conditions is in reality a work of abstraction of the concept from its objects and mediums until all that remains is the power of rational choice itself, called "humanity." Humanity is then set against a world that is disenchanted through the very processes of formation (and deformation) which have given humanity its abstract independence. Only then can the strong impositional thesis in which reflective evaluation is legislative and constitutive of value become operative: " . . . rational choice itself *makes* its object good," thus giving rational choice "a value-conferring status."[32] What then makes us ends in ourselves is that we are value-conferring, we bestow value on things, give it to them, even though they have become mere things, mere means, only through the detachment of humanity from them.

The idea of value-conferment, the power of setting ends, is a figure of mastery. The source of this power, what makes rational choice into this power, is the abstraction of value from the world, an abstraction that is both the purification of reason and the concept, and the simultaneous disenchanting of the object. However, even if Kant's double abstraction from world and body are not well founded, even if there is no overriding reason why there must be a single, positive criterion for sufficiency and hence a single source of value, even if the isolation of our humanity from

32 Korsgaard, "Kant's Formula of Humanity," p. 122.

our embodiment is deeply implausible, and finally even if there is a dependency on body and world that is inappropriately and inadequately acknowledged (as the material support for choosing and providing the "matter" for legislative activity), it does not follow that all this is intrinsically self-defeating. For that another angle of argument is necessary.

4. Independence: The Constitutive Subject

The effectiveness of moral reason turns on its reasoning, the practice of universalization, coming to constitute the worth of maxims of actions. Presupposed by this reflective procedure is the identification of the self with its capacity for rational deliberation; that capacity represents for Kant our "humanity." There is thus an equivalence between the supervening logic of moral reason and the idea that transcendental or rational subjectivity is constitutive. Adorno construes rationalized reason and constitutive subjectivity as equivalent expressions. This does no more than take idealism at its word since it is an operative premise of Kant's idealism that the unity of the concept is the same as the unity of the "I"; this is why the "I think" that must accompany all our representations has no independent existence beyond being the unity of conceptual consciousness. Hence the growth of conceptual consciousness, the rationalization of reason, must simultaneously provide for the increasing unification of the self, its individuation, to the point at which as conceptual unity becomes self-determining, and thereby determinative for what falls under it, the self becomes a vehicle of conceptual unity reflectively in a way that is analogous to it becoming the simple bearer of rationalized social forms. Hence, the central semantic thesis of idealism, that the unity of the concept and the unity of the "I" are the same, is for Adorno both the pivot of the account of the genesis of the self, and the key to unlocking the abstractive and dominating character of rationalized social forms. For Adorno it is the idealist semantic thesis that best explains the inner unity of idealism and rationalized modernity, and equally explains why, finally, only transforming idealism's construction of conceptual unity can provide emancipation for the self.[33] Hence, tracking the self-defeating char-

33 I owe the label "the semantic thesis of idealism" to Robert Brandom, "Some Pragmatist Themes in Hegel's Idealism: Negotiation and Administration in Hegel's Account of the Structure and Content of Conceptual Norms," *European Journal of Philosophy* 7/2 (Aug. 1999): 164. Brandom's intention, of course, is to defend the thesis. One short way of coming to see how this idea works in Brandom would be to track, even in just this essay, how what he calls the "pragmatist semantic thesis," the thesis that the use of concepts determines their content, becomes unhinged by the semantic thesis when the latter is interpreted wholly in terms of commitments and entitlements of inferences established through intersubjective negotiation. What thus drops out of the notion of *use* is its connection to complex *practices* that possess both material and nonmaterial aspects.

acter of autonomous subjectivity is diagnostic for what must become an immanent critique of the rationalized concept.

Although both the supervenience of instrumental reason (in its narrow and wide senses) and constitutive subjectivity are figures of mastery, of claimed independence and disavowed dependence, in the first instance Adorno pursues the claim for independence through the idea of constitutive subjectivity. His argumentative strategy involves making two claims: first, that what is thought of as objective reason or rationality, precisely because it is constitutive, meaning- and worth-bestowing, is in truth subjective, a construction of experience from the perspective of the needs of the human subject; but, second, because the construction occurs at the behest of the needs of the subject as a rational outgrowth from the drive for self-preservation, then what takes itself to be "humanity" is in fact all the more just a bit of nature, more of a thing or object than what it emerged from through rationalization, hence more heteronomously controlled and constituted. The master, constitutive subjectivity, is mastered by what it seeks to master.

Because Adorno embeds these two claims in a wider strategy, it is easiest to begin with the wider strategy. Adorno's anthropomorphism thesis is at one with contemporary naturalism in one fundamental respect, namely, in seeking to remind idealism that human conceptuality is part of the natural world: "In truth, all concepts, even philosophical ones, refer to nonconceptualities, because [concepts] on their part are moments of the reality that compels their formation, primarily for the purpose of controlling nature" (ND, 11). It is the natural desire for control over nature that leads conceptuality to offer primacy to generality over particularity. Abstraction from qualitative differences that would correspond to bound affective states has been the method of the concept whereby this increase in the control over nature has been achieved. On the side of the object, the result of abstraction is, finally, the idealized object of mathematical physics and rationalized institutions; on the side of the subject, that same process of abstraction yields the identification of subjectivity with its capacity for rational self-determination and, by extension, with reason itself. Adorno thus contends: "Abstraction, which in the history of nominalism ever since Aristotle's critique of Plato the subject has been rebuked for its mistake of reifying, is the principle whereby the subject comes to be a subject at all, it is the [transcendental] subject's essence" (ND, 181). Because the modern subject *is* abstract, an abstraction, in virtue of its placement in rationalized institutions and its encountering the world only through rationalized regimes, then any going back to the nature from which it emerged, as imaged for instance in the thought of the inclinations as being heteronomous inducements to action, must now strike it as being "external and violent" (ibid.).

In perceiving a correlation between the abstractive processes of rationalization and the rational subject, Adorno genealogically reconstructs the Kantian idea of what is transcendental accordingly.

> The definition of the transcendental as that which is necessary, something added to functionality and generality, expresses the principle of the self-preservation of the species. It provides a legal basis [*Rechtsgrund*] for abstraction, which we cannot do without, for it is the medium of self-preserving reason. . . . It is not true that the object is a subject, as idealism has been drilling into us for thousands of years, but it is true that the subject is an object. The primacy of subjectivity is a spiritualized continuation of Darwin's struggle for existence. The suppression of nature for human ends is a mere natural relationship, which is why the supremacy of nature-controlling reason and its principle is an illusion [*Schein*]. (ND, 179)[34]

Elsewhere, Adorno makes the same point when he claims: "Self-preservation is the constitutive principle of science, the soul of the table of categories, even when it is to be deduced idealistically, as with Kant" (DoE, 86–7).[35] No sense can be made of the presumed necessity of the categories apart from what they functionally accomplish, namely, our capacity to engage with the world in a manner appropriate for satisfying our most basic natural ends. Conceiving of objects as, essentially, substances in space and time all of whose characteristics are to be understood as ideally explainable within a unified system of causal laws is to regard things from the angle of what we can do with them, how they can be used, altered, employed. Hence the original motive for the demythologizing processes examined in Chapter 2 is the drive for self-preservation, and in the same way in which the motive of fear is indelible in explanatory ordering, so too is the drive for self-preservation; they are equivalents seen from different angles. Calling that stance on the world "transcendental"

34 I want to here flag and then drop a large issue. If the argument of the previous chapter that Kantian practical reasoning involves "social survival" is correct, then one might argue that the naturalistically conceived drive for self-preservation is not so natural. One might claim that fully animal drives are not "self" preserving since at the animal level the preservation of the individual and that of the species are fully intertwined. Not so with us: we seek the good of our "selves" in relation to competing selves, and how those competitions link with that of community and species is an open question – in part the very question of ethics. Properly taking account of this would complicate Adorno's story – talk of regress to the "natural" would have to drop out – without changing its fundamental shape. Of course, Adorno always opposed the thought that we could neatly factor within the human what was natural and what historical, above all because what defines the baldly natural, causal law-governedness, derives from reason and infects human sociality.

35 As I say something about in the next section, Adorno's hermeneutical thesis that Kantian idealism should be genealogically understood from a naturalistic perspective must be framed within an overcall contestation about the nature of modernity; in urging genealogical and naturalist perspectives against idealism Adorno is implying a conception of modernity that is not a given achievement, but a result (of critique) to be struggled for.

is, at one level, to do no more than acknowledge that mode or form of interacting with the natural world is not optional. We could not do otherwise and survive. Hence, nothing is wrong with the abstractive achievement in itself or considering the stance a necessary or unavoidable one – survival is an end which is best served by the method of abstraction – but for its claim to *exhaust* the possibilities of cognitively encountering the empirical world. That exhaustion occurs by transforming natural fact (or even natural necessity – DoE, 32) into transcendental necessity, the ultimate "right" of the categories. With that gesture the necessary or minimum conditions of experience (= necessary conditions for animal survival processed cognitively) become exclusive, *constitutive* of what it is for something *to be* an object in the world. In transforming a partial if necessary perspective on the world into what makes it the world, other possible forms of encounter are eclipsed. Functionality becomes absolute.[36] This is the same functionality that we saw was the suppressed meaning of the moral reasoning that takes action coordination amongst a plurality of agents as its terminus.

The twist in Adorno's account is that in offering a naturalistic reminder to idealism, he is simultaneously claiming that the abstract conception of self and reason with which idealism operates, because it is a continuation of the drive for self-preservation, is faulty in being too naturalistic. But that rational fault is equally a social fate: the abstractions that form the rational self are equally processes that deprive that self of its (animal) subjectivity. Because the natural impetus motivating the suppression of unreduced subjectivity remains unacknowledged, the belief arises that moral, rational, and societal unities that result from the operation of the principle of identity represent triumphs of the modern subject. This is the delusion of classical idealism; what it thinks of as the transcendental subject is, tendentially, object: "The more autocratically the I rises above entity, the greater its imperceptible objectification and ironic retraction of its constitutive role" (ND, 177). Earlier, and at somewhat great length, Adorno writes:

> The subject is spent and impoverished in its categorial performance; to be able to define and articulate what it confronts, so as to turn it into a Kantian object, the subject must dilute itself to the point of mere universality, for the sake of the objective validity of those definitions. It must cut loose from itself as much as from the cognitive object, so that this object will be reduced to its concept, according to plan. The objectifying subject con-

36 While Kant's conception of the categories of the understanding as constitutive of the objective world, making objectivity finally co-extensive with a closed causal order, is a vivid way of stating this thesis, as we shall see in the next section, any account of knowing that makes natural science paradigmatic or hegemonic with respect to knowledge must be implicitly transforming functional priority into transcendental necessity.

> tracts into a point of abstract reason, and finally into logical noncontradictoriness, which in turn means nothing except to be a definite object. (ND, 139)

Adorno is here attempting to comprehend the Kantian "I think" as an abstract *result* of the very processes of abstraction it is carrying out on the object. Adorno is hence asking after the cost to the subject of objectifying experience through categorial synthesis, and contending that the cost is the dislocation and separation of the I as logical agent of abstraction from I the living animal with a psychological life: my empirical life is always nonidentical with the I think, and from the perspective of that I think my empirical life becomes rigidly causally determined. If anthropomorphism is to be avoided, then the object must be constituted as object in a manner that abstracts from the peculiarities and particularities of subjective experience; this is what categorial constitution enables. In considering the object in abstraction from projective coloring (as enlightened reason conceives it), the experience of that coloring must also be diluted, abstracted from, supervened on. As Adorno states the thesis elsewhere: "For the sake of mastery, subjectivism must master and negate itself. Just to avoid mistake – since that is how they promote themselves – they abase themselves and at best would like to eliminate themselves. They use their subjectivity to subtract the subject from truth and their idea of objectivity is a residue" (AE, 15).[37] In bald terms, the disenfranchisement of how things appear in ordinary experience to a merely subjective take on the world must finally discount the ordinary experiences that are overcome and explained through scientific advance. The differentiation between the empirical subject and the I that thinks is the form that discounting takes. The separation between the two makes the real, empirical subject of experience object, and the I that thinks its empirical life as only object an etiolated point of view on the proceedings it observes; the subject is thus transformed from an embodied being in the world into "at most geometrically in the world."[38]

Hence the path that leads from immersion in the natural world to the self as subject, the position which constitutes the world as world, follows a path of abstraction; but since the path of reiterative abstraction and ascent is just the systematic enlargement of the drive for self- preservation in its cognitive form, then the so-called transcendental subject is a function of the living nature it suppresses in the course of its emergence. The consequence of that emergence is the self epistemologically excising

37 This will entail, as we shall see in Chapter 6 below, that for Adorno those properties of objects typically seen as mere correlates of our sensibility, and hence as subjective, secondary, are in truth at the core of their objectivity.

38 John McDowell, *Mind and World* (Cambridge, Mass.: Harvard University Press, 1994), p. 104.

from itself its animal life. By this route the transcendental self becomes what it beholds: more object than subject.

Adorno construes transcendental subjectivity as both a maddened response to the world (the moral law is a "rationalized rage at nonidentity" – ND, 23), and lacking in self-consciousness, since the very move to a notion of transcendental or constitutive subjectivity blocks awareness of how that self-conception came to be formed. Transcendental reflection necessarily inhibits reflection, abstracting subject and its reasoning from history and nature. Because the subject considers that control through identifying as its own achievement, and not the rationalized form of the drive to self-preservation, it fails to perceive its entrapment, its imprisonment within its survival mechanism (ND, 180).

> The practice of its [the transcendental subject's] rule makes it a part of what it thinks it is ruling; it succumbs like the Hegelian master. It makes manifest the extent to which in consuming the object it is in bondage [*hörig*] to it. What it does is the spell of that which the subject believes under its own spell. The subject's desperate self-exaltation is its reaction to the experience of its impotence [in the face of nature and society], which hinders self-reflection; absolute consciousness is unconscious. (ND, 180)

The transcendental subject, the agent of centralist morality, in withholding acknowledgement of the separation of the object from itself, and thus in denying the object's nonidentity with the regimes of rationalized reason, deprives itself of "recognition," that is, the affirmation of its subjectivity since "world" has become solely a function of its self-determining thought: instead of living objects it perceives only the etiolated outline of its own categorial performances.[39] But the withholding of acknowledgement is itself an outgrowth of nature in the subject; hence the goal of mastering nature as the formation of rationalized reason in its first-person and institutional forms becomes a mastery by the slave nature has become.

Now while Adorno repeats this thought in a variety of ways, and routinely insinuates it into the course of his arguments, he never says much more to directly support the claim that rationalized reason is self-defeating in this way. Without question, then, this whole basic line of thought in Adorno is presented almost formally, at a high level of abstraction, and with a significant element of metaphoricity rather than argumentatively.

39 And while this sounds metaphorical as an account of everyday cognition, it sounds much less so when we conceive of the objects being considered as functional placeholders in or as the products of rationalized institutions. And once that step is made, fully specifying objects that are the correlates of transcendental subjectivity, rationalized reason becomes substantial. In fine, for Adorno this is another way of stating the implications of inhabiting social practices which have been shaped or supervened on by rationalized reason. So again, the first-person experience at stake here is best reflected in the aporiae of *Minima Moralia*.

Worse, the whole self-defeating narrative is abstract and thin in comparison, for example, with the narrative of self-defeating forms of consciousness offered in Hegel's *Phenomenology of Spirit.* More simply, Adorno's presentation does not quite do what it appears to promise to do, namely, sketch an unfolding causality of fate whereby the nonrecognition of nature within and without, in severing our immanent connection or unity with anthropomorphic nature, leads us to mistakenly see as the historical necessity of fate (i.e., the institutional experiences of rationalized modernity) what, again, "is actually only the reactive force of a life that has been suppressed and separated off." This failure is, in fact, comprehensible and inevitable since its dialectical pivot, the standing of living nature in social practice, is the one element of the account to which we have no direct access; we know about it, to the extent we do, through the effects of its suppression. Because anthropomorphic nature has at least been made all but invisible, and at worst eliminated, become a residue, then all Adorno can do is point to the original setting of reason and subjectivity, itself a highly speculative gesture, point to the mechanisms which explain how invisibility or elimination were effected, and finally redescribe the result, the present end point, accordingly. This is not to deny that there could be detailed histories of the suppression of anthropomorphic nature; but for those histories to carry epistemic weight, we would have first to accept the premises and conclusions of Adorno's account, that is, his metacritique of idealist reason, the genealogical demonstration that it is a form of instrumental reasoning that in its unfolding becomes existentially self-defeating. Historical genealogy *explains* the suffering of the present only by offering an alternative interpretative framework; but since a fundamental element of the framework concerns the elimination or disappearance of the framework itself as the explanation for the misery, then evidently only a very abstract redescription of the present will be possible, inflecting it so what has become normatively compelling can be comprehended as simultaneously pain-inducing.

5. Independence: The Simple Concept and Linguistic Determinacy

To contest the hegemony of reiterative cognitive ascent, Adorno must contest "the notion that all knowledge can potentially be converted to science" (NL1, 8). For Adorno's argument to work, ordinary empirical judgements and everyday assertoric statements must not be indeterminate or loose somethings that become determinate and justified through being explained scientifically. Ordinary perceptual judgements and statements must be shown – ideally or under optimal conditions – to *lack nothing* in the way of objectivity or rationality, or at least nothing that cannot be corrected by further reflection and refinement *at the same level.* The hegemony of scientific reason over rationality and objectivity is thus what must be critically undermined. To accomplish this end, Adorno must demonstrate that the basic mediating forms of everyday cognition – concepts, judgements, and ordinary language – do not intrinsically operate in accordance with the principle of immanence; and further, that when they are so constructed, when reason is rationalized, then their own immanent claim to objectivity and rationality is destroyed. When ordinary judgement and language are constructed and employed in the image of identity and independence, they become irrational and subjective. The first step in such an argument must thus be to see precisely what concept and language look like when they are constructed and rationalized in terms of the principle of immanence. What does the ideal of independence – thus far expressed in the autonomy of reason, constitutive subjectivity, the platitudes governing the principle of immanence – come to in the concept of the concept and in the understanding of ordinary language? How does anti-anthropomorphism manifest itself in conceptions of the concept and language?

Concepts and language are the fundamental mediums of cognition, the minimal mediational forms without which there could not be knowledge at all. Hence after the more obvious unreliable mediational forms of tradition and status authority were removed by enlightened scepticism, an adequate account of how reason could be independent of its objects, autonomous and self-determining, came to focus on those minimal forms themselves. While it is not difficult to conceive of the claim that objectivity is grounded in a synthesis governed by categories that are a priori, universal, and necessary because owing nothing to experience, as a direct way of satisfying the desire for rational independence from the natural world, it has seemed to many that the linguistic turn in philosophy is incompatible with the dominant intentions of idealism, while itself critical of the ideal of independence: concepts are dependent on language. The ideal of independence cannot be so literally construed; within the analytic tradition the role of rational autonomy was resurrected in the ideal of the determinacy of linguistic meaning. Mark Sacks succinctly states the thesis: "If the world is fully determinate, the perfect target for scientific inquiry, it is necessary to ensure that we approach it with implements that are as finely tuned as possible, to make sure that it is not the insensitivity of the mapping mechanism that produces an inaccurate picture."[40] Notice the premise of this construction of language: the world as fully determinate. So this conception of language is being tailored to a conception of the world that is abstract and idealized; novelty, indeterminacy,

40 "Through a Glass Darkly: Vagueness in the Metaphysics of the Analytic Tradition," in David Bell and Neil Cooper (eds.), *The Analytic Tradition: Meaning, Thought, and Knowledge* (Oxford: Basil Blackwell, 1990), p. 174.

ineliminable contingency, are conceived from the outset as perspectival takings on what is in itself fixed and determinate. Such abstractions and idealization must seep into the pores of the account that is constructed through them.

If language is the tool with which we map the world, then any ineliminable vagueness in language entails that the world will remain unmapped and unknown. Hence, only by demonstrating that in principle linguistic meaning can attain to complete determinateness ensures that the enlightenment project of knowing can succeed. The dominant criterion for determinacy of meaning, and indeed a motive behind the desire to attain it, is transparent communicability or, to keep the thought in touch with the claims of idealism, discursivity without remainder. Here is a pointed passage in defense of this ideal from Michael Dummett.

> Thought differs from other things also said to be objects of the mind, for instance pains or mental images, in not being essentially private. . . . It is of the essence of thought that it be *transferable,* that I can convey to you *exactly* what I am thinking. . . . [In which case] I do more than tell you what my thought is like – I communicate to you the very thought. Hence any attempt to investigate thought which culminates in a study of what is in essence private, that is, of inner mental experience, must have missed the mark.[41]

One might feel that something has gone terribly awry in this passage since one of the undoubted contributions of Wittgenstein's philosophy is the claim that pains and mental images are not essentially private, albeit they are not sharable in the same way or to the same degree that the thought "two plus two equals four" is communicable. How does Dummett get from the reasonable thesis that thought cannot be essentially private, to the quite different thesis that it is unrelievedly public? Why come to believe that it is constitutive of thought that it be intersubjective in the sense that two or more people can have the identical (same) thought, where this itself involves the claim that my thought is *fully* expressible, fully capable of being borne by the sentence that expresses it?[42] If my thought about an object is somehow dependent on a mental image, if my experience of an object enters essentially into my thought about it, then any proposition about the object will include something not transparently communicable or fully expressible. My thought, under this condition, will not be able to be either handed over to like a trinket or directly

41 M. A. E. Dummett, "Frege's Distinction between Sense and Reference," in *Truth and Other Enigmas* (London: Duckworth, 1978), pp. 116–17. I came to see the relevance of this passage for my purposes with its appearance in David Bell's important essay, which I return to, "The Art of Judgement," *Mind* 96/2 (1987): 223–4.

42 Note how Dummett's requirements of intersubjectivity and expressibility are operating here: intersubjectivity requires determinacy, and determinacy requires expressibility (discursivity without remainder).

shared (like a blanket) with another. So thought cannot be either contingently or essentially object-involving. For a theory of meaning, this requires that the sense of a proposition be capable of being fixed independently of the object it is about (or, what is the same, fixing the object, determining it, solely through the statements about it). Nothing fits this requirement better than statements about nonempirical or abstract objects, although orders determining a unique behavioral response ("Company, attennn . . . tion!") come a close second.

The ideal of the determinacy of linguistic meaning is the direct successor and the linguistic analogue of the belief in the autonomy of reason: only if meaning can be made determinate can reason be self-sufficient. Just as the drive of idealism is to render the inner structure of reason independent of the world (a priori) and determinate for it (synthetic), so the fundamental presupposition of the analytic project is the thesis that "there is a tenable dichotomy between language and the empirical world, such that it makes sense to think of one as a description of the other."[43] Linguistic determinacy is thus beholden to the independence thesis and is a version of it. Indeterminacy (arbitrariness) is to reason as vagueness is to language; vagueness and indeterminacy translate one another, so reciprocally translating the discourses of reason (concept) and language into one another. The project of enlightenment would be fulfilled by the provision or discovery of a determinacy that would demonstrate and secure independence.

One might hope to quickly overturn these dual projects by pointing to the false inference on which they are both premised: because some false beliefs (myths, superstitions, metaphysical hypotheses, etc.) are subjective projections, then the medium of those projections (sensory images, social practices, historical traditions) must themselves be systematic sources of error. But this distrust of unreliable mediums could not have persisted so long and so powerfully unless its own premise, namely, that concept and language are essentially tools or instruments for grasping the world, itself contained a partial truth (DoE, 39). That partial truth and its inflation into the whole truth about the concept is contained in the ideal of the simple concept. For Adorno, the ideal of the simple concept is historically defined with Kant's dichotomy between concepts and intuitions: intuitions without concepts are blind, and thoughts, concepts, without intuition are empty (A 51/B 75). The separation between concept and intuition, while calling for a coordination between these two stems of cognitive life, is for Adorno nonetheless a dualism (a represen-

43 Sacks, "Through a Glass Darkly," p. 176. Idealism, of course, is distinctive in seeking to overcome or dissolve the dichotomy between cognition and world; but it achieves this end by first defining the world in the image of the concept, by specifying a priori the concept of an object in general.

tation of the dualism between culture and nature) that requires overcoming: "In the relationship of intuition and concept, philosophy already discerned the abyss which opened with that separation [between sign and image], and again tries in vain to close it: indeed, philosophy is defined by this very attempt" (DoE, 18).

What notion of the concept would evince its ideal independence from anthropomorphic coloring? What notion of the concept expresses the *ideal* independence of the concept? Conceptual independence takes its lead from the problem of affection: if concepts are bound to the items giving rise to restrictedly affective states, then those concepts will map how the world contingently appears to individuals rather than how it is. Passivity or receptivity, the contingency of affection, requires overcoming. Hence, the more concepts of objects are independent of affective states, the more "true to" an independent world they will be. The ideal of the simple concept is formed from what will satisfy the need to avoid affective contamination as the general conception of anthropomorphic projection. Three ideals capture this ideal of independence: (1) truth should be "imageless," unmarked by the subjective perspective; (2) vertically, the more general a concept is the more rational it is; (3) horizontally, the meaning of a concept should be independent of, its sense insulated from, its application to future cases. Vertical unconditionality, we saw earlier, is itself a part of the principle of immanence. The cognitive value of concepts lies in their generality, with cognitive progress occurring through conceptual ascent to higher levels of generality; what lacks absolute generality is relatively particular and hence arbitrary. Ascent to the unconditionally general is the path of removing arbitrariness, passivity, the subjective factor; hence, what best approximates being a product of pure spontaneity, if universal, best approximates independence from affection. It is in this way that the space of reasons comes to be identified with autonomy and freedom. In Kant unconditional generality is coextensive with the a priori, which itself is coextensive with pure self-consciousness, the transcendental unity of apperception and the fact of reason. Hence the path of removing the subjective factor becomes ironically equivalent to the Copernican turn, constituting nature in the image of idealized reason.

Horizontal unconditionedness, in which the meaning of a concept or theory is independent of its application to future cases, requires that the lines of projection from concept to world be internal to the concept, fully given with it, and thus invariant. This thesis is equally necessary for the demonstration of the determinacy of linguistic meaning. If the extension of a sentence could change in the future, then its intentional meaning now could be indeterminate between its present and future sense on the hypothesis that two speakers were using the sentence in accordance with its two senses: same extension, altered extension.[44] Only horizontal invariance permits sense to determine reference and guarantees that the same sentence used by two speakers now has the same meaning. Conceptually, horizontal invariance is a corollary of vertical generality; if the point of moving to higher levels of generality is to remove dependence on contingent experience, then future new cases are as troubling as bound affective states. No conceptual ascent would be progressive if conditions of application systematically altered. All novelty is thus equivalent to bound affective states; history and embodied subjectivity are equally incompatible with the ideals forming the simple concept.

Concept-intuition dualism is defined by the ideal independence of nature from the human, and the ideal independence of the concept from dependence on contingent states of affairs that are detectable only through experience. Adorno interprets the search for generality and invariance in the simple concept as "archaic [mythic] features which cut across rational ones" (ND, 153), that is, the static cognitive ideal expressed by the principles of vertical generality and horizontal invariance ill consort with the dynamic character of consciousness that the move from a theological to a historical and secular conception of the world implies, for scientific as well as ordinary understanding. "The [simple] concept in itself," Adorno states, "previous to any content, hypostatizes its own form against content. With that, however, it is already hypostatizing the identity principle: that what our thinking practice merely postulates is a fact in itself, solid and enduring. Identifying thought objectifies by the logical identity of the concept" (ND, 153–4). Adorno is here explicating how conceptual activity can be the bearer of rationalized practice. How, given the dynamic character of conceptual activity, even or especially for Kant, can we make sense of its objectifying outcome, its reduction of experience to determining judgement, its framing of judgmental indeterminacy within scientific practice, and its conception of scientific practice as a search for unconditionality? Kant knows, Adorno states, that a concept's logical identity, what can be revealed about it through analysis, is, finally, a "postulate," that no concept now possesses an uncontestable logical identity. Indeed, part of Kant's point in making unconditionality ideal is to keep experience open, to require continuing dependence on empirical experience. How is that openness to experience related to Kant's excision from experience of anthropomorphism, and ultimately to a conception of empirical reality as a closed causal order?

Kant argues that ideally all concepts ought to be fully determinate (A 571–2/B 599–600): insofar as a new content could conceivably require

44 For this application of Nelson Goodman's paradox of induction to the problem of meaning determinacy, see ibid., pp. 178–9.

the alteration in the sense of a concept (what is given through logical analysis), then that concept is indeterminate (vague); hence, if we do not know that a concept is determinate, then it could mean other than it now means, and hence now be defective or false. Hence a concept is only true, possesses a determinate logical identity, if no content could alter it. But if no content or intuition could change or redetermine a concept, then ideally the concept *by itself* gives reality independently of empirical experience. Hence the logical identity of a concept is ideally self-sufficient, that is, for a true concept its logical form alone would be cognitively indistinguishable from the cognitive value of the concept-and-content of indeterminate concepts. If the ideal of determinacy is built into the simple concept, then all normativity comes from the concept and intuitions become *only* their matter or filling; if determinacy is achievable only through ascent, then what makes for particularity either stands outside conceptuality or becomes, again, just the "filling," token, example, specimen of the concept. The ideal of determinacy, in language and concept, is what logically secures independence and thereby what logically generates the concept-intuition dualisms. If abstraction is the mechanism of the simple concept, determinacy is its logical anchor. Determinacy, whether of concept or meaning, is, I am contending, the logical pivot of identity thinking. *Determinacy is the logical figure of independence.*

This is the way in which the ideal of the simple concept aims at the extinguishing of experience (albeit in the name of keeping experience open). From this perspective, the goal of conceptual ascent is to drive out dependence on the world since the world is conceived of prospectively as only a potential falsifier. Kant says too little about everyday judgement to interpret how he conceives of the significance of this ideal for it. What is evident, however, is how the claims of a scientific rationalism are inscribed even in the innocent work of conceptual identification. Given this notion of conceptuality, how could there be a fully rational ethical knowing? How could there be a fully rational knowledge of the ordinary that was not further translatable?

6. Dependence: The Guilt Context of the Living

What is the ethical significance of the claim to independence by moral reason, constitutive subjectivity, the simple concept? And how can dependence on anthropomorphic nature be thought as a *claim* lodged by *it* against the concept? Is it not persons rather than things that raise claims? To ethically redescribe the meaning of the claim to independence we must return to the grammar of moral insight sketched in the Introduction, for the question of the claim of anthropomorphic nature, if there is one, and the problem of the demand of the good are, at least, structurally synonymous. There it was argued that two of the distinguishing features of practical as opposed to theoretical reason are, first, that practical reason contains a moment of ineliminable passivity that is expressed in the idea of individuals assenting to the good as a condition for cognizing it; and thus, second, that the good becomes determinate only through the ethical performances that it makes possible. I then offered in a footnote Aristotle's negative version of this doctrine: in acting in accordance with the bodily drives of pleasure and pain the objects of theoretical reason remain as they were, for example, two plus two equals four whether I am drunk or sober; however, practically, for a person in this state the origin or goal fails to appear: vice is destructive of principle, vice corrupts the origin. If the good becomes determinate only through the performance that it makes possible, then a fortiori, immoral or unethical action will corrupt and destroy the good (and not simply make a subject blind to its being there). The most difficult element of this doctrine is to imagine what the good could be such that it can have these properties and characteristics. Adorno's hypothesis is that anthropomorphic nature within and without is the (ground of) the good. To accurately capture the repercussions of this hypothesis, let us step back for a moment.

A presupposition of the debate between Kantian modernizers and Aristotelian reactionaries is that the attunement between mind and world, subject and object, must itself be either subjective or objective, either subjectively established and constituted through the synthetic achievements of the transcendental unity of apperception (or some collective version of it: "we think" must accompany all our representations), or objectively grounded in the becoming of the world itself. For the latter position it matters little whether that becoming, that metaphysical teleology, is theologically understood or theoretically explained as a continuation of natural evolution (naturalized, evolutionary ethics being just the continuation of theology by other means). In either case the thesis the subjects confront a world always already colored in values pertaining to what is subjectively meaningful is objectively secured as something beyond acceptance or rejection by the subjects for whom there is such an order, and hence beyond whatever stance we might take toward it. We might, individually or collectively, turn our back on God's gift or, misguided by philosophy itself, seek legitimation for morality beyond the natural order, but come what may the existence of such an order exists and is there to be found if we but look in the right place. The lineaments of morality are ontologically secure. However, ontological security is arguably logically incompatible with practical reason. Worse, such views dissemble the destructive and sceptical consequences of progressive disenchantment: if there has been disenchantment, and if disenchantment actually destroys the ethical attunement of mind and world by destroying anthropomorphic nature and the mediums through which it is apprehended, hence if reflection has disintegrated the possibilities of meaningful action, then ethical life cannot be unconditionally objective or unconditionally grounded.

Sceptical demythologization is thus not ethically neutral. Disenchanting the world is the progressive disappearance of anthropomorphic nature; as this process reaches its modern phase desires and motives are decoded until they become, in Kant's term, "pathological," one and all bound to the naturalistic anthropology of self-preservation in which the counters of pleasure and pain, desires and aversions, refer always to "one and the same life-force" (CPrR, 23). That one and the same life force can only be the drive for self-preservation. As Dieter Henrich has claimed, the drive for self-preservation represents "the extreme counter-instance to all anthropological teleology, for it is the only subjective motivational impulse that is by definition without a goal. It forms in psychology the predecessor of Newton's force of inertia . . . that is, the force that ultimately liberated physics from the Aristotelian teleology of 'natural locations.'"[45] While it is tempting to perceive self-preservation as a goal of sorts, Hobbes pointedly construes his reduction as demonstrating that there is no highest good or good that all men seek, but only a greatest evil: the threat of violent and sudden death. Death, however, is only the state of the object (which is the subject) whereby it is at rest and remains at rest. Whether it is conceived of as a decoding or work of supervenience (where these are extensionally equivalent), every modern subject is installed in a space in which anthropomorphic nature within has been neutralized and naturalized, reduced to the rudiment of desires and aversions. This is how the first ledger of the double accounting system in which every action could be thought to be motivated by selfish desires is opened.

When Aristotle states that vice destroys principle, he must be construed as claiming that acting in accordance with the raw feelings of pleasure and pain (the life of the sensualist) not only leads to immoral action but decays ethical principles themselves such that not only does the world appear to the immoral agent to lack moral values, but, at least for that agent, they are no longer available.[46] If principle can decay or be corrupted or destroyed by vice, then the good can disappear from the world. Conversely, it is supposed, acting ethically affirms the reality of the good in the world and thereby entails a world whose ontological shape is distinct from the world of the immoral man.

Enlightenment disenchantment is the collective vice that destroys principle by corrupting anthropomorphic nature. More precisely, the vice of disenchantment is the attempt to secure the independence of reason and concept

45 "The Concept of Moral Insight," p. 67.

46 I have no answer to the question of how Aristotle thought he could square this thesis with rest of his naturalist metaphysics. In his anti-platonism, he should have believed that the good, the noble, could disappear from existence.

from anthropomorphic nature. As the various characterizations of moral reason, constitutive subjectivity, and the simple concept have shown, each is formed so that its fundamental characteristics and operations are independent of its objects. Such independence is logically incompatible with moral insight, practical reason, as such. By seeking independence, rationalized reason tendentially destroys practical reason as such by making the standpoint of practical reason, with its ineluctable moment of passivity (the demand of the good), always not rational and not objective. Hence, those versions of morality that embrace the idea of independence, as does Kantian moral reason, fail to be moral because, in truth, they are works of theoretical and not practical reason.[47] And that is the nub of the complaint over externalism; the products of rationalized reason are, finally, products of theoretical reason. *Rationalization in its movement to independence transforms or reifies practical reason into theoretical reason,* which in attempting to be practical and moral can do so only from "without." The question of motivation is thus not extrinsic to questions about the nature of morality; motivation must be considered a thin representation of the role of passivity (affection and assent) in ethical cognition. Hence, any attempt to construct a conception of morality that leaves out or passes over the question of motivation on the grounds that it can be supplied from elsewhere, or, ultimately, it is just a question of habituation and internalization of what anyway must originally appear as external, mistakes the contours of the problem of the relation between practical and theoretical reason. What thus makes the destruction of anthropomorphic nature simultaneously complete and undetectable is theoretical reason becoming absolute. To describe the process by which that occurs as a form of vice, a vast, collective act of immorality through which we have lost sight of the good, anthropomorphic nature, largely by losing

47 From this it equally follows, what I have been implying throughout, that instrumental reasoning is *not* a form of practical reasoning. One might say that instrumental reasoning is a form of *causal reasoning* that is applied to practice or applied to practical questions, viz., what are the at least sufficient things I must do to bring about a desired end, and ideally the most efficient of the sufficient ways of achieving that end given my resources and other wants and needs. The question is practical enough; the reasoning itself, as far as I can see, theoretical. But since the question is analytical for action – without it one could not be thinking of achieving an end as opposed to wishing for it to come about, for example – then none of the distinctive features that Henrich brings to our attention concerning that kind of practical reason that follows on from the idea of moral insight is bound up in instrumental calculations. The idea that instrumental reasoning should be a model of practical reasoning is the most perverse of doctrines, although consistent with enlightenment demythologization, since it offers as the model of practical reasoning just a low-grade form of theoretical reasoning, applied theoretical reason. I should say here that Kant was not insensitive to the issues being raised in this paragraph for it is they which lie behind his question of how pure reason can be practical, and the doctrines of the primacy of practical reason and the fact of reason. Insensitivity is not the issue; the claims of moral reason are, finally, theoretical and not practical, and Kant's desperate attempts to show otherwise inevitably fail.

sight of the kind of sight ethical cognition demands, is a first resistance to that process.

It is equally the key to Adorno's fundamental stance. He routinely appropriates a phrase of Walter Benjamin's to characterize the ethical disposition of the world: "the guilt context of the living."[48] As a context of guilt, the world inhabited is purchased through vice, albeit not explicitly moral vice, but the generalized vice of acting in accordance with principles and forms of reasoning that are themselves incommensurable with a proper regard for the sensuous particulars composing anthropomorphic nature to the extreme in which that nature has been lost to sight, and life reduced to having a contemplative stance toward it even when it is most vigorously pursued.[49] Because it is a context of guilt, it is a default on true existence which infects all, even those most opposed to it. Yet, if it is a guilt context we inhabit, then we are not utterly lost to the good: remnants and remainders persist. Guilt is an obscured consciousness of the good in the performance of what contradicts it. Hence, theoretical consciousness, identity thinking, must itself in its most standard performances and elaboration be bearing witness to what it obscures and denies. And indeed, this must be the case if anything like the idea of a disenchanted world is true and a recuperation of moral consciousness is possible.

If the guilt context of modern life is a product of instrumental reason which is itself capable of registering and acknowledging the ethical failure involved in its claim to absoluteness, then the faulty character of the claim must derive from a feature of instrumental reason that it shares with practical reason. Further, that fault must be both theoretical and ethical. The most natural place to look for this fault would be in theoretical reason's characterization of reason, of itself. Looking at reason as such, however, would be of little avail since theoretical reason is certainly a *part* or *form* of reason whose claim to self-sufficiency is internal to its constitution – once again, the platitudes of the principle of immanence.

Because he wishes to return the ethical to cognition, Adorno chooses for his focus the medium of all reflection and reasoning, theoretical and practical (if there is such): the concept. Nonetheless, working out this

48 Walter Benjamin, *Reflections*, trans. Edmund Jephcott (New York: Harcourt Brace Jovanovich, 1978), p. 308.

49 The reduction of practical reason to theoretical reason, and the consequent dominance of a contemplative stance toward the world, which is central to the critique of instrumental reason, is an idea Adorno inherited from Georg Lukács, *History and Class Consciousness*, trans. Rodney Livingstone (London: Merlin Press, 1971), pp. 83–110. However, once the issue is framed this way it becomes possible to reconstruct a large part of European philosophy according to it, from Kant, Fichte, and Hegel, through Marx, Nietzsche, and Kierkegaard, to Heidegger and Levinas. Each can be understood as attempting to diagnose modernity as a reduction of practical knowing or activity to the theoretical, and to reinstitute the broad ontology of moral insight itself.

project requires pursuing the problem on two different fronts: arguing against the transformation of ethical cognition into moral reasoning, and arguing against the narrowing of cognition to theoretical or scientific cognition, where it is assumed that the latter narrowing is responsible for the former transformation. This is the explanation for the constant shuffling in this work between questions of ethics and questions of epistemology, with the continual effort to perceive failures or problems in one domain as repeating or echoing problems in the other. The repeating pattern of failure has been the claim to real or ideal independence, and if the autonomy of reason is the fullest and best expression of this ideal, and the self-defeating character of constitutive subjectivity most expressive of its failure, both, I have claimed, are borne by and within the ideals of the simple concept: imageless truth, vertical unconditioned generality, and horizontal invariance. In the concept, and in language, those ideals can themselves be characterized by or supplemented with the ideal of determinacy. It is the simple concept and linguistic determinacy so defined that Adorno will contend are both theoretically false and ethically condemnatory. To do so, he must demonstrate that all these ideals are necessarily extrinsic and inapplicable to the concept in everyday empirical judgements, and to ordinary language. To demonstrate that, Adorno will need to show that concepts, as vehicles for cognition and with respect to meaning, are *dependent* upon, and hence not detachable from, what they are about. His concept of the concept I will entitle "the complex concept." Since one can actually be dependent upon only what possesses independence, then acknowledging the independence of the object, its nonidentity with its concept, becomes the theoretical and ethical drive of critique. Adorno entitles the critical procedure whereby the acknowledgement of dependence elicits a simultaneous acknowledgement of independence "dialectics": "The name of dialectics says no more, to begin with, than that objects do not go into their [simple] concepts without leaving a remainder, that they come to contradict the traditional norm of adequacy" (ND, 5).

The claim that objects must transcendentally, as a condition of their possibility, "conform to our knowledge" (B xvi) defines the Copernican turn as espousing the independence of concepts, most perfectly those a priori concepts, the categories, which are not derived from experience but provide the conceptual conditions that make knowledge possible. Because the negativity of any concept with respect to what falls under it is a necessary moment of conceptuality – without it concepts could not apply to more than one object – then there is an enormous half-truth, a platitude, in the idea of the simple concept. What makes this enormous half-truth best expressed in Kantian terms is the recognition that the generality of the concept is an expression of the mind's capacity for negativity with respect to mental contents: the capacity of the mind to order, classify, connect depends upon not submitting to the givenness of what appears to the senses. One expression of the negation of givenness lies, then, in generality: what is given to the mind, no matter how unique, also exemplifies what that item shares with other items (color, shape, texture, smell). Concepts are the mediation of objects through their marks or characteristic features, their qualities, that they have in common with other objects (actually or potentially). In this respect, the *appearance* of identity, the appearance of every object being the token of a type, identical with other objects in some fundamental respect, is inherent in the pure form of thought: "to think is to identify" (ND, 5). However, if the correct understanding of the power of concepts to identify is as an expression of the negativity and spontaneity of the intellect, if conceptualizing must be conceived as an *active* power of resistance to what sensorily appears, and if, finally, each act of negation that permits identification, subsumption, is aptly conceived of as also abstracting from what is given, then the independence of concepts from their objects in itself does possess a potentially sceptical moment. The scepticism of enlightenment is thus grounded in an intrinsic feature of conceptuality: concepts are vehicles for the negativity of consciousness. Exploiting the moment of negativity in the concept is what enables abstraction and its reiteration. Hence, the claim for the a priori independence of concepts from objects, the claim that what appears is subject to and appears in accordance with the mind's own activity of determination, hence the claim that there is normativity all the way down, are all grounded in and reifications of the negativity of the concept with respect to objects, making human conceptuality, so stated, sceptical – the very scepticism of which realists and naturalists have accused idealism. It is the scepticism that Kant's critics continue to find in the claim that we know appearances only and not things in themselves, no matter how carefully elaborated. Normativity *all* the way down, without remainder or remnant, nothing outside, is invidiously idealist. However, if to think is to identify, then Adorno must agree that there is normativity all the way down. Overcoming sceptical independence can be effected only as an act of consciousness, and hence through "a second Copernican turn" (SO, 249). However, if the independence of the concept from its objects is an illusion, then, in part, the ground for this axial turn must come *from* the object.

Dialectics cannot be a "standpoint" (ND, 4–6), an a priori method or an independent project of reason, for were it so it would be in contradiction with the claimed dependence of concept on object. The subject's guilt, which in accordance with the concept of moral insight is the cognitively opaque experience of its refusal of the good consequent upon choosing against it (in this case consequent upon the adoption of a theoretical stance toward the world), is the ethical ground of the critical reflection of rationalized reason upon itself, hence the ground of its attempt to free itself from its reified stance. What *motivates* critical thinking, dialectics, is "its own inevitable insufficiency," my "guilt [*Schuld*: debt, need, responsibility] with respect to what I am thinking about" (ND, 5). To experience such a guilt, debt, or need with respect to the object of thought is a tacit acknowledgement that what gives me to thought, arouses me, draws me to reflection, is not itself thought but its object. It is precisely the recognition that the object of thought has a claim against me. Only because the object has already showed itself as what is to be thought about (which will entail the object being already mediated, not a dumb in-itself) can thought occur. I need the object not as a mere filling for or confirmation of concepts spontaneously produced, pure idealities within the space of reasons, but as the very substance of the concept. Thought lives off what it thinks about; and so living off its objects, it incurs a debt to them.

Putting the matter this way might well be construed as, at least, tendentious, and, at worst, utterly figurative and metaphorical (although it takes literally and exploits the idea that there is normativity all the way down). Why speak of debt, guilt, living off the object when all that is occurring is, say, perceptually judging "This chair is blue"? Am I in debt to the chair and its blueness through my judging? In what sense could it be correct to say there is a claim here? To see that these questions, the questions as to whether my factual dependence on the objects of judgement is more than factual, whether what I owe the object (say, the truth about it) is not only a self-imposed end (seeking to accurately and correctly judge), but something that might be claimed by the object, hence coming to see the question as to whether the moments of independence and dependence in conceptualizing possess a distinct ethical dimension alongside their factual dimension, is well posed and pivotal with respect to limning the figure of a human life in a human world that is central to Adorno's whole endeavor. To be able to be *moved* by these questions, perhaps in the way in which a painter might be thought to be moved by a blue chair, wanting her painting to be an acknowledgement of that blueness, to be able to see that mere factual dependence somehow misses something significant about what is involved in thinking, judging, and perceiving is already to have entered into the space of moral insight, its (ethical) necessity. Or, to state the same thought from the opposing direction: if we are willing to agree that there is something wrong-headed in the idea of reason being value-conferring, then must not analogous considerations weigh for conceptuality – concepts do not constitute the meaning of their objects? But once this is conceded, has not some notion of *conceptual normative dependence* become compulsory? And will not acknowledging a previous failure of acknowledgement have to be spelled out, somehow, in terms of owing something to the object, of being responsible to it and for it?

To feel indebted to the object of a concept would be to acknowledge that a self-sufficient, self-determining reason in its self-sufficiency loses the very aboutness of its activity, its being directed to articulating what is other than and thereby separate from itself. Or rather, more accurately, when reason acts self-sufficiently it is redetermining what its activity is about, what concerns it; and in this redetermination of the point of its activity, providing an explanation of what is there, it is ignoring or turning its back on one aspect of its doing for the sake of another. Prosaically, reason would not be without its particular objects; but as reason becomes more autonomous, it can make less sense of the dependence the aboutness of its activity involves. And this is comprehensible: everyday acts of judgement are object-involving in a manner that explanatory activity is not. But my reasoning's guilt and debt is more than this prosaic point, for what *now* appears as *its* objects have already been shaped, reduced, and imposed upon: they have become mirrors of rationalized social practice, and so have lost their emphatic distance and separateness from reason. This loss, the loss of anthropomorphic nature, the loss of aura, is reflected in claims to immediacy (in retreats from reason to inwardness), and in the feeling of indifference: in judging neutrally, impartially, disinterestedly, I am dishonoring the object, failing to take *it* seriously. Hence, the guilt or debt of thought to its objects, its insufficiency, first and dominantly emerges as the claim of an ethical remainder, that there is *more* to the object and more involved in thinking about it than what my present thinking acknowledges, and thus a feeling of remorse and a desire to make reparation: "Pure identity is that which the subject posits and thus brings up from the outside . . . . The subject must make good what it has done to nonidentity [that in the object that exceeds its reified concept]. In doing that it becomes free of the appearance of its absolute being-for-itself" (ND, 145–6). To say pure identity is an "outside" is to claim that it is a posit, an idealization of conceptuality. The feature of conceptuality idealized, the concept of the concept at issue, is its claim to "order-creating invariance as against the change in what it covers" (ND, 153) – a restatement of the principle of immanence. In Kant's lexicon: " . . . reason has insight only into that which it produces after a plan of its own, and that it must not allow itself to be kept, as it were, on nature's leading-strings, but must show the way with principles of judgement based on fixed laws, constraining nature to give answer to the questions of reason's own determining" (B xiii). Such "constraining" "injures" what is heterogeneous by abstracting from change and difference, and imposing on it a unity and sameness, "fixed laws," whose only model is an ideal of reason. If we can acknowledge what harm has been done in the name of invariance, we can glimpse the requirement for reparation.

Without a sense of indebtedness, this pathos of reason, thought would have no motive to seek reconciliation with anthropomorphic nature. Reason comes to self-consciousness about its limits through the experience of dissatisfaction with its achievements (ND, 186); this dissatisfaction, in its unqualified affectivity, is an exemplar and component of the particularity and actuality that reason in its universalistic ambition excises. So moved, reason must turn upon itself, must perform a self-critique through which actuality can be reendowed with ethical substantiality. The practice of this autocritique, because an *approving response* to the claim of being damaged, is itself ethical. If progressive rationalization and acting in accordance with rationalized reason is a form of vice, corrupting the origin, *then critique in response to what has been injured is ethical in itself.* It is this that makes Adorno's philosophical practice as a whole ethical, the reflective after-image of an ethical life no longer to be lived ("Wrong life cannot be lived rightly"), despite its lack of a positive ethical teaching.

For Adorno, philosophical thought is lodged in a guilt context, in a space of ruins, and hence in a space where all that appears ethically are remainders about which remorse (confession) and the need to make reparation are demanded. As a guess, it is this all but complete ethical orientation toward the past which explains both Adorno's fragile utopianism as its counterpoint, and above all his seeming and actual indifference to the needs for present action. If the main bearer of vice is rationalized reason, then Adorno believes that *philosophy* itself, philosophical thought, must be the locale, the first respondent to the claims of the remainders. It is, I think, no accident that Adorno's central term for specifying the remainder of anthropomorphic nature is "nonidentity," a conception of the damaged object in the light of its relation to the rationalized concept. But this egregiously abstracts reason from those subjects whose reasoning it is, inflating the centrality of philosophy and its conscience in art practices in a specious way.

To state the same point another way, Adorno is torn between two demands. On the one hand, in order to give the Copernican revolution an axial turn toward the object through critical reflection he must demonstrate that what is arbitrary, contingent, particular, even evanescent are not opposed to reason, that "there is no origin save ephemeral life" (ND, 156). But, as he equally insists, the medium of philosophy is the concept, and conceptuality now *is* abstract; only art as a practice systematically acknowledges the claims of sensuous particularity. Philosophy cannot be concrete in an abstract culture, a culture formed through abstraction; it cannot, in the manner of artistic collage, paste scrapes of concretion into its texts. Philosophy must thus abandon itself to the very abstraction it is taking against. But in seeing this constitutive ethical demand on philosophy, Adorno does come to consider concrete ethical action outside the scope of what philosophy can even talk about. It is difficult not to see this line of thought as conflating the nature of philosophical self-consciousness and actuality with everyday self-consciousness and actuality. There is no obvious reason to think that philosophy's form of ethical action, critique as a form of reparation, exhausts ethical action.

Nonetheless, for Adorno the reconciliation of reason and devotion, subject and object, general and particular, is not a matter of abandoning reason for the sake of something else, say, Heideggerian "being" or Nietzschean affirmation; nor does he want to reduce reason to a tool or instrument, to go pragmatist, above all because secretly reason has been just that all along. Rather, the transformative self-critique of reason is to offer to particularities and contingencies composing our lives all the weightiness that reason sought in necessity, universality, unity, and eternity. The essay, for example, as a form of writing that accedes to the entwinement of particularity and universality, "does not try to seek the eternal in the transient and distill it out; it tries to render the transient eternal" (NL1, 11). The oxymoron of rendering the transient eternal is figurative; the transient, Adorno will claim, can have all the weight, all the substantiality, all the objectivity and bindingness that was once believed to be the prerogative of the necessary and universal. And further, only in the acknowledgement of such transiency and contingency can there be ethical life, a life in which the good is performatively realized. To render the transient eternal is to secure for it the dignity which once only eternity could provide, and which finds it echo in the privilege accorded explanations with the widest possible global reach. That is what is involved in finding the "origin" in ephemeral life, anthropomorphic nature. The vehicle for coming to that realization is the lowly medium of thought, the concept.

However, before turning to the concept, it is necessary to take a step back. Throughout this chapter I have insisted upon the comprehension of nature as anthropomorphic nature. Self-evidently, access to anthropomorphic nature cannot be had directly through immanent critique. Yet it is anthropomorphic nature, in the guise of nonidentity, that governs Adorno's critical procedures. Consider this extravagant passage from *Dialectic of Enlightenment*:

> Enlightenment is more than enlightenment – the distinct representation of nature in its alienation. In the self-cognition of the spirit as nature in disunion with itself, as in prehistory, nature calls itself to account; no longer directly as *mana* – that is, with the alias that signifies omnipotence – but as blind and lame. The decline, the forfeiture of nature consists in the subjugation of nature without which spirit does not exist. (DoE, 39)

It is certainly a theoretical advance to transform the conception of nature as "blind and lame" into nonidentity with the concept. But nonidentity is nonetheless a claim from anthropomorphic nature. Hence, we are still left with the question of the methodological presuppositions underpinning Adorno's access to and employment of this idea of nature.

5

INTERLUDE: THREE VERSIONS OF MODERNITY

Although the whole impetus of Adorno's thought is to raise the possibility and rational necessity for a radical transformation of modernity, he nowhere provides a philosophical analysis of modernity in the sense of how modernity is to be distinguished from and is an achievement with respect to what preceded it. So, on the one hand, Adorno is engaging in a critique of modernity, and presupposes that no philosophical thinking can be legitimate unless it is elaborated in relation to the characteristic institutions and practices of the modern world; on the other hand, he nowhere offers an explicit account of the modern world in its self-conscious differentiation of itself from the theological and metaphysical past. Yet this reluctance to provide an affirmative account of modernity must trouble his critical strategy since in its naturalistic and genealogical aspects it conflicts with the strong conception(s) of modernity in Kant, Hegel, and, to a certain degree, Marx. I think the best one can do here is to say that although Adorno does possess an affirmative conception of modernity that *implicitly results* from his critical endeavors, from immanent critique, it is equally plausible, and almost certainly necessary, to see him as presupposing this affirmative account.

Nonetheless, the reason he remains sanguine, even oblivious, to this question is that the critical object of his thinking is, in a curious way, distinct from the implied and presupposed affirmative account of modernity. Modernity, as what is to be transformed, is not modern but old; modernity as an achievement is yet to be realized. Those two modernities are intertwined in the texts of idealism and their aftermath, in the repetitions of idealism in the philosophies that seek to displace it and in what is promised through the critique of those repetitions. Because of that entwinement, Adorno did not believe he could, legitimately, propound a conception of modernity except as a result. His practice says otherwise.

I begin this chapter by attempting to locate Adorno's conception of modernity in relation to his general views about the role of any putative philosophy of history in a critical theory. In the second section I argue that Adorno's critical practice presupposes, and there are prima facie reasons to believe, that there are at least three logically distinct and irreducible fundamental orientations that can claim to constitute secular modernity: (1) no belief (action, norm, etc.) can be valid apart from our authorizing of it, self-legislating it; (2) that we must be capable of viewing and comprehending human practices as practices of animals of a certain kind who belong to or are parts of the natural world; (3) that we must conceive of significant human values, practices, and institutions as emerging historically as the intended or unintended consequence of particular human activities. We can think of (1) as "modernity as autonomous self-legislation"; (2) as some form of naturalism or vulgar materialism; and (3) could be titled "genealogical particularism." Each of these, I want to claim, is a basic way of thinking about the modern world as a wholly secular one, and further represents the actual standpoint or orientation that governs Adorno's critical practice. What does not appear on this list is instrumental reason; but as Adorno keeps repeating, it is not modern but old.[1] Finally, in the final section of the chapter, I briefly trace Adorno's critique of Kant's account of freedom as a way of showing how standpoints (2) and (3) are both thought of as resulting from immanent critique and yet presupposed in the carrying out of that critique. Because I am here mostly concerned with the problem of anthropomorphic nature that emerged in the previous chapter, Adorno's naturalism is my primary concern. Particularism has its moment in the succeeding chapters.

1. Modernity and the Philosophy of History

As we have seen throughout, the object of critique is rationalized institutional life and the rationalization of reason that generates and reproduces those institutions. A rationalized social world and rationalized reason, however, are the product of a form of thinking and reasoning that is nearly as old as human society; they are the developed form of instrumental reason, the form of reasoning that humans first adopted in order to deal with threatening nature. As Adorno bluntly states the thesis: "[h]uman history, the history of the progressing mastery of nature, con-

1 My idea of three fundamental orientations owes something to the late Cornelius Castoriadis's idea that modernity is governed by two dominant imaginary significations: rational mastery and autonomy. As an account of the dynamics of modernity, I think Castoriadis's account remains compelling. Hence, my use of the idea of fundamental orientation is not his dynamic one, but rather intends an account of what standpoints we must adopt toward the world in order to think the world in wholly secular terms. The best place to go for the fundamentals of Castoriadis's thought remains his *The Imaginary Institution of Society,* trans. Kathleen Blamey (Oxford: Polity Press, 1987). For a thoughtful defence of this aspect of Castoriadis's thought, especially in relation to Habermas, see J. P. Arnason, "The Imaginary Institution of Modernity," *Revue Européenne des Sciences Sociales* 27/86 (1989): 323–37.

tinues the unconscious history of nature, of devouring and being devoured" (ND, 355). In making this remark Adorno neither is denying that this history has had massive progressive features and achievements to its name, both technical and human, nor, as noted before, is he propounding a negative philosophy of history. It is not a negative philosophy of history because he does not think the past was ideal nor that the present is a necessary or inevitable outcome from its raw beginning; things might have gone otherwise (ND, 323), the hopes of the past might have been realized and still might. But there are no grounds for a progressive philosophy of history either, since "after the catastrophes that have happened, and in view of the catastrophes to come, it would be cynical to say that a plan for a better world is manifested in history and unites it" (ND, 320). There are no systematic practices in the present, practices central to the reproduction of society, that can be regarded as the working out or realizations of past dynamic processes, nor, in their turn, do modern practices represent a dynamic potentiality for a better world. This does not mean that there are no "progressive" ideas and ideals in the present; only that they cannot be accounted for through a philosophy of history that will itself, given the disposition of contemporary institutions, be actualized in some now foreseeable future.

"History," Adorno states, "is the unity of continuity and discontinuity" (ND, 320). For the most part history is best seen as discontinuous, as "chaotically splintered moments and phases." Only retrospectively, and only from here, can we "construe" a kind of unity: "the unity of the control over nature, progressing to the rule over men, and finally to that over men's inner nature . . . from the slingshot to the megaton bomb." This is a "construal" in the weak sense that it interpretatively unifies the past in relation to the disposition of present institutions and forms of rationality without claiming that what provides that unity has been an active agent continuously operative in history. The exclusivity of this unity, its interpretative priority for us, is that *now* no other forms of social and historical practice are evident as real alternatives. The combination of Weberian rationalization and the spread of capital have driven out competing forms of sociation and cultural orientation. In fine, there is no deep or dynamic unity in history; what unity it has can be retrospectively constructed only in the light of the (negative) totalization of experience that is occurring. Other readings of the unity of history hence must overplay its unity, generating a philosophy of history thereby, whether it is the dynamic of forces and relations of production leading to the ideal communist future or the history of spirit, while ignoring or misdescribing the present. In a polemical vein, then, following Walter Benjamin's contention that every document of civilization is equally a document of barbarism, Adorno asserts that the Hegelian "transfiguration of the totality of historic suffering into the positivity of the self-realizing absolute . . .

would teleologically be," if it were to be anything real at all, "the absolute of suffering" (ND, 320). Although Hegel too believes that history has been a slaughter bench, and that his goal is to elicit the actual rationality *in* that process, nothing now could vindicate that full reflective separation of reason from the slaughter.

While Adorno does not perceive in present social practices a plan for a better world working itself out, he does regard both contemporary institutions and the reflective comprehension of the present, our own time in thought as represented by idealism, as *also* manifesting or expressing ideals and commitments that he believes we cannot circumvent or forgo. As we already have seen, he regards the practices of the intimate sphere as aporetic because they imply or promise forms of intersubjective experience that they cannot now realize; without the promises implied in the practices of romantic love or marriage or home-owning there would be nothing that could misfire. Equally, Kant's moral philosophy promises or projects certain moral ideas, universalism and others as ends in themselves, which its conception of moral reason retracts. Even capitalist practices are like this: "exchange as a process has a real objectivity and is objectively untrue at the same time, transgressing against its own principle, the principle of equality" (ND, 190). The principle of equality is not to be rejected because it is not actually achieved in capitalist exchanges – this would be regression below the level capital has achieved. Rather, the goal must be to generate a condition in which exchanges are fair and equal. To be sure, these ideals are not ideas of reason, pure and unproblematic in themselves; if the ideals of enlightenment are borne by and/or embodied in practices that are dominating, then the ideals must bear in themselves that dominating moment. No neat separation between historical actuality and cultural ideality can be drawn: "The concept of progress is dialectical . . . in that its organon, reason, is one; a nature-dominating level and a reconciling level do not exist separate and disjunct within reason, rather both share all its determinations."[2] The ideals of the enlightenment, as they have come down to us, are a mixture of domination and promise: the equality of individuals in the market is also their reduction to their labor power, and the reduction of labor power to labor time;[3] the concepts which enjoin the freedom of the moral law –

2 "Progress," in Theodor W. Adorno, *Critical Models: Interventions and Catchwords,* trans. Henry W. Pickford (New York: Columbia University Press, 1998), p. 152. When Adorno goes on to claim that the moment of domination transforms itself into the moment of reconciliation "only in that it [reason] literally reflects itself, in that reason applies reason to itself and, in its self-restriction emancipates itself from the demon of identity," (ibid.), he is claiming that identity thinking is built into the ideals we have as the moment of domination in them, and only through critical reflection on that element can the truth content of the ideal be released.

3 The exchange principle is not only a social exemplification of the universal over the particular, and hence an instantiation of identity thinking, it is its model and fullest expres-

respect, fear, and so on – are also repressive. Reason, as identity thinking, dialectically produces the ideals whose expression through this production is dominating. The actuality of reason is both domination and idealization.

Nonetheless, and perhaps ironically, where Adorno is at his most historicist and complaisant is with respect to the achievements of modernity, the ideals of enlightened liberal thought. Wherever these ideals are challenged, Adorno will contend that the challenge is atavistic, regressive, that the critic mistakes ideals for actuality. What ails modernity is that its own premises, ideals, and aspirations are not actual in its practices, and this failure cannot be an accident: something must be untoward in their very articulation, in the reason that gives and withholds them at the same time.

How emphatically Adorno takes this as the case is expressed in the opening section of *Negative Dialectics,* "The Possibility of Philosophy." Because of his historicism, Adorno does not take it for granted that philosophy has an automatic right to exist or that what the fundamental aims and motives of philosophy are or ought to be can be read off from its history. In his earliest writings, Adorno contended that philosophy was anachronistic, its problems so remote from social reality and the urgency of its problems that the best course of action would be for philosophy to liquidate itself, ceding its place to culture criticism.[4] Recent philosophical developments – he was thinking of Heidegger, but the emergence of positivism also would have been relevant – had shown that idealism's aspiration to give a unified and systematic account of reality was no longer possible, and that philosophy was returning to the plu-

sion: "The exchange principle, the reduction of human labor to the abstract universal concept of average working hours, is fundamentally akin to the principle of identification. Exchange is the social model of the principle, and without the principle there would be no exchange; through it [exchange] non-identical individuals and performances become commensurable, identical. The spread of the principle imposes on the whole world an obligation to become identical, to become total" (ND, 146). Again, the key to instrumental reason is not means-ends logic, but the primacy of the abstract over the concrete, the universal over the particular. For a fine, detailed reading of Marx that comes close to Adorno's position, see Moise Postone, *Time, Labor, and Social Domination: A Reinterpretation of Marx's Critical Theory* (Cambridge: Cambridge University Press, 1993).

4 In "The Actuality of Philosophy" (1931), *Telos* 31 (1977): 124, Adorno states: "By "actuality" is understood not [philosophy's] vague "maturity" or immaturity on the basis of nonbinding conceptions regarding the general intellectual situation, but much more: whether, after the failure of these last great efforts, there exists an adequacy between the philosophic questions and the possibility of their being answered at all; whether the authentic results of the recent history of these problems is the essential unanswerability of the cardinal philosophic questions. . . . Every philosophy which today does not depend on the security of current intellectual and social conditions, but instead upon truth, sees itself facing the problem of a liquidation of philosophy." The relation between this early essay and the opening of *Negative Dialectics* is acutely handled by Max Pensky in his editor's introduction to *The Actuality of Adorno: Critical Essays on Adorno and the Postmodern* (Albany: State University of New York Press, 1997), pp. 1–12.

rality of practices (science, history, ethics, logic, etc.) which had once been its task to unify.

By the time of *Negative Dialectics,* Adorno interprets the failure of idealism more pointedly: "Philosophy, which once seemed obsolete, lives on because the moment to realize it was missed" (ND, 3). The philosophy which once seemed obsolete is idealism; it had seemed to Marx, but not just him, to provide a more or less adequate account of the nature of human reason, and how that same reason displayed itself in the two great modern enterprises: natural science and universalist morality (including liberal political thought). Because idealism appeared correct in its essentials – ongoing disputes being merely quibbles about details – the task of ceasing to interpret the world and to change it, to bring it into accord with reason was not, after all, a critique of idealist rationalism but its affirmation. After a century and a half (now two) of failure in which these ideals were not realized, the judgement that we have failed reason, that we have lacked only the political will and insight to bring about its ideals, is unjustified; the consideration that perhaps it was an inadequate interpretation that forged the promise that it would be translated into practice cannot be indefinitely avoided. Philosophy "lives on" *because* it broke its pledge to be at one with reality, because its (proper) time was missed.[5] Its living on is an afterlife, the reflective form of its "disappointment."[6] There is then a concrete sense in which tradition conditions contemporary philosophical thought: not simply in general is philosophy beholden to what is handed down to it, but specifically its sole mission now is to criticize the tradition of idealism.[7] Hence, no philosophical defense of the

5 Eva Geulen states the thesis well: "Philosophy's afterlife is not a life after the end nor is it the uninterrupted resumption of a previous life. Since philosophy survived its own apocalypse it has become untimely – it comes, from now on, always too late, it will always be a philosophy *post festum,* a postmodern philosophy, as it were. However, only because philosophy paradoxically survived the experience of outliving itself, is there yet a faint chance of one day arriving in time. The 'no longer,' so to speak, holds open the possibility of the 'not yet;' the negative telos sustains the positive." "Theodor Adorno on Tradition," in Pensky (ed.), *The Actuality of Adorno,* p. 180.

6 The word is Max Pensky's in his editor's introduction to ibid., p. 11. In the light of Adorno's views on life, one should hear in the "living on" thesis something more literal and darker than its natural metaphorical interpretation would involve: philosophy can "live on" only because the vital connection between emphatic living and reflection has been severed. Philosophy moves in the shadow world of concepts that are themselves cut off from objects which it unknowingly "lives off."

7 Throughout Adorno one finds this sort of double inflection of a thesis: the presentation of it that accords with the tradition in arguing for it as a general philosophical truth, a truth revealed to and through reason itself, as it were; and elsewhere that same thesis is presented as a concrete response to a concrete situation. The decontextualized, abstract argument convicts the tradition in its own terms, while the contextualized presentation replays the thesis in terms of the particularities the original criticized thesis abstracted from. Unless the second, concrete version of a thesis were possible, Adorno's construal of the primacy of the particular in relation to the general could be accused of being contradictory. The primacy of the object over the subject, the particular with respect to the

ideals of liberal modernity is owed, no further elaboration of the goodness of autonomy or equality or universality or scientific practice, or how all those must be placed within self-determining social practices is owed because they have already as full and articulate a defense (apart from details or issues of presentation) as they could receive. Idealism, sympathetically interpreted, accomplishes all of this more than sufficiently, and there is no intelligible way back from the heights it achieved; idealism, again, is, for all intents and purposes, the philosophical material a priori of modernity, our quasi-transcendental starting point. But it is this because it is its promises that have not been realized, or rather, because *its* promises have been realized but not its ideals. For Adorno rationalist idealism is *the* philosophical articulation of the shadow hanging over the modern world; it continues to loom because in reality it has been neither realized nor replaced. The vacuum between these two possibilities is the reality and experience of nihilism.

Hence the ideals of idealism, and their placement within institutional practices, are not by-the-way commitments for Adorno: their failure to be realized *is* the disappointment of the present, the fundamental cause of our nihilism, and thereby the condition through which we come to philosophical self-consciousness. More specifically, the failure of realization bespeaks a power that was to be reason's, its capacity to determine reality, that it has been shown not to possess. Yet the power that reason lacks is equally a power of reason, the precise power of rationalized reason and its institutional embodiment to prohibit the realization of the ideals of reason. Because rationalized reason is the presumptive source of those ideals and their failure to be realized, reason is divided within itself. Immanent critique is the prolongation, exacerbation, and working through of this division.

2. Idealism, Naturalism, and Particularity

Commitment to the ideals of idealism, however, is insufficient to explain Adorno's critical practice which does not proceed only through immanent critique, only through the comparing of a practice with its normative premises, or the logic of a text with the ideals it promotes. Nor is this an idle point since, not only does Adorno employ the alternative critical vocabularies of naturalism and genealogy in lodging his critique of idealism, but those critical perspectives also token substantive commitments: to a form of naturalized anthropomorphism and the priority of the object. To get some leverage on these premises and commitments, it helps to begin by examining the affirmative account of modernity in idealism.

universal, etc., are not a priori philosophical claims, but specific judgements that bind, are true, only in relation to the context of criticism.

What is the core claim of idealism as philosophical modernism?[8] Roughly something like this: With the coming of modernity – with the emergence of a disenchanted natural world as projected by modern science, a political language of rights and equality, a secular morality, a burgeoning sense of subjective consciousness, and autonomous art – the task of philosophy became that of providing a wholly critical and radically self-reflexive conception of reason and rationality that would demonstrate the immanent ground for our allegiance to these new ways of being in the world. Or better, what these distinctly modern forms of practice evince is an ideal of human freedom and autonomy in which the worth of our pursuits is dependent upon their being self-legislated and self-authorized; only these distinctly modern forms of practice (at least in relation to previous forms of social practice) can be self-legislated without a dogmatic residue, and only what can be so authorized is rationally deserving of our allegiance. What makes philosophical modernism a form of idealism is its radical self-reflexivity: nothing can "count as" a reason (or a piece of evidence or a motive for an action or an intention or a belief, etc.) unless we so count it, normatively authorize it. And what makes this version of idealism "Hegelian" is that in place of Kant's "I think" which must accompany all my representations, there is a "we think" that must accompany all our fundamental practices; and in place of a transcendental deduction of the categories necessary for the possibility of experience (and finally for rational self-determination), we are offered an historical narrative of the self-defeating character of the antecedents to modernity's self-authorizing institutional forms.

Phrased in this way, idealist modernism can appear a daunting claimant since its fundamental critical gesture, derived from Kant, treats all of its opponents as falling into some version or other of the Myth of the Given, some version of providing a ground or authority for what we do in a source beyond our doing that is given to us, and hence either lapsing into some form of dogmatism or pretending to an authority that it can have only because we have already, reflexively, tokened that authority. Yet there is massive difference between, let's say, the Kantian *appeal* of the argument for self-legislation and the actual Hegelian defense of it. The Kantian version of the self-legislation, self-authorization thesis, in which only formal reason itself is truly self-determining, depends on the belief that reason in itself provides the necessary, and arguably constitutive conditions, for what is to *count as* a reason that we *could* self-legislate and share. Adorno, following Hegel, denies that reason on its own can accomplish this end, that there is an atemporal or historically immutable reason that from within its own resources can determine what makes a

8 I am here summarizing, fast and brutally, the core contentions of Robert Pippin's defence of philosophical modernism in his *Idealism as Modernism*.

reason a good one. But this says only that reason is not a spontaneous product of our intellects which can and must be legislative for our activities because it represents who we truly are. In broad terms then the claim for autonomous self-legislation is not equivalent to a claim that we possess a given rational essence whose dictates would govern our pursuit of the great ends of acquiring knowledge and attaining moral worth.

Once, however, the strong Kantian version of autonomous self-legislation is set aside, how much is left of the argument against heteronomy? How strong is the claim that any prereflective attachment to the world, an obeisance to a law that is not "our law," must be invidiously heteronomous? What is the force of the idealist reminder that nothing can count as a reason unless we so count it? And again it is worth noting that the sound or appeal of this argument against heteronomy derives much of its force from the critique of religion, from the metaphysical beliefs that seek to ground human practice in divine law. And there are some modern views – forms of naturalism that believe the whole story about human cognition can be given in, broadly, causal terms (nature's law), or the Heideggerian idea that Being provides or sends the clearing within which human activities can be pursued – that inevitably strike us as attempting to go behind the back of reason and locate some ultimate authority that is antecedent to it. However, to argue that nothing beyond human practice can ground or found it since only through our practices and their capacities for justification can an item come to have an authorizing role, and *in that sense* nothing outside reason grounds or founds it, says less than it might first appear. As we saw in the case of tradition, while we can no longer regard traditional authority as self-sufficient, doing something only because it is the tradition, obeying tradition on the grounds of tradition, we can come to see tradition as a necessary condition for reflective and rational activities by coming to recognize the historical and social character of all such activities. Because something is thus handed down and given to us does not make it heteronomous in any invidious sense – a thesis Hegelian idealism insists upon rather than denies; it is the core of Hegel's critique of the radicalism of the French Revolution. In terms of the argument being presented, any collective independence and capacity for self-legislation would require our acknowledging our collective dependence on the materials and institutional practices (the norms governing those practices) handed down to us by the historical tradition: we must start in the middle, from where we are. And where we are, rationally and institutionally, is equally, for Adorno, *who* we are, who we have become. Hence, Adorno's reliance on what he takes to be the best sociological accounts of our modern institutions, and the best philosophical articulations of the present standpoint, and his project of using the strength of the constitutive subject, who we are, to overcome it. Might not there be other "items" that figure *in* our practices the way tradition does? And might not these other items claim a kind of equality with the self-authorization thesis?

Hegelian self-legislation seems a secular ideal in which the ultimate authority of an item depends upon its fit and suitability for having a place within a series of practices for which we are ultimately responsible; nothing is good or worthy in itself but only in virtue of its enabling of self-determining social practices whose authority in this respect is absolute.[9] This, again, is a weaker thesis than it appears, because it is not presented by Hegel or his defenders as a foundational philosophical thesis, but rather as one that emerges from, what is argued to be, the self-defeating character of its historical antecedents. But in emerging in this way what it provides are not criteria for present practices but, rather, as one defender states it, "with a sort of original '*orientation*.'"[10] The notion of "orientation" as used here is apt since its expresses the kind of nondogmatic, criterionless, normative commitment that is involved in the claim for Hegelian self-legislation. Although I say more about this notion of original orientation below (it possess a wider significance than its use here evinces), for the present let us accept that it specifies the way in which in virtue of our reflective grasp of the history that has brought us here nothing can make a claim on us accept through those social practices of justification, and the norms governing them, that enable the item to lodge its claim. No facts, objects, persons, gods, or demons, in themselves and apart from how they are taken up, can matter. Mattering is something that transpires through social practice and is empty outside it.

Now insofar as this is what is at stake, this is an orientation that Adorno accepts. Even where he is defending the priority of the object over the subject, Adorno insists that this priority is not restored by any form of direct awareness, or by insisting on some putative facts, or by flat appeals to experience. "The primacy of object," Adorno asserts in a complex formulation, "means rather that the subject for its part is object in a qualitatively different, more radical sense than object, because object cannot be known except through consciousness, hence is also subject" (SO, 249). By this intentionally clumsy formulation, Adorno is asserting the reflexive character of our becoming aware of our placement in a natural world of which we are a part, but a part that has the characteristic of re-

9 Much of the force of Hegel's own thought is packed into the word "enabling" as used in this sentence. For Hegel what the constraint on such enabling involves is that the practices concerned must secure the fact of there being social practices we share while acknowledging that the only ultimate bearers of such social practice are individuals each of whom has a life that is not synonymous with the life of the institution, his or her own good, and who possess the capacity to transform given practices. While the great weakness of Adorno's ethical and philosophical utopia is that it is presented almost wholly negatively and, above all, without consideration of its institutional realization, nothing in this aspect of the Hegelian picture conflicts with what Adorno thinks is worth affirming.

10 Pippin, *Idealism as Modernism*, p. 147; emphasis mine.

lating to other parts through cognition. As knowing subjects we reflectively become aware that we are also objects among other objects, and must hence consider our status as knowing subjects, what separates us from other objects, as a characteristic that is intelligible only as that of an object of a certain kind. In a more directly idealist vein, and almost immediately after this last statement, he says: "The object's primacy is the *intentio obliqua* of the *intentio obliqua,* not the warmed-over *intentio recta*; the correction to the subjective reduction, not the denial of a subjective share" (SO, 250). Even the primacy of the object for Adorno is something that arises only through critique and reflection, and hence is something that requires rational assent and acknowledgement. There is no going below or behind the back of reason. All immediacies are mediated.

By conceding these points one might think that Adorno is conceding that the collective self-legislation thesis is modernity's fundamental orientation, however otherwise elaborated. Yet conceding this thesis is not equivalent to agreeing to its exclusivity; on analogy with the example of history and tradition, Adorno plainly believes there are at least two further "original orientations" – had he access to this idea – which we cannot conceive surrendering. First, as implied by the priority of the object thesis, against the backdrop of the achievements of natural science, against the backdrop of the discoveries that the world existed long before us and that we have evolved out of lower life forms, but in so evolving come on the scene in the same way they do, we must conceive of ourselves as being *parts* of the natural world, however much social and cultural practices transcend their natural setting and develop forms of normativity that cannot be derived from anything natural science (in its search for laws of nature) could explain. Adorno thinks the correct non-reductionist way to approach naturalism is via piecemeal demonstration of how what first appear to be purely cultural or intelligible phenomena are dependent upon what they presume to transcend, culture is a way of inhabiting the natural world and outgrowth of it.[11] *The* piecemeal exemplar of this in Adorno is, of course, the demonstration that what we think of as pure reason is an outgrowth of the drive for self-preservation, something more than that drive but still bound to it. Naturalism, in the sense of conceiving of the human form of life as emerging within and from nature, is not for us an optional or arbitrary orientation; in the same way in

11 So far as I am aware, Adorno had no access to modern ethology. But it is almost inevitable that we should see his genealogical naturalism as adumbrating a practice of genealogical reflection that would be ethologically informed. Not having access to ethological findings, Adorno's genealogical naturalism thus becomes highly speculative. Equally relevant here, although I do not elaborate it, is Adorno's employment of psychoanalytic thought. In that stretch of his work it is fair to say that he was interested, precisely, in psychoanalysis's conception of the transformation of the natural (drive theory) into the social, and the recurrent interplay between those two levels.

which heteronomous forms of authority have become unintelligible, dogmatic, so metaphysical conceptions of ourselves as created, as wholly immaterial substances, as disembodied souls, as fully autonomous and rationally self-legislating, as essentially end-setters, as not animals of any kind, have become unintelligible – not as pieces of abstract argument, but as a consequence of the orientation of naturalism, of naturalism as an horizon of intelligibility. Our animal embodiment, our ways of living it out, and its role in all our practices, is the mark of our belonging to nature, a part of the "prehistory of reason" (ND, 289), that is at least as historically noncircumventable now, an orientation, as reason's constitution through social practice and its correction.[12] Even more emphatically, nothing for us can count as an account of reason or practice unless it is in broad terms compatible with some form of naturalism, however expanded, our aporetic condition of being parts of the natural world without a naturally given niche in it. Hence, reason itself is answerable to the demands of naturalism in some yet to be identified version. One might even suppose that the authority of the self-legislation thesis – nothing to count unless we so count it – is dependent on the naturalist orientation; is it not our creatureliness, that we are not created beings, that abandons us to reason as the only resource we possess for determining our existence (ND, 381)?

Second, modern historical awareness tells us that nearly all of our most fundamental values and ideals are subject to a level of constitutive contingency both in their historical emergence (hence our penchant for genealogy), and individually (the meaning or worth of a life can be grounded in what is no more than the contingency of events). This is a different aspect of the priority of the object. Apart from his consistent employment of genealogical materials (which in part owe their rationality to the natural history thesis), this orientation is realized most explicitly in Adorno through the critique of abstraction and a quarrying after what might count as concretion in philosophy and cognition generally. So, very near the opening of *Negative Dialectics,* Adorno states that what is of the most interest to philosophy now – he is thinking of Heidegger, Husserl, Bergson, and others – are those things in which Hegel and the tradition preceding him expressed a disinterest: "the nonconceptual, individual, and the particular – that which ever since Plato used to be dis-

12 As Simon Jarvis, *Adorno: A Critical Introduction,* pp. 35–7, 217–22, correctly points out, this is the crux of an Adornoian answer to second-generation critical theory which attempts to neatly separate a cultural sphere of intersubjectivity as communication from material nature: "For a materialist theory, to dominate other humans – since humans are not pure culture – is *already* domination of nature as well as social domination, not social domination instead of or 'modelled upon' domination of nature. Only a theory which itself presupposes mastery of nature can regard intersubjectivity as a separate sphere which has somehow separated itself from the natural" (p. 35).

missed as transitory and insignificant . . . Of urgency to the concept would be what it cannot reach, what escapes its mechanism of abstraction, what is not already an instance of it" (ND, 8). Since this thought is central for Adorno, and one whose full force does emerge best as a result, I will elaborate it at length below. However, even the Hegelian story about the modern orientation, insofar as it does not conceive of Spirit as a moving force in history beyond the activities of individuals, depends on major achievements being the unintended consequences of action, of the necessity of our being where we are as a retrospective construction that could have turned out otherwise, and so in reality dependent on accident, contingency, and the like.[13] But historical self-consciousness thinks this can be pressed further: in the light of historical discovery, are we now not normatively enjoined to consider the possibility that *all* significant human things have their origin in concrete states of affairs that could have been different or in themselves not produced what they in fact did, including our normative practices? Would not denying this end up denying the significance of history and the role of individual human efforts in it? But if anything like this critical, genealogical perspective is commanding for us, an original orientation that explicates our experience of ourselves as belonging to or in a wholly secular world, a world without providence or divine forces, then must it not equally affect how we conceive of future practice, of what social practices are or can be? If the lesson of genealogy is that our highest ideals emerge through particular actions and events, in

13 However the history of spirit is thought, the claim that past social practices, when seen through the lens of phenomenological reconstruction, were practically self-defeating is not the same as claiming that those practices empirically collapsed because they were structurally self-defeating. The collapse of the Roman empire had very little to do with structural faults in its normative self-understanding. Whether its distance from empirical history must be a mark against Hegelian history is a matter for dispute. Given that some of the stakes of history are normative, then it is not obvious to me that Hegelian retrospective reconstruction in which it is demonstrated that past forms of practice were, endogenously, doomed to collapse, and that there is a way of construing the path of multiple collapses as informing our present, are obviously methodologically faulty. What Adorno insists upon is that we cannot accept the whole of that story in its own terms; what occurred in the past is not *reducible* to the triumphal story – its bracketing of "the discontinuous character of blighted life [*zerrüttete Leben*]" (ND, 319) – nor is the present the *concrete* actualization of its orientational result (few modern practices in fact operate in accordance with those normative self-understandings). In Hegelian language, we might say that its normative story in highlighting the rational rose in the cross of the present is too much rose and too little cross, and, more important, seems unable to regard the cross of the present as anything other than our failure to realize those normative ideals. The two are not yet so separately identifiable. History itself forces us, Adorno contends, to question whether the failure may not be in part due to how those norms have been expressed and elaborated. So Adorno is also attempting to locate the rose in the cross, but is going to find it elsewhere than where Hegel looked. Adorno, then, is reapplying to Hegelian modernity the accusation of formalism it lodged against Kant, and he finds in Kant some of the individuality and particularity, and some larger sense of what is lost in virtue of what is actualized that is needed to rebut Hegel.

how ideals and norms are *instantiated* and thus taken up and exploited, if, then *actuality precedes possibility* (*the* modal linchpin upon which particularism turns) in this way, then must not that matter to how we conceive of the role particularity, the weight and burden of singular events and actions in ethical life?[14]

Contingencies, sensuous particulars, events, like the elements of anthropomorphic nature that Adorno aims to rehabilitate or uncover, are not brute facts, self-sufficient in themselves; they do require rational acknowledgement. However, saying that is not equivalent to agreeing to the claim that the perspective of rational self-determination is self-sufficient, either. What the perspective of autonomy reveals is that contingency and belonging to nature as a whole are *claims* that require appreciation and normative validation; but *the contents of those claims exceed normative self-validation*: from the perspective of those contents it is not true that it is normativity *all* the way down; that is just the mistake of the constitution thesis. Tautologically, because an item cannot now be accepted as having worth unless it is recognized as having worth, that is, its worth would be idle, vacuous, unless it played a role in our cognitive life, it does not follow that its worth is *constituted,* conferred upon the object through our activities – which was my point about the appearance of the apple and the value-conferment thesis in the preceding chapter. Arguably, this is the most consistent element of Adorno's critique of the concept: "What is known through consciousness must be something; mediation applies to something mediated [and not the given]. But subject, the epitome of mediation, is the 'How,' and never, as contrasted to the object, the 'What' that is postulated by every conceivable idea for a concept of subject" (SO, 249). Exercises of spontaneity may indeed be the *way* in which we actualize ourselves as animals, but *what* is so actualized is in the first instance our animal life, and thereafter objects whose material embodiment contributes to their meaningfulness in a manner that outpaces our powers of value conferment.[15] Thus, even if it is true that nothing can count as a claim unless realized through social practice, in the same way in which tradition conditions practice from within and from without and the attempt to eliminate it is necessarily self-defeating (the example of the French Revolution again), so our anthropomorphic nature and contin-

14 In saying this, I do not mean to deny that there are *constraints,* one might even say transcendental constraints on, human practices; to deny that would be to deny that forms of activity could be existentially self-defeating. As becomes clearer below, the thought is rather that the force of any such constraint, and hence what it might mean to heed it, is irrevocably bound to its instantiation.

15 The first clause of this sentence paraphrases John McDowell's conception of the relation between spontaneity and animality, which the rest of the sentence is implicitly criticizing. See *Mind and World* (Cambridge, Mass.: Harvard University Press, 1994), p. 78. I take up McDowell's arguments in the next chapter.

gency condition practice from within (in what is taken up and acknowledged) and from without (as material conditions of it that are not now recognized in their role in practice, generating thereby the self-defeating enterprises of rationalized culture and society). If anthropomorphic nature and attachment to practices in the light of contingent conditions do play the role in our lives here being ascribed to them, then they have as much a claim to be counted as (components of) "who we unavoidably are" as any unavoidable rationality requirements. That is the reason why Adorno takes such pains, despite the dangers involved, to explicate that the wrongness of identity thinking is *existentially* self-defeating – a revocation of our constitutive embodiment and constitutive contingent conditioning – and not simply or merely irrational or bad theory or insufficiently explanatory or not corresponding to all the facts.

Equally, *as orientations,* naturalism and genealogical particularism may each be regarded as *constituting* the secularizing movement of modernity, as providing it with its only historically specific productive normative resources. As becomes evident below, Adorno does not believe we can surrender any of these orientations, nor does he believe that they can be synthesized into one large philosophical system that would provide *the* modern orientation.[16] Adorno is most misleading in not explicating and acknowledging that his philosophizing depends on and presupposes these orientations, and hence, that while their *ultimate* claim must pass through and emerge from work on the concept, because it is the minimal unit of cognition, and must be shown as belonging *to* the concept, for the same reason, that immanent critique of the concept is not free-floating, wholly immanent. In attempting to show the role of contingency and nature *in* the concept, he has already brought these competing perspectives to it. Adorno is not unaware of this; natural history and genealogy, as we see below, are what make possible "metacritique" – historical and naturalizing genealogy. But it is the status and meaning of metacritique which is at issue here. On my reading, because Adorno fails to suf-

16 For Adorno, philosophy becomes self-reflection and critique. The idea of a grand synthesis of these orientations would belong to the ideal of philosophy as system; but that ideal cannot be sustained except through a "synthesis of diversity" (ND, 20) which hence would hand over priority to the universal over the particular (ND, 20–28). If the object is going to have priority, however this is spelled out, then what results must be intrinsically not self-sufficient, and hence intrinsically answerable to other perspectives and views.

I was emboldened to spelling out Adorno's view in this way after hearing Bernard Williams's "Genealogy and Naturalism" at Vanderbilt University in February 1998. Although I would guess that Williams is far less sympathetic to the claims of idealist modernism than either I or Adorno is, his conception of genealogy and naturalism as irreducible, overlapping, and competing paradigms of social explanation and self-understanding (or so I understand the thrust of his argument) helped solidify my view that Adorno was operating with critical perspectives that were irreducible to one another but differently and jointly necessary.

ficiently or accurately acknowledge that his critical practice has accepted particularity and naturalism as original orientations, he fails to adequately distinguish the sense in which idealism is central because its concept of the concept is the dominant one with its role as one (progressive) orientation amongst others. Idealism is the dominant of modernity in that its concept of the concept is the one that is normatively standard and actual in social reproduction (assuming that bureaucratic rationalization and the domination of use values by exchange value can both be regarded as employing the same assumption, the principle of immanence, as operative in the concept); idealism is not the dominant of modernity, however, as the exclusive orientational horizon of self-understanding; there naturalism and genealogy are equal competitors and collaborators. Indeed, as orientations they may be said to have been more efficacious in modern thought than idealism, however much their thought misfires because it pursues those orientations, unknowingly, under the flag of identity thinking.[17] Adorno has and employs more critical perspectives than his self-description of his activity appears to acknowledge.

3. The Metacritique of Freedom

Consider very briefly, and only for example, Adorno's immanent critique of Kant's conception of freedom and free will. While extended and elaborate, covering nearly 100 pages, near the center of this critique is the immanent attempt to show that the will, pure reason, apart from bodily impulses cannot be a source of movement or action (ND, 240). For Adorno, the real response to Kant's question of whether pure reason can be practical is to show the unintelligibility of the idea of pure reason: "By

17 This is the crux of Adorno's critique of reductive naturalism – the absolutist conception of knowledge, or the ideal of a perspectiveless knowing. His brief critique is worth stating in full: "Identity thinking, the screen-image of the dominant dichotomy [between subject and object], in the age of subjective impotence no longer poses as the absolutization of the subject [as it did in Kant, Fichte, Hegel, and Husserl]. What is taking shape instead is a type of seeming anti-subjectivist, scientifically objective identity thinking, what is called reductionism. . . . It is the characteristic form of reified consciousness at present, false, because of its latent and therefore all the more fatal subjectivism. The residue [of anthropomorphic nature, hence raw nature] is molded according to the standard of the ordering principles of subjective reason [= the categories of the understanding], and being abstract itself, it agrees with the abstractness of that reason. Reified consciousness, which mistakes itself for nature, is naive: a historical formation and itself mediated through and through, it takes itself, to speak with Husserl, for an "ontological sphere of absolute origins" and takes the thing confronting it, which it itself has trussed up, for the coveted matter itself. The ideal of depersonalizing knowledge for the sake of objectivity retains nothing but the *caput mortuum* of objectivity" (SO, 252–3). The final argument is exactly the same as one of his arguments against Kant: naturalized epistemology as the reflexive or self-implicating form of the philosophical claim for the privilege of scientific knowing, the claim that what mathematical physics and its circle capture of the world *is* the world, mistakes the achievement of science, with all its social and historical presuppositions, as its self-sufficient ground.

allowing no *movens* of practice but reason, Kant remained under the spell of that faded theory [of the isolation of reason and consciousness from material experience] against which he devised the primacy of practical reason as a complement. This is what ails his entire moral philosophy" (ND, 229).

The strongest element of the Kantian thesis is its plausible contention that a desire or impulse on its own is not a reason for action. Unless a desire is *taken* as a reason for action, incorporated into a maxim, it will not move me to action. The best evidence for this is that we can have a desire at a time which, no matter how strongly it is felt, does not by itself lead us to act on it. Feelings of murderous rage can strike us as having no worth, and hence as not even considerable with respect to action; feelings of fear, which naturally incline us to flee or protect ourselves, may be ignored when the occasion requires. By itself, however, this much of Kant's incorporation thesis shows that while reason is not reducible to inclinations, the reasons for action we develop nonetheless can be viewed as an outgrowth from natural ends: courage as the need to master fear; patience as the need to control immediate desires for the sake of those desires or for longer term ends and so on. And, by a series of transformations, reasons for action, above all those elaborated within complex institutional practices, can emerge that have no direct natural antecedents (however much those institutions themselves are grounded in our animal nature). Reason, in this light, is again how we actualize our animal lives.

Reasoning activities, as normative, are not reducible to drives and inclinations; and drives and inclinations on their own are not, for rational animals, unconditionally self-authorizing reasons – which, at this level of generality, is not to deny that they are nonetheless reasons. This much of what has come to be called the "incorporation thesis" is granted by Adorno.[18] But it is not sufficient for Kant. For him, if reasons are to be truly reasons and not secretly articulations of our animality, then there

18 In *Religion Within the Limits of Reason Alone,* trans. Theordore M. Greene and Hoyt H. Hudson (New York: Harper & Row, 1960), p. 19, Kant states that the freedom of the will, *Willkür,* is "of a wholly unique nature in that an incentive can determine the will to action only insofar as the individual has incorporated it into his maxim (has made it a general rule in accordance with which he will conduct himself). . . . " For a defence of the doctrine, see Henry Allison, *Kant's Theory of Freedom* (New York: Cambridge University Press, 1990), pp. 40–41. Of course, the extant to which I have conceded something to the incorporation thesis – that the sorts of desires that are reasons for action are essentially hospitable to rational criticism – is weaker than the actual Kantian view in which a desire is only a *reason* for action if incorporated into a maxim and thereby subject to the constitutive demands for something being rational provided by the hypothetical and categorical imperatives. My weak statement of thesis is intended to capture the thought that desires and inclinations as reasons for actions belong within the space of reasons generally, without dragging with that concession any commitment to purely (a priori) rational standards.

must be reasons that are pure, without any natural antecedent, and equally there must be a capacity to act that is not naturally conditioned: our willing must be of such a kind that it is wholly independent from natural determination, an unconditioned capacity for self-movement. For this to be the case reason must be capable of exhausting the will without remainder (ND, 228). One side of this argument depends on the purity of reason as a spontaneous product of the intellect; an idea we have already found grounds for doubting. What worries the other side, immanently, is the intelligibility of something purely mental realizing itself in action and in the world. Adorno avers that the phenomenological basis for Kant's thesis is the self-experience of the moment of freedom depending on consciousness: "the subject knows itself to be free only insofar as its action strikes it as identical with it, and that is the case in conscious actions only" (ND, 227). My actions are free only if irreducibly mine, and what is irreducibly mine is what follows from being consciously chosen. There is some truth in this since only in what is consciously chosen can "subjectivity laboriously, ephemerally raise its head." But, Adorno continues, consciousness or rational insight is not the same as the free act. Nor is conscious insight a sufficient guarantor of the independence of the will from inclinations; only the presumed distance of the laws of reason from natural determination can fully distance consciousness from desire. Ignore the issue that we have reason to think that pure reason is an outgrowth from the drive to self-preservation; there is here a Humean worry that Adorno accepts: how might pure reason, logic, consistency, move us to act?

"Logic," Adorno asserts, "is a practice insulated against itself. Contemplative conduct, the subjective correlate of logic, is the conduct that wills nothing" (ND, 230). For rational insight to be just that and nothing else, it must *abstract* itself from the demands of practice. The withdrawal from practice is what *forms* the practice, the conduct of theory, the ideals of a purely knowing consciousness and rational insight. Adorno thus believes that the protocols of theoretical reflection emerge in a two-step process: in the first step, the flickering withdrawal from practice implicit in practices of reasoning, finding suitable means to accomplish a given end, for example, is extended and exacerbated at first circumstantially (because the problem faced has no obvious solution), and then self-consciously. It is withdrawing from action in this self-conscious mode that first makes reasoning a new mode of conduct, a new orientation on the world. What holds this new mode of conduct in place as non-action is achieved in the second step through institutionalizing that withdrawal into reflective practices on their own, and then codifying the rules of those now separate activities. If the reasoning governing everyday practices is conceived of transpiring in accordance with rules of material inference, then the self-conscious withdrawal from the action-orientation of those inference structures in order to make them explicit will operate through a process of abstraction and decontextualization, and thence the reinterpretation of those rules into self-contained patterns, eventually, after the failures of patterning by myth and metaphysics, the patterns of science and pure logic. But this is as much as to say that the protocols of contemplative reason, pure reason, are formed in part for the sake of sustaining the activities of reasoning apart from the pressures of action. Once this mode of conduct is established, it equally follows that "each act of will breaks through the mechanical autarky of logic; this is what makes theory and practice antithetical" (ND, 230).[19] This conception of breakthrough, apart from the intermediaries of those affects that are to flow from reason, troubles Kant's account.

The mystery of the breakthrough is resolved if we turn the matter around; rather than moving from the question of how pure insight can move us to action, we should see conscious insight, reason, and logic, and the idea of the autonomous will, as developing from a repression or withdrawal from the demands for action. Hence, Adorno's belief that what Kant has done is taken the part of action that differs from pure consciousness, what in Kant's eyes "compels the action, the part that abruptly leaps out" (ND, 229), namely, the spontaneity of action, and transplanted it into pure consciousness. Two theses support this idea. First, "pure consciousness – 'logic' – itself has come to be; it is a validity that has submerged its genesis. It [its genesis] lies in a moment Kantian doctrine suppresses: in the negation of the will, which according to Kant would be pure consciousness" (ND, 230). Not only has contemplative conduct and logic come to be, possessing a validity that cannot be fully detached from its genesis, but that genesis involves a negation of the will, a sublimation and hence redirection of the impulses to act into the conduct of thought. For a will exhausted by reason alone to arise, embodied willing must have been already negated: "What the great rationalist philosophers conceived of as the will is already, without accounting for it, a denial of the will."

This gives on to Adorno's second thesis. He calls what I have just termed the embodied will the "addendum [*Hinzutretende*]," on the grounds that for now this is all it is – an addendum to pure consciousness. Developing consciousness requires that the addendum become increasingly sublimated, and only with that increase can the will "as something substantial and unanimous [*Substantiellen und Einstimmigen*]" be formed. Since Adorno is not opposed to the will as something "substantial and unanimous," this sublimation is not to be decried. Nonetheless, "if the motor form of reaction were liquidated altogether, if the hand no longer

19 Not for nothing, Adorno believes, is the radically self-reflective Hamlet the first example of a *self*-emancipating modern subject; in him "we find the divergence of insight and action paradigmatically laid down" (ND, 228).

twitched, there would be no will." We cannot even conceive of willing except as a further elaboration of motor reactions, instinctual responses (sucking, grasping, patterns of eye movement), spontaneously enjoined response mechanisms like infant imitation, and on. These examples, reminders, support the idea that reason "has genetically evolved from the force of human drives as their differentiation."

By stating this Adorno is not offering a philosophical *theory* about the connection between mind and matter; he has none. Rather, he means his remarks to be taken as emerging from the immanent critique of the idea of pure will. So, the idea of the addendum works throughout the small section on it (ND, 226–30), as an emblem of anthropomorphic nature that is conceived as both a necessary supplement to the idea of pure will and as a figure reconciling the mind (culture) and nature. In its first guise, it can be the necessary supplement to pure will because it is "the name for that which was eliminated" (ND, 229) in the formation of pure practical reason. In reality, this elimination was an incomplete abstraction, and only in idea, in philosophical reflection, does it come to appear as downright otherness to pure practical reason. In its second guise,

> the addendum is an impulse, the rudiment of a phase in which the dualism of extra- and intramental was not thoroughly consolidated, neither volitionally bridgeable nor an ontological ultimate. This also affects the concept of the will that contains so-called facts of reason, which at the same time, pure descriptively, are more than that; this lies hidden in the will's transition to practice. The impulse, intramental and somatic in one, drives beyond the conscious sphere to which it belongs just the same. With that [impulse] freedom extends to the realm of experience; this animates its concept as a state in which nature would be neither blind nor oppressed. Its phantasm, which reason will not allow to be withered by any proof of causal independence, is that of a reconciliation of mind and nature. (ND, 228–9)

Taken at face value, this could well strike one as naive, crude, fanciful, or all three. At one level, Adorno is pursuing what could have been a plausible philosophical hypothesis, namely, that what we have come to think of as pure reasoning and free willing emerged from a state in which "voluntary" actions were just "responses" to external stimuli and bodily drives. In such a state there is no reason to press a sharp distinction between what is somatic in character and what belongs to the domain of consciousness. This is not offered, however, as an hypothesis that might receive theoretical vindication. Nor is it a prelude or anticipation of theory. Rather, the remark is entered as an attempt to relieve the transcendental anxiety that emerges from the duality which Kantian doctrine introduces between the demands of reason, on the one hand, and the apparently wholly extraneous embodied action, on the other. When we are not in the grip of such an idea, we naturally suppose the somatic and the rational cohabit in action. But, and it is here that Adorno's remarks press beyond forming an account of how reasoning could eventuate in empirical action (because they, reasons, are just reified bits of somatic life), we cannot be fully relieved and disabused of our anxiety by the transcendental reminder because there is an actual, historic aspect to the duality. It is not an accident that at the center of his account Adorno employs a concept – the addendum – that is an invention, a neologism. Relief fails to follow from insight because the relation of mind and nature expressed in the folk psychology which is the social actuality of self- understanding, which philosophical reflection tracks, has already radically come to conceive of mentality as nature's other (or, more exactly, of nature as the absolute other of mentality); and, on the other hand, we have come to think of nature as a realm of causal law.[20] No juggling with these dichotomous vocabularies will put an end to the anxiety or comfortably express the mind and body's belonging together; too much damage and abstraction has occurred to both sides. Hence, the notion of addendum both refers back to a point when the duality between mind and body had yet to get a grip, and hence when there was no problem about the relation between the two which called for philosophic resolution (which is why one might think that the purport of Adorno's genealogy is transcendental), while simultaneously acknowledging that we do not inhabit that point, thus curtailing the force of the transcendental claim. To claim that the actuality of the position which would be a dissolution of dualism is an addendum is to offer and withdraw relief from the dualism at the same time.

By lodging his immanent critique of the pure will, Adorno is not unaware of alternative and more ameliorating strategies in Hegel, Nietzsche, Freud. But he cannot see those strategies as other than ameliorating, as attempting to revoke the extremes which the Cartesian and Kantian philosophies have already lodged; and to the extent to which they propose a theory of the unity of mind and nature, they leap over the

20 Adorno subjects the idea of nature as a realm of pure causal law-governedness to the same sort of critique as he subjects the idea of the pure will (ND, 247–9, 265–70). The notion of law-governedness is modeled after identitarian reason. Actual causal episodes occur not in chains (X causes Y causes Z), but in causal contexts or fields, and can be singular. When so conceived, it becomes possible to perceive that causal necessity owes more to reason's self-understanding of order than to natural fact. Hence the hostility of nature to human freedom is a construct of free self-determining reason. While this is crude, at least some of its drift is operative in recent analytic work on scientific law and causality. In particular see Dupré, *The Disorder of Things,* chapters 8 and 9, and the challenging works of Nancy Cartwright: *How the Laws of Physics Lie* (Oxford: Oxford University Press, 1983), and *Nature's Capacities and Their Measurement* (Oxford: Oxford University Press, 1990). Dupré's work, which extends Cartwright's, is significant here since its impulse is to attempt to conceive of how the nature described by mathematical physics can be brought to actually accommodate the reality of living systems where the latter cannot be reduced to the former.

disenchanted and dualist disposition of pre-theoretical thought and practice. The extremes, Adorno consistently claims, the exaggerated elaboration of a problem, are truer to our difficulties than what pretends these problems can be resolved or overcome by immediate theoretical fiat. Hence, the addendum is figured as an ancient impulse, suppressed, sublimated, withered, but necessarily weakly present if real willing is to be intelligible; and as such, it figures as a promise of a reconciliation between mind and nature that is *not* now actually conceptualizable: "It is a flash of light between the poles of something long past, something grown all but unrecognizable, and what some day might come to be" (ND, 229). The addendum is, and is only, the *figure* of something that would be neither mental, as now conceived, nor natural, as now conceived. Its validity is negative; it is nothing other than an excrescence of the pure will. What might be different, as the unity of mind and nature, can be conceived only through a transformation of the practices in which our folk psychology and our conception of the natural world are embedded.[21]

The notion of the addendum perfectly images particularity and anthropomorphic nature emerging, however fragilely and indeterminately, as the *results* of immanent critique: in acting we must be depending upon the particular impulse that is neither somatic nor mental in character if the mystery of how pure reason can be practical is to be resolved. In reality, however, this critique is not as independent as my account, which could be filled in far more extensively, makes it appear. Well before Adorno has proposed the idea of the addendum, he has already genealogically delegitimated the idea of the pure will. From the outset Adorno denies that *a will* that is monadologically insulted from the outside world is intelligible: " . . . countless moments of external – notably social – reality invade the decisions designated by the words 'will' and 'freedom'; if the concept of the rationality in the will means anything at all, it must refer precisely to that invasion" (ND, 213). All the ideas, con-

21 The torturous movement of this paragraph aims to pick out a general feature of Adorno's philosophizing, namely, a two-step procedure in which, first, the attempt is made to *dissolve* a philosophical problem by providing a genealogical account of its emergence from a state of affairs in which the dialectical anxieties of the present could not so much as get a grip. Because Adorno is not offering theory to explain some possibility (how reason could eventuate in bodily action, for example), but historically redescribing what appears to call for theoretical resolution such that the elements seem to "naturally" fit, I am here calling this step "transcendental." In the second step, which of course in Adorno is almost always offered simultaneously with the first step, the transcendental relief offered in the first step is withdrawn, shown somehow to be more like a memory or anticipation (hope), thereby making the first step problematic – what should provide transcendental relief is posed within a conditional setting: we would feel (transcendental) relief if . . . As continuous with philosophy, Adorno provides the possibility of the kind of transcendental insights that dissolve rather solve traditional dilemmas; as critic of philosophy, he conditions insight, and hence the satisfactions and relief insight offers, to positions we do not in fact inhabit.

cepts, opinions, ways of weighing them that an individual employs in deliberating are already socially formed, hence not neutral counters in the game of reasoning, hence already outside the individual's "will" while helping to form it. These factors are, Adorno believes, far weightier difficulties in thinking an autonomous will, an individual's free willing, than the ones Kant considers; what an action means, what action an individual can be thought to perform, is not fully "up to" the individual, his or her intention. No clear theoretical boundary can be drawn between "my will" and the social facts that invade every decision I make.[22] Actions do not mean monadologically.

But the social preformation of individual will must, in fact, lead back to the formation of will and freedom themselves. After quoting Kant's acknowledgement of the historical delay between the state in which individuals considered themselves bound by the laws of duty, and his unearthing of the truth that they are bound only by laws that are self-legislated, Adorno states: "By no means, however, did it occur to Kant whether freedom itself, to him an eternal idea, might not be essentially historical, not merely as a concept but also in its empirical substance [*Erfahrungsgehalt*]. Whole epochs, whole societies lacked not only the concept of freedom but the thing" (ND, 218).[23] In accordance with this thought, throughout his considerations of Kantian freedom Adorno offers scattered mini-genealogies about how we should conceive of the ideas and reality of freedom and individual independence being formed, from their historic archetype in "he who is topmost in hierarchies, the man who is not visibly dependent" (ND, 220) through the collapse of feudal roles to the need of increasingly isolated individuals who were deprived of the freedom from domination that the collapse of feudalism and absolutism promised to narcissistically inflate their sense of self and worth – the Hegelian thought of inner, stoical freedom as an individualist strategy for preserving self-worth in conditions denying it.

Although he nowhere offers anything like an Hegelian account of how the conception and reality of the autonomous self or free will were formed, Adorno frames his immanent critique of Kant on freedom within a genealogical conception of the will as an historic production whose reality is negatively parasitic on the history producing it. Only the experi-

22 Which is not to deny the obvious: there are hosts of ways in which we practically discriminate what I am doing or what I am responsible for and what actions I can call my own that do not involve an essential me.

23 This is one of the places in which one cannot help but wishing that Adorno had taken more note of Aristotle, for his handling of the problems of the voluntary and involuntary as finely tuned to the contexts of action and the ways in which we account for or excuse what is or is not reasonably within an agents' control might have helped Adorno to frame his claim that we do not need the extensive, transcendental notion of freedom urged by Kant.

ence of unfreedom provides purchase for its affirmative positing: "By introspection, we discover neither positive freedom nor positive unfreedom. We conceive both in their relation to extramental things: freedom as a polemical counter-image to the suffering brought on by social coercion, unfreedom as its [coercion's] image" (ND, 223). A freedom that matters is always negative; but if this is correct, and it is correct to argue that freedom arose at a moment in time, then equally "freedom . . . might be wholly extinguished again, without leaving a trace" (ND, 218). Not for a moment does Adorno give the solely conceptual problem of freedom and determinism a chance.

Equally, and nearly from the outset, Adorno helps himself to a natural history of the subject – this one of Freudian pedigree. So he opens the fifth section of the "Freedom" chapter, "The Pre-Egoic Impulse [*Der vorichliche Impuls*]," thus:

> The dawning sense of freedom feeds upon the memory of something archaic, impulses not yet steered by any solid I. The more the I tries to curb them, the more chaotic and thus questionable will it find the pre-temporal freedom. Without an anamnesis of the untamed, pre-egoic impulse, later banished to the zone of unfree bondage to nature, it would be impossible to form the idea of freedom, although it in turn ends up reinforcing the I. In spontaneity, the philosophical concept that does the most to exalt freedom as a mode of conduct above empirical existence, there resounds the echo of that by whose control and ultimate destruction the I of idealistic philosophy means to prove freedom. (ND, 221–2)

This is bad speculative anthropology, especially the thought that it is an anamnesis of the spontaneity of the pre-I impulse that forms the model for the spontaneity of the free will. If that thesis seems dubious, its background assumption is not obviously so: if humans were first truly parts of nature, then there must be a natural history of their emergence from nature. In this natural historical account, the conception of the self is formed through a curbing of natural impulses and, in time, contrasting the split-off power of repression with what is so curbed. To tell this story with any conviction, although it would remain speculative, one needs a far more complex armory of psychological mechanisms and concepts than Adorno here employs: identification, projection, idealization, introjection, and the like. Since Adorno has this vocabulary at his disposal, and in other contexts is happy to employ it, his eschewing it here is calculated. The most plausible hypothesis about his calculation is that, in the light of the fragmentation of philosophical knowing from social scientific (including psychoanalytic) knowing, he intends it as a critical reminder, one that depends upon the idea of employing natural history as an original orientation in order to undermine the self-sufficiency of Kant's account, and, more problematically, to make an appeal to our pre-theoretical intuitions about what in the nature of the experience of spontaneity lodges an affirmative claim for us. Is the naive conception of spontaneity as acting impulsively, out of character, transgressively, on the spur of the moment, unreflectively, without deep appeal and significance? Is not some of our conception of freedom as spontaneity modeled on experiences where the either/or of reflective choosing or being passively determined seem otiose, for example, in play, "rough-housing," making art (creating), or making love? Is not a wholly deliberative conception of freedom tied to a concept of self-control, and thereby to instrumental choosing? And is it obviously wrong to consider the appeal or claim of the ideal of spontaneity as exemplified by activities that cannot be easily labeled as deliberative choosings or passively determined behaviors (the way neurotic acts are determined "from without") as anamnestic, as somehow a remembrance of something past, at least our childhood and what it innervates with respect to our collective past?

Throughout the freedom chapter the perspective of natural history is used in this twofold manner. First, we must consider reason as something which intelligibly has a natural origin, as belonging to our "natural" way of coping with the environment. In this light we are enjoined to consider the force of reason as something derived from its prehistory in which it was both a moment of nature and something else. Reason remains natural as "the psychological force split off for purposes of self-preservation" (ND, 289); once split off, it can reassure, interpret, and form itself as what is other to nature. It is that process that the perspective of natural history permits us to question: " . . . if the nature in reason itself is forgotten, reason will be self-preservation running wild and will regress to nature. It is only as reflection upon that self-preservation that reason would be above nature." The fact that the question of nature in reason is a matter of what is forgotten or remembered defines the first-person, reflective, nontheoretical status of Adorno's comments. What is being asked for is not a better theory of reason, but a reflective acknowledgement by reason that its force is not its own, and that it cannot utterly transcend its natural context without self-defeat. Because natural history belongs to self-reflection in this way, the pointing to the moment of nature in reason is quasi-transcendental.

If the distortions of reason originate from the suppression of anthropomorphic nature, then, conversely, something within what is repressed must image a restored anthropomorphic nature. In this second sense, natural history is used to project or promise a reconciling of nature and reason. Occasionally, as in his treatment of the addendum, Adorno is careful in his handling of this thought. Equally often, bereft of how to handle the idea of anthropomorphic nature as that with which we need to be reconciled, he runs an argument that illicitly stretches from the plausible idea of spontaneity and the restless of thought, our minds routinely and randomly active, to diffuse nature as forming the "lineaments of an intelligible being, of that self which would be delivered from the I; contemporary art innervates some of this" (ND, 277). Even as a rhetorical flourish this is incoherent: art might well innervate a depiction of anthropomorphic nature; what it cannot do is innervate an image of nature in its diffuseness as providing the lineaments of an intelligible being delivered over from the narrow confines of autonomy.

It must be conceded that Adorno's employment of natural history is intensely repetitious, thin, and gestural. He makes the same remarks about a more integral state becoming split, and that split becoming reified into a debilitating dualism of constitutive subjectivity, freedom and the will, reason, the person, all standing opposed to a mechanical nature. While not above suspicion, it is I think necessary to see the thinness of this natural history and its gestural character as due to caution and care on Adorno's apart. After all, the real substance of the thesis finally depends upon the analysis of instrumental reason in terms of the principle of immanence (identity thinking), and then coming to be able to recognize current formations of reason as exemplifying identity thinking. The further demonstration that identity thinking is irrational will depend on showing there are material elements of the concept that it denies, hence issues that belong to a critical epistemology. What the addition of natural history adds to all of this is, narrowly, that it helps explain why the domination of identity thinking should be experienced as damaging, how it can be conceived of as self-defeating, and hence how some conception of anthropomorphic nature is necessary if any conception of reason as abstracting *from* anything is going to be intelligible. Because, however, Adorno takes seriously, perhaps too seriously, the obliteration of anthropomorphic nature, the only direct philosophical use he can make of natural history is the gestural one concerning the origins or prehistory of reason, will, subject. To do more would, again, overstep what his own diagnosis asserts: anthropomorphic nature is not now available.[24]

24 The best recent attempts at natural history begin with the infant rather than the beginnings of the species. See, for example, Jean Laplanche, *Life and Death in Psychoanalysis,* trans. Jeffrey Mehlman (Baltimore: Johns Hopkins University Press, 1976), and Jonathan Lear, *Love and Its Place in Nature: A Philosophical Interpretation of Freudian Psychoanalysis* (New York: Farrar, Straus & Giroux, 1990). While such attempts narrowly give force to Adorno's critique of reason, because they abstract from the history through which this idea of self, subject, was formed, they make the difficulties of the present narrowly and implausibly available to therapeutic intervention. For a better go at all this from a psychoanalytic perspective, see Julia Kristeva, *Black Sun: Depression and Melancholia,* trans. Leon S. Roudiez (New York: Columbia University Press, 1989), and her *New Maladies of the Soul,* trans. Ross Guberman (New York: Columbia University Press, 1995). Another strategy is to use Greek thought as a form of resistance to the idealist anthropology. The best example of this genre is Bernard Williams, *Shame and Necessity* (Berkeley: University of California Press, 1993). A suspicion worth exploring is that Kristeva's works contain the rudiments of a psychoanalytic theory that would match the directions of Adorno's critical theory.

But there is more to Adorno's use of natural history, and, as it turns out, genealogy. He subtitles the chapter on freedom "On the Metacritique of Practical Reason." Metacritique, classically, was meant to demonstrate the nonreflective conditions of possibility of the categories that Kant contended were the transcendental conditions of possibility. As I have indicated, throughout the chapter on freedom Adorno presupposes the metacritical vantage points of natural history and genealogy. Indeed the most plausible way of reading the chapter is as an implicit reworking of the metacritiques of Kant that Schelling, Hegel, Marx, and Nietzsche had already provided. These metacritiques need to be performed again because in their first attempt they were infected by identity thinking. Modestly, Adorno thinks he cannot assess Kant directly, but only in the light of these earlier metacritiques. *What these earlier metacritiques make available to Adorno is natural history and historical genealogy as original orientations that compete with idealism.* In considering his own activity metacritique Adorno is then doing nothing other than acknowledging the tradition through which natural history and historical genealogy have become for us original orientations. This makes the critique of idealist reason far from wholly immanent. If anything deserves to be called a moment of immanent critique in this context, it is only the moment in which freedom is internally brought into contact with the exteriority that natural history posits, say, the moment of the addendum.

What distinguishes Adorno's practice of metacritique is that he pursues it without system, without the thought that the three fundamental orientations we have noted can be put together into a unified account of the nature of reason or freedom. Adorno acknowledges each of the three original orientations that belong to our idea of modernity, philosophically attempting to honor each, without reducing any one orientation to its competitors, against identity thinking. For him these orientations, however, are not to be thought in terms of the constituting achievements of modernity since, in a profound but obvious way, they are not yet constitutive of who we are. Their weight and significance as original orientations are best vindicated, and only vindicable now, by employing them in the first instance metacritically (and not theoretically). What metacritique presupposes and then illuminates is that the ultimate force of these perspectives, their unavoidability, turns on their showing who we unavoidably are, where who we unavoidably are *can* be avoided, but at the cost of self-defeat. As we have seen, further, in making the claim for who we unavoidably are, even assuming the metacritical perspectives on offer, what is offered is not a given or determinate human essence, and hence not the alienation of some essence, but an indeterminate horizon of possibility that emerges only negatively. If anything stronger can be said about to what acknowledging anthropomorphic nature (within and without) and particularity amounts, it can transpire only through some consideration of how we go about acknowledging or failing to acknowledge, that is, through some account of how we could, possibly, acknowledge, cognize, differently. What more is thus needed now is to see whether the critical perspectives that spell out who we unavoidably are can be honored in the concept.

6

DISENCHANTING IDENTITY: THE COMPLEX CONCEPT

The goal of this chapter is to begin providing an account of conceptuality that can answer to the diverse but interconnected set of demands that have arisen in the light of the failures of rationalized reason. Formally, we are seeking a conception of ethical reasoning that will enable reasons for action to be intrinsically motivating. But equally I have contended that reasons for action, ideally, would emerge from cognitive awareness of states of affairs; and in order for that to be the case a state of affairs itself must be capable of lodging a claim. While it is obscure how this might work out in general, in our "fallen state" each particular object we face – each person and thing as set within the institutional frameworks of the modern world – is a rationalized version of itself, hence damaged, hence not as it could be. The desocialization of society that is a consequence of disenchantment makes each object a moral remainder; no particular within rationalized society is, existentially and conceptually, what it could be as a consequence of "our" collective participation in the rationalization of reason and experience. If sensuous particulars are raising claims, then a fortiori there must be a "material" or "sensuous" moment *in* the concept that rationalization leading to the simple concept suppresses, and, equivalently, something about each object that rationalized concepts have left out of account. Such a conceptual moment, Adorno must presume, when rightly acknowledged, when reintegrated into the concept, would answer to the motivational thesis. Finally, such a reformed conceptuality would be normatively indebted to and so dependent on its objects.

My implicit contention in the preceding two chapters has been that the distinction between rationalized reason and some other conception of reason can best be comprehended as the distinction between a reason regulated by the norms of reasoning itself, call it logical reason, and a reason governed by some conception of material inference structures.[1]

1 For my first go at making a conception of material inference structures central to ethical

Within an account of material inference, the goodness of inferences depends on the logical powers of the concepts employed and not on their conforming to the purely logical forms of inference, the latter restricting empirical content to the truth of the implicit premises of an inference. Hence, for a material inferentialist what makes the inference from "Nashville is to the South of New York" to "New York is to the North of Nashville," or from "Lightning is seen now" to "Thunder will be heard soon" valid is the contents of the concepts of *South* and *North*, or *lightning* and *thunder*. To have possession of the concept of *lightning* is precisely to believe that if there is such now then soon there will be thunder (which equally involves mastery of the relevant temporal terms). If this were the right story, then one might believe that practical inferences would work in the same way: the inference from "He is bleeding badly" to "I'll apply a tourniquet," or from "I borrowed ten dollars from her yesterday" to "I will return her ten dollars now" equally depends on the content of the relevant concepts: *bleeding badly, applying a tourniquet, borrowing,* and *returning*. Anyone who does not see how applying a tourniquet is the (or an) appropriate response to someone's bleeding badly (where the bleeding cannot be stanched by pressure to the wound or placing an absorbent material over the wound or by holding the injured limb up in the air, etc.) has not understood what it is to recognize, see, that someone is bleeding badly under conditions in which no one else is available to render aid. Actual material inferences are not enthymemes; hence there are no suppressed general laws or rules from which they derive. On the contrary, the thesis motivating this conception of material inference is that the attempt to ground first-order material inferences by making them the conclusions of syllogisms (or the like) with universal premises mistakes the source of the linkage between the relevant statements. At best, the conditionals related to particular material inferences – for example, If someone is bleeding badly from one of their limbs, then, ceteris paribus, one

experience see *Recovering Ethical Life*, pp. 168–70. Since writing that, indeed, since writing the first draft of the present work, Robert Brandom has published *Making It Explicit*. For the foreseeable future this will be the touchstone for accounts of and debates over material inference. And since, at least at the level of discriminating the relative roles of logical and material inference my earlier account and Brandom's converge, I tailor my account here to his. Nonetheless, I radically disagree with Brandom over two utterly central aspects of material inference: what counts as making a material inference (or material inference structures generally) explicit (Brandom's theory of logical expressivism), and how to regard singular cases (Brandom's account of anaphora). The combination of those two divergences entails a different weighting and characterization of first-person experience to the one Brandom provides. Implicitly, the argumentation of this and the following chapter contests Brandom over these issues. In "Mimetic Rationality and Material Inference," forthcoming in a volume edited by Henry Pickford, I have extended the following pages in order to clarify my critique of Brandom. The account of material inference in the present paragraph tracks the introduction of material inference in Brandom on pp. 98–101.

should (ought to) apply a tourniquet[2] – make *explicit,* and hence clarify the logical connections of the particular inference without altering its validity one way or another. In a material inference the universal is realized only through the particular that exemplifies it; and the particular appears only as determined, thus universal. This is why Adorno thinks the antithesis between universal and particular is deceptive; neither can exist without the other, "both of them are and are not" (SO, 257). What he calls "nonidealist dialectics" becomes intelligible as the promotion of material as opposed to logical inference.

Nonetheless, Adorno believes that the issue between accounts of inference as logical or material cannot be adequately grasped in purely theoretical terms, however useful such theoretical accounts may be, and this for two reasons. First, because to understand the claim, appeal, and authority of logical inference in relation to material inferences one must have an understanding of the history through which that authority established itself not just conceptually but culturally and institutionally. What is at stake in the debate between accounts of reasoning in terms of logical and material inferences is a social actuality as well as a theoretical difference; for Adorno, the theoretical debate must be seen as tracking and reflecting a social fate (the fate of reason). (Ultimately, the propriety or urgency to regard certain inferences as materially licensed must itself be material; say, because I feel a sense of guilt or responsibility toward objects as a result of responding to them through abstractly rational means, and hence come to perceive them as, so to speak, bleeding badly. This would make metacritique and its corollaries conceptual tourni-

2 I am intentionally leaving it ambiguous whether this rule is a technical one (If you want to stop the bleeding, then . . .) or an ethical rule (When someone is bleeding badly, then the right, appropriate, human thing to do is . . .) since that separation is disastrous for thinking about actions in response to human injury. What should be already evident in virtue of the "remainder" thesis, and is elaborated more below, for Adorno ethical action is paradigmatically a response to *injury*; doings in response to injury do not actually have separable technical and ethical aspects (ethical ends and technical means): the point or meaning of the technical action, and hence its meaning *überhaupt,* is its work of repairing, healing. To be sure, the technical and the ethical portions of the commitments in a concept can become systematically separated; I am, so to speak, routinely faced with persons bleeding badly under conditions in which either the resources for applying the tourniquet or other demands interfere. Under such conditions, which are a fair image of our own, other kinds of practical issues arise, e.g., how can we best reconstitute the conditions of action so that the ethical and technical aspects of a conceptual commitment can be univocally satisfied? Second here, there are no "oughts" or "musts" in the first-order inference; while in a particular context there may be reason to employ an "ought" or a "must," those terms are not responsible for the primary demandingness and hence the normativity of the inference. Finally, Brandom construes first-order or primary material inferences as shorn of explicitly logical language, and hence the addition of logical language as a component of the reflective work of making the inferential commitments explicit. While this strategy certainly makes vivid the autonomy of first-order material inferences from their logical elaboration, I can see no other reason for thinking that such language is not a part, however routinely abused, of first-order practices.

quets.) Second, because as a matter of "social fact" the most significant practical material inferences have been supervened upon by logical inference structures, and hence are not themselves fully or adequately available. Material inference seems remote theoretically because practically the material inferences that had been the empirical bond amongst subjects have been dissolved through the supervenience of instrumental forms. It is these historical exigencies that dictate the direction of Adorno's *critical rescue* of material inferences.

And right from the outset that direction diverges radically from the standard defense of the priority of material inferences over formal inferences as being a consequence of the fact that non-logical content-based reasoning is determined by the situated character of our linguistic *practices*. For Hegel or Heidegger or Wittgenstein, it is the situated practical character of language, the weaving of language into our social practices and the social practice of language itself, that is the primary bulwark against formalism and abstraction. However valid this is, and however much the framework of social practice is presupposed by Adorno as a condition for metacritique, the sheer normativity of social practices cannot be central for him since our social practices themselves have become instances of formal reason. In actuality, even "concrete" activities, activities that are situated, can occur in accordance with rules and norms that are formal and abstract – the contextual, say, buying an object, is decontextualized by the system of relations in which it is submerged. The local is so determined by the universal that it is local no more. But if some instances in which formal rules supervene on practical interaction are legitimate, say, in routine economic exchanges, then why not rationalize all interactions? The sociality of human reasoning may well provide a necessary condition for securing the propriety of material inferences, and hence *calling* us back to those practices, or at least some of them, may form one limb of a strategy for resurrecting or reactivating some structures of material inference, but by itself will not provide sufficient resources for displacing logical reason. To make Adorno's divergence from the standard account perspicuous, I want to begin with a marginal moment in Adorno's analysis that will lead us, however awkwardly and uncomfortably, to see how a standard material inferentialist and the formal Kantian account of conceptual content might partially overlap, both equally passing over Adorno's concern about content.

1. Conceptual Content

Even as sympathetic and astute a reader as Albrecht Wellmer badly misinterprets Adorno's critique of the simple concept as a critique of conceptual knowing as such. This argument presupposes that simply in virtue of the fact that concepts are general and discursive they are thereby always an imposition upon and a violation of the uniqueness of whatever objects to which they are applied.

> As Adorno conceives it, this "violation" of the "non-identical" by the concept also constitutes the *untruth* of the conceptual judgement. He takes on board the paradox that what we normally call "true," namely linguistic propositions, is at the same time supposed to be "untrue." But not only does this mean that the *emphatic* concept of truth, which . . . Adorno brings into play *against* the truth of propositions, can no longer be set in any obvious connection with what we call truth; it also means that we are unable to *say* in what the general concept does an injustice to the individual particular. . . .[3]

If the emphatic conception of truth is now posed as beyond what we can say, then truth is beyond history, and the critique of the concept becomes a critique of historical existence: "But if history has to become the Other of history in order to escape the system of delusion that is instrumental reason, then the critique of the historical present moment turns into a critique of historical being – the latest form of a theological critique of the earthly vale of tears."[4] Directly continuous with this objection to Adorno is the claim that he contrasts the instrumental rationality of the concept with a, presumably, aconceptual aesthetic rationality. Whatever aesthetic rationality is supposed to represent, its realization too is to be located beyond the parameters of historical existence. Hence, the aesthetic critique of modernity eventuates in, despite itself, a critique of historical existence as always damned by the ineliminable necessities of con-

3 Albrecht Wellmer, *The Persistence of Modernity: Essays on Aesthetics, Ethics and Postmodernism*, trans. David Midgley (Oxford: Polity Press, 1991), p. 72. This is curious since nowhere does Adorno identify rationalized reason's suppression of sensuous particularity and uniqueness with the simple invocation of conceptuality and discursivity. Identifying an object *as* such-and-such does not reduce the object to the concept it comes under, and hence does not by itself "violate" the object. What I called in Chapter 1 "the platitudes" underlying the principle of immanence employ subsumption as a guiding thread in order to erect a conception of rationality. The impression that Adorno is making this gross error probably derives from the concatenation of the fact that Adorno seeks to undo the domination of rationalized *reason* through an interrogation of the simple *concept* with the fact that his critical practice is so resolutely "negative," hence leading to the perception that the critique of the simple concept (an understanding of conceptuality from the perspective of rationalized reason) is the epistemological equivalent of a negative theology. Of course, rationalized reasoning operates with rationalized concepts; but that would hardly justify the crudeness of Wellmer's interpretation. Nonetheless, it seems right to begin with this charge because it forms the nucleus of all second-generation critical theory critiques of Adorno, and hence explains how these readers myopically construe Adorno's aesthetics, i.e., aesthetic rationality as "the other" of conceptual rationality. But if second-generation critical theory begins from this palpable misreading of Adorno, then the question might well arise as to how it can ever rationally begin its reconstructive enterprise. For Habermas's version of this complaint, see his *The Philosophical Discourse of Modernity*, trans. Frederick Lawrence (Oxford: Polity Press, 1987), chapter 5.

4 Ibid., p. 63.

ceptual mediation and instrumental rationality; only beyond history can the utopia of aesthetic interaction be found. The proposed explanation for this aporetic conclusion is that Adorno repeats the "very forgetfulness of language" which is characteristic of European rationalism.

While this whole critique is transparently wrong, the final thesis that Adorno's rationalism emerges through a forgetfulness of language is particularly breathtaking since in the closing paragraph of the Introduction to *Negative Dialectics* we find the following thoughts: "The alliance of philosophy and science aims at the virtual abolition of language and thus of philosophy, and yet philosophy cannot survive without the linguistic effort"; dialectics in its literal sense is "language as the organon of thought"; and it is "only in language that like knows like" (ND, 56). Why, against the background of Adorno's patent insistence that all thought is linguistically mediated, would Wellmer contend that he forgets language? Two thoughts are likely to be motivating Wellmer's contention. First, while Adorno concedes that every judgement of the form "S is P" is mediated by language because we learn the concepts "S" and "P" only through learning their linguistic equivalents, he does not think perceptual judgement, the cognitive act, can be understood through the exposition of (the content or truth conditions of) the assertion "S is P." Since we know already that Adorno regards some notion of experience as fundamental to cognitive life, it follows that he must believe that something gets lost or overlooked if one attempts to replace or displace the role of cognitive activities, including perceptual experience, with linguistic analysis; to that extent he does remain within a "philosophy of consciousness."

Second, Adorno's defense of the essential role of language just cited occurs in the context of a defense of "rhetoric," where by rhetoric Adorno means, roughly, the expressive and performative aspects of language. Adorno proceeds to contend, without argument, that dialectics involves the attempt to provide a "critical rescue" of the rhetorical aspect of language, and achieving that rescue is equivalent to finding through language a "mutual approximation of thing (*Sache*) and expression to the point of indifference"; hence in dialectics "the rhetorical element is on the side of content" (ND, 56). This all sounds deeply puzzling. What Wellmer hears when the two theses are placed together is that what we think of as ordinary conceptual grasping is equivalent to what is expressed by standard assertoric statements, and these essentially "violate" the object judged by subsuming it. Only rhetorical discourse which bypasses the conceptual in language in favor of its expressive power can put us in touch with the content the concept disallows. If one replaces the role of "rhetoric" with "aesthetic materials," then the logic of the remainder of this fallacious view slides into place: aesthetic rationality achieves an apprehension of things which standard conceptual and assertoric discourse prohibits.

It will help to begin simplistically and reductively.[5] Consider: from the assertion "The chair is red" we can infer the speaker believes that there is a chair, not a couch or a stool, before her, that it is really spatially here and not elsewhere, that it is red and not purple or orange, and that any ordinarily equipped perceiver would perceive the chair as red in standard lighting conditions, and so on. Compare that with: "The chair is red like a ripe plum tomato" or even simply "The chair is *red!*" Nothing in the rhetorical version of the assertion denies or cancels the inferential commitments of the first non-rhetorical version; hence nothing about the rhetorical version suggests that one can grasp something as red without understanding it as not purple or orange. If both the rhetorical and non-rhetorical versions of the statement share the same inferential core, then Adorno cannot believe that intrinsically or *essentially* ordinary predicative judgements or ordinary assertions somehow violate the sensuousness particularity of things.[6]

Conversely, in claiming that rhetoric sides with content Adorno means to assert that the simile or the exclamatory emphasis are not mere or reductively psychological extras that, as might be said, make the assertion "persuasive." (Although both rhetorical versions have "psychological" analogues: "The chair's redness reminds me of . . . " and "Gosh, I do find that chair very red indeed.") Rather, what the rhetorical statements do is to direct our attention toward the concept's experiential content: the chair's redness; that is, the rhetorical statements *orient* our attention away from the inferential commitments implied by the bald assertoric version and toward the matter of the judgement itself, they inflect the statement toward its own emphatic content. This is not to say that the original assertoric version necessarily orients us away from the content; all by itself, the assertion appears neutral. But if one thinks the epistemic meaning of the original judgement is best grasped through either tracking the ma-

5 What makes the following example simple and reductive is that it deals with color, hence with a domain of experience that we suppose, because it concerns nothing more than the surfaces of objects, and hence is as "thinly" attached to them as a coat of paint, is least subject to rationalization. While this view is wrong – for living things their colors are internally related to their waxing and waning, their ripeness and dying, their anger or shame or numbness; and even outside that context colors have more semantic "depth" than is typically believed (at least if, say, the results of Matisse's and Barnett Newman's "investigations" are thought valid) – its wrongness can be bracketed for the moment. See, however, note 9 below.

6 It is here worth recalling that in Chapter 2 we agreed standard empirical concepts are bound to the sensuous appearings of the properties they signify, and that even reiterative ascent on its own would not force a dismissal of the relevance of such properties (because the gods too are explainers). Only the whole concatenation of criteria, including causal explanation as involving in principle manipulability, would secure the principle of immanence as entailing both the disenchantment of nature and the rationalization of reason. And, again, the force of that argument was to demonstrate just how the principles securing the "good" of disenchantment were the flip side of the principles generating the rationalization of reason.

terial inferences it implies or, the Kantian view, the properties denoted being tokens of types that are ideally subject to scientific explanation,[7] then in comprehending and evaluating the goodness of the judgement one's cognitive attention will be directed away from the state of affairs itself and toward the surrounding space of reasons (inferential commitments or general laws). On Adorno's view, the rhetorical versions inflect the original semantic and epistemic core of the statement toward its object, forming thereby a reflexive resistance to its being submerged or fixed through the diacritical and doxastic relations to other words or beliefs (wherein the original statement as a whole operates as a premise for a body of inferential commitments) or fit for explanation (wherein the original statement is finally a conclusion to an explanatory argument). This is straightforward in the emphatic, exclamatory version where there are no new linguistic elements, extra words, or concepts. What could the standard material inferentialist interpretation or Kantian explanatory rationalization make of rhetorical emphasis? Since for them those elements would be literally invisible, they must identify content with the statement's role as premise or conclusion in the space of reasons, literally disembodying the judgement thereby. If all the exclamatory version does is focus on the actual experiential content of the perceptual judgement, then in acknowledging no space for it, the inferentialist acknowledges that the original judgement was without content on its own. Pressed far enough, taken literally, inferentialism thus appears to be concepts without intuitions.[8] Again, it is because the rhetorical emphasis disappears al-

7 Stated baldly, for Kant it is finally "only a metaphysics of nature [that] can fully justify the move from a [merely subjective] judgement of perception to a [truly objective] judgement of experience." Béatrice Longuenesse, *Kant and the Capacity to Judge,* trans. Charles T. Wolf (Princeton: Princeton University Press, 1998), p. 175. This doctrine, needless to say, precisely overlaps with the idea of increasing objectivity through permitting only items that can possess a wide cosmological role. Longuenesse's book does better than previous accounts in demonstrating Kant's general commitment to a reiterative ascent model of objectivity, and hence of the connection between the account of judgements of perception and experience with the arguments of the first *Critique.*

8 Gregg Horowitz alerted me to this "inference" of my account. Needless to say, I do not think that tracking the inferential commitments implicit in a particular use need go in this "flattening" direction, otherwise Adorno would be unable to avail himself of a logic of material inferences at all. To anticipate: if one were to go on to make explicit the implicit commitments of the rhetorical version of the statement, one would, I think, produce what Adorno calls a "constellation" (in which, doubtless, some of the "facts" I cited in note 4 above that I claimed had no part in our ordinary accounting of "red" would suddenly become relevant). At any rate, the "disembodying" of the original judgement should be taken literally, not metaphorically. For Kant, as we saw at the conclusion of the previous chapter, the ideal of the complete concept is, finally, to void the role of intuitions in concepts. In his "Reply to Commentators," *Philosophy and Phenomenological Research* 58/2 (June 1998), John McDowell makes the same objection to Brandom: "How could multiplying what are, considered by themselves, blind responses, to include blind responses to how the blind responses of one's fellows are related to the circumstances to which they are blind responses, somehow bring it about that the responses are after all not blind?" (pp. 408–9).

together in these forms of interpretation that they relegate the rhetorical to the merely psychological; but so doing relegates content too to something below the cognitive level.

In the simile version of the statement the orientation toward the content is equivalent to inviting the hearer to "bring to mind" the chair's redness by associating it with a sensory image (one available to the hearer in the absence of the chair and what it is like). One might say the simile interprets or articulates or informs the original predication, that its work of orientation is equivalent to, perhaps, securing the concept's intuitional content by providing a linguistic exposition of it. But now, insofar as the word "red" is inflected toward the chair's redness in virtue of the simile, then that "expression" of the chair's color can, legitimately, be thought to "approximate" (*nähern*: approach or draw near) its object. The simile reorients the word so that it can be conceived of as being in the service of the very object that it alone enables us to discriminate. Finally, since physical contiguity or proximity are dumb, speechless facts, then, in however thin a fashion in this case, the redness of the chair and that of the ripe plum tomato only "know" one another, achieve likeness, in language.[9]

9 Placing the tomato on the chair might "show" the likeness, but only in circumstances where the simile was already operative; otherwise the gesture would be utterly baffling. Hence, placing the tomato on the chair immediately after uttering the assertoric version would be the effort of finding a trope adequate to the meaning of the original expression. The act of placing in the appropriate context is the physical performance of a simile. This is the force of Adorno's contention that it is in language alone that like knows like. If a physical act can be a simile, then (some) art works too might be construed as rhetorical versions of assertoric statements. For example, one could interpret Matisse's *The Red Studio* as a rhetorical version of the statement "The chair is red" (there is a chair in the front right corner of the painting). A dialectic around this disturbing painting might take the following form. The painting could be considered an answer to the question: What would it be like to conceive of objects as adhering to properties, things themselves becoming qualities, and secondary properties, above all, color, substance? I do think Matisse is doing just such a conceiving in this painting, but the intelligibility of the attempt does seem curious. Why pursue such a patent inversion of the logic of object and property (substance and attribute)? After all, is not the color of an object just or only its surface, and hence is not the representation of things in painting through line and color a dismal pretence to reduce the substance of objects to that surface? Not too far down this road is the thought that the color of things is not essential to them, that color is *merely* sensible, an object of mere liking (Kant), and hence merely of decorative significance. What is considered merely sensible in life begins the train of argument that will first condemn certain features of painting as merely decorative until, as painting finds itself with only line and color as its subject matter, painting as a whole is condemned as merely decorative. Hence, with the stigma of the "mere" and "merely" anticipating the conclusion, the role of "decorative" here comes to parallel in the logic of painting the dismissal of rhetoric in standard and narrow material inferentialist accounts of language.

Matisse's painting is the beginning of a response to both charges (about color in and outside painting). The redness of *The Red Studio* cannot be decorative since it is the substance (matter or content) of the painting, what holds our attention, and can bear the weight of being an object of continuing visual attention – one presumptive criterion for an object being a work of visual art. In the light of the painting being able to discharge its responsibility for being such an object of attention can we be confident about what is

On the material inferentialist and Kantian interpretations of "red" it is difficult to see what else other than making the concept determinate could be at stake for them. For the former, ideally, the goodness of the singular judgement would be vindicated just in case we all could agree to it as a token instance of the series of judgements in which we call "these" things red and no others red. If we were worried by this agreement, perhaps it is just a matter of agreement and nothing more, then we could shift into the explanatory mode and be further vindicated by the discov-

merely decorative and what is essential (to a work of art)? But if this dissolution of the distinction between what belongs to art proper (objects capable of bearing the weight of visual attention) and what is merely decorative can occur in painting, what then is the force of the claim that color relates *only* to the surface of objects? What notion of surface is operative here? Does it follow that because the chair could have been blue or yellow or beige (and remain the *same* chair?) that its redness is *only* a (secondary?) property, and hence relates *only* to its surface? Is the fact that its color could have been different and yet the chair still be there enough to discount the color as composing an element of the content of our perception of it, what makes the chair something "there" in our perceptual environment? How "deep" is the surface of things if we are to have a seen-world at all? If the scene would have been different if the colors were different, and hence would have yielded a different painting, does that make the *whole* scene just appearance? And is the chair we sit on thus unrelated to the one we see? Matisse's painting does not so much answer these questions as, pointedly, ask them. In asking them (in the light of the way in which analogous questions were asked and assertions made by, say, Cezanne), Matisse's painting *exposes* – through the rhetorical space painting is, through an insistent redness that takes on the value of substance in opposition to our anticipation of both what categorially counts as substantial and what categorial role color can play – the patterning of inferential commitments, within and outside paintings, that attend the bald assertoric statement and interrogates the propriety of those commitments. But, an objector will want to insist, all this is surely just painting (just rhetoric). This is a thought that Matisse himself underlines and thereby questions by having the only nonred things in the studio (Matisse-like) paintings and other "decorative" objects (except, of course?, the pencils which are the tools of his art); the paintings in the painting "decorate" a painting that is not decorative. Because Matisse cannot do otherwise than to *paint* painting as decoration and substance, hence painting both objection and answer to painting (as the tropic agent of color) in his painting, he is powerless to make his interrogation of the material inferentialist and Kantian accounts of the assertoric statement directly bear on the reflective understanding of it. Because the painting's reflexivity is itself painted, the magic circle of semblance is never quite broken through. To perceive that his painting does bear on those accounts one would have to "find" in it an alternative orientation to the subject matter it is about; but even appreciating the painting well, finding it compelling and disturbing and ravishing all at once, does not immediately require finding oneself (reflectively) reoriented. And how might one discover that one's appreciating does (necessarily) involve such a reorientation? Only by tracking the inferential commitments implied by the painting's tropic assertion and one's own assent to that assertion (finding the painting compelling and disturbing and ravishing all at once). But that demonstration can never be fully compelling because the magic circle of semblance, art's autonomy, entails the possibility of withdrawal and retreat, of thus opting out of the inferential commitments implied by a judgement by opting out of art's normative claiming generally. That possibility of retreat is the price art pays for its autonomy and hence the kind of normative claiming of which it is capable – the precise powerlessness, poverty, of art's modern potencies.

Adorno's *Aesthetic Theory* should be understood as taking up the burden of the powerlessness of art for it – conceptually. But for that project to even get off the ground, Adorno ery that everything we call "red" in fact reflects light waves falling within a specifiable span, with those cases in which we find ourselves disagreeing nicely located at the outer limits of the span. With such a discovery we might believe we have cognitively mastered "red" – which at a general level is where we left the simple concept at the end of Chapter 4. Again, it is this predetermination and eventual mastery that Adorno believes is mythology, and it is in protest against the predetermination or closure of content so understood that dialectics, in its mode of being a rescue of the rhetorical element of language, what is equivalent to a rescue of material inference itself, operates (ND, 56). The content to be rescued through rhetorical reorientation is not the other of conceptual understanding, but that part of the content of the concept which is passed over and abstracted from in the disenchantment of the world and the rationalization of reason; it is the suppressed mimetic moment of the concept.

And not only does Adorno not think that this content is utterly outside the concept, but, rightly or wrongly, one of his central criticisms of Hegel is that he attempts to secure concreteness in thought through his notion of "spirit" while bypassing the necessary mediations of language and concept (ND, 162–3). In opposition to Hegel, Adorno argues that the indissoluble content in previous thought survives as the nonidentical; but the nonidentical "communicates" with what it is separated from, the rationalized object of rationalized thought, *by the concept.* The nonidentical is thus only an ideal content of, for example, the rhetorical version of the assertoric statement. But that it is now only in the rhetorical expression of an assertoric statement that the nonidentical is glimpsed is what marks out the original assertoric statement as, in historical truth, not neutral but rationalized; inferential and explanatory analyses of assertoric statements are *historically true,* an accurate accounting of the fate of assertoric stating and empirical judging, and that is precisely the problem. It is because rationalized reason rationalizes conceptuality that the *simple* concept appears as if it were the whole of conceptuality. Accepting the synechdocal conceit of the simple concept, Wellmer hears Adorno protesting against history rather than simply *this* history. Adorno's response to Wellmer's charge could not be more unequivocal: *nonidentity "is opaque only for identity's claim to be total*; it resists the pressure [of that claim]" (ND, 163; emphasis mine). When the exchange between conceptual determinacy and

must first show, from the perspective of the concept, that there is room in the concept that can accommodate art in this way. And in order to show that, he must generate a conception of material inference that is an alternative to what I am agreeing, and Matisse's painting agrees, is the standard one. (Conversely, unless one did find *The Red Studio* or its like "aesthetically" disturbing, there would be a theoretical claim about conceptual content but no experiential basis for the claim, no turning or reorientation that would manifest the *stakes* of the conceptual difference. The dislocation of the concept of conceptual content from the question of the human, orientational significance of different possibilities of content is one aspect of the simple concept.)

rhetorical protest is over "red," it might be difficult to appreciate the stakes; if we were speaking of "vicious," "cruel," or "torture" then perhaps the stakes of the debate would be sharper.

Nonetheless, what Adorno's brief riff over rhetoric highlights is the question of orientation; and that there is a question of orientation, a question about in what "direction" a conceptual determination is oriented, and hence a question about what the "content" of a concept is should now have become more insistent and problematic than it at first appeared. Adorno works through the complexity of the concept at four distinct levels of analysis: first, he is interested in the relation between the simple concept, or what I call the *logical* aspect of the concept (what a "flattened" and regimented material inferential analysis perfectly captures), and its *material* aspect or, more familiarly, its intuitional aspect or moment (what rhetoric orients us toward). The logical aspect of the concept corresponds to identity thinking, and its material aspect corresponds to the nonidentical. At this level of analysis Adorno wants to argue that identity *depends* on nonidentity, that identity thinking "lives off" the nonidentical. I pursue this thesis under the slogan: *no predicative identification without non-predicative identification.* Non-predicative identification is that portion of the concept that ties predicative identification to experience. Yet the materialist reminder that rhetorical inflection offers to the logical concept does not in itself qualify as an orientation. Second, then, Adorno construes the interplay between the logical and material moments of the concept to imply that each *mode* of identifying, predicative and non-predicative, has associated with it a distinct cognitive orientation, a distinct conception of what cognizing something is or amounts to, and thus a distinct conception of what cognitive activity involves. On the schema with which Adorno is operating, the critical uncovering of the material component of the concept is what is to generate in rationalized reason an axial turn toward the object, to reorient it, where that new orientation is to be actualized in or through this alternative manner of cognizing, a form of material inferential accounting. In this respect, the identification of two different axes in the concept and the two competing cognitive orientations corresponding to the concept's differential components is a *critical* conception of the concept, not a theory of the concept; it is how we (ethically) must think about the concept, interpret it, in the light of the insufficiency of thought, the guilt of thinking, that emerged at the end of Chapter 5. Third, to secure the material content that is dislodged by the logical interpretation of assertoric statements, Adorno will have to argue that assertoric statements contain a now suppressed performative or rhetorical moment through which the orientation toward the object is displayed; every normal statement of, for example, "The chair is red" is thus to be construed as a now suppressed claiming (also), "The chair is *red!*" Sustaining the performative dimension of assertoric statements is what requires that inferences drawn from statements remain material. As we see below in Chapter 7, Adorno signals this fact by employing a paratactic as opposed to a hypotactic form of writing. Finally, the different cognitive orientations implied by the axial differentiation in the concept are actualized in the two fundamentally different patterns of reasoning: logical and material.

In the next section I offer a brief overview of Adorno's dual axis analysis of the concept in just the terms he provides. In section 3 the standard problem of color perception is used to inaugurate an analysis of the way in which concepts may be said to depend on objects; while in section 4 Kant's conception of reflective judgement is exploited in order to theorize a distinctive cognitive orientation belonging to the material axis of the concept. Other features of the complex concept are dealt with in the next chapter. I, however, conclude this chapter by attempting to show how the account of the complex concept thus far elaborated answers directly to Henrich's account of the structure and nature of moral insight outlined in my Introduction.

2. Communication versus Naming

> But although art and science became separate in the course of history the opposition between them should not be hypostatized. (NL1, 7)

Adorno's indictment of the simple concept would be more than questionable unless its cognitive norms and ideals were not exhaustive for what cognition might be. Conversely, unless the simple concept did embody a real and legitimate cognitive end, its development and hegemony would be unfathomable. Finally, unless the cognitive ideals implied by the logical and material axes of the concept were both necessary and not fully or ideally commensurable, not directed along the same lines and hence not capable of receiving an ideal simultaneous articulation, then no story about how there could be development (enlightenment) and regression (disenchantment) at once, formation and deformation at once, could be lodged.

The ideals of the simple concept that come to fruition in science, rationalized reason, and the rationalized practices of the dominant institutions of the present are a formation of the complex concept that gives priority to just one of its axes.[10] Equally for Adorno the practices of aesthetic modernism are a formation of the complex concept that give priority to just one of its axes; aesthetic modernism is for him a reaction formation in response to the experience of identity thinking as total.

10 Where the thought of the concept in terms of competing axial orientations is itself a consequence of rationalization.

Because it is essentially a reaction, then artistic modernism is as partial and one-sided in its way as rationalized reason is in its. The *duality* of art and science, not the sheer existence of different practices that we think of under the labels "art" and "science" but the experience of these activities as opposing one another, as somehow in competition with one another, is for Adorno expressive of competing cognitive orientations that, if truly cognitive, must articulate a potential for cognition latent in conceptuality that has yet to find a mode of articulating itself.[11] We thus come to understand the genealogical and historical significance of these different practices through comprehending them as displays of potentials grounded in the axial structures of concept and language themselves.[12]

Consider again the contrast between the inferential and rhetorical articulations of the plain assertoric statement. In seeking determinacy, the inferential articulation equally moves toward determinacy and full or replete discursivity: what is implicit in the original statement is made fully explicit in tracking the full set of commitments we must agree to if we agree that the original statement is true. Anything less would entail that there are inferences entailed by the original statement that remain unknown; to the extent they are unknown we cannot know if we do actually think the original statement is true; a suppressed or unknown inference we could not agree to would necessarily rebound onto the original assertion.[13] In such a case either we are not in agreement with one another or,

11 What this somewhat cumbersome way of expressing the problem is attempting to avoid is stating that art is directly or immediately the form of cognition that science overlooks, a thesis that is patently false. If it were true, then the division of labor between art and science would be wholly rational in itself, and only a fuller appreciation of art necessary. Artistic practice is an orientation that points to a potential for cognition in the concept that is not at present actualized. But if this is how Adorno thinks of the significance of art, then however heuristically significant art is for recovering that potential, it presupposes that the simple concept is deficient in itself, and hence that only in the context of an account of the concept as complex, and hence as composed of competing axes, can the "aesthetic" defence of artistic practice be vindicated.

12 Because for Adorno the duality between art and science is the paradigmatic expression of the opposing cognitive orientations, which hence refer to the lacuna in the standard concept of the concept, reference to modernist art in this section is unavoidable. However, I have tried to construct my account so that these references are of only *heuristic* significance; that is, even if it should turn out that Adorno is profoundly wrong in his interpretation of the relation between modernist art and the rationalization of reason – if, say, Matisse's *The Red Studio* should be discovered not to stand in a determinate relation to a body of assertions in which the concept *red* is employed because art as a practice is more autonomous from other social practices than Adorno's account allows – nothing in that discovery would require an alteration to the general line of argument being developed. Of course, if art really were that detached from ordinary conceptual practice, then one might wonder how we could care about art at all; but since philistinism is one inflection of the scepticism built into the simple concept, and hence indigenous to modern philosophy's self-understanding, critiquing it must follow from the critique of rationalized reason.

13 This is another way of stating the logical pressure that binds together vertical ascent and complete determinacy as spelled out in Kant's notion of a complete concept.

more important, we are not in agreement with ourselves. Full determinacy and full discursivity are the same. In contrast, the rhetorical version in reflecting the statement back toward its content has the effect of resisting full discursive articulation in the standard inferentialist sense. The rhetorical statement implies that the experience of seeing the chair as red, and by extension the chair's redness, has a *role* in its cognition that is repressed in the movement toward full discursive articulation. Without as yet attempting to articulate what is involved in such a claim, we can simply note that Adorno identifies the impulse to orient ourselves toward the object in this way as the impulse to *name* the object, *as if* naming were not labeling (or pointing or referring) but an always complex perfected expression of the thing itself.[14] The temptation to consider the hope or ideal or impulse to name in this way expresses the cognitive orientation of the material axis of the concept. Whether any actual cognitive activity or linguistic performance approximates to that cognitive hope, the imaginary significance attached to the act of naming, is what is to be discovered.

Throughout his writings Adorno contrasts the impulse to name or express an object with the impulse to classify, order, and explain. These two impulses are transmitted through a recurrent series of dualities: *sign and image, concept and intuition, concept and object, rationality and truth, communication and expression, communication and naming, function and substance, universal and particular, form and content, reason and mimesis, identity and nonidentity, philosophy (or science) and art.* While these dualisms operate at different levels, each possessing its own contextual appropriateness,[15] each equally refers back to the axial structure of the complex concept and the different cognitive orientations associated with each axis.[16] In

14 Metaphorically, *The Red Studio* names red.

15 In what follows I focus on the dualism between communication and naming, letting it *stand in for,* as it were, the whole series. But this is a reduction and simplification of Adorno's practice since a significant part of the weight of his argument turns on our coming to seeing how these different dualisms both overlap with one another, rehearse an analogous impasse, while each nonetheless enters in a quite specific conceptual terrain.

16 Despite the fact that I think it is correct to speak about the dual axes of the concept, I consider the alternative to the simple concept the complex concept because the formation of the simple concept occurs through a *series* of abstractions from a series of items that mediate the simple concept, and hence through a reflective dissolution or disavowal of a series of items on which the simple concept depends: object (anthropomorphic nature), image, experience, language, social practice, and history. For Adorno, each of these is both a material *condition* of the simple concept and a material *component* of it. Each item abstracted from contributes to, plays a role in, in part determines what material inferential powers any particular concept has. Conversely, if one does abstract from each of these then one will disable a concept's material inferential powers, producing, again, a flattened or thinned-out version of the concept concerned in which the connections we naively believed the concept to possess do not obviously pan out. Once this occurs, then the "panicky metaphysics" exemplified by moral centralism is called upon in order to reinstitute the lost connections. While the idea of the complex concept is implicit in much writing on Adorno it is rarely explicit. Three exceptions are Rolf

each case, then, the contrast turns on a rationality which seeks to master the particular by revealing how it is the same as others versus a rationality which seeks to comprehend the particular itself: "This [dialectical] cognition seeks to say what something is, while identitarian thinking says what something comes under, what it exemplifies or represents, and what, accordingly, it is not itself" (ND, 149). If one thinks of dialectical cognition on analogy with the rhetorical versions of the bald assertoric statement, then the temptation to hear Adorno suggesting that dialectics wants the thing itself apart from conceptual discrimination can be resisted. In passages such as the following, the idea of an alternative cognitive orientation is perspicuous.

> The world is unique. The simple repetition of the aspects which constantly recur in the same way is more like a vain and compulsory litany than the redeeming word. Classification is a condition for cognition and not cognition itself; cognition in turn dispels classification. (DoE, 220)[17]

> What is abandoned [in logical formalism] is the whole claim and approach to knowledge: to comprehend the directly given as such; not merely to determine the abstract spatio-temporal relations of the fact which allow them just to be grasped, but on the contrary to conceive of them as the superficies, as mediated conceptual moments which come to fulfillment only in the unfolding of their social, historical, and human meaning (*Sinnes*). The task of cognition does not consist in the mere apprehension, classification, and calculation, but in the determinate negation of each immediacy. (DoE, 26–7)[18]

Throughout *Dialectic of Enlightenment* Horkheimer and Adorno tend to present their position in these unsatisfactory terms in which the potentialities for different cognitive orientations are reduced to a condition for

Tiedemann, "Concept, Image, Name: On Adorno's Utopia of Knowledge," trans. Ellen Anderson and Tom Huhn in Tom Huhn and Lambert Zuidervaart (eds.), *The Semblance of Subjectivity: Essays in Adorno's Aesthetic Theory* (Cambridge, Mass: MIT Press, 1997), pp. 123–45; and Christoph Menke, *The Sovereignty of Art: Aesthetic Negativity in Adorno and Derrida*, trans. Neil Solomon (Cambridge, Mass: MIT Press, 1998); and Espen Hammer, "Minding the World: Adorno's Critique of Idealism," *Philosophy and Social Criticism* 26/1 (2000): 71–92. Completely independently, Hammer works Adorno's claim through its overlap with McDowell.

17 Horkheimer and Adorno cannot be thinking of science here, where classification might be thought an appropriate preliminary to explanation, but those contexts in which classification is being inserted in place of a situated accounting. Their penchant for hyperbole, however rhetorically justifiable, can be misleading. In the present passage, for instance, they are attempting to explicate conceptual identification as not the end of thinking, but as a moment in a process.

18 Given that this passage concludes with determinate negation as the mode or manner in which dialectical thinking is to proceed, it is a fair surmise that "apprehension, classification, and calculation" refer to the modes of cognition examined in the opening three chapters of Hegel's *Phenomenology of Spirit*: sense-certainty, perception, and (deductive scientific) understanding.

cognition, classification, coming to be erroneously accepted as the whole of cognition. This is unsatisfactory as it stands since it implicitly denies that the modes of cognitive activity which emerge from classification, explanation and instrumental reasoning, are legitimate modes of cognition; a fact which neither Horkheimer nor Adorno ever meant to deny, although Adorno is denying that the rationalist conception of such reasoning could be cognitive – instrumental reason cannot be what its defenders take it to be. Yet if both cognitive orientations are legitimate, and further if the process through which just one of them becomes dominant and exclusive is internal to the formation of reason itself, then it is unclear how Horkheimer and Adorno could make their critique work without simply dismissing the instrumentalist orientation as nonknowledge.

The critique of rationalized reason cannot be sustained at the level of cognitive orientations, something both Horkheimer and Adorno must have known since at no point do they directly avail themselves of the standard neo-Kantian distinctions between explanation and interpretation, nomothetic and idiographic, and the like, however much their own claims appear to insinuate just them.[19] As the role of abstraction throughout the critique of rationalized reason demonstrates, what Adorno wants to claim is that non-instrumental cognition is somehow primary, indigenous, or intrinsic to cognitive experience, and hence that instrumental reasoning, however necessary and legitimate, is, at some level, secondary or parasitic.[20] To secure the primacy of non-instrumental cognition, Adorno retreats to the concept as the minimal unit of cognition.[21] Some interaction of *both* the logical and material axes of the complex concept forms the condition of any and every cognitive episode, and it is only in virtue of that interaction that any concept can be said to possess its inferential powers. Almost at the beginning of *Negative Dialectics,* Adorno poses the claims for the complex concept, its dual axial structure, in dogmatic terms.

19 For an account of Adorno's rejection of these distinctions, see Simon Jarvis, *Adorno: A Critical Introduction,* pp. 45–8.

20 There can be little doubt that Adorno came to appreciate this way of structuring the argument as a consequence of his early reading of Heidegger's *Being and Time,* above all the account in sections 15–16 of the relation between the ready-to-hand (*zuhanden*) and present-at-hand (*vorhanden*) in which the latter (the object of instrumental reasoning) arises through the decontextualization and recontextualization of the former. It would not be an exaggeration to say that *Negative Dialectics* attempts to procure for itself the structural sets of dependencies and emphases of *Being and Time* without reference to Heidegger's overall framework relating to the meaning of Being, and within the context of the critical concept-object dialectic of Kant and Hegel. For an attempt to appropriate the insights of *Being and Time* directly for a conception of material inference, see Robert Brandom, "Heidegger's Categories in *Being and Time,*" in Hubert L. Dreyfus and Harrison Hall (eds.), *Heidegger: A Critical Reader* (Oxford: Blackwell, 1992), pp. 45–64.

21 To place the concept in this way is not to deny that concepts have meaning only in the context of judgements (statements), but only to assert that it is concepts themselves that are the operative units which judgements (statements) order.

> Concepts such as "Being" at the beginning of the Hegelian logic, first of all emphatically mean nonconceptualities; they mean, as Lask remarked, beyond themselves. Dissatisfaction with their own conceptuality is part of their meaning, although the inclusion of nonconceptuality in their meaning makes it tendentially their equal and thus keeps them trapped within themselves. Their content (*Gehalt*) is not only immanent to them, as mental, as ontical (*ontisch*) it is to them transcendent. Through self-consciousness one is in a position to be rid of concept fetishism. Philosophical reflection secures the nonconceptual in the concept. . . . Insight into the constitutive character of the nonconceptual in the concept would end the compulsive identification which the concept brings unless halted by such [negative dialectical] reflection. (ND, 12)

Notice the slide within this passage from referring to the nonconceptual as extrinsic to the concept to the effort of securing the nonconceptual in the concept. The first locution locates the nonidentical from the perspective of the simple concept, and hence as definitionally nonconceptual. The second locution portends a transformed understanding of conceptuality itself. Compulsive identification signifies the dominion of the simple concept. The nonconceptual in the concept is its intuitive moment suitably enlarged. Adorno adopted the range of dualities listed above in the attempt to adequately characterize that enlarged intuitive moment: as content, as cognitive orientation, as linguistic form. As its title suggests, in *Negative Dialectics* the nonconceptual is quarried as the negation of the hegemony of the simple concept, hence as its suppressed other. This can make that other methodologically appear like the mysterious other of negative theology, reenforcing the belief that nonidentity is nonconceptual and ineffable. It was in order to avoid that belief that this chapter opened with the example of the rhetorical second reflection of a assertoric statement.

As the diverse series of dualities through which Adorno constructs the complex concept makes evident, each version arises as part of some wider dialogue with the philosophical tradition. The following remark on the relation between language as expression and language as communication is situated in a discussion of Hegel in which his philosophical practice is defended as exceeding its results.

> Language as expression of the thing itself and language as communication are interwoven. The ability to name the matter at hand is developed under the compulsion to communicate it, and that element of coercion is preserved in it; conversely, it could not communicate anything that it did not have as its own intention, undistracted by other considerations. This dialectic plays itself out within the medium of language itself; it is not merely a fall from grace on the part of an inhumane zeal that watches to make sure that no one thinks anything that cannot be communicated. Even a lin-

> guistic approach of the utmost integrity cannot do away with the antagonism between what is in itself and what is for others. (HTS, 105)

In this passage communication speaks for the logical axis of the concept, while expression relates to the material axis. As its final sentence underlines, Adorno believes the dual axes of the concept are "antagonistic," oriented differently, and that the antagonism is not local but structural. If Adorno is correct about the structural character of the antagonism, then there is nothing in the structure of the concept that, even as a regulative ideal, points toward identity or determinacy or closure or fulfillment or completion. On the contrary, part of the reason Adorno turns to Hegel is for an account of conceptuality and language that is "dialectical" in the sense of having structural features that are never wholly theoretically unified and synthesized into a whole, but are understood through an interaction that is never permanently resolved. Crudely, each axis is permanently both independent of and yet dependent on the opposing axis; and this in part because each axis possesses a distinct orientation and hence unique ideal of its own, despite the fact that each is impossible without the other. Structural antagonism within the concept is what keeps concepts open, receptive to unanticipated futures, never fully determinate but always only a determination of an indeterminate set of possibilities. Understanding how the axes do oppose and yet depend upon one another is the consistent charge of Adorno's thought.

Surprisingly, but consistently with the claim that rhetoric is on the side of content, the expressive pole of language is said to relate to truth, the truth about the matter to hand; language is to express the thing itself, to grasp it, present it, show it. To call this axis of language "expressive" indicates that it concerns subject and object: subjects express themselves about objects, but they do so in order to express the object. Adorno's anthropomorphism can be located here: the object itself is expressed, presented, through subjects expressing themselves about their experience of it. Adorno will sometimes state this as the claim that the thinking subject is the object's agent, lending the object voice; or that the goal of thinking, its creative activity, is the exhibition of its dependent moment.

The function of the expressive pole of language is hence to "name" the matter to hand itself. To think the naming function of language Adorno will occasionally retreat to the more extreme duality between sign and image: language as conceived through the sign provides calculation without any likeness to the object, without anything sensible, and hence without substantive material/sensible mediation; while language as reduced to images provides a mirroring of the object without knowing, and hence without the mediation of the negating powers of the intellect. (This is Adorno's version of Kant's concept/intuition dictum: signs without images are (nearly) empty; images without signs (almost) blind.)

Mimetic imaging, like silent pointing, is not naming but expresses the desire which the naming function of language is to satisfy. Naming is an articulated, linguistic- conceptual mediated extension of the image-bound mimetic impulse: "Concepts alone can achieve what the concept [as simple] prevents . . . . The determinable flaw in every concept [viz., its generality] makes it necessary to cite others; this is the font of the only constellations which inherited some of the hope of the name. The language of philosophy approaches that name through negation" (ND, 53). If the hope of the name is to be realized, it is through the concept, through further and more elaborate conceptualization. Cognition approaches naming through canceling the claims and rigidities of the logical axis as they become manifest in thought.

The effort of naming is developed "under the compulsion to communicate." To communicate, even with myself, the givenness of the object must be negated and re-articulated. Negation and re-articulation refer to the moment of universality that is the logical axis of the concept, the moment in which the generality of a word, its applicability to more than one instance, trumps its naming function. Adorno considers this aspect of language in terms of "compulsion" and "coercion" because it represents the disciplining of the expressive/naming ideal: "To philosophy, expression and stringency are not two dichotomous possibilities. They need each other; neither one can be without the other. Expression is relieved of its contingent character by thought, on which it toils as thought toils on expression" (ND, 18). Or: "Coercion (*Zwang*) is inherent in philosophy; yet coercion alone prevents it from regressing into arbitrariness (*Willkür*)" (ND, 48). Adorno underlines the divergence of the logical axis from the naming axis by writing the former in terms of compulsion, coercion, stringency – thought's own ascetic ideal (as if the naming function were thought's own eudaimonic or hedonic ideal; which in a way it is for Adorno); acknowledging all the while that without coercion the naming function would lapse into arbitrariness. Adorno denominates the appropriate balancing of expression and communicative coercion "presentation" – *Darstellung*. Presentation is to be conceived as an alternative to narrowly logical argument, deduction, system, and so on. To express oneself about the matter to hand is to find a linguistic form that can embody, present, one's experience of it, not as a matter of what one privately or subjectively feels about it, but rather as the correlative of a reflective attending whose aim is to give voice to the object. Perhaps one could think of this as an interweaving of first- and third-person perspectives such that the factual demands of the latter would be coordinated with the sensuous and sentimental demands of the former.[22] But this is equally to sug-

22 For an approach taking off from thinking through the matter in terms of subjective and objective in this way, see David Wiggins, "Objective and Subjective in Ethics, with Two

gest that the first-person/third-person distinction is structurally dependent on the axes of the concept itself, its duality, and hence that the unequivocally third-person ideals of pure logic and ideal scientific explanation, the anti-anthropomorphic ideals, are partial. It is equally to suggest that naming is not the expression of first-person understanding – that is exactly the false belief which generates antagonism to anthropomorphism, and hence provides hegemony for the third-person simple concept. Cognition, as Adorno conceives it, is the surmounting of the dualism between first- and third-person perspectives.

To better comprehend the antagonism between "what is in itself" (naming) and "what is for others" (communication), and hence to attempt to demonstrate the existence of the dual structure itself, Adorno looks to the extreme of each axis. The extreme of the axis of communication would be the exact language of the natural sciences and its philosophical imitations. Adorno construes the communicative axis of language, the striving for transparent, intersubjective communication without loss or remainder, the complete fitting of language to the demand for intersubjective consensus, as nothing but the tendential abstracting from linguistic meaning of its expressive, sensible, truth-oriented relation to the world. It is this thought which lies behind his reiterated ironic thesis, joke really, that the more readily a thought is communicable, the more untrue it must be (HTS, 106; NL1, 263; NL2, 98; etc.). While this is hyperbole, its substantial sense is not difficult to locate: the more a thought abstracts from concrete subjective experience, from our bodily response to things in seeing, hearing, feeling, touching them, experience that is thus forever beholden and in debt to those worldly matters, with that abstraction equally requiring abstraction from the sedimented record of those experiences elaborated in sensibility and tradition, the more unambiguous, precise, and determinate thought becomes, the more capable it thus becomes of intersubjective agreement. Perfectly communicable thought without any sensory accompaniment is equally thought that in leaving behind the individual's response to experience leaves the sensuously particular, concrete "thing" behind; in leaving concrete things behind, it leaves behind the world of individuated things, so the world; the discourse that arises through these abstractions must hence be perfectly "false" – untrue to every concrete thing in the world. One might thus explain why the wholly disembodied abstract language of mathematics has remained a model for truth as ideal consensus; which is not a critique of mathematics but of its role as model. The natural tendency, the gravitational pull of the axis of communication, derived from the platitudes of the principle of immanence, is toward

Postscripts About Truth," in Brad Hooker (ed.), *Truth in Ethics* (Oxford: Blackwell Publishers, 1996), pp. 35–50.

the shadowless determinacy of ideal languages: sign without image, rationality without truth, concept without object, citation without reference. Pure communicability can arrive when there is almost nothing to communicate about, when the perfected syntax of language becomes its semantics, and hence when the difference between the monologue of self-sufficient reason and ideal dialogue lapses.[23]

In opposition, Adorno sees the axis of language as expression being idealized in the practices of the arts in their most modernist forms. Typically, Adorno considers the arts as a corrective to the high abstraction of exact languages since the former's languages are materially bound, bound to their own material and formal conditions of possibility: color, line, space in abstract painting, sound in the new music, the word in modernist poetry. These practices are as extreme in their way as mathematical physics is in its.[24] What gives point to looking in this direction is that these practices present, in their turn, a reminder or a claim about the axis of expression by, however abjectly, revealing a potentiality for sense-making in the very materials which the disenchantment of reason and world has left behind. For Adorno, the claim of artistic modernism is thus simply that there is a stratum of material meaning and an ideal of truth which belong essentially to human cognitive experience.

While exorbitant, the narrow, technical point of Adorno's turn to the material languages of the arts is to support the idea of a weighty conception of material inference by showing that there can be transitions between items that are rational but non-logical, thus escaping from the dictates of an a priori or fixated logical syntax. But this is equally to claim that at least some of the logical powers of a concept, what enables a transition, are to be located in the materials themselves (recall "bleeding badly"). Adorno's focus on the problem of transition hence derives from the claim, from the perspective of the simple concept and hence the philosophical tradition, that while contents may be worldly, nonconceptual, things referred to, syntactical ordering and logical connection – inference – belong exclusively to form and reason. Hence, if it can be demonstrated that there can be *structures of order and inference that are themselves sensible and material, then the categorial duality between concept and intu-*

23 Expressing the ideal of communication this way is, of course, expressing it from the perspective of the opposing ideal. Its more positive formulations are synonymous with philosophical rationalism in all its most hopeful forms. Neither way of stating the achievements of logic and mathematics, what they in truth are and accomplish, is accurate.

24 These extremes are not equal; mathematical physics really is a massive cognitive achievement, fully exploiting the logical axis of language, while artistic modernism is a record of our collective failure to acknowledge or exploit the material axis of language, the material sign, and hence of what has been left behind in virtue of our one-sided development.

ition can be challenged and defeated and a portion of the inferential powers of a concept can be located in its enlarged material/intuitional, mimetic moment.

To say that the transitions in question are non-logical is not to claim that they are contrary to logic, but only that whatever linkage occurs, it is not compelling *because* of a topic-neutral law of logic. This is what Adorno means by "aconceptual": a transition or synthesis is aconceptual only in terms of the conception of logical linkage presumed by the simple concept. Obedience to the laws of logic might be necessary for rational thought, but it is not sufficient; and obedience is not made sufficient for rationality by recourse, say, to true empirical premises – especially since both "empirical" and "premises" are problematic notions. What more is involved in rational linkages if not some combination of valid empirical premises and topic-neutral logical laws? To ask this question is to ask how there is a materialist moment of dependency in conceptuality "all the way up."

Adorno's beginning point for thinking through this problem remained modernist music. Since in many ways music is the most difficult of the arts to engage critically, for our purposes this point of departure can be regarded as simply heuristic. The premise of Adorno's view is that there is a nontrivial analogy between music and language.

> Music resembles languages in the sense it is a temporal sequence of articulated sounds which are more than just sounds. They say something, often something quite human. The better the music, the more forcefully they say it. The succession of sounds is like logic: it can be right or wrong. But what has been said cannot be detached from the music. Music creates no semiotic system. (QF, 1)

A semiotic system is one in which the meaning of an occasional sign is determined strictly by its negative differences with equally differential signs. In the case of natural language – sounds meaningful by convention – this entails a radical autonomy of language from nature and materiality. Semiotics, despite the fact that it tends toward a relativity of linguistic practice rather than rationalism, is nonetheless a version of the simple concept precisely because it accepts the radical separation between sign and image as final, reducing language to the communicative axis. Although music is a system of differences, it is not a true semiotic system because what its sounds say is not detachable from the sounds themselves. In it the signs are "looked at" or, rather, "listened to," not through.

The analogue of simple concepts in music are the "recurring ciphers" established by tonality: "chords which constantly reappear with an identical function, well-established sequences such as cadential progressions," And so on (QF, 2). Classical tonality, Adorno contends, functions like rationalized concepts in coming to only formally or extrinsically be related to the intuitions filling its protocols. Because of their unchanging identity, forming our musical second nature as it were, consciousness finds it difficult to "bid farewell" to the concept of classical tonality. Classical tonality is the shadow of the syntax of musical discourse. The new music operates as an immanent critique of this reified musical language. Necessarily the critique is reflexive and grammatical: it concerns the kind of language music is.

The subtitle of his book on Alban Berg indicates the orientation of Adorno's concerns: *Master of the Smallest Link (Übergangs).* On Adorno's reading, Berg's greatness derived from his dissolution of the musically given: the historically a priori forms of classical tonality and the consequent reduction of other musical sounds to blind intuitions filling those forms (hence receiving all their sense from the forms). To accomplish this end, Berg needs to make each sound more than immediate and singular thises; each must itself also be a transition. If each sound is itself a transition, then musical form, the conceptual or logical element in music, is determinately located in a purely sensuous element. That is how I understand a passage such as the following: " . . . structurally his music does not consist of elements in any commensurably traditional sense. It is, by its inherent nature, in a constant process of disintegration. It strives toward the individual element as its goal, that is, toward a threshold value bordering on nothingness."[25] I take the "constant process of disintegration" to refer to the practical deconstruction of existing forms. The music does not begin with sounds as either forms or intuitions, but with dead forms that are to be renewed through de-composition that would set its elements free to be sound and sense, material and meaningful, semantic units and logical connectives.[26]

Looking at this procedure from the perspective of the result: if no logical laws, that is, traditional musical forms, guide composition, then equally sounds can no longer be regarded as contents for those forms. Sound emerges autonomously when it stops being the raw matter or

25 *Alban Berg: Master of the Smallest Link*, trans. Juliane Brand and Christopher Hailey (Cambridge: Cambridge University Press, 1991), p. 37. For a philosophical critique of Adorno's treatment of Berg, see Raymond Geuss, "Adorno and Berg," in his *Morality, Culture, and History: Essays on German Philosophy* (Cambridge: Cambridge University Press, 1999), pp. 116–39. Although Geuss is certainly correct in noting how severely Adorno must understate the "affirmative" and formally retrograde circular forms in Berg, those criticisms do nothing to the logical basis on which the interpretation turns. Indeed, if Adorno's own views elsewhere are properly noted, above all, his sharp sense of how constrained modernist practices were in virtue of their social determination, then what is surprising is that he believed there could be any cases that satisfied the negative ideal. Here, as elsewhere, Adorno seems unsteady about the status of his own claims.

26 As Geuss, ibid., p. 129, nicely states the thesis: "So the basic structure of Berg's music is not 'tension/resolution' but 'construction/deconstruction' ('Aufbau/Abbau'), or one of asserting and taking back what was asserted. This 'taking back' is the opposite of traditional forms of musical affirmation."

Kantian intuition that can fill an antecedently validated formal mode. Given the prominence of classical form, the art of composition becomes the negative art of resisting historical a priori forms while nonetheless making each transition compelling: rational. *If each sound is a transition, a logical link, then there is normativity all the way down: no sound is a blind given. If transitions can be located at the micrological level of the individual note, then there is dependency all the way up: the work as a whole is nothing but a configuration of sounds.* Adorno takes this to be the risky project of the new music. Appreciation of such music is bound to the internal demands that each work sets for itself, thus forcing us to relinquish reliance on previous musical concepts for our comprehension. In giving assent to works of this kind, we are responding to the deliverances of our senses. Because the assent would not be forthcoming from an haphazard concatenation of sounds, then our assent tokens the intrinsic rationality of what is sensibly given. Because the work is not a semiotic system, if it names anything, it names itself. Because the sounds release an affective response, say, of sadness, it names that emotion not as something independent of its sound patterns but as what they are. It names its object materially.

3. Non-Predicative Identification: Dependency All the Way Up

Adorno's conception of a work of art in which there would be normativity, logicality, all the way down (or out) and materiality all the way up (or in) models how the axes of the concept might be reconciled with one another. Although the model is structurally perspicuous, its status is ambiguous since, first, the model is provided in the material language of one of the fine arts, and, second, since works of art are semblances, then there is no guarantee that the form of reconciliation promised is satisfiable outside art practices.

The material axis of the concept is the mark in the concept of its actual dependence on its object. Dependence on the object for Adorno tracks the primacy of the object. Primacy is always introduced by Adorno through an implicit naturalistic presumption: "Not even as an idea can we conceive a subject that is not an object; but we can conceive an object that is not a subject. It belongs to the meaning of subjectivity to also be an object, but not to the meaning of objectivity to be subject" (ND, 183). Despite the fact that we never know nature or object other than through consciousness, we can make no sense of consciousness unless it is the consciousness of a subject who is also an object akin to the objects of which it is aware. In this and like statements, rather than attempting to secure our insertion in nature demonstratively, say in the manner of Kant's "Refutation of Idealism," Adorno is reflectively acknowledging the a priori of modern naturalism: there is nothing else for a consciousness to be if not the consciousness of an object of a certain radical kind, one capable of becoming aware of its indelible objecthood. Showing that not even as idea can we conceive of a subject that is not an object can involve subtle argumentation; but as we noted in Adorno's critique of Kant on freedom, the guiding thread of argumentation, and part of what makes it a "metacritique" is that it presupposes modern naturalism as a material a priori orientation, an horizon of intelligibility. Hence, in the same place in which he asserts the priority of the object, he explicitly comments that the consciousness that has achieved independence (in the form of transcendental subjectivity) when considered genetically "has branched off from the libidinous energy of the species . . . . Consciousness is a function of the living subject [*des lebendigen Subjekts*]" (ND, 185).[27]

Here is Adorno beginning to play out that thought in more explicitly epistemological terms, to transform ontological priority into epistemological priority:

> If one wants to [cognitively] attain the object . . . its subjective determinations or qualities are not to be eliminated: precisely that would run counter to the primacy of the object. If the subject has a core of object, the subjective qualities in the object are all the more an objective moment. For object becomes something at all only through being something determinate. In the determinations that seem to be affixed to it by the subject, the subject's own objectivity comes to the fore: they are all borrowed from the objectivity of the *intentio recta*. . . . [T]he supposedly pure object, free of any added thought or intuition, is the very reflection of abstract subjectivity: only it makes the other like itself through abstraction. *Unlike the indeterminate substrate of reductionism, the object of undiminished experience is more objective than that substrate.* The qualities the traditional critique of epistemology eradicated from the object and credited to the subject are due in subjective experience to the primacy of the object. . . . (SO, 250; emphasis mine)

I take the turning point in this argument to be the claim that if subjects have an objective core, if the subject thus is something other than a transcendental subject, more than a geometrical location in space, then this will be due to just those sensory/perceptual qualities which it shares with objects that traditionally have been designated as merely subjective. What

27 Even more explicitly in the same paragraph: "[Physicality, *Körperlichen*] emerges as the ontic pole of subjective cognition, as its core. This dethrones the guiding idea of epistemology: to constitute the body as the law governing link between sensations and acts, in other words, to constitute it spiritually; sensations are already in themselves what the system would like to set forth as their formation through consciousness" (ND, 193–4). One can privilege consciousness as unique and constitutive only through the disarticulation of embodied experience. Conversely, the idea of the body as machine is, ironically, its dematerialization, its subsumption within an idealization of embodiment. The utterly idealized body subject to unrestricted lawful analysis is a dead body – not even that, since it analytically shows no signs of its former life it is a mere thing.

makes those qualities more objective than, say, the microscopic or abstract primary qualities of things are that for conscious states they alone provide objects with their actual material specificity and concreteness (as manifest to consciousness). Abstraction is always abstraction from a qualitatively dense awareness of *this*; the qualitatively dense *this* cannot be eliminated from experience of the world because I can come to awareness of myself solely through and in relation to the qualitatively dense phenomena presented to consciousness; there are no alternative sources since there are for animal bodies constructed like our own no other originary ranges of objects to which we are perceptually attuned. Hence, I must consider myself qualitatively like what I am primarily consciously aware of. It is only in virtue of those palpable, sensory properties of objects that are the content of sensory states that subjects are epistemically inserted into the object world, and it is in virtue of that insertion that subjects are always also objects.

While traditional secondary qualities, narrowly understood, are part of this story (ND, 187), the thicker protocols and proto-meanings of anthropomorphic nature, all those properties that might be subject to the libel of being merely projected onto nature, animal life in all its differentiation and practical complexity, are necessary in order to make the argument hold. If one halted the argument at the level of attunement between macroscopic features and secondary qualities, on the one hand, and our perceptual apparatus, on the other, then the former could be merely perceptually necessary, something a bald, reductive naturalist could happily concede. For sensory objects to be *more objective* than their micrological counterparts, perceptual attunement must be symptomatic of a wider and deeper macrological structuring: the system of living and animal nature of which we are a part. We are epistemically inserted in the world via the sensible features we share with perceptual objects because that always reflexive insertion is not purely epistemic; reflective self-insertion recapitulates the contextualization of animal life in its living environment: "the originary production of consciousness presupposes precisely what it promises to establish: actual, living individuals" (SO, 247). Not merely location in space, not merely the comprehension of my experiences of the world as carving a unique route through it as a condition of self-awareness, which by itself certainly requires the epistemological primacy of sensible experience, but my insertion in a living/practical habitat marked out by objects of need, threat, attraction, objects to be grasped or tripped over or bumped into, objects edible and inedible, loved and feared, objects useful for shelter or for protection, above all composed of entities, living and animal organisms, which *are macrological wholes* constitute the most primitive sense in which any individual has a world; one has a world, epistemically, synonymously with being in a context of actual macrologically specifiable relations bodily and practically.

One way in which this might be pursued quite generally would be through explicating how self-conscious experience is nonetheless the experience of an animal of a certain kind. This would call for a wider and more systematic strategy of genealogical naturalism than the one Adorno actually pursues. What would enable us to identify those aspects of our cultural life that have their origin in our animality is their comparability with the behavior of the higher mammals: seeking out food, hunting, protecting our young, wanting, mating, bonding, clustering into families, interacting ("socializing" and acting in concert) with nonfamilial others, displaying forms of aggression and territoriality, feeling pain and protecting ourselves from hurt, learning mature forms of behavior through play, displays of strength or desirability, and so on.[28] To agree that human forms of nurturing the young, for example, are not reducible to the behavioral patterns through which our nearest animal relations nurture their young is not, for all that, to accede to the claim that our nurturing is *sui generis*, wholly formed or uniquely comprehensible through the demands of reason. *Nurturing* is neither a product of reason nor a raw given, but a pattern of behavior that, in the course of evolution, is transformed, elaborated, and becomes ever more plastic in its satisfaction. Plasticity (complexity?) of satisfaction anticipates nurturing becoming a social practice, but still, a practice that is bound to our animality. Animal forms of behavior, if I can so put it, are meaningful or proto-meaningful, certainly purposive, without as yet being conceptual; conceptuality, spontaneity, exploits and elaborates a potentiality for explicitly conceptual meaning that is already there.[29] To suppose otherwise, to suppose that exercises of reason are utterly *sui generis*, would be to literally cut human meaningfulness off from natural meaning.

28 I mean this somewhat random list to, in part, evoke the complex animal context and related forms of behavior to which the experience of pain, but not it alone, of course, belongs. Alasdair MacIntyre's *Dependent Rational Animals: Why Human Beings Need the Virtues* (Chicago: Open Court, 1999) arrived too late for me to accommodate its claims. If I find MacIntyre's concern for the virtues untoward, I nonetheless must acknowledge that his emphasis on our animality (on the basis of analogy with higher mammals; for him, especially, dolphins), our consequent vulnerability and thus indefinite dependency pointedly articulates one version of the very constellation of items I perceive Adorno attempting to make salient. Exactly how to parse the sameness and difference of their accounts I am not yet in a position to say.

29 It is well to remember that with the higher mammals, at least, purposive activities are "learned" and hence "taught"; the young are "trained," their behavior, when appropriate, "punished" and "corrected." Hence, the young of the higher mammals do things "correctly" and "incorrectly." (One follows the same route to get to Carnegie Hall as one follows in learning to capture one's prey: practice, practice.) Not all purposiveness is like this – the purposive activities of frogs and spiders is not – but some is. So one way of pushing the thesis I want to achieve would be to ask: Can we make sense of rational activity apart from purposive activity? And can we make sense of purposive activity (what is subject to learning and correction) apart from purposive routines (unlearned behavior)? And can we make sense of purposive routines apart from (their emergence from) purposive systems?

Adorno does not employ genealogical naturalism in this way for two distinct reasons. First, he thinks the task of explicating the natural presuppositions of cultural practice belongs to science, above all, psychoanalysis. Following Nietzsche's example, philosophy is to employ genealogical naturalism critically, not systematically. Second, Adorno does think that human meaningfulness has been cut off from natural meaning. As a consequence, when Adorno is considering the issue of our likeness to the rest of the natural world, he adopts a very circumspect approach that is always fundamentally critical, a reminder to be posted against the self-inflation of concept and self-consciousness. He entitles the likeness of the human and the natural "affinity."[30] In typical fashion, Adorno deploys affinity both as if already established and as a result to be achieved: "affinity is the point of the dialectics of enlightenment" (ND, 270). The point of the latter claim is to halt an identitarian employment of our relation to nature, as if it could be established now as a firm piece of knowledge.

> . . . affinity is no positive ontological determination. Once affinity is turned into an intuition, into an immediately, empathetically known truth, it will be ground to pieces by the dialectic of enlightenment as a warmed-over myth; as something in accord with mythology which reproduces itself out of pure reason, with domination. Affinity is not a remnant, which cognition could have securely in its hands once the identificatory schemas have been excluded; rather, it is the determinate negation of those schemas. (ND, 270)

While affinity can thus not be used to theoretically fix our relation to nature, it is still pivotal for Adorno, a fulcrum, ontologically and epistemologically: "[Dialectics of enlightenment] no sooner cuts completely through affinity than it will recoil into delusion [of being epistemically and axiologically omnipotent], into a conceptless execution from the outside. Without it there is no truth . . . ." (ND, 270) Affinity represents the indeterminate idea of our immersion in and being parts of nature, ontologically and epistemologically. In this respect, it is what identity thinking can be conceived as recoiling from; affinity is a counter-image to anthropomorphism as a structure of projective illusion. In this light, identity thinking is conceptless, an execution from the outside, pure spontaneity, a *sui generis* positing of an order that owes nothing to the nat-

30 Adorno is presumably referring back to the strange moment in the "A Deduction" of the *Critique of Pure Reason* in which Kant appears to be claiming that the operations of consciousness by means of which a manifold can be united, "so far as it lies in the object, is named the *affinity* of the manifold" (A 113). One can read this as either a preparatory statement which gets overtaken a few pages later with the claim that the possibility in question is located in the transcendental unity of apperception, or as pointing forward to what becomes in the *Critique of Judgement* the demand that nature in fact conduce toward the kind of order we impose upon it.

ural – the critical point of my fable concerning the apple. The denial of affinity is the fantasy of reason. Affinity, thus, must be conceived as a condition of possibility of conceptuality in general. Whatever that thought amounts to ontologically, epistemologically it must, I think, turn on establishing that the concept has a material axis, where this amounts to establishing full objectivity for sensible knowings.[31]

If the partial re-enchantment of nature is the rehabilitation of anthropomorphic nature, the question arises as to how we can conceive of perceptual takings of sensuous particularity in its qualitative density as significantly objective, as something upon which the subject *depends,* and hence as sustaining the priority of the object, without losing the normativity of the space of reasons. How can the space of reasons be a repository of protomeanings it does not originate? How is the very idea of a space of reasons, rational demands, compatible with naturalism and the priority of the object? And, again, for Adorno the crux of this story is to show how the coordination between the axes of the concept, alias concept and intuition, is *not* seamless since if it were there would be no way of halting the simple concept from devouring the object: conceptuality all the way out without resistance from the object would make its representation a mirror of the simple concept's comprehension of it.

In *Mind and World* and "Having the World in View: Sellars, Kant, and Intentionality," John McDowell pursues a line of thought whose governing aim is to secure our routine cognitive engagement with the world from the disenchanting consequences of reductive naturalism, and indeed to do so in a way which would legitimate the thesis that "perceptual demonstrative content is *object dependent.*"[32] Given this proximity of McDowell's defense of the autonomy of everyday experience and knowledge with Adorno's, and his presumption that so securing everyday experience would be to re-enchant the world (MW, 85), I want in this section to think with and against McDowell as a way of fleshing out some of the epistemological issues in the idea of object dependence.[33]

31 Again, while Adorno is not a reductionist, he clearly believes that our folk psychology has been deformed by its need to resist reductionism. Hence, our picture of objective nature is too mechanical and our picture of subjectivity too anti-naturalist.

32 "Having the World in View: Sellars, Kant, and Intentionality," *Journal of Philosophy* 95/9 (September 1998): Lecture III, p. 475. For the purposes of my argument here, I assume that the refinements of these lectures are consistent with the claims of *Mind and World,* at least the small stretch of it I borrow from here.

33 The source of the difference between McDowell and Adorno is that McDowell thinks that disenchantment is only a mistaken epistemological theory and not either a feature of worldly experience or even a formation of reason. Since he does not think there is a formation of the concept that needs to be resisted, he is content to explicate how ordinary perceptual experience and what is continuous with it operates without being either beholden to or in need of support from science for its intelligibility. For an account of how the indifference to the actuality of disenchantment affects his view, see my "Re-Enchanting Nature," *Journal of the British Society for Phenomenology* 31, no. 3 (October

I need to think against McDowell because for his Kant-inspired project the key that needs unlocking is the demonstration that "receptivity does not make an even notionally separable contribution to the co-operation" (MW, 9) between receptivity and spontaneity; unless that was true, he thinks, it could not be the case that there was no outside to the space of reasons, and hence it would not be true that there is normativity all the way down. But, if receptivity can be seamlessly incorporated in the spontaneity of thought, then features of the world can be regarded as wholly within the space of reasons; what is manifest in experience is always already categorially articulated, and thus a component of a meaningful whole. For Adorno this Kantian vision is historically too true; it is the success of enlightened rationalism and thus the claim of identity thinking; nothing demonstrates the limitlessness of reason better than the success of mathematical physics, which was Kant's own view of the matter. Further, once the passive, experiential moment of human thought is fully incorporated into full-blown conceptuality, where full-blown conceptuality includes reason's explicit capacities for discursive justification and criticism, self-consciousness, then, as McDowell himself underlines, there will be no overlap between human experience and the experience of animals lacking the capacity for conceptual thought (MW, 114); in the phrases "human experience" and, say, "gorilla experience," but also "human infant experience," the term "experience" does not mean the same. And while this is difficult if not absolutely impossible to comprehend for perceptual experience, it becomes as good as impossible when the experience is of pains, especially those pains that are occasioned in the same way. Something in the nature of pain experience *prima facie* aligns us with, at least, the higher mammals, making us one of them rather than inhabiting a world apart.[34] Keeping this thought in mind governs what I say here, although its full consequences are not unpacked until my discussion of compassion in Chapter 8.

Conversely, if one detaches passivity and sensibility from the routine

2000): 277–300, the second half of which is more or less identical to the remainder of this section.

34 This worry about McDowell is widespread. For criticism of McDowell on this point that is lodged from, unexpectedly, a Kantian perspective, see Alan Thomas, "Kant, McDowell and the Theory of Consciousness," *European Journal of Philosophy* 5/3 (1997): 283–305. Of course, McDowell does not wish to deny the obvious: that animals and infants feel pains; he intends only to mark the difference between theirs and ours, and hence thinks the worries on this point are scholastic. Dialectically, however, the discriminating move appears to block the insight that it is precisely in the domain of vulnerability, pain, and the like that our status as dependent animals is most insistently in view. It is I think no accident that in cases of extreme pain our intentional comportment *toward* the world collapses and we become, so to speak, worldless, our animal existence emphatic. The must nuanced phenomenology of this remains Elaine Scarry, *The Body in Pain: The Making and Unmaking of the World* (New York: Oxford University Press, 1985).

synthetic achievements of the intellect, then will not the deliverances of sensibility collapse back into raw sensation or its like? Hence, I must think with McDowell to the extent that Adorno too is committed to the autonomy of everyday knowledge and linguistic practice from science; and that thought requires that experiential input be, validly, coordinate with its sensory appearing – the very thesis about secondary and sensory qualities that we just surveyed in "Subject and Object."

In the above-cited extended passage from that essay Adorno entitles the richer, not seamlessly incorporated notion of receptivity "undiminished experience [*Erfahrung*]"; hence, he thinks that the deepest consequence of the rationalization of reason is the reduction and epistemic disenfranchisement of experience, and that a future, utopian philosophy would be "nothing but full, unreduced experience in the medium of conceptual reflection" (ND, 13). Experience, then, is for Adorno the crucial epistemic intermediary, that item which will have the "intrinsic potential to command a certain conceptual response from a suitably endowed thinker" without that conceptual response constituting its "very being."[35] Unless experience had the intrinsic potential for conceptual response it would be only externally related to ordinary knowing and speaking; an external relation between experience and conceptuality would entail the dependence of ordinary knowing on something extrinsic to ordinary consciousness, say, some causal mechanism for transmitting "information" from one place (objects) to another (subjects), rather than a relatively autonomous form of interaction with the world. Conversely, unless experience had a foot outside its conceptual uptake it would have no means of resisting its indefinite transformation into conceptual articulation, and hence possess no features upon which the logical axis of the concept might be said to depend.[36]

In fact the question of whether experience is reducible to conceptuality shows up perspicuously in McDowell in his treatment of visual experiences that are prima facie richer and more fine-grained than our conceptual vocabulary either acknowledges or can easily account for. For example, the field of color experience that we possess simply in virtue of our animal embodiment is more fine-grained than any individual's or culture's conceptualization of it. Color awareness is a thin but intrinsic feature of our animal, bodily attunement to the world; and here, as elsewhere throughout modern philosophy, it stands in for much else. Its richness or fine-grained character raises a problem for McDowell since if

35 Crispin Wright, "Human Nature?," *European Journal of Philosophy* 4/2 (1996): 245. This is a review article of *Mind and World.*

36 What Adorno requires for dependence is weightier, so to speak, than the dependence McDowell pursues.

color experience were really a potentiality for conceptuality that was *not exhausted* by it, it would follow that passivity would be making a separable contribution to cognition; if it were making a separable contribution then its intelligibility could not be explained wholly in terms of our conceptual capacities. In tackling this issue I want to split the difference between McDowell's claims and those who want to say "that the content of experience is *partly* non-conceptual" (MW, 56).

McDowell's intriguing and suggestive claim is that with the help of demonstratives such as "that shade" we can give expression to a concept of a shade no matter how fine-grained. "Why not say," McDowell asks, "that one is thereby equipped to embrace shades of color within one's conceptual thinking with the very same determinateness with which they are presented in one's visual experience, so that one's concepts can capture colors no less sharply than one's experience presents them?" (MW, 56) All that is required in order to ensure ourselves that what we have in view here is a genuine conceptual capacity is that the capacity employed to embrace a color in mind that is activated in the presence of the original sample as designated by "that shade" is that it be able to persist beyond the duration of the experience itself.[37] What holds for color can then be generalized: if anything is to count as experience it must be such that in becoming an object of attention it simultaneously can be demonstratively designated. So long as what is demonstratively designated is such that its recognition satisfies the criterion of being able to persist beyond the duration of the experience itself, then it seems legitimate to say that the experience is intrinsically a potential for conceptuality, and that the power of recognition at stake is indeed conceptual.

But this does not show, quite, what McDowell claims: even if conceptual understanding *can,* in principle, be as fine-grained as experience, that does not entail that experience is conceptual all the way out. Actual experience is always more fine-grained, complex, and richer than any actual individual or collective conceptual grasping of it. There is no feature of my current view, for example, of the honeysuckle before me, that is in principle not capable of being attended to and thereby appropriately

37 In "Reply to Commentators," McDowell acknowledges that the expression "that shade" does not quite accurately express the point since it sounds as if it is about the concept of the associated object rather than its presentation. Hence, he now wants to express the thesis, which better states how I took the original claim, in this way: ". . . the fact that anyone who has the idea of a way of being colored can be credited, on some occasion when the grain of her color experience is supposedly finer than the discriminative power of her conceptual repertoire, with a conceptual capacity whose content is expressible by ' . . . is colored *thus,*' where the demonstrative expression enables the very fineness of grain in experience itself that is supposed to escape her conceptual net to be partly constitutive of the net" (p. 415). I hence use the formula ". . . is colored *thus*" from here on.

conceptualized; but my *experience* is, at least, more dense and complex than I can, in fact, now in any delimited temporal stretch of time attend to such that all its features would be grasped in the manner of "is colored *thus*." The in principle possibility of *any* portion of my experience being conceptually attended to does not entail, due to density, that *every* portion can be so attended to. Part of what distinguishes experience from its explicit conceptual grasp is just this complex density, that conceptualization, no matter how complex, is a refining and simplifying of an experiential field. Fine-grainedness is an aspect of density, and density (the fine-grained multiplied and diversified) part of what distinguishes the experiential from conceptual response *to* it. It is the saturated density of experience, in itself an anticipation of auratic uniqueness, that leads us to naturally think of conceptual response as unsaturated, partial, a report, hence always a perspective on and a slicing up of experience. Phenomenological density is the feature of experience that distinguishes it from explicit conceptual awareness. Density does not contradict the idea that experience is of a kind that can be responded to conceptually – all the way down; but it does oppose the claim that we should think of the experiential as always already conceptual in everything but name.

Even this presumes, however, that all features of my experience are ones I, or those in my culture, might here and now attend to. We know, however, that features of experience become prominent through interest; and not all cultures share all routes of interest. It is not just the density of experience that makes it presently concept transcendent, but that capacities for attending even in the manner of "is colored *thus*" are not capacities that are strictly one-to-one corollaries of portions of experience. Experiential *indeterminacy* runs deeper. Attending is not indifferent to questions of salience; and salience is socially and historically relative. Hence, while there is no reason to deny that experience is, intrinsically, a potential for conceptual articulation, it equally seems that experience is, both individually and socially, subject and concept transcendent. To state the same thesis from another angle, *conceptualization is the determination of an intrinsically indeterminate but essentially determinable, albeit never fully determinate fine-grained and dense experiential base.* Unless this were the case we could not explain why, as a matter of fact, different cultures operate with quite distinct conceptualizations of color (or snow or coconuts or trees or types of insult or forms of aggression or kinds of sadness). Experience, then, is the permanent indeterminate condition of determinacy; since the demand for determinacy is the logical anchor for identity thinking, then it is unsurprising that identity thinking should drive out experience. Equally, I think it is the desire for determinacy that pulls McDowell toward the seamless incorporation thesis, where determinacy and conceptuality translate one another. Unless sensory experience were saturated and dense it could not be indeterminate; but its being indeterminate is the precise condition for the differentiation of conceptual responses across times and cultures, as well as individually.[38]

That concepts can be, in principle, as fine-grained as experience provides the right kind of intimacy between experience and conceptualization; unless experience and conceptuality could be so coordinated, experience would lose its mediated, proto-cognitive character, its aboutness and form of claiming. Said otherwise, unless the correlation between experience and conceptuality was such that experience could be transformed into the fully conceptual via the rather simple mechanism of demonstrative reference, then what conceptuality took up would be outside or below the level of consciousness itself, hence making the appropriate story not one that could be told from within conscious experience itself. Demonstrative reference as the simplest form of non-predicative identification gives to sensory experience precisely the kind of authority it appears to have from the inside, that is, it confirms sensory experience as our connectedness to the world without absorbing it. The conceptual content of a perceptual demonstrative is nothing but the discriminated object of experience; discrimination and reapplicability ensure that the grasping is conceptual, while the content of the concept remains in the appropriate sense "material."

What forces McDowell toward his tight aligning of conceptuality, determinacy, and experience is the belief that the order of the space of reasons is *sui generis*; part of my purpose in above discussing the relation between human and animal nurturing was, in anticipation, to throw some doubt on the intelligibility of the space of reasons being *sui generis*. Experiences can be anticipations of conceptual activities if conceptual activities are themselves developments from plastic animal routines. The choice is not between conceptuality on the one side and causal structures

38 In a reply to my essay "Re-Enchanting Nature," McDowell complains that this account begs the question against his claim that there are actualizations of conceptual capacities that are not exercises of them: "An aspect of experiential content need not be conceptualized to be conceptual." While no phenomenological argument is decisive, there is something phenomenologically and logically counterintuitive in the idea of experience being fully determinate all the way down – for that is the claim. But even if one were to concede that nothing is yet decided between me and McDowell here, the setting should be telling: (1) in presuming determinacy all the way down, McDowell makes disenchantment epiphenomenal, a mere failure of attending and not an actual occurrence; (2) symptomatic of this failure is the fact that McDowell's view disallows us from distinguishing between *Erlebnis* and *Erfahrung*; but (3) the idea of determinacy all the way down is, I have argued, following the line of Sacks's "Through a Glass Darkly," the dialectical linchpin of identity thinking; (4) if my acknowledgement that what *determination* enables is demonstrative reference which makes ". . . is colored (shaped, etc.) *thus*" to be partly constitutive of the conceptual net, then there is no dialectical advantage in urging full determinacy all the way down. Further considerations in favor of indeterminacy emerge below. Nonetheless, the reason I am employing McDowell here is because the overall trajectory of his attempt to secure the cognitive import of experience strikes me as correct.

on the other, in which case conceptuality would be related to experience only by throwing a conceptual cloth over a preexistent structure indifferent to it, the very idea McDowell wants to avoid. But it can be avoided by denying that the categorial cut is between the conceptual and the causal. Adorno's underlying hypothesis, again, is that the cut, if anywhere, is between the living and the non-living; within the sphere of animal life, there are likenesses and differences throughout, as I say more about in the next section. Nonetheless, the simple assumption as to why we should expect experience to anticipate conceptuality is that all experience is mediated by either our animal embodiment, with its forms of order, or previous cultural mediation. McDowell himself insists that exercises of "spontaneity belong to our way of actualizing ourselves as animals" (MW, 78); but if this is going to be a form of naturalism, then *what* is so actualized must have as great a speaking role as the manner, the *how,* of its actualization. The *what* has no independent content in McDowell. The mediations of animal embodiment will provide even the most "immediate" experiences with a meaningfulness or proto-meaningfulness; but this is just to say that the indeterminacy of dense experience is not the absolute other of conceptual meaning.

Experience, then, must itself be mediated either bodily or through previous conceptualization; but if it is to be experience, then its demandingness must be either sensible or analogous to the sensible. The internal coherence of conscious experience from within is an obvious condition for its insulation from a wholly external, scientistic accounting. However, that experience, in fact, is *always* richer than its current conceptualization, even highly elaborated and mediated cultural experiences (e.g., I can fail to notice how thoroughly I have been just insulted although all the phenomenal signs are there), gives experience the immediacy and independence from conceptuality we normally suppose it to have while providing it with the right kind of material and causal credentials. But now, if experience is essentially dense, then is it a mere device to employ the mechanism of demonstrative designation such as " . . . is colored *thus*" to capture the fine-grained quality of an actual experience, or is the case of " . . . is colored *thus*" exemplary, what conceptual consciousness of experience is fundamentally like? Density pleads for the latter solution. If we are to consider conceptualization as fundamentally a *further* determination of experience rather than, as in identity thinking, the subsumption of particulars under universals, then we need to consider *all* empirical general concepts (like "red" or "sad") as particular elaborations and extensions of cases like that in which the concept in question is grasped like " . . . is colored *thus*" is grasped. General concepts enable the discrimination and recognition of experientially dense but, at least, anthropomorphically articulated, bodily relativized, phenomena. But this does not quite accurately state what is needed. One reason for thinking that the paradigm of conceptually grasping something is a case where that grasping is expressed through demonstrative reference is that in those cases the experiential content of the concept is, via demonstrative reference, *a component of it.* If this were not so, then, first, a conceptual episode would not *intrinsically* differ had its object differed; nothing less than this is necessary to secure the role of the object in a perceptual judgement.[39] But, second, unless the object were a component of the perceptual judgement of the experience of it the empirical content of a perceptual experience would be *exhausted* by all the true inferences that could be drawn from it, in which case perceptual experience itself would reduce to "blind" input.[40] And this, of course, brings us back to the problem of the specificity of perceptual experience.

Adorno's way of attempting to capture what it at issue here is to say, again, that all empirical concepts must be organized along two different axes: sign and image, communication and naming, function and substance, and so on. We should now probably want to state Adorno's thesis as claiming that *all (empirical) predicative identification incorporates (presupposes) a moment of non-predicative identification.* And while acts of non-predicative identification are expressed with the aid of demonstratives, non-predicative, perceptual judgements themselves are not *fully* discursive, where full discursivity is fleshed out in the thought that the empirical content of a judgement is equivalent to the totality of the true inferences it licenses. As McDowell rightly comments in a slightly different context: "a perceptual demonstrative thought surely homes in on its object not by containing a general specification, with the object figuring in the thought as what fits the specification, but by virtue of the way this sort of thinking exploits the perceptible presence of the object itself" (MW, 105). Non-discursive cognition, I am suggesting, is what in the first instance distinguishes perceptual demonstrative thought, it is what perceptual attending achieves. The notion of perceptual demonstratives having objects (properties) – in their mode of appearing – as contents displays precisely how context itself can be justificatory (and unless context is justificatory, then empirical content itself is jeopardized).

McDowell would not, I think, agree with my discursivity thesis. For him it would be sufficient to say that the specificity of perceptual judgements as opposed to judgements that issue from routine acts of reflection is that

39 "Having the World in View," pp. 476–82.

40 My point in putting the matter this way is to drive a wedge between McDowell's version of normativity – which, like Adorno's, follows Kant (against Hegel) in attempting to preserve a privilege and specificity for first-person experience – and that found in Robert Brandom's *Making it Explicit.* A wholly intersubjectively constituted account of normativity, which I am bound to say is not quite Hegel's own, inevitably makes first-person experience *mere* entry and exit points (transitions) with respect to the discursive realm, and the discursive realm identical with conceptuality and normativity. The idea of entry and exit points is the fate of animal embodiment in discursive idealism.

the former are "constrained" by the objects they are conceptually of.[41] But this is a way of, finally, discounting experience by incorporating it fully. If we are to consider object dependence as axial, as something that would or could mark a concept "all the way up," then there needs to be an analogue of perceptual constraint in ordinary conceptual understanding; it is this analogue of the perceptual constraint as non-predicative identification that I am designating as being cognitive while not being fully discursive. Something of this is implied in Adorno's claim that "priority of the object means making qualitative discriminations among things which are themselves mediated" (ND, 184). Qualitative discrimination opposes conceptual ascent; it is the route down toward what is sensuously particular – toward Berg's smallest link. Its relative autonomy can be established only if its cognitive mode can be discriminated from identity thinking in a manner other than simply saying that a judgement is perceptual. Below, I attempt to redeem this thought as one of reflective judgment providing intransitive understanding. Reflective judgement is the mode of cognition that is not fully discursive.

But before getting there, an issue is still hanging. One might find the argument to here hopelessly circular. What difference does the claim of object (experience) dependence make? After all, even if true that there is no predicative identification without non-predicative identification, nonetheless the converse will, generally, hold, and hence the claims of identity thinking can seamlessly unfold, that is, non-predicative identification is only a preparation for a possible ordinary predicative concept. The problem with the example of color is that routine perceptual judgements *are seamless* in the incorporation of the passive into the coordination between receptivity and the spontaneity of the intellect, social facts that are no more than "*shadows* cast by the syntax of our discourse;"[42] identity thinking has there already triumphed, and challenges to it hence always arise from the outside, as it were, in the space of rhetoric or art, and thus in those modes in which the issue of whether the experience is cognitive is in jeopardy from the outset – is appreciating Matisse's *The Red Studio* cognitive or non-cognitive? In fine, the line of argument from McDowell presupposes that there is no distinction to be drawn between emphatic experience and its withered shadow; but the argument that predicative identification presupposes non-predicative identification does not entail that ordinary judgements perspicuously bare the mark of that presupposition. On the contrary, if cognitive orientation of the axes is different, then ordinary perceptual experience will be a form of nonexperience, a way of forgetting emphatic experience, and the recovery of the latter, for us, something requiring an extra conceptual effort – only Ma-

41 "Having the World in View," pp. 472–5.
42 Wright, *Truth and Objectivity*, pp. 181–2.

tisse, for example, offering us an arguably actual perception of red that eludes conceptual devouring. And that, contrary to tradition in which it is assumed that if anything is experiential it is color awareness, speaks against using color as an example of experience.

4. "Is Living" as a Material a Priori Predicate

In order, then, to make the idea of object dependence stick I need an account of why routine perceptual judgements should be regarded as experientially idle, an argument I begin in the next section and complete in Chapter 7; and a case in which an ordinary predicative concept *must* be thought on the basis of its non-predicative sense if its empirical content is to be grasped at all. I do not know of any passage in Adorno that would help here, although the argument I am going to trace is only intelligible as a piece of negative dialectics. Intriguingly, the best and perhaps only perspicuous case for the dependency of predicative on non-predicative identity equally returns us to the issue of embodiment, pain, and animal life. The relevant case appears as part of Wittgenstein's private language argument.

> And can one say of the stone that it has a soul and *that* is what has the pain? What has a soul, or pain, to do with a stone?
>
> Only of what behaves like a human being can one say that it *has* pains . . . .
>
> 284. Look at a stone and imagine it having sensations. – One says to oneself: How could o ne so much as get the idea of ascribing a *sensation* to a *thing*? One might as well ascribe it to a number! – And now look at a wriggling fly and at once these difficulties vanish and pain seems able to get a foothold here, where before everything was, so to speak, too smooth for it.
>
> And so, too, a corpse seems to us quite inaccessible to pain – Our attitude to what is alive and to what is dead, is not the same. All our reactions are different. . . . [43]

As I read him, Wittgenstein is here attempting to question the Cartesian (and Kantian) picture of interiority by contending that it is not souls or minds that feel pain but bodies. But in order for this to have the force he wants, Wittgenstein attempts to show, *from the outside,* that bodies cannot be the dead or lifeless or unfeeling or mechanical *things* that the picture that drives one into Cartesian interiority makes them appear to be; or, more precisely, the intelligibility of the grip of Cartesian interiority (as an underpinning for modern asceticism) is that consciousness cannot be the

43 *Philosophical Investigations,* trans. G. E. M. Anscombe (Oxford: Basil Blackwell, 1953), sections 283–4.

locus of subjectivity without the relegation of the body to a machine; that mode of thinking subjectivity is what reifies the body, assimilating it to the inanimate.[44] By pressing the issue of whether a stone can feel, have sensations, suffer pain, Wittgenstein is attempting to return the idea of mere things versus living ones to the domain of experience, to make the idea of a living body, the wriggling fly versus the stone, into an *emphatic experience* once more.

One might say that Wittgenstein's demonstration here begins from the insight that from a restrictedly first-person perspective, at least ours, the relation between pain and consciousness of pain is so intimate that there is barely room for the body to enter. What thus distinguishes this run of thought is its second- or third-person construction; it is about the *perception* of bodies rather than about being possessed of one; or rather, it is from the perception of other bodies that the place of one's own becomes epistemically perspicuous – the very argument with which we commenced the preceding section. This is an argument about affinity in exactly Adorno's sense. Atypically, Wittgenstein is here contending that there is something basic, categorial in our apprehensions of mere things, dead things, and living ones, and that in making these discriminations we are not blindly subsuming these different kinds of objects under different (categorial) concepts, but that our apprehensions are somehow experiential *responses* to the objects, guided and governed by their forms of appearing – too smooth, wriggling, inaccessible to pain.[45] In these cases the smoothness or motionlessness of the stone, the wriggling of the fly, and the inaccessibility to further hurt or pain in the corpse are not external properties of these objects, not mere empirical predicates picking out properties capturable in a normal predicative judgement or assertion ("the fly is wriggling"), but, at least here, features of those objects *experienced* as marking them off from one another, and hence as providing us with utterly different and incommensurable orientations toward them – "All our reactions are different" in the different cases. Hence, my judgement of the fly as living *orients* my relation to it in the sense of regulating the appropriateness or inappropriateness of other conceptual responses. In judging the fly as living, "is living" is not a simple determining or classifying of the experiential manifold, but a judgement that attunes us to that manifold generally; it is presupposed in all our reactions to things

44 It is the "from the outside" take on this problem – let's call it the problem of "other bodies" as opposed to "other minds" – that makes this passage moderately unique. The usual treatments of this problem, very much in the tradition of Merleau-Ponty, emphasize how much "I" must be a living, embodied being for perceptual experience to be possible. Wittgenstein approaches the problem from the other direction; which is why, I believe, his treatment of the problem of "other minds" has remained so influential.

45 For simplicity, I am taking Wittgenstein's metaphorical "too smooth" as descriptive of the stone; even if the stone were rough, however, nothing would change in the basic story, it would be just harder to lay out quickly.

like that, it orients the kinds of meaningfulness our application of predicates to that kind of object have. As Wittgenstein says in rebutting the interlocutor who thinks that stones and flies are just things that, as it so happens, behave differently, "I want to intimate to him that this is a case of the transition 'from quantity to quality'." To let a little enchantment in: wriggling is something like or a component of the material form of the fly, it is a bit of nature's cipher that we decode or determine into the categorial predicate "is living"; wriggling thus possessing the exact valence of a Berg sound/note: a material "this" and a transition. "Is living" has an experiential content that, qua orientational, underlies but is not exhausted by its explicit conceptual content, and thus "cannot be the result of any inference or application of, or even obedience to, a rule."[46] If the logical axis of the concept is identified with a rule-like aspect, then evidently the *content* of the concept cannot be exhausted by it logical axis.

In this instance "is living" is a *material* a priori predicate. What makes the predicate a priori is its controlling of "all" our reactions. What makes it material is that its a priori power is not detachable from the exemplary instances through which it is experientially announced. It is an a priori distinction that imposes itself on us.[47] Or, as we might now be tempted to say: it is *the* a priori distinction that is here imposed on us, for in controlling the direction of "all our reactions" it is equally announcing or introducing into our reactions the very idea of normative appropriateness (toward the object), of our having attitudes that are normative.[48] The sense in which all our reactions are at stake here is that there is no more emphatic divide than between what is living, animate, and what is not, inanimate: I might express my rage at a chair, but I can only kill what is living, and can only mangle, torture, maim those living things which can

46 "Avoiding German Idealism," p. 147. Pippin is here stating what he takes to be the orientational meaning of reflective judgement, where he is adopting Kant's conception of spatial orientation – "To this purpose, I require above all the feeling of a difference in my own person" – to the wider purposes of the *Critique of Judgement.*

47 Which is why, of course, it is so fragile; because it is so experience-dependent it possesses no powers of resistance to a rationalized reason that demands objects fit patterns of rational articulation that emerge solely from reason itself (on the presumption that there are such).

48 This would be the beginning of a critique of Brandom's contention that normativity is instituted through the taking up of a normative attitude, and that nothing lies behind this attitude (hence it is a form of "normative phenomenalism") other than the attitude and the practices consequent upon having it. See *Making It Explicit,* pp. 32–7, 47–50, 626–7. What Wittgenstein is here claiming we cannot even imagine is that the susceptibility to pain of living bodies is not *itself* the categorial divide in virtue of which it makes sense to speak of taking up a normative attitude. If there is a sense in which I "cannot" respond to stone, corpse, fly in the same way it is not, finally up to me – although, of course, nothing is easier than to *ignore* the difference or, worse, for the difference to wither. Its tendential withering is part of disenchantment, the disappearance of aura; and for Adorno nothing makes that withering more likely than the thought that how the other is treated, deserves to be treated, is finally up to me, just my attitude or stance.

feel pain. Wittgenstein's severe depiction of the (experiential?) ludicrousness of a stone having sensations, the stone's sheer thingness as inhospitable to sensations as bodiless abstract entities like numbers are, his subtle thinking of the corpse as what is no longer susceptible to harm, the categorial jolt of the wriggling fly are hence precise: susceptibility to pain is the initial and controlling axiological cut in experience; but that cut tracks bodies of kinds and in states, not "consciousness."

If normativity is more than the thin notion of having a reason for a belief and being responsible for beliefs via reasons, this is because there are kinds of objects in the world, the living ones, where living is being construed experientially and narrowly (the vegetable is here outside consideration[49]) as susceptibility to pain, that *demand* to be responded to differently than other things, the mere ones and the dead ones.[50] Below I argue that one "natural" form in which this demand arises is through spontaneous feelings of compassion. Wittgenstein is here pressing the case more generally via perceptual awareness. What is involved in appropriately seeing the fly wriggling, say, in desperately attempting to break free of the spider's web or as it whirls about on the ground after a boy has torn off one of its wings? I am minded to say here that the demand in such cases is a response to or a feeling of the "aura" of such objects; objects have aura just in case their appearing can orient response, where an oriented response prefigures or adumbrates "having a reason" to respond differentially. Nothing can be made of the boy's viciousness, the pleasure of wing tearing, if not the pleasure of transgression. But the "law" transgressed is not elsewhere than in the fly's aura; and the fly's aura is its oneness as what is susceptible to damage, pain, suffering. What has aura is what can suffer, and by extension what can suffer loss. *Not differential response itself, but what organizes it, categorially, is the material condition of having reasons.* If differential response mechanisms are taken as the only

49 Korsgaard, *The Sources of Normativity*, p. 156, plausibly suggests that Kant's argument that our duties to animals derives from duties not to do things harmful to our own moral character, while implausible for animals, is plausible for plant life. I pick up Korsgaard's nuanced claims about animality and pain, completing the above argument, in Chapter 8 in my discussion of Adorno on compassion.

50 Because the dead ones are not susceptible to *further* hurt, then they remain within the circuit of the living as *its* etiolation. Hence death is not the opposite of life – mechanical nature is that – but rather a mode of it, entangled with it. Eventually I want to argue that the living/dead distinction is relative, a matter of degree. And indeed this must be the case otherwise reification could not be literally the encasement of the living in the dead mechanism of rationalized practice. The attempt to preserve ourselves, despite everything, creates death as not mode of a life, and *thereby* removes life from the living. This is why the crux of recognition of the living is not some vital principle, but irremediable vulnerability, pain. The emphasis on suffering in Adorno is hence not sentimental moralism, merely the identification with the victims of domination, but bears categorial significance. An animistic auratic individual does not refer merely to the uniqueness of an emphatically living being, but is that in virtue of being the locus of injurability.

connection between experience and conceptuality, then conceptual difference would be uniform throughout: the difference between what can elicit the judgement *blue* as opposed to *red* utterly continuous with what can elicit the difference between *inanimate* (smooth like a stone) and *animate* (buzzing like a fly). Conceptuality without material/orientational experience thus levels all objects into the inanimate, which was the core argument against conceptual ascent and identity thinking: enlightenment assimilates the animate to the inanimate. Equally, there is no thought of uniqueness, in the first instance, the other element of aura, without the uniqueness of living bodies: only that which whose surface is also a normative boundary can be unique, a one. But what makes a surface a boundary and limit, the outside *of* an inside, which means the outside of what is vulnerable to violation, what can suffer pain, is not "up to us," hence not constituted by an attitude or stance. It is not because I take up an attitude or stance that the fly is living, but because it is living it solicits a normatively structured response, whether respectful or transgressive (sadistic). Again, there are stances and attitudes because there is the living and the not living. The introduction of normativity is "intuitive" just like the distinction between left and right is a matter of intuition – what can be pointed to but inevitably misrepresented when construed as merely discursive, our way of classifying and categorizing. That there can and must be such material a priori predicates is thus what demonstrates that the concept's empirical meaning outruns its discursive employment.

But that Wittgenstein is having to *introduce* the auratic body – with a fly! – as a *reflective* counter to ordinary conceptualizations of soul and consciousness in fact presses toward interpreting his claim here as precisely a moment of negative dialectics, a making of qualitative discriminations in order to secure the qualitative dimensions of concepts that have lost their experiential meaning for us. If we are struck by Wittgenstein's discriminations, if they have the power to give consciousness an axial turn toward the object, this can only be because we need turning. The force of Wittgenstein's claim is in direct proportion to the preponderance of what it opposes.[51]

While Wittgenstein's big game here is to contend that the distinction between the psychological and the merely physical lies in the division between the living and nonliving, and not between inner (first person) and outer (third person),[52] and hence the key to establishing the intimacy of

51 The same needs to be said for my claims about animal life at the beginning of this section; nothing could be further from the truth now than that we are inserted into a living environment.

52 I am here following the conclusion drawn by Marie McGinn, *Wittgenstein and the Philosophical Investigations* (London: Routledge, 1997), p. 153. I am grateful to my former colleague Stephen Mulhall for bringing this portion of Wittgenstein's thought to my attention.

the relationship between inner and outer is to reanimate (and so re-enchant) the body, he is simultaneously concerned to show how this reanimation requires non-predicative forms of identification. For example, he states just a few lines later, "one can imitate a man's face without seeing one's own in a mirror"; a remark that I interpret, in the context of the above, as claiming that mimetic behavior is a form of (intransitive) understanding that has its source in the structures of meaningfulness that animate objects possess. To think of perceptual judgement on the model of mimetic behavior is prescient since in the latter case we can make no sense of the idea that one could grasp the meaning of a thing in that way without the presence of the object governing one's response utterly. The presence of a mirror, that is, mediation through internal reflection, would make mimetic understanding non-mimetic, so removing the object from its controlling role and replacing it by an internal self-relation. If the model of mimetic response is how Wittgenstein intends us to interpret our understanding of the fly's wriggling, our non-predicative identification of it, is there any reason not to suppose that more mundane empirical concepts have their empirical meaning in just the same way? As I shall suggest below, the good reason to think that ordinary empirical concepts ideally (utopianly) operate in fundamentally the same manner is because emphatic experience is the fundamental condition of concept acquisition and learning.

5. Reflective Judgement as Intransitive Understanding

> If the universal (the rule, the principle, the law) is given, then the judgement which subsumes the particular under it is *determinative*. . . . *If, however, only the particular is given and the universal has to be found for it, then the judgement is simply* reflective. (CJ, 179)

When the dependent moment of a perceptual judgement does enter seamlessly into its spontaneity, then, even if we allow the object itself to be what constrains application of concepts to it, the judgement is nonetheless identitarian.[53] Nothing could be more routine than the non-emphatic judgement that the fly is wriggling. Wittgenstein's fragment uncovers the emphatic experience underlying that judgement, its material a priori status, by rhetorically shifting the orientation of the judgement toward its object in just the manner in which the judgement concerning

53 I have adopted the notion of intransitive understanding from David Bell, "The Art of Judgement," *Mind* 96, no. 2 (1987): 221–44. My thinking throughout this section is indebted to Bell's important essay. For an analogous argument urging the claims of intransitive meaning against transitive communicability, see Alexander Düttmann, "On Translatability," *Qui Parle* 8, no. 1 (1994): 29–44.

the red chair was rhetorically reoriented in section 1. The logical and material axes of the concept collaborate in each judgement, but since each axis possesses its own orientation, then what has been judged in a judgement is not transparent in the judgement itself; only the setting and aftermath reveal the stakes and orientation. My suggestion in the previous section was that the seamless incorporation of the dependent moment presupposes a nonseamless one (predicative identification presupposes non-predicative identification). To underwrite that thesis two questions need answering: If the orientation of judgements can be different along the two axes, then there must be a cognitive difference in the result. What is that difference? If, seemingly, judgements can all run along identitarian lines, then where is there space in the life of the concept for the material orientation apart from being a rhetorical flourish?

In response to both questions, I want to employ a fundamental idea of Kant's as a clue. The clue concerns the relation between aesthetic judgements and empirical ones, and is self-evidently the hinge by means of which Adorno connected the empirical and the aesthetic in his mature thought.[54] For Kant routine empirical judgements are "determinative" judgments in which particulars are subsumed under general concepts. Determinative judgement on its own is exemplary of identity thinking. But determinative judgement cannot be all there is to judgement for at least two reasons: First, even if a concept provides criteria for what falls under it, it cannot provide rules for the application of those rules; rules for the application of rules would generate an infinite regress (B 171–2). Especially in new instances the question can arise as to whether *this* is an instance of X. But if the question can arise, then there must be a way of my relating to *this* which comprehends its unity without presupposing that the unity in question is given through determinate concept X (or Y or Z). Second, there are cases when novel items appear and we have no concept available to judge them, and hence must search one out. To Kant's two primary cases in which determinative judgement is in need of supplementation and support, there is an obvious implied third one: concept acquisition and learning. The conceptual neophyte is faced with phenomena for which she lacks a determining concept, yet if learning is to be possible then the phenomena must mean for her in some way, must somehow be available to her. The subjective conditions of concept acquisition parallel those of concept formation as Kant sees it. In each of these cases, Kant avers, the faculty of reflective judgement is operative.

Here is the clue I wish to track: In the First Introduction to the *Critique of Judgement* Kant claims that aesthetic judgement is to be understood as "none other than reflective judgement," that is, our capacity for aesthetic judging is a specific version of that more general capacity of reflective

54 I argue for this thesis in *The Fate of Art*, chapters 4 and 5.

judging which is not itself limited to the issuing of aesthetic judgements. Kant amplifies this thesis as follows:

> . . . we must regard the feeling of pleasure (which is identical with the representation of aesthetic purposiveness) as attaching neither to the sensation in an empirical representation of the object, nor to the concept of that object, but consequently as attaching to – and as connected with, by means of an a priori principle – *nothing but the reflection and its form (the essential activity of judgement) by which judgement generally strives to proceed from empirical intuitions to concepts as such.* (CJ, First Introduction, 249; emphasis mine).

The phrase in italics is the clue: aesthetic judging is nothing other than the mental activity through which we interrogate indeterminate phenomena in a manner that enables us to proceed from awareness of them to the formation, or acquisition, or application of a concept. In aesthetic judgments themselves no concept is formed, acquired, or applied; that is what makes them distinctive. In an aesthetic reflective judgement what occurs is the process of conceptualizing without a conceptual result. Identitarian thought holds fast to the result and eliminates its formation; it is determinative judgement without (explicit) reflective judgement.[55] *My answer, then, to the question of where in the life of the concept is there space for the material axis will hence be: in processual activities of concept acquisition, formation, and application,* in other words, in all those places where something new prima facie asserts itself, where a full concept has not already secured its authority and validity, and in which *conceptualizing* as process is an explicit feature of what results from the process. In just those places where a concept is either not present or uncertain, conceptuality is exposed to and dependent on its object. Cognitive exposure to an object in the absence of a (full) concept would be sheer cognitive terror unless we had the cognitive ability to engage with objects under those circumstances. Reflective judging is that ability.

But to urge that concept acquisition, formation, and application to new instances (concept extension) belong to the concept itself is equally to claim that concepts are in themselves historical, that the history of a concept belongs to the *life* of the concept; concepts emerge, change, solidify, congeal, wither, and die. For the simple concept, for which determinacy is criterial of cogency, these eventualities are extrinsic to the meaning of the concept; the ideal of determinacy, horizontally and vertically, is what makes good concepts ones for which all change has been

55 Menke, *The Sovereignty of Art: Aesthetic Negativity in Adorno and Derrida,* argues that aesthetic negativity is precisely process as opposed to result or product, what he calls "automatic understanding." As an account of Adorno's aesthetics this is far too formal; nonetheless, the processuality of artworks and aesthetic judgements is fundamental to Adorno, and Menke's work usefully elaborates that moment.

eliminated. Reflectively, only if the full comprehension of a concept must include its acquisition, formation, application to new instances does genealogy become essential to its comprehension. Genealogy uncovers the life of the concept against its identitarian form. But this becomes plausible only if Kant is correct in arguing that determinative judgement presupposes reflective judging as its condition of possibility, and that the relation of determinative judgement to reflective judgement reflects features of concepts themselves; if reflective judgement did not articulate a feature of conceptuality, it would degenerate into a merely psychological condition for our possessing the cognitive states we do. *The orientational judgement that announces the wriggling fly as living exemplifies the role of reflective judgement in a determinative judgement.*

Tracking down the details and complexities of Kant's own analysis would lead us too far astray for the purposes to hand.[56] It is his clue that needs elaborating. Here is a passage from Adorno which I construe as encapsulating at least part of how he construes aesthetic judging or estimation:

> If that concept [of understanding] is meant to indicate something adequate, something appropriate to the matter at hand, then today it needs to be imagined more as a kind of following along afterward [*Nachfahren*]; as the co-execution [*Mitvollzug*] of the tensions sedimented in the work of art, the processes that have congealed and hence become objectified in it. One does not understand a work of art when one translates it into concepts . . . but rather when one is immersed in its immanent movement; I should almost to say, when it is recomposed by the ear in accordance with its own logic, repainted by the eye, when the linguistic sensorium speaks along with it. (NL2, 97)

This passage of Adorno's can usefully be compared with a run of remarks by Wittgenstein:

> . . . understanding a sentence lies nearer than one thinks to what is ordinarily called understanding a musical theme. Why is just *this* the pattern of variation in loudness and tempo? One would like to say "Because I know

56 For my own views on Kant's account, see *The Fate of Art*, chapter 1; and "Judging Life: From Taste to Experience, from Kant to Chaim Soutine," in *Constellations* 7, no. 2 (June 200): 157–77. Amongst the large literature on this topic, I have been most influenced by Howard Caygill, *The Art of Judgement* (Oxford: Basil Blackwell, 1989); Rolf-Peter Horstmann, "Why Must There Be a Transcendental Deduction in Kant's *Critique of Judgement?*," in *Kant's Transcendental Deductions*, ed. Eckart Förster (Stanford: Stanford University Press, 1989); Rudolf Makkreel, *Imagination and Interpretation in Kant: The Hermeneutical Import of the Critique of Judgement* (Chicago: University of Chicago Press, 1990); Hannah Ginsborg, "Reflective Judgement and Taste," *Noûs* 24 (1990): 63–78; and her "On the Key to Kant's Critique of Taste," *Pacific Philosophical Quarterly* 72, no. 4 (1991): 290–313; Robert Pippin, "Avoiding German Idealism"; and his "The Significance of Taste: Kant, Aesthetic and Reflective Judgement," *Journal of the History of Philosophy* 34, no. 4 (1996): 549–69.

> what it's all about." But what is it all about? I should not be able to say . . .
> 531. We speak of understanding a sentence in the sense in which it can be replaced by another which says the same; but also in the sense in which it cannot be replaced by any other. (Any more than one musical theme can be replaced by another.)
>
> In the one case the thought is the sentence says something common to different sentences; in the other, something that is expressed only by these words in these positions. (Understanding a poem.)[57]

In both passages what is at stake is the contrast between a form of understanding in which what is to be understood is grasped through means which are logically independent of the object – different sentences expressing the same thought – as opposed to a form of understanding in which the object – the work of art, the sentences – must be understood intrinsically. And while Wittgenstein refers to a poem as the prime example of sentences of the latter kind, any instance in which it is discovered that what is said cannot be said in words other than just the ones used in the order in which they were used without loss of meaning, where translation and paraphrase do involve significant loss of meaning, can be substituted. In cases of nonparaphrasability the words and their ordering are not mere vehicles for what is expressed, but are that expression. Hence, Adorno's construction of a "linguistic sensorium": the understanding is bound to just those words in those positions in a manner directly analogous to the binding of the eye to the visual array in the understanding of a modernist painting, for example.

Aesthetic experience is the experience of unique items where precisely the material conditions of meaning and meaning itself are fully joined; this was the radical thesis of the Berg example (as well as the underlying presumption about the conceptualization of experience in the preceding section). Hence in aesthetic experience we are invariably radically dependent on the object for our understanding of it; repainting with the eye is a matter of visually scanning the canvas, noting the intrication of details, searching out patterns of color and line until the diverse elements appear, satisfyingly, as a whole. In these instances, satisfaction arises not because the pattern revealed enables the application of a concept ("It's a fish"), or because we pick up a transitive sense ("Love is painful"), although both moments can be components of a fuller aesthetic comprehension; rather, satisfaction arises because what is discovered is a patterning *in the material itself* without the presumption of a concept giving the material that shape or pattern. There is in such cases the kind of patterning or integrity or structure that indeed enables concept formation or application, but which in these cases is barred – imagine you

57 *Philosophical Investigations,* sections 527 and 531; emphasis mine.

are looking at a work of Abstract Expressionism, a Pollock or a de Kooning.[58] In such cases the material elements – say, color contrasts – are not a prop or support for conveying something else, but what require comprehension in themselves. Because meaning here is nothing other than an arrangement of material elements – recall, again, Adorno's analysis of Berg – our grasping of the meaning remains sensory, remains bound to the acts which accomplish it, remains something accomplished *in* the very act of hearing or seeing (and not through it). (Modernist art works are those which explicitly prohibit being treated as representations of something else beyond themselves.) A translation of a modernist work of art, a paraphrase or an interpretation of it, misses out on the form of understanding involved, its object dependence, and its completion in the object, so to speak. Because understanding of the work is sensorily bound, it cannot be communicated without remainder. I can aid and inspire you to see what I see, but the comprehension is the seeing itself (*thusly*), and hence nondetachable from the experience which gives rise to it. (Equally, of course, I can make no sense of *seeing* what I see unless I presumed that you should, ought to, see the same. Otherwise my judgement would not be a case of finding or discovering or understanding *it* – the object.)

Notice how first-person experience operates in reflective judging. In the first instance what is before my eyes makes no sense *to me*; knowing it is a painting (because hanging on a museum wall) is insufficient since I cannot see it *as* a whole of any kind (apart from being an arbitrary object hanging from the wall); hence its claim to be a painting is initially honorific. And in the worse case scenario, the scenario that modernist works routinely court, the disorder of the novelty will be permanent for me, hence the work for me will never be a true painting.[59] When, however, the diverse elements begin to appear to belong together, to somehow fit, since what is occurring is aconceptual, orderly but not through a concept, and remains in the domain of the sensory, then the unity in question must be grasped and *felt*; what is there appears whole and integral *to me*. Since there is no concept to hold that unity together, to represent that unity and articulate it, then what unity there is must be held in mind (the way "is colored *thus*" must be held in mind), to be meaningful to me. There is no getting around the *to me* because there is nothing else that can be the

58 For an elaboration of this case, see my "The Death of Sensuous Particulars: Adorno and Abstract Expressionism," *Radical Philosophy* 76 (March/April 1996): 7–18.

59 I am assuming here that modernist works really do raise questions of the form "Is it painting?," "Is it art?," and that the honorific answer given by museum space is not enough "for me": if I can find no pattern or sense to it, then for me it is not just a bad painting, but one which I do not know how to attach to the practice of painting as it traditionally has been. Hence, nothing I can recognize as a painting. This may oversimplify matters a lot, but not in ways that effect the core of the argument here.

bearer of unity (meaning, significance). Reflective unity is always felt precisely because it is non-predicative; the feeling of unity, its appearing unified and meaningful to me, is a condition of whatever else may be said (meaningfully) about it. And although what is meaning here is meaning to me, there is nothing essentially private about this meaning – it is the integrity of the object after all. While, again, I cannot directly communicate its meaning to you, we can share its meaning by you coming to see the object as I do. When my understanding is sensorially bound, reflective, then affect and understanding are necessarily united.

Meaning that is discovered *in* the object is not its meaning in terms of something else, through something else, in virtue of something else. If *this* object reflectively means at all, it means intrinsically or intransitively; its meaning is articulate, structured, but not further articulable. As David Bell has noted, Wittgenstein provides a host of examples of such intransitive understanding – "understanding a picture, a face, a pattern, a piece of music, a poem, an attitude or posture."[60] If we think of a poem as a prime example, then it would be curious to claim that what is understood (about what the poem is about, say, love or death) is understood only metaphorically, only "as if," but in truth there was nothing to understand, only the experience of understanding but with nothing understood. Or, in understanding a poem I learn nothing about what the poem is about. Understanding when applied to artworks cannot be regarded as a metaphorical extension of real understanding. That is the exact prejudice of claiming that all understanding and meaning is transitive – identitarian – and all judgement determinative. Nonetheless, it is commonly said that aesthetic experience is non-cognitive, which raises the largest challenge to what I am claiming here. Let me, however, hold off that worry for a moment.

Following Kant's clue, Adorno's notions of "following along afterward" and "coexecution" are (among) the forms of reflection involved in cases where one is beginning without a concept that would identify a case. In aesthetic instances, the goal is not to reach a general identification, but to cognize the elements as configured in their own right, to see or hear that there is order and meaning. The activities of reflection without determination, of following along afterward and coexecution, are what Adorno means by mimetic conduct. *Mimetic cognition is understanding intransitively*; reflective judgement is the heir of mimetic understanding. Adorno sometimes elaborates the cognitive operations at stake in this idea through the Hegelian trope of "freedom toward the object" or, more dubiously, "simply looking on [*reines Zusehen*]":

> Hegel is able to think from the thing itself out, to surrender passively, as it were, to its authentic substance .... Hegel everywhere yields to the object's

60 "The Art of Judgement," p. 242.

> own nature, which everywhere become something immediate for him again, but it is precisely this kind of subordination to the discipline of the thing itself that requires the most intense efforts on the part of the concept. Those efforts succeed at the moment in which the intentions of the subject are extinguished in the object. (HTS, 6–7)

The notion of immediacy here is not the direct opposite of what is mediated and conditional, and hence not a return to the myth of the given. Immediacy signifies the overcoming of or resistance to transitivity, automatic understanding, and the attempt to discover an order or meaning in the object that is not wholly bound to discourse about it. More simply, immediacy means only that what unity is found is not there solely in virtue of a covering concept, solely in virtue of a predicative concept's work of ordering or synthesizing. This is equally what is at issue in the claim that, in intransitive understanding, the subject's intentions are "extinguished in the object": the intentional activities of reflection – articulating, scanning, estimating, integrating – are not realized in a final intentional action, the application of a covering concept, the subject's appropriating the unity of the object for himself through the concept, but in the acknowledgement or realization of the object's internal integrity, its material sense.

In language, the axis of communication is the carrier of transitive understanding, while the axis of naming and expression carry intransitive understanding. Because intransitive understanding is not directly communicable, then typically intransitive meaning and understanding is communicated performatively or rhetorically; the performative/rhetorical dimensions of language are employed precisely to halt transitive comprehension and reorient understanding toward the object itself – or when the object is absent to insinuate the experience which is being drawn upon. I take it that this work of performative reorientation, exemplified by the procedure of negative dialectic and the forms of writing to be examined in the next chapter, is what Adorno has in mind when he says that subordination to the object requires "intense efforts on the part of the concept." Adorno's goal is to find the mark of the object in the concept, the intransitive meaning of a concept through the performative employment of other concepts. The myth of the simple concept is the myth that all understanding must be transitive; this is the myth of a pure semiosis, of language spinning out its meaning by endlessly referring us from one negatively differential sign to the next – all mediation without anything being mediated. The intransitive understanding of reflective judging explicates how that dizzying possibility, the possibility of a wholly disenchanted world, can be, at least in principle, halted, bound, riveted to the world through eye and ear, skin and flesh, memory and imagination.

Does the instance of the intransitive understanding involved in reflective judging show that concepts themselves must possess a material axis? Are we so sure that intransitive understanding is truly understanding? This is where Kant's clue becomes relevant once more. Concept acquisition, formation, and application to new objects or events all necessarily presuppose our capacity for reflective judging and hence for intransitive understanding. The narrow notion of aesthetic reflective judgement enacts the subjective element presupposed by objective judgements. Precisely those powers of judging that are involved in our appreciating works of art underlie our acts of determinate conceptual judgement. How else other than through coming to see a regularity or significance or orderly patterning of a perceptual array might it be possible to explain that there is a cognitively significant relation to a material that *anticipates* its logical-conceptual grasp but is not reducible to or explainable through that grasp? This anticipation is necessary otherwise there would be no basis for applying *this* concept to *this* new perceptual complex. The case of the conceptual neophyte is an extreme version of this. As Stephen Everson has suggested:

> . . . what is changed in the acquisition of concepts is a subject who does not *start out* with that ability. The actions and objects to which the subject is perceptually exposed thus have an effect on him even at the state when he cannot recognize them for what they are. The reason why it is important to emphasize the role of ostension in the acquisition of concepts is that one cannot get a grip on the norms governing the application of concepts without standing in a direct cognitive relation to instances of the kind of thing that falls under that concept.[61]

The neophyte lacks the concepts necessary to grasp a novel array until they are supplied by her elders; prior to their intervention she might have experienced intense sensory unities – the grimaced and red face, eyes slightly bulging, teeth clenched, the loud voice with familiar sounds "nn-oooo!," the threatening/frightening posture, all there for her awaiting what will become their coordinator: "Daddy is *angry*." *Angry* is the final synthetic operation, what gives or provides the material/sensory array stability by offering criteria for sameness, replacing sensory ("is colored *thus*"-like) memory, and relating the state identified to other relevant states and surrounding events ("Daddy is angry because you have . . . "). The cases of abstract art we have been employing are ones that place each of us in the position of the neophyte, the learner for whom the world is not yet coded and closed; but the position of the neophyte is equally the position

61 S. Everson, "Aristotle and the Explanation of Evaluation: A Reply to David Charles," in Robert Heinaman (ed.), *Aristotle and Moral Realism* (London: UCL Press Limited, 1995), p. 198.

of each of us before any radically new or unexpected perceptual array which exceeds the bounds of our standing conceptual repertoire.

Is it wholly contingent that the institutional bearer of reflective judging and intransitive meaning is in the non-practical practices of art and aesthetic judging? Even if concept acquisition and change require reflective judgement, is there any reason to suppose the everyday acts of concept application do so as well? If for mature adults the universal is, for all intents and purposes, always given, then is there any reason to believe that we are ever faced with particulars for which a concept is lacking? Routine concept application, where concepts are possessed and the world routine and law-like in its presentation of phenomena, would seem to *not* call into operation our capacity for reflective judging. Ordinary perceptual judgement only wants from the object judged its familiarity, its fit within the conceptual order as a step within practical life; which is why "conceptual order is content to screen what thinking seeks to comprehend" (ND, 5). More exactly, if the logical axis of the concept displaces the "holding in mind" of the unity of the array, and further displaces sensory awareness of the object into conditions for applying the concept, then concept possession routinely overtakes and displaces the cognitive relatedness to the object that distinguishes reflective judgements on their own, objects thus becoming merely *occasions* for triggering the appropriate conceptual response. (Because objects are *occasions,* they are perceptually present, hence there is experience in its weak, *Erlebnis,* sense. Hence the slide into emptiness can occur without any phenomenologically distinctive sense of emptiness, of anything being amiss.)

Because routine concept application proceeds all but automatically, without calling forth reflective judging or intransitive understanding (or not calling it forth in any significant way), then routine practices can operate on the presumption that transitive thinking is all, that all meaning and understanding are transitive, and further have an interest in being so: automaticity of identification is instrumentally rational for practical purposes. Identity thinking, the law of the simple concept, is transitive understanding without explicit intransitive understanding. That is the truly seamless incorporation of the passive moment into the spontaneity of judging – the very thing, normativity all the way down, that McDowell considers the path to re-enchanting experience. Indeed, since concept *possession,* in opposition to concept acquisition, *can,* but need not, in accordance with the ideals of the simple concept, be thought to require the automatic or spontaneous or immediate determination of phenomena, subsumption, then concept possession can, but need not, be thought to necessitate forgetting the experience of concept acquisition, hence forgetting the intransitive sense of the concept, suppressing the role of intransitive meaning in transitive understanding. And what can occur for each individual can, under suitable conditions, happen for a community as a whole; it can construe the meaning of its most urgent and central concepts in wholly transitive terms. For Adorno, this is in fact what has happened to us – as I rehearse in the next chapter: "all reification is a forgetting" (DoE, 230); and that is why art and aesthetic reflection appear extrinsic to the veridical cognitive life of concepts. If the axes of the concept each possess its own cognitive orientation, then discounting or forgetting intransitive sense is a structural tendency within the complex concept.[62] In virtue of its communicative axis, human conceptuality is a priori exposed to the degeneration of emphatic meaning into the mechanical meaning of transitive understanding. Disenchantment is the epitome of concept degeneration, even if degeneration is a structural feature of the concept while disenchantment is not.

Kant's clue was meant to restore to cognitive experience the life of the concept which routine transitive understanding had suppressed and eliminated: "It is true that the regularity leading to the concept of an object is the indispensable condition . . . for apprehending the object in a single presentation and determining the manifold in the object's form; this determination is a purpose [we pursue] with regard to cognition" (CJ, 242). Reflective judging conceives of the object as possessing the kind or type of unity or integrity which the concept will transitively state; reflective judging connects the visual array *as* a unity fit for conceptual articulation, say, this sensory manifold possesses the regularity and unity fit for the purpose of cognizing it as a chair. If intransitive understanding anticipates logical grasp in this way, then it must be presupposed, if only for the neophyte, by logical grasping. However, even if the interpretation of aesthetic reflective judgement as rehearsing in an unconstrained and explicit way the implicit work of reflective judgement required for concept acquisition, formation, and application to new phenomena is accepted, and hence it is granted that reflective judgement involves the subjective conditions for determinative judgement, the case for all this being thought to be a form of nondiscursive *cognition* and thereby an axis of the concept is still not made. Above all, Kant himself did not see matters this way.

While Kant insists upon the indispensability of reflective judgement, he nonetheless regards it as non-cognitive. The two fundamental reasons

62 See Heidegger, *Being and Time*, sections 34–38. It is this structural case which I think opens up Adorno's thought to a purely logical, ahistorical and nonsociological interpretation. Unless something in the nature of concept possession itself truly enabled the forgetting and/or suppression of the intransitive sense of concepts incurred in concept acquisition, it would be inexplicable as to how such a catastrophe could happen to our conceptual life and go, for the most part, unnoticed. At one level, then, ordinary concept degeneration phenomenologically converges with notable aspects of reified modernity. However, one needs the wider sociological canvas in order to explain how and why our state of degeneracy is not subject to renewal in the way that Heidegger thought authenticity would provide renewal.

for claiming that judgements of taste, and hence by extension reflective judgements generally, are non-cognitive are, first, they are criterialess, and, second, they are merely aesthetic.[63] The first reason is question-begging since it amounts to no more than the thesis that judgement is cognitive only if it is subsumptive; only an object's concept can provide the criteria in virtue of which the concept applies to it. (The question of criteria equally shows how indeterminate demonstrative reference is; after all, nothing is criterial for something being "colored *thus*" other than it being so colored. That would empty the notion of criteria; but it would not show that we would not, on occasion, have all the reason in the world for thinking of some color that it was "*thus*" again, namely, because it was.) The second reason falsely identifies the intransitive understanding which features in aesthetic judgment as the complete or fulfilled concept of reflective judgement. A judgement of taste, for example, the judgement that "F is beautiful," is according to Kant a response to the feeling incited by the reflective survey of the object: "What is strange and different about a judgment of taste is only this: that what is to be connected with the presentation of the object is not an empirical concept but a feeling of pleasure (hence no concept at all) . . . " (CJ, 191). Since only the appropriate feeling of pleasure is at issue in a standard, pure judgement of taste, then it is legitimate to claim that such judgements do not contribute to our knowledge. Of course, only rarely are aesthetic judgements so pure that only beauty is at issue; for the most part aesthetic experience as channeled through the arts involves complex hermeneutical efforts on our part of the kind that Kant himself specified in the notion of an aesthetic idea: " . . . a presentation of the imagination which induces much thought, but to which no determinate thought whatsoever, i.e., [determinate] *concept,* be adequate, so that no language can express it completely and allow us to comprehend it" (CJ, 314). Since beauty is but the tip of the aesthetic iceberg, the issues concerning aesthetic judgement itself are more complex than are here being acknowledged. Nonetheless, let us grant that pure judgments of taste are non-cognitive, that in judgments of taste proper intransitive understanding is itself being harnessed to a non-cognitive end: the appreciation of beauty. That tells us nothing about reflective judgements that are not being harnessed to the end of the appreciation of beauty.

Nor, more important, is Adorno wed to thought that the material axis of the concept should be interpreted in narrowly "aesthetic" terms; on the contrary, even aesthetic cases involve a moment of logicality. Which

63 I am here following Bell, "The Art of Judgement," pp. 234–5, who supports Kant in this. Bell is speaking for the majority in simultaneously urging the indispensability of reflective judgement for determinative judgement while denying that reflective judgement is itself cognitive.

is as much to say that he is everywhere attempting to deny the duality of active conceptuality and passive intuition, and hence to deny that the material axis is wholly without logical form, a pure *this*. The axes of the concept are axes of a complex whole with opposing orientations within it which enable different cognitive functions to be satisfied. Adorno is opposing the rigid opposition of passive reception and active conceptualization, and hence of universal concept versus singular intuition. Reflective judgement is hence being construed as expanding intuition and apprehension; it expands intuition by revealing how sensory manifolds themselves – in virtue of anthropomorphic nature or culture – can constrain, limit, and invite discursive conceptualization. In this respect the range of examples – listening to Berg's piano sonata or looking at Pollock's *Lavender Mist* – employed in order to highlight the existence of intransitive understanding exacerbate the thought that it is non-cognitive. If the diet of examples is altered would the situation look the same?

Is the neophyte merely gaining a subjective, psychological acquaintance with cruelty, say, as she coolly, one by one, pulls the legs off the spider? As we watch the torturer coldly applying the lit cigarette to the arm of the victim, smell the singed hair and flesh, are the olfactory and perceptual images mere *accompaniments* to the real, transitive concept – "the willful and knowing causing of pain to others"? The coldness of the branding, the smell and imaged pain, our empathic identification are not accompaniments to the concept of cruelty but components of it, its material sense, its material inscription. Because cruelty can be detached from just these material inscriptions, the temptation is to think that its meaning must be detachable from its material sense and inscription *tout court*. But that *tout court* detachment, which we now know is a tendency and temptation implicit in concept possession, is just the separation of transitive from intransitive understanding, turning the latter into something automatic, mechanical, cruel in itself. The configuration of an olfactory and a perceptual image (the burned hair and flesh, the cool branding) is not created *ex nihilo* by something different from it; nor, oppositely, is Adorno wanting to contend that the configuration of the two images exists in complete independence from their discursive articulation. There is no "first": an immediacy that is forever unmediated or a pure mediating without reference to an immediacy, something to mediate (ND, 171).

Ideally, but remembering that the ideal is routinely suppressed by the concept's own degenerative tendency, possessing the concept is coordinate with the natural history of its acquisition, stretching from the merely curious cruelty of youth to scenes of torture, the vocal reminders about pain, the explanations that permit the ethical neophyte to identify with a sufferer (animal or human), the deployment of moments of empathic identifications in socialization and the way that history shapes the individual undergoing it. The history of concept acquisition is material and rational, affective and cognitive at the same time. Without the material-sensory element conjoined with empathic identifications, it would remain unintelligible how concept and motive *could* be joined. But within that natural history there is a psychology (our spontaneous propensity to cruelty, our spontaneous reaction to intentional harm to ourselves and others, our capacity for empathy, etc.) and the experiences – sensory, psychological, motor – which articulate into the cognitive and motivational formation of the self that would lead it to eschew cruelty at all costs. Without the sensory and tactile elements sensitivity to "harm" would be unintelligible; being sensitive to such harm is alertness to others' vulnerability and fragility, their easy mortality, and the consequent motivational set that moves an agent to act in a particular manner. Without a conception of its emotional "coldness," the indifference and methodicalness of cruelty – slowly, one by one, tearing the legs off; carefully pressing the lit cigarette to the arm – its "willful and knowing" character, the meaning of those terms, would lack substance. "Willful and knowing" code affective indifference and coldness. Cruelty would not be eerie, uncanny, and frightening without material "coldness," its sensible palpability, as if the touch of another human being was not warm and fleshy but literally cold, inhuman. Nothing outside all this, and the complications that permit its extension into the more refined forms of cruelty, can give cruelty its *normative* sense, its ethical meaning – which is just, ideally, its sedimented and formed empirical sense, neither more nor less.[64] Nor is it too difficult to comprehend how one could move from a sense of cruelty as a certain treatment of others' bodies to psychological cruelty; or how adding pleasure in doing cruel deeds turns cruelty into sadism. What now could a golden rule or a divine commandment or principle of universalizability add if nothing within the natural history of cruelty suffices to *move* an agent, if that history is not one in which the agent can be said, truly, to come to possess the concept? (Of course, a threat of eternal damnation or social ostracism might lead an individual to obey the prohibition against cruelty; but would she possess the concept if that were the only reason for compliance? Would not responding for those reasons be equivalent to adapting from "without," and hence "externally"?)

64 I am here construing the "thickness" of thick concepts as in part the sedimented meaning of the intransitive sense. I am equally presuming that included in a concept's sense is its horizontal connection to adjacent concepts: vicious, nasty, mean, insensitive, cold, brutal, kind, gentle, attentive, warm, sympathetic. To truly possess, understand, a concept is to understand a huge portion of the world. But, equally, it is noticeable how the family of concepts that surround *cruelty* can be regarded as logical articulations of its material sense (or its opposite); and that each such term will have its own material sense that will require further logical identifications for its adequate conceptual grasp.

6. The Complex Concept as Moral Insight

In learning and coming to possess the concept of cruelty our neophyte becomes a self of a certain kind and with a certain ethical identity in which the dispositional set to avoid cruelty at all costs is partially constitutive of who she is. In a slightly more complicated narrative, say, one including moments of sadistic treatment by one of her parents, she would perhaps become a self for whom love and cruelty were intertwined, so that loving or being loved included (the dispositional sets to inflict or seek to suffer) acts of cruelty, hence leading to her judgements diverging from those around her in systematic and important ways. Or imagine a narrative where she first learns and becomes a self for whom cruelty is to be avoided at all costs, and then on maturity is plunged into an environment of extreme competitiveness in which inflicting a certain measured harm on one's competitors is a necessary condition for economic and social survival. One might say that in the first two narratives concept acquisition and attaining a mature identity converged, while in the third scenario, treating the fate of cruelty as representative for what happens to majority of her "ethical" concepts, all the concepts acquired in the formation of her self became subject to systematic rearticulation on achieving adulthood. In the third case, our own, another system of order supervenes on original concept acquisition and identity formation which, a fortiori, breaks the intimate connection between them. Once this occurs, the disenchanting of the world as experienced from within by Habermas's adolescent, for example, then not only does it become impossible to perceive how concept acquisition is intrinsic to the meaning of concepts possessed, but that connection *is* broken; with the breaking of that connection the whole apparatus which enables ethical concepts to be compelling collapses as well, and the self becomes for itself abstract, someone for whom the goodness of a path of action must be calculated through some reflective schema, either the new supervenient competitive one or some other, say, the moral law.

The point of offering these mini-narratives is twofold: first, to indicate, however briefly, how the turning point in the third, modernity narrative is best understood as a deformation in the structure, function, and operation of our leading concepts, but a deformation in our conceptuality that is so radical that it comes to redetermine what a concept is – the ideal simple concept of concept possession for which the moments of concept acquisition and transformation become wholly extrinsic – thereby making the catastrophe itself invisible (how can we perceive a radical deformation of our conceptuality when the notion of conceptuality presupposed by the deformation itself is a victim of it?); and second, to at least indicate how a familiar, Aristotelian/Hegelian conception of ethical identity, and its historic collapse, is coordinated with the account of conceptuality being offered.

Helping myself to the coordination of ethical identity with the complex concept, I am now in a position to outline how the very idea of moral insight as analysed by Henrich can be reconfigured as itself an articulation of the logic of the complex concept. Recall the four moments of Henrich's analysis: (1) a structure of demand and approval entailing a moment of ineliminable dependency; (2) a cognition consequent upon and internal to (1); (3) the grounding of the self in the spontaneous act of approval; (4) the ontological dependence of the good on the performances of the selves who constitute themselves in relation to it. Historically, what has made moral insight most suspect is (4), since it affirms anthropomorphism; but enlightened conceptuality and rationality are wholly poised against (1) with its affirmation of radical dependence.[65] But without (1), the rest of the logic collapses.

The whole weight of Adorno's project, which, following on from the idea of the primacy of practical reason, was arguably also the original project of post-Kantian German Idealism, is to deny that there is a separable logic of the morally good. Rather, *what has been conceived of as the logic of moral insight is nothing other than the unfolded logic of the complex concept;* human conceptuality is subject-involving and property-involving, and only a triumphant instrumental rationality has made the normal case in which concepts align ordered pairs, (property, response), into deficient cases that can be stigmatized as anthropocentric and subjective. If concepts are complex in the manner thus far described, then value predicates are, were, ideally just ordinary modes of conceptual response to experience. What David Wiggins has claimed for value predicates matches what I am claiming for them exactly with the proviso that where Wiggins speaks of "attitude" and "response" we should have in mind reflective judging and intransitive understanding:

> . . . for each value predicate φ (or for a very large range of such), there is an attitude or response of subjects *belonging to a range of propensities that we actually have* such that an object has the property φ stands for if and only if the object is fitted by its characteristics to bring down that extant attitude or response upon it and bring it down *precisely because* it has those characteristics.[66]

Ethicality on this account is not a separate sphere or domain of human existence, or a separable logic that developed for certain narrow pur-

65 I have replaced the Henrichean locution of passivity with dependence since, as by now should be clear, episodes of radical dependence both experientially (the synthesis of the animal body) and in terms of reflective judgement are anything but passive.

66 David Wiggins, "A Sensible Subjectivism?," in his *Needs, Values, Truth: Essays in the Philosophy of Value*, 2nd ed. (Cambridge, Mass.: Blackwell, 1991), p. 206. Paragraphs 8 and 9 of this essay provide the core of Wiggins's thoughtful defense.

poses (e.g., the coordination of human actions); although both eventualities befall ethical experience. Ethicality, what we think of as ethicality, is an historically emergent configuration of human conceptuality as such, that is, ethicality, ideally, was or would be nothing other than what is involved in conceptualizing human activity and experience in a living, social environment, our conceptual awareness of the world and our socially significant others in a context in which we are jointly agents and patients. This is why, despite Adorno's philosophy lacking an explicit ethical theory, it appears ethical as a whole. In responding to the claims of the nonidentical and in attempting to restore to the concept the dignity of the material, naming axis, all of which can be conceived of as dryly dealing with questions of rationality and epistemology, Adorno is simultaneously eliciting the formations of dependence and independence, of responsiveness and reflection, of demand and affirmation through which our entanglement in the lives of others is announced and elaborated. The simple reason why this reversal had to wait upon late modernity for its discovery is that the logic of the complex concept is materialist (naturalist), historical, and temporalizing; hence, until both the old gods and the eternalistic ideals of enlightened rationalism could be contested, it could not emerge.

The manner in which (1) through (4) are articulated is altered and complicated by their alignment in the complex concept. Above all, the logic of the complex concept dispenses with the idea there is moral insight into *the* good. The most persistent difficulty with moral insight into the good has been identifying what, precisely, the good is that *it* can make demands which can be approved. The very idea of "the good" smacks of either theology or Platonism. But, of course, there is no "the good" into which we might have insight; there are, or were, only the particular forms of awareness of the living world and living others afforded by "ethical" concepts and the forms of action picked out and incurred, via structures of material inference, by those forms of awareness. I have claimed that the bindingness of moral claims is to be understood primarily as nothing other than material inferences from awarenesses of a state of affairs, from (the appreciation of) *bleeding badly* to (the response) *I will apply a tourniquet.* Material inferences of this kind do not operate in a void. On the one hand, I have conceded that material inferences are articulations of the experiences of auratic individuality, that is, of living beings that are injurable, and hence that there are practical demands at all depends on being aware of vulnerable life and developing modes of response that acknowledge vulnerability. For Adorno, the minimum and necessary conditions of ethicality are bound to injurable life; and further, human practical identities are themselves always elaborations of the auratic body such that all moral harm is injurability on analogy with injury to the auratic body.[67] "Enchantment" is nothing other than a conceptual scheme that elaborates forms of practice that acknowledge, protect, and foster the integrity of injurable selves in an environment of other injurable life forms. On the other hand, I have acknowledged as well that, not directly or immediately, but indirectly and mediately, the demandingness of an ethical claim, what I discover I must do, *sometimes* does have the force of "a reaction against the threat of a loss of identity."[68] But this, while essential, is derivative. It is essential because my practical identity is constituted by those ethical beliefs, the structures of material inference, that specify my connectedness to and separation from those around me; hence, were I to routinely or in an emphatic way act in opposition to those beliefs I would be acting in opposition to the conditions through which I have a self at all: such action would be, finally, practically self-defeating. Becoming aware of that can certainly be a spur to appropriate action. But ethical demands are not demands *because* to act against them would be to threaten me with loss of identity; that, finally, will end up in the Kantian dilemma of making duties to others derivative of duties to myself. The demand not to injure you is just and only my appropriately seeing you as one who is not to be injured, and when injured to help, to apply the tourniquet.

Putting these thoughts together: complex concepts that possess both material and logical axes are a form of conceptuality that is capable of responding to injurable bodies as themselves imposing demands to respond in a particular way. Ethical concepts jointly articulate, give expression and shape to the originary demandingness of auratic individuality. Equally, as specified in the first two mini-narratives, *practical identities* are formed through learning and internalization of complex concepts of the appropriate kind. The moment of demand and approval (or disapproval) was, originally, nothing other than the material axis of the concept, the moment through which learning, formation, and transformation occurred; what we originally were demanded by and spontaneously offered our approval or disapproval to was just our intransitive understanding of a state of affairs of other living (auratic) beings like ourselves – an experience of love or cruelty or pain, for example. And of course this moment of demand and approval must indeed have been a moment of insight and cognition; but the moment of cognition is complex since it is divided between a moment of nondiscursive cognition, logically having the form of a demonstrative designation, coordinate with the experience of demand and approval, and the taking up of that primary identification in the logical moment of the concept. Coming to truly possess the concept is learn-

67 For the suggestion that bodily injury forms the pattern for all moral injury see Axel Honneth, *The Struggle for Recognition: The Moral Grammar of Social Conflicts,* trans. Joel Anderson (Oxford: Polity Press, 1995), p. 135.

68 Korsgaard, *The Sources of Normativity,* p. 102.

ing the mode of appropriate response. Because the first moment is not wholly discursive, it always seems suspect. But the suspicion is misplaced; there cannot be anything like what we have imagined ethical demandingness to be like without an address *to me*; the first-person moment is just that only in virtue of its lack of full discursivity in which a cognitive state is dependent on the experience of the object the experience is about – an appreciation of an auratic body or its disruption. But lack of replete discursivity does not entail that the moment of undergoing the demand is not cognitive; the intransitive understanding that is aligned with non-predicative identifications is how the neophyte, or us as perpetual learners, *come* to awareness of new features of the world. And it is because a reflective judgement is cognitive that it can become elaborated through its further conceptualization, through its uptake in the logical axis of the concept and the whole complex concept's entanglement with other related concepts. Because routine conceptual identification is so unlike having an originary experience, because determinative judgement is so unlike reflective judgement, then it is easy to both dismiss the latter as non-cognitive and to deny the structural role of the originary non-predicative identification in the operation of the normal predicate. But neither denial is compelling.

And now if one were to acquire a vast battery of concepts through the dialectic of dependent and independent thought, reflective and determinative judgement, then, in line with our first two mini-narratives relating to the formation of the ethical identity of our neophyte, the self would be grounded in the very conceptualities she had antecedently given her approval to as a condition for acquiring those concepts; she became the self she was in part because she learned and incorporated (through the impetus of parental or tribal training, no doubt) into her dispositional set just those concepts that would govern her forms of awareness and consequent forms of activity with respect to others. Her "ethics" is as deep as that, it is who she is and her way of perceiving the world, cognizing it; and as perfectly groundless as that, nothing actually supporting or grounding or explaining those concepts other than the recognitions offered in tribal practice even if the tribe proposes otherwise – sustaining a vast body of "ethical" concepts is not socially easy since there are massive pressures from diverse sources that can trouble them; there are reasons for gods and shaming and punishment. Finally, there is such an "ethics" only for as long as and on the condition that she and her cohort continue to perceive the world in accordance with those concepts and act accordingly. Were they to stop conceptualizing the world in those terms, as in the third narrative scenario above, then apart from limit cases those features of experience and forms of activity would gradually disappear from the world. (How radically they can disappear is the grain against which Wittgenstein's fragment rubs.) While the potentiality for ethical experience in the sense being canvassed is given with the human form of life, which is how and why there are (anthropomorphic) limit cases, unless the world and its inhabitants are routinely perceived and treated in accordance with complex "ethical' concepts, concepts attuned to and which elaborate and structure auratic experience, there is no ethics, or at least very little, and that little deformed in ways we have learned about. There is the ethical, the good, only through the performances it makes possible – and vice destroys origin. The moments of this outline perfectly coordinate with, in the mode of spelling out the underlying presuppositions, the earlier account of a world in which there was ethical knowledge which we have now lost. Only through something like the complex concept was ethical knowledge and ethical experience (as preserved in the material axis of the concept) possible.

All this is painfully simplistic and skeletal; still, this skeleton is recognizable, and, arguably, recognizably accounts for some of our most basic intuitions about ethical experience. That the skeleton can stand, if it does, is due wholly to its articulation through the complex concept since it unties the systematic, philosophical conundrums about ethical experience: the nature of demandingness; the role of conceptual dependency; the commensurability between demandingness, acceptance, and cognition; why we should consider the ethical and personal identity as somehow internally related; and how the ethical can systematically disappear from human experience. Moreover, even in this bare-boned account, there is no puzzle about ethical motivation since it is at one with our having motives to do anything whatsoever in the light of our epistemic appraisal of the world; being moved to help another in distress is no more mysterious than being moved to avoid stepping in poison ivy whilst wearing only shorts: one perceives and acts accordingly. From within the purview of the complex concept the problem of motivation does not exist; from the perspective of the simple concept it is irresolvable since in accordance with simple moral concepts motivation is logically extrinsic to their meaning.

7. The Complex Concept as Authority

The complexities of Adorno's philosophy are a consequence of attempting to enact, perform, the mediations demanded by complex conceptuality under conditions in which it has been institutionally, practically, and ideologically undone. Exactly how Adorno seeks to recover the material axis of conceptuality under conditions of its suppression and tendential disappearance is the work of the remaining chapters of this book. Before taking up that argument, I want to offer a skeleton analysis of the relation between authority and the complex concept which runs parallel to, and is a moment within, the mutual implication of the complex concept and moral insight just sketched. Authority, again, comprises three forms: legal-rational, charismatic, and traditional. These three forms, I now argue, are to be deciphered by each representing or being coordinate with an element of the complex concept itself. Legal-rational authority corresponds to the logical axis of the concept; taken on its own, it follows the path of the ideals of the simple concept. Pure legal-rational authority is the authority of the simple concept, the authority of identity thinking in which universality determines the meaning of whatever might rise through external determination; above all, legal-rational authority is the authority of transitive understanding. That we have discovered that morality when conceived in terms of the simple concept devolves into a form of instrumentalism is what should be expected if, on the one hand, even in its own terms rational morality is thought to be for the sake of action coordination, and, on the other hand, Weber is correct in contending that the point of bureaucratic order, as the institutional embodiment of legal-rational authority, is to provide a system of rules oriented toward "the satisfaction of calculable need with ordinary, everyday means."[69]

Historically, charismatic authority emerged in times of social distress; it was always, in its operation, an interruption of the economic order of everydayness. As the revolutionizing and creative force of history, charismatic authority was what alone enabled communities to transcend their instrumentally rational attachment to everyday practices and meet the extraordinary needs of the time. What distinguishes the operation of charismatic from legal-rational authority, we learned, was that the former operated by revolutionizing attitudes from within, while the later transformed patterns of activity from without – social "externalism," as it were. Episodes of charismatic authority were transformative and reorienting. Because episodes of charismatic authority involved the institution of new rules, they could sanction themselves solely through their appearing in the performance, personal and/or linguistic, of the charismatic leader. *In brief, charismatic authority is about the formation, institution, or novel extension of concepts; its specific sphere of operation overlaps, exactly, with the sphere of operation of the material axis of the concept.* Weber's difficulty with charismatic authority is that he could not offer any rational characterization of it apart from its creative effects; for him it was always proto-religious in character, and for that very reason ultimately incompatible with secular modernity. The simple hypothesis that makes immediate sense of charismatic authority is that it not only functionally overlaps with the material axis of the concept, but equally overlaps with it in terms of content. Concept formation, transformation, and acquisition all require a material display and the capacity for intransitive understanding; because the understanding of new concepts must occur initially through reflective

69 *ES*, p. 1111.

judgement, then they can achieve their effect only through conversion – the ineliminable first-person quality of reflective judgment. Conversely, it is the necessarily intransitive quality of reflective judgement that explains why the transmission and institution of new ethical rules can occur only performatively. Charismatic authority is the authority of the material axis of the concept; it relates to that component of ethical concepts in which they relate directly to worldly experiences, and where those experiences are imposed upon the perceiver as demanding a response of a certain kind. Charisma is the creative force of history because it picks up that aspect of concepts which enable them to transform and move agents. And just as Weber contends, its eventual incorporation in social practices involves its routinization, that is, its being possessed and transmitted intransitively through tradition and even, eventually, becoming wholly transitive through becoming a legal-rational rule.

If one sees traditional authority through the lens of the complex concept, then its difference from charismatic authority decreases radically. In Weber traditional authority is said to operate through *personal* loyalty to the master; it is thus natural to think of it as the mechanism for transmitting either the novel concepts which originate in a charismatic episode or, more simply, the intransitive sense of routine ethical concepts. Either way, traditional authority is the mechanism for instituting and transmitting complex ethical concepts that possess as part of their meaning an indelible intransitive sense. Loyalty, love, veneration are the modes of acceptance and dependence which, as the bonds connecting master and neophyte, provide the logical space for the transmission of what itself requires acceptance as a condition for its intelligibility in general. It is for this reason that the family has always been at least a mechanism for the transmission of ethical knowledge, and that in bourgeois societies the role of the traditional master was for a time filled almost uniquely by paternal and/or, more than is usually conceded, maternal authority – mom and dad as domestic traditional masters, remembering that masters are just miniature and routine charismatic leaders.[70] Traditional authority is, was, just the authority of *essentially complex* ethical concepts as understood through the mechanism of their routine social reproduction.

At the end of the discussion of Weber the question arose as to why Weber believed that there were only three forms of authority. An answer to

70 The devaluation of women and the presumption that the ethical was to be understood in terms of (deontological) moral principles made maternal authority more difficult to sustain and perceive, but given what I have been claiming about the ethical, those factors should not blind us to its operation. I suspect there is a significant history here waiting to be written. In connecting parental authority with the traditional master on the one hand and the charismatic leader on the other, I mean to be implying that some of the mechanisms for the reproduction of complex concepts can and are analysable in psychoanalytic terms.

this question can now be provided: the analytic of authority is nothing other than the articulation of the components of the complex concept as sources of value. Not only does the orientation of each axis of the concept have its corollary in a mode of authority, but the complex concept as whole as it is historically transmitted also possesses a distinct mode of authority. To put the matter more directly: *there is nothing else for authority to be but what in human conceptuality demands and secures rational obedience.* Although nothing makes the manifestations of any of the three modes of authority intrinsically rational, there is no rationality apart from what they jointly enable. To perceive how the modes of authority are joined in the complex concept thus enables us to explain why the domination of any one mode at the expense of the others will be, finally, irrational and socially stultifying. Still, the three modes of authority, the complex concept writ large, are modes, and nothing in their characterization points toward any ideal synthesis, a utopia of authority; the different orientations that each axis of the concept and, now, its reproduction through time invokes equally point toward different cognitive needs; and the different cognitive needs coordinate with different social needs: for order and routine, for solidarity, for social renewal, for the perpetuation of meaning over time.

From a naturalistic perspective it would be odd indeed if the big story about human conceptuality were not honed to the needs of human sociality; conversely, it would be strange if the conceptual structure of human forms of order, the sociology of authority, were not just the flip side of intrinsic features of human mentality and activity. The one-to-one correlation among the features of the complex concept and the ideal types of rational authority should not be regarded as a surprise or felicitous theoretical outcome; rather, that coordination, or better, theorization of the same phenomena from two contrasting perspectives, is what we should have been looking for and demanding from philosophical accounts of conceptuality all along.[71]

Conversely, it now becomes very tempting to argue that there are no sources of value other than those provided through the axes of the complex concept and its historical transmission. To give this thought its most upbeat statement: secularity is not the end of significant meaningfulness,

71 I am not here suggesting that modern philosophers have ignored this problem; it is palpable in the philosophies of Kant, Fichte, and Hegel; although seeing those philosophers in this way is not done consistently enough. Rather, my complaint is that with the emergence of a theoretical sociology, the fine-tuning of that two-sided activity changes. We must harmonize our accounts of language and conceptuality with the best sociological theories of order and change we have. I am gambling that Weber's theory is still the one the most demands attention. Thinking about Weber on authority is, I am claiming, a better guide to thinking through the meaning of conceptuality than, say, attempting to square human conceptuality with computational languages.

but the condition of its becoming intelligible *überhaupt*; only with the fall of traditional metaphysical meaning does the truth-content of metaphysics become available. Adorno does think this; but he equally regards this thought as momentous, as the difficult result of immanently criticizing everything that opposes it; and what opposes this second secular vision, this materialist conversion of the enlightenment, is, most of all now, the reign of identity thinking and instrumental reason – legal-rational authority within and without.

7

TOWARD AN ETHIC OF NONIDENTITY

1. Introduction

Disenchantment as procedural demythologization is sceptical and irrational because it operates with an illegitimate, partial concept of the concept; disenchantment is sceptical and destructive because the logic of the simple concept destroys the very structures through which human cognition becomes sensitive to those features of experience that bear on human happiness and misery as internally correlated with the possibilities of human action. By seeking to eliminate the materiality and dependency of the concept, the reflective mechanisms of the simple concept tendentially disintegrate an independent ethical world. Conversely, the trajectory of Adorno's argument is to show how, if matters are understood from the perspective of the complex concept, then the logical moments comprising moral insight become instantiated in the world not through the taking up of a special moral point of view or as a special domain of practice within a complex world, but as somehow constitutive of the conceptual binding of the self to the world *überhaupt.* Put another way, if Adorno's conception of the complex concept is anywhere near correct, then there is no original distinction between practical and theoretical reason to be drawn, even if specific practices of reasoning develop which elaborate, extend, clarify, and rationalize different portions or aspects of or perspectives on ordinary experience.

Stating Adorno's original insight in this manner is, in two respects, deeply misleading. First, to assume the standpoint of the complex concept would be to assume a certain theoretical stance toward our conceptuality, as if, from insight into the nature of the complex concept it follows that we *ought* to bring about a world in which it would be actualized. To read Adorno in this way is take the complex concept as another theory of concept and morality, another rational structure determining what ought to be the case; hence to construe the complex concept of a concept as an emergent *theory* of the concept is to interpret it from the standpoint of the simple concept, as Hegel routinely complained that Kant interpreted Reason from the perspective of the Understanding. Second, then, it is no accident that Adorno nowhere directly provides an analysis of the complex concept of the more or less direct kind offered in the previous chapter, for to do so would be in contradiction with its central orientation. Ethical necessity, the bindingness of the good, is not derivable from theoretical insight or necessity. What demands approval is not the complex concept, but the nonidentical, that in the object which has been buried, repressed, disavowed, cut off from experience through the operations of the simple concept theoretically and practically, reflectively and institutionally. *Only (moral) remainders remain; hence to think the ethical now, which is what thinking now must be, is to respond to the claim of those remainders. Philosophically to heed the claim of moral remainders is to reflectively undo the concepts and the concept of the concepts that has produced the condition of damage.*

It is just this fact that generates the aporetic character of Adorno's writing: disenchantment has destroyed the forms of object-relation which would make the dependent, material moment of cognition routinely socially available; since reflective possibilities are socially conditioned, then there cannot be in Adorno's thought the rational necessity, which, again, would be an ethical necessity, that meets the standards set by its own claiming. Hence his thought is rationally underdetermined and necessarily overreaches itself. It begins not from the binding character of a cognition of an object's claim, from the demand of some sensuously particular object, but from its *felt* absence, from the logical concept's "own inevitable insufficiency," its "guilt" or indebtedness (*Schuld*) with respect to what it is thinking about (ND, 5).

This sense of the insufficiency and indebtedness is a normatively inflected awareness of dependence on sensuous particularity, in general, in its absence and unavailability. The logic of this claim is, again, a reprise of Hegel's notion of the causality of fate which forms the model for Adorno's dialectic of enlightenment. Just the slightest addition to Hegel, in square brackets, enables us to perceive the confluence between Adorno's epistemological construction with that of an experience of what occurs to a subject as a consequence of acting against the other on whom it is ethically dependent:

> The trespasser intended to have to [rationally and epistemically] do [away] with another's [anthropocentrically conceived] life, but he has only destroyed his own [anthropocentric life], for [anthropocentric] life is not different from [anthropocentric] life. . . . When the trespasser feels the disruption in his own [now repressed, voided anthropocentric] life . . . or knows himself (in his bad conscience [in his guilt]) as disrupted [reified], then the working of his fate commences, and this feeling of a [anthropocentric] life disrupted must become a longing for what has been lost.[1]

1 "The Spirit of Christianity and Its Fate," pp. 229–30.

Instead of explicating the refusal of dependence on an explicit ethical act of transgression, Adorno traces it to the rational development of progressive domination over nature; but that development is, *implicitly*, but all the more emphatically, a movement of transgression. But this can only have the repercussions Adorno identifies through the medium of the concept and conceptual experience: cognition of the object through the complex concept which would be our ethical binding to the world is incrementally and processually displaced by the distanced and distancing machinations of rationalization. The eschewal of intransitive understanding and the ascent to transitivity is the production of the so-called autonomous subject. This is "inhuman" (the autonomous "self is what is inhuman" (ND, 299)) because instrumental reason operates through forming the subject, as world-manipulator and as executor of the causal logic of instrumental reason, after the – inanimate – object to be controlled. Both subject and object are thinned out to their lowest common denominator.

It is this thinned out, modern subject who must take the place of the Hegelian transgressor, suffering its loss of the world, longing for another. But because the world has become intolerably thin, reified, because the major institutions and practices have been corralled by a fragmented conceptuality and rationality, then no simple acts of confession or reparation are available. In the first instance, what is required by the impasse of the present is critical work on the simple concept, turning it against itself, opening it up to its repressed other. Yet if this is going to have ethical weight, then philosophy must break from the demands of the simple concept and begin approaching the form of understanding concomitant with the claims of the nonidentical. But what precisely does this mean? What is it to acknowledge in philosophical practice a dependency on the object? How does one write philosophy in a manner that encourages and enables the moment of intransitive understanding? What would be the bindingness of such writing, its criteria of success or failure? To answer these questions, I want to follow a path that shows how the basic gestures of Adorno's philosophy – his conceptions of negative dialectic, philosophical writing as paratactic, constellations – can be seen as accomplishing three tasks: (1) as giving form and substance to the idea of the complex concept; (2) as providing a critical rescue of material inference in opposition to logical inference; (3) as providing an outline of the field of an ethics of nonidentity – an ethics *now* that sides with the nonidentical and an ethics conformable to what is projected by the recovery of it. For reasons that become apparent below, I begin somewhat abstractly with an account of the nature of radically conditioned reasoning, and from there proceed to accounts of negative dialectic and aphoristic writing. I conclude the chapter with an account of the status of moral norms that responds to what has preceded. In pursuing this argument it will become evident that there is a tension in Adorno's argument between the austerity of his vision of negative dialectics itself (section 3) and the requirements of material inference (section 4) that his form of writing employs. This theoretical tension, essentially between the self-critique of the simple concept and the inferential powers of complex concepts, directly bears on Adorno's understanding of the recuperative possibilities available to us. Thinking through the two sides of this dialectic between negative dialectic and material inference in explicitly ethical terms is the work of Chapters 8 and 9, respectively.

2. Reasoning in Transitions

In accordance with the legislation of the simple concept, ideal knowing crystallized in the image of the unfolded analytic judgement, eliminating further contribution from the world as redundant. Worldly contribution to the complex concept appears in two dimensions: the relatively stable position in which it appears as tradition, memory, sensibility (bodily memory), or, its most degenerated form, habit – the concept as the sedimentation and repository of encounter; and the dynamic moment when it appears through the explicit transformations of concept (self and world). If there is no single, overarching telos to conceptual practice, no ideal or complete synthesis of the axes of the concept, then the stable dimension of knowledge is only a frozen image, a narrow time slice in the life of the concept. The life of the complex concept is located, like life itself, in change and transition. Only if transition is constitutive of cognition will concepts have to be affirmatively conceived of as intrinsically indeterminate. The movement of the concept is not from indeterminate to determinate, but always a movement of contextual redetermination. Formation, de-formation, transformation for the sake of and in response to the claims of the object is what reasoning with the complex concept amounts to.

In order, then, to secure the role of the material axis of the concept in it, concept possession must be not only supplemented by concept acquisition but, so to speak, displaced by it. Neophytism can be intrinsic to conceptual practice because we are (might yet become) perpetual learners, not transcendent knowers; that is, to regard the moments of acquisition or formation or extension as essential to conceptuality is to contend that concept and language need to be regarded from the vantage point of tension, conflict, and change, from the perspective of those places where thought is disarmed and must reconstitute itself. Only in those places where thought is forced to go beyond itself can its internal dynamic be understood, and it is that dynamic, and not the places of cognitive rest, assurance, success, repetition (all the places in which receptivity is seamlessly incorporated into the coordination of receptivity and spontaneity), that is thought's moving essence. Rather than thinking of ordinary acts of awareness as the model for cognition, we should instead look to those events in which cognition happens, to the new rather than the old as exemplary of knowing and reasoning: knowing as event should displace knowing as achievement. In honor of Marx, one can think of this as a conflict model of reason as opposed to a teleological, success model.[2]

In considering the stakes of this claim, it can usefully be compared to Crispin Wright's conception of superassertibility.[3] Although moral truths cannot attain the standards required of truths bound to the ideals of the simple concept, Wright thinks they nonetheless can be superassertible. Superassertibility is an absolute notion; a statement is superassertible "if it is assertible in some state of information and then remains so no matter how that state of information is enlarged upon or improved."[4] The crux of such a notion is that a statement now, rather than at some mythic end of inquiry, be able to endure assertion under ideal and continuing investigation and argumentation.[5] If it is so, then despite the fact that it belongs to an anthropocentric domain of discourse and hence is barred from being truly representational, it possesses everything in the way of truth we might hope. Although this idea makes sense of some inductive ethical claims, for example, "Slavery is wrong," it makes little sense of standard ethical claims which are made under conditions of partial information in situations of ethical complexity, or, for different reasons, ethical norms and concepts themselves. If superassertibility were even ideal, then remorse, regret, remainders would point to ideally eliminable moral failure rather than the temporality of ethical experience.[6] But this is not surprising since the notion of superassertibility begins with the ideals of the simple concept, and then cobbles together an anti-realist, language game-relative *analogue* of anti-anthropomorphic realist truth, so denying the anthropocentric in the very gesture that is meant to acknowledge its difference from ideal scientific explanation. How this denial reverberates, we come to below.

2 Honneth, *The Struggle for Recognition,* chapter 4.

3 For a condensed expression of this with respect to morality, see Wright's "Truth in Ethics," in Hooker (ed.), *Truth in Ethics,* pp. 1–18. I am here focusing on Wright since I have been throughout expressing the ideal of the simple concept and instrumental rationality in terms of his notion of wide global reach. For Wright, although the items cited in moral beliefs, intrinsically, cannot attain to wide global reach, that is, be explanatory of states of affairs other than those they directly give rise to, they are truth apt in virtue of being superassertible.

4 Ibid., p. 10.

5 To make the investigation suitable for superassertibility, Wright naturally enough thinks of it as being "ideally prosecuted" (ibid.). With this condition in place, not much will separate superassertibility from the goals and assumptions of Habermasian communicative rationality.

6 For a quick contesting of Wright's view, focusing on his antirealism, see Wiggins, "Objective and Subjective in Ethics, with Two Postscripts About Truth," pp. 44–50.

In opposition to superassertibility, we can say that for an open-ended, conflict model of reason all reasoning is a "reasoning in transitions," borrowing a phrase from Charles Taylor.[7] Reasoning in transitions is the model of reasoning that emerges in place of reiteration and ascent or its anti-realist analogues once we permit the material axis of the concept to determine cognitive orientation. Reasoning in transitions is a way of expressing the Hegelian notion of determinate negation that Adorno occasionally points to. Here is Taylor:

> [Practical reasoning] aims to establish, not that some position is correct absolutely, but rather that some position is superior to some other. It is concerned, covertly or openly, implicitly or explicitly, with comparative propositions. We show these comparative claims to be well founded when we can show that the *move* from A to B constitutes a gain epistemically. . . . The nerve of rational proof consists in showing that this transition [from A to B] is an error reducing one. The argument turns on rival interpretations of possible transitions from A to B, or B to A.
>
> This form of argument has its source in biographical narrative.[8]

While this passage harmonizes with Adorno, its restriction to practical reason and its excision of experience is noteworthy, especially since Taylor derives his account, in part, from an analysis of Hegel's notion of a "way of experience" (*Erfahrungsweg*). The first way in which the excision of experience is manifest in Taylor's model is that he, apparently, places the reasoner outside the transition, as if neutrally poised, hovering, above A and B. If conceptual practice defines a world for a subject, with the world thereby always appropriately colored, then transitions are moments in which self and world have fallen apart (however partially). The movement through de-formation and into transformation is the movement of experience, a *turning* from A to B. Second, then, the *need* for reasoning in transitions arises when our conceptual grasp of the world fails and we are returned to the position of the conceptual neophyte, a position of encountering a configuration in which reflective judgement is called for. Without recourse to situations of epistemic collapse, frustration, inadequacy or dissatisfaction, the idea of a B which challenges A becomes overly abstract and rationalized. A wholly externally appearing B might, of course, be itself the source of the extremity of a dissatisfaction; but that is hardly the standard case. It is no accident that Adorno, in its very first sentence, relativizes the whole of *Negative Dialectics* to a state of crisis

7 Taylor, *Sources of the Self*, p. 76. In this section I merge some of Taylor's conception of reasoning in transitions with Adorno's; both, of course, are adapting or explicating Hegel. Taylor restricts reasoning in transitions to practical reason; working from the perspective of the concept, that restriction seems unnecessary.

8 Ibid.

and failure; and further, throughout the "Introduction" relativizes the claims of the practice of negative dialectics to an immanent critique of rationalist idealism.

While Taylor offers a good description of the idea of reasoning in transitions, its underlying rationale has gone missing. It is best to construe the idea of reasoning in transitions as a condensed formula for a bundle of epistemological theses all of which are oriented toward eliciting the meaning of another general thesis, namely, the only unconditioned of rationality is its universal conditionedness; this is the counter-thesis to the motive for reiterative ascent, the converging of the anthropomorphic with the relative and conditioned. If that ascent is driven, originally in actuality but presently only logically, by fear of overwhelming nature, then the acceptance of conditionedness is equally acceptance of natural belonging. That thesis of universal conditionedness might equally be stated as claiming that the state of information relevant to the assertion of an ethical statement is necessarily partial, a determination of how things are, making the statement itself necessarily subject to (further) redetermination. Adorno unpacks this through four theses.

1. Truth and error are internally related to one another; error is not privative, the simple absence of truth.
2. Truth is (bound to) the movement of overcoming illusion.
3. If the movement of overcoming illusion is part of the content of truth, then the genesis of a truth is essential to its validity.
4. If the genesis of a truth is part of its content, then the cognition of truth is , also, an act of memory.

Adorno's employment of metacritique, genealogy, and natural history all presuppose these four theses. Collectively they project the possibility of a perfectionist epistemology, an epistemology which in being forward-moving (overcoming illusion) is teleological, but in being always conditioned, always for the sake of a particular state of affairs, remains open-ended, without a final end or goal.[9] Teleology without a *telos* can be regarded as the formulaic structure of Adorno's perfectionist epistemology.

9 I am here adapting Stanley Cavell's conception of moral perfectionism to epistemology. For Cavell's account of perfectionism, see his *Conditions Handsome and Unhandsome: The Constitution of Emersonian Perfectionism* (Chicago: University of Chicago Press, 1990). The precise point of contact is the idea in moral perfectionism that the self be considered "as always attained and always unattained" (p. xxxi). One requires some such notion in order to figure present knowledge as not a mere means to future, ideal knowledge while nonetheless granting the essential openness of present knowledge to future revision. If Adorno's conception of the ethical is cognitive in the way I am asserting, than it is more than plausible to infer that it will also be a version of moral perfectionism. Both inference and the decipherment of the version in question are matters for some other occasion.

In urging thesis (1), Adorno quotes a central passage from Hegel's *Encyclopedia Logic*: "Only out of this error [whereby present appearances take on the illusion of truth] does truth arise. In this fact lies the reconciliation with error and finitude. Error or other-being, when superseded, is still a necessary dynamic element of truth: for the truth can be only where it makes itself its own result."[10] Truth is not robust correspondence in part because, familiarly, robust correspondence on its own, an unmediated measuring of the relation between a representation and its object, is not possible. But equally, truth is not a *static* representational correspondence, but fundamentally what is error-reducing, hence a further determination of a concept or of our knowledge of a situation. This is not the weak thesis that reasoning in transitions is also a question of truth. Rather, the very idea of truth is bound to overcoming illusion, otherwise reason and truth fall apart and become only externally related to one another; once the connection between reason and truth is presumed to be external, the presumption of the classical robust correspondence notion, then the reasons that can be offered in order to somehow close the gap, making good reasoning a path toward or conducive of the truth, will suffer the same externality that calls them into being in the first place. But it is not merely this general idealist thesis, reason must be constitutive of the truth relation, intrinsic to it, which Adorno is urging here; it is reasoning in transitions as the unending and processual overcoming of illusion, that he is urging.

On Adorno's scheme, what is "for others" (hence for some subjects) and what is "in itself" (with respect to the object), as axes of the concept, are perspectivally and contextually defined. Hence, what is "in itself" is not a trans-conceptual thing-in-itself, but a bound moment of nonidentity or a claim of an object or state of affairs in some here and now. Illusion, then, is equally not an abstract believing true what is timelessly false, but a believing true what is – has become – inadequate to this present, what has become or will retrospectively appear as untrue. Truth is its own result when it shows itself to be different from the illusion it was thought to be, when the distinction between what is merely for others (illusion) and in itself is a reasoned component of what is claimed as true. In maintaining that error belongs to truth, truth is thus bound to the path of its emergence. Keeping truth so bound is the path through which we are constituted as perpetual learners, and past appearances are transformed from being mere means to present truth to components of it: we are dependent upon the very illusions we have overcome, and "owe" our truth

10 G. W. F. Hegel, *Encyclopedia Logic*, trans. William Wallace (Oxford: Oxford University Press, 1975), section 212, p. 275. I take the defence of these four theses to be fairly near the core argument of Adorno's *Hegel: Three Studies*, trans. Shierry Weber Nicholsen (Cambridge, Mass: MIT Press, 1993).

to them. The process of overcoming illusion, then, gives us all the truth we can have; its moments are moments of truth, moments in which we have learned and do know, and yet remain incomplete (open to the discovery of further illusion and more knowledge).

And it is the process of overcoming illusion as ingredient in the truth of a claim that ties together genesis with validity. What would most plausibly make genesis irrelevant to truth would be a case in which a state of information *could* be complete. Although such a claim has numerous presuppositions that might be challenged, the most implausible for our purposes is that what is to be known is itself an atemporal and unconditioned state of affairs. But if what is to be known is itself intrinsically temporal, and our knowing of it interested, purposive, then the presumption of a standpoint of unchanging validity distorts the practice it is to govern.[11]

Validity is not determinable independently from the path through which it arises. If reasoning in transitions is the space of epistemic advance, then both transition (genesis) and validity must be phrased as having equal weight: "The measure of . . . objectivity is not the verification of assertions through repeated testing [as in the correspondence or superassertibility model] but rather individual [or collective] experience, maintained through hope and disillusionment. Such experience throws its observations into relief through confirmation and refutation in the process of recollection" (NL1, 8). These two sentences are a fair description of Hegel's elaboration of the way of experience (*Erfahrungsweg*) as appropriated by Adorno. Hope governs the search for truth as much as the search for the good life; disillusionment can fall on either. Adorno frames the problem of objectivity in terms of hope and disillusionment in order to explicate knowledge as always a wholly human pursuit, thus binding the meaning of knowing to the self-understanding of the knower as seeker. Even anti-anthropomorphism is bound to the hope of living free of anthropocentric illusion; and a significant element of Adorno's critique of it involves exploring the kind of hopefulness it involves (e.g., the desire to be rid of all otherness), including its desire to be beyond hope and despair. Unless knowledge is bound to knowledge-seeking, making knowledge itself a practice, the place of history is eclipsed and a

11 Implicitly, I am here contending that the ideal of unchanging truth is best understood not as a free-standing epistemological thesis, but as derivative from a domain of objects that are (relatively) subject and context independent and unchanging. Seeking for superassertibility, it might be said, makes sense of the nonorganic, physical universe, but not otherwise. For an argument to this effect, see my *Recovering Ethical Life*, op. cit., pp. 103–10. For an argument that biological knowing cannot meet the standards of context independence because there is no single time framework for living things (e.g., the time of evolution and the time of an ecological habitat), see Dupré, *The Disorder of Things*, chapter 2. Dupré's work is helpful for my purposes since he potently argues against essentalist and reductionist views whilst holding to an empiricism that resists sceptical nominalism.

wholly idealized endpoint is substituted for the process through which it could arise and in virtue of which it could matter.

Epistemic "mattering," how we care and are concerned for the truth, is located and evinced in the moments of advance; the validity of B can carry no independent cognitive value apart from its being an advance beyond A. This is not to reduce validity to genesis: the new standpoint is error-reducing; it explains the failures of the previous position; it licenses more predictions or provides richer and more realistic hopes; it provides for greater lucidity or more sensitive responsiveness to individual cases; it enables the making good of past failures; it is better than any other interpretation of this situation I can provide here and now; and so on. All that, at least, is compacted into the idea of overcoming illusion. Transitions lead to comparisons, and comparisons involve, indeed are, retrospections. Only if comparison transpires through recollection, where recollection construes the items being compared as formations and re-formations of the concept-world nexus occurring as a consequence of changing praxis, can the worth or good of knowing be secured without prejudice in favor of instrumentality. As retrospections, epistemic comparisons relate to self and world equally: the redetermination of the object is also, given the essentiality of illusion to truth, a redetermination of the relation of the self to the object.

It is against the background of this emphasis on recollection as the epistemic form of comparative evaluation that weds truth with illusion that the epistemic component of Adorno's notorious statement about forgetting needs to be understood: "Loss of memory as the transcendental condition for science. All reification is a forgetting" (DoE, 230). We can consider this statement as the ethical expression of the more familiar idea that teleological conceptions of knowledge, that is, any form of knowledge that detaches validity from genesis, necessarily treat the past as a *mere means* to present insight; such conceptions of knowledge and truth thus instrumentalize the past for the sake of the present or future, and hence necessarily instrumentalize the human embodiment of that past. That our most familiar conceptions of truth – as stable, unchanging, transcendent, superassertible – should *directly* contradict our most widely accepted moral principle should be disconcerting.

What is forgotten, according to Adorno, is not only the past, but the struggle, suffering, and loss constitutive of the past as a path of learning. If truth (concept possession) becomes detached from learning, then the suffering through which we have learned becomes detached from what we have learned. "Oblivion of suffering" is the price paid for (unconditionally or ideally) determinate truth or moral superassertibility. If the very intelligibility of a present insight is misconceived if it is detached from the path through which it arose, then the elements belonging to the genesis of that insight, their untruth, are components of the insight achieved. Science, physical and ethical, by regarding illusions as sheer false belief (anthropomorphic illusion, say) forever on the wrong side of a unchanging divided line, must count for nothing the suffering through which it arises: "The suspicion would then arise that our relationship with human beings, indeed creation in general, was like our relationship with ourselves after having undergone an operation – oblivion (*blind gegen*) of suffering. For cognition the gap between us and others would have the same meaning as the time between our present and past suffering: an insurmountable barrier" (DoE, 230).

The ideal of fully determinate truth is what erects the "insurmountable barrier" since such truth is a mode or way or form of forgetting, an epistemological anaesthetic (the conceptual resistance to what in being disavowed is conceived as only "aesthetic"). For Adorno, classical epistemology is to be understood and condemned as a form of anaesthetic, as the way of eliminating pain (and happiness and desire) from cognition. In the same way in which, in virtue of an anaesthetic, the agony suffered when being operated upon becomes no part of present well-being, so ideally determinate truth puts itself beyond the journey of hope and despair, the suffering and illusions, through which it arose; it corresponds or fails to correspond to what is the case, is or is not superassertible. If we can only construe our relation to others and creation through the plateau of achieved and ideally determinate truth (validity), then past suffering (genesis) is no element of present truth: there logically can be no moral remainders, or, better, what moral remainders there are must be determined by the standpoint of the truth achieved rather than from what enabled that truth to arise. So, past suffering cannot logically matter if the plateau of present insight is, even fallibly, ideally determinate and superassertible. But, then, *present suffering* cannot matter either except as it accords or fails to accord with superassertible moral truth. Universalistic or superassertible determinate truth does not exclude the facts of human suffering, but carefully weighs their significance through determinate measures unformed by it. That is how the epistemological assumptions, those of the ideal of the simple concept or its anti-realist analogue, that produce an insurmountable barrier that cuts past suffering off from present mattering introduce, in the same gesture, a barrier between me and those around me. Moral centralism, the kind of morality that relies upon what is ideally superassertible, is itself a barrier between me and others; which, of course, is another way of expressing how moral centralism is, whatever its intentions, a form of externalism, which is to say, immoralism. Hence part of what it would mean to give the concept an axial turn toward the object is that the particular would be the source and measure of the universal, and the construal of past suffering in the moral present a component of the meaning of that universalistic moral claim; a position we see below concretely elaborated in Adorno's thinking the event of Auschwitz.

Nonetheless, here is a provisional set of considerations. Even for an optimum case of a superassertible moral truth, say, "Slavery is wrong," that wrongness can be understood in two quite different ways. One way of construing it would be to claim that necessarily or a priori all men are equal and free, or all persons are possessed of indelible natural rights, and the state of slavery contradicts those atemporal or a priori norms. Slavery would then be a contingent human practice that contradicted a timeless truth, and once the contradiction is seen then the thesis becomes superassertible. From an Adornoian perspective, nothing about this story is coherent. There are no a priori ethical truths nor do humans possess mysterious properties such as natural rights that somehow ethically cloak them. The universalistic ideals of equality and liberty are in part *formed* through the appreciation of the awfulness of slavery; finding slavery awful, intolerable, by slaves themselves and the opponents of slavery gives a sense to what *we mean* by liberty and equality that they would not possess without it. But if those senses of those concepts depend upon the contingent practice of slavery and its overcoming, then the content of those norms is not atemporal. If the content of those norms is not atemporal, then neither can be the statement of the wrongness of slavery of which they are the presumed ground.

The modern *force* of ideals and values which make slavery wrong have been shaped by the awfulness that slavery was (is). Now for the superassertible version of the thesis, the misery and suffering that slavery was, the struggles against slavery, the history through which the thesis became recognized and acted upon, all that belongs only to the history of slavery but not the truth of the moral claim. But then, now that we have the truth of the claim, that history is surely redundant, properly "antique." Conversely, if the suffering and injury of slavery is a component of the values and ideals of freedom and equality, for example, then both increasing knowledge of slavery and changing understanding of the values of freedom and equality matter to the understanding, validity, of the bald wrongness thesis. How could seeking superassertibility not come to function, finally, as an anaesthetic? Is not seeking superassertibility looking in the wrong direction? The import of the statement that slavery is wrong is not what it states but what it remembers; unless its statement is a form of remembrance that gathers or re-gathers a *prise de conscience* the danger is that the truth of the claim will become subject to competing rationalizations making it seem not the human accomplishment it is but a fragile bit of ethical theory.

Suppose now that it is agreed that "slavery is wrong" is an inductive truth, as Adorno would insist; would not making it superassertible hence become desirable and plausible? Not if inductive truth is seen as second-best deductive truth, since then it would carry on the liabilities that I have claimed for timeless truth. But precisely what makes superassertibility an "absolute" notion is its seeking to surmount its contingency and be timeless in manner utterly analogous with the way in which ideal cosmological truth is timeless. As long as superassertibility aims to detach genesis from validity, then it will forfeit the kind of historical immanence Adorno understands to be implied by inductive truth. The ethical force of the statement, indeed, what makes it an *ethical* truth would be lost if it were to be treated as some second-best theoretical truth. Again, for a statement to be ethical, there must be the structure of demand and assent, as well as the implications for self-identity. It is unclear how superassertibility can support those series of grammatical requirements. The point, then, is not that the statement "Slavery is wrong" does not meet the criteria for superassertibility; it plainly does. It is rather that if its force is understood in terms of superassertibility, its significance becomes depleted. And this is because the goodness of the thesis epistemically is not captured in its being superassertible, even if it is. Attempting to approximate the epistemic goodness of cosmological truth disorients anthropocentric truth; which is equally to say that designing the truth concept in absolutist terms, presumably in order to defeat the relativist and sceptic, moves in the wrong direction. Defeating the sceptic becomes a self-defeat; but that is always Adorno's view of anti-anthropocentric epistemology.

The logic of the complex concept construes the given universal as for the sake of the particular – only this fully inverts identity thinking rather than simply finding an analogue of cosmological truth for anthropomorphic phenomena. Because for the sake of the particular, the universal, the complex concept, is subject to perpetual redetermination. Redetermination is the response to intramundane experience, suffering, for example. Reasoning in transitions is the recollection of experience. Making conceptual neophytism trans-conceptual, implicated in all conceptuality, is what requires the connecting of genesis and validity. The internal connection or ratio or dialectic between genesis and validity is just the relation between the axes of the complex concept writ large. If it is the principle of determinacy, in meaning or concept, that generates disenchantment by disembedding cognition from its material-conceptual context, so permitting a view of the "whole" from the outside, then the complex concept reveals this standpoint as impossible, as a posit, and when posited and pretended a massive distortion of knowing and object. The abstractions of the simple concept are abstractions from learning and genesis. But if these abstractions are from what the concept is necessarily dependent upon, then the sceptical attitude is dependent on the nonsceptical, and the meaningless disenchanted world is derivative, a specific de-formation of meaningfulness itself, a modality of embedded meaning. And that conclusion gives substance to a common perception, namely, disenchantment is *experienced* as loss, destruction, fragmentation, or disintegration. Coming to comprehend disenchantment as a privative modality of enchantment, of anthropomorphism, is one part of enlightening Enlightenment about itself.

3. Negative Dialectic

The philosophical aim of *Negative Dialectics* is to break through the insurmountable barrier that separates our present from past suffering that is the precipitate of identity thinking, hence to engender a form of thinking that is geared to moral remainders. Even more precisely, it is to reform the identitarian concept of metaphysics in the light of the suffering at Auschwitz, to restore to the concept of metaphysics both the suffering that its identitarian form denied and helped to produce, and to transform what it means thereby. But this very specific end is approached through a highly formal set of considerations. We cannot reason in transition until the present becomes transitional; if the present is reified, an iron cage, then in part the issue of transitionality is itself practical. But if part of the reason why the present appears an iron cage is because rationalized reason espies no future for reason, then there is an antecedent conceptual blockage that needs undoing – again the claim and call of the first sentence of Adorno's book. Both the "Introduction" and "Part Two: Negative Dialectics. Concept and Categories" of *Negative Dialectics* take aim against the idealist simple concept as the formal condition for the substantive redetermination of the concept of metaphysics that is the conclusion of the book.

In broad terms, negative dialectic is the procedure for seeking out in existing (philosophical) concepts, and in the existing concept of the concept, their material axis and intransitively understood moment. Adorno, again, denominates the suppressed moment in the object "the nonidentical"; it is the aspect or formation of an object that would be named and expressed, were such possible, rather than exhaustively communicated. Said otherwise, the nonidentical stands for what would be released in an object were it considered through a regime in which the complex concept held sway. For the thought of the nonidentical to become significant some premonition of it must be found in existing conceptual practices. Consider the following account of "definition":

> Regression of consciousness is a product of its lack of self-consciousness. Consciousness is capable of seeing through the identity principle, but cannot think without identifying; any definition is identification. But definition also approaches that which the object is as nonidentical [with its simple concept]; in placing its stamp on the object its allows itself *to be stamped* by the object. Nonidentity is the secret telos of identification; it is the part that can be salvaged [*Rettende*]; the mistake in traditional thinking is that identity is taken for the goal. The force that shatters the appearance of identity is the force of thinking; the use of "it is" undermines the form of

> that appearance, which remains inalienable just the same. *Dialectically, cognition of nonidentity lies also in the fact that it identifies, to a greater extent and in other ways than identity-thinking.* (ND, 149; emphasis mine)

Although routinely denied in the literature, here as elsewhere Adorno affirms that knowledge of the nonidentical, *Erkenntnis des Nichtidentischen,* is possible, and indeed that such knowledge itself is a form of identifying. I understand this passage as seeking to unravel how the axes of the concept relate. That cognition wants to let itself be "stamped by the object" must refer not only to there being a dependent moment of responsiveness in cognition, but to the requirement that this passiveness should iterate in the concept "all the way up." Acceding to be stamped by the object is identifying differently, non-predicatively or demonstratively. But non-predicative identification, I have suggested, is able to bear ongoing cognitive significance in virtue of something being explicitly experientially formed and intransitively rather than transitively understood. As Adorno is here depicting the process, intransitive understanding is the not the beginning of the process of reflection, but its result. The nonidentitical in an object is that about it which can only be understood, in the first instance, intransitively, and hence what is not understood at all or understood wrongly when the object is grasped transitively.

One unproblematic version of identifying otherwise is identifying through exemplification, for example, a swatch of cloth has and refers to the properties (color and weave) in a roll. Exemplification is a limited version of identifying otherwise since, as normally construed, it depends on exact resemblance. Exact resemblance is unnecessary, however: the sensible-material inscriptions of cruelty, for example, can be exemplifications without what they exemplify, cruelty, resembling them (whatever that might mean), or, more obviously, mimetically resembling one another in some naive way. In accordance with Adorno's account of definition, cruelty can be considered from two perspectives: formally, in terms of what all cruel acts have in common, or intensively, so to speak, through an exemplification of what cruelty "is." In both definitions, cruelty is identified. Hence, it is not identification as such that is being objected to; it is identifications that halt at the moment of the common and communicable. The formal definition defrauds the knower since it provides the concept of cruelty without the experience – intuition – of cruelty. On being told the standard, verbal definition of cruelty, could one not go on to demand some account of what cruelty *is*? Once a corresponding intuition or exemplification is provided, perhaps through the use of historical or fictional narratives (say, *Uncle Tom's Cabin*), once cruelty becomes experientially bound – "*That* is cruelty!" – , thereby satisfying the desire to know what cruelty "is," the definition would no longer be fully transitive. Stating "it is" brings the naming axis of the concept "secretly" into play;

it intrigues the idea of a proper name. The exemplification and intransitive understanding of cruelty would capture its nonidentity with its formal concept. Hence, nonidentity is the secret telos of identification.[12]

Now the narrow and historically delimited role Adorno assigns negative dialectic must be sharply distinguished from the rationality and cognitive claims being made for the complex concept as just illustrated; the two are not equivalent extensionally or intensionally. Again, Adorno does not believe that we can now provide for ourselves fully conceptually complex understandings of what confronts us; nothing within our purview can be systematically, routinely, and confidently intransitively understood. Negative dialectics is a route *toward* such understanding. By assimilating the aspirations of the complex concept to Adorno's actual practice of negative dialectic, critics mistakenly narrow the cognitive aspirations of the concept to what is just its preparatory phase, thereby making the whole appear as an epistemological version of negative theology. From within the disenchanted world of modernity, the fundamental issue is *returning* to concepts their power to name, to open a possibility for intransitive understanding, and so returning to objects themselves the possibility for meaning which their reality within rationalized society has cheated them (ND, 52). Within these circumstances, Adorno claims, not altogether accurately, philosophy remains tied to the legality of the simple concept. As we see below, it would be better to say that negative dialectics *begins* with the legality of the simple concept only to find itself always beyond it.

Dialectic operates though contradiction; the type of contradiction salient for dialectic is that which transpires through the occlusion of the moment of sensuous particularity. Negative dialectics aims, therefore, to bring about the possibility, in principle, of cognizing in accordance with the logic of the complex concept, but is not itself such a cognizing. Negative dialectics broaches, aims at, reveals the possibility of a regime of the complex concept, but always remains this, disenchanted, side of it. Dialectics does not partake in the depth or wealth of experience promised by the complex concept; rather, it points to the absence of experience in the concept, and thereby remains itself experientially impoverished (ND, 6). Dialectics eschews the satisfactions of content for the sake of interrogating the possibility of there truly being content. Dialectics is a reflective asceticism of the concept for the sake of a different conceptuality: "Its

12 This account can run only if exemplification can be disentangled from the offering of examples. As we see in Chapter 8, exemplary instances are those instances which themselves, in part, determine what a concept is to be rather than, as with examples, fulfilling a blueprint determined independently of them. Equally, exemplarity is what establishes the charismatic authority of a complex concept. One could, I suspect, run the whole argument concerning identity and nonidentity via a working-out of the different logics of example and exemplarity.

agony is the world's agony raised to a concept" (ND, 6). For Adorno any pretense at actual concretion would be illusory; as if we could conjure into existence a substantiality of meaning which the unfolding of modern social experience has in fact ruined. Adorno's insistent negativity, the formality, abstractness, and poverty of his philosophy, the world's agony "raised to a concept," is for the sake of a concreteness that philosophy cannot now have.

Dialectics, Adorno states, is neither a standpoint nor a method (ND, 4); it is the reflective turning of the simple concept on itself, a "striving by way of the [simple] concept to transcend the [simple] concept" (ND, 15). In precisely the same way in which the formal definition of cruelty could be seen as reverting into and requiring an intensive definition, so the simple concepts of philosophy and its dominant concept of a concept reflectively announce their own inadequacy and emptiness.

> The name of dialectics says no more, to begin with, than that objects do not go into their concepts without remainder, that they come to contradict the traditional norm of adequacy. Contradiction is not what Hegel's absolute idealism was bound to transfigure it into: it is no Heraclitean essentiality. It is the index of the untruth of identity, the fact that the [simple] concept does not exhaust the thing conceived. Yet the appearance of identity is inherent in thought itself, in its pure form. To think is to identify. Conceptual order is content to screen what thinking seeks to comprehend. The semblance and the truth entwine. The semblance cannot be decreed away, as by avowal of a being-in-itself outside the totality of cognitive determinations. (ND, 5)

Begin with the end of the passage: "To think is to identify. . . . " Adorno is here tracking the resilience not only of identity thinking and the ideology of the simple concept, but more emphatically the logical root of the belief that the world is always our world, that facts are a shadow of syntax, that the routine form of appearance of the world as proffered by identity-thinking is somehow "inalienable" despite nonidentity being the telos of conceptual activity. The possession of a coherent conceptual order, the world appearing as the world we comfortably know, is a *necessary* semblance, it is the inevitable precipitate of routine and hence routinely successful cognitive and linguistic practice. Its necessity is one part of the explanation of how success became origin and paradigm for the understanding of truth and meaning: closure, in the aspect of identity thinking, belongs to thought's "pure form." Having a communicable order is synonymous with a conceptual scheme having always already and necessarily secured a world for itself. Once established, a conceptual scheme can insinuate its repetition (and for the purposes of self-preservation must do so): if communal policing is efficient enough, "going on" in new circumstances can always become a matter of going on as before. Because under these conditions the world appears as determinably given, our consciousness feels this world is "natural" and "immediate."

As urged earlier, the communicative moment in every concept, and the way in which that moment is socially secured and reproduced, entails a degenerative tendency that is structurally built into all conceptual and linguistic practice. If communicative identifying is an element in all identifying, then potentially every act of identification lodges the possibility of being leveled down to what it would be for communicative identifying on its own. Communicative identification is not merely a structural property of the concept, its generality, it is continuously motivated by the *drive* to communicate, to make what is thought communicable. Neither the structural feature nor the drive is itself degenerative: they are constitutive of cognition. Nonetheless, they are also, and precisely in their constitutive capacity, degenerative since they license and promote the leveling down of experience to the unconstrained repetitions of the same that deprive the concepts they govern of intensive meaning. Instrumental rationality, itself motivated by the drive for self-preservation, is in part a productive employment of that degenerative tendency, and in part, in virtue of its own elaborated forms of practice, an intensification of it.

What makes degeneration ordinary, to return to the argument of the preceding paragraph, is that it is structurally in place, and hence potentially operative, even in contexts that mean to oppose it. Within a standing conceptual order, then, there are no a priori grounds for differentiating between those elements of it representing valid cognitive achievements and those representing impositions, mythic identifications. Thus "semblance and truth entwine" in two respects: first, in the sense just mentioned; second, in the precise Kantian sense that we know appearances only and not things in themselves. This phrase is the truth of the communicative axis of language: insofar as the world is known it is equally true to say that language reflects it as to say it is a reflection of language. Wherever the world is viewed from the axis of communication, there will be an emphatic correlation between conceptual scheme and world, collapsing as meaningless the distinction between "for us" and "in itself"; wherever there is such an emphatic correlation truth will be definable in deflationary and minimalist terms.

Adorno's anti-Kantian point in the final sentence of the passage is that one does not escape the transcendental scepticism, the precise fear of anthropomorphism, by asserting the reminder that we do not know things in themselves. Hence, Adorno continues the passage: "It is a thesis secretly implied by Kant – and mobilized against him by Hegel – that the extra-conceptual (*Begriff jenseitige*) 'in itself' is void, being wholly indeterminate." To comprehend the communicative axis of language as only a pole of linguistic/conceptual practice, as the moment of sanguine immediacy to which thought inevitably returns after its confrontations with experience, is to dissolve the temptation to reify either appearances (what is "for us") or things in themselves. The Kantian thesis – against its own best judgement, as we see below – halts the dialectic at the moment of success, thus dispatching things in themselves to an indeterminate beyond. Kantian idealism, the *seamless* incorporation of receptivity into the cooperation of receptivity and spontaneity, is the necessary moment of determinacy raised to a transcendental level.

Kant's transcendentalizing of appearances is, however, the truth of our disenchanted world. Dialectics is not another theory about this state of affairs, but its immanent (re-)activation, a bringing of it to self-consciousness through siding with the object against its identifications (ND, 406). Siding with the object can occur, philosophically, only through the discovery of contradictions. Adorno's statement about contradiction does not confuse it with falsification as it might appear to do, since on that account identitarian and nonidentitarian thinking would each be theories about an independent object domain. To view identity thinking as a false theory would assume some version of conceptual scheme-world dualism. Identity thinking is for us constitutive of the worldhood of the world, it is both the internal dynamic principle governing societal reproduction, and reflectively therefore a summarial and hyperbolic auto-representation of the world itself as a constricted space of human habitation. If it is the "world" that is wrongly disenchanted, then the world is in contradiction with itself, we with ourselves ("The whole is untrue"); it, we, are less and other than we could be. But this "could" is not to be gathered from a transcendent perspective, from an idea or principle of what we, or the world, "ought" to be. There is no transcendent "ought." To conceive of the position of a utopian "ought" is to take up a standpoint outside society and its (now frozen) becoming. This stance too turns on identity thinking, only now a version of it opposed to the existing societal one. By its lack of inwardness, sympathy, and attention to particulars, transcendent criticism is at one with domination: "In wishing to wipe away the whole as with a sponge, transcendent critique develop[s] an affinity to barbarism."[13]

In the first instance, only contradiction provides the "index" of untruth of an identitarian, disenchanted world. For contradiction not to slip into what Hegel made of it, the form of becoming which is "the concept's" essence, then the force of systematic contradiction needs to be localized. If the identity principle provides a "form" of world, so to speak, the very form which gives to contradiction its centrality, then implied by the limiting of contradiction to "this" world is the thought of one in which contradiction *could not* have this function. What would make Adorno's claim

13 Theodor W Adorno, *Prisms*, trans. Samuel and Shierry Weber (Cambridge, Mass: MIT Press, 1981), p. 32.

come out consistently would be the, wholly formal, conception of a world of pluralized differences, a world that could not be thought in terms of a unified and internally coherent system. Adorno conceives of this possibility in terms of what a future philosophy would be like, a philosophy which would displace his own. A changed philosophy, he asserts, would be "infinite" in the sense of "scorning solidification in a body of theorems"; its substance "would lie in the diversity of objects that impinge upon it and of the objects it seeks, a diversity not wrought by any scheme . . . " (ND, 13); or: "Utopia would be above identity and above contradiction; it would be a togetherness of diversity" (ND, 150); or, he claims that the happiness of reconciled philosophy would lie in the fact that the "alien" would, in its proximity remain "what is distant and different, beyond the heterogeneous and what is one's own (*des Eigenen*)" (ND, 191). What such a particularistic pluralism might formally look like in explicitly ethical terms, we come to below. The more immediate question is how are we to logically distinguish a pluralistic particularism from the either/or of unitary system or contradiction?

Identity-thinking secures itself against its objects by requiring conceptual and linguistic determinacy, banning vagueness and indeterminacy. Particularistic pluralism could come about only with the dissolution of the principle of determinacy, bi-valence. Adorno begins to broach this alternative in the continuation of the previous passage.

> Since the totality is structured to accord with logic . . . whose core is the principle of excluded middle, what will not fit this principle, whatever differs in quality, comes to be designated as a contradiction. Contradiction is nonidentity under the aspect of identity; the dialectical primacy of the principle of contradiction makes the thought of unity the measure of heterogeneity. As it [the thought of unity] collides with its limits it exceeds itself. Dialectic is the consequent consciousness of nonidentity. . . . What we differentiate will appear divergent, dissonant, negative for just as long as the structure of our consciousness obliges it to strive for unity. . . . (ND, 5)

Compulsory "either true or false" portends determinacy for every statement, and hence for what would correspond with every statement: the world is determinate, the world is all that is determinately the case. As Weber showed, for complicated reasons we have *made* the lived world determinate by requiring objects and practices to be stamped by determinacy: every piece of every manufactured object must determinately be or not be what its concept requires, say, being a door handle for a Toyota Camry; a working day is to be exactly H hours long; and a casual chat between friends when done on the telephone is of an exact duration (to the second), for which an exact amount is to be paid. Determinacy can be manufactured; but is it anything else? Is there anything logically or rationally deep here? Anything outside the instrumental and practical demand for determinacy that makes it constitutive for rationality?[14] Genealogically, I suggested earlier, bi-valence is to be understood as representing the most emphatic of all either/ors: life or death. Bi-valence feeds into instrumental reason under the governance of the most pressing demand: either control threatening nature and survive or submit and die. The genealogical root of bi-valence colors it still despite the fact that the demand is no longer operative as it was. What, then, if the image of the world as a determinate whole is what falsifies what lies within? What if the principle of determinacy projects a conception of the world that tendentially eliminates what would make it a human one after all? For instance, might not the determinacy requirement be what cuts an object off from future possibilities, from becoming different?

In the previous section I claimed that the point of Adorno's considerations of reasoning in transitions was to elaborate the thesis that the only unconditioned of reasoning is its conditionality. Adorno is here approaching that problem from the inside, so to speak, from within the ideal of determinacy. In asserting that when the thought of unity collides with its limit, which is the principle of contradicition in operation, it "exceeds itself," Adorno is claiming that in such contexts identity-thinking becomes a thinking of nonidentity, language as communication itself insinuating the possibility of language as expression. In "unfolding the difference between the particular and the universal, dictated by the universal" (ND, 6), the particular is revealed as being more than what its simple concept legislates. To say there is a more, as there is more to the concept of cruelty than what its formal definition stipulates, is not yet to say what that more is; but it is to say that in belonging to the object of a concept, it belongs to the concept itself. The determinacy of the simple concept is the denial that there could be more in the particular than what it is ideally determined to be by the concept. Hence, in opening the critical difference between reified concept and pacified object the indeterminacy of the identitarian concept is revealed; *indeterminacy in the concept corresponds to possibility in the object.*

There are three aspects to this claim. Let us begin with the conclusion concerning "possibility in the object." In defending the idea of reasoning in transitions it was claimed that, in part, the reification of concept and object derived from separating validity from genesis; this has ontological implications for the comprehension of the relation between (natural) object and history. In separating process from product, identity thinking gives priority to determinate or invariant actuality over possibility. Pri-

14 In a forthcoming book, Elijah Millgram argues that the ideal of determinacy is an idea belonging to a narrow but now pervasive feature of man-made things – the car example is his; outside that domain it is not only the case that we can manage with truths that are only approximate, more or less, but indeed that is all there is. Even for the natural sciences it can be argued that determinacy is a product of idealization.

macy of actuality over possibility is equivalent to the excision of history from concept and object; in its turn this is another fetishizing of determinacy, another modeling of the concept-world nexus after the image of a disenchanted natural universe. If the analysis of reasoning in transitions focused on the historical element in knowing, then in accordance with the schema of a concept-world nexus in which each side is both independent and dependent of the other, the object too becomes, and in becoming, as being in history, it escapes the rigidity of the law of the excluded middle.

> What dissolves the fetish [of the irrevocability of things in being] is the insight that things are not simply so-and-not-otherwise, that they have come to be under certain conditions. This becoming fades and dwells within things; it can no more be stabilized in their concepts than it can be split off from its own results and forgotten. Similar to this [becoming] is temporal experience. It is when things in being are read as texts of their becoming that idealist and materialist dialectics touch. (ND, 52)

This thesis challenges our naive scientistic naturalism. We should be familiar with how this form of naturalism works itself out: if, for example, water existed before there were human beings, then there must be something that water *is* independently of what human beings say about it. While there may be a history of ideas (concepts) about what water is, water itself remains outside that history. Natural science tracks this subject-independent object. But why should this decontextualized and unconditioned view of water be the truth of water, especially if water so conceived is an idealization of the actual stuff? Why should not being found drinkable or undrinkable, becoming polluted, being desalinated, purified, dammed, becoming scarce or being abundant be considered truths of water? Nor need such thinking itself be considered subject-dependent, merely anthropomorphic. Even prior to the existence of human beings water entered into "significant" relations with other objects: being nutrifying or poisonous, freezing, flooding, becoming abundant or too rare to support life. This natural history – think of the significance of the ice age – is not other than the natural history of water that occurs in which human beings play a part; rather, we are part of the history that occurred prior to the introduction of self-conscious historical existence. What then makes the "Water = H_2O" account the truth about water and everything else a mere interested accounting? What makes the microscopic and significance-neutral theory emphatically knowledge and the historical accounting in which macroscopic predicates are fundamental (e.g., is rare in region R) subjective valuing, merely anthropomorphic? Why is the classification of a sample as (more or less) H_2O knowledge rather than a preparation for knowing? Why are not the predicates "too rare to support vegetation," "polluted," and "no longer drinkable except in bottled form" every bit as objective as "boils at 212 degrees"? Despite the fact that none of the states of affairs to which they apply needed to have come about, once such states of affairs exist, are they not explanatorily unavoidable? Would not lacking them be lacking what was explanatorily necessary, even without the backing of microscopic knowledge of the underlying structure? Does the fact that water need not have had those properties vitiate their explanatory significance? If "pure" water is an idealization, nothing that any actual sample of water ever is, should we not say that the decontextualized knowledge of water is only that, and that this knowledge itself belongs to the natural history of which the history of water is a part?[15]

Second, then, if this conception of objects is accepted, then seeking determinacy in the concepts of objects becomes otiose.[16] If context and condition are constitutive of concept and object, then the hope of determinately fixing concept or meaning is bound to be defeated. The defeat is no failure, but a recognition of constitutive indeterminacy and vagueness.[17] As I say more about in the next section, the mark of indeterminacy in thought is that actual relations of material inference will, from the perspective of the simple concept, always appear to leave gaps and fissures, to suffer from logical inconclusiveness. Logical compulsion and conclusiveness belong to the regime of identity thinking; they can be attained only by the exclusion of empirical conditionality. Logical compulsion is unconditioned transitivity. Conversely, the empirical will appear to lack normative and binding force just so long as binding is conceived as what tolerates no gaps.

15 The suppressed premise of this conception of objects as "texts" of their own becoming is its reliance on "life" contexts, ecological habitats and their history. At least with the introduction of "life" significant macroscopic relations among objects are introduced because some living organisms, the evolutionary more recent ones, are actual macroscopic unities, with boundaries (an outside that mediates between the environment and inside) that are in actual relations of dependence and independence with their environment. Again, for Adorno the complaint about anthropomorphism can get started only by ignoring the fact that consciousness is but another adaptive mechanism of a living being, another way of relating inside and outside.

16 Because water belongs to inorganic nature, then as a matter of fact it makes sense to ask after what it timelessly is. But if every organic object is a product of evolution, then at best accounts of what something is represents only an extended time slice. For further complications that would deny even that level of surety, see Dupré, *The Disorder of Things*, Part I.

17 Sacks, "Through a Glass Darkly," p. 188, argues that this same espousal of constitutive indeterminacy is the deep trajectory of Wittgenstein's thought. Rather than attempting to answer the sceptical paradox which arises from the thought that there could still be meaning variance despite the satisfaction of all criteria for something's being G, Wittgenstein means to endorse ineliminable vagueness. So, for example, in section 181 of the *Philosophical Investigations* we read: "But here we must be on our guard against thinking that there is some *totality* of conditions corresponding to the nature of each case (e.g. for a person's walking) so that, as it were, *he could not but walk* if they were all fulfilled."

Third, because now the totality is "structured to accord with logic," then whatever emphatically does not accord with the totality, whatever is in emphatic contradiction with its concept, can only *appear* as "divergent, dissonant, negative." For Adorno, the *systematic appearance* of what is negative and dissonant occurs in modernist art, whose task is the production and reproduction of sensuous particulars that demand recognition but cannot be understood conceptually. Modernist art, again, could be considered as the material reproduction of the idea of material things as moral remainders. But there must be more to the idea of negative dialectics than, on the one hand, immanent critique of the identitarian concept, and, on the other, the philosophical defense of artistic modernism. What makes this either/or look compelling is that negative dialectics cannot secure an intransitive truth-content for a reified concept against its existing transitive content; it is limited to undermining the appearance-form of identitarian concepts, opening them up to their material sense: "From philosophy we can obtain nothing positive that would be identical with its construction. In the process of demythologization, positivity must be denied all the way down to the reason that is the instrument of demythologization" (ND, 145). But that material sense must nonetheless be in part cognizable, and the cognition in question cannot itself be simply negative. Adorno contends that his philosophy is not itself a full philosophy of experience – "What would be different has not begun as yet" (ND, 145); and therefore he is consistent in claiming that determinate negation does not yield a positivity: even when immanent critique does reveal particular untruth (e.g., formal equality masks real inequality), the significance of this is not the implied determinate negation of the particular claim ("Let's create real equality now!"). That determinate negation would itself be identitarian, another simple concept. Adorno thinks we do not know what the determinate negation of particular untruths would be so long as the practice and regimes (economic, political, social) of identitarian thought remain in control. The idea of *negative* dialectics is determined by this belief; its intention is to maximize critical agency while forestalling precipitous concretion. Precipitous concretion primarily refers to the consequences of determinate negation. If the belief is that all concretion "this side" of disenchantment is precipitous, illusory, then the temptation will be to insist that only negative dialectics honors the nonidentical. Yet there is an implied either/or here which is false: simple concept and its negation here, complex concept only in the utopian future. This is false because *no concept is, as yet, unrestrictedly simple; the simple concept is a reification or stultifying of a complex concept*; and, to be sure, a consequence of that is disenchantment, a withering of the experiential material itself. That is why reactivating a concept cannot immediately put us in touch with what its rationalization destroyed. Negativity aims to set the concept, necessarily complex, in motion. Contradiction is how negative dialectics begins; but it cannot be restricted to this, nor is it.

In the concluding sections of the "Introduction" (from the section "Argument and Experience" on) and in important sections of "Concepts and Categories" ("Constellation," "Constellation in Science," etc.) Adorno should be interpreted as beginning to inscribe an approach to material inference as it operates in the context of negative dialectics itself. Better, the issue of method that Adorno raises turns on how in a context in which they have been displaced, the material inference structures of philosophical concepts can be, at least in part, reactivated. Whenever Adorno discusses forms of discursive writing the implicit issue is always moving away from formality and a structure of purely logical inference toward a conception of material inference. To think the nonidentical, the moral remainder as moral remainder, as damaged sensuous particular, is thus always going to involve more than pointing to a contradiction: showing a contradiction, a heterogeneous and suppressed content, by means of genealogy or metacritique, for example, presupposes the possibility of making empirical and contingent material formative for philosophical conceptuality; and this will itself only be possible if what is demanded of and appropriate to conceptuality, including philosophical conceptuality, is other than what the simple concept demands. Adorno's various explorations of dialectic, the essay, aphorism and fragment, parataxis, are each an account of a form of reactivating material inference as what would enable the thinking of the nonidentical. As we see in Chapter 9, there is still a question of negativity in Adorno; but whatever that question is, it is not equivalent to the claim that philosophy speaks only in negatives, for example, "This is not freedom." If philosophy is to "lend a voice" to unfreedom, and that voice be objective, then the material axis of the concept, its "mimetic moment of expression" in language must be reactivated (ND, 18); but such reactivation is, formally, the practice of reasoning materially.

4. Reactivating Material Inference

> But the concept itself is identified with the particular constellation of material inferential transitions the concept is involved in.
>
> Robert B. Brandom

Aphorism, fragment, model, constellation, essay, dialectic, and their anticipation in eighteenth-century encyclopedic thinking each represent a form of writing in which relations of material inference predominate over deductive demonstration and its analogues; but for Adorno it is these forms of writing that alone enable thinking unique particulars. The ambitions of his view are perspicuous in the following elaboration of constellations:

> The unifying moment [of the concept] survives . . . because the concepts do not progress step by step to a more universal cover-concept, but enter into a constellation. The latter illuminates what is specific in the object, that which is burdensome or a matter of indifference to a classificatory procedure. The model for this is the procedure of language. Language does not merely offer a system of signs for cognitive functions. Where language appears essentially as language, where it becomes an exposition, it does not define its concepts. It lends objectivity to the concepts through the relation into which it places them, centered around a subject matter. Language thereby serves the intention of the [naming axis] of the concept, wholly to express what is meant. Only constellations can represent from outside that which the [simple] concept has cut out inside. . . . (ND, 164)

Resting somewhere between a notion of an actually complex conceptual discrimination of an object and a form of argumentation, the notion of constellation has something in common with the Wittgensteinian notion of family resemblances and the Peircean notion of argument as a cable whose fibers can be ever so slender so long as they are sufficiently numerous and interconnected. What is striking about this paragraph for us is the extent to which it replicates what we have already traced in Adorno's account of the role of rhetoric in dialectic at the beginning of the previous chapter. For Adorno the logical and material axes of the concept relate to literal (logical) and performative (language appearing "essentially as language") dimensions of language, respectively. The necessity for the material axis of the concept to appear in the performative dimension of language derives, on the one hand, from the way in which the material axis of the concept is bound to the experience of the object, its intransitivity, and, on the other hand, from literal discourse's temptation to make itself transparent. Language's appearing as language is not, however, a supplement to language's appearing; our forgetfulness of language's ineliminable performative dimension is another version of the degenerative tendency of the concept. Adorno's emphasis on language here derives not from a general theory about the relation between concept and language, but only as the condition of possibility of expressing a complex concept.

Since pressing the role of language would only replicate what was already said about rhetoric and material inference, let me instead employ Adorno's comments on the nature of aphorism and essay to try and deepen the relation between material inference and cognizing particulars. As we recall, the aphorisms of *Minima Moralia* were to take upon themselves the duty "to consider the evanescent itself as essential" (MM,

"Dedication"). To consider the evanescent as essential is to provide what is merely contingent, say, *this* form of marriage and divorce, with a significance equal to the unconditioned. Such a consideration is necessary to the extent to which the functional order of society cannot explicate the worth of the particular except functionally – from the perspective of the whole. What is evanescent and particular is essential to our lives; particulars are monads, opening themselves up to "monadological insistence" in which something individual is "objective as sedimented history" (ND, 163). The aphoristic treatment of evanescent items must, if it is not going to betray the claim that the essential really is evanescent, partake or participate in the contingency and particularity they report.

Aphorism and essay both begin "in the middle" with a cultural artifact or practice that is imbued with a history, including the history of what has been said about it. For this focus to be maintained, aphorism and essay must dispense with definitions, grounds, first principles; but equally, they must dispense with the syntactic markers through which the legal-rational authority of first principles and logical rules is transmitted to what falls under them. Aphoristic or fragmentary writing is hence premised on the refusal of the operations that establish logical connections between statements in standard theoretical discourse (inference, entailment, deduction) and their linguistic representatives ("therefore," "if . . . then," "because," "if and only if"). "Parataxes," Adorno states, "are striking – artificial disturbances that evade the logical hierarchy of a subordinating syntax" (NL2, 131)

Part of the reason for so dispensing is that logical syntax is conceived of as belonging wholly to the domain of language as communication. If this language is always dependent on its material inscription, on intransitive, material sense and its material mediation in language, then leaving the syntactic markers of transition in place will automatically invoke an illusion as to the ground of the connection between A and B. Removing syntactic markers for connectedness is the beginning to dissolving that illusion, of making explicit the connections of material inference that logical syntax presents as its own. For Adorno, parataxis is the linguistic equivalent, far more extensively than traditional rhetorical tropes, to the aconceptual art of transition analyzed above with respect to Berg. Parataxis involves placing concepts or propositions or larger trains of thought one after the other without indicating relations of coordination or subordination between them. Paratactic orderings are subversive of the force of logical syntax: the lack of a guiding connective forces the reader to establish the linkage between propositions, or larger blocks of text, substantively rather than relying on the familiar connectives to do the work for her. So, again, the logically expressed rule "If P is bleeding badly from an external limb, and it cannot be stanched otherwise, then you should apply a tourniquet" is but the formal expression of what is the material connection between the experience of humans "bleeding badly" and everything about our experience of that situation – how awful, painful, threatening it is; how urgent is the requirement for response; how we aid one another in this way, and hence what giving aid is and how and why we do it; how different forms of damage require different forms of aid, and the role of tourniquets in those forms of emergency aid – that makes "applying a tourniquet" the thing to do. Resisting logical subordination and coordination thus orients reading toward the object of reflection by urging discourse as a whole in an intransitive direction. For Adorno, parataxis releases the structures of material inference that in orienting attention to the phenomena simultaneously insinuates a demand for a moment of intransitive understanding within the transitive whole, a moment Adorno likens to the flying open of the lock of a well-guarded safe-deposit box in response not to a single key or single number, but to a combination of numbers (ND, 163).

Paratactic orderings aim to present or express their objects, and in that way to let the objects be present to thought without implying that the meaning of the object reductively derives from thought about it, from a theory which would explain all.

> Dialectical thinking . . . means that an argument should take on the pungency of a thesis and a thesis contain within itself the fullness of its reasoning. All bridging concepts, all links and logically auxiliary operations that are not a part of the matter itself, all secondary developments not saturated with the experience of the object, should be discarded. In a philosophical text all the propositions should be equally close to the center. (MM, A44)

What bridging concepts and formal linkages do is offer to what is being thought a shape that is neither that of object or experience about it. By dispensing with the difference between thesis and argument (argument and conclusion), individual statements must bear the full weight of their content rather than merely being truth-preserving; what is merely truth-preserving falsifies content. By devolving inferential connections down to their most emphatic level, we regain touch with experience and object: "Because it acknowledges no first principle, it ought, strictly speaking, to know nothing secondary or deduced; and it transfers the concept of mediation from formal connections to the substance of the object itself, thereby attempting to overcome the difference between the latter and an external thought about it" (MM, A44). Logical criteria are not abrogated but displaced by this procedure; only the essence of an aphorism's content, "not the matter of its presentation, is compatible with logical criteria" (NL1, 22). Parataxis is the syntactic expression of dependency going all the way up; it is the manner or mode in which concepts can reveal how they are stamped by object and experience, hence a mode of writing and expression that presents objects as if from the experience of the neophyte; paratactic ordering thus sustains the interplay between determinative and reflective judgement: parataxis turns each determination back into its reflective condition of possibility. Paratactic orderings reveal structures of material connection, and Adornoian material inferences express conceptual content only if conceptual content is a relation between the logical and material axes of the concept.

Because Adornoian structures of material inference, an essay or aphorism, are object-oriented and object-involving, because they eschew first principles (whether subjective or objective), then their conceptual substance is marked by irremediable contingency. Adorno runs this thought through a series of registers. Initially, he is content to note the role of writing itself, a densely textured prose, as the attempt to compensate for what is lost in departing from formalism: "The manner of expression is to salvage the precision sacrificed when definition is omitted, without betraying the subject matter to the arbitrariness of conceptual meanings decreed once and for all" (NL1, 12). Arbitrariness is here considered to be a function not of contingency, but rather of the desire for or presumption of conceptual determinacy failing to acknowledge its own conditionedness. This is a provocation about the scope and meaning of arbitrariness; in neither case is the merely subjective being affirmed. But when contingency is extruded from material argument, a second-level arbitrariness emerges. The essay "wants to heal thought of its arbitrary character by incorporating arbitrariness reflectively into its own approach . . . " (NL1, 19). The untruth of conditionality, which is just its finite character, belongs to the essay's truth.

Still, even the reflective incorporation of conditionality into thought does not overcome contingency, but only pleads its case. Essays and aphorisms raise a difficulty for us because we cannot make sense to ourselves of why we should feel *compelled* to acknowledge their truth even when we lack grounds for doubt. Part of the difficulty here derives from an image of what we take rational compulsion to be, namely, transparent premises combined with transitions from step to step in accordance with logical laws whose validity makes what accords with them rationally transparent. Reason's self-image of impervious righteousness and legitimacy looks different from the unruly entanglement of charismatic, traditional, and legal-rational authority. Yet, to the degree to which the complex authority relations of the past have fallen into disrepute along with the traditional ethical practices and the forms of social bond that supported them, then to that degree reason's self-image becomes our own image of what having rational beliefs involves. For us logical compulsion is freedom from the arbitrariness of the charismatic and the traditional, from what is heteronomous. We now take it to be the case that truth involves demonstration, and demonstration involves logical compulsion. This compulsive-ness is manifest in Kant's belief that the morally obligatory and forbidden are exhaustively captured by procedures containing only universalization and contradiction as elements.

In locating the functional organization of thought implied by identity thinking, we are pointing toward what gets ruled out, namely, judgement's necessary reliance on the unreduced (if highly mediated) experiences of the judger: " . . . knowledge comes to us through a network of prejudices, opinions, innervations, self-corrections, presuppositions and exaggerations, in short through the dense, firmly founded but by no means uniformly transparent medium of experience" (MM, A50). The desire to weed these out, to reduce what can be judged true to what can match the claims of transparent reason, makes experience redundant for knowledge; and, of course, that makes sense only if how things are in the world is detachable from how they are experienced.

Adorno is not insensitive, however, to how the "gaps" in structures of material inference disappoint in comparison with what might have been anticipated, what we hope from "honest ideas."

> For if honest ideas unfailingly boil down to mere repetition, whether of what was therefore beforehand of categorical forms, then the thought which, for the sake of the relation to its object, forgoes the full transparency of its logical genesis, will always incur a certain guilt. It breaks the promise presupposed by the very form of judgement. . . . Every thought which is not idle . . . bears branded on it the impossibility of full legitimation, as we know in dreams that there are mathematics lessons, missed for the sake of a blissful morning in bed, which can never be made up. Thought awaits to be woken one day by the memory of what has been missed, and to be transformed into teaching. (MM, A50)

The demand for honest ideas is the demand that there be no gaps, as Descartes desired that trains of reasoning have the same self-evidence as the simplest clear and distinct ideas (NL1, 14–16). The form of judgement – S is P – appears to promise this same level of transparency; the application of a predicate to a subject appearing as seamless as the simplest deduction. Yet if a judgement is not mere repetition, if it actually seeks to say what is true of the object and not repeat what is already stored in the mind or community (in the form of an object's concept), then it will exceed previous judgements and cases, leaving gaps thereby. If an object is qualitatively distinct from others, then what can truly be said of it will extend beyond what is already known; if true judgements extend beyond what is already known, then no full legitimation of them is possible – conceptuality must learn to meet qualitatively distinct phenomena, rather than the phenomena meeting stored-up conceptuality.

To seek full legitimation involves suppressing the qualitative moment of rationality, a moment that calls for the ability to "discriminate" (ND,

43). Discrimination allows for the experience of an object beyond what is stored in its concept. Discrimination, Adorno claims, "is the experience of the object turned into a form of subjective reaction" (ND, 45). Discrimination converges with the capacity for reflective judgement: without the power of discrimination, experience would be flattened; without the power of reflective judgement, given structures of discrimination would be final. Reliance on discrimination entails there will be gaps in the presentation of an object, since presupposed in presentation is subjective exposure to the item being presented as if a component of it. Presentations do not directly communicate the object, but aspire, through language, to let the reader have the same discriminating reaction to it: "What resembles writing in constellations is the conversion into objectivity, by way of language, of what has been subjectively thought and assembled" (ND, 165). Adorno is happy to compare the activity of producing constellations, essays, and the like to "composing" a musical work; and equally to think of what is produced as like a composition (ND, 165). Compositions are objective structures imbued with subjectivity. Hence, in the same way in which "getting" a musical work can require coming to hear in a new way, and this really the only route to it, so for Adorno every significant piece of philosophical writing is soliciting from the reader a "conversion," a coming to see/experience/understand the object in a new way. Knowledge that is dependent on experience cannot be achieved through a course of neutral reasoning; coming to understand is learning *to* reason correctly rather than something effected *by* reasoning correctly.[18] But this difference, between right reasoning as a means to the truth and right reasoning as its expression, is just the difference between logical and material inference in operation and aspiration. Aphorisms, constellations, and others, are for Adorno linguistic performances of reason; in being performative they not only give space to the material axis of the concept, but in so doing attempt to reconnect the charismatic with the legal-rational.

The ideal of the aphorism is "bindingness [*Verbindlichkeit*] without system" (ND, 29). Aphorisms (et al.) are not mere perspectives on the world, how things might or could be seen; they bind. Adorno does not regard what is shown in the aphorism or essay as rationally or cognitively inferior to what we regarded as true in virtue of its place within a totalizing conceptual system. Nonetheless, it is noteworthy that Adorno uses a term whose natural habitat is the ethical to explicate the kind of normative authority aphorisms possess. A truth claim does not float above either

18 I am here paraphrasing John McDowell's account of moral deliberation: ". . . the transition [from not being so motivated] to being so motivated is a transition *to* deliberating correctly, not one effected *by* deliberating correctly; effecting the transition may need some non-rational alteration such as conversion." "Might There Be External Reasons?," in his *Mind, Value, and Reality,* p. 107.

the logical-material configuration the aphorism is or our comportment toward it. Rather, if the aphorism is an *expression* of right reasoning about an object, then it is itself a mode of conduct; and if there is no appreciating the mode of conduct apart from coming to see in accordance with its inflections of experience, then coming to an understanding is heeding a demand placed on one by the aphorism. Bindingness without system is thus an expression of the normativity of material inferences. Material inferences bind in the same way as ethical claims do, they are cognized structures of demand and approval; thus responding to them must traverse the same entanglement of orientation and cognition. But this is just to say that aphorisms express nothing other than the normative authority of the factual.

5. Conclusion: The Indexical Binding of Moral Norms

Negative dialectics as a whole is a response to damaged sensuous particularity, giving voice to the moral remainders produced by rationalized reason. The double gesture of Adorno's practice involves inaugurating (or reinaugurating) the very form of normativity which his practice presupposes: the normative authority of the factual is the source and goal of his philosophizing. Adorno thus intends to stake his position, finally, on the claim of damaged particulars themselves: only if we could *know* the claim of some particular as what, in and of itself, demands response, the performance which *Negative Dialectics* is, would the authority of the simple concept be truly contested.

> What the system used to procure for the details can be sought in the details only, without advance assurance to the thought: whether it is there, or what it is. Not until then would the steadily misused word of "truth as concretion" come into its own. It compels our thinking to abide with minutiae. We are not to philosophize *about* concrete things; we are to philosophize, rather, *out of* these things. (ND, 33; emphasis mine)

The particular that Adorno will, finally, philosophize out of is the event given by the geographical place name for one of its occurrences: the event of the Nazi genocide as exemplified by what occurred in Auschwitz. In anticipation of Adorno's treatment I want to exploit a suggestion of Albrecht Wellmer's about the status of moral norms and principles that, I argue, overlaps with the conception of material inference and normativity that has been emerging.

In one respect, it is odd to offer here an account of moral norms and principles at all since my contention is that what demands a response are the moral remainders – events, objects, states of affairs – of disenchanted modernity appropriately conceptually depicted and grasped, and that the connection between such a demand and the requisite action is a material inference no different in kind than that which connects different portions of reality, lightning and thunder, say. While this is the direction of argument, it cannot eliminate the palpable fact that there are moral norms and principles – stealing is wrong, tell the truth, do not kill – however faded their authority; further, Adorno does not think that his particularism entails that there are no valid moral principles; finally, even for the thick empirical-ethical predicates which I am assuming to be of primary ethical importance, one can associate with each and every one an implied norm or principle (avoid acting cruelly at all costs, be loyal to your friends, keep your promises). First-order ethical-empirical predicates that provide for either the interpretation of a situation or for the action that materially inferentially follows from it or the two connected raise an issue of rational authority exactly akin to faded moral norms because for us *no* predicate or norm has unproblematic natural or immemorial authority. To say of these predicates and material inferences now that they compose *our* second nature both rushes the question, as if we knew what having a second nature of reason amounted to, and, in the light of actual societal disenchantment, is whistling in the dark.[19] Asking after their authority is asking how, in the context of disenchanted experience, we can begin to conceive of how they could *acquire* authority, how material inferences might be (non-Kantianly) reactivated or introduced.[20] While the answer to the question of the *status* of concepts and norms I offer below will not itself answer that question, it will imply the answer I elaborate in Chapters 8 and 9. I here adopt a slightly idealizing approach, with appropriate corrections emerging below.

A consistent focus on the priority of the object entails that the validity of any moral norm, moral principle, or concept is *dependent* on the validity of its application to a particular instance. If the judgement "This is cruel" is true, then we would have all the evidence possible for the claim that cruelty is wrong or evil or bad, that it deserves and has a legitimate place in our ethical repertoire. As Wellmer states the thesis: " . . . the validity of moral norms stretches as far as the validity of the moral judgements that can be – not grounded, but – expressed through those norms. The norms themselves carry, so to speak, a situational index which binds them to the situations in which they have their origins."[21] Let us denom-

19 However much I am persuaded by the shape of ethical life McDowell argues for, his reliance on second nature strikes me as having just the undue sureness this sentence means to question. See, for example, "Two Sorts of Naturalism," in *Mind, Value, and Reality*.

20 This shows why Kant's project is truly the alternative to Adorno's: Kant understood that overcoming disenchantment required the reactivation of the material inference structures that had been dissolved by instrumental reason. His rationalism involved his believing that this could be accomplished by a further work of supervenience.

21 Wellmer, *The Persistence of Modernity*, p. 204. In context, Wellmer is arguing, *pace* Haber-

inate this as the "principle of the indexical binding of moral norms" or "the indexical principle" for short; it is the immediate corollary of the inversion of logical and material inference, itself a corollary of the thesis that predicative identification presupposes non-predicative identification; equally it makes sense of the relation between norms and the thesis that the ground of ethical claims is states of affairs themselves. There are two aspects to the indexical principle: (1) norms carry within themselves a situational index referring to a place of introduction; (2) the cognitive validity of a moral norm or concept is *exhausted* in the true judgements that can be made employing it. Austerely interpreted, (2) would entail (1).

The immediate appeal of the indexical principle is evident. For example, it explains why the employment of problem cases and counterexamples in moral argument can be both compelling and utterly artificial at the same time. They are compelling because they do demonstrate something rigid or blind in almost every moral norm; there are innumerable cases where lying is the thing to do, where killing is necessary, where you have to be cruel to be kind which makes the presumption of the principle as itself commanding look arbitrary. Conversely, counterexamples of this kind strike us as artificial since, intuitively, we know that they do not touch the operative scope of the norm or concept; a thick conception of lying will support notions of honesty, truth-telling, trust, reliability, loyalty, promising. sincerity which together and with related notions define, like so many strands of a cable, the nature of our connectedness to those around us. What creates the dilemma is the presumption that moral authority belongs to the norm, that it is the norm we are following when we act appropriately, and that the norm would be ruined if there were striking counterexamples to it in just the way that scientific generalizations are ruined if falsified.

Part of Wellmer's thought in proposing the indexical principle is that to attempt to avoid these and kindred problems by claiming that a theory of moral norms will need supplementation by a theory of moral judgement looks in the wrong direction: if you do not know how to apply the norm, then you do not know what accords with it and what not; if you do not know this, then you lack the norm. Equally, then a consensus or a demonstration that a norm "ought" to be adopted independently of actual cases in which the employment of the norm appears rationally compelling can only mean wanting to *impose* a norm on individuals without concern for fit or appropriateness. Conversely, if you can judge that *here* lying would be wrong, for all the reasons that would make it wrong, then there is no separate or higher appeal that will show the goodness or

mas, that moral discourse is properly a discourse concerning the application of moral norms and that there is no separate discourse of grounding. Wellmer embeds this worthwhile thesis in a very much less convincing setting: a theory of universalizable moral interpretations, which I criticized at the end of Chapter 3.

badness of lying. Roughly, then, if no true judgement can be made employing a particular norm, then that alone would show employing the norm to be irrational. Conversely, if a true judgement or ethical action can be accomplished employing the norm or concept, if here that is the thing to do, say, an act of heroic self-sacrifice, then the existence of fictional or real counterexamples, examples of self-righteously making oneself a martyr, do nothing to impugn the rationality of the first, true act. *Situational truth is the index of what is rational and what not.* The indexical principle fulfils the thought that it is states of affairs that are the source or ground of claims by insisting that what makes for an ethical claim is all that can make for the validity of the concepts through which that claim emerges.

To ask a moral norm to show its goodness apart from the particular situations it can illuminate is to suppose the validity of norms to be answerable to something other than particular situations, say, to some idea or ideal of truth or reason or goodness or humanity, or some collated version of human flourishing that (instrumentally?) requires a particular set of virtues. In fact, Wellmer himself posits a "deep" theory that he thinks is if not the ultimate ground, then at least a significant complement orienting and so in that sense explaining the rationality of the operation of the indexical principle.

> . . . a dimension of moral judgement and self-judgement is constitutive of all forms of human community. That is to say that a categorical "ought" is built into the structure of reciprocity that characterizes human social relations, and that the commands of this "ought" can only be violated at the price of moral condemnation and self-condemnation (feelings of guilt). We are unable to withdraw from this dimension of moral judgement *as such,* and this implies that we are unable to withdraw from the conditions of living in mutual recognition of each other.[22]

This is inspirational, and very close to Hegel's own early theory of the causality of fate, but, at least in this form, theoretically sheer bluff. Routinely human beings do withdraw from conditions of reciprocity without either self-condemnation or the condemnation of those about them; and if they are condemned by their victims or remote spectators, that is not going to say much for the robustness of moral structures and relations. Wellmer here simply ignores both the pervasiveness of disenchantment and the even more radical evidence of cases of the social collapse of moral order that strew our murderous century. We can all too easily withdraw from the conditions of living in morally significant mutual recognition of one another. In proposing a categorical "ought" characterizing human

22 Ibid., p. 207.

social relations that stands above and beyond moral claims and norms, Wellmer retracts the substance of his initial situational thesis.

Perhaps Wellmer could be supported by a very much weaker theory, but one that appears to be underlying a good deal of Adorno's own thought given that he too wants some claim about how the abrogation of the norms of reciprocity that are the substance of enchanted experience entails forms of activity that are existentially self-defeating. How can Adorno maintain that thesis, and not, finally, propound some version of a super-categorical "ought" that hovers over all forms of human interaction? The weaker, naturalistic thesis might run as follows: all forms of reproducible social existence *functionally* require structures that bind social agents together, structures of connection, and structures that acknowledge the separateness of human agents from one another. Societies that lack adequate means for sustaining human connectedness (dependence) and separateness (independence) will follow forms of activity that are existentially, functionally or structurally, self-defeating. I suppose that both psychoanalytic theory and the classic sociology of Marx, Weber, and Durkheim all converge around this quasi- or socially naturalist hypothesis. These theories have the force they do because they fall upon this naturalist thesis from out of an experience of its failure, micrologically in individual pathology and macrologically in social pathology (alienation, reification, anomie, rationalization, and disenchantment), experiences then not simply of wrong or evil or injustice or unhappiness or irrationality, but, however theorized, of injury, damage, and suffering. Perhaps, from the height of a social naturalism, one wants to say that in the annals of human history only religious and ethical practices have been able to secure adequate social forms and practices enabling recognition of connectedness (love, solidarity, cooperative action) and separateness (individual human worth and/or autonomy).[23] All this seems to be true enough, and Adorno's dialectic of enlightenment theory is evidently one version of such a theory; his version of the causality of fate an expression of a history in which rationality increasingly finds itself unable to acknowledge separateness (interpreted in terms of sensuous particularity), and as a consequence destroys the deepest nondominating structures of human connectedness.

Nonetheless, even this more modest and naturalized conception of the "unavoidability" of structures of mutual recognition, as it might be expressed, will not ground, explain, or give rational sustenance to ethical experience. First, and most directly, if ethics is conceived of as a *means* for realizing ends that are not themselves ethical, sustaining naturalisti-

23 For an attempt to connect the moral ontology of reciprocity with the devolution of religious into secular forms of life, see ibid., pp. 209–25, and, for a comparison, my *Recovering Ethical Life,* chapter 3.

cally or functionally defined relations of separateness and connectedness, then ethics as a whole is instrumentalized and ethical concepts have no independent authority or rationality. Indeed, the instrumentalization of the ethical for "natural" ends was just Hobbes's way of dissolving ethics.[24] Replacing Hobbes's naturalistic ends with a more generous set, be it some notion of human flourishing or the requirements of separateness and connectedness, does not change the shape of the reduction. On the contrary, all the standard problems of Hobbesian theory, exemplified by the free-rider problem, will surface for the new functional set. Second, the presumption of external naturalism is premised on a kind of optical illusion derived from the luminous quality of cases of failure: *lack* of individuation or the *failures* to form bonds with others leads to the belief that the concepts of separateness and connectedness have an independent, naturalist, theoretical pedigree. But this would be to measure the meaning of success in terms of failure. However, the failure is the lapse of certain practices; once lapsed, what originally appeared as an intrinsic ethical good now appears as an unsatisfied quasi-natural need. The external naturalism is a product of socio-historical failure; to now read the meaning of the ethical in terms of the perspective of its failure is to make the torturer the hermeneutical authority over the meaning of the screams of the victim.

Together those two thoughts point to a third: there is no reason to believe that human separateness or connectedness can be – ethically – understood apart from all the complex conceptual ways, the social forms and practices, in which they have been articulated. The *substance* of the notions of separateness and connectedness are the actual practices and institutions which sustained material inferential relations between states of affairs and human activities. Consider, for example, my contention about how the thick conception of lying embeds and is entwined with a host of related notions all of which *together* provide a formation of connectedness, how our lives are normatively bound together. Ways of generalizing over failure can make the imperatives of material inferences appear merely functional and external, which, again, was the "trick" of Hobbesian supervenience. Negative dialectics, in contrast, works from the inside out: it begins with an experience of ethical guilt, of the concept's debt to its object, and makes sense of that experience as one in which damaged sensuously particularity is raising a claim which can be

24 For a thoughtful critique of external naturalism that disallows ethical concepts from revealing actual features of experience, see John McDowell, "Two Sorts of Naturalism." In McDowell's Aristotelian jargon, my point here is that to say, "We need the virtues" is not to say that the virtues are necessary for helping us to achieve an end, human flourishing, characterizable independently of them; on the contrary, "We need the virtues" in the sense that human flourishing is characterizable only as a life lived in accordance with them. The virtues are not a means to a flourishing life but constitutive.

acknowledged only by undoing the form of conceptuality in which the claim arises. Adorno hence attempts to show how the naturalistic appearing outside belongs to the ethical inside, how it is a failure of rationality and recognition that is *existentially* self-defeating, without presuming that what is existentially self-defeating causes systematic hurt, damage, and pain, need appear neutrally as ethically untoward (guilt feelings), or assuming that forms of life which forsake ethical forms of separation and connectedness as essential be altogether incapable of reproducing themselves; social order need not be a strictly ethical product. The structural parameters of human experience, separateness and connectedness, independence and dependence, cannot give external support to the indexical principle because it is only from within that what is realized through those parameters can ethically and rationally matter. More severely, if the validity of a norm is situationally indexed, then so must be the philosophical validity of norms *überhaupt*; that is why Adorno will recapitulate the whole course of his philosophical argument for the complex concept at the conclusion of *Negative Dialectics* from *out of* the experience of Auschwitz. There is neither a moral outside, a super-categorical "ought," nor a functional demand and natural outside that might be, so to speak, satisfied by our as a matter of fact adopting ethical practices. Both external perspectives rationalize the ethical beyond the particulars that are its substance.

From an Adornoian perspective, the indexical principle is a version or application of the notion of the complex concept. In fairly evident ways, if the axes of the concept represent the relation between concept possession and concept acquisition, then one can possess a concept only in the light of its acquisition. The situational indexing of a moral norm or concept thus binds the meaning of a concept to its material inscription, implying that concept possession carries with it the intensive meanings embedded in the intransitive grasp of the concept; the indexical principle formalizes and reproduces the perspective of the neophyte. Equally, the contention that norms are situationally indexed entails that their authority is always charismatic as well as legal-rational. In a situational index we are offered not a bare concept, but a person exemplifying the employment of the concept. The indexical principle thus embeds the idea that authority is established through exemplification. Exemplarity in ethics is a way of harmonizing first- and third-person perspectives. Finally, if ethical concepts and norms are, routinely, about how to act in a kind of situation, what acts to perform or not to perform in relation to one's others, then ethical concepts and norms are themselves, again, just structures of material inference. The fullest intent and support for the indexical principle would thus be to say that it is the mode for expressing ethical concepts that adequately acknowledges them as principles of material inference in Adorno's sense.

One way of fleshing out the indexical principle would be to see it in the light of Adorno's cognitive ideal in which the transient is to be regarded as if eternal, an ideal which means to protest against "the partition of the world into the eternal and the transient" (NL1, 11). Situational indexing, and the corresponding idea that the cognitive validity of norms is exhausted in the true judgements made through them, are precisely the claim that all authority is derived *from* transient states of affairs; in shifting the direction of the derivation, the transient takes on the garb of the eternal. Further, if cognitive authority does not stretch beyond the true judgements made employing a norm, then formally at least each further instantiation of a norm can itself be a situational indexing of the norm. This is why I said that the exhaustion thesis entails the origin thesis; if the validity of the norm is exhausted in the true judgements made using it, then formally the norm has no validity apart from its employment here. The austerity of this thesis is necessary if only states of affairs can raise moral claims. What prevents this idea from collapsing into a form of ethical amnesia is that the common way to justify the employment of a concept *here* is through a process of analogical reasoning: if this *too* is not lying, then lying cannot be what we claimed it to be originally. Analogical reasoning, so conceived, reiterates without subsumption.[25]

Conceiving of the relation between an indexical origin and further instances of it as also, in formal terms, origins enables us to say that no state of affairs is being subsumed under the norm in question, but rather each instance is a cognitive/ethical *complete* realizing of the norm (and not a case, instance, token, or example of it) – complete but for the fact that no context is closed and no one norm or concept independent of others. One might consider this notion of completeness as a way of interpreting Adorno's claim about a true philosophy (a true ethics) scorning solidification in theses and principles, its true substance being the diversity of things (the diversity of situations), and hence "there is no origin save in ephemeral life [*Leben des Ephemeren*]" (ND, 156). If a concept or a principle is cognitively exhausted through its employment *here*, then its truth does not lie in some remote future, even if what has its origin here is a directive for future action. In the latter case, we are realizing a demand whose claim is found not in the end to be realized but in its source, what

25 That this still sounds painfully hyperbolic, that it seems to disallow routine reapplications of a concept is to be understood sociologically rather than philosophically. Structurally, neither the indexical principle nor the thesis that claims emerge from states of affairs entails that there cannot be routine reapplications of a concept, so long as reapplications are rationally motivated by the demands of the situation. Only under the dual condition of disenchantment of the world, its becoming motivationally inert, and the withering of moral norms and concepts does the exacerbated form of indexing and reindexing that my notion of analogical reasoning propounds come into effect.

responding here and now to this state of damage, say, requires of us. Concrete demands can require temporally extended forms of response; that fact does not loosen the tie between particular and norm. Satisfying claims can take the longest time.

If moral norms and concepts are cognitively exhausted by the true judgements made through them, then what can be said about norms and principles in their traditional form? In themselves traditional norms and principles are best conceived of as memorial, as summaries of the true judgements that have been expressed through them. On their own, they are neither valid nor invalid; they have functions and uses, but not truth. Principles stand between the particularistic extremes of their situational indexing and their future employment. As such, they are stopping places in the loop that runs from particular situation through them to further particular situations. Within this loop their most evident functions are memorial and communicative; they allow us to carry about moral concepts as potentialities for interpreting experience, and to communicate those concepts within and across generations. Moral principles are the durational form of ethical concepts, hence they express the traditional authority of the concept. The indexical principle as the elaborate form of the complex concept in relation to ethically significant concepts, without any weighty conception of autonomy, explicates why traditional authority is both (functionally) ineliminable and always (cognitively and rationally) derivative.

Because moral principles are neither true nor false, valid nor invalid, in themselves, then neither coherence nor rational consensus is necessary in order to validate them, at least as those notions typically operate.[26] Moral principles possess authority; that authority is created and recreated through struggles around particular states of affairs, by making those states of affairs appear in a particular light, as requiring a particular interpretation. In finding a moral principle or concept authoritative, one includes it on one's repertoire. Such an inclusion will involve the principle giving an agent a motive or disposition to act on the principle, and as a consequence a certain orientation in action. By these mechanisms a principle, whether possessed as a conceptual schema or character trait, can focus the attention of the agent, make certain features of states of affairs salient or nonsalient. In themselves, however, principles are not explanations for action, and when they are something untoward is occurring. If the authority of norms is situational, then the ground of my action had better be, for example, the awfulness of this situation – and not the

26 The *web* of thick ethical concepts, on the one hand, and ethical complexity on the other will separately and jointly engender efforts of reflective rationalizing; consider, for example, the endless efforts to clarify the relation between the demands of liberty and those of equality. But this is not a matter of philosophical validation or legitimation, but simply an extension of ground-level acts of deliberation.

belief that cruelty is wrong. *Situationally indexed moral norms, were there any, would be the facts of our reason.*

What is worrying in the idea of the indexical principle is that it so pointedly converges with what Adorno thinks of as a utopian philosophy, one which would scorn solidification in theses and principles, finding its true substance in the diversity of things and situations. If the full flowering and deployment of the indexical principle in fact converges with a transformed ethical situation, one in which experience will have become motivationally significant, then it cannot adequately describe our ethical situation. There must be far fewer recuperative possibilities in experience than what the indexical principle projects for its routine operation. Nonetheless, when Adorno does forward a new categorical imperative it does operate in precisely the manner demanded by the indexical principle. That is the core argument of Chapter 8. The interrogation of what further possibilities there are for ethical action beyond the new imperative and yet short of utopia is the object of Chapter 9. That division of labor corresponds to the terrain we have just traversed: the new imperative encapsulates negative dialectics in its narrowest and most austere sense, while further possibilities presume the isolated, punctual, nonsystematic reactivation or activation of particular relations of material inference.

8

"AFTER AUSCHWITZ"

1. Introduction

"Meditations on Metaphysics," in which Adorno's most famous discussion of Auschwitz takes place, is the third of three models that make up the final part of *Negative Dialectics*; the other two models being "Freedom: On the Metacritique of Practical Reason" and "World Spirit and Natural History: An Excursion to Hegel." Models, themselves composed of aphoristic fragments, are another of the forms of writing Adorno identifies as a critical successor to the system. The term itself is appropriated from Schöenberg.[1] Adorno describes models in *The Philosophy of Modern Music* thusly:

> Now, in association with development, variation serves in the establishment of universal, concretely unschematic relationships. Variation becomes dynamic. It is true that it still strongly maintains the identity of its initial thematic material – what Schöenberg calls its "model." Everything remains "the same." But the meaning of this identity reveals itself as nonidentity. The initial thematic material is so arranged that preserving it is tantamount to transforming it. There is in fact a way in which it no longer exists "in itself," but only with a view towards the possibility of the whole composition.[2]

This description makes models sound akin to Hegelian *Aufhebung*, sublation as canceling and preserving since here too an original concept is shown to be "dynamically" or internally related to what originally appears as heterogeneous to it. So, again, Kant's notion of freedom is shown to require the very somatic and causal moment it is originally designed to escape. In the "Meditations," metaphysics, which traditionally concerned unchanging things beyond experience, are shown to now necessarily con-

1 For a discussion of this, see Fredric Jameson, *Late Marxism: Adorno; or, The Persistence of Dialectic* (New York: Verso, 1990), pp. 61–2.

2 T. W. Adorno, *The Philosophy of Modern Music*, trans. Anne G. Mitchell and Wesley V. Blomster (New York: Seabury Press, 1973), pp. 55–6.

cern first temporal and transient things, then material things, and even, finally, materially imagined things. If there is a difference between Adorno's models and Hegelian sublation it is that the former follow no stipulated procedure, and the result of the variation is "universal, concretely unschematic relationships" – constellations of material inferences.

"Meditations on Metaphysics" is a compressed, transfigured précis of *Negative Dialectics* as a whole. It begins with Adorno's terse reflections "After Auschwitz" and, after issuing a new categorical imperative in the light of Auschwitz, quickly moves first to a series of meditations on nihilism, and then to a consideration of Kant's "Postulates of Pure Practical Reason." What connects these apparently disparate items is the question of the need, meaning, and possibility of metaphysics itself "after Auschwitz," with Kant's "Postulates" forming the paradigm for metaphysical speculation in a secular context, indeed, precisely as a necessary supplement to a categorical imperative. For Adorno, the question of the possibility and status of philosophy now, the very question with which he opens *Negative Dialectics,* becomes the question of the possibility of metaphysics after Auschwitz because the disenchantment of the world is fully realized in Auschwitz as a concrete historical event. We have already seen that the question of the possibility of philosophy is answered in part by the necessity of enlightened reason becoming enlightened about itself, by, that is, the practice of negative dialectics. If the possibility of philosophy is minimally satisfied by negative dialectics, then metaphysics must denote something more than negative dialectics, and thus a further inflection in our understanding of philosophy, its possibility and limits.

I say more about what lies beyond negative dialectics in relation to the structure of the "Meditations" as a whole at the beginning of Chapter 9. In this chapter I want to offer a commentary on Section 1 of the "Meditations" in which Adorno provides a philosophical characterization of the meaning of Auschwitz, and the opening several sentences of Section 2 in which he announces the new imperative and explains its status. After providing that commentary I complete the chapter with a discussion of Adorno's contention that the affective condition for Auschwitz occurring was a "coldness" that, by means of its being the affective correlate of instrumental reason, has become the fundamental principle of bourgeois subjectivity.

2. Auschwitz as Negative Theodicy

> Their life is short, but their number is endless; they, the *Muselmänner,* the drowned, form the backbone of the camp, an anonymous mass, continually renewed and always identical, of non-men who march and labour in silence, the divine spark dead in them, already too empty to really suffer.
>
> Primo Levi

> Like the pile of corpses, the *Muselmänner* document the total triumph of power over the human being. Although still nominally alive, they are nameless hulks.
>
> Wolgang Sofsky

Since the writing of *Negative Dialectics* two terms have come to replace Auschwitz for denoting the Nazi genocide: the Holocaust and the Shoah. The main connotations of the term "holocaust" "derive from the use in the Septuagint of *holokaustoma* ('totally consumed by fire') – the Greek translation of the Hebrew *olah,* which designates the type of ritual sacrifice that was to be completely burned."[3] While it might appear thoughtless and cruel for critics of the Nazi genocide to employ this term, as if for us too these events were sacrificial, nonetheless the word has a certain morbid propriety. The Nazis were enacting a ritual cleansing, a removing from their midst of what they regarded as impure; and sacrificing, totally consuming by fire, a part for the sake of the whole. The sacrifice of the particular to the universal, which Adorno consistently identifies as the deadly logic of enlightenment, becomes a genocidal ideology with the Nazis. Descriptive accuracy and moral perversion syncopate in the name "the Holocaust."

The name "the Shoah" equally possesses fitness and misdirection. In Hebrew *shoah* means, variously, destruction or wasteland; its Yiddish equivalent picked up the sense of a destruction, with the further implication of the destruction of the Temples. "Shoah" hence came to designate a destruction that was a "breach or turning point in history."[4] While employing the term "Shoah" to name the Nazi genocide fails to imply the intentional actions which brought it about – indeed, both "Holocaust" and "Shoah" are victim rather than perpetrator terms – the whole weight of "Meditations on Metaphysics" is to elaborate the meaning of what happened as a certain kind of turning point and breach in history. Quite differently, finally, using the place name "Auschwitz" as a metonym to refer to these events underlines the specificity, the historical actuality of what happened: in this place Jews were first barbarously imprisoned and then systematically exterminated. "The Holocaust," "the Shoah," "Auschwitz": each name implicitly presents a perspective on the Nazi genocide that, from an Adornoian point of view, is fundamental to its philosophical comprehension, including the fact that what happened matters to philosophy.

So the very first sentence of the "Meditations" should be read as fol-

3 Berel Lang, *Act and Idea in the Nazi Genocide* (Chicago: University of Chicago Press, 1990), p. xxi. For a severe critique of the use of "holocaust," see Giorgio Agamben, *Remnants of Auschwitz: The Witness and the Archive,* trans. Daniel Heller-Roazen (New York: Zone Books, 1999), pp. 28–31.

4 Lang, *Act and Idea in the Nazi Genocide* ibid.

lowing on directly from the title of the fragment: "[After Auschwitz] we can no longer assert the unchanging is truth, the mobile and the transitory are appearance, the mutual indifference of temporal items and eternal ideas . . . " (ND, 361). Exploring why Auschwitz should be so understood is the dominant leitmotif of Section 1; its elaboration and the tracking of its consequences for metaphysics ("eternal ideas") the work of the remaining sections. To this juncture the antagonism between unchanging truth and transitory existence has been pursued as the reflective comprehension of the limit and contradictoriness of identity thinking against the background of a generalized sense of the failure of the Enlightenment project. Now the indifference or self-sufficiency of enlightened reason, including its earlier metaphysical avatars (eternal ideas, an immobile God; a utopian kingdom of ends), is punctured directly by what we can and cannot claim as a consequence of the Nazi genocide. Our unwillingness to affirm unchanging truth, that serious truth concerns, properly, what is unchanging, what is purely ideal, is a response to what occurred. Hence there emerges a sense that there would be a massive impropriety in affirming a moral truth to which the occurrence of these events would be a matter of indifference, that moral norms and ideals could have meaning and truth independently of these events, so an impropriety in affirming any moral truth or idea of meaningfulness to which these events would be related as only tokens or examples or applications positively or negatively.

> After Auschwitz, our feelings resist any claim for the positivity of existence as sanctimonious prating, as wronging the victims; they balk at squeezing any kind of sense, however bleached, out of the victim's fate. And these feelings do have an objective side after events that make a mockery of the construction of immanence as endowed with a meaning radiated by an affirmatively posited transcendence. (ND, 361)

Throughout this fragment, albeit as a consequence of everything that has preceded it, Adorno registers our "feelings" about Auschwitz as directly pertinent to what rationally can or cannot be said about transcendence: the Holocaust destroys and consumes the idea that human existence is essentially or a priori good, or that we can affirm that despite the exorbitant evil and suffering that occurred in Auschwitz human life contains, even if only ideally or as a logical possibility, a meaningfulness that derives from a transcendent source, one that would be somehow forever reflectively safe from the disintegrating forces of disenchantment. Once these metaphysical ideas have been dismantled, then Adorno presumes with them must go as well the general conception of transcendence on which they rely.

Metaphysically transcendent ideas wrong the victims in their indifference: how can these lives and their extermination not be *formative* for what good and evil *are*? How could the meaning of meaning not be "touched" by the events at Auschwitz? If notions of the good or human meaningfulness are left as logically transcendent, as in the moral law or in the shape of regulative ideas of human flourishing, then our feelings of horror become mere accessories to an insight forever beyond them. That possibility is something we now find intolerable. Thus, that our feelings, in all their transitoriness and specificity, now matter, "have an objective side," is itself a consequence of not permitting claims for transcendence to be determinative for what is and is not meaningful, what is or is not a rational response. Our conscientious repugnance at metaphysical transcendence simultaneously makes the question of metaphysics a question of conscience in general.

The recurrent and problematic circle operating here should be underlined. We have already seen Adorno forwarding philosophical arguments about the significance and role of particulars and responses to particulars in cognition. Yet it might reasonably be complained that Adorno commits the error of which he accuses Hegel, namely, of transposing particulars into particularity, defending particulars by categorically insisting upon them, without there being any actual particulars instanced (ND, 326–8). Adorno can be partially defended against this charge by noting that his argument is framed from the beginning by guilt feelings about the nonidentical that are thence specified as a condition of negative dialectics. But even this, it could be argued, is still abstract and categorial; no concrete objects are shown. With the phrase "After Auschwitz" as the condition of all that is to follow Adorno raises the stakes of his argument to the level an actual particular. Not only the object of philosophical claiming, the transition from immutable truth to a transitory event, but the mode and possibility of that claiming, his or our feelings balking, also become philosophically relevant. Exactly how we can make our feelings pivotal about what is rationally or not rationally sayable is not immediately stated. But those feelings themselves insist upon their placement – they make the thought that there is a stratum of meaningfulness that could be untouched by these events *rationally intolerable* because emotionally intolerable, where, again, it is assumed that what is or is not rationally tolerable, heretofore rationally vindicable, is itself set in motion by event and response.

In one respect, Adorno is not here saying anything other than what he has been saying throughout *Negative Dialectics,* only now he is saying it concretely; but in accordance with the reversal in question, what is being said here is not the illustration or culmination of what he has been saying, but, rather the converse: finally, the argumentation that leads to the instancing of metaphysics after Auschwitz becomes the expression of what philosophy is called to think about itself in the light of Auschwitz, a point Adorno underlines by closing Section 1 with first a reprise of the thesis that philosophy now begins in guilt and indebtedness, and then a restatement of the general task of negative dialectics, a self-reflection of thinking that is equally thinking against itself, only now set firmly within the frame of the Nazi genocide: "If thought is not measured by the extremity that eludes the concept, it is from the outset in the nature of musical accompaniment with which the SS liked to drown out the screams of its victims" (ND, 365). Whether or not the prose needs to be this purple, the thought is the same as that marked by the title of the section: unless reason considers what does not affirm its claim to autonomy, it will become not simply idle in the face of the worst, but its accomplice. "After Auschwitz" flags a caesura in reason itself since in the light of Auschwitz what is to count as a reason and as a philosophical claim must change.

Making sense of Adorno's thought here is nonetheless not easy. The overall trajectory of the "Meditations" is fairly clear; it is to argue both for the continuing relevance of metaphysics, some idea of human transcendence, and that what is transcendent must be nonetheless immanent and concrete. How the highly rhetorically charged argument of Section 1 feeds into that trajectory is less clear. What is Adorno ruling out as a consequence of Auschwitz and why? Directly after saying our feelings balk at squeezing any kind of sense out of Auschwitz he comments that the Lisbon earthquake "sufficed to cure Voltaire of the theodicy of Leibniz, and the visible disaster of first nature was insignificant in comparison with the second, social one, which defies human imagination as it distills a real hell from human evil" (ND, 361). From this it is at least evident that Adorno thinks that any philosophical theodicy, that is, any attempt to demonstrate how despite and in the light of the existence of evil we are at home in the world, is "refuted" by Auschwitz. This has two sides: no affirmative metaphysics, whether of the wholly transcendent kind or of the historical, Hegelian kind, can avoid, side-step, or discount Auschwitz as irrelevant to it – were it to do so it would face the charge of being a musical accompaniment; but equally Auschwitz cannot be included in a philosophical theodicy of modernity in the way, for example, Hegel included the terror of the French Revolution into his theodicy of human freedom. Auschwitz can neither be avoided (the proximity thesis) nor recuperated (the anti-theodicy thesis) by or for metaphysics. As becomes evident below, the impossibility of recuperation is sufficient for establishing proximity.

One way in which one might be tempted to squeeze sense from the victims' fate would be to place it within a progressive narrative of moral and societal learning in which human failures of different kinds, including those exemplified by Auschwitz, became so many lessons through which and at the end of which moral truth would emerge. Adorno does not explicitly pitch an argument to that effect in the "Meditations" because in the previous chapter he had already offered a highly inflected critique of Hegel's philosophy of history. Those considerations, which we touched on in the opening section of Chapter 5, form the immediate backdrop to his argument here. With the Enlightenment metaphysics became historical, above all with Hegel, "who transfigures the absolute [the object of metaphysical speculation] by equating it with the total passing of all finite things" (ND, 360). Enlightenment thought construes itself as the reflective appropriation of an historical learning process, a maturation from servitude (where priests and monarchs do our thinking for us) to maturity (where we think for ourselves). Without denying either the significance of the history of nations and groups or the existence of historical trends as partially determining what historically has happened (ND, 301), Adorno was intent on demonstrating the abstraction involved *in counting* only the macroscopic – nations and trends – as of philosophical significance; and further, in showing how Hegel's positive account must now be construed as part of natural history: "Human history, the history of the progressing mastery of nature, continues the unconscious history of nature, of devouring and being devoured" (ND, 355).

However exorbitant, although in reality no more than a restatement of the dialectic of enlightenment thesis itself, this passage should remind us that Adorno is not an opponent of the philosophy of history as such or of the employment of historical trends for understanding particular facts. After noting the "discontinuous character of blighted life" as the counterpoint excluded by the continuum of progress in universal histories, Adorno goes on to argue that "discontinuity and universal history must be conceived together. To strike out the latter as a relic of metaphysical superstition would spiritually consolidate pure facticity as the only thing to be known and therefore to be accepted" (ND, 319–20). So Adorno believes that it would be nitpicking to deny "the fact that the French Revolution, for all the abrupt diversity of some of its acts, fitted into the overall course of bourgeois emancipation" (ND, 301). For Adorno, part of the movement of history is to be understood in terms of the formation of the modern autonomous subject and then the various modes by means of which it became eclipsed in the course of, at least, this past century. To accurately comprehend this occurrence requires that universal history be

> construed and denied. After the catastrophes that have happened, and in view of the catastrophes to come, it would be cynical to say that a plan for a better world is manifest in history and unites it. Not to be denied for that reason, however, is the unity that cements the discontinuous, chaotically splintered moments and phases of history – the unity of the control over

> nature, progressing to the rule over men, and finally to that over men's inner nature. (ND, 320)

Conscientious resistance to progressive philosophies of history should not blind us to macro trends and eventualities. Auschwitz evinces the history that must be construed and denied – its construal being seeing it in the light of the dialectic of enlightenment, its denial, as we see below, the new categorical imperative.

While he thinks that history itself refutes speculatively progressive philosophies of history – it would be "cynical" to claim otherwise – what Adorno objects to logically is that in discounting the significance of particular suffering, the discontinuous character of blighted lives, they turn suffering and defeat into victory, counting only the progress achieved as truly meaningful – recall the argument about instrumentalizing past history in the previous chapter. Hegel's account of the French Revolution, terminating in the Terror, is chilling:

> The sole work and deed of universal freedom is therefore *death,* a death too which has no inner significance or filling, for what is negated is the empty point of the absolutely free self. It is thus the coldest and meanest of all deaths, with no more significance than cutting off a head of cabbage or swallowing a mouthful of water.[5]

The moment of these deaths, the coldest and meanest Hegel could conceive, is approached as a moment in the formation – deformation and reformation – of human freedom and self-determination. The experience of these deaths *as* cold and mean is itself the mechanism through which we come to understand human freedom as something that cannot be had directly or immediately, as thus requiring mediation within itself and in its relation to others. Hence these cold and mean deaths appear, first, as ethically surveyable, as having a meaning in a progressive narrative whose dominant thought, the maturation of human freedom, supervenes on them, giving them a salience or weight beyond what they mean in themselves; and second, as disappearing in the realization of the supervening claim. In terms of the logic of the concept, it is tempting to read these theses as equivalent to the claims that: (1) concept possession supervenes on the process of concept acquisition; and (2) ideally, the learning process can disappear once concept possession is achieved.[6]

Jointly (1) and (2) make up the logical infrastructure of speculative

5 G. W. F. Hegel, *Phenomenology of Spirit,* trans. A. V. Miller (Oxford: Oxford University Press, 1977), Section 590.

6 Although this is not the only reading of Hegel possible, one perspicuous way of seeing his commitment to (2) is simply via his view of the *Phenomenology* as merely preparatory to the *Logic,* with the *Logic* as the truth of the system as a whole, its pivot.

metaphysical thought in which history and subject-transcendent meaning are united. The events of Auschwitz "shatter" the basis – the logical infrastructure of metaphysical supervenience – "on which speculative metaphysical thought could be reconciled with experience" (ND, 362). One might think that it is the sheer magnitude of the event that suffices for this conclusion: no savagery on that scale could fit into an affirmative metaphysical narrative. Maybe not, but Adorno pushes a far more refined thought, one having to do with, exactly, the fate of human individuality and particularity as it is actualized in Auschwitz.

In Auschwitz, Adorno argues, "it was no longer the individual who died but a specimen"; because it was specimens, not individuals, who died, then even death, "the poorest possession left to the individual," what was once thought to be indefeasibly "mine," mine even if nothing else is, is "expropriated." Hence death as a condition or site of individuality, the natural terminus of a human life, closing it the way in which an end closes a narrative, is expropriated: "There is no chance any more for death to come into the individual's empirical life as somehow conformable with the course of that life" (ND, 362). The idea of the conformability of a death to the life lived is indigenous to our moral picture of human lives: full, cut short, wasted; and it is transmitted from there to our telling of lives and thence to philosophical history. Adorno construes the expropriation of death that occurred to individuals in Auschwitz – their death removed as their own because their "administrative murder" involved the systematic elimination of any "ownness," any individuality – as reverberating on the concepts and categories through which we attempt to comprehend it. The idea that a death belongs to a life, is tellable in relation to it, is part of the categorial syntax through which process (life) and result (death) are connected. Here the result overtakes the process itself, leaving it without result: "Once again, the dialectic motif of quantity into quality scores an unspeakable triumph. The administrative murder of millions made death a thing one had never to fear in just this fashion" (ND, 362).[7]

A speculative philosophy of history, history as a narratable if horrific learning process, presupposes ethical surveyability as its condition of possibility. What, then, makes Auschwitz not ethically surveyable? Or better, why with Auschwitz do we sense that acts of ethically surveying, philosophical theodicies, would be a betrayal, another wrong to the victims? Ethical nonsurveyability does not deny the obvious: that we can write a history of these events. We can write the political history of the rise of fascism, and the slow genesis of the final solution; we can patiently docu-

7 The most well-known defence of the claim that the Holocaust must be understood through rationalized modernity is Zygmunt Bauman, *Modernity and the Holocaust* (Oxford: Polity Press, 1989), esp. chapter 4.

ment the construction of the camps, their procedures, the events that occurred in them. We can write biographies of the leaders in order to better understand their motives and self-understanding. We can search out and record the name of every victim. In short, nothing in Adorno's claim that it would be wrong to squeeze sense from Auschwitz is meant to deny that it cannot be both explained and understood, that somehow evil on that scale is distorted if understood. Writing before the debates about the uniqueness of the Holocaust and anticipating it, Adorno nonetheless cannot be aligned with the thesis that what is resistant to recuperation in Auschwitz entails its incomprehensibility since so saying would detach it from the history of which it is a part. On the contrary, at least part of the intelligibility of Auschwitz is that it is utterly continuous with, fulfils and exemplifies the destruction of individuality and particularity that the disenchantment of the world and the rationalization of reason have been preparing from the beginning of the modern epoch.[8] That level of explanation does not restore the possibility of metaphysical theodicy.

For Adorno, Auschwitz is the event in which the particularity of human beings was obliterated in a manner – rationally, systematically, and ritualistically – and on a scale that makes those features, the means of the extermination, overtake whatever ends they might have been meant to serve. But the intelligibility of those means is not haphazard: they are identity thinking itself. Not only, then, were millions of people murdered, but before their extermination their humanity was systematically eradicated while their bodies were left alive; what occurred was hence the most elaborate and extreme literal process of reification. For the most part both the treatment and response of the victims occurred in the absence

8 I do not here compare Adorno's views with the range of others available. Nonetheless, I think the most balanced, nuanced, and subtle view is to be found in Inga Clendinnen, *Reading the Holocaust* (Cambridge: Cambridge University Press, 1999), chapter 2. I read her account as compatible with Adorno, underlining exactly how much we can understand while nonetheless emphasizing two features: on the one hand, the administrative, industrially organized, systematic character of the extermination intended to wipe out an entire people; and, on the other hand, that "we did it," that it was done by people whose lives and culture is so proximate to our own that the attempt to make "them" somehow wildly different from us can be accomplished only by self-deception. These two thoughts do not leave much room for anti-Semitism in the overall account, and indeed Adorno does not in the "Meditations" take up the issue of the specific character of the Jews in the events. The best justification for that lacunae is given by Hannah Arendt: "Had the court in Jerusalem understood that there were distinctions between discrimination, expulsion, and genocide, it would immediately have become clear that the supreme crime it was confronted with, the physical extermination of the Jewish people, was a crime against humanity, perpetrated upon the body of the Jewish people, and that only the choice of victims, not the nature of the crime, could be derived from the long history of Jew-hatred and anti-Semitism." *Eichmann in Jerusalem: A Report on the Banality of Evil* (New York: Penguin Books, 1977), p. 269. For a thoughtful account of Critical Theory's handling of the Jewish question, see Martin Jay, "The Jew and the Frankfurt School: Critical Theory's Analysis of Anti-Semitism," *New German Critique* 19 (1980): 137–49.

of the language of act description and evaluation that provides lives with a distinctly human shape. Only by negation were the victims treated as centers of agency, their methodical humiliation for the sake of making creatures incapable of suffering further humiliation. Every determination through which a life is more than life itself was voided. But life without the applicability of evaluative predicates to it is a kind of death, a collapse into a kind of meaninglessness. Reducing life to this level voids death of its ultimate significance. When life becomes a function of the administrative system, then death too dies. It was not this or that individual who died, but, again, a numbered specimen.

Nowhere else in history has the terrifying proximity of spiritual death and physical death been so emphatically realized; that realization is non-detachable from the rational method and industrial means employed. Although American slavery anticipates Auschwitz in its routinely attempting to spiritually kill the slaves while leaving their bodies alive, the prosecution of that end was neither industrially organized to a significant degree nor methodically pursued nor oriented toward extermination;[9] while the fire-bombing of Dresden and the dropping of bombs on Hiroshima and Nagasaki achieved a technological distancing and coldness that fully exploited the potentials of enlightened rationality, and perhaps harbor thereby something even more awful than Auschwitz,[10] nonetheless the victims there were not first erased as singular human beings before being industrially exterminated. What then strikes Adorno in the case of Auschwitz is its realization of the destruction of aura, its obliteration of aura, in precisely the manner that is logically and rationally continuous with how it had been being destroyed previously. The emphatic realization of the proximity between spiritual and physical death, on this industrial scale and in this technological manner, is the legacy of enlightenment in Auschwitz.[11]

Because spiritual death is here so proximate to physical death in its systematic achievement, then the idea of considering death a point of closure is dissolved. With respect to these administratively eradicated lives, there is no "life" that receives it final determination or culmination with death, no teleology that is either realized or failed. Murder, even genocide, can bring a life to an abrupt and undeserving end, can make us

9 Orlando Patterson, *Slavery and Social Death* (Cambridge, Mass: Harvard University Press, 1982).

10 For a thinking through of this suggestion, see Julia Kristeva's powerful reflections on the writings of Marguerite Duras, including *Hiroshima Mon Amour,* in her *Black Sun: Depression and Melancholia,* trans. Leon S. Roudiez (New York: Columbia University Press, 1989), chapter 8.

11 While we have numerous representations of this proximity, the most telling is Primo Levi's description of the *Muselmänner* in his *If This Is a Man,* trans. Stuart Woolf (London: Abacus, 1987).

grieve over it as something tragically "cut short," eclipsed before it had a chance to begin. The administrative effort of the Nazi genocide was to make of its victims meaningless organisms, walking bits of flesh and bone with a number attached, to which the forms of predication proper to the human were no longer applicable. The point here is not that these individuals were not given the moral regard they deserved; such a lack of regard is a massively routine event in human history. Rather, what was made of the victims of the Nazi genocide was that they were disenchanted in exactly the same way in which anthropocentric nature had been disenchanted previously. The mechanisms of the final solution perfectly supervene on the remnants of the structures of material inference that still bound Germans and Jews; hence, not the acting against moral norms, but acting to remove the conditions through which moral predicates apply distinguishes the Nazi genocide. Thus to say of the victim of the genocide that her life was tragically cut short would subsume it under a form of moral accounting – lives tragically cut short – that presumed there remained in this case a general moral intelligibility through which we could evaluate what happened. No doubt, part of the continuing appeal of Anne Frank's diary is that it sentimentally permits us to view her as so intensely alive while still knowing her fate that we are enabled, precisely by being shielded from the details of her dying, to consider that fate in traditionally moral terms. Once the shielding is removed, and it is this which Adorno is insisting upon, then as aura is lost so are the conditions of the particular applicability of evaluative predicates; what makes local patterns of understanding inapplicable to individual victims equally makes macro patterns of understanding inapplicable to the event of Auschwitz as a whole.

As Tom Huhn usefully states the thought, when Adorno said one could not write poetry after Auschwitz he should be understood literally: "since extermination entails the absence of death, the project of poetry as recuperation has no more deaths upon which to erect meaning."[12] The generalized impossibility of erecting meaning as a consequence of the dying of death is, I take it, the core of the anti-theodicy thesis. By undoing the categorial distinction between life and death, the Nazis equally dissolved the syntactic and semantic means that traditionally thought their connection, human lives as narratable; in destroying the syntactic and semantic rules for connecting life and death, they destroyed the conditions through which the meanings of lives and deaths can be ethically interpreted.

12 Private correspondence with the author. When Adorno came to retract the claim about writing poetry he was not retracting his original thesis; rather, he was acknowledging other possibilities of carrying on short of recuperation; that is the force of the general presence of Samuel Beckett's works in Adorno's thought.

Hence, the unprecedented practice of the Holocaust, its methodical inexorability, its industrial scale and form of organization, its administrative precision, do not become ethically intelligible by being harnessed to identifiable collective ends, conceived nationally or racially. On the contrary, the ends of national grandeur or racial purity or brute power lose their teleological significance in virtue of the means employed to realize them. Ethical narration presumes a commensurability between means and ends; the means of Auschwitz, the dying of "human" death, render void any ends which may be suggested to explain them as simply means to those ends. The difficulty thus posed by Auschwitz is the demand to hold together its socio-historical occurrence, its empirical narrative, and the utter evacuation of speculative, moral, and metaphysical meaning from it as a consequence of its method. What perhaps truly explains Auschwitz empirically is nonetheless ethically vacuous. The overlap and internal connection between socio-historical dynamics and explanation, on the one hand, and progressive speculative meaning, on the other, which formed the cornerstone of the grand philosophies of history, including and above all those that argue for modernity in its moral and political forms as a rationally self-sufficient achievement, the achievement of Enlightenment, is exploded with Auschwitz. The oft-cited "unspeakability" of the Holocaust receives a partial vindication in its dirempting of explanatory and ethical intelligibility.

Adorno does not quite say that mechanisms of narrative supervenience that underwrote speculative philosophies of history operate in accordance with the same logic of sacrificing the individual to the universal which occurred in the "expropriation" of the victims' death. Rather than directly making this anti-theodicy point, something more or less accomplished in the earlier discussion of Hegel, Adorno's construction of Auschwitz as fulfilling the logic of disenchantment is his "construing" of Auschwitz in terms of identity thinking. More than an anti-theodicy, always implied, Section 1 supplies a negative theodicy. Adorno thus focuses directly on how the absolute negativity of Auschwitz – its bespeaking "the indifference of each individual life that is the direction of history," its affirmation of "the philosopheme of pure identity as death," the brutal recognition that "genocide is absolute integration" (ND, 362) – paralyzes our ability to go on operating with the mechanism of metaphysical supervenience. The expropriation of death, the making of death systematically continuous with life is the expropriation, the disenchantment of lives as human lives. This is the precise sense of "absolute negativity" which makes Auschwitz a negative theodicy.

We cannot bleach any sense out of the victims' lives because, first, the traditional mechanism of bleaching sense is a logic of supervenience that makes particular suffering a means to collective good, and, at the very least, we will not tolerate that use of the victims since it logically converges or formally overlaps with their logical annihilation by the perpetrators of the genocide. Second, the actual shape of the genocide destroys the existential conditions of meaningfulness: particularized selves each to suffer his or her own death. But this destruction is nothing historically or sociologically unique; it is the direction of modern societies as a consequence of rationalization.

> Even in his formal freedom, the individual is as fungible and replaceable as he will be under the liquidators' boots. Since in a world whose law is universal individual profit, the individual has nothing but this self that has become indifferent, the performance of the old, familiar tendency is at the same time the most dreadful of things. (ND, 362)

Adorno is not here saying that possessing only a formal freedom is the same as being reduced to a specimen or that the treatment of individuals as just bits of labor power is the same as the practice of the camps; it is not the practices that are the same, but the relation of universal and particular *in* those practices, and hence the *structural* indifference of particular lives to logically subsumptive practices that is the same. That in the case of liberal democracies and market economies there are still countervailing forces is thus not being denied. What is being insisted upon, however, is that there is a structural and logical overlap, and as a consequence that we see *in* the still moderated practices "at the same time the most dreadful of things." Hence, the destruction of the conditions of metaphysical meaningfulness, how lives have point and worth, that occurred in the camps is the hyperbole, the exaggerated fulfillment of the instrumental rationality that forms the infrastructure of modern societal rationalization and rationalized reason. Recognition of that calls for, demands a reorientation in our thinking.

3. "A new categorical imperative . . . "

Adorno's anti-theodicy argument in Section 1 of the "Meditations" turns into a negative theodicy. But a negative theodicy, unlike an anti-theodicy argument, presupposes the proximity thesis. It is because Auschwitz evinces disenchantment of the human subject itself and the destruction of aura through a practice that is, for all intents and purposes, continuous with processes of disenchantment and rationalization that have been the dominant of the modern desocialization of society, the supervening of instrumental rationality on what were the material inference structures that formed the empirical bonds among subjects, that it offers an apotheosis of identity thinking, the negative theodicy of the modern (which is not modern but old).

Without preliminary, Adorno opens Section 2 of the "Meditations,"

"Metaphysics and Culture," with the only explicit statement of a moral norm in the text: "A new categorical imperative has been imposed by Hitler upon unfree mankind: to arrange their thoughts and actions so that Auschwitz will not repeat itself, so that nothing similar will happen" (ND, 365). After a few brief statements about the status of this claim, Adorno turns to what is evidently the main business of the section, a discussion of the connection between metaphysics and culture, and the materialistic transformation of culture necessary consequent upon Auschwitz. From the fact that Adorno does not spend a great deal of time elaborating the new categorical imperative, it should not be inferred that he in any way doubts either its validity or significance; it is here not central because, although the immediate response to the negative theodicy canvassed in Section 1, it announces without itself partaking in the transformation of metaphysics called for by Auschwitz; or better, its validity, when understood aright, is what calls for the radical transformation of metaphysics. Metaphysics is the necessary complement of a wholly negative moral norm since ethics without transcendence is necessarily incomplete, incomplete in the way in which negative dialectics in its narrow construction is incomplete; this is why for Adorno it is metaphysics and not ethics that is at stake here. How justified this is we see in Chapter 9.

Once the argument of Section 1 is seen as a negative theodicy, Auschwitz's "construal" as a "real hell" that is the apotheosis of identity thinking, then the new imperative arrives immediately as what it is to "deny" it, a concrete and particular recapitulation of the thesis that universal history must be "construed and denied." Instead of a lesson learned, a drawing out of the meaning as placing us in an ethical space beyond it, the new imperative is the simple determinate negation of the negative theodicy itself. It could be argued that such an imperative could be asserted even without the negative theodicy of Section 1, that simply as a consequence of the suffering and slaughter that happened at Auschwitz we would want to assert that nothing like it should occur again. But to so urge while humanly comprehensible would be idle since unless one had grasped *why* Auschwitz occurred and *what* occurred there, then the imperative to arrange our thoughts and actions to prevent it or its like reoccurrence could not even begin to specify what imaginably so arranging our thoughts and actions amounted to. As the denial of the apotheosis of rationalized reason, the new imperative calls for, at least, the critique of reason, the enlightening of enlightenment about itself – just the thought with which Adorno had ended the previous section. The closing sentences of Section 1 and the new imperative state the same thought differently, the new imperative itself nothing but the thought of negative dialectics reconfigured around the event of Auschwitz. In this respect, Adorno's statement about the justificatory grounds for the new imperative are partial.

> This imperative is as refractory to rational grounding as the Kantian one. Dealing discursively with it would be an outrage: it gives us a bodily feeling of the moral addendum. Bodily, because it is now the practical abhorrence of the unbearable physical agony to which individuals are exposed even with individuality about to vanish as a form of mental reflection. It is in the unvarnished materialistic motive only that morality survives. (ND, 365)

This is partial because although Adorno does not seek to provide a discursive vindication of the new imperative, the *cognitive component* of the new imperative is provided by the intelligibility of Auschwitz as the apotheosis of rationalized reason. Adorno's statement here does not mean to deny that. Rather, in claiming that dealing with it discursively would be an outrage he is referring not to its cognitive content, but to its status *as a categorical imperative*; the issue is *how* it moves us to action, and with what *rational force*. The force of the *not* and the *ever* in "Not that ever again!" is transmitted by our "practical abhorrence" at the "unbearable physical agony" which the victims of Auschwitz suffered, and to which, in the light of Auschwitz *as* apotheosis of rationalized reason, each individual is now potentially exposed. Physical agony is the ground of the imperative; abhorrence the response to the ground. It is, again, a question of feeling.

As we can recall from Adorno's discussion of Kant on freedom and the will, the notion of the "addendum" was introduced as a dummy term, an X, for what would be neither strictly somatic nor purely mental, but "something physical which consciousness does not exhaust" (ND, 229). Adorno contended there that without some notion like this the will in relation to consciousness would be unintelligible, but that for now the connection between body and consciousness was so eviscerated, actually and conceptually, that the connection could be thought of only as an addendum. That addendum has now become a moral addendum; it is our practical *abhorrence, Abscheu,* at physical agony.[13] This is an addendum in both directions: a somatic addition to conscious understanding, and a cognitive addition to physical reaction. The abhorrence at *that,* and what *that* tokens for other individuals, makes it practical: a categorical imperative. Hence, the new imperative states what we must do simply in the light of a full appreciation, cognitive and affective, of Auschwitz; reasons for acting otherwise are "silenced altogether – not overridden – by the requirement."[14]

We might say that what the new imperative both accomplishes and

13 Abhorrence includes the sense of horror and disgust, where the notion of disgust has the sense of what cannot be taken in or incorporated. Thus a feeling of abhorrence has the sense of a response to something that sketches out a limit to our capacity for response; thus abhorrence is, precisely, the feeling attendant to a limiting condition; in this case the human as inhuman. On this sense of the "inhuman" see note 15 below.

14 John McDowell, "Are Moral Requirements Hypothetical Imperatives?," in his *Mind, Value, and Reality,* p. 90.

evinces simultaneously is a reorientation, a mode or way of proceeding and thinking that will govern "all our reactions" in the same way as we earlier said that the buzzing of the fly could come to function as a material a priori – it changes the meaning of all our reasons, attuning them to it. And there is more than similarity here; abhorrence at unbearable physical agony is the experience of bodily suffering as the determining ground for *all* future action. To arrange our thoughts and actions so that Auschwitz will not recur is to arrange them so that no group of individuals is exposed to physical agony of the kind suffered there. If individuality is vastly more than physical integrity, it is at least physical integrity, not as condition for something else, but as a stratum of existence of each individual. Abhorrence sees, feels, *in* the agony the destruction of the auratic body; abhorrence is an experience of auratic animism at the precise sight of its destruction. What we find abhorrent is the suffering occasioned by the lapse of the body being a vehicle for individuality; but that lapse is the point at which the body as the constitutive medium of individuality becomes morally visible. The abhorrence that introduces the auratic body is the perception of the protection of bodily integrity as the sufficient condition for future valuing. But since this arises in the context of the eclipse of the moral, a space of utter disenchantment, then morality survives in letting this unvarnished material motive dominate. It is hence not just that our practical abhorrence indeed provides governance for our actions – why should it not? – but that in these circumstances the fact of its so doing images a fundamental shift or conversion in our self-understanding. Our abhorrence at Auschwitz is at the physical agony suffered there, a bodily reaction to the fate of those bodies. In context, that bodily reaction feels itself a sufficient reason to become *the* reason for our self-understanding. In becoming *the* reason for our self-understanding, the addendum as connecting physical response with rational action becomes a moral addendum, an X belonging neither to the system of bodily reactions nor the self-moving terrain of autonomous reason, but a lightning flash connecting the two. In connecting the two, morality is rematerialized.[15]

15 Giorgio Agamben's moving and thoughtful *Remnants of Auschwitz: The Witness and the Archive,* arrived too late for me to fully incorporate his findings. However, his argument is so proximate to the one being pursued here, I must say something. Like Adorno, Agamben regards Auschwitz as a negative theodicy of modern life (p. 49); he equally construes the mechanism of the camps, as exemplified by the *Muselmänner,* as the utter disenchantment of the individuals, their removal from the space in which standard moral predicates have application (Chapter 2, passim); this equally has the sense for Agamben of the dying of death (p. 70ff). Hence, what I have referred to in terms of the lapse of the auratic body, Agamben succinctly captures with the thought that the "human also endures the non-human. . . . This means that humans bear within themselves the mark of the inhuman, that their spirit contains at the very center the wound of non-spirit, non-human chaos atrociously consigned to its own being capable of everything"

In the light of our practical abhorrence, it would be an "outrage" to allow moral theory, the principle of identity, proprietary rights in determining whether and in what sense the new categorical imperative was valid since to do so would be to deny that our abhorrence was practical, a moral addendum. What might it mean to claim that the imperative was valid because it was compatible with the golden rule or the principle of utility? The outrage would be to think that the new imperative's validity depended on these, that our understanding and abhorrence at

(p. 77). I presume it is the spectacle of the nonhuman that generates abhorrence – horror and disgust. Because horror and disgust – which appear as modalities of shame in Agamben (pp. 105–7) – then it is a response that builds meaning on a moment of the absence of meaning, "the non-language to which language answers" (p. 38). Thinking the character of this responsiveness is what Agamben means to think in his notion of "witness." But this notion of witness is meant to exactly capture, as a practice, the naming and material axis of the concept: ". . . only if language is not always already communication, only if language bears witness to something to which it is impossible to bear witness, can a speaking being experience something like a necessity to speak" (p. 65). If the idea of "impossible to bear witness" has the sense of what can never be unrestrictedly communicated, what language as communication always and necessarily falsifies, then Adorno and Agamben agree formally in terms of their conceptions of meaning, and substantially in regarding the sight of the disenchanted body as the marker for the necessity of this moment. Is there then a difference between the two accounts? I am uncertain, but I suspect there is since I suspect that Agamben intends his argument concerning the non- or inhuman in the human as a kind of transcendental marker, the inhuman having something like the role of *differance* in Derrida: a necessary condition for the possibility of meaning that is equally its impossibility. (For a full consideration of this issue one would need to compare the idea of "impossible to bear witness" with the idea of infancy in *Infancy and History,* where infancy is thought in relation to a "transcendental history" in which experience is "the simple difference between the human and the linguistic" (p. 50). Sometimes this sounds to me like my notion of learning and the position of the neophyte, and sometimes, say, when Agamben talks about this moment in terms of "the ineffable" (p. 51), as transcendental in a more suspect sense.) Consider the following: "The *Muselmann* has, instead, moved into a zone of the human where not only help but also dignity and self-respect have become useless. But if there is a zone of the human in which these concepts make no sense, then they are not genuine ethical concepts, for no ethics can claim to exclude part of humanity, no matter how unpleasant or difficult that humanity is to see" (pp. 63–4). I agree with the first half of Agamben's claim here, but disagree with the inference. Dignity and self-respect cannot be the *grounds* of our response since these are human creatures without it; our abhorrence is precisely abhorrence at human lives to which these forms of predication no longer apply. And this does entail that dignity, self-respect, and the like are not foundational, they do not self-sufficiently ground the possibility of ethical response. But in saying this Agamben supposes we are responding *directly* to the inhuman; Adorno supposes that we are responding to the *in*-human, the canceling or disappearing or stripping away of the human, its negation or disenchantment. Hence, while Agamben and Adorno share the inference that the human is not self-sufficient (autonomous), that it necessarily partakes of the inhuman (otherwise there could not be disenchantment), and further that without inhuman *life,* bare life, there could not be ethically significant *human* life, Adorno construes this as revealing the contingency of ethical predication (concepts like dignity and self-respect, for example, as forms that make good on the experience of abhorrence, as what we ethically must ascribe to others if our response to them is going to be anything other than sheer abhorrence), Agamben wants the inhuman itself to be the fund or fount of ethical response. But if the experience of the in-

Auschwitz could have moral significance only if vindicated by discovering such compatibility. So, again, the "outrage" is premised on the thought with which the "Meditations" open: after Auschwitz we will not tolerate or accept, we find it unconscionable and therefore unintelligible that what occurred there should not matter to the weal and woe of what were taken as "universal" truths and ideas; our feelings demand that *this* matter and matter to the possibility of mattering *überhaupt*. The new imperative's lack of rational grounding appears "irrational" only from the perspective of a reason that withholds acknowledgement of what might judge it, from what "tests" our reason or standing in the world. The extremity of the new imperative as an instance of the principle of the indexical binding of moral norms derives from the fact that both imperative and principle are being announced by Auschwitz, it becoming thereby a fact of and for our reason.

Earlier I claimed that a summary statement of the task of *Negative Dialectics* was to make good on the statement that "there is no origin save in ephemeral life" (ND, 156). The new imperative partially accomplishes that task – only partially because, as we see more fully below, its authority lies almost wholly in what it negates. What distinguishes the new categorical imperative from the old is that its cognitive content and form of necessity are bound to what is contingent, factual, empirical. In making Hitler the source of this new imperative, Adorno is, with brutal irony, removing from the conditions of ethicality the need or presumption of purity or freedom, as well as insisting that the imperative has no source or origin other than our response to these events. In technical terms, the distinction now is that what is a moral principle contains a proper name; it is indexically bound. That it is so transforms what we might mean by

human is not the experience of the *loss* of the human, its eclipse, how might the experience of the inhuman cause abhorrence? For Adorno there is something anamnestic in our response, a response at the loss and absence of aura, hence a response to the claim of aura in *its* precise lapsing and consequent absence – a process that occurs quite naturally in certain extreme forms of aging or illness. Because of this, the inhuman is *also* human but appears as its sheer cancellation because of the indifference of rationalized reason to it. Hence for Adorno there is a *dialectic* of the inhuman: it is both the abject and the nonidentical (the nonidentical appearing as abject), poles within the inhuman that cannot be further synthesized. Adorno handles the phenomenon of death in an analogous manner. However, the two sides of the inhuman are the two sides they are only in context. Hence, the double movement of repulsion, horror, and affirmation is contextual, that is, it is only in this social and historical context that the inhuman possesses its role as negation and remnant. Hence, there is no *intrinsic* designation of the inhuman (it is not a self-sufficient dimension or stratum); and it is just such an intrinsic designation that I hear in Agamben's treatment. How significant a difference this is I find hard to measure or determine; only in what follows from Adorno's and Agamben's different analyses might the significance of their disagreement be measured. Still, Agamben's summarial contention that "human beings are human insofar as they bear witness to the inhuman" (p. 121) potently captures the leading idea of Adorno's response to Auschwitz.

being obliged or acting on a principle since in elaborating our ethical orientation we must make essential reference to *this* object, *these* circumstances. Of course, the immediacy of the obligation, our practical abhorrence, is itself mediated: by the identities of the victims (Europeans like us), the identity of perpetrators (Europeans like us), by our identities (it would not arise or arise in this way for non-Europeans or for those in societies not integrally tied to European culture like those in North America and Australia), by the manner and mode in which "the final solution" was carried out, by how that manner and mode connected with wider social practices (bureaucratization, capital reproduction, a commanding culture industry), and so on. Without those mediations our abhorrence would not be *ours* or the abhorrence an abhorrence at *that.* But these mediations, including the ideals of enlightenment, are not the grounds of the imperative, but components in its emergence and elaboration; they form a constellation around the name "Auschwitz" through which it comes to be seen and appreciated, and in being seen and appreciated like *that,* our finding it abhorrent, we find ourselves with the new imperative imposed on us. I am bound by the new imperative because it asserts and expresses what I take those events to mean as they bear on how I must conceive of myself if that conceiving is not to descend into the depths of self-deception, self-betrayal, and self-dissociation.

None of this is simple or innocent. If you think that Adorno is wrong to interpret Weberian rationalization and capital in terms of instrumental reason (understood widely), or wrong in seeing the Holocaust as in any way bespeaking instrumental rationality, then whatever your abhorrence at the events there, you will be unpersuaded by the claim of the new categorical imperative. And for me to change your mind, I would have to get you to see it and yourself differently; and I may well be unable to do so. My failure does not prove you right or me wrong. There are no demonstrable proofs here; the force of the imperative, via practical abhorrence, depends on its being not logically demonstrable: structures of material inference leave gaps from the perspective of rational demonstrability; from the inside, conversely, there is no sense of a gap to be filled: right reasoning, again, occurs only from within ethical understanding and is not a route to it. The distance between experience of an unsatisfiable gap in our reason, and the conclusiveness of a logical inference is the gap between material and logical reason – a second-order gap which is now not systematically bridgeable. As should be evident, my strategy is to interpret the new imperative in precisely the way moral realists interpret moral judgements generally, the only differences being that for Adorno Auschwitz is a particular event possessing orientational significance, where the condition of the material inference in question is not the experience of precious human lives, each radiant in its significance, being morally infringed upon, but the physical jolt at the perception of the utter evacuation of auratic inviolability; the abhorrence, again, our horror not at lives ruined, but at life not living. With these differences conceded, the pattern of argument is nonetheless morally realist.

This being so, we should be alerted to what is a presumption or indiscretion or failure of precision in Adorno's original statement. When he states that Hitler has imposed on "unfree mankind" a new imperative, he is presuming that the new imperative is imposed on all of us. And he is not wrong to so believe; on the contrary, he cannot interpret Auschwitz as he has and conceive of himself as simply one of us in the way he does and not think that what leads him to believe that he must arrange all his thoughts and actions so that it will not happen again is equally true for each of us since the grounds for his accepting the new imperative are ones that do not discriminate him from the rest of us. But what is important is that the logic of the claim be put this way. Adorno's being bound by the new imperative, its bindingness on him, is not detachable from his relation to object and circumstances. Unless this were the case, the force of the new imperative could not lodge in practical abhorrence. If his relation to the event is particular, then so will be any other individual's. There is no external standpoint from which the debate can be prosecuted and the validity of the imperative judged. Hence, even if it is correct to say that Hitler has imposed a new imperative on "us," nonetheless the imperative possesses an ineliminable intransitive sense, making its comprehension a matter between any individual and the event itself, and it is only via or through relation to the event that anything like a categorical imperative arises.

But this indicates a peculiarity with Adorno's view. I have already suggested that Adorno's negative theodicy argument assumes that Auschwitz is not unique, that it is all too understandable and predictable: it is in what is most horrifying about it, the systematic, industrially organized, technologically efficient disenchantment and extermination of a people, the apotheosis of instrumental reason. At the same time, I now seem to be arguing that, understood aright, Auschwitz eventuates in the new imperative, which fundamentally reorients self and reason at once even though the imperative can emerge only via a one-to-one encounter with those events. Adorno's employment of Auschwitz hence appears paradoxical: as apotheosis it manifests features and characteristics that are pervasive, structurally and reflectively, in modern social life; as a reorientation of reason itself, a conversion of the self through which a single event becomes orientational, it parades as unique, *the* turning point in Western metaphysics, *the* turning of reason, *the* rebinding of reason to experience. And is not that sense of Auschwitz as turning point, Shoah, implied by Adorno's phrasing "after Auschwitz"? Would not making Auschwitz such a turning point be, almost, a kind of immanent moral centralism, Auschwitz becoming the reason which gives sense to our reasoning generally?

There can be nothing untoward in the thought of a single event possessing orientational significance for a life; on the contrary, that is exactly what is required by the claim that there is no origin save ephemeral life. Hence, there is nothing untoward in Adorno finding Auschwitz having that force *for him*; and if the new imperative indeed manifests the indexical principle, then its having that force for him is a necessary condition of its having force, it being a categorical imperative. And there is a level of first-person experience reported in Section 1 that underlines how, not only reflectively but psychologically, Auschwitz came to have pivotal significance in Adorno's life: "By way of atonement [for having been spared without merit] he will be plagued by dreams such as that he is no longer living at all, that he was sent to the ovens in 1944 and his whole existence since has been imaginary, an emanation of the insane wish of man killed twenty years earlier" (ND, 363). Notice how in this passage, the most intimate and yet histrionic in the entire text, Adorno nonetheless writes of himself in the third person although the sense of the passage is irremediably first-person. Hence his sense of atoning for his mere survival by dreams that continually call that survival into question, de-realizing the life given back, is meant to have an extrapersonal significance, of us too being survivors, our mere existence unmerited, fortuitous, and hence within the black halo of Auschwitz. I take up the issue of guilt and survival in the next section. What holds for this single passage could be widened for the whole of Section 1: although arguing for something structural, Auschwitz as negative theodicy, its prose consistently castes that argument as one from experience. Hence, the compellingness of the new imperative turns implicitly on our finding it compelling for Adorno. As we read through Section 1 and reach the abrupt introduction of the new imperative our initial acknowledgement is bound to Adorno's own: how, given his beliefs, at the very least plausible in themselves, and his experience, which is hardly idiosyncratic, could he think and believe otherwise? Would not I too, if I were he, necessarily come to think that all my thoughts and actions must be reoriented in the light of Auschwitz? But then this implicit first-person accounting is simultaneously being caste in a third-person form. What is this logic connecting first- and third-person experience, the fading of the difference between them, in relation to not just what is to be done about some singular state of affairs, but in response to those affairs proposing, offering, demanding a new imperative, a new norm of action which is to reorient experience utterly?

By recasting his experience into a form which enables us to participate in that experience, come to appreciate the event as he himself understood it, Adorno is making, attempting to make, his response *exemplary*. I intend exemplarity here to carry its full Kantian sense: an item is exemplary only if although derived from no previous rule, principle, or idea, it makes original sense, that is, provides a new rule for a practice: from now on the practice is to be understood from out of the exemplary instance. Exemplary instances are not explainable or derivable because they are to be what gives a rule, what will be the model or origin or explainer for what is to, normatively, follow it. Exemplarity establishes a form of successiveness, horizontally, for items that are themselves normatively constituted; it is the establishment of a new rule of material inference. The litmus test for exemplarity, the way in which we know that the new item is original sense and not nonsense is, as Kant insists, succession. Succession, Kant states, is not *imitation,* but "to create from the same sources out of which the former himself created, and to learn from one's predecessor only the way to proceed in such creation oneself" (CJ, 283). Exemplarity thus provides an account of the *form* of objectivity and universality applicable to indexically bound norms. The authority of the new imperative is that it is exemplary, exemplarity being the form of rational authority that conspicuously entwines the logical and material axes of the concepts involved. Exemplarity is the logical form of charismatic authority.

Will regarding the new imperative as exemplary shift the sense that Adorno is claiming that Auschwitz is *the* turning point in Western metaphysics? Not without one further thought. Almost all of the sense that Adorno is claiming Auschwitz as the turning point derives from what it instantiates; only insofar as Auschwitz is the apotheosis of identity thinking and instrumental reason, and that reason is the dominant force theoretically and practically in Western societies, is it the case that in saying "never again" to Auschwitz are we being reoriented generally. *The more than exemplary generality of the new imperative derives from what it opposes, and not from anything about it in itself.* The generalized denial of Auschwitz has a more than exemplary force only because Auschwitz itself is to be understood as the apotheosis of instrumental reason, as a negative theodicy of reason. So saying, agreeing that Auschwitz is but the "first sample" of a lurking doom, acknowledges that other events could be equally perspicuous as actualizations of instrumental reason at its worse. One could argue, for example, that Hiroshima and Nagasaki are at least as good realizations, and perhaps better since the ease with which we accepted the immediate erasure of hundreds of thousands of innocent lives speaks more emphatically to the racism and provincialism that has systematically accompanied Western universalism throughout its history, as well as the technological indifference to life that is becoming the most threatening form of instrumental reason. But even a case like that is unnecessary. After all, the fundamentals of Adorno's own stance toward the world were fairly fully in place prior to, at least, his knowing what had occurred at Auschwitz. Understood in a certain light, the sight of a hungry child on a street corner could generate an imperative having all the reorientational significance of the one actually offered; indeed, unless this was possible, the new imperative could not mean what it is intended to mean. If Adorno's view about the scope of instrumental rationality is true, and hence his thought that *each* particular which now faces us as a moral remainder, as the damaged face of what it could be, is true, then necessarily the smallest event, a singular object (a buzzing fly?) must be capable of bearing the weight of possessing orientational significance, of providing the jolt that forces us to say "Not this ever again!," where the force of the claim involves a transforming of reason.

Auschwitz is a radical but not unique instance of instrumental rationality; there are other instances that might be thought to be as radical; but radicality is not necessary for an event to precipitate an imperative having the reorientational significance of the one Adorno offers. What gave Auschwitz its focal role in Adorno's writing was, first, its status as negative theodicy, it being one version of the completion of disenchantment; and second its historical and public character, it being literally an occurrence in and to the European West as a whole, and hence its social vividness and perspicuousness for his generation. But unavoidability here has only the significance that Adorno believed his audience generally would accept or could be quickly brought to agree that it was an event which needed to be encountered, explained, responded to. It is natural to suppose that what Adorno thought he was doing was not so much drawing it to their attention, but, differently, casting it in a specific light – it was not some historical monster, but a horrific instantiation and intensification of the dominant sociological and reflective trends of modernity. For Adorno, if *it* were not sufficient as a call to change our lives, to arrange our thoughts and actions so that *it* would not happen again, then it was unclear what could make that claim and appeal. But that sense of unavoidability is weakened by time, distance, and the transformation of European identities. Agreeing to that does not change the status of the new imperative, only its capacity to be communicated.

If, as a consequence of *this,* I cannot do other than to attempt to change my thoughts and actions so that it will not occur again, then, at the very least, anything like it will raise an analogous imperative, and any practices, states of affairs, events, objects that I can come to understand as contributing to or being the consequence of what contributed to and eventuated from Auschwitz would equally raise a reorienting categorical claim. The movement from the exemplary instance given by the new imperative to further instances is the lateral or horizontal universality implied by the imperative itself, what it would be to arrange our thoughts and actions so that Auschwitz is not repeated. But, as I argued above, if indexically bound moral norms are exhausted in their performative realization, then logically each realization can be an indexical origin. That thought is more oblique here because the norm in question possesses orientational significance; nonetheless, the announcement of the new imperative is only exemplary. Hence, despite the commanding authority of Auschwitz, its interruption of the reign of the simple concept and instrumental reason, its providing the Copernican turn with an axial revolution toward the object, its binding us to its horror as what must not be repeated, it is not *the* categorical imperative, *the* law, but an imperative, a law, of which necessarily there can be others with equal force and commandingness or it could not be the law it claims to be. Said another way, in responding to the text, we are responding to Adorno's exemplary performance; the validity of the new imperative for us as readers is bound to the compellingness of the ethical performance through which it emerges. And indeed, Adorno can do no other than to make his own response to the disaster exemplary for what responding to the disaster is.

This would be a trivial thought were it not for the fact of the stakes: the issuing of the new imperative is not the issuing of just another moral judgement or another moral principle; it occurs in a context in which it is simultaneously the issuing of a moral norm in opposition to what moral norms and principles have been, giving the announcement equally the second-order sense of "this is what a categorical imperative must be if there are to be categorical imperatives." By extension, then, the exemplary status of the new imperative gives it a strange double character: an announcement of a content and a reflexive announcement about the nature of contents. Because the imperative possesses a specific cognitive content, then it is possible to disagree with the imperative, to not believe that Auschwitz is the apotheosis of instrumental reason (say, because you thought that the camp practices were dehumanizing but in a ritualistic rather than instrumentally rational way), and still to agree that Adorno's performance is exemplary of what ethical responding is, and hence that the argument is fulfilled in its reflexive announcement only.

This indicates two ways, then, in which the new imperative is weaker than the climatic phrase "after Auschwitz" would appear to require. First, the conditions which give the new imperative not its objectivity but its reorientational significance equally requires that other instances and events can possess reorientational significance. Auschwitz is not metaphysically or epistemically privileged; even as negative theodicy, Auschwitz is not unique but, horrifyingly, exemplary. Second, because the form of objectivity of the new imperative lies in its being exemplary, its being bound to the performance through which it is issued, in a context in which moral norms have had a quite other status, then the issuing of the new imperative has a second-order exemplarity: it is exemplary of the exemplarity of ethical principles. And this second-order exemplarity can be sustained even if one has particular objections to the new imperative itself.

In a context in which identity thinking remains practically dominating and reflectively hegemonic, any exemplary instance will have the extra or reiterative sense of being exemplary of exemplarity, of indexically binding the principle of indexical binding, of being ethically binding and the binding of ethical binding, of charismatically and rationally authoring the union of charismatic and rational authority. The logical momentousness of the eruption of the new imperative in Adorno's text depends on it having this reflexive feature: its claim simultaneously a transformation of what claiming is. In showing that the new imperative is exemplary, I am claiming that its logical momentousness, the transformation of reason, can be had without that instance being unique. The darkness of our time is that every instance in which an ethical material inference comes into force, is activated or reactivated against the supervenience of instrumental reason, is simultaneously a claim for ethical material inferences as such. The "as such" owes nothing to what is exemplified and everything to that from which it is departing.

4. Coldness: The Fundamental Principle of Bourgeois Subjectivity

There is an idea in Section 1 of the "Meditations" that relates sufficiently directly to an ethical understanding of Auschwitz that it deserves extended discussion. Adorno concedes that he might have been wrong to say that one could not write poetry after Auschwitz, but a noncultural extension of that question arises, namely, "whether one who escaped by accident, one who by rights should have been killed, may go on living. His living on requires coldness, the fundamental principle of bourgeois subjectivity, without which Auschwitz would not have been possible; drastic guilt of one who was spared" (ND, 363). Although it is coldness that I want to address here, its mode of introduction calls for a little comment. The two sentences just quoted do not transparently add up; the first concerns survivor's guilt, the second guilt at having to sustain oneself through the very stance of coldness that is the precondition for Auschwitz. Survivor's guilt is complex and many-sided: guilt for having survived while others died; guilt at the sheer fortuitousness of having survived; guilt through a sense of having failed in solidarity; guilt at finding oneself plagued by a desire to survive. How are we supposed to connect those thoughts with the issue of coldness, which looks free-standing? In a parallel investigation, Habermas has come close to mapping out the structure of the inference.

> But since that moral catastrophe doesn't the survival of all of us stand under the curse, in attenuated form, of having merely escaped? And doesn't the fortuitousness of unmerited escape establish an intersubjective liability – a liability for distorted life circumstances that grant happiness, or even

> mere existence, to some only at the cost of destroying the happiness of others, denying them life and causing them suffering?[16]

In Section 1 we find Adorno himself issuing an extension of survivors' guilt into a consideration of the "guilt context of the living" very like this one from Habermas; it is almost certainly the origin of Habermas's thesis.

> The guilt of a life which purely as a fact will strangle other life, according to statistics that eke out an overwhelming number killed with a minimal number of rescued, as if this were provided in a theory of probabilities, this is irreconcilable with living. And the guilt does not cease to reproduce itself, because not for an instant can it be made fully, presently conscious. (ND, 364)

While it makes sense for Adorno to consider himself an unmerited survivor, and to a lesser extent Habermas too, nonetheless it is unclear how the generalization of that experience into a "guilt context of the living" thesis is supposed to occur. Might not one think just the opposite, that it would be a gross self-deception, a plea for victimhood, for me to identify myself with actual survivors? And why think the proper lines of identification for those not immediately involved is with the victims rather than the perpetrators? Part of the strangeness of the survivors' guilt thesis is that via mere survival potential victims become perpetrators. Some teasing out of that idea is required.

Following Tom Huhn, I urged that the sense in which one could not write poetry after Auschwitz was that, with the dying of death, there were no more deaths on which to erect affirmative meaning. Analogously, to ask the *question* whether one has a right to survive is to ask after the basis of one's survival: on what can it be erected? And in the same way one cannot erect affirmative meaning out of extermination, then the ground of continuing existence can be nothing affirmative either. Rather, what enables one to survive is, on the one hand, nothing but the drive for self-preservation, and the coldness and indifference, structural in both our institutions and personal comportment, intrinsic to instrumental rationality as the rational form of the drive to self-preservation, and, on the other hand, unmerited good fortune – unmerited simply because a matter of luck only. In acknowledging that coupling of luck and the coldness necessary to make use of it we acknowledge both complicity and indebtedness. Hence, the point is not, as Habermas believes, that we are survivors of Auschwitz albeit in attenuated form; but rather that the experience of the survivors, what is revealed as their *categorial* ethical landscape,

16 Jürgen Habermas, *New Conservatism: Cultural Criticism and the Historians' Debate,* trans. Shierry Weber Nicholsen (Cambridge, Mass: MIT Press, 1989), p. 252.

is equally our categorial ethical landscape. It is not Auschwitz that places us under a curse, but, again, what Auschwitz stands for and represents.

There are two aspects to this that deserve comment. First, to say that categorially we should interpret present life as "survival," as "living on," as Adorno opens the whole of *Negative Dialectics* by claiming that philosophy is now only a "living on," an afterlife, is to say that in the light of societal rationalization there is a guilt context of the living that cannot be escaped. We do live off the misery and deaths of others; in so living off the misery and lives of others where nothing other than luck explains our being in a position to do so, then our life, its survival, is without unconditional right or merit – it can be nothing affirmative. The rule of self-preservation rules even when its rule is not necessary. It is equally to say that as a consequence of disenchantment, with Auschwitz as the apotheosis of disenchanting life, the semantic resources for affirmative life are not available. There are no longer the resources, structurally or semantically, on which to construct an affirmative conception of life. But since there is no unconditional life, full living, without the forms through which to acknowledge it, then emphatic life has been left behind (or not yet arrived): we are, precisely, survivors. Present life is a living on or afterlife or one of being a survivor. These expressions can all be construed as extensions, by way of making the thoughts concerned literal, of where we began in Chapter 1: life does not live, there is no true living in a wrong world, and there is no right living in a wrong world. Via the relation between (the absent) semantic forms and what those forms are of or enable, it now becomes possible to perceive the depth of mutual implication amongst what at first appeared to be quite distinct aspects of those ideas: wrong life is life enmeshed in death, which we survive in and as.

Second, living on certainly manifests the depth of the drive to self-preservation, and even more the shape that drive now takes, instrumental reasoning. While that will do for unavoidable complicity, something more specific is at issue: not only guilt at living off others, but guilt at having as one's fundamental resource for both living and thinking the coldness that is the fundamental principle, *des Grundprinzips,* of bourgeois subjectivity. In Chapter 1 I persistently circled around what I called Adorno's suspended stance. That suspension can now be identified as the reflective coldness of the theorist against the conditions requiring it. Because the conditions of coldness have not passed away, then an ethics responsive to sensuous particulars in their diversity is not possible. In what way is coldness or indifference the fundamental principle of bourgeois subjectivity? And in what way does it makes sense to say that without it Auschwitz would not have been possible?

Before attempting to unpack Adorno's claim, let me instance it. In a short, popular essay originally given as a radio talk, "Education After Auschwitz," Adorno considers the meaning of education in the light of the new imperative: "The premier demand upon all education is that Auschwitz should not happen again" (EAA, 191). After working his way through some familiar terrain on administered society, the temptation to replace civic republican nationalism with an ethnically based form of nationalist bonding after the lapse of the autonomous individual, a process that has become rampant over the past decade beyond Adorno's imagining, the continuing withering of experience and reification of consciousness, he turns to modern technology, which has become the fetishised means for the self-preservation of the species. This fetishisation occurs because "the ends – a life of dignity – are concealed and removed from the consciousness of people" (EAA, 200). [17] There then occurs the following series of comments on coldness (EAA 200–203), some of which are undoubtedly sentimental in tone, a fact of which Adorno is aware. Sentimentality, I presume, is here the discourse of sentiment under conditions of its exclusion.

> With this type, who tends to fetishize technology, we are concerned baldly put, with people who cannot love. This is not meant to be sentimental or moralistic, but rather describes a deficient libidinal relationship to other persons. They are thoroughly cold, deep within themselves they must deny the possibility of love, must withdraw their love from other people before it can even unfold. And whatever of the ability to love somehow survives in them they cannot apply except as a means.
>
> . . . if people were not profoundly indifferent towards whatever happens to everyone else except for a few to whom they are closely bound, and, if possible, by tangible interests, then Auschwitz would not have been possible, people would not have accepted it. . . . [the "lonely crowd" is] an aggregate of people completely cold who cannot endure their own coldness and yet also cannot change it. . . . The inability to identify with others was unquestionably the most important psychological condition for the fact that something like Auschwitz could have occurred in the midst of more or less civilized and innocent people. . . . The coldness of the societal monad, the isolated competitor, was the precondition, as indifference to the fate of others, for the fact that only very few people reacted. The torturers knew this; and they put it to the test ever anew.
>
> One of the greatest impulses of Christianity, not immediately identical with its dogma, was to eradicate the coldness that permeates all things. But this attempt failed; surely because it did not reach into the societal order that produces and reproduces coldness. . . . If anything can help against coldness as the condition for disaster, then it is the insight into the conditions which determine it and the attempt to combat those conditions, initially in the domain of the individual.

17 This is perhaps an overstatement; it would have been sufficient to claim that even if a life of dignity is not concealed from people, nonetheless the economic and technological means for achieving it inexorably make the pursuit of means primary.

> The first thing therefore is to bring coldness to the consciousness of itself, of the reasons why it arose.

This emphatic focus on coldness would be of merely psychological interest were it not for Adorno's forwarding of it as the fundamental principle of bourgeois subjectivity, a thesis that this run of statements illustrates. In the first instance, the idea of coldness as the fundamental principle of bourgeois subjectivity echoes not only the obsessive concern for efficiency and order in the puritan, but quite generally the self-portrayal of liberal moral and political theory as conditioned by and premised upon mutual disinterest. Mutual disinterest, as I have interpreted it, is transmitted into bourgeois moral theory by the actual supervenience of instrumental rationality upon the material inference structures that had previously formed the empirical bonds among persons. Modern moral theory, nonetheless, took mutual disinterest as the condition of morality and justice (rather than as what makes either unintelligible). If the very idea of a moral norm is constructed upon the presupposition of lack of interest (often now coded as value pluralism), if it presupposes that what moral norms *do* is to correct my self-interest (or my as opposed to your idea of the good life), then moral and political practices built on that foundation will secretly transmit coldness as a morally legitimate stance toward others since they will presuppose that others are of no concern to me as what moral deliberation must override. Hence, the very idea of such deliberation has already neutralized and displaced others as a condition for the way in which they will eventually be counted in. Centralist morality is forged in coldness. Hence, even as bourgeois morality does, undeniably, urge appropriate moral "counting" of the existence of others, its *method* of counting contains an original indifference to them that is a "dis-counting" of them in the very gesture of their being counted in. Under such conditions, it is not surprising that some recipients have found the moral attention focused on them a perplexing form of denial; and more generally, that those addressed by moral principles and norms so forged should feel that those principles are intrinsically "external" to them. What I claim is that the coldness of bourgeois moral norms and principles, the moral point of view, is the affective source of the complaint against externalist morality.

As an inference from his naturalist locating of cognition, and by extension the material axis of the concept, Adorno presupposes that all cognition is conditioned by desire and need, mood and affect. So, for example, he comments that "the moment called 'cathexis' in psychology, thought's affective investment in the object, is not extrinsic to thought, not merely psychological, but rather the condition of its truth."[18] With-

18 "Opinion Delusion Society," in Theodor W. Adorno, *Critical Models: Interventions and Catchwords*, trans. Henry Pickford (New York: Columbia University Press, 1998), p. 109.

out affective investment, a concern for the object of cognitive attention, the affect of attending, Adorno contends that there occurs a blindness to the difference between the essential and inessential, between, we might say, what of the object must be appreciated intransitively and what transitive understanding licenses. Attending to an object is not a mechanical operation akin to turning a camera on a pivot or focussing a lens; on the contrary, some of what is uncanny about the mechanical look of the camera is its indifference to what lies before it, its not looking back. And that should serve as a clue as to what affective looks require. Affective investment, cathexis, is the sensuously active corollary of the sensuous impact of the object; the joining of cathexis and mimetic reaction form the full pull and tug of the object, its intrinsic cognitive mattering. Adorno equates object cathexis with "freedom toward the object"; again, it is the form of investment in the object that does not want to control or subsume, but to attend, interrogate, discover. If dependency is a condition of cognition, then acknowledging such dependency requires a reversal of standard conceptions of desire and freedom; object cathexis is desire against appropriation and a freedom "for" not "from." If cathexis is a primitive form of love, then Adorno's thesis comes down to the claim that all knowing that can take on the complexity of singular objects, events, and states of affairs is lover's knowledge, knowledge as guided by loving attention. In one of his few explicit statements in this direction, Adorno comments:

> Unbroken and all to human slogans lend themselves to new equations between the subject and what is not its like. Things congeal as fragments of that which was subjugated; to rescue means to love things. We cannot eliminate from the dialectics of remainders what is experienced by consciousness as an alien thing: negatively, coercion and heteronomy, but also the marred figure of what we should love, and what the spell, the endogamy of consciousness, does not permit us to love. (ND, 191)

Given that this is almost immediately followed by one of Adorno's phrasings of the state of reconciliation, it is fair to infer that a rejoining of love and knowledge, eros and cognition would belong to utopia.

Adorno rarely discusses the lover's knowledge thesis, since identity thinking's claim to independence, its curtailment of the material axis of the concept in all its moments, is fundamental to our own image of the self-sufficiency of reason. And at one level, given the real triumph of identity thinking, there is a reality to that curtailment: there has been, generally, a withdrawal of affect, of cathexis, from the object, and when it does occur now it tends to be mediated by a cathexis originally directed at the self. This is how object-directedness now comes to be narcissistically constituted, a wanting of the object, and an investment in it, as a reassuring mirror of the self. Instrumental knowing is the universalized form of the narcissistic derangement of object cathexis. What occurs in this movement is a withdrawal and a curtailment of affective investment, a drawing back and in, a redirecting of affective bonds toward the self, with the object as ever only its passing reflection. When all this is set in a practical context, there emerges an underlying lack of concern for the object in its specificity, a material a priori indifference toward the object which is the precise affective analogue of the indifference of the simple concept and what is governed by it to what falls under it; it is the same indifference in its logical and materially inscribed form. Coldness is the material inscription of logical indifference; coldness is the mood, the *Stimmung*, of identity thinking in its exploded bourgeois form.[19]

This thesis first emerges in *Dialectic of Enlightenment* in the context of a discussion of bourgeois morality's critique of pity and compassion, and its affirmation of stoical hardness. We can come to understand the moral significance of coldness as the fundamental principle of bourgeois subjectivity if we follow out Adorno's conceptual construction of it in relation to bourgeois morality's critique of compassion. For Adorno it is the way compassion is displaced that best reveals the coldness in bourgeois morality, and by extension the subject that is in part formed by that morality; always remembering that bourgeois morality is only a part of the rationalization of society through which bourgeois subjectivity is formed.

The prelude to the discussion of the critique of compassion in the text is Nietzsche's contention that regret and remorse, as backward-looking emotions, refuse the temporal conditioning of human action, that what is done cannot be undone – a thought which by itself would dislocate moral remainders from the domain of morality. The Marquis de Sade joins Nietzsche in this thought and extends it:

> If repentance is senseless, then pity is sin pure and simple. Whoever surrenders to compassion "perverts the general law; whence it results that pity, far from being a virtue, becomes a real vice once it leads us to interfere with an inequality prescribed by nature's laws." Sade and Nietzsche recognized that after the formalization of reason, *pity still remained as, so to speak, a sensual consciousness of the identity of the general and the particular*, as naturalized mediation. (DoE, 101; emphasis mine)

Compassion is the historical archetype of what now appears, even more remotely, as only a moral addendum; on Adorno's telling, compassion, as the sensual consciousness of the identity of general and particular, was already in the nineteenth century fast becoming only a remnant.

Remarkably, both rationalist and Nietzschean, affirmative moralities

19 Heidegger, *Being and Time*, section 29, explores the interconnectedness of mood and understanding. Adorno adopts a Freudian way to prosecute this idea.

consistently manifest a severe distrust of the form of responsiveness to the suffering of others exemplified by compassion. For Spinoza, "pity, in a man who lives under the guidance of reason, is in itself bad and useless," since the goal of pity is to relieve the victim from misery, and only "at the dictation of reason are we able to perform an action, which we know for certain to be good."[20] For Kant, compassion was "softheartedness" and without the "dignity of virtue." Susceptibility to compassion is likened to "the communication of warmth or contagious diseases . . . since it spreads by natural means among men living near one another." The analogy to contagious disease sets in place the identification of man with misfortune which is to be rejected: "When another person suffers and, although I cannot help him, I let myself be infected by his sorrow (by means of my imagination), then the two of us suffer, though evil actually (in nature) affects only one."[21] Passive compassion produces two evils, two instances of suffering, when there was only one before; thus, it cannot be a duty to feel compassion since there cannot be a duty to increase the amount of suffering in the world. Suffering that cannot be eliminated, which must be borne and suffered, removes human dignity because only the rational part of the rational animal provides humanity. Thus no value can be ascribed to the mere sharing of suffering, animal solidarity. Almost from compassion, Kant sides against nonpractical sympathy. Only in relation to what is not suffering, the moral law itself, can suffering be meaningful.

Coldness may thus arise from a desire to strengthen virtue or from a pained screening from consciousness of the limitless character of suffering beyond control and endurance. Because spontaneous compassion does not necessarily calculate or prepare for action, but in the first instance finds its worth in identification itself, it appears to threaten both the claim to dignity which resides in rational or self-legislating action alone, and to ensconce us within an overwhelming and finally humanity-destroying merely sentient world. By means subtle and moral, coldness becomes the necessary condition for morally surviving in a cold world. The radical abrogation of compassion plausibly thus becomes the categorially affective condition through which the body can be de-animated, mechanized, and consciousness elevated, making ensoulment not a formation of animal embodiment but the unique prerogative of the uncontaminated spontaneity of consciousness. Without the generalized suppression of compassion as a fundament for ethical action secular subjectivity would not have been able to sustain the categorial depreciation of the animal body – a depreciation which, granted, Western subjectivity has been working away at since its inception.

20 Spinoza, *Ethics,* trans. R. H. M. Elwes (New York: Dover Publications, 1951), book 4, proposition. L.

21 Immanuel Kant, *The Metaphysics of Morals* in *Practical Philosophy,* trans. Mary J. Gregor (Cambridge: Cambridge University Press, 1996), section 34, p. 575.

The coldness of bourgeois morality is its removal of compassion as a governing reason for action, as if to respond as compassion requires goes against what is properly moral.[22] The rationalization of this belief depends upon a variety of familiar and not very plausible theses: emotions are blind and arbitrary, non-rational and non-cognitive; because arbitrary, compassion lacks the ability to generate the requisite consistency morality is meant to supply; passions, as emotions, infringe upon the autonomy of the subject; only what is under my immediate control can be essentially mine, a thesis integral to the Cartesian and Kantian conceptions of subjectivity. This last thesis is the most invidious since it intimately connects the idea of instrumental rationality with subjectivity, what is essentially mine or me, as such, as if what cannot be immediately determined or controlled by me will eventually figure in what can bring me, my life, to ruin; anything that can so figure is hence intrinsically "not me." This is the logical expression of the negation of this thesis that living is susceptibility to pain and injury. In its converse form, that is, only the determinations of instrumental rationality itself can count as products of spontaneity since only they are truly not heteronomous; this thesis is responsible for the way in which instrumental rationality comes to absorb spontaneity and autonomy. The linkage is unsurprising. It is also this last thesis which must be responsible for the transformation of the idea of things we suffer or undergo from being neutrally composed of things both pleasurable and awful into a wholly negative category, the overwhelming sense now that anything "suffered" is something negative or destructive. The suppression of compassion thus belongs to the syndrome of rationalizations through which, more generally, animal embodiment is read out of human normative self-understanding.

The metaphysical excision of passivity, dependency, heteronomy, the animal and responsive body has a precise moral equivalent. For Horkheimer and Adorno the deepest moral source for the eschewal of compassion and the source of bourgeois morality's categorial coldness is its unwillingness to "equate man with misfortune," that is, to equate human life with its constitutive vulnerabilities and indefinite susceptibility to injury. These philosophers, they argue, "looked on the existence of misfortune as an outrage. The very sensitivity of their impotence could not suffer man to be pitied. In despair, they lent their voices to the celebration of power, but disclaimed allegiance to it in practice – while constructing the causeways of power" (DoE, 103). Vulnerability and injury cannot be indefinite without curtailing the rationality of experience as a whole. The dignity of man as a rational being would be permanently infringed upon if life were equated with misfortune. So the power of rea-

22 Although it would require detailing, almost certainly the direction of formation runs from the depreciation of animal embodiment to the depreciation of compassion.

son (the Baconian equation) is introduced in order to bring the removal of pain within the ambit of an instrumental rationality that can act with certainty, thereby proposing the ideal elimination of the threat. Ideal elimination becomes constitutive, however, only if compassion itself is supplanted; suffering matters only as an object of rational action, of what moral action can cope with, and not otherwise. In this way, suffering is not seen unless it is "morally" seen, that is, seen in the prospect of the certainty of removing it and not from my co-suffering. Replacing or displacing compassion by reason is what constitutes the latter's coldness, a coldness, a denial of the appropriateness of responsiveness, which is both a part of the neutralization of reason (and its object), their disenchantment, the assimilation of the animate to the inanimate, and an unintended preparation for colluding with and promoting what it was designed to remove.

When Zarathustra proclaims, "So much justice and compassion, so much weakness," he identifies terms, justice and compassion, that initially conflict:

> [Compassion] confirms the rule of inhumanity by the exception it practices. By reserving the cancellation of injustice to fortuitous love of one's neighbor, compassion accepts that the law of universal alienation, which it would mitigate, is unalterable. Certainly, as an individual, the compassionate man represents the claim of the generality – that is, to live – against the generality, against nature and society, who deny it. But the unity with the universal, as with the heart, which the individual displays, is shown to be deceptive in his own weakness. It is not softness but the restrictive element in pity which makes it questionable; for compassion is always inadequate (DoE, 102–3).

Compassion's inadequacy, its being restricted to just this suffering here, can lead to its abuse: its substitution for justice or the narcissistic self-congratulations of the philanthropist. It is the former complaint that is primary for Horkheimer and Adorno; compassion is inadequate since its cancellation of injustice is limited, leaving both the breadth and causes of misery standing. Compassionate relief aid to the starving helps some but not all, and leaves the causes of hunger unaltered. This is the real problem with pity, and not its "softness" to which stoical coldness is the antidote. But in saying this, Adorno and Horkheimer must have an affirmative view of compassion that contrasts with its displacement by rationalized reason. Their affirmative conception of compassion, which again I am construing as the historic archetype for the moral addendum, must enable the material motive which Adorno contends is the premise and upshot of the moral addendum. Arguably, a reasonable logic of compassion can support that perception.

Compassion expresses a solidarity of human beings which is a part of the "solidarity of life in general."[23] Horkheimer and Adorno are not attempting to promote compassion over justice – compassion is "always inadequate." Rather, they are diagnosing and revealing the coldness of rationalist morality, and its consequent distrust of contingency, sensuousness, and vulnerability as constitutive conditions of human experience in the very midst of the attempt to remove what such may bring. Seen aright, compassion's fortuitousness enunciates a naturalized mediation of universal and particular since in immediately taking your pain as a reason for my acting I treat your suffering as equivalent with my own; and hence even when acting is impossible, my co-suffering with you functions as a bond between us, a *valuing* of your hurt as what should not be. But it is a premise of the simplest forms of compassionate bonding that the suffering which is the object of the emotion is perceived as what is antithetic to what is the good of an other's animal body. Hence, compassion immediately figures the integrity of the body, its freedom from pain and suffering, as of value.

The most direct route to supporting this conception of compassionate perception is by a considering of our animal relation to our pains, that is, primitive human responses to pain on analogy with how the higher animals respond to their pains. From the perspective of animal behavior, it can be argued that acting in response to one's own pain, seeking to remove it, *is* the valuing of bodily integrity. The pattern of animal pain behavior is purposive; it intends not just the silencing of the pain, on the anaesthetic model, but its prevention and removal. Hence, bodily integrity is shown to be something valued by the fact that the pattern of response to pain and suffering is toward their elimination when possible. So pain is naturally perceived as injury to body integrity, as a negative value, and hence as a reason for action. But this is equivalent to saying that the mere having of an animal life in and of itself is a work of valuing. Seeking its pleasures and well-being, and seeking to avoid its suffering and injury is how the animal body expresses its valuing of itself, even when no other values are circulating, hence even in the case of non-human animal bodies.

If seeking to remove pain is an expression of valuing life, then compassionately responding to another's pain is valuing it as the other does and thereby expresses that value. Hence compassionate action is the natural valuing of life, in the light of life as valuing, as shared and social. Compassion as natural mediation between universal and particular is one of the most primitive material inference structures creating an empirical bond between living beings; natural nurturing and protection of the young are other such bonds. By mediating the value of life that value it-

23 Max Horkheimer, "Morality and Materialism," trans. G. Frederick Hunter and John Torpey, *Telos* 69 (Fall 1986): 107.

self comes to form a bond; the bond is normative since it establishes the valuing of life as what draws us together and regulates interaction. When I said earlier, in discussing Wittgenstein on living bodies, that the discriminating perception that categorially distinguishes the living from nonliving cognitively experiences the material a priori that is the condition for normativity, as opposed to stance taking, it was this thought about life, pain, and valuing I had in mind. Valuing is natural; it emerges with, at least, those forms of life that can suffer pains and pleasures, and can seek to remove and have them.[24]

Only in virtue of having vulnerable animal bodies that can suffer pain and which spontaneously seek to remove pains is there valuing, an expressing of what ought and ought not to be; and in compassion the singular condition of animal embodiment, one's striving to protect the integrity of one's own body, is presented or expressed as a generality. That generality is always, again, inadequate, but it adumbrates and anticipates the generality that justice would be. Full justice, Adorno and Horkheimer imply, receives its sense from the "injustice" it would correct, suffering and the causes of suffering, from compassion *and* the correction of its "unjust" limitation. Pain behavior reveals the value of life and life as valuing; compassion's generality turns suffering into injustice, as what ought not to be generally, and its arbitrariness reveals the unjustness of its limitation. Full or political justice corrects the unjust limitation of compassion, that only this one here because here and not elsewhere is rescued. There is nothing amiss in either the rescue or its particularity, only the arbitrariness of the limitation. I cannot mean your suffering is deserving of alleviation as a consequence of compassion without recognizing that it could have been another here and they would have been rescued and not you, or that no one was about to do the rescuing and hence no rescue occurred. Political justice completes the small justice of compassion; the unjust limitation of compassion unfolding, as if for the first time and however haltingly, the simultaneous indexicality and generality of ethical life. Whether or not a conception of justice can be constructed along these lines, I do not know. But at least the hint of compassion as primitive justice, and political justice the correction of compassion's natural injustice indicates how Adorno and Horkheimer conceive of the animal solidarity represented by compassion as prefiguring political justice in its weighty sense.

No simple path leads from compassion to justice. Perceiving the injustice of compassion would depend upon being able to acknowledge the accidentality of compassionate rescue. Compassion requires reason for

24 I am condensing a far more complex set of connections. For some splendid pages elaborating these connections that, appropriately tailored, would fill in the gaps, see Korsgaard, *The Sources of Normativity*, pp. 147–56.

its completion; there is no intrinsic contradiction between them. How could there be if compassion is ethical reason in naturalized form? Yet, as Rousseau's diagnosis underlines, the association of compassion with human weakness and unlimited dependency and of reason with independence has led to the latter displacing the former. Reason, which is here being understood much as Adorno and Horkheimer understand it, opens the space through which commiseration – "a sentiment that is obscure and strong in savage man, and developed but weak in civilized man"[25] – can be evaded, its claims silenced. Since it so aptly and powerfully construes the coldness of bourgeois reason, Rousseau's account is worth instancing.

> Now it is evident that this identification [with the suffering animal] must have been infinitely closer in the state of nature than in the state of reasoning. Reasoning engenders vanity and reflection fortifies it; reason turns man back on himself, it separates him from all that bothers and afflicts him. Philosophy isolates him; because of it he says in secret, at the sight of a suffering man: Perish if you will, I am safe. No longer can anything except dangers to the entire society trouble the tranquil sleep of the philosopher and tear him from his bed. His fellow-man can be murdered with impunity right under his window; he has only to put his hands over his ears and argue with himself for a bit to prevent nature, which revolts in him, from identifying with the man who is being assassinated.[26]

However apparently hyperbolic this chilling passage, its structure of avoidance demonstrates the possibility of there being an utter intimacy between rational morality and moral indifference that is for Adorno the presupposition for the intelligibility of how Auschwitz could happen.

In Auschwitz "it was no longer the individual who died but a specimen." The methodical, procedurally refined, administrative handling of the victims deprived them of their sensuous particularity as the preparatory condition and form of their slaughter. Again, Adorno is not saying that the brutal proceduralism of the death camps is the same as the proceduralisms of enlightened moralities. Rather, what binds those proceduralisms together is their structure of indifference, the logical indifference of universal to particular and the affective coldness secreted by that logical indifference. Affectively, for others to not matter is neither an automatic presupposition of everyday experience nor when it occurs always of the same stripe. Others cannot matter to me because my attention and affect are directed elsewhere, or because they lack characteristics I presume necessary for mattering, or because they are irrele-

25 Jean-Jacques Rousseau, *The First and Second Discourses,* trans. Roger D. and Judith R. Masters (New York: St. Martin's Press, 1964), p. 132.
26 Ibid.

vant to my concerns, or because I am dumbly self-consumed. And others can matter negatively by being objects of hate, spite, resentment, fear, threat. Coldness is the specific form of not mattering that attends instrumental rationality.

We now know that the call to coldness and hardness, the stoical virtues celebrated by Spinoza, Kant, Nietzsche, and which Adorno will impose upon himself (there are no innocents here), was at the center of Himmler's Posen address of 1943 to the SS in which he sought to prepare his elite core for the task of carrying out the work of the final solution. The ethical core of Himmler's address could be paraphrased as follows: "Each member of the SS, and by extension each German citizen, will know of a Jew that is an exception to the rule of them as a race of vermin. If we allowed each of us to have their own 'good Jew,' then the extermination of the Jews would not be possible. We must harden ourselves against compassion for the odd, but indefinitely multiple, good Jew. Each member of the SS, and by extension each German citizen, would be revolted and horrified at the piles of bodies which mass extermination requires. You, the SS, have been hardened by experience to be able to stand the sight of heaped corpses and yet remain decent. You must take on this hardness as the necessary means for completing your task. It is terrible, a task which ordinary human compassion would prevent. It is a task that ordinary consciousness could not carry out. Your training in coldness prepares you for the act. As a consequence, the SS must take on the responsibility for carrying out the Final Solution for the German people, and you must take the secret of having done so to your grave."[27] That Himmler presupposes that it is not ordinary morality but compassion that would be the greatest bar to the carrying out of the administrative murder is telling if Adorno is right in considering compassion itself, in the midst of bourgeois morality, as a remnant. Ordinary morality apparently presents no particular obstruction.

Hence we can consider this address as offering the inverse of compassion's unjust limitation: since the rule of compassionate exception can be multiplied, then potentially each Jew could be an object of compassionate rescue. No administrative policy could succeed if each individual who is its object can be considered in the light of any other individual's judgement of their appropriateness or inappropriateness. Administrative handling presupposes abstraction from sensuous particularity, each German having their own "good Jew," and must operate in a wholly mechanical

27 An edited version of Himmler's address appears in Lucy Davidowicz (ed.), *The Holocaust Reader* (West Orange, N.J.: Berman House, 1976), pp. 130–40. For a telling treatment of Himmler's address, see Peter Haidu, "The Dialectics of Unspeakability: Language, Silence, and the Narratives of Desubjectification," in Saul Friedlander (ed.), *Probing the Limits of Representation: Nazism and the "Final Solution"* (Cambridge, Mass: Harvard University Press, 1992), pp. 277–99.

manner if it is to be effective. For that to be possible, compassion must be silenced. Silencing compassion requires becoming cold, where coldness is the affect of indifference toward sensuous particularity. Further, it is the same coldness that is the condition of abstraction from particularity that is necessary in order to carry on acting methodically and consistently in the midst of revolting carnage. The coldness that enables this is the condition of remaining "decent," that is not being ruinously affected by the sight of carnage, and hence remaining a self-determining and rule-observing agent, mindful of all the moral distinctions that organize the world. In this extreme case, but it is the extreme case of those directly responsible for carrying the genocide, duty, coldness, and industrially organized slaughter congeal into a brutal but intelligible constellation.

A moralized coldness, secrecy, and a hidden shame (extreme coldness is not without cost on its subject) gather in Himmler's speech. Whatever was done in the name of the German people and in the midst of the Polish nation, it was not an absolutely secret venture.[28] Adorno's thesis can thus be interpreted as claiming that the extreme case of the SS, where coldness becomes an explicit affective ingredient in the prosecution of the Jewish genocide, cannot have arisen and become effective for them unless it was prepared for, and that preparation is equally central to the comprehension of the willingness of the rest of the population to collude. The preparation is the pervasiveness of identity thinking, from rationalized morality to bureaucratic rationality and capitalist economic calculations, and the coldness it exudes; it is coldness as the fundamental principle of bourgeois subjectivity.

What is at issue here is typically misfocused in commentary on the Nazi genocide, as if we needed to discover in the Nazis and the German people as a whole some demon, call it "radical evil," or some punctual reflective failure, call it "thoughtlessness," or some ideology or form of false consciousness, call them "race hatred" and "scapegoating," that would explain the horror. Part of what is wrong with these responses to the Shoah is that they are looking in the wrong place, as if the emergence, carrying out, and national complicity in the Jewish genocide could be explained through a single, unidirectional, and simple narrative. Even at the level of asking how people could be brought to carry out the details of the final solution it does not make sense to look for a one-note answer, if for no other reason than for a range of individuals there will be different answers: some willing, some unwilling; there will be military rules to be obeyed and fear of punishment for not obeying; there will be questions of solidarity and shame before one's comrades; there will be in all cases habituation, a practice at killing, and a getting used to it; there will be guilt feelings for some

28 See Daniel Jonah Goldhagen, *Hitler's Willing Executioners: Ordinary Germans and the Holocaust* (London: Little Brown, 1996).

and not others, and the use of alcohol to deal with those feelings.[29] And versions of what can be said about those directly involved can be modified for the surrounding populace. Adorno's thesis is that coldness was the *pre*-condition for the host of complicating factors to kick in; and coldness could serve as a precondition precisely because it is integral to bourgeois subjectivity independently of particular circumstances and conditions. Consider again Himmler's address: race hatred is not enough because, apart from the very few of whom Himmler supposes that SS themselves do not belong, it will be riddled with exceptionality. Thoughtlessness presupposes indifference, and cannot be used to explain it. Fear of reprisal assumes there are not countervailing moral pressures that could silence fear. In each case we need to see how other explanatory factors contribute to and depend on the constellation of coldness, rationalized experience, and bourgeois subjectivity. The coldness necessary to complete the task, to participate directly or indirectly or to just to let it happen without resistance, tapped a coldness already there.

Let me pursue this thought from the opposing angle.[30] Late in September 1943, after taking over the government, bureaucracy, police, and military of Denmark, the Germans set in motion preparations to arrest all of the country's Jews on October 1 and 2. For whatever reasons, word of this was leaked to the Danes. Within a few weeks 7,500 of the 8,000 Danish Jews had been carried to safety in neutral Sweden. For this to occur, the vast majority of the Danish people had to participate, directly or indirectly: hiding, feeding, transporting, keeping silent. Nor is that all. Danish officials convinced Adolf Eichmann that the unfortunate 481 Jews who were captured should be kept in Theresienstadt, away from the Polish extermination camps. Through the intervention of the Danish civil service and church groups, almost all of those captured survived with 700 packages a month of clothing, food, and vitamins being sent to the Jews in the camp. When the Jews returned to Denmark after the war they returned to homes and shops in perfect order.

There are historical complexities aplenty here: Unlike others, the Danes offered almost no resistance to the Germans when they were invaded in 1940, and 17,000 Danes fought for Germany on the Eastern Front. On the other hand, and almost in exchange for their quick capitulation, the Germans let Denmark maintain its sovereignty, becoming

29 For a fine, complex sense of how ordinary people could become killing machines see Christopher Browning, *Ordinary Men: Reserve Police Battalion 101 and the Final Solution in Poland* (New York: HarperCollins, 1992). For a helpful comparison of Browning with Goldhagen which attempts to extend the complex answer view, see Clendinnen, *Reading the Holocaust,* chapter 7.

30 I owe the historical details and argument of this and the following paragraphs to Judith Goldstein, "Facts and Myths: The Holocaust, The Rescue of Danish Jewry and 'Schindler's List,'" unpublished ms.

Hitler's "model protectorate." Nonetheless, and throughout it all, the Danes refused to forsake their tradition of toleration; the Jewish population remained protected. And that protection turned into the far more substantial and heroic collective act of rescuing nearly every member of the Danish Jewish community. So we have here a systematic and national act of rescue. Rescue was possible, and in Denmark it was accomplished. How? In this case, it would appear that a unique synthesis of Christian and democratic ideals was formed that was sufficient to mobilize the entire Danish population. According to Frode Jakobsen, the leader of the Danish resistance movement,

> Moral indignation was the true origin of the Danish resistance. . . . And nothing created so much anger as the persecution of our good compatriots, the Jews. . . . The Jewish people became a symbol to us of tortured mankind. And those who treated other human beings like that – there could be no doubt in our hearts that we had to fight them with all our power. . . . What we experienced was the suffering of humanity, concentrated in the suffering of the Jewish people as so many, many times before. . . .[31]

In Jakobsen's words I hear exactly the great impulse of Christianity to "eradicate the coldness which permeates all things." More pointedly, the impulse converges on the suffering of others as being unconscionable, as if the "bodily sensation of the moral addendum" did not here have to await painful retrospection but was able to emerge in the midst of the disaster. That the Danish rescue effort was both national and all but complete, and that it was, arguably, moved by passionate indignation at suffering must be telling.

Himmler's Posen address and the Danish rescue are contrasting poles, the one explicitly calling for coldness as the affective condition for the carrying out of genocide, the other moved by the sight and anticipation of suffering to secure rescue. I am unsure what, in short compass, would secure the contrast between coldness and compassion as forming the categorial stakes of bourgeois subjectivity at a certain moment, but the contrast between the Himmler address and the Danish rescue, two events which are arguably exemplary for each side of the equation, fit uncannily with Adorno's diagnosis.

Coldness is part of the "grammar" of rationalized conceptuality, having a place in both its institutional operation and its reflective employment. The union of the two in practice must be formative for the subject using and subjected to it. Which is why Adorno considers coldness the fundamental principle of bourgeois subjectivity. Instrumental reason can

31 Quoted in ibid., p. 10.

secrete coldness and indifference because it disengages the connection between responding to the world from thinking about the world. Insofar as the disengagement of response and cognition occurs, and I have argued that it is explicit in the very idea of acting on universalist moral principles, coldness is a consequence. Coldness is the affective correlate of a conceptuality that wants to secure knowledge, meaning, order, and self-possession independently of the vicissitudes of contingent experience. The cost of withholding responsiveness is always the defeat of the withholder; as a consequence of disenchantment and the rationalization of society, that cost is all but universally incurred. Adorno's "bodily sensation of the moral addendum," which I hear as the operative force of the Danish rescue, hence forms a counter-image, and counter-pressure, to the coldness secreted by identifying reason.

What is awkward for the reader here is Adorno's concession to coldness, its necessity and continued place. The disengagement of reason and response cannot be undone at will, their reconciliation achieved by force. If abhorrence is the sufficient material motive for the new imperative, it does not follow that from henceforth we can simply trust our empathic projections and compassionate reactions. If the reach of the culture of identity thinking and instrumental reason is all but universal, and disenchantment all but complete, then conduct must be governed by the extremes of cold reason and passionate response; the radical separation of reason and response must inform the reason that would think that separation and the conditions of its dissolution. It is the structural block between reason and response, which he construes as being equivalent to the claim that there are no oases of innocence in social experience, that leads Adorno to enjoin on the intellectual "inviolable isolation" as the only way of showing "some measure of solidarity": "All collaboration, all the human worth of social mixing and participation, merely means tacit acceptance of inhumanity. It is the sufferings of men that should be shared: the smallest step towards their pleasures is one towards the hardening of their pains" (MM, A5). The second sentence is what prevents the first sentence, and what leads up to it, from collapsing into the elitist, self-righteous priggishness it forebodes.

Adorno knows that the distinction is conceptual and not practical: there is no humanly sustainable route to sharing in general suffering but not sharing in general pleasures. The point rather is to circumscribe the meaning of the isolation and the reflective effort of distancing necessary for serious intellectual work. Adorno knows as well that the isolation of the intellectual, their "privileged" ability to attempt to frame a "private life" resembling one "worthy of man," is illusory just by the fact that it is withdrawn from general realization (MM, A6). Nor does standing aloof make the intellectual better.

> The detached observer is as much entangled as the active participant; the only advantage of the former is insight into his entanglement, and the infinitesimal freedom that lies in knowledge as such. His own distance from business at large is a luxury which only that business confers. That is why the very movement of withdrawal bears features of what it negates. It is forced to develop a coldness indistinguishable from that of the bourgeois. (MM, A6)

Coldness, like fidelity earlier, is imposed and affirmed; it is affirmed against its imposition as the unavoidable means of undoing that imposition.

The imposition of coldness is just the existence of a guilt context, that is, a context in which the activities of thought unavoidably deploy the very forms they seek to transfigure. What distinguishes the coldness of the philosopher from that other coldness is just the guilt that makes it, mediately, a response. Nothing for us is new in this thought. In the "Meditations," however, Adorno does broach a new question, namely, is this context of guilt all? If the coldness of philosophy has any meaning, if not participating in easy solidarity is vindicable, then this must be because this form of life is not definitive. To say that this form of life is not definitive is to contend that, say, a wholly naturalistic and pragmatic understanding of life does not exhaust its possibilities. If Adorno is right in interpreting rationalized reason as but the transformation of self-preservative drives into mentality, then in pragmatically seeking the amelioration of the world's ills we are acting in thrall to a conception of life, mind, and reason that denies that there is anything "more" than (human) life and death. In asking this question, then, Adorno means to place metaphysics back on the agenda, where by metaphysics he does mean what was once upon a time understood as providing life with just such a meaning beyond its own immanent terms of reference. For Adorno there is no prospect of a resolution to the problem of nihilism without metaphysics and its transformation.

9

ETHICAL MODERNISM

1. Introduction

If the inference from Auschwitz, understood in terms of a negative theodicy, to the new categorical imperative is sound, it nonetheless falls well short of demonstrating, even in principle, that a wholly secular form of life can be rationally compelling and intrinsically motivating. The eschatological destruction of meaning in Auschwitz casts a shadow over the new imperative which can only say "never again!" to it. Even if we could conceive of arranging our thoughts and actions in a manner ensuring that Auschwitz would not be repeated, and it remains quite unclear what *in detail* this would amount to, how we could *ensure* this without utterly transforming our present form of life, even so there is no obvious reason to believe that the virtuous lives of individuals corresponding to such an arrangement would be happy, satisfying, meaningful. Thus one can say either that the new, contextually defined imperative on its own because negatively constructed is so indeterminate about what a form of life resistant to a repetition of Auschwitz would look like that its satisfaction would require the depiction of a new form of life, or, more simply, that the new imperative shares the meaning deficit of all negative versions of moral principles: "It heeds the prohibition of graven images, refrains from positive depiction, and . . . refers negatively to damaged life instead of pointing affirmatively to the good life."[1]

Although tempting, the indeterminacy and incompleteness of the new imperative must not be understood grammatically in terms of the distinction between the moral and the ethical, the former being concerned with the *limits* of individual (or collective) human action demanded by, what it is to acknowledge and respect, the presence of others, and the latter being concerned with the *ends* of human action.[2] However this dis-

1 Habermas, *Moral Consciousness and Communicative Action*, p. 205.

2 Jürgen Habermas, "On the Pragmatic, the Ethical, and the Moral Employments of Prac-

tinction is conceived – as between the moral and the prudential (widely understood), categorical imperatives and hypothetical imperatives, deontological considerations versus consequentialist considerations – there are both substantive and formal reasons to set it aside. Substantively, the cleaving of normative experience into the structural differentiation between what is good for me and what is demanded in order to respect the presence of others genealogically looks like a product of the supervening of instrumental reason on the previous structures of material inference. Until that moment of supervenience, I have suggested, there was no clear distinction to be drawn between civilization as humanity (morality) and civilization as instrumentality (prudence). Honesty can be indeterminately both the right thing to do and a prudentially good policy until there is a wholly separate accounting system; once there is such a system, then Kant's bewildered grocer needs an autonomous moral logic to enable him to act honestly on principle rather than from self-interest. It is inconceivable that the distinction should not drive morality inward, leaving it permanently exposed to sceptical erosion. To support the grammatical distinction between the moral and the prudential is to reify the destruction of the empirical bonds that earlier material inferences represented, making the grocer's dilemma, as it may be put, permanent.

And if we inquire of our paradigm inference from *bleeding badly* to *I'll apply a tourniquet,* should we say that it is moral or prudential? Since it is not directly about my limiting my actions, my not harming or interfering with others, then it is not directly moral. Since it is not directly concerned with my realizing my individual ends, unless I so happen to desire to help those in distress, then it is not directly prudential. There are fairly simple ways that would permit either moral or prudential interpretations of the inference, but, against the background of the directness of the material inference interpretation and a reasonable genealogy, choosing one in favor of the other and thereby the distinction between limit and end appears ethically otiose. An argument that contrived a conception of justice from compassion would have a similar result. Quite generally, one may think that if ethical material inferences depend on the sight of injurable bodies, then they are going to be neutral with respect to the prudence/morality distinction or, better, indifferently entwine them. Insofar as others are bodies, then in noting their injurability we are simultaneously acknowledging their intrinsic being for themselves, hence their possession of ends that are unique to them – the experiential premise of animism. Insofar as suffering and injury are immediately (prima facie or defeasible) reasons for responding to others, then others are fundamen-

tical Reason," in his *Justification and Application: Remarks on Discourse Ethics,* trans. Ciaran Cronin (Oxford: Polity Press, 1993), pp. 1–17. For a refutation, see my *Recovering Ethical Life,* chapter 4.

tally open and exposed, and thereby to be aided. Injurable bodies are intrinsically both independent and dependent; hence material inferences that recognize them are *simultaneously* both a recognizing of their being for self and of their infinite exposure and vulnerability. Only when those streams are sundered does morality become imponderable and prudential self-interest inexorable.

The formal issue concerns the ontological possibility of an enchanted world; specifying that thought will take a moment. I have claimed that the new imperative is nothing other than an explicitly ethical formulation of the normative movement of negative dialectics itself, a reflective acknowledgement of the excess of damaged objects beyond their identifications grounded, in this case, not on guilt but abhorrence. The necessity of the new imperative presupposes not only the logical and existential non-self-sufficiency of identity thinking, but far more tendentiously that animistic auratic individuality and a form of thinking appropriate to it are possible, otherwise abhorrence would not be abhorrence at individuals turned to specimens. To demonstrate that the transformation of individuals into specimens is intolerable is not to demonstrate that a materialistically premised, animistic, auratic individuality is rationally intelligible. Narrowly, this means only that, as Adorno continuously reminds us, negative dialectics is determined by identity thinking and draws its strength from it; if the new imperative is only an ethical articulation of the reflective movement of negative dialectics, then it too is bound to identity thinking. More than anything else, it is this which makes the imperative "negative." And it is why the final section of the "Meditations" insists upon dialectics turning against itself. Critique, Adorno states,

> destroys the claim of identity by testing and honoring it; therefore, it can reach no farther than that claim. The claim is a magic circle that stamps critique with the appearance of absolute knowledge. It is up to the self-reflection of critique to extinguish that claim, to extinguish it in the very negation of negation that will not become a positing. Dialectics is the self-consciousness of the objective context of delusion; it does not mean to have escaped from that context. Its objective goal is to break out of the context from within. (ND, 406)

This thought in context has two sides. On the one hand, it means to point to the limits of philosophy. Dialectics is only the self-critique of the identitarian concept, that form of conceptuality that contends that it can retrieve the intelligibility of experience reflectively; the claims of the simple concept and the conception of philosophy as a grounding or founding enterprise, the reflective grasp of the inherent intelligibility and meaning of existence are one. Dialectics spoils that claim. But the spoiling is ambiguous; if the force of dialectics depends on identity thinking, then its medium is essentially and necessarily the concept. If philosophy now attempted to become concrete, to paste bits of reality into its texts, it would forfeit its own powers while pretending that another form of conceptuality had already appeared. Philosophy as dialectics lives on because the moment to realize it was missed.

On the other hand, critique is not logically or rationally self-sufficient, most directly because the concept is not, in truth, self-sufficient. With the new imperative, which again is itself just an ethical statement of negative dialectics (or even, more weakly, a statement of its necessity), that lack of self-sufficiency takes on a specific shading: the negativity of the imperative presupposes what a pure conceptual demonstration cannot show, namely, that a cognition of auratic individuality on materialist premises is *possible*. Nothing to here has demonstrated the *actual possibility* of enchanted experience, auratic individuality. On the contrary, it is premise of Adorno's enterprise – the guilt context of the living, the whole is the untrue, there is no right living in wrong life – that there are no actual possibilities in contemporary experience that point toward a future structurally discontinuous with it; identity thinking has poisoned both the institutions and general practices of modern social existence. The need to demonstrate the possibility of a cognition of auratic individuality dovetails now with the fourth element of Henrich's concept of moral insight, namely, that moral insight into the good has ontological implications, and hence the account of the good projects a conception of the world in which the reality of the good (and its possibility of occlusion through evil) is accommodated. Thus far nothing in Adorno's argument has demonstrated that accommodation.

But we now know as well that such a demonstration is going to be inherently problematic. Evidently, a demonstration of logical possibility is insufficient. But equally, it is a premise of the entire analysis that there are no actual possibilities of what would be different. Hence, the space of demonstration that Adorno's analysis seeks to inhabit is one lodged somewhere between logical possibility and actual possibility, where actual (causal) possibility is the strong one of realizing structural tendencies in present practices through identifiable steps. Adorno makes four initially surprising claims about this space between logical and actual possibility: (1) because it will "transcend" the closed context of immanence of identity thinking, that is, transcend the narrow confines of a world construed in reductively naturalistic terms, then, *qua* transcendence, it will overlap with the space of traditional metaphysics; (2) the most compelling demand for metaphysical thought from within a secular perspective is that found in Kant's "Postulates of Pure Practical Reason" (Adorno's new imperative requires its "postulates" for all but the same reasons as Kant originally did); (3) the joining of immanent and materialist critiques of Kant's "Postulates" shows that their truth content is an imagining of otherness that transcends "empirical" experience, an imagining that would allow empirical experience as specified by the understanding to be united with moral experience as demanded by reason; (4) but the *imaginary* space between logical and real possibility which the critique of the "Postulates" elaborates is precisely the space of modernist art practices. Hence, actual art practices, which are *material* practices producing "auratic individuals" but in an autonomous domain (making the individuals produced only "semblances" – imaginary), are the supplement to dialectical reason and the new imperative that demonstrate the "possibility" of a cognition of auratic individuality. Or rather, a sophisticated aesthetics will need to make claims of that order about contemporary art, but it is art that shows the possibility, not philosophy (if the concept is not self-sufficient, then neither can be philosophy).

My interest here is not in detailing Adorno's aesthetic theory; rather I want to claim that once the conceptual space art practices inhabit on Adorno's analysis is understood, and with it is understood as well the precise modal status of such works, it becomes at least plausible, and I think necessary, to claim that some empirical events themselves can have an equivalent status, possessing a kind of unreal reality, or, more exactly, as making a promise about what is empirically possible as a form of life which is implied by their mere existence but which cannot be further specified or justified. Certain empirical events have the status of both actualizing a possibility and in so doing making a promise about the future; it is this notion of an event that is a *promise* that I want to claim as filling the space between logical and actual possibility. Since such events both flee from ordinary empirical experience and are intrinsically ephemeral and transient, I consider them "fugitives."

Fugitive ethical events, so conceived, are Adorno's conception of the experience of normativity in late modernity: the domain of the normative, when fully, which is to say more than negatively, thought, is a domain of emphatic yet material experience; such experience is an experience of transcendence, and hence overlaps with what used to be thought under the title of metaphysics. That Adorno thinks that the vexed modern question of normativity overlaps, finally, with the even more vexed questions of metaphysics and modern materialism is disturbing; but given that throughout our argument the intelligibility of ethics has been bound to the limits of disenchantment, we should not be surprised. What I have not yet mentioned, although it might have been anticipated, is that Adorno explicitly claims metaphysical experience would be extensionally equivalent to what would demonstrate that the claims of the complex concept are satisfiable. Hence, the stakes of fugitive ethics will turn on what would satisfy the complex concept; because in fugitive ethical experience the axes of the complex concept can be reconciled with one another, then it is the complex concept itself which provides the key that explicates how the components of the analysis – metaphysics, transcendence, materiality, and experience – are bound together in thought of normativity. Because the structure of fugitive ethical events is generated on analogy with modernist works of art, it seems appropriate to think of it as a form of ethical modernism, of what modernism in ethics is. Modernist ethics is not an ethics that, so to speak, conveniently fits the contours of late modernity; rather, the fugitive character of ethical experience now makes perspicuous for the first time the truth of ethics, and thus what the normative force of ethical norms and actions has always been. Modernism is the truth of ethics; it is precisely the fact that fugitive ethical experiences satisfy the demands of the critical rationality of the complex concept that makes this claim compelling. The fugitive character of ethical modernism refers thus only to its rarity, the way in which ethical actions and experiences in late modernity are enclosed on all sides in rationalized institutional structures and social practices. Hence the fugitive character of ethical experience is the experience of the ethical as withdrawn from the possibility of general circulation.

Modernist ethical experience, if there is any, is the experience of transcendence; modernist ethical experience, if there is any, is the experience of the promise of a form of life escaping nihilism. So far as ethical modernism accords with the inner impulses of Adorno's thought, then it will confirm what he has to say about nihilism, transcendence, metaphysics, culture, materialism, possibility, and, above all, conceptuality. Since I intend my account of ethical modernism to fit tightly within that Adornoian space, then my procedure is to present it in the context of a continuing exposition of the Adorno's "Meditations."

2. Experience as Metaphysics

In section 2, after the offering and brief exposition of the new imperative, as an extension of the claim that morality survives only in the unvarnished materialistic motive, the abhorrence of the moral addendum, in what is a pointed continuation of his anti-theodicy argument Adorno states: "The somatic, unmeaningful stratum of life is the stage of suffering which in the camps burned every soothing feature out of mind [or spirit] and its objectification, culture, without any consolation. The point of no return has been reached in the process which irresistibly forced metaphysics to join what it once was conceived against" (ND, 365). Culture is here understood as the relatively autonomous domain of objects and practices containing the mind's objectifications of its separation from the needs of the body and the requirements for individual and societal reproduction. How did the camps "burn" every soothing and consoling feature out of culture? It cannot be the raw, unmediated character of suffering that is responsible for this burning. Suffering becomes the limit of intelligibility when we can no longer distinguish between cruelty to the body and cruelty to the self, when the mechanisms of cruelty are meant to leave no self to suffer physical pain as its mode of attacking the self. Auschwitz was the systematic joining of materialism and culture because, first, it employed the products of culture to make the horizon of material existence, bare life, absolute for the victims. Second, a version of the anti-theodicy argument, Auschwitz practically refuted the division between the sensible and the intelligible, making the fate of culture as something independent of the material stratum of existence a gross deceit. The cultural two-step whereby physical suffering is given intelligible meaning becomes insupportable, inconceivable, and intolerable, when we no longer know where physical suffering ends and cultural meaning begins. When suffering can no longer be made ethically intelligible, then the claim and meaning of culture as conditioned by but independent of material existence must be reconsidered.

The direct argument for the joining of materiality and culture returns suffering to its purely somatic location. Suffering so understood enjoins an anamnesis of childhood experience in which the lowest elements of life – sex, death, excrement, violence, and decay – are sensed as being of ultimate importance, as being closer to absolute knowledge than Hegel's chapter on it. Adorno complements his direct argument with an indirect one: "Auschwitz demonstrated irrefutably that culture has failed" (ND, 366). Adorno's aporetic comment on this thesis deserves to be given in full. Comments in square brackets are my elaborations.

> That this [Auschwitz] could happen in the midst of the traditions of philosophy, of art, and of the enlightening sciences says more than that those traditions and their spirit lacked the power take hold of men and work a change on them. [Culture did lack this power. And to say this is to raise the question of formation and motivation: what is it about our cultural ideas that explains their remoteness from our motivational sets, that having those ideas and yet not acting on them should become so routinely and horrifically compatible?] There is untruth in those fields themselves, in the autarky that is emphatically claimed for them. [Culture not only failed motivationally, but the radicality of that failure inclines to the thought that it was not something accidental or wholly external to culture. The "untruth" of culture in itself is its claim to self-sufficiency, be it the autonomy of reason or the self-sufficiency of aesthetic beauty or the value neutrality of scientific thought. The rationalization of culture, of science, morals and aesthetics, whereby their validity becomes an internal matter, a matter of self-legitimation, cuts them off from, to deploy a Nietzschean or Rousseauian formula, their "usefulness" for life. Only by being put back into relation with life in its most basic, material aspects can culture be evaluated and reformed. Or better: Auschwitz transforms the theoretical claim that culture should be useful for life into an urgent ethical matter because Auschwitz realizes the connectedness of culture to life, it brings about the measuring of culture by life: culture has failed.] All post-Auschwitz culture,

> including its urgent critique, is garbage. [Since even the urgent critique of culture transpires through the very same self-sufficient cultural forms that proved themselves inadequate, then despite itself critique is part of the culture that failed, that proved itself empty at the very moment in which it claims might have mattered most.] In restoring itself after the things that happened without resistance in its own countryside, culture has turned into entirely the ideology it had been potentially – had been ever since it presumed, in opposition to material existence, to inspire that existence with light denied it by the separation of the mind from manual labor. [Culture becomes ideology by continuing on in practices that have already shown themselves to be complicit in the very barbarism they deplore. The only legitimate cultural practices now would be ones that reflectively put themselves and their past in question. The potentiality for culture to lapse into ideology, the false consciousness of satisfaction and metaphysical security, was implicit in the origins of culture when, as a consequence of wealth and leisure, a division of labor could emerge between manual and mental activity.[3] Under the aegis of this division, the objectifications of the mind's transcendence over the body became reified into a world apart. As a world apart, culture leaves material existence in darkness, despised as lowly and unredeemed.] Whoever pleads for the maintenance of this radically culpable and shabby culture becomes its accomplice, while the man who says no to culture is furthering the barbarism which our culture showed itself to be. (ND, 365–6)

The final aporetic neither/nor of this paragraph returns us to Adorno's self-suspending stance: one can neither affirm culture because it has failed, nor deny it because it contains all the resources we possess for understanding that failure and combating the barbarism that failure permitted.

What can be said of culture equally holds for metaphysics because, as a consequence of Auschwitz, "metaphysics has merged with culture" (ND, 367). Auschwitz, we might say, accomplished what was promised in Nietzsche's declaration that "God is dead": "After Auschwitz there is no word tinged from on high, not even a theological one, that has any right unless it underwent transformation" (ND, 365). Culture's espousal of the mind's independence is at one with metaphysics' affirmation of ultimate truth; both now are answerable to material existence; their answerability, again, a consequence of the intolerableness of their not being answerable. Any form of meaningfulness or method of counting for which Auschwitz is not formative must by that very fact fall; hence nothing transcending material existence in general is, as a matter of conscience, rationally acceptable. However, exactly what might be meant by conceiving

3 Alfred Sohn-Rethel, *Intellectual and Manual Labour: A Critique of Epistemology*, trans. Martin Sohn-Rethel (London: Macmillan, 1978).

of material existence as a necessary ingredient in culture and hence as providing an ultimate horizon of intelligibility cannot be thought directly. The belief that it can be thought directly, that we can with a single gesture reunite human finitude with human transcendence, is attempted by Heidegger. *Being and Time* attempts to turn what was always the greatest challenge to metaphysical meaning, the exorbitant negativity of human death, into something to be affirmed. This, Adorno argues, is not truly materialist in its understanding of death, it spiritualizes death too quickly, and despite itself is in thrall to the elimination of traditional metaphysical meaning carried out philosophically by enlightenment and practically by the Nazi genocide.

In section 3 of the "Meditations," "Dying Today," Adorno is intent on making a variety of points. (1) Death is not just a biological category, but undergoes transformations: "The manner of people's coming to terms with death varies all the way into their physical side, along with the concrete conditions of their dying" (ND, 371). (2) Two traditional forms of death – the classical "beautiful death" in which finite life is sacrificed for an infinite idea (glory, virtue, etc.) and Christian death in which finite life is redeemed or compensated for in eternity – have become unavailable to us. Both those forms of death sacrifice mortal life for what is not itself finite or living. (3) Heidegger's death metaphysics in comprehending the meaning of human finitude through an active being-toward-death colludes with the naturalism it opposes, making death, as the condition or horizon of meaning (culture), too acceptable. In saying this, I take Adorno to mean that Heideggerian "resoluteness" that acknowledges death as the horizon of one's activities is akin to Nietzchean affirmation wherein negative elements of experience (especially suffering) are canceled by being freely accepted; as a reconciliation of freedom and necessity is achieved through making the recognition of necessity the meaning of freedom, so the affirmation and negation of life are reconciled by making the free acceptance of death the condition of authentic living.

For Heidegger only death conceived as the endpoint and horizon of an individual's projects makes possible their individuation as the individual's "own." Because only my death is truly non-exchangeable, no one can die my death for me (although of course another may die in my place), then only through my relation to my death are my projects individuated from their socially shared equivalents, becoming thereby indissolubly "mine." By resolutely comprehending my projects in relation to the indefeasible character of my death, my projects are torn out of their always already socially legitimated form to become truly mine. The very absoluteness and meaning-canceling negativity of death is thus reversed so as to become the necessary condition through which I can call anything "mine" at all. Hence Heidegger's characterization of death as "one's ownmost possibility, non-relational, not to be outstripped, and – above all – *certain*."[4] These characteristics are meant to articulate how it is that my relation to my death can uniquely provide the condition for radical individuation. By implication, Heidegger is contending that only the radical individuation given through an "authentic" being-toward-death can return to our acts and projects what enlightened accounts of autonomy claimed for self-legislation and modern social life continually deprives them of.[5] Heidegger audaciously takes what has been conceived of as the opponent of all meaning and shows it to be a condition of possibility for meaning, conferring on our relation to death all the anti-sceptical power that Descartes conferred upon the sceptically achieved certainty of the *Cogito*.

In "Dying Today" Adorno does not explicitly elaborate nor, in detail, refute Heidegger's death metaphysics; throughout the section the critique of Heidegger recurs in fragmented bursts. However, near the center of Adorno's critiques lies one central thesis: Heidegger illegitimately abstracts death from dying, the stark negativity of death itself from its biological substratum. Pain, suffering, decrepitude are extracted from the meaning of death (ownmost possibility, non-relational, etc.). The negation of meaning that is death's mastery over life occurs in life in the process of dying. If death and dying cannot be detached from one another, then the negativity of death as the absence of meaning cannot be isolated so as not to infect life itself; death's capacity for individuation cannot be detached from dying's work of de-individuation.

> In the camps death has a novel horror: since Auschwitz, fearing death means fearing worse than death. What death does to the socially condemned is anticipated biologically in old people we love; not only their bodies but their egos, all the things that justified their definition as human, crumble without illness, without violence from the outside. The remnant of confidence in their transcendent duration vanishes during their life on earth, so to speak: what should be the part of them that is not dying? (ND, 371)

The most radical consequence of disenchantment, the withering of continuous experience, is the loss of the emphatic experience of life. That loss is not only epistemic, it affects the object as well; the assimilation of the living to the non-living that is the structural mechanism of enlightened rationality non-naturally infects the living with their death. Adorno's diagnosis of disenchantment as the destruction of the animistic,

4 *Being and Time,* p. 302.

5 For a lucid defense of this stream of Heidegger's thought in relation to a practical conception of the self, see Ernst Tugendhat, *Self-Consciousness and Self-Determination,* trans. Paul Stern (Cambridge, Mass: MIT Press, 1986), lectures 8–10.

auratic individual is not intended metaphorically; it will sound metaphoric only if we consider life and death absolutes. Dying happens to the living; it is the process of their disintegration that, even before the heart stops beating, will have destroyed anything that might have individuated them from any other. The sting of death is not an abstract, absolute negativity, but its organic insistence, its being a force of disintegration within life. The abstractive mechanisms of enlightened thought transform the disintegrative forces of dying into a social practice. Auschwitz is the epitome of that practice. What is worse than death is the eternity of suffering that is the reduction of self to its de-individuated form, a specimen, in life. The violent insertion of death into life shows death to be extrinsic to the good of life. Without defiance of death, right down to the outmoded wish for immortality, life cannot be affirmed.

While we cannot return to the "beautiful" or Christian sublations of death, Heidegger's dialectical ruse of making the negative positive does not provide an answer to or diagnosis of what made it a plausible philosophical move in the first instance. Heidegger's dialectical transformation of death into a condition of meaning is a speculative sleight-of-hand.[6] So Adorno replies to Heidegger: "At a final stage, in despair, death itself becomes a property ["my death" becomes non-exchangeable]. Its metaphysical uplifting relieves us of its experience [being-towards-death takes the dying out of death]. Our current death metaphysics is nothing but society's impotent solace for the fact that social change has robbed men of what was once said to make death bearable for them, of the feeling of its epic unity with a full life" (ND, 369). For Adorno, what makes death again an object of metaphysical speculation is the decay of the experience of life, life's decay. The very formalism of Heideggerian authenticity, a tearing of the self loose from decaying life through being-toward-death, unintentionally cooperates with the forces of decay since its poses nothing existing beyond them. The dissolution of metaphysics, the dialectic of enlightenment that places a ban on any meaning beyond what can be rationally known, is simultaneously a descent into nihilism and despair.

Adorno's critique of Heidegger represents only a ground clearing within the wider survey of dying today; the point of the survey as a whole is to explicate why our fascination with death and inability to experience it portends an aporetic space between the unthinkability of death (we cannot affirm its epic unity with life) and the unthinkability of immortality (the only eternity available to us is the worse-than-death eternity of

6 Christopher Fynsk, *Heidegger: Thought and Historicity* (Ithaca: Cornell University Press, 1986), p. 38. And for convergent concerns over the absence of physical embodiment in *Being and Time*, see Michel Harr, *Heidegger and the Essence of Man*, trans. William McNeill (Albany: SUNY Press, 1993).

suffering of the de-individuated self). If we are not to succumb to Heidegger's totalization of death as horizon, then the transcending impulse of traditional metaphysical ideas must become relevant once more. Picking up and underlining the already claimed materialism and cultural belonging of metaphysics, Adorno poses the question that will provide the guiding thread for the remainder of the "Meditations": "In place of the Kantian epistemological question, how is metaphysics possible, steps one from the philosophy of history, whether metaphysical experience [*metaphysische Erfahrung*] in general is still possible. That [metaphysical experience] was never so beyond the temporal as [implied] in the textbook word metaphysics" (ND, 372). What is focal here is not metaphysics, but experience, the very thing which, in general, sceptical demythologization destroyed. Adorno's twist, we might say, is to raise the question of the possibility of experience after Auschwitz to the level of the question of the possibility of metaphysics, of what lies beyond or outside disenchanted life, outside the universal guilt context of existence. Thus, if the joining of the rationalization of society and the rationalization of reason brings about the destruction of experience, then the possibility of experience for us can be conceived of as only what *transcends* rationalized everyday life. From the other side, the closed context of empirical life requires something beyond it in order to think the possibility of a meaningful life; the beyond which is the supplement or vindication of empirical life is what traditionally has been thought under the heading of metaphysics. After Auschwitz, however, that beyond cannot be beyond the temporal and finite. Therefore, to think the possibility of metaphysics now is to think the possibility of metaphysical experience. Hence, the problem of the possibility of experience and the problem of the possibility of metaphysics converge; they are the same problem. *If there is a recuperative moment in Adorno's otherwise negative philosophy it is to be located in the insistence upon the question of the possibility of metaphysical experience: only as a temporal experience is metaphysics possible, and only as metaphysics, as what transcends existence now, is experience possible. Because in thinking metaphysical experience Adorno is thinking what would answer the problem of nihilism, then metaphysical experience inscribes the space of the ethical.*

The urgency of the question of metaphysics relates to the question of what lies beyond or departs from the totality represented by Auschwitz. For Adorno, to deny the question of metaphysics would be to deny "my own consciousness as well" (ND, 372) since it is sustained almost solely in defiance of Auschwitz and the despair it intones. Minimally, metaphysics is necessary if I am not to deny my own consciousness because my consciousness contains a transcending impulse, the very impulse that is abrogated in identity thinking; the transcending impulse of consciousness is the orientation of the material axis of the concept, the impulse to name, the impulse toward truth as opposed to communication. One fate of the transcending impulse in its traditional guise was into metaphysics, placing what was of ultimate significance beyond time and experience. The dialectic of enlightenment, for which the critique of religion is not an inconsiderable moment, revealed what was traditionally thought to be metaphysical as a work of projection. However, in the light of the sceptical denouement of the dialectic we cannot rest satisfied with pure immanence; if pure immanence, as specified by identity thinking, were all, then the guilt context of existence would be all; disenchanted immanence in suppressing the transcending impulse cuts the concept off from its object. Hence the truth content of metaphysical ideas, what is legitimately at stake in their transcendence, becomes both germane and perspicuous at the very moment in which traditional metaphysics "falls" (ND, 408); the very experiences that rightly tear down the metaphysical ideas and their eternity, because they have become unconscionable and thereby inconceivable, simultaneously make the thought of transcendence they contained unavoidable.[7]

In the wake of the rise of modern science and the thoroughgoing socialization of the world of practice, the question of metaphysics requires an immanent answer, one tied to temporal existence and the possibility of encounter. If the world is constituted as disenchanted, as a universal guilt context, then there is a potential antinomy between the requirement to think what is outside existence and the requirement that metaphysics must now be a matter of experience. Unlocking this antinomy is pivotal in the progress of the "Meditations." In section 4, "Happiness and Waiting in Vain," Adorno begins circumscribing metaphysical experience through interrogating how it might be visualized if we disdain from projecting it upon "allegedly primal religious experience" (ND, 373). Childhood, with its potential for experience still unchallenged, with its openness to the world and its sense of fulfilled presents and promised futures, is Adorno's first resource for reflection; given that the material axis of the concept aligns with the experience of the conceptual neophyte, this

7 Menke, *The Sovereignty of Art,* pp. 216–23, provides an interesting commentary on the role of death in making out the claim that the "modern occurrence of its [metaphysics'] fall does not mean a complete departure from the metaphysical, but quite the opposite, unveils and grounds for the first time its truth contents" (p. 218). While there is much that is pointed and right in his account, Menke appears to think that the purpose of the interpretation of modern death is to demonstrate how nonaesthetic experience of disintegration raises an infinite claim against the competence of ordinary discourse. While there is a crisis of reason that is manifest in our experience of death, which thus requires a return to the transcending impulse traditionally expressed by the metaphysical ideas, Adorno does not turn to death to demonstrate the irresolvable crisis – that would again make death the measure of life, which is the precise objection to Heidegger. That Menke goes on to criticize Adorno for using death as an experience of "total negativity" makes his strategy all the more perplexing. Narrowly, the mistake arises because Menke pulls the analysis of death out of context; but more broadly, his presumption that the rationality of the aesthetic is structurally extrinsic to the concept is the source of the problem.

choice is hardly accidental. It is in the writings of Proust that Adorno finds a presentation of childhood retrospectively understood as a source for the idea of metaphysical experience. It resides in the promise of village names that resound with an emphatic sense of place; the promise of those names is the promise of unconditional happiness. If travelling to those places makes "the promise recede like a rainbow," still one is not disappointed, "the feeling now is one of being too close, rather, and not seeing it for that reason" (ND, 373). Metaphysical experience is adumbrated in being entranced, enchanted, by one place "without squinting at the universal."

To the child who has such a favorite place, it is evident that the enchantment found is available only there. This is a mistake, but, Adorno continues, "his error creates the model of experience [*das Modell der Erfahrung*], its concept, that will end up as of the thing itself, not as a poor projection from things" (ND, 373). The child's error is to make absolute what is but his own idea of fulfillment; but it is just that illusory absolutization, an inflating of a singular instance to self-sufficiency, that forms the concept of experience. The child's illusory experience of the name as a promise of unbroken fulfillment forms the concept experience, and it is this concept of experience that Adorno is identifying as metaphysical experience. But if we consider what is being promised, namely, an encounter with a sensuous particular where that particular is experienced in its own right and not as an example or token of anything else, then it would appear that the emblem of metaphysical experience is no more than the promise of an instance of the complex concept – of the concept fulfilled. Which is what Adorno goes on to say:

> Only in the face of absolute, indissoluble individuation can we hope that this, exactly this has existed and is going to exist; *fulfilling this hope alone would fulfill the concept of the concept.* But the concept clings to the promised happiness, while the world that denies our happiness is the world of the reigning universal, the world stubbornly opposed by Proust's reconstruction of experience. (ND, 373–4; emphasis mine)

Somewhat later, an equally downbeat, conceptual/epistemic note is struck: "The mind, for all its mediation, shares in existence, the substitute for its alleged transcendental purity. Although its moment of transcendent objectivity cannot be split off and ontologized, that moment is the unobtrusive site of the possibility of metaphysics" (ND, 392–3). Adorno's conception of metaphysical experience, itself verging on being an oxymoronic concept, has now been qualified one step further: what would fulfil the concept of metaphysical experience is nothing other than a version, an emphatic realization of the way in which the mind participates in reality generally; since the mind does not participate in reality other than through conceptualizing it, then what would meet the requirements for metaphysical experience would of necessity simultaneously fulfil the concept of the complex concept. Because the stakes in the "Meditations" are so high, this claim is always overlooked. The transcendence located in metaphysical experience concerns not what exceeds ordinary conceptuality, but what would correct the rigidified conceptuality of the present. If this were not the case then Adorno's insistent cognitivism, his claims for material inference, his work on the concept would become utterly separated from what is meant to be the conclusion of his argument. Hence the point of lurching into the problems of metaphysics, transcendence, and experience is precisely to give back to human conceptuality that potentiality which enlightenment destroyed. Only with respect to ordinary conceptuality can the themes of metaphysics, transcendence, and experience matter.

Given what we have claimed about the complex concept, both in terms of its axial structure and in terms of its destruction at the hands of rationalization, the convergence of metaphysical experience with it could have been anticipated. The guilt context of existence is the block dividing the concept from its object (making the object but a reflection of the concept), thereby making the naming axis of the concept inaccessible to its communicative axis. It is thus no accident that Adorno's first attempt at visualizing metaphysical experience should be through the happiness – what "gives us the inside of objects as something removed from them" (ND, 374) – promised in a child's conjuring of proper place names: Atlas Springs, Lake Forest, Oakville, Martha's Vineyard. Those names, in the happiness and fulfillment they promise, recall for us the hope of the naming axis of the concept; in so doing they promise counter-names to the name "Auschwitz."

3. Metaphysical Ideas: Possibility as Promise

We are not yet finished with section 4 of the "Meditations"; in continuing his exposition of metaphysical experience, Adorno takes the notion that it would satisfy the complex concept and ratchets that notion up to its inevitable conclusion. Adorno is in the midst of criticizing the lament over "reification" as naively projecting a return to pure immediacy when he states that deposited "in the objectivity of the metaphysical categories was not congealed society alone," which was the claim of left Hegelians; that objectivity also deposited "the priority of the object as a moment of dialectics" (ND, 374). This is but another way of saying that the metaphysical ideals were also suppressed or distorted expressions of the naming axis of the concept which construes the object as the condition for what is to be said about or known of it – again, Adorno's anti-idealism. Pressing the case for immediacy against reification hence threatens to relinquish "the element of otherness in dialectics" (ND, 375). Adorno continues:

> The surplus over the subject, which a subjective metaphysical experience will not be talked out of, and the truth moment in thingliness [*das Wahrheitsmoment am Dinghaften*] are extremes which touch [*berühren*] in the idea of truth. (ND, 375)

The extremes that touch in this idea of truth derive from competing conceptions of metaphysical experience: the reification of truth in objective theological categories (e.g., thinking of God as "the absolute" or as himself "the truth"), and the negation of those categories in claims that immediate experience itself delivers the truth. Adorno's emphatic conception of truth emerges out of the dialectical negation of both metaphysical reification and immediacy. Contemporary analyses of truth consider some complex of linguistic mediation as sufficient to accomplish both tasks. Yet the truth concept that emerges from the simple concept fails both extremes: its reductive conceptuality denies there is a moment of truth "in things" (only in language is truth to be found), and, by the same movement of mediation, it eliminates subjective experience as cognitive. The middle ground occupied by standard correspondence theories does justice to neither impulse, which is not to deny that the space so occupied is in need of occupation; routine judgements and statements are indeed either correct or incorrect, true or false, in some ponderable and not very taxing way. Such correctness, I have claimed, is no more than obeying the rules of whichever game is presently being played.[8]

While if espoused directly Adorno's defense of some robust or emphatic idea of truth would be worrying in the extreme, in context it should at least be considerable since it says no more than that there is a difference to be drawn between the withered and deracinated experiences (*Erlebnisse*) of everyday life in modern society and emphatic experience, *Erfahrung*, between McDowell's perception of red and Wittgenstein's perception of the wriggling fly, which has been a premise of the entire analysis. It might sound as if with the idea of a truth moment in things, as a secularized version of god as truth, Adorno is adding something to the notion of metaphysical experience. But the idea of emphatic experience has throughout been expressed as being essentially object-involving, and hence being indexed to an event that is bound to a place and a time. So although Adorno is insisting on the need or necessity for

8 Which is not to deny that social correctness may represent a consolidation or sedimentation or routinization of a more fundamental "truth experience" – so much is presupposed in the dialectical movement of the categories of authority from charismatic to traditional to legal-rational. Truth as correctness is legal-rational truth without its charismatic introduction, or so what follows assumes.

an emphatic conception of truth, we should hear this as a further elaboration of metaphysical experience, rather than the other way round. If we are to have any conception of experience that eludes the rule of identity thinking, and hence restores or resurrects anthropocentric nature as a self-sufficient domain of knowledge and practice, then it will be possible now only as metaphysics, as an experience of transcendence; what satisfies that will reconcile the axes of the complex concept; and what satisfies the concept of the concept will, a fortiori, be emphatically true. Metaphysical experiences cannot now, at least, be merely correct or incorrect because in part their validity is determined by their breaking from the norms determining correctness or incorrectness, not merely as a matter of fact, but in refusing that determination of their validity and claiming otherwise. Metaphysical experiences bespeak their fugitive quality. While Adorno insists that the idea of truth is "supreme among the metaphysical ideas" – "It is why one who believes in God cannot believe in God, why the possibility represented by the divine name is maintained, rather, by him who does not believe" (ND, 401–2) – he says little more about it.

Appreciating the shape of Adorno's argument to here is important if his exposition of Kant's "Postulates" in sections 6–9 is not to be misunderstood. On the whole, although not completely, these sections recapitulate what has already been argued within the narrow context of Kant's treatment of the traditional metaphysical ideas, what he thought we must think but cannot know. The focus on Kant here is inevitable since for Adorno Kant's Copernican turn in which the necessary and thereby "transcendental" conditions of possible experience are made immanent to the mind is the philosophical nail in the coffin of metaphysics. Equally, the Categorical Imperative as what constitutes maxims as worthy or worthy makes the necessary conditions of morality immanent to the mind, dependent on nothing external. Nonetheless, scattered throughout Kant there are references to what lies beyond the framework constituted by the categories and the work of reason. What almost all writers on Kant want to read out of his philosophy for Adorno is the sign of its integrity, the deepest concession that the mind cannot encapsulate what is on its own terms. Hence for Adorno the notion of the thing-in-itself forms a memory of nonidentity; in so doing Kant is tacitly affirming "nonidentity as the premise of possible identification," which essentially eludes identification (ND, 291). In the "Meditations" Adorno thus turns from the immanent critique of the Kantian concept and the disembodiment of freedom which have been the guiding elements of the entire argument to a rescue of Kant's own transcending impulse.

In the "Postulates" the positioning of what is transcendent to mind but necessary for it is more explicit and the stakes higher than in the doctrine of the thing-in-itself. We must think the metaphysical ideas of freedom, God, and the immortality of the soul, because they are sources of the possibility for realizing the highest good, the proportioning of happiness to virtue, which itself is the necessary object of moral striving. Only in the light of the idea of highest good is the negative determination of the moral law made systematically compatible with both the natural desire for happiness, which is the general orientation of our inclinations, and the teleological structure of human action generally. Actions not only must accord with the rules of morality, but equally they have ends or goals, which are generally supplied by the inclinations, and those ends or goals must be capable of being brought into harmony with moral principles as well as being realizable. Kant's depiction of bringing all these considerations together is his notion of the highest good in which I realize my moral ambitions by bringing my inclinations into harmony with morality and receive happiness in proportion to my success in that endeavor. The highest good depicts then both my moral self-realization and the satisfaction of my desire for happiness that is proportional to that. The nub of the problem is that empirical reality is, in fact, unaccommodating: life is preciously short for realizing oneself morally, the inclinations rebellious; and even if those conditions are met, in this world as a matter of fact the evil flourish and the good and the innocent suffer. Hence, the dilemma: the highest good is the necessary object of moral volition but in accordance with the principles governing empirical experience it is not possible to realize it. If ought implies can, then something more is required. The thought of the immortality of the soul (which is to enable us to achieve a harmony between morality and inclination) and the existence of God (who will reward virtue with happiness) are postulated in order to make the highest good possible.

The highest good is an object of striving only if *possibly* real, and it is possibly real only if the metaphysical ideas are conceived of as real. To conceive the highest good as possible is to conceive of empirical reality, the total context of immanence, disenchanted nature, as making room for, accommodating, the demands of reason; if empirical reality were really a fully causally determined order, on the one hand, and the evil flourished while the good suffered, there being generally no morally intelligible connection between virtuous action and the flourishing of the embodied agent on the other, then morality, or what we think of morality, would come to appear to be a chimera. It is this train of thought that makes Kant so pertinent: he did radically conceive empirical reality as inhospitable to the demand of morality while nonetheless wanting to preserve the latter's possibility. For that he concocted his doctrine of two perspectives or two worlds view: the empirical world as the knowable object of the understanding, and the intelligible world as thought by reason. For Adorno, the account of empirical reality as radically disenchanted and therefore radically inhospitable to moral life is truer to our predicament than the more ameliorating representations of post-Kantian philosophy.

But it is just that which equally makes Kant's insistence that empirical reality must be conceivable as different, and as not inhospitable, and the metaphysical ideas as the fulcrum for conceiving of the unity of empirical reality and ethical experience telling.

Where Kant's argument misfires according to Adorno is in thinking that the metaphysical ideas as mere ideas might be sufficient: "as mere ideas they would be empty if they were not conceived from the point of view of possible experience, that is, an objective reality that is at least *possible*."[9] The metaphysical ideas can reveal possibility only if by their own concept they are things in being, where to be such requires "matter"; and if they possessed matter, then they would become objects of possible experience (ND, 391). Ideas cannot reveal possibility if that possibility is forever cut off from intelligible realization;[10] the immortality of the soul and the existence of God solve the problem not by showing how nature and morality can be brought together but, essentially, by denying the conditions that originate the problem. If the metaphysical ideas are to represent a possibility for the unification of the sensible and intelligible realms, then they must do so as an historical possibility; this is what makes the notions of God and immortality figures or images of something other than what is claimed by their traditional content. Their real truth content points to the idea of "another" nature, rather than to a domain beyond the natural. But this thought converges with a criticism of the Kantian system that can be lodged independently of consideration of the metaphysical ideas, namely, that the cause of Kant's "block" between the empirical reality and the intelligible world derives from his depreciation of sensuality, the making of intuition a shadow of the concept, and making the concept identitarian (the concept of a closed causal order under unchanging natural law): "The separation of the sensual and the intellectual realms, the nerve of the argument in favor of the block, is a social product; by the *chorismos* [separation], sensuality is designated as a victim of the intellect because, all arrangements to the contrary notwithstanding, the state of the world fails to content sensuality" (ND, 389). If the sensual is conceived as blinded intuition, then it shall never be compatible with the demands of reason.

The possibility of removing the block between the empirical and intelligible realms depends on changing the *content* of the sensual realm, of

9 Albrecht Wellmer, "Metaphysics at the Moment of Its Fall," in his *Endgames: The Irreconcilable Nature of Modernity,* trans. David Midgley (Cambridge, Mass: MIT Press, 1998), p. 184.

10 A thought that has become legible in Kant scholarship in arguments that seek to show how the "Postulates" achieve their fullest articulation in Kant's philosophy of history. Although this is an older Marxist view going back to Lukács and Lucien Goldmann, for a contemporary statement, see Yirmiyahu Yovel, *Kant and the Philosophy of History* (Princeton: Princeton University Press, 1980).

conceiving of the sensual realm as itself accommodating to what Kant believes belongs solely to the intelligible realm; to conceive of this possibility would be to conceive of the relation between form and content changing, of perceiving the forms of reason as possessing a social content that is transformable, and that when transformed would simultaneously provide a different concept of empirical content (ND, 386). Adorno thus contends that the ideological untruth in the idea of transcendence, everything that makes the notion of transcendence both suspect and conservative, is "the separation of body and soul," and hence what all hope clings to is "the transfigured body" (ND, 400). So, as Albrecht Wellmer has rightly commented, in arguing simply for the transformability of the relation between form and content Adorno is critically shifting the weight of the Kantian argument from "we cannot know what is depicted by the metaphysical ideas" to "we do not know it yet."[11] But that can hardly be the totality of Adorno's claim as Wellmer presumes it to be since nothing in the doctrine of a possible knowable future that is categorially discontinuous with the present feeds back into how the metaphysical ideas themselves demonstrate possibility. On the contrary, while we can reflectively make an argument to the effect that the relation between form and content must be conceived dynamically, the very argument that Fichte and Hegel did make in opposing Kant, if some idea of metaphysical experience is to be enlarged or elaborated through recourse to Kant's ideas, then Adorno must think that the very effort of conceiving of them portends an experience of transcendence. Wellmer's account simply dismisses the guiding question of the "Meditations": Is metaphysics still possible as an experience?

Metaphysical experience must be the experience of a possibility that transcends current actual possibilities and is capable of bearing the weight of the idea of the transfigured body, that is, of a nature, including human nature that is not conceived of in reductively naturalistic terms. And for that to be an experience, then it must satisfy the individuation requirements set out in the account of childhood names; it is presumed that this requirement is the same as or overlaps with the transcendence requirement. What satisfies those requirements ought, all other things being equal, to satisfy the concept of the concept. While the terms of the argument are far-reaching and complex, the issue is narrowly modal: the possibility of a transfigured nature must be stronger than logical or conceptual possibility, since those possibilities can be had through the mechanisms of negative dialectics on its own, and must be weaker than actual possibility since if such were actually possible metaphysical demonstration would be neither relevant nor necessary. It is necessary because logical and conceptual possibility are insufficient, and actual possibility un-

11 Albrecht Wellmer, "Metaphysics at the Moment of Its Fall," p. 190.

attainable. Of course, all this presupposes the Hegelian dictum that there is no possibility without actuality. But that premise is given directly with the thought that the relation between form and content is dynamic, historical, and transformable. It is that the Hegelian requirement cannot be fully met which entails that Adorno's modal conundrum contains one further twist; since we are asking how the idea of a transfigured nature is conceivable as an *experience,* where an experience is some kind of worldly event, then we appear to be asking, how can an actual event demonstrate possibility without demonstrating something to be actually possible? Or, what is the same, how can we have an experience of something that is neither fully actual nor fully nonactual? Adorno thinks this is the space of the metaphysical ideas: "The concept of the intelligible realm would be the concept of something which is not, and yet is not merely nothing" (ND, 393).

In pacing out this space between logical and fully actual possibility Adorno traces two lines of thought. The first, which is the conclusion to the analysis of Kant, begins with the contention that what we say about transcendence is but its semblance, an appearing and showing of transcendence; but, as Kant urges, it is a necessary semblance: we must postulate the metaphysical ideas if the necessary conditions for rational action are to be shown to be internally consistent (ought implies can). This is the real, metaphysical relevance of aesthetics: it is the theoretical reflection that attempts the rescue of semblance, *die Rettung des Scheins,* that is, aesthetics seeks to demonstrate how art works as semblances can reveal the possibility of a transfigured nature. Set aside the thesis about aesthetics for the moment. Adorno does want to claim that the truth content of metaphysics is that it offered a semblance, an appearing of otherness, and it is its status as semblance that explains its power to move and orient action. This is why the "neturalization" of metaphysics over the past three centuries, the topic of section 9 of the "Meditations," has been so debilitating spiritually.

Artworks, especially modern ones, are paradigmatic semblances because they self-consciously pose their unreality while simultaneously underlining their materiality. As material things they are fully actual. As material things without purpose, function, or practical use, they are not fully or practically actual. Artworks can be non-fungible material objects of attention only in virtue of their not being beholden to the norms that govern the rest of social practice. What Adorno hence means by semblance, the showing, shining appearance that is not as such the appearing of an unconditionally actual empirical object, is a material object that is "more than" an object in the world in being unique, non-fungible, non-derivable, and claiming or demanding attention/appreciation simply as what it is, while simultaneously being less than any factual thing in adding nothing to the practical social totality. Adorno hence wants to underline rather than dodge how modally anomalous works of art are; in some way he thinks their power and significance is utterly bound up with their modally anomalous status.

If artworks are not semblances of anything actual, what they are semblances *of*? Although he says it movingly and lyrically, the precise claim is that semblance is the promise of nonsemblance (ND, 405), or a promise of otherness, *des Anderen,* to revert to the title of section 11. The notion of the promise of semblance is clearly an echo of Stendhal's contention that aesthetic pleasure is a "*promesse de bonheur*"; Adorno would assume that the Stendhalian promise could be heard in the more austere promise he proposes. There are two aspects to Adorno's proposal here. First, he is claiming that if works of art are semblances, then they must be semblances of something; and once art is no longer representational, then the temptation to suppose that the semblance is of an existing real thing or the idea of such a thing lapses. Thinking again of paradigmatically modernist works, music by Berg, abstract expressionist art, the claim would be that *this* is a semblance or appearing of an ordering of material stuff that owes nothing to the simple concept, that is, *this* is a concatenation of material stuff which is meaningful and orderly in itself without the meaning or order being owed to anything but the medium and the matter. This side of the argument thus states that *here* is the possibility of another nature, of the transfigured body. Second, in the same light, Adorno is contending that works of art say that nature *can* be like this. And what now is the status of that *can*? It is a promise.

I presume that the notion of promise was carefully chosen to capture the anomalous modal status of the kind of possibility, the kind of relating of present to future, which semblances project. Like a promise, a work of art is a fully (materially) substantial present object; like a promise, a work of art "intends" a future that is not legible from the present other than through its very being, only providing a sign that a certain nonpredictable future will come to pass; and finally, like a promise, a work of art is impotent in the face of future reality. While promises are certainly iterable, in promising to be there tomorrow I am also promising that my promise will be kept, they are equally fragile: in promising that my promise will be kept I cannot guarantee that it will be; forces beyond my power, say, the forces of causal nature, may prevent its being kept. Part of the majestic beauty of promises, vows, and pledges is that they pose human determination and hopefulness in the teeth of intransigent reality. Artworks on Adorno's accounting partake in that kind of emphatic claiming and impotence. In experiencing works of art we are experiencing a material event that *is* incompatible with the present social order of the living, and in so being *promises* another social order of the living.

These are, I know, massive claims about works of art that would take, did take Adorno a huge volume on its own to substantiate. However, at least on this account, it is the modal shape of semblances that is the heart of the matter; if so, then one may legitimately ask whether anything other than artworks has the structure and modal shape Adorno attributes to semblances and which simultaneously satisfies the other requirements for metaphysical experience. There are losses and gains in taking this path. The loss is that no domain of social practice *systematically* sustains human transcendence in the way that art does according to Adorno; on the contrary, the philosophical importance of art is that it systematically, that is, in accordance with the demands of the practice itself, works at sustaining human transcendence. And this means as well, that only from within art can the necessity of semblance be inferred since only in making out why there is art at all in its present disposition in relation to the rest of social reality can the role of semblance in social reality as a whole (including art now) be shown to be rationally necessary. The gain is twofold. First, it has proved consistently difficult to demonstrate how the achievement of artworks can be interpreted as satisfying the concept of the concept; which has made the whole cognitive side of Adorno's aesthetic theory an invitation that no one seems quite sure how to accept or reject. In asking after more worldly events, the conceptual and cognitive aspects of the claim about semblance should be able to come into view. Second, in focusing on the modal shape of Adorno's conception of metaphysical experience, it becomes possible to see that his attention to aesthetics need not be considered as being at the expense of the possibilities of ethical action.

I said above that in pacing out the space between logical and fully actual possibility Adorno traces out two lines of thought; the dominant one concerning semblance, art, and aesthetics we have just looked at. The second, much less developed line of thought concerns possibility in reality. Following it out will form the bridge to Adorno's ethical modernism.

4. Fugitive Experience, Ethical Modernism

There are a few passages in the "Meditations" where Adorno hints at the idea that the promise of otherness he attributes to works of art can be found in social experience, and hence that it is only art's systematic working at the promise of otherness that gives it its special status. In fact, Adorno must think otherness can be found in experience or else he would be committed to the belief that the guilt context of the living is absolute and all. Not everything can be shaped by the negative whole without making even the statement of that fact unintelligible.[12] This thought comes through in the "Meditations" in Adorno's contention that the

12 For a vigorous and telling defense of Adorno on this point, and responding fully thereby to Michael Theunissen's charge that in his metaphysical, speculative moment Adorno

world's course is not conclusive, entailing absolute despair, but that only despair makes the world's course conclusive (ND, 404). It is at just this juncture that Adorno introduces the motif of the promise that becomes at the end of the section the promise of nonsemblance:

> However frail is every trace of otherness in it, however much all happiness is marred by revocability, in the breaks that belie identity, what exists is still interspersed by the ever-broken promise of that otherness. All happiness is a fragment of the total happiness which men are denied and are denied by themselves. (ND, 404)

The world is disenchanted, but it is not utterly closed in on itself: there are moments of happiness (and not just pleasure or illusory happiness), and there are the fragmented and heterogeneous that do not fit with the course of the world. In not fitting, these negative others promise otherness – the world enchanted. Hence in the preparation for the idea of semblance promising nonsemblance, the model is not art but fragmented reality; art's promise is the world's promise, the one evinced in fragments of happiness and the shards of heterogeneity scattered in the world, become thematic. If fragmented reality did not promise otherness, there would be no otherness for art to thematize. Metaphysical experience is the generic bridge connecting world and art, making art's already well-known promise of happiness bear on the deepest structures of experience.

Metaphysical experience is an epistemological necessity for Adorno since "consciousness could not even despair over the gray, did it not harbor the notion of a different color, whose dispersed traces are not absent from the negative whole" (ND, 377–8). If despair were truly total, we would not be speaking of despair, reflectively conceiving of ourselves *as* despairing, just as if life were meaningful we would not be asking after the meaning of life (ND, 376). Hence, even the assertion of total negativity belies it, necessarily bespeaking the hope that is denied.[13] And while the claim for the necessity of there being another color is compatible with only art being that different color, Adorno urges that he "who reduces what is to nugatoriness without differentiation, and without a perspective of possibility, he aids and abets the dull bustle . . . . [F]or transcendence feeds on nothing but the experiences we have of immanence" (ND, 398). In this passage Adorno is elaborating the idea that the modern, Enlightenment "neutralization" of the metaphysical impulse has itself led to the discounting of transcendence generally, and hence a perceiving of reality without possibility. The same nihilistic process of our highest values

shows himself to be simply dogmatic and hence not negative enough, see Jarvis, *Adorno: A Critical Introduction*, pp. 211–16.

13 Ibid., p. 214.

devaluing themselves that has emptied the metaphysical ideas has simultaneously neutralized the truth content of those ideas, and with it the legitimate impulse toward immanent transcendence that belongs to conceptuality generally. Hence, the experiences of otherness in immanence are not recognized as such. Recovering that impulse is the telos of the "Meditations" as a whole, a thought resoundingly pronounced in the famous concluding sentences of *Negative Dialectics.*

> Represented in the inmost cell of thought is that which is unlike thought. The smallest intramundane traits would be of relevance to the absolute, for the micrological view that cracks the shell of what, measured by the subsuming cover concept, is helplessly isolated and explodes its identity, the delusion that is but a specimen. There is solidarity between such thinking and metaphysics at the time of its fall. (ND, 408)[14]

The smallest intramundane traits, the merest object or event that is perceived in its helpless isolation as thereby eluding what its concept otherwise determines it to be reveals itself other than a specimen, and hence as containing more possibility than what is contained in its identifying concept. Insofar as the event cannot be subsumed, it forges a promise about what an event or object can be. This is only a promise because nothing dictates that what is so helplessly isolated, fugitive, what falls between the cracks of social determination, eludes and thereby breaks them open, can be generalized into a socially reproducible practice. Nonetheless, in occurring the event is actual; in being isolated, nondeterminable in accordance with principles and rules of social practice, it possesses a kind of unreality; an unreality that it transmits to its status as in being actual it must thereby project future possibility – it is a semblance, something more and less than what is factual, more because it is not a mere fact (its sensuous particularity promises otherness), less because its factuality is untethered from both social generalizability and reproducibility. We presume that if an empirical event occurs, events like it must be actually possible. Because their occurrence is a leaping or falling out of social practice, fugitive events do not unqualifiedly carry that potential.

In section 5 of the "Meditations," "Nihilism," Adorno is considering the ideality of total nihilistic despair, and conjectures that a man in a concentration camp might reasonably believe that it would be better not to have been born; but even in that context there might be a hesitation:

14 This is the same thought that is urged at the conclusion of *Minima Moralia* (MM, 153), only there the emphasis is more activist: "Perspectives must be fashioned that displace and estrange the world, reveal it to be, with its rifts and crevices, as indigent and distorted as it will appear one day in the messianic light. To gain such perspectives without velleity or violence, entirely from felt contact with objects – this alone is the task of thought."

"And yet the lightening up of an eye, indeed the feeble tail-wagging of a dog one gave a tidbit it promptly forgets, would make the ideal of nothingness evaporate" (ND, 380). These are certainly intramundane traits, and in the case of the dog's animal gratitude, although abruptly humane in a way that camp life sought to vanquish, not otherwise breaking from the rule of self-preservation. What is more telling, in context, is how Adorno is nonetheless marshalling the lightening up of an eye or some tail-wagging as fractures in total negativity that point beyond themselves; they are the color. The dog's tail-wagging like Wittgenstein's fly disperses the context of immanence, creation, and in revealing an animal solidarity (affinity) opens a space of possibility which no intentional doing can by itself bring about; creaturliness as the material a priori of humanity. What these cases thus urge, especially in the light of Adorno's remark excoriating the reduction to nothingness of what is through a lack of discrimination, of failing through lack of attention to perceive a possibility in things that reality has cheated them of, is that metaphysical experience can occur anywhere, and can be as slight and ephemeral as can be imagined; it is a matter of coming to see such events aright that is Adorno's challenge, not their occurrence.

Despite the clear indications that Adorno did think there were intramundane traits revealing possibility that satisfy the requirements of metaphysical experience, they play almost no role in his philosophy. Again, formally, this is perfectly intelligible. An exposition of actual intramundane metaphysical experiences could have no systematic basis other than the negative one Adorno actually provides in arguing against the intelligibility of total despair, absolute negativity, and unmitigated nihilism. Beyond this negative determination there is nothing further to say *philosophically or conceptually*; there is something further that can be said about art because as a practice it does involve a systematic transformation in the relation between concept and object, form and content. But even in his aesthetic writings, Adorno only *mentions* particular works of art, and offers no concrete analyses of those works.[15] Aesthetics for him was a wholly conceptual affair; to introduce concreteness into it by building conceptual arguments on the basis of the analysis of particular works would presume that philosophy could make the concrete its own, rather than, those objects, the works themselves, being the demonstration of possibility. Conversely, if works were offered as illustrations of the aesthetic theory, then it would appear that the demands of the theory were determining

15 Conversely, Adorno produced numerous works of musical and literary analysis. Whether this is regarded as overfastidious or not, it derives from the consistent insight that under the reign of the simple concept work on the concept and the appearing of what exceeds it are opposing perspectives. Adorno's dual practice underlines the concept's claim to self-sufficiency and its actual non-self-sufficiency.

the meaning of the works, so apparently subsuming the works under the theory – the very domination of the concept which the theory itself was intending to undermine. From Adorno's perspective the situation of metaphysical experience outside art is even more difficult since apart from the negative there would be no conceptual supports, and any concrete offerings, in the absence of such support, would be wildly underdetermined. The point of the doctrine of metaphysical experience is that it cannot be conceptually prescribed, that the sort of meaningfulness such events reveal cannot be conceptually or rationally grounded because *they* represent all the grounding that is possible: the dog's tail-wagging itself the reason for any further reasons one might have for wishing to live and live a human life. Not only is philosophy powerless before fugitive events, and hence should concede this fact by not seeking to incorporate them into itself, but, further, although the whole effort of the "Meditations" is to conceptually articulate the color which makes the gray of the world intelligible, as becomes evident at the end of Section 2, Adorno thought that any attempt to provide consolation could only help adjust individuals to the world as it is and thus deprive them of their due (ND, 368); if an empirical metaphysical experience offers hope, and that is just what it does, the parading of such would undermine the strategic ethical orientation of the writing.

Once it is conceded that metaphysical experience is not restricted to art, rather it is art that systematically thematizes indigent intramundane metaphysical experiences, then there is no reason to think that ethical actions and events cannot themselves be amongst those intramundane metaphysical experiences. On the contrary, Adorno argues that the possibility of metaphysical experience is akin to the possibility of freedom in that freedom requires the breaking of the bonds of domination, and, equally, only an "unfolded subject," that is, a subject who has already escaped from the bondage of tradition and feudal hierarchy, can have a metaphysical experience that is not based on delusion (ND, 396–7). *Metaphysical experience is possible only with the fall of metaphysics*; prior to that the experience of transcendence remained, despite itself, entangled in dogmatism – almost a positivism of transcendence. But the link between freedom and metaphysical experience runs deeper: "The instants in which a particular frees itself without in turn, by its own particularity, constraining others are anticipations of the unconfined, and such solace radiates from the earlier bourgeoisie until its late period" (ND, 306). Acts of liberation, almost by definition, are departures from the context of total immanence; and if their mode of coming to be do not explicitly involve the domination of others, then whatever transpires from them – and, alas, what does typically transpire is a normalization that, finally, will succumb to standard societal rationalization – they nonetheless anticipate, promise, a state of freedom generally. It would be difficult to deny that the French and American Revolutions and the civil rights movement innervate in this way. If the logical character of ethical modernism is just that of metaphysical experience, and metaphysical experience possible only with the fall of metaphysics, then it is comprehensible why ethical modernism, the meaning and being of the ethical, the devolution of the ethical down to particular events in which the material inferences which are the content of ethical concepts are activated or reactivated, should begin to emerge in its own right only at the very moment in which it might have been thought that the ethical was impossible. The emergence of particular ethical acts in the precise context in which the social actuality of ethical life had been ruined through rationalization, on the one hand, and all the metaphysical and transcendental props which had been regarded as providing the ground of the ethical found idle because implausible, on the other hand, jointly provide those acts with their modernist shape. Ethical action and experience thus only become palpable at the time of the fall of the ethical; only when ethical life seems most impossible can its true possibility emerge. Although this idea of ethical modernism is nothing but an elaboration of Adorno's conception of metaphysical experience, it is fair to hazard that Adorno never had the idea of ethical modernism clearly in view although he can, must be interpreted as broaching it all the time and everywhere.[16]

Would we want to now deny that the Danish rescue of the Jews too, like the French and American Revolutions or the civil rights movement, satisfies the broad modal requirements for metaphysical experience? If we take Frode Jakobsen at his word, the resistance was borne of moral indignation at the sight of the suffering of the Jewish people which was experienced as the suffering of humanity. Whatever the preconditions that enabled the Danes to experience the persecution of the Jews in this way, Jakobsen's account frees the episode of any metaphysical presuppositions, and thus of any non-materialist, non-universalistic assumptions. In a context in which the major European nations did not distinguish themselves,[17] the Danish effort "leaps out" – remains fugitive; even now, with the history of failure ever more visible, there is little to contravene the belief that rescue is the exception and not the rule. To say it is an exception is precisely to claim that no rule anticipates it, nor is there a conceivable rule which would enable its replication as appropriate. Against bourgeois self-immersion, against the ordinary dictates of self-preservation, against

16 I have no deep explanation of why Adorno failed to see the immediate overlap of metaphysical experience and ethical action and experience.

17 This is central for my claim here since had rescue been the norm of European response to the Nazis, then the credit for rescue might reasonably be tied to Enlightenment ideals in their standard shape. The rarity represented by the Danish rescue effort is thus being interpreted as the flip side of the failure of enlightened morality to be effective when most needed.

the ethical bonds to family, friends, and those who shared their ethnic identity, against the harsh glitter of Nazi propaganda, the Danes experienced the suffering of European Jewry as destructive of humanity, and in response to the threat to the local Jewish community mounted a rescue. In virtue of its isolation, is not what radiates from that rescue the promise of rescue and an end to suffering? Is not that event exemplary? Does it not innervate the name "rescue"? Is not the concept of rescue there fulfilled, the material inference linking Jewish suffering and the necessity for rescue there (re-)activated, and in being fulfilled and (re-)activated exemplary of the ethical as such? Of course, this is a strange exemplarity, namely, exemplarity without succession. It is standardly assumed that the exemplary is only exemplary through succession; only by an actual following event does an exemplary event become, retrospectively, exemplary. Fugitive events cannot satisfy this criterion; that, in part, is what makes them fugitive. Yet their emphatic actuality makes them appear as if they *must* contain the possibility of their succession. It is the absence of the actual succession and the lack of the social conditions which would underwrite future succession, hence the sense that the rescue ran against the grain of social actuality, that de-realizes these events; they contain succession only in the mode of a promise.

Again, metaphysical experience does not belong to philosophy; philosophy can only reveal or explicate that kind of significance that should be understood as implied by particular worldly events. In the case of fugitive ethical experiences this is even more radically so since there is nothing in philosophy's own mode of conduct that even conceivably could anticipate, forecast, or legislate ethical action of the kind that, I am suggesting, it is nonetheless committed to affirming. What is so affirmed is what reveals that the course of the world is not final, and that experience could be otherwise. To be sure, no ethical event will be so utterly negative in its complexion, or so utterly ungrounded in its emergence that one could not interpret it more conservatively. Purity, however, is not to be looked for in this area – ethical actions are not undertaken in order to make theoretical points, but in response to damaged life.[18]

Working in from a Weberian perspective, it becomes possible to make more perspicuous why ethical experience can be only fugitive for us; why fugitive ethical experience is, in a sense, privileged in making perspicuous the logical form of ethical experience *überhaupt,* and hence why, in the light of those two claims, there are grounds for believing that there is more ethical experience about than Adorno seemed to think. Mod-

18 Adorno does not believe that artworks can be fully negative and noncomplicitous, either; indeed, the very being of autonomous artworks, the condition that enables them to carry their critical charge, simultaneously implicates them in what they are opposing. In a total guilt context, there is no innocence.

ernist, fugitive ethical experience makes optimal sense of the Weberian structure of authority. On Weber's model, again, charismatic episodes revolutionize society, and the lessons of those revolutionary episodes are then transmitted into tradition, and from tradition can be further rationalized until they become elements of a legal-rational order; while legal-rational order traditionally was equivocal in being both the institutional routinization of practices necessary for social reproduction and what demanded obedience from without, in late modernity that equivocality becomes radical, its two sides experientially distinct: rationalized institutional order experienced as unequivocally both what is necessary for social reproduction and as the wholesale imposition of instrumentalized rules that dominate subjects and remain indifferent to their real needs and ends. Traditional authority has faded; where it remains it looks suspiciously like either dogmatic cult or simply the rules of a particular community. And it is probably not be hoped that charismatic episodes will truly revolutionize our society. Rather, under the conditions of late modernity, the permanent crisis of society is its rationalized order that, in supervening on ordinary practices, thus colonizing them, systematically drains authority from ethical norms and values. This, again, is the social and institutional actuality of nihilism. Yet, thus far, the crisis has never been quite complete, the despair total.[19] Fugitive ethical episodes, charismatic episodes under the conditions of late modernity, interrupt the context of immanence, to innervate new norms or re-innervate the authority of faded norms and reveal the possibility of otherness.

What gives this account its structure is its denial that there is some habitable space between the ever-closing context of immanence (the all but uninterrupted spread of societal rationalization and thus legal-rational authority) and what interrupts it (charismatic authority); that is the real bite in the collapse of traditional authority: what ethical experiences and norms exist are withdrawn from generality and routine, everyday reproduction. But this is just a restatement of the governing argument of *Minima Moralia.* Even if private existence, remote communities, peculiar institutions like those dedicated to education, can, occasionally, be construed as refuges from the full impact of societal rationalization in that their forms of practice have not been completely systematically regimented via supervenience to the demands of instrumental rationality, nonetheless, again, those practices are conditioned by being both set

19 Although I cannot argue the point here, my hunch is that the moment in which the crisis was most visible and hence in which the despair nearly total was in and around World War I. Much of twentieth-century history thus has been a replay and disavowal, covering over, of that moment. A good way to begin teasing out this claim would be to read John Keegan's *The First World War* (London: Hutchinson, 1998) next to Pat Barker's stunning *Regeneration* trilogy: *Regeneration, The Eye in the Door, The Ghost Road* (New York: Plume, 1992, 1993, 1995).

within the systematic whole (families and schools have a functional role in the reproduction of society), and are subject to the supervening hegemony of instrumental rationality that has, at least, fractured the material inference structures that had previously been the empirical bonds among subjects. In Chapter 1, I contended that the practices of private existence possessed a surplus of ideality and hence normativity that eluded instrumental reduction. I am here insisting, on the back of Weberian theory, that the remnant ideality cannot be explained *directly* by the practices being partially insulated from the direct glare of instrumentality, as if distance from immediate social functionality alone might enable a practice to continue as if it were the practice of a traditional society – the idea of latter-day Aristotelians. Distance is a condition for an ideality that is not instrumental, but under the conditions of modernity cannot itself be the source of ideality. Although then I am still required to say something about the ideality of practices in the private sphere, structurally it seems most plausible to suggest that we are caught between the unmediated extremes of the charismatic and the legal-rational, the fugitive and bureaucratic.

This state of affairs possesses an enabling aspect. I have argued that in accordance with the logic of the concept ethical norms must be conceived of being indexically bound. Under the governance of the idea of the indexical principle, traditional authority is to be understood as the temporalization and societal generalization of charismatic episodes, indexically bound ethical truths. Hence, what the collapse of traditional authority emphatically tokens is, precisely, the withdrawal from generality and reproducibility of ethical truths. Yet there remains some ethical experience and ethical truth. Hence, it is precisely the fugitive character of ethical experience in late modernity which reveals the event-character of ethical truth, that ethical events disclose ethical truth (by activating or reactivating material inferential relations) and that there is no ethical truth without the event structure of a charismatic episode.[20] It is not then the remnant communal forms, interpreted through either the notion of practices of mutual recognition or through enabling practices embodying the virtues, that explains why those communal forms contain still ethical experience; rather, what makes those forms locales of ethicality is that they make optimal the possibility of fugitive ethical episodes. Only as ethical experience is forced to take on a wholly modernist stance are its true lineaments revealed.

Nothing I have said about fugitive ethical experiences entails that they need be large or collective events like the Danish rescue effort. Given

20 I have not in these pages said anything about the notion of truth as disclosure; that notion has here been taken up in terms of the indexical principle. For my earlier attempt to link disclosure and exemplarity in ethical experience, see my *Recovering Ethical Life*, pp. 207–20.

what Adorno says about the fragmentary and the heterogeneous as promissory, it becomes plausible to think that scattered throughout ordinary experience, showing here and there in unpredictable and unforseeable ways, fugitive ethical events occur, leaping out from the routine of everyday life: there a spontaneous act of generosity, a promise kept improbably, an act of cruelty so emphatic that the ban on cruelty is experienced as if for the first time, a patient stance of dignity that given the circumstances is without support and reason other than the space it carves out for itself, and so on. The difficulty of our ethical predicament is that there is no room or space in ordinary life for what might be thought to be ordinary ethical action: the functional context of modern life draws everything into its orbit so that we are endlessly in some version of the predicament of Kant's grocer – our actions, even for ourselves, structurally indistinguishable from what is self-serving and instrumentally rational, from what suits the nonbenign ends of social reproduction. This means there is no habitable space between the fugitive and the rationalized. What nonetheless makes even complicitous action in these circumstances *more* than what rationalized form dictates, what supports and gives life to the ideality nonetheless sedimented in everyday practices, our sense that in keeping our routine promises, for example, we are not just capitulating to the dictates of social regularity, can only be their likeness to their fugitive counterparts (and not tradition or virtue or deontological principle, or being utility maximizing); *fugitive counterparts alone offer to everyday practices both a fragile rational authority and a sense of surplus, call it a promise or sense of transcendence, which their placement in rationalized society continually undermines.* Adorno's thought that identity thinking lives off the nonidentical becomes explicit and substantive in late ethical experience: rationalized ethical action lives off its fugitive counterparts. But according to Weberian doctrine, *this has always been the case,* that is, routine ethical action has always been dependent upon the exemplary actions of charismatic leaders and traditional masters, and thus routine ethical actions always counterparts to those instances in which the norms in question are emphatically, charismatically, first activated (the charismatic leader) or reactivated (the traditional master). What distinguishes late modernity from premodern and utopian social forms is that now charismatic ethical events are precisely fugitive, possessing no possibility for routine, that is, traditional uptake; nothing mediates between fugitive, charismatic episodes and everyday practice. Which is the precise thesis concerning the collapse of the bourgeois family and the chilling rise of the culture industry. The lack of the possibility of routine uptake is our misery, and it is this misery that can bring about the optical illusion that ethical truth resided in communal practice (of mutual recognition or the life of the virtues). But that is only a sentimental illusion. Only an unconditional ethical modernism can secure a secular ethics without depending on premodern ideas of community.

Fugitive ethical action is not supererogatory; rather, it is forged in resistance.[21] So the single mother who quietly and undramatically manages in the face of poverty and social disintegration to raise her children so that they escape the fate that awaits them, without their escape demanding the repression of others, if exemplary is not doing other than what, all other things being equal, the circumstances require. That the achievement of this bit of ordinary nurturing is extraordinary, fugitive, bespeaks its conditioning, the apparent impossibility of experience it contravenes. To be able to do the ordinary, to make a promise and mean it beyond all its multiple instrumental meanings, all its ways of furthering selfish ends or oiling the wheels of cooperative arrangements, is never simply ordinary; the ordinary, when it occurs, is an achievement, something still rare and sublime (ND, 364). The secular everyday promised by enlightenment is still far off, and when it appears it does so against the machinations of the spellbinding rationalized whole. It is because it is forged in resistance that fugitive ethical experience is as discomforting as it is innervating since it illumines the depth of complicity in our ordinary doings. Its power to innervate is coordinate with its power to dissolve spell of the security which the legal-rational order itself provides.

Resistance is always resistance to disenchantment; the material inferences that are enacted in resistance commence with the sight of damaged life and injurable bodies, that is, they take their start from the experience of moral injury. Fugitive ethical experience is attuned, so to speak, to extant moral injury as what needs to be responded to – "Signs that not everything is futile come from sympathy with the human, from the self-reflection of the subject's natural side . . . " (ND, 397). Not communally sanctioned virtuous lives nor the grace of human flourishing nor the model of unbending principled action can count or possess authority within the functional whole; rather, fugitive ethical life has its touchstones in its resistance to what now appears to us as explicit violations of the integrity of the animistic auratic individual: child abuse, rape, racism, torture, cruelty, starvation, and their like. It is not an accident that these have become so salient in our ethical self- understanding for they are in

21 If we could take sufficient account of what is at stake here, namely, the difficulty of there being any ethical actions at all under conditions of disenchantment, what makes for the fugitive character of ethical modernism, then we might come to appreciate how that huge conundrum in Kantian ethics, namely, nothing can count as a moral act unless done from the motive of duty, is nothing other than a reified expression of the utter difficulty and rarity of the ethical in modern conditions. The conundrum thus should not be written off, as if a theoretical embarrassment, but embraced as symptomatic of a real dilemma squarely faced.

small what the Nazi genocide was in large: cases of the appearing of animistic auratic individuality in its negation or palpable violation. As the more conventional sources of moral authority disintegrate and the crisis in value is felt, these extreme cases leap out from the reproducing whole, providing the orientation toward injurable nature that is the condition for non-self-defeating ethical action. In saying this I do not mean to claim that fugitive ethical experience is restricted to the exorbitant cases of resistance to embodied moral injury, only that such cases are for good reason ethically perspicuous, that they implicate the thought that all moral injury is akin to or modeled by embodied moral injury, and that the orientation they provide can feed into the understanding and innervation of less perspicuous cases and their traditional conceptual understanding – patience, dignity, fortitude, respect, self-respect, and so on.[22]

Fugitive ethical experiences, ethical modernism in its fugitive appearance, extend the model of the ethical that emerges from the new categorical imperative to everyday occurrences. What makes the new categorical imperative compelling equally should make more routine ethical actions compelling since the latter realize in nonexorbitant form the kind of responsiveness to sensuous particulars that was emphatically realized in the case of Auschwitz. Fugitive ethical experiences *disclose and promise* ethical concepts, understood in terms of material inference, com-

22 I am here assuming that the virtues can be understood on analogy with the principle of the indexical binding of moral norms. Nor is this very contentious since, prima facie, virtuous action is equally a matter of material inference: the best (most virtuous) thing for me to do in this situation is *this*. Put another way, once we recognize that virtuous action, so-called, and moral action, so-called, are both essentially explicating what is called for by a situation, and hence come to see that the connection between the description of the situation and the way *it* demands *this* response, is all best thought in terms of a material inference, and that the establishing of structures of material inference logically must commence from and be bound to particular circumstances, then we can acknowledge that a conception of material inference under the aegis of the indexical principle captures best what the core phenomenon of what was wanted from traditional conceptions of the virtues and (nonempirical) moral principles. Still the issue might be pressed from the side of virtue theory: do not you still need some overall account of the human good, some account of flourishing, some account of what is best for us? My fundamental response to this question, which would need elaborate defence, is that insofar as any such considerations ever impinge upon practical deliberation they emerge from the bottom up, as reflective adjustments demanded by particular states of affairs, and do not structure those deliberations even from afar. A subsidiary response would thus be: the image of ethical life suggested by that picture is wholly unrealistic; human lives are not teleologically oriented, do not follow life plans, but struggle under adverse conditions to respond to the diverse commitments and demands to which we discover ourselves to be subject. Response to imposing demands (to make a living, to protect our dearest, etc.), on the one hand, and contingency and accident, on the other, is what *shapes* lives. Lives are typically messier, more fragmented, more responsive to rapidly changing conditions, more a matter of finding ourselves burdened in this or that way than the picture that gives onto the idea of human flourishing suggests. Again, this is not to deny (some) the forms of activity that have traditionally appeared as virtuous, it is to deny only a certain picture of how they fit in our lives and how they may thus be vindicated.

ing-to-be in rationally compelling ways. The fugitive character of the ethical under conditions of late modernity, that is, in the absence of the possibility of traditional authority, makes perspicuous how the axes of the concept are actualized in ethical actions. Fugitive ethical experiences strike us, to use the analogy with modernist works of art, as authentic appearings of ethical concepts. What rationality our own ethical actions may have is parasitic upon these authentic episodes; again our ethical concepts receive whatever rationality they have beyond their identitarian form only in relation to their fugitive counterparts. Thus, it is fugitive ethical experiences that are the main bulwark against further societal rationalization. However, precisely because such experiences are fugitive we are unable to judge whether the form of life they implicitly project is really possible. The difficulty here is the same as it is for Adorno with authentic works of art, namely, we cannot subtract from the rationality of fugitive ethical experiences their *critical* function; an indeterminate portion of the rationality of fugitive ethical experiences derives from their resistance to societal and moral rationalization. So every appearing of an ethical concept in a fugitive context has the sense of affirming that concept against its reified and rationalized form; without the breaking open of the rationalized form of the concept the fugitive one could not attain to its charismatic appearance and authority. Recall how Adorno vindicates fidelity *against* (rationalized) fidelity, or cold rational deliberation *against* bourgeois coldness. Or we may conceive of the Danish rescue as reactivating the idea of rescue *against* its desuetude throughout the rest of Europe. The fugitive character of these ethical experiences gives to them a critical significance which is partially constitutive of the rational authority of the material inferences they enjoin.

When I said that fugitive ethical experiences *extend* the model of the ethical from the Auschwitz model, I also intended the thought that while the new categorical imperative responds to auratic individuality through the moment of its utter *collapse,* fugitive ethical experiences disclose individuals as, in the light of the actions responsive to them, *possessing* auratic individuality. The activation or reactivation of a material inference – a complex concept fulfilled – is an enchanting or re-enchanting of an individual. If only *this* action fully and adequately responds to the individual in this situation, if thus this is what perceiving or judging this individual requires, then the descriptive portion of the material inference as requiring the action it does a fortiori treats that descriptive designation as sufficient grounds for the action so entailed (demanded). To respond *thus* to *this suffering* (*this need, this lack,* etc.) is to regard a state of affairs as normatively demanding; but to find an individual or group of individuals *demanding* to be responded to *thusly* is what it is to regard their appearing in the way the action responds to as the ground of the action. (Conceptual content is the material inferential nexus linking descriptive state and appropriate action; each side of the inference makes essential reference to the other without it being the case that inferences exhaust contents – if they did, then there would be nothing for an inference to mediate.) To perceive the individual appearing *thus,* the individual as a locus of claims upon me, is to perceive the individual's aura. The appearing of individuals as lodging claims is the appearing of those individuals as possessing animistic auratic individuality. Aura is nothing more than this – the appearing of individuals as in their sensuous particularity lodging claims – but equally it is nothing less. To find in an episode in which a material inference is activated or reactivated, where individuals appearing as lodging claims to which particular courses of action are the only rational response, is thus to naturalize aura. This is naturalistic in the sense that nothing supports the practice other than the practice itself; ordinary descriptive predicates as applied to empirical states of affairs and the forms of action that articulate them (the meaning of bleeding *badly* is articulated by the actions appropriate to it, hence the inference *I'll apply a tourniquet*) is what it is to regard the world as ethically colored. The material inferential nexus connecting descriptive account and appropriate action is what having an enchanted world amounts to. Hence, in extending the model of the new categorical imperative to fugitive everyday occurrences (thus to a certain promise of the everyday), we come to perceive both the possibility of aura and how, in the light of this possibility, a wholly secular form of life can be rationally compelling and intrinsically motivating. So an ethical modernism in its fugitive appearing promises.

At this juncture the complaint might be lodged that my characterization of the occurrence and dispersal of fugitive ethical experience, ethical modernism in its fugitive occurrences, offers more in the way of consolation and hope than the negativity of Adornoian doctrine can tolerate. Am I not, implicitly, denying that there are no more deaths on which meaning can be erected? This would attribute to fugitive ethical experience more than it in fact delivers. What may give the impression that my characterization of the occurrence and dispersal of fugitive ethical experiences diverges from Adornoian doctrine is that I am suggesting that there is more experience of the metaphysical than Adorno appeared to believe there was; that the metaphysical experiences I am highlighting belong to the field of action about which Adorno is worse than silent; and one consequence of there being more metaphysical experience and its being ethical is that there is more vindicable rational authority about than he appears to have acknowledged. And to be sure, by its very existence, fugitive ethical experience, by converging with our need to regard ourselves as autonomous agents whose lives are meaningful through our choices and doings, can dull the sense of crisis, contributing to the acceptability of the negative whole it explicitly refutes. But that the form of hope given in fugitive ethical experience can provide for forms of consolation and solace that tendentially undermine resistance is an *empirical sociological* claim about the effects of fugitive ethical experience. The sociological worry about the empirical effects of fugitive ethics might explain Adorno's reticence. However, that fugitive ethical experience can empirically effect consolation and thus undermine resistance does not entail that the form of hope it typically, conceptually, enjoins is consolatory. Is not the structural ambiguity in fugitive ethical experiences being not transparently iterable, that they can only *promise* otherness, just their withdrawing from hope its power to console? Fugitive ethical experience would be intrinsically consolatory only if it could show that a different future is really possible or this present truly livable. It does neither; hence its power to console must derive from a mistaken interpretation driven by psychological need. If philosophically fugitive ethical experience is non-consolatory, then there is no reason to think that it must undermine resistance. Is the tail-wagging something that would structurally undermine resistance? Only for the hopeless, that is, those within the total context of immanence, is hope given. *The promissory character of fugitive ethical experience is its logical detachment from consolation.*

Fugitive ethical experience is forged in resistance, it is determined by the sight of the disenchanted body as suffering that disenchantment. Because the experiences are fugitive, then nothing supports the claim that they will be socially reproducible. Because there is no habitable, living space between the fugitive and the rationalized, I am saying neither that wrong life can be lived rightly nor that wrong life emphatically lives.[23] What makes such events fugitive is their isolation and hence desolation; at most, their actuality entails that right living is *possible in the mode of a promise,* but that, as Adorno states it, is a promise which at every moment reality breaks.

5. Conclusion

Ethical modernism in its fugitive form relates to the operation of thick ethical concepts in a state of not only fragmentation and dispersal, but in which whether or not we have, possess, such concepts and what is entailed by that possession remain unsettled matters. But that is equivalent to saying that we are unsure if what is purportedly represented by our thick

23 The innervation provided by fugitive ethical experience is not equivalent to unqualified resuscitation but the mechanism whereby the undead "live on" after true living has ceased or has not yet occurred. I am thus presuming that the defense of fugitive ethics is compatible with the darkest strain of Adorno's thematic of enlightenment as the assimilation of the animate to the inanimate. For a brilliant thinking through of this issue independently of Adorno, see Gregg M. Horowitz, *Sustaining Loss: Art and Mournful Life* (Stanford: Stanford University Press, forthcoming).

ethical concepts is anything in the world whatsoever. Within this context fugitive ethical events occur that install, disclose, and innervate a concept and its object, reactivating or activating for the first time structures of material inference that are the empirical bonds among subjects.

Adorno's account of ethical life gives to it a broad naturalist backdrop: valuing belongs to life; the valuing of the living is nondetachable from their sense of themselves as injurable; the perception of animal others as injurable and compassion as a natural response to injury are basic experiences of others as of worth – the perception and the feeling, which is also a perception, are the experience of aura and its attribution; the sustaining of animistic aura requires practices, structures of material inference, that acknowledge the independence (separateness) and dependence (connectedness) of each individual in relation to its significant others; no set of ethical practices can be viable unless it sustains structures of separateness (independence) and connectedness (dependence). What these and kindred bits of theoretical knowledge can provide is rational confidence that the possibility of the ethical is natural; that acknowledging humans as belonging to the natural world is necessary in order to correct the self-defeating elements of enlightened rationalism; and that, at least in principle, in theoretical terms, a wholly secular form of ethical life is logically possible. So much ethical theory can offer to ethical practice.

However, knowing these bits of theory will not take us far since, above all, what will in fact count as recognizing another's separateness or connectedness, acknowledging their worth, is given solely through the material inferences constituting ethical concepts and is not practically available otherwise. Hence despite the discovery that there are certain limiting conditions that must be satisfied if a set of practices is going to be adequate and endure – not be intrinsically self-defeating – and hence probably a small core set of moral injuries that any secular ethical practices will converge on, there is nothing in Adorno's account to lead one to expect that there is just one ideal ethical language that will be viable across cultures and over time. What I claimed about the density and indeterminacy of experience in relation to conceptuality, together with the multiple social and historical sources of value give every reason to suppose that there is a high level of relativity built into ethical life and that there is no persuasive way, in a theory of human nature or human flourishing or the virtues, to nonarbitrarily regiment that relativity.[24] Even the notion of self-defeat, I argued, is finally ethical and normative; although there is a functional outside to human practice, that outside has significance only internally because there are systematic and reproducible practices, or maybe only "practices," in which humans are treated in a man-

24 For a sceptical canvassing of the possibilities, see Bernard Williams, "Who Needs Ethical Knowledge," in his *Making Sense of Humanity*, chapter 17.

ner that takes no account of their animistic auratic individuality, and in not being taken account of the individuals subject to those practices tendentially cease to possess the property of animistic auratic individuality. Nothing ensures that the processes of discounting will not become total, just as nothing ensures that fugitive ethical experiences will continue to occur, or if they occur, that they will be understood appropriately. Adorno is a self-limiting rationalist in that he thinks that the idea of a rational whole is intelligible, but – and this is the self-limiting bit – that intelligibility is not something that philosophy can provide. The philosophical comprehension of the possibility of a free and meaningful life emerges only through philosophy's self-dispossession. Fugitive ethical experience, and its artistic thematization, is the experience of possibility and meaning in the only mode such is available.

The reasonable question at this juncture is whether in conceding variability and openness Adorno has undermined the plausibility of his own cognitivism. In fact, Adorno was not much moved by the problem of relativism. He thought that relativistic views could be asserted only in the abstract, "from without," and that as soon as some definite thing raised a particular claim, then any sense that one's response was accidental dissolved (ND, 36); if context is justificatory, and there is no possibility of non-contextual justification, then the "from without" doubt flounders.[25] The social conditioning of thought makes implausible the actual conceivability of social judgements being haphazard. And equally, since there is no leaping over the conditioning of one's own thought, then the fact that from some other place or other time a different description or judgement could be issued about the state of affairs in question must be idle: I, we, can act and judge only from where we are. Adorno further thought that relativism, even when it had some progressive bearing as a reminder of social conditioning, nonetheless always also was linked with reaction, since its overall tendency is to except social phenomena from criticism (ND, 36–7).

Standard worries about variability and relativity in a sense come too late. Although truth for Adorno is emphatic – "Truth is objective and not

25 This thought might be pursued in relation to Michael Williams's *Unnatural Doubts: Epistemological Realism and the Basis of Scepticism* (Princeton: Princeton University Press, 1996). I hope at some future time to show the connection between the claim that scepticism involves an effort of decontextualization with the thesis that rationalized social practices, practices in which local structures of material inference are supervened upon by instrumentally rational structures, have their nihilistic consequence because what occurs in bureaucratic rationalization is equally a matter of decontextualization. This, at any rate, is how I perceive the connection between the apparently narrow analytic problem of scepticism and the social problem of nihilism. Equally, it should be noted, that societal rationalization is a work of decontextualization explains why one might suppose that it was community itself that was the victim of rationalization rather than, as I claim, structures of material inference.

plausible" (ND, 41) – it is equally, due to its temporal substance, its contextual and conditioned character, always suspended and frail (ND, 33–4). Frailty, the fact that any ethical truth is temporally bound and indexed, and hence is something that can be missed or lost, belongs to the kind of truth fugitive experiences provide. Because statements or expressions of ethical truth are indexed material inferences, then from the perspective of identity thinking and its absolute truth concept, they will appear inconclusive. The shock of inconclusiveness, Adorno states, which is the negative experience of truth in the context of the system of total immanence, "is untrue for untruth only" (ND, 33), that is, we will experience inconclusiveness, the gaps that material inferences leave, as a symptom of untruth only under the conditions in which identity thinking reigns. But since these are the conditions of our thinking, then our thinking is beset by an experience of inconclusiveness which both is and is not telling against it. We can have the experience of a fugitive ethical truth as emphatic, as, perhaps, to borrow an idea of David Wiggins, leaving us nothing further to think than that *P*.[26] So of a particular occurrence, if asked whether it was cruel, we would emphatically claim it to be cruel. But under the conditions in which any such thought might arise for us, there *is* something else to think, namely, what is thought in those surrounding experiences in which the fugitive concept either does not appear or appears only in its degraded form. If only here does an event like that appear suddenly but emphatically cruel, then there remains all those events like and surrounding it where cruelty was not stated because, say, it never occurred to us prior to the emphatic event to think of events like it in terms of cruelty or not. And we are in no position to separate this dialectic of the emphatic and its relativisation from what Adorno *hopes* would be its benign form under utopian conditions in which whatever there was further to think would be immediately silenced; under ideal conditions in which identitarian claims no longer had rational appeal one might suppose that the lack of the concept cruelty, for example, was a wholly contingent matter, and for those who appeared to possess it but remained unmoved that there was something untoward in their possession, a blockage or irrationality. So the thought is that for us the emphatic experience contains both the idealizing understanding and its nonbenign relativisation, and we are in no position to fully insulate the former from the latter; we are always *also* struck by inconclusiveness. Roughly, for us the "inside" experience in which inconclusiveness is compatible with being emphatic is now always subject to a counter-experience

26 David Wiggins, "Moral Cognitivism, Moral Relativism and Motivating Beliefs," *Proceedings of the Aristotelian Society* 91 (1990–91). My criticism of Wiggins follows Bernard Williams, "Who Needs Ethical Knowledge?," p. 212. For a continuation of their exchange on this issue, see their essays in Hooker (ed.), *Truth in Ethics.*

that inconclusiveness is a symptom of untruth. We can of course say that such untruth is untrue for untruth only, but that saying is only a hopeful mantra not truly separable from fugitive ethical experience itself. I suspect, because this aporetic condition for the time being is ineliminable, that Adorno thought it unproductive to try and elaborate an emphatic conception of truth beyond the adequation family. Too much of the kind of emphatic conception of truth that fugitive experience presupposes is bound to the inconsolable hope such events provide. For Adorno, even the idea of truth is had in the mode of promise.

Fugitive ethical experiences are the facts of our social reason, collectivity via the exemplary charismatic episodes of late modernity (Martin Luther King, Jr., and the civil rights movement, for example), and individually from scattered and always improbable everyday occurrences. Some history writing and some literary fiction sense this. If ethical modernism and its display in fugitive ethical experience could be provided with wider currency, then perhaps alternative forms of history writing and social criticism might emerge that would see themselves as limning the intelligibility of social life. That might come to matter to the intellectual conscience of our age. But I suspect that it is the more mundane sources of fugitive ethical experience that are more significant. Because the opportunities in ordinary life for fugitive ethical experiences are not many, it is likely that for most of us it is in watching and interacting with children that the promise of another nature is most vocal in the course of everyday experience. Children's unformedness, their vulnerability and radical dependence, the necessity by which they must love, accept, trust as a condition of survival, the intensity of their conceptually unsaturated experience of the world, all can always feel like the opportunity of a new beginning, one which they bring to their interactions with adults, so almost providing a new beginning for them too, albeit one which is forfeit over and over again. It is not only the history of suffering that has been hardly noticed by philosophy; childhood, in which vulnerability is most perspicuously in evidence, is not much in presence, either.[27] In retrospect the official Enlightenment view that poses childhood as what is to be permanently overcome appears terrifying in its disavowal of the trust and dependencies that make lives minimally livable where they manage as much. If the position of the neophyte is intrinsic to human conceptuality, then a more continuous presence of the standpoint and meaning of

27 There are exceptions, most notably Rousseau's *Emile*, and the espousal of natality in Hannah Arendt's *The Human Condition* (Chicago: University of Chicago Press, 1958). That there is something more than a family resemblance between fugitive ethics and Arendt's conception of the political is not an accidental feature of my argument. Because philosophy has not seen fit to consider childhood experience as formative and thereby, to certain extent, unsurpassable, psychoanalysis has come to seem to many as a replacement for philosophy.

the neophyte in philosophy might shift its outlook, making some of what childhood innervates a more established component of our self-understanding. Seeing the fit among vulnerability, helplessness, trust, and love in the formation of the self may make what appears most remote in fugitive ethical experience less alien. Society's constant initiation process can make the reminder of our vulnerability and dependence unwelcome; yet no fugitive experience is more insistent than that initiation process is not complete, each emphatic presence of a child and each emphatic childlike experience a reminder of "the child," injurable, vulnerable life present in each.

INDEX

(References to Max Horkheimer as the co-author of *Dialectic of Enlightenment* have not been included.)